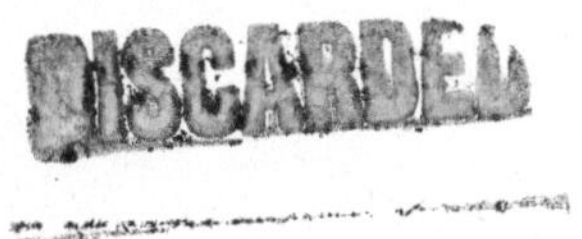
DISCARDED

D1558528

THE
Complete Writings of
ROGER WILLIAMS

PUBLISHER'S NOTE

All the new matter contained in this edition, including Prof. Miller's essay, will be found in VOLUME SEVEN. This arrangement was adopted in order to retain the original pagination of the first six volumes and thereby maintain the integrity of the voluminous references to the *Narragansett Edition* in the literature about ROGER WILLIAMS. The reader is directed to the inclusive Table of Contents for guidance.

THE *COMPLETE WRITINGS* OF ROGER WILLIAMS

VOLUME FOUR

NEW YORK
RUSSELL & RUSSELL · INC
1963

THE COMPLETE WRITINGS OF ROGER WILLIAMS
Issued in Seven Volumes in a Limited Edition
of Four Hundred Sets
Published in 1963 *by Russell & Russell, Inc.*
Library of Congress Catalog Card Number: 63-11034
Printed in The United States of America

THE COMPLETE WRITINGS OF ROGER WILLIAMS

IN SEVEN VOLUMES

VOLUME I

Biographical Introduction
by Reuben Aldridge Guild, A.M.
Key into the Language of America
Edited by James Hammond Trumbull, A.M.
Letter of Mr. John Cotton
Mr. Cotton's Letter Examined and Answered
Edited by Reuben Aldridge Guild, A.M.

VOLUME II

John Cotton's Answer to Roger Williams
Queries of Highest Consideration
Edited by Reuben Aldridge Guild, A.M.

VOLUME III

Bloudy Tenent of Persecution
Edited by Samuel L. Caldwell

VOLUME IV

The Bloody Tenent Yet More Bloody
Edited by Samuel L. Caldwell

VOLUME V

George Fox Digg'd out of His Burrowes
Edited by Rev. J. Lewis Diman

VOLUME VI

The Letters of Roger Williams
Edited by John Russell Bartlett

VOLUME VII

Publisher's Foreword
Roger Williams: An Essay in Interpretation
by Perry Miller
Christenings make Not Christians
Experiments of Spiritual Life and Health
The Fourth Paper Presented by Major Butler
The Hireling Ministry None of Christs
The Examiner—Defended in a Fair and Sober Answer

THE

BLOODY TENENT YET MORE BLOODY.

EDITED BY

SAMUEL L. CALDWELL.

EDITOR'S PREFACE.

——o——

THE reply of Mr. Cotton to *The Bloudy Tenent* was publifhed in London, May 15, 1647.[1] It is a work of 195 pages, and is bound in the same volume with his *Reply to Mr. Williams his examination*, which was written earlier, and is inferted after it with a different paging. It is in feventy-nine chapters, criticifing and traverfing *The Bloudy Tenent* chapter by chapter, ftopping however when it reaches Williams's examination of *The Model of Church and Civil Power*, as Corton difclaimed any part in the compofition of that work, and therefore refufed to defend it. The nature of its argument may be gathered to fome extent from Williams's rejoinder contained in the prefent volume, and now foɿ the firft time reprinted.

In November, 1651, the author failed from Bofton,[2] for England. His companion there, and probably on the voyage,[3] was John Clarke of Newport, who was joined

[1] 3 *Mass. Hift. Coll.* viii : 287.

[2] His petition for permiffion to embark there is in 3 *Mass. Hift. Coll.* iv : 471.

[3] "I do not think it likely that Clarke came to Maffachufetts to embark with Williams, confidering the treatment experienced by him in that colony only a fhort time before." Palfrey, *Hift. of N. E.* ii : 355. Yet Mr. Palfrey reprefents that Clarke went there and pro-

with him in an effort to ſecure the repeal of Coddington's commiſſion, and the confirmation of the Charter. It was also a part of Clarke's buſineſs in England to make known the proceedings of the authorities of Maſſachuſetts in their treatment of himſelf and his companion Obadiah Holmes, on their viſit to Lynn the previous ſummer.[1] This he did in his *Ill Newes from New-England: or a Narrative of New-Englands Perſecution.* [2] As will be ſeen, Williams made uſe of their caſe to give point to his argument.

"In the ſecond Moneth, 1652," according to the title-pages, Williams publiſhed *Experiments of Spiritual Life and Health*, and *The Hireling Miniſtry None of Chriſts.* According to the Julian calendar, then in vogue, this was in April. On the tenth page of the Addreſs to Parliament, which precedes the following work, there is a reference to the war with Holland, which broke out in May, and which would therefore indicate that this book was not printed till after the other two.[3] In the "Epiſtle Dedicatory" to *The Hireling Miniſtry*, however, he ſpeaks of his "late unwaſhing of Mr. Cotton's waſhing of the Bloudy Tenent," as if it had already been publiſhed. But it

voked ſuch "treatment" in order to procure a grievance to carry with him to England. On that theory, neither his fears, nor his reſentments would have prevented his going to Boſton for the convenience of ſailing with Williams. Beſides, his fine was paid, he was liable to no charge, and he had made a propoſition for a public diſpute there three times, profeſſing his willingneſs "through the help of God to come from the Iland to attend it." Williams himſelf had ſome queſtion in regard to embarking at Boſton, ſeeing that he had been baniſhed from the juriſdiction. He writes to John Winthrop, jr., "Being now bound reſolvedly (if the Lord pleaſe) for our native country, I am not certain whether by the way of the Engliſh, (you know the reaſon) or by the way of the Dutch." Knowles, *Memoir*, 248.

[1] See pp. 52, 53 *infra*.

[2] 4 *Mass. Hiſt. Coll.* ii.

[3] p. 10 *infra*. This is alſo ſuſtained by an alluſion to it in his firſt letter to Mrs. Sadleir. "Since I landed, I have publiſhed two or three things, and have a large diſcourſe at the preſs, but 'tis controverſial." Elton, *Life*, 89.

appears by a marginal note to the Letter to Governor Endicott, which follows this treatiſe, that "this Rejoynder was ſent to England long ſince, and hoped to have been publiſhed."[1] In the Table of Contents at the end of the Book, there is a ſimilar ſtatement: "This Rejoynder formerly ſent out of N. Eng. but not till now publiſhed."[2] As his reference to the caſe of Obadiah Holmes is inſerted in the margin rather than in the text, at page 3 *infra*, it may be reaſonably inferred that the treatiſe was written, and perhaps ſent to England, prior to the date of Holmes's arreſt, July 19, 1651. The title-page alſo ſpeaks of the Letter to Endicott "as a Teſtimony to Mr. Clark's Narrative," as if that had been already publiſhed. The *Ill Newes* was iſſued, according to Mr. Savage, May 13,1652.[3]

When in England before, he had had the ſervices of Gregory Dexter, eſpecially in printing the *Key;* who was now living in Providence, and to whom Williams wrote under date of October 7, 1652, "It hath pleaſed God ſo to engage me in divers ſkirmishes againſt the prieſts, both of Old and New England, ſo that I have occaſioned uſing the help of printer men, unknown to me, to long for my old friend."[4] He intimates that his intention had been to print with this an Examination of Cotton's *Reply*, which was printed with *The Bloudy Tenent Waſhed*, but that he was prevented by "ſtreights of time,

[1] p. 505 *infra*.

[2] In 1650, Williams writes to John Winthrop, jr., "You may pleaſe to remember that I have bene large (in the Bloodie Tenent) in the difference betweene that land of Iſraell and all others. It is in diſcuſſing of the modell. Mr. Cotton refers the anſwere to the reſt of the elders, whoſe answer or reply I yet here not of, and pray you if you doe, to intimate. 'Tis a controverſie wherein I am deeply engaged, of which you will (if God pleaſe) ſee more." 4 *Mass. Hiſt. Coll.* vi: 282.

[3] 3 *Mass. Hiſt. Coll.* viii: 287.

[4] Knowles, *Memoir*, 253.

being conſtantly drunk up by neceſſary labours for bread for many depending on me, the diſcharge of Engagements, and wanting helps of tranſcribing."

As in the previous work, he prefixes an addreſs to Parliament, in which praiſe and religious dehortation and appeal are mingled. The Editor has inferred from an alluſion at the top of the tenth page, that this addreſs was written during the progreſs of the Dutch War, and after the conflict between Blake and Van Tromp, May 18, 1652, ariſing out of neglect in "ſtriking of colours." In the original work the three addreſſes with which it is prefaced are not paged, are in ſlightly different type, and were probably printed, and perhaps written, in England, after the remainder of the work had been put to press.

The work is followed by a letter to Governor Endicott, in reference to the caſe of Clarke and Holmes, which furniſhed ſo pertinent an illuſtration of the ſubject of the preſent diſcuſſion. This letter was apparently written in the course of a correſpondence with Endicott in regard to Indian affairs, and ſent to him the previous ſummer, ſhortly after the events to which it refers.[1] Its ſtyle ſeems more as if it were a continuation of the preſent treatiſe, or a formal addreſs, than a friendly letter. But as it is ſpoken of as a "Copie," and begins with an allusion to another letter, or a previous part of this, it is moſt reaſonable to ſuppoſe that it was firſt ſent to Endicott,

[1] Endicott writes to John Winthrop, jr., "Salem the 15, 6, 51. I have written to Mr. Williams an anſwer to his letter you were pleaſed to bring mee, and I hope to ſatisfaccon as much as lyes in mee. And I heartilie deſire that you will labour with the Sachims of the Narraganſetts, Ninecroft and Mixam, that they will be peaceable with their neighbour Indeans till their complaints be heard and anſwered, which I ſhall endeavour to effect the next generall Court." 4 *Mass. Hiſt. Coll.* vi: 153,

and for immediate remonſtrance, and was taken to England to be publiſhed with this work, as adding force to it, and alſo to Clarke's own plea for the ſame principle.

Williams alſo adds, in an Appendix, an addreſs "to the cleargie of the foure greate Parties, viz: The Popiſh, Prelaticall, Preſbyterian, and Independent." This appears to have been written after his arrival in England, and probably while this work was paſſing through the preſs, as alluſion is made to "Mr. Clark's Narrative," as "lately publiſhed," which, as has been mentioned, was iſſued as early as the 13th of May, 1652. And in another ſentence one hears the echoes of the guns in Dover roadſtead five days later, when he ſpeaks of "the Treacherous Dutchmen, who Capitulate of Leagues of Peace and Amitie, with their neighbor English, and in the midſt of State Complements (ſome ſay, out of malicious wrath, others ſay twas out of drunken Intoxications at the beſt) thunder out Broad-ſides of Fire and Smoake of perſecution."[1]

The author, though engaged in a miſſion which would induce him to conciliate the ruling powers, does not heſitate to ſpeak very boldly, and to charge upon all of them complicity in the doctrine and the practices he is aſſailing. He arraigns the Independents, then the ſtrong party, who through Cromwell were riſing to power, as guilty with all the reſt, notwithſtanding they were charged with being friendly to toleration. Other incidental references are to be noted. The laſt page of the addreſs To the Reader, contains his confeſſion of faith in

[1] p. 526 *infra*. "Which was the aggreſſor in the action which enſued between theſe two admirals, both of them men of ſuch prompt and fiery diſpoſition, it is not eaſy to determine; ſince each of them ſent to his own ſtate a relation totally oppoſite in all its circumſtances to that of the other, and yet ſupported by the teſtimony of every captain in his fleet." Hume, *Hiſt. of Eng.* vii: 220.

regard to the Church. On pages 191 and 380 alſo are ſtatements in regard to the church and miniſtry, ſimilar to thoſe contained in *The Hireling Miniſtry*. More than once he refers to the Six Principles or Foundations alluded to in Hebrews vi : 1. 2., which were adopted as a baſis of fellowſhip by many of the Baptiſts of Rhode Iſland in his day and ſince.[1] That he was not fully ſatisfied with any exiſting Church, although abiding ſubſtantially by his principles as a Baptiſt, is tolerably clear from the incidental alluſions ſcattered through his works published at this period, and perhaps more diſtinctly from his letter to John Winthrop, jr., written Dec. 9, 1649. He there ſays, "At Secunck a great many have lately concurd with Mr. Jo: Clarke and our Providence men about the point of a new Baptiſme, and the manner by dipping: and Mr. Jo: Clarke hath bene there lately (and Mr. Lucar) and hath dipped them. I believe their practice comes neerer the firſt practice of our great Founder Chriſt then other practices of religion doe, and yet I have not ſatisfaction neither in the authoritie by which it is done, nor in the manner: nor in the prophecies concerning the riſing of Chriſts Kingdome after the deſolations by Rome, &c."[2] On pages

[1] In the note on p. 21, it is ſuggeſted that Williams may have been the firſt who advocated impoſition of hands, and the Six Principles as eſſential to church fellowſhip. The Rev. W. Perkins, publiſhed in London, in 1606, a work called The Foundation of the Chriſtian Religion gathered into Six Principles, to which John Robinſon publiſhed an Appendix. But it had no reference to the paſſage in Hebrews, or to the impoſition of hands. D'Anvers ſtates that the practice commenced in England about the year 1646. Evans, *Early Engliſh Baptiſts*, ii: 146.

[2] 4 *Mass. Hiſt. Coll.* vi: 274. Oct. 18, 1649, the General Court of Maſſachuſetts write to Plymouth, "Particularly wee underſtand that within this few weeks there have binn at Sea Cuncke thirteen or fourteen perſons rebaptized (a ſwift progres in one towne.) The infection of ſuch diſeaſe being ſo neare us, are likely to ſpread into our jurisdiction." *Mass. Col. Rec.* iii: 173.

44-47 he has further allufion to his views on thefe prophecies.

The NARRAGANSETT CLUB, in reprinting this work, have had the ufe of a copy of the firft edition, which was bequeathed to the Library of Brown Univerfity by the Rev. Ifaac Backus, the Hiftorian of the Baptifts, and which was prefented by Williams to John Clarke. On a fly-leaf is the following infcription in Williams's handwriting: "For his honoured and beloved Mr. John Clarke, an eminent witnes of Chrift Jefus, ag'st ye bloodie Doctrine of perfecution, &c."

S. L. C.

PROVIDENCE, March 2, 1870.

THE

BLOODY TENENT

YET

More Bloody:

BY

Mr *Cottons* endevour to waſh it white in the BLOOD of the *LAMBE*;

Of whoſe precious Blood, ſpilt in the Blood of his Servants; and

Of the blood of Millions ſpilt in former and later Wars for Conſcience ſake,

THAT

Moſt Bloody Tenent of Perſecution for cauſe of Conſcience, upon a ſecond Tryal, is found now more apparently and more notoriouſly guilty.

In this Rejoynder to Mr *Cotton*, are principally

I. *The Nature of Perſecution,*
II. *The Power of the Civill Sword in Spirituals* } Examined;

III. *The Parliaments permiſſion of Diſſenting Conſciences* } Juſtified.

Alſo (as a Teſtimony to Mr *Clarks* Narrative) is added a Letter to Mr. *Endicot* Governor of the *Maſſachuſets* in *N. E.*

By R. WILLIAMS of *Providence* in *New-England.*

London, Printed for *Giles Calvert,* and are to be ſold at the black-ſpread-Eagle at the Weſt-end of *Pauls,* 1652.

TO THE

MOST HONORABLE

THE PARLIAMENT OF THE

Common-wealth of ENGLAND.

Most Noble Senators,

ONE of the greatest *Spirits*, and as active as later times have yeelded, *Charles* the fifth, tired out with *Affairs* of *State*, resigns up all, and sits down to end his dayes in quiet *Contemplation*. I doubt not but many of your Honorable *Heads* have felt the thorny *Crown* (of these late *years* troubles) so *sharp*, so *weighty*, that your *tired* Spirits would joyfully embrace, if not (with *Charles* the fifth) a totall *Cessation*, yet like some faithfull tired *Judge*, (after so long and troublesome a *Tearm*) at least some breathing short *Vacation*.[1]

The Parliaments Labours and Labyrinths,

[1] The Long Parliament had existed since Nov. 3, 1640. Of course it had changed, and in fact had been greatly reduced in that time. Williams perhaps saw the signs of its coming dissolution. It had voted Nov. 18, 1651, just before his arrival in England, and probably under the constraint of the victory at Worcester, Cromwell's "crowning mercy," that at the end of three years it would give way to a new Parliament, to be seasonably summoned. But Crom-

Although I dare not (as to *Englands* peace and ſafety) admit deſires of your *Totall Ceſſation*, or long *vacation:* yet common *Gratitude* for ſuch incomparable labours, expences, hazards, &c. from whence the God of heaven hath vouchſafed ſuch rare and incomparable preſervations, deliverances, enjoyments, &c. I ſay common gratitude cannot onely wiſh you heartily & pray for earneſtly your eternal *Reſt*, and moſt joyfull *Harveſt* in the Heavens, but also, all the poſſible breathing hours, and cool retired *ſhades* of Contemplation and ſelf-enjoyment amidſt the ſcorching *Travels* [travails] of ſo many vexing and tedious *Actions.* You cannot (ever renowned Patriots) but like ſome grave Commanders of *Fleets* and *Armies*, who have brought their *Ships* and *followers* through tempeſtuous *ſtorms* and bloody *fights*, to joyful *Reſt* and *Harbours*! You cannot but look back with Admirings, with Praiſings, with Reſolvings to caſt you Crowns, and Heads, and Hearts, and Hands, (for the remaining *Minutes* of the ſhort Candle of your life) at his *Feet*, in whoſe moſt High and moſt gracious Hands have all your *Breaths* and *wayes* been.

Two Subſidies granted by the Parliament to the King of Kings.

In the review of the multitude of your *Actings* and *Sufferings*, your *Battells* and *Victories*, *Dangers* and *Deliverances*, you cannot, (no man can) but obſerve and ſee (a naked) Arm from Heaven fighting for you, but moſt eſpecially ſince the times and houres you gratified the moſt *High Eternall King of Kings* (now more then ever *Englands King*) with

well finiſhed it before that, diſſolving it by force April 20, 1653. Guizot, *Cromwell and Eng. Commonwealth*, i: 315–318.

Charles V. abdicated Oct. 15, 1555, retiring to Yuſte, in Spain. Robertſon, *Life, &c.*, iii: 201; Stirling, *Cloiſter Life of Charles the Fifth.*

theſe two famous *Subſidies* (if I may in humble Reverence ſo call them.)

The firſt, of *Mercy* and *Moderation* to the poor oppreſſed Conſciences of the *Engliſh Nation*, amidſt the throng of which he graciouſly will, yea he hath acknowledged, that *ſome* of his own dear *Children* (the Sonnes and Daughters of the God of Heaven) have been relieved and ſuccoured by you. *The firſt Subſidy.*

The ſecond your high and impartiall drawing of the Sword of *Juſtice* upon the great and *higheſt* offendors:[1] Since which two wonderfull Subſidies, the moſt wilfully blind muſt be forced to ſee the glorious *Goings* of the God of Heaven with your *Councels* and *Armies*, and the diſcharge of his holy promiſe in honouring you, who have ſo highly, (in ſo rare and unparalleld *Travels* [travails] and *Hazards*) honored him. *The ſecond Subſidy.*

Concerning the firſt of theſe *Subſidies*, I was humbly bold ſome few yeares ſince, to preſent you with a Conference between *Peace* and *Truth*, touching a moſt bloudy Murtherous *Malefactor*, the bloody *Tenent* of *Perſecution* for cauſe of *Conſcience*: (a notorious and common Pyrate, that *takes* and *robbs*, that *fires* and *ſinkes* the (*Spirituall Shipps* and *Veſſels*) the *Conſciences* of all men, of all ſorts, of all *Religions* and *Perſwaſions* whatſoever. *The Bloody Tenent a common Pyrat.*

[1] One of the firſt acts of this Parliament had been to impeach the Earl of Strafford, Nov. 18, 1640. He was executed May 12, 1641. McDiarmid, *Brit. Stateſmen*, 391. Archbiſhop Laud was ſent to the Tower March 1, 1641, under articles of impeachment for high treaſon. Theſe were not followed up for a long time. But in March 1644, he was brought to trial, and was beheaded Jan. 10, 1645. Neal, *Hiſtory of Puritans*, i: 501–526, gives an abſtract of the trial. Charles I. was beheaded by order of a High Court of Juſtice conſtituted by this Parliament, Jan. 30, 1649. Clarendon, *Hiſt. of Rebellion*, v: 2387; Guizot, *Eng. Revolution*, 1, 450.

Mr. Cottons Reply. It hath pleaſed Maſter *Cotton*, (a Man incomparably too worthy for ſuch a ſervice) to attempt the waſhing of this bloody *Tenent*, (as hee ſpeakes) in the blood of the Lamb CHRIST JESUS (though one part of the *Conference*, to wit, the *Examination* of a N. *Engliſh Modell* of *Church* and *Civill Power*, he leaveth to the waſhing of ſome other of the N. *Engliſh Miniſters*, the *Authors* of that *Modell*, of whoſe *waſhings* as yet I have not heard of:)[1] This preſent diſcourſe preſents your *Honours* with the ſecond part of the *Conference* between *Peace* and *Truth*, and hath examined Mr. *Cottons Reply* and *waſhings*.

I ſumme up the multitude of my *Thoughts* touching your *Honours Conſideration* of this point, in theſe three moſt humble *Petitions*.

The firſt Petition. Firſt, I moſt humbly and earneſtly beſeech your *Honours* to mind the *Difference* between State *Neceſſity* of *Freedome* to different *Conſciences*, and the *Equity* and *Piety* of ſuch a Freedome.

Difference betweenthe Piety and Mercy, and State-neceſſity of granting State *Policie* and *Neceſſity* of *Affairs* drew from great *Conſtantine* (with his Colleague *Licinius*) that famous *Edict* of *Freedome* to all mens *Conſciences*, whom yet afterward he perſecuted:[2] But a *Succeſſor* of his (of late years) *Maximilian* the ſecond, comes

[1] Cotton gives but one chapter to his conſideration of Williams's examination of the *Model*, proteſting that he was not the author of it. He ſays, "But wherefore doe I put my Sicle into the Harveſt of my Brethren? my Brethren, who penned that Modell, are richly furniſhed by Chriſt with ability to defend it. I therefore leave it to them, whom it chiefly concerneth, to maintaine the Truth, which themſelves have witneſſed in that Modell." *Bloudy Tenent Waſhed*, 195.

[2] "Either in the ſpring or ſummer of 312, Conſtantine, in conjunction with his eaſtern colleague, Licinius, had publiſhed an edict of religious toleration, now not extant. Soon after, in January, 313, the two Emperors iſſued from Milan a new edict (the third) on religion,

neerer the *Life* of the *Businesse*, when he conscientiously profest in a solemne *Speech* to the Bishop of *Olmuts* in *Bohemia*, *There is no sin ordinarily greater against God*, said he, *then to use violence against the Consciences of men.*[1]

freedom to mens Consciences. Constantines and Maximilians acts compared,

Your *Honours* will find (if the *Father* of *Spirits* please to spare you time and *Spirits*, to mind this *Cause* and *Controversie*, that all violence to *Conscience* turns upon these two *Hinges*.

First, of *Restraining* from that *worshipping* of a *God* or *Gods*, which the *Consciences* of men in their respective worships (all the world over) believes to be *true*.

Two wayes of oppressing conscience in Religion.

Secondly, of *Constraining* to the *practising* or *countenancing* of that whereof their Consciences are not perswaded.

In the *practice* of both these, the *Histories* of our own *Nation* will tell us (besides the forraigne) how *sharp* and *zealous* the *strongest Swords* of *England* have ever us'd to be.

And yet of the practice of both, what a *Propheticall passage* of our late troubles and *King*, did the foresaid *Maximilian* expresse to *Henry* the third of *France*, (in his passage from *Poland* to *France* to claim the *French* Crown) to this effect, Sir, remember that when men think to get Heaven by using violence to the *Consciences* of men, they oftentimes lose that

The late King Charles *his conscience to oppresse the consciences of others, no small occa-*

still extant both in Latin and Greek, in which, in the spirit of religious eclecticism, they granted full freedom to all existing forms of worship, with special reference to the Christian." Schaff, *Hist. of Christ'n Ch.* ii: 29; Neander, *do.*, ii: 12, 13; Milman, *Hist. of Christianity*, ii: 356.

[1] Maximilian II. (1527–1576) became Emperor in 1564. His sentiments and his acts were all in favor of toleration, although he adhered to the Catholic Church. Coxe, *House of Austria*, ii: 19, 62.

sion of the ruine of him and his.

The Bishops kild the King.

Hollands policy.

which they might peaceably have kept on *Earth.*[1] Some have said that *worldly policie* perswaded, as well as *State-necessity* compelled the States of *Holland* to a prudent permission of different *Consciences.*[2] And that the said *State-policie* perswaded some *Dutch* to wish that *England* might not tolerate, least a permission of Conscience in *England* should break down the *Bridge* and *Passage* into their parts of *Freedome* in causes of Conscience.

The permission of conscience in Holland.

Those prudent and prosperous *States* have gone far (though driven by *Spanish* persecution) to it) in taking off the yoak from the necks of *Dutch* & *English*, *French* yea, *Popish* & *Jewish* consciences. For all which (though but Mercy, though but Justice and humanity to fellow mankind) he that runs may read the truth of Gods never failing *Promises*, *Blessed* are the *Mercifull* for they shall obtain *Mercy*.

Gods wonderful goings in Holland *from* Stafore, *undone by Pride and unthankfulness,*

Their own *Chronicles* tells us of a wonderfull walk of the God of Heaven between three of their most eminent Towns or Cities, First *Stafore* was the wondrous Wealthy *City*, their *golden Citie*, til a proud wealthy, *Merchants widow*, caused a whole ships loading of wheat (which her ship brought home and she despised) to be thrown over into the Harbour, which (with other Accidents of water and weather, Gods most righteous providences) so choak'd up the *Haven*, that Vessels of Burthen durst never frequent that *Citie* (by this occasion) most wondrously impoverish'd since.

[1] Coxe, *House of Austria*, ii: 29; Wraxall, *Hist. of France*, ii: 129, 131.

[2] The effects of toleration upon the prosperity of Holland are well treated by Sir William Temple, in his *Observations on the Netherlands*, Works, i: 61. See also McCullagh, *Industrial History of Free Nations*, ii: 299.

To Enchuyſin, *undone by the bloody Tenent of Perſecution:*

From *Stafore God* carries all the *Shipping* and *wealth* to *Enchuyſin*, whoſe Zealous, over-zealous and furious *Clergie* provoke the *Civil Magiſtrates* to perſecute *diſſenting, non conforming conſciences:* Amongſt the reſt 'tis rare (if ever) that the moſt glorious *Son* of *God* himſelf eſcapes.

From Enchuyſin *to* Amſterdam,*raiſed to its preſent hight and glory, by mercy to the perſecuted.*

From *Enchuyſin* therefore (a Den of perſecuting *Lyons*, and mountain of *Leopards*)[1] the *perſecuted* fled to *Amſterdam*, a poor fiſhing Town, yet harborous and favourable to the *flying*, though diſſenting *conſciences:* This confluence of the perſecuted, by *Gods* moſt gracious coming with them, drew B*oats*, drew *Trade*, drew *Shipping*, and that ſo mightily in ſo ſhort a time, that *Shipping, Trading, wealth, Greatneſſe, Honour* (almoſt to aſtoniſhment in the Eyes of all *Europe*, and the *world*) have appeared to fall as out of Heaven in a Crown or Garland upon the head of that poor Fiſher Town.

Englands ſhip got into Harbour.

O ye the prime of Engliſh men and Engliſh *worthies*, whoſe *ſences* have ſo oft perceived the everlaſting Arms of the Invincible and Eternal King, when your Ships *Hold* hath been full with water, yea with *Blood*, when ſtorms without, fires and mutinies within, when ſhe hath beaten upon ſome Rocky *Hearts* and *paſſages*, as if ſhe would have ſtaved and ſplit into a thouſand pieces; yet this ſo neer ſtav'd, ſo neer fired, ſo neer ſplit, foundred, ſinking Nation, hath the *God* of *Heaven* (by your moſt valiant and carefull hands) brought ſafe to *Peace* her *Harbour*! Why now ſhould any duty poſſible be impoſſible? yea, why not impoſſibilities poſſible? Why ſhould your *Engliſh* Seas con-

[1] *Song of Solomon*, iv: 8.

Striking of Colours. tend with a neighbour *Dutchman* for the motion of a piece of *Silk,*[1] *&c.* and not ten thouſand fold much more your *Engliſh* Spirits with theirs for the Crown of that State-piety and Wiſdome which may make your faces more to *ſhine*, not only with a common luſtre after a *Dutch* Preſident, [precedent] but (if it be the holy will of God, and I humbly hope it may be) with a *glory* far tranſcending all your faireſt neighbours Copies.

The States of Holland yet to ſeek in the matters of liberty of Conſcience. The States of *Holland* having ſmarted deeply, and paid ſo dearly for the purchaſe of their freedomes, reach to the neighbour Nations and the world, a *taſt* of ſuch their dainties. And yet (with due reverence to ſo wiſe a *State*, and with due thankfulneſſe for mercy and relief to many poor oppreſſed Conſciences) I ſay their Piety nor Policie could ever yet reach ſo far, nor could they in all their School of Warre (as their Countries have been call'd) learn that one poor *Leſſon* of ſetting abſolutely the conſciences of all men free.

Touching abſolute freedome to 'Tis true, they vouchſafed to the Papiſts and Arminians the *liberty* (as I may ſo ſpeak) of the priſon, and ſometimes to go abroad (as I may ſay) with a *Keeper*, *&c.* But why ſhould not ſuch a parliament as *England* never had, (and who knows whether ever will the like) why ſhould not the piety and policie

[1] May 18, 1652, the Dutch Admiral, Van Tromp, with a fleet of forty-two veſſels came into the roadſtead at Dover, where Blake lay with a ſmaller fleet. The Dutch Admiral neglected or delayed to ſtrike his topſails and flag as England required of foreign men-of-war in its own waters. This led to a bloody engagement, which precipitated actual war between the Commonwealth and Holland. Hume, *Hiſt. of England*, vii: 220. This indicates that this work was publiſhed later in 1652 than May.

every mans conſcience impar-tially.

of ſuch *Stateſmen* out-ſhoot and teach their Neighbours, by framing a ſafe communication of freedome of *Conſcience* in worſhip, even to them to whom with good ſecurity of *Civill peace*) it is as due as to any other Conſciences or Worſhippers in the World) the *Papiſts* and *Arminians* themſelves. Of the Piety and Policie of ſuch a freedom I have diſcourſed more largely in the anſwering of ſome Objections of Mr. *Cotton* in Chapter 59. of this Book: and proved that ſuch a freedom of the Conſcience of each member of the Commonweal, and ſuch a Commonweal as *Englands* now is, eſpecially, cannot in all probability prove ſo dangerous and prejudiciall as many do imagine and diſcourſe, but contrarily many wayes prove beneficiall, and marvellouſly advantageous.

Freedome of Popiſh conſciences. *See Chap. 59, more particu-larly.*

Your Honors know what bloody bickerings and bloodſheds have been in later times in *Germany*, in the *Low-Countries*, in *France*, in *England*, in *Polonia*, in *Hungaria*, *Bohemia*, *Tranſilvania*, *&c.* about the Freedome of mens Conſciences and Worſhip?

The God of Heaven may alſo pleaſe graciouſly to remember you, that it hath been the fatall errour of all Reformers that *England* or other States have ſeen, to doe as the *Portugals* did in the *Eaſt-Indies*, who pull'd down the Images of the *Pagans* whom they conquered, and ſet up their own Images of *Portugall* in their ſtead and places.[1]

Old images puld down, and new ſet up.

[1] The Portugueſe through the great Albuquerque took poſſeſſion of Goa in 1503. It became a great focus of proſelytiſm, and hundreds of thouſands of converts were made. But ſucceſs came in a great meaſure by conformity to exiſting pagan practices. Later, the Jeſuits, and eſpecially Father Nobili, carried this to exceſs, until it was checked by the briefs of ſucceſſive Popes. Ranke, *Hiſt. of Popes*, 302; Nicolini, *Hiſt. of Jeſuits*, 96–128. See alſo Hough, *Hiſt. of Chriſtianity in India*, ii: 248; Tennent, *Chriſtianity in Ceylon*, 14, 20.

It is agreed on all hands that ſubſcribe to one God, that his worſhip is but one, and that all beſides that one true God, are idols, and all worſhip beſide his own (but one) are Images: And you know the fiery jealouſie of the *Eternall* will not ever endure an Image (though never ſo fair) his Rivall: Hence in the many former *Changes* of eſtates, and *State-worſhips* (by Gods juſt and jealous permiſſion) the childrens work hath been to tumble down their fathers buildings. Nor can your moſt prudent *Heads*, and potent *Hands* poſſibly erect that *Fabrick*, which the next *Age* (it may be the next *Parliament*) may not tumble down. And yet ſo may the God of Heaven ſo pleaſe to guide you in the high matters that concern the *worſhip* of *God*, and the *Conſciences* of men, that (what ever be the preſent or future conſequences) your own Conſciences may reap the joyfull harveſt of their preſent and eternall *Requiems*.

All Images muſt down.

The *Pope*, the *Turk*, the King of *Spain*, the *Emperour*, and the reſt of Perſecutors, build among the Eagles, aud the Starres,[1] yet while they practice violence to the Souls of *Men*, and make their *Swords* of Steele Corrivals with the two-edged Spirituall *Sword* of the Sonne of God: the *Baſis* of their *Higheſt Pillars*, the *Foundation* of their glorious *Palaces*, are but *Droſſe* and *Rottenneſſe*. And however in our poore Arithmeticke, their Kingdomes *Number* ſeem great, yet in the onely wiſe account of the Eternall, their Ages are but Minutes, and their ſhort Periods are neer accompliſhed; for herein the *Maxime* is moſt

All violent courſes

1 "Though thou exalt thyſelf as the eagle, and though thou ſet thy neſt among the ſtars, thence I will bring thee down, ſaith the Lord." *Obadiah*, 4.

true, (in the matters of Religion and Confciences of men, efpecially:) the *violent* motion muft break. *muft break.*

But *Light* from the *Father* of *Lights* hath fhined on your eyes: Mercy from the Father of Mercies hath foftned your breafts, to be tender of the tendereft part of Man, his Confcience: for indeed there is no true Reafon of *Policy or Piety* (as this Difcourfe difcovereth) why that man that will fubfcribe (and give affurance for honeft meaning) to that moft prudent Act of Civill Engagement,[1] (what ever his Confcience be) fhould be depriv'd and rob'd of the liberty of it, in *Spirituall* and *Religious* matters. *The Act for Civill Engagement of great neceffity.*

I have (I fear) been long in my firft Petition, my fecond fhall be brief, is this.

I moft humbly and earneftly befeech your *Honours* in all the ftraits and difficulties which yet you are to paffe (concerning this great point of mens *Confciences*, or other high affairs) fteere carefuly off from one funk *Rock*, on which fo many gallant Veffels have mifcarried. This *Rock* lies deeper then others, and feldom hath appeared but at fome Deadlow water, when the moft high *Judge* of the whole world reckons with Men or States, in low conditions and debafements. *The fecond Petition.*

I humbly beg from *God* the gracious continuance of his mighty *Angels guard* about your fitting, to preferve your Honours from the flames of *Wars* abroad, and from fuch flames at home: from *Rifings*,

1 This was a part of the legiflation by which the authority of the Government of the Commonwealth was to be eftablifhed. It was adopted Oct. 11, 1649, and required every fubfcriber to be "true and faithful to the Commonwealth of England, as the fame is now eftablifhed without a King or Houfe of Lords." *Parliamentary Hiftory*, iii: 1334.

Worldly wiſdome in ſtraits a moſt dangerous rock.

from *Tumults*, from *Mutinies*, from *Piſtols*, from *Stabs*, from *Powder-plots*, from *Poyſon*, *&c.* but above all, from your own *Wiſdoms* and *Policies* in ſtraits and difficulties.

The holy Hiſtory tells, that on this *Rock* (in a State ſtrait) ſtrook the great Statiſt *Jeroboam*, to the ruine of himſelf and his poſterity.

On this Rock ſplit that famous and zealous Reformer *Jehu*.

This pluckt the Crown from *Sauls* high head, when his own wiſdome in ſtraits made him preſumptuous about the worſhip of God.

This pluckt off the Crown, and pluck out the eyes of *Zedekiah*, when in a ſtrait he truſted not in God, as *Solomon* ſpeaks, but leaned to his own underſtanding for his ſafety.

The third Petition.

To which purpoſe my third Petition is, that in the midſt of ſo many great *Negotiations* of *Juſtice*, of *Mercy* to the Bodies and Eſtates, or Spirits & Conſciences of ſo many thouſands and ten thouſand, you forget not to deal *juſtly*, & to ſhew *mercy* to your ſelves: Oh how lamentable and dreadful wil it prove, if after all your high *Employments* (as the *State-Agents* & *Factors* for the *Commonweal*!) if in the midſt of all your cares and fears, and toſſings about the *Souls* and *Conſciences* and *ſalvations* of others, your own moſt dear and pretious ſelves make an *eternal ſhipwrack?*

Soul ſhipwrack.

Your *Honors* know, that although men have choſen and cull'd you out as *wiſe* and *noble*, yet *God* hath not choſen (if *Paul* ſay true) many *wiſe* and *noble* to eternall *life* and *bleſſedneſſe*.

Who can love and honor you, and not cry to the *God* of *Heaven* for you, and to your ſelves for your ſelves: Be not ſo buſie about the *Earthly* eſtate, no nor the *Heavenly* eſtate of others, as to forget to make ſure your own *vocation* and *election*, & to work out your own *ſalvation* with *fear* and *trembling*.

Oh let not this bold *cry* offend, and though offend, yet let it throughly *awake* your noble *ſpirits* to know your dangers & hindrances (more then other mens) from a world of *diſtractions* from without, from *pride* & *ſelf-confidence* from within, from the flatteries of ſuch who (hoping for rewards & morſels from you) proclaim abroad (that you may hear it) O bleſſed *Chriſtian Magiſtrates, Chriſtian Kings* & *Queens, Chriſtian States, Chriſtian Parliaments, Chriſtian Armies*, ſo lulling your pretious ſouls into an *eternall ſleep*.

Dangers of Parliament men.

I need not remember your *Honours* of that moſt wonderful *ſumma totalis* of all the caſtings up of *Solomons* choice particulars (his *wiſdom, works, riches, peace* and *pleaſures*,) *Vanity* and *vexation* of *ſpirits*. I need not remember you of that wonderfull *Confeſſion* of *Philip* the 2nd of *Spain* (neer his laſt) to his ſucceſ-
"ſor and ſon *Philip* the 3rd, to this effect: I have had
"and expended (about the time of theſe 30 years) 594.
"millions of *Treaſure*, and yet gained nothing for my
"ſelf but *heart* ſorrow, and vexation of *Spirit*.[1] Your

Wonderfull Confeſſions of two mighty Kings.

[1] Watſon, *Hiſtory of Philip II.*, 440. Gayarré, *Philip II., of Spain*, 2–11. Mr. Motley gives a detailed account of the death of Philip II. *Hiſt. of Netherlands*, iii: 503–511. He ſets a low eſtimate on what was then conſidered his enormous revenue. He ſays: "His income was eſtimated by careful contemporary ſtateſmen at what ſeemed to them the prodigious annual amount of ſixteen millions of dollars. He carried on a vaſt war without interruption during the whole of his forty-three years reign, and in ſo doing is ſaid to have expended a ſum total of ſeven hundred millions of dollars—a ſtatement which made men's hair ſtand on their heads. Yet the American Republic during its civil war

own obſervant *eyes* and *ears* (in the late moſt wonderfull changes and toſſings of all affairs and things) cannot but read a thouſand *Lectures* to your moſt ſerious midnight and morning *Thoughts* of the moſt *certain uncertainties* of Friends, Treaſures, Revenues, Armies, Forts, Magazines, Caſtles, Ships and Navies, Crowns and Lives.

True Heavenly wiſdome.

Why then ſhould your renowned *wiſdom* & *prudence* excel the folly of others as much as *light* excelleth *darkneſs*, in ſearching of the root and cauſes of *matters*, in fore-ſeeing Events and Conſequences, in raiſing Monies and Armies, in chooſing Agents, in framing Laws, in managing great affairs at home & abroad, in diſcovering *plots*, in preventing *dangers*, & finall overthrows by ſure retreats, &c. If yet, alas, that wiſdome make not out a ſaving diſcovery of the moſt holy and only wiſe, the *Alpha* & *Omega*, the firſt of *cauſes* and *laſt* of *Ends* (in whoſe hand is all your *breath* and *ways:*) in raiſing *ſpiritual ſupplies* againſt your ſpiritually devouring *adverſaries*, in diſcovering their *methods*, *deſignes*, *deceits*, in preventing that (that) fatall overthrow, and eternall defeat (*remedileſs*, *hopeleſs*) where the *worm* never dies, and the *fire* never goes out?

The onely valour or cowardize.

O why ſhould your renowned *valors* ſo glory in the conqueſt of *Cities*, *Caſtles*, *Ships* & *Armies*, if your ſelves are led captive in the ſpiritual chains of *luſts* & *paſsions*, a more lamentable, and more to be deplored object, then the pooreſt *ſlaves* in the *Spaniſh* aud *Turkiſh Gallies*.

to repreſs the inſurrection of the ſlaveholders, has ſpent nominally as large a ſum as this every year; and the Britiſh Empire in time of profound peace ſpends half as much annually." iii: 519.

What ſhall avail your admired *diligence* and *activity* in managing & quick diſpatching ſo many and ſo high *affairs*, by day and night, catching hold of all occaſions, redeeming all opportunities, improving all advantages, if you loſe the fair *Gales*, and oreſlip and ſleep away the pretious and ineſtimable ſeaſons and calls, and knocks and offers of your own eternal *Mercies?*

True and *beſt diligence.*

What boots your exemplary and impartiall *juſtice* on ſo many and ſo high *Delinquents*, if your own boſomes are found traiterous to the State of *Heaven*, rebellious to the *King*, to the *God* of *ſpirits*, and if in that moſt high Court of *Juſtice* from Gods moſt dreadful *tribunal* you hear that thunder (which oh that you may never hear) *Go ye curſed, &c.* [*Matt.* xxv: 41.]

True *Juſtice and* R*ighteouſneſs.*

'Tis true your *mercies* have been eminent to the poor, to the oppreſſed, to the captive, to the maimed, to the wounded, to the fatherleſs, widows, &c. But will you now be cruel to your ſelves, incompaſſionate to your own bowels, inſenſible of your own wounds, and miſeries? O ſearch and ſee, and be perſwaded of your infinite want of *Crummes* falling from your *Table* of *Mercy*! of the infinite *price* and *value* of the *wine* & *oyl* of the mercifull (though deſpiſed Samaritan) to eaſe and ſupple, to cleanſe and heale your broken Hearts and wounded Spirits.

Heavenly mercy.

The flames of your *Zeal* for the *God* of *Iſrael* [2 *Kings*, x: 16.] (as that famous *Iehu* ſaid) have been ſo bright, and mounted ſo high againſt two mighty Factions of the Kings and Queens (the *Prelats* & the *Popes*) that thoſe *flames* have not only dazled and amazed all

Late zealous Reformations.

Britiſh eyes (the *Engliſh* & the *Scotch*) but or'e the *Seas*, and or'e the *Alps*, and or'e the P*irenean mountains*, and *Romes* own 7 hils have flown & fild all Proteſtant and Popiſh ears, and hearts, and tongues, with either admiration & exulting, or furious rage and indignation! Yet what avails theſe glorious *flames*, and furious whirling of your zealous Chariots, if yet they are but *Jehu's?* If *Sathan* the *God* of this world poſſeſſe the Throne of *Pride* and *Oſtentation* in your boſoms (Come ſee my zeal which I have for the *God* of *Iſrael*) yea though you ſhould go on where *Jehu* left, and ſhoot home where he fell ſhort, yet what avails it that the God of *Iſrael* be in *Iehu's* mouth, when *God-ſelfe*, *God-honour*, &c. fill his breaſt & heart? What gains he by the ſlaughter of Princes, Prieſts and Gods, when *Iſrael* it ſelf is but an Apoſtate ſtate from the true worſhip of the God of *Iſrael*, and *Iehu* himſelf (according to the purity of *Gods word* and *ordinances* at *Ieruſalem*) reformed not ſo much as his *own privat heart* & *conſcience?*

Jehu his zeal and reward.

Alas, what ſolid joy (moſt zealous W*orthies*) ſhall a *Crown* of *leaves* (a temporal reward, *Iehu's* wages) bring to your Noble *Heads* & *Breaſts*, if you heare not at laſt that ſaving *Call* to all humble and ſelfe-denying *Followers* of *Jeſus*, *Come ye bleſſed* of my *Father*, inherit the *Kingdom prepared for you from the foundation of the world*. [*Matt*. xxv: 34.]

Your admired publick patience ſo wonderfully aſſaulted, ſo wonderfully loaden with ſuch mightie *Trials* from *Mans*, from *Gods* hand, with ſuch mighty *Loſſes*, mighty *Defeats*, mighty L*abours* & *Hazards*, mighty *Reproaches*, *&c*. I ſay your unwearied Patience hath ſtood (like ſome mighty *Rock*, or *Anvill*) invincible: Yet who can ſtile this *Patience*, or State-policie! if your private *Howſes* and *Breaſts* ſwell and ſwarm with rebellious Paſſions, Impatiences, Revenges! If in the furnaces of your own private afflictions, aud in the powrings out and changes of the moſt *High* upon you, your *Droſſe* and *Lees* of unmortified, unſanctified Spirits remain uncleanſed! if you moſt humbly kiſſe not the *Rods* of the moſt *High* chaſtiſing you by *ſickneſſes*, by *loſſes*, and other *trialls*, humbly thankfull, and longing to declare the Spirits of true Children, truly deſiring more and more to partake of his Divine Nature and Holineſſe?

Of the Parliaments patience.

Yea, what avails the *Crown* of your enduring Conſtancy that have rid out ſo long a *ſtorm*, held out ſo long a *ſiege*, not fainted in ſuch tedious *Travels*, *Labours*, *Oppoſitions*, *Treacheries*, *Diſcouragements*, but glorioully caſt *Anchor* in the Port of *Patience*; if yet your perſonall Righteouſneſs paſſe away as the morning dew melted with the warme beams of victorious and proſperous *Succeſs?* If your own profeſſions of *Chriſt Jeſus* prove but a fading colour, and not died in the right Grain of the pretious *blood* of the *Son* of *God*?

Of the Crown of true Conſtancy.

Your Honours well remember, that the main point of *Luthers Reformation*, (and before him of the *Huſsites* in *Germany* and *Bohemia*, and before them of the *Wickleviſts* in *England*, and before them of the W*aldenſes* in *France*, conſiſted chiefly about Repentance and Faith in the blood of *Chriſt*: That the main Contentions of *Calvin*, and ſince him of the moſt Reformers, have turn'd upon the hinge of the

The Controverſies of late years about Religion.

Form of the *Church*, and the Adminiſtrations thereof, the lamentable though pretious *Fuell* of thoſe fires of ſtrife among the wiſeſt, holieſt, and learnedſt of the Followers of *Chriſt Jeſus* in theſe times. You know the Lord *Jeſus* propheſied, That many *falſe Chriſts* ſhould ariſe, and the Scriptures more then once give the *title* of *Chriſt* to the *Church*; whence it is evident, That every ſeverall *Modell*, *Platform*, and *profeſsion* of a *Church*, is the profeſſion of a various and different *Chriſt*. Your Honours alſo know he ſpake moſt true (being *Truth* it Selfe) that ſaid, That which is moſt highly *eſteemed* amongſt men, is abomination in the ſight of *God*, *Luke* 16. [15.] Hence, ſuch may the glorious profeſſion of *Chriſts* or *Churches* be, as may raviſh the eyes and hearts of men, and from which the jealous eys of the true Lord *Jeſus* turn away as from the falſe and counterfeit with *indignation*. Beſide the *Counterfeit* in holy Scripture, how famous was the *Pageant* of that counterfeit King of *England*, which ſo haunted with long vexations one of the wiſeſt of *Englands* Kings (*Henry* the ſeventh?) How wonderfully (even to aſtoniſhment) did the impoſture of *Richard* Duke of *York* (proclaiming *Henry* an uſurper and falſe,) I ſay, how wonderfully did that monſtrous impoſture take, that not onely Foraigners where that *Counterfeit* moſt kept (the Arch-Duke, the King of *France*, the King of *Scots*, the King of *Romanes*, the *Iriſh* Nation, &c.) were deceived with that feigned King, but alſo ſo many gallant men of our own *Nation*, even to the *wiſeſt* and *higheſt* (as that famous *Stanley* Lord Chamberlain, the *Preſerver* and *Raiſer* of King *Henry* him-

So many oppoſite Churches, ſo many oppoſite Chriſts to the onely true.

The Pageant of Perken Warbeck in K. H. 7. his dayes, a picture of falſe Chriſts, or Churches.

ſelfe) lamentably loſt their *Heads* and *Lives* about that pretended King?[1] Now counterfeit *Spirituall deluſions* of falſe and counterfeit *Chriſts*, as they are *deeper* and *ſtronger*, ſo they find more eaſie *poſſeſſion* of the *Ears* and *Souls* of men, ſo wofully prepared by naturall *ſelf-deceivings*.

On ſix principall Pillars or* Foundations (ſaith the holy Spirit, *Heb.* 6. 6.) is built the fabrick of of true Chriſtianity: On R*epentance*, on *Faith*, on *Baptiſmes*, on *laying on of Hands*, on the *Reſurrection*, and the *Eternall Judgement*.

* *θεμέλιον.* *The ſix fundamentals of Chriſtian* R*eligion.* *Heb.* 6.

Concerning the two middle ones of theſe there are and have been mighty and lamentable differences among the Scholars of *Jeſus*, who yet agree in the other foure, of *Repentance* and *Faith*, the *Reſurrection* and *Eternall Judgement*.[2]

Whatſoever your Honours apprehenſions are of the

[1] Henry VII., the firſt of the Tudors, gained the throne of England on the field of Boſworth, and mainly by the defection of Lord Stanley from Richard III., who thus turned the fortunes of the day. Perkin Warbeck claimed to be Richard Plantagenet, the younger of the two ſons of Edward IV., ſuppoſed to have been murdered in the Tower of London, but whom he alleged to have eſcaped. Among thoſe accuſed of complicity with him was Stanley, "the preſerver and raiſer of King Henry himſelfe," who was arraigned for high treaſon, condemned and beheaded. Bacon, *Hiſt. of Henry VII., Works* i: 347–370. (Montague's edition.) Williams follows the partial judgment of Lord Bacon as to Henry's wiſdom, who calling him the "Solomon of England," ſays he "was one of the beſt ſort of wonders, a wonder for wiſe men." But Sir James Mackintoſh ſays, "No generoſity lent luſtre to his purpoſes; no tenderneſs ſoftened his rigid nature. His good qualities were uſeful but low; his vices were mean; and no perſon in hiſtory of ſo much underſtanding and courage is ſo near being deſpiſed. He was a man of ſhrewd diſcernment, but of a mean ſpirit and a contracted mind." *Hiſtory of England*, 205.

[2] Williams was the firſt in this country, if not indeed in England, of thoſe who have ſince been known as Six-Principle Baptiſts, who hold the impoſition of hands to be as eſſential as baptiſm for any church fellowſhip. Cf. *Bloudy Tenent*, 21; *Pub. Narr. Club*, iii: 65; *Hireling Miniſtry*, 6.

With or without the firſt two, ſalvation or no ſalvation.

foure laſt, I beſeech you (as you love your lives to *Eternity*) make ſure of the two firſt, and ply (with *Sails* and *Oars*) day and nights, and give not reſt to your ſouls till you have anchored in ſome bleſſed *aſſurance*, that although you find not ſatisfaction in the many frames of *Churches* pretending; yet that you have ſaved (as once you know a wiſe and honorable perſonage ſaid) the *Bird* in your *Boſome*: and that thoſe your very eyes which have ſeen ſo much of Chriſt Jeſus, and ſo many wonderfull changes, and have been rotten awhile in their holes (in *Death*) ſhall joyfully poſſeſſe, and fill their holes again, and be glorioufly bleſſed with the ſight of a *Redeemer*, when theſe *Heavens* and this *Earth* ſhal paſſe away. For which humbly and unceſſantly prayes

Your Honours moſt unworthy,
yet unfainedly devoted,

Roger Williams.

Your Honours (wanting time to read much) may pleaſe to view in a few minutes the *Portraicture* and *Map* of the whole *Bloody Tenent* in the latter end of the laſt Chapt. Chap. 79.

To the ſeveral Reſpective General Courts, eſpecially that of the Maſſachuſets *in* N. ENGLAND.

Honored and beloved Friends and Countreymen,

N, England Priviledge.

WHile You ſit drie on your ſafe *American Shoars* (by *Gods* moſt gracious *Providence*) and have beheld the dolefull *toſſings* of ſo many of *Europs Nations*, yea of our deareſt *Mother*, aged *England*, in a *Sea* of *Tears* and *Bloud*, I am humbly bold to preſent your E*yes* and *Hearts* with this (not unſeaſonable) diſcourſe of *Bloud*, of the *Bloudy Tenents* of *Perſecution, Oppreſſion*, and *Violence*, in the Cauſe and matters of *Conſcience* and *Religion*.

Whole Nations of Lyons or Perſecutors.

It is a Second *Conference* of *Peace* and *Truth*, an Examination of the worthily honoured and beloved Mr. *Cottons Reply* to a former *Conference* and *Treatiſe* of this Subject. And although it concern all Nations, which have perſecuted and ſhed the *Bloud* of *Jeſus*, the Bloudie *Roman Empire*, with all the *Savage Lyons* thereof, *Emperours* and *Popes*, the bloudie *Monarchies* of *Spain* and *France*, and the reſt of *Europs Kingdoms* and *States* (which under their ſeveral *Vizards* and *Pretencss* of Service to *God*, have in ſo many thouſands of his *Servants*, *Murthered* ſo many thouſand times over, his dear *Son*) yea although it concern that *Bloudie Turkiſh Monarchy*, and all the *Nations* of the *World* who practiſe *violence* to the *Conſcience* of any *Chriſtian*, or *Anti-chriſtians*, *Jews* or *Pagans*; yet it concerns your ſelves (with all due reſpect otherwiſe be it ſpoken) in ſome more eminent degrees: *Partly*, as ſo many of yours of chief note (beſide Mr. *Cotton*) are engaged in it; partly as *N. England* (in reſpect of *Spiritual* and *Civil State*) profeſſeth to draw nearer to *Chriſt Jeſus* then other *States* and *Churches*, and partly as *N. England* is believed to hold and practiſe ſuch a *Bloudie Doctrine*, notwithſtanding Mr. C*ottons Vails* and *Pretences* of not *perſecuting men for conſcience*, but puniſhing them only for ſinning againſt *conſcience*! and of but ſo and ſo, not *perſecuting*, but *puniſhing Hereticks*, *Blasphemers*, *Idolators*, *Seducers*, &c.

The Bloudy Tenent more eſpecially concerns N. E.

It is Mr. C*ottons* great *miſtake* and *forgetfulneſſe*, to charge me with a *publick examination* of his *privat Letter* to me; whereas in Truth, there never paſſed ſuch *Letters* between himſelf and me about this Subject; as he alledgeth: But the *Priſoners Arguments* againſt *Perſecution*, with Mr. *Cottons Anſwer* thereunto (which I examined) I ſay theſe were *unexpectedly*, and *ſolemnly* ſent to me, as no *privat* thing, with earneſt deſire of my *conſideration* or *Animadverſions* on them.[1]

The occaſion of the preſent controverſie.

Theſe *Agitations* between Mr. C*otton* and others, ſo ſent unto me, as alſo the *Model* of C*hurch* and C*ivil Power* by *Gods Providence* coming to hand, I

[1] This ſtatement is made more explicitly in Chapter I., *infra*.

ſay they ſeem'd to me to be of too too *Publick* a nature: And in which my ſoul not only heard the dolefull *cry* of the *ſouls* under the *Altar* to the *Lord* for *Vengeance*, but their earneſt *ſollicitations*, yea and the command of the *Lord Jeſus* for *Vindication* of their *blouds* and lives ſpilt and deſtroyed, by this *Bloudie Tenent*, though under never ſo Fair and Glorious *Shewes* and *Colours*.

This Conteſtation is not wih perſons, but againſt their bloody Doctrins and Te*nents.*

The moſt *holy* and *allſeeing* knowes how bitterly I reſent the leaſt *difference* with Mr. C*otton*, yea with the leaſt of the *followers* of *Jeſus*, of what *conſcience* or *worſhip* ſoever: How mournfully I remember this *ſtroak* (as I believe) on Mr. C*ottons* eye, and the eyes of ſo many of *Gods* precious *children* and *ſervants*, in theſe and other parts; that thoſe eyes ſo *peircing* and *heavenly* (in other holy and precious *Truths* of *God*) ſhould yet be ſo over-clouded and *bloudſhotten* in this: I grieve I muſt *conteſt*, and maintain this *conteſtation* with (in other reſpects) ſo dearly *beloved* and ſo *worthy Adverſaries*.

And yet why mention I or reſpect I man that is but *Graſs*, and the children of men that muſt *die*, whoſe *Brains*, *Eyes* and *Tongues* (even the *holyeſt* and the *higheſt*) muſt *ſhortly ſink* and *rot* in their *skuls* and *holes*.

Without remembring therefore who my *Adverſarie* is, nor all the *Wormwood* and the *Gall* ſo frequently in Mr. C*ottons* Reply againſt me; I fully and only level with an upright and *ſingle eye* (the *Lord Jeſus* graciouſly aſſiſting) againſt that fowl and monſtrous bloudie *Tenent* and *Doctrin*, which hath ſo ſlily (like the old S*erpent* the *Author* of it) crept under the ſhade and ſhelter of Mr. *Cottons* Patronage and Protection.

The *end of this* Treatiſe.

My end is to diſcover and proclaim the crying and horrible guilt of the bloudie *Doctrin*, as one of the moſt *Seditious*, *Deſtructive*, *Blaſphemous*, and *Bloudieſt* in any or in all the *Nations* of the *World*, notwithſtanding the many fine *Vails*, *Pretences* and *Colours* of not perſecuting *Chriſt Jeſus*, but *Hereticks*, not *Gods Truth* or *Servants*, but *Blaſphemers*, *Seducers*: not *Perſecuting* men for their *Conſcience*, but for ſinning againſt their *Conſcience*, *&c.*

The *cry of the Lord Jeſus.*

My end is to perſwade *Gods Judah* (eſpecially) to waſh their hands from *Bloud*, to cleanſe their hearts and wayes from ſuch *Unchriſtian practices*, toward all that is *man*, capable of a *Religion* and a *Conſcience*, but moſt of all toward *Chriſt Jeſus*, who cries out (as he did to *Saul*) in the ſufferings of the leaſt of his *Servants*: *Old England*, *Old England*, *New England*, *New England*, *King*, *King*, *Parliaments*, *Parliaments*, *General Courts*, *General Courts*, *Preſbyterians*, *Preſbyterians*, *Independents*, *Independents*, &c. Why perſecute you me? It is hard for you to kick againſt the Pricks.

My end is to prepare the *Servants* and *Witneſſes* of *Jeſus* (what *Truth* ſoever of his they teſtifie) for that *great* and *general* and moſt *dreadfull ſlaughter* of the *witneſſes*, which *I* cannot but humbly *fear*, and almoſt *believe*, is near *approaching*, and will be *Uſhered* in, *provoak'd* and *haſtned* by the *proud ſecurity*, *worldly pomp*, *fleſhly confidence*, and *bloudy violences* of *Gods* own children, wofully exerciſed each againſt other, and ſo rendred wofully *ripe* for ſuch an *Univerſal* and *dreadfull Storm* and *Tempeſt*!

My end and ſcope is to put a *Chriſtian barr*, and *juſt* and *merciful Spoaks* in the *wheels* of ſuch zealous reforming *Jehues*, who (under the *Vizard* and *Name* of *Baals Prieſts*) may poſſibly be induced to account it good *ſervice* unto *God*, to kill and burn his precious *Servants*.

A Bar againſt Perſecution.

My end is, that the greateſt *Sons* of *Bloud* (the Papiſts) may know, when ever (as the Saints in Queen *Maries* days confeſſed) when ever it ſhall pleaſe the jealous *God* for the ſins of his *Saints* to turn the *Wheels* of his moſt deep and holy *Providences*, and to give the P*ower* to the *Paw* of the *Beaſt*, againſt his *Saints* and *Truths*, for their laſt dreadfull ſlaughter (as *Daniel* and *John* do clearly ſeem to tell us)[1] I ſay thoſe *Sons* of *Bloud*, the *bloudie Papiſts*, may know, that their *bloudy Doctrin* of *perſecution*, was diſclaimed by ſome, whom they call *Sectaries*: That *equall* and *impartiall* favour was pleaded to the *Catholicks*, as wel as to their own or other mens S*ouls* and *Conſciences*: And that if that great *Whore* ſhall yet proceed not only to drink the wine of their carnal *Jollitie*, in the *Bowles* of the holy *Ordinances* of *Chriſts Temple* and *Sanctuary*; but alſo to drink more drunk in the bloud of his *Saints* and *witneſſes*! This *Teſtimony* may ſtand as a *Character* of *Bloud*, fixed by the hand of *Gods* eternal *Truth* and *Peace*, upon the *Gates*

Or a T*eſtimony againſt it, eſpecially in the Papiſts.*

[1] "Then I would know the truth of the fourth beaſt, which was diverſe from all the others, exceeding dreadful, whoſe teeth were of iron, and his nails of braſs: which devoured, brake in pieces, and ſtamped the reſidue with his feet: and of the ten horns that were in his head, and of the other which came up, &c. I beheld, and the ſame horn made war with the ſaints, and prevailed againſt them." *Daniel*, vii: 19–21.

"And when they ſhall have finiſhed their teſtimony, the beaſt that aſcendeth out of the bottomleſs pit ſhall make war againſt them, and ſhall overcome them, and kill them." *Revelation*, xi: 7.

A double priſon, of prejudice and Conſcience.

of their bloudie *Courts*, and upon the *forehead* of their bloudie *Judges*, who (under what pretence ſoever) hunt and perſecute the *Souls* and *Conſciences* of any Child of *God* or M*an*.

My truly honoured and beloved Countrimen, vouchſafe me I beſeech you that humane and Chriſtian Libertie to ſay, that I fear your *Spirits* are lock'd up in a double priſon from any ſerious *Audience* to ought of mine preſented to you. The firſt of *Prejudice* againſt *ſuch* and *ſuch* a *perſon*. The ſecond of *Conſcience*, againſt *ſuch* and *ſuch* a *matter*; and that while my *Conſcience* or another mans ſaith, Let me be *Heretick*, *Blaſphemer*, *Idolater*, *Seducer*, with *Chriſt Jeſus*, with his *Apoſtles*, *Saints* and *Witneſſes*: Let me (for his ſake) bear *Frowns*, *Cenſures*, and *Perſecutions*, from men ſo *dear*, ſo *excellent*, ſo *holy*! Your *Conſciences* plead for equall *Libertie* of *oppoſing* in your way, all ſuch erroneous or wandring *Conſciences*.

For anſwer, It is but *Humanity*, it is but *Chriſtianity* to exerciſe *meekneſſe* and *moderation* to all men: It is humane and Chriſtian *Wiſdom* to liſten to a ſerious *Alarm* againſt a *Common Enemy:* Prove the *Alarm* falſe, it may be but troubleſome: Prove it true, it may be *Deſtruction* to have *deſpiſed* it.

As the *wounds* of a *Lover* are better then the *Kiſſes* of an *Enemy*: So ſaith the ſame *Spirit*, an open *Rebuke* is better then ſecret *Love*. [*Proverbs*, xxvii: 5.]

2 Foundamentall Hints againſt Perſecution.

But yet your *Conſciences* (as all mens) muſt be ſatisfied, I have therefore in all theſe *Agitations* humbly preſented (amongſt others) two *Foundamental Hints* or Conſiderations.

Firſt that the *People* (the *Original* of all free *Power*

and *Government*) are not invefted with *Power* from *Chrift Jefus*, to rule his *Wife* or *Church*, to keep it *pure*, to punifh *Oppofites* by force of *Armes*, &c.

Secondly, that the *Pattern* of the *National Church* of *Ifrael*, was a *None-fuch*, unimitable by any *Civil State*, in all or any of the *Nations* of the *World* befide: In this latter hint I infifted more largely in my former *Confiderations* upon *Church* and *Civil Power* in *N. E.*[1] unto which Mr. *Cotton* replyed not (and of any other *Replyes* of any (to whom Mr. *Cotton* refers it) do I yet not know of:)

I Add, it is a glorious C*haracter* of every true *Difciple* or *Scholler*[2] of C*hrift Jefus*, to be never too *old* to *learn*.

It is the C*ommand* of C*hrift Jefus* to his *Schollars*, to try all things: And *Libertie* of trying what a *Friend*, yea what an (efteemed) *Enemie* prefents, hath ever (in point of C*hriftianity*) proved one efpeciall means of attaining to the *truth* of C*hrift*.

For I dare confidently *appeal* to the *confciences* of *Gods* moft *knowing fervants*, if that *obfervation* be not true, to wit, that it hath been the common way of the *Father* of *Lights*, to inclofe the *Light* of his holy *Truths*, in dark and obfcure, yea and ordinarily in *forbidden Books*, *perfons* and *Meetings*, by Sathan ftiled Conventicles.

Libertie of trying forbidden Books, &c.

New Englifh Voyages, have taught moft of our *Old*

[1] *Bloudy Tenent*, Chap. cx–cxii. *Pub. Narr. Club*, iii: 317–324.

[2] "Firft, as to the name *Schollar*, although as to *humane learning*, many wayes lawfull, yet as it is appropriated to fuch as practife the Miniftry have been at the *Univerfitie* (as they fay) It is a *facrilegious* and theevifh title, robbing all *beleevers* and *Saints*, who are frequently in the Teftament of Chrift, ftiled Difciples or Schollars of Chrift Jefus, and only they as Beleevers." *Hireling Miniftry*, 14.

Engliſh ſpirits, how to put due prices upon the moſt *common* and ordinary *undervalued mercies*; how precious with ſome hath been a little *water?* how dainty with others a piece of *bread*: How welcome to ſome the pooreſt *howſing?* Yea the very *Land* and *Earth*, after long and tedious paſſages?

New Englands Leſſons.

There is one *commoditie* for the ſake of which moſt of *Gods children* in *N. England* have run their mighty *hazards*; a *commoditie* marvellouſly *ſcarce* in former times (though in ſome late years by *Gods* moſt gracious and mighty hand more *plentifull*) in our *native* Countrey: It is a *Libertie* of ſearching after Gods moſt holy *mind* and *pleaſure*.

Out of this moſt precious and invaluable *Jewel*, if you ſuffer Sa*than* (that grand *thief* and *cheater* to bereave you, and that it ſhall be a *crime*, humbly and peaceably to queſtion even *Lawes* and S*tatutes*, or what ever is even publickly taught and delivered, you will moſt certainly find your ſelves after all your long *Run* (like that little *Frenchman* who kill'd the *Duke* of *Guiſe*, and was taken next morning neare the place from whence he had fled upon a ſwift horſe all night)[1] I ſay you will moſt certainly find your ſelves, but where you were, *enſlav'd* and *captivated* in the C*hains* of thoſe *Popiſh Darkneſſes*, [to wit, *Ignorance* is the *mother* of *Devotion*, and we muſt believe as the C*hurch* believes, &c.]

Liberty of ſearching out Truth, hardly got, and as hardly kept.

Jan le petit.

Remember therefore (O ye the C*ream* and *Flower* of *Engliſh* Plantations in *America*) what a black and

[1] Francis, Duke of Guiſe, was killed before Orleans by Jean de Poltrot, or Poltrot de Merey, a Huguenot, February 24, 1563. The aſſaſſin on a ſwift horſe eſcaped to the neighboring woods, and after wandering all night was apprehended the next morning. Davila, *Civil Wars of France*, i: 148.

direfull a *cole* it was with which it pleaſed the Spirit of *God* in *Habacuck*, to brand the *Aſſirian* Monarchie, to wit [a *Bitter* and *haſtie Nation*][1] but in the *ſpirit* of *meekneſſe*, in the *meekneſſe* of *wiſdom*, be pleaſed to remember that poſſible it is for *Gods viſible*, only people in the *world* to have very foul and bloudie hands, full of *Bloud* (*Iſa.* 1.)! [15.] To build up *Zion* and *Jeruſalem* (that is, to erect the *Viſible Church* and *Kingdom* of *God*) with *Bloud* (*Mic.* 3.) [10.] and with *Iniquitie*: That the *Heads* and *Judges* of *Gods People*, may judge for a *reward* (and the deceitfull heart of man graſpeth at *rewards* more then of one ſort) that the *Prieſts* and *Prophets* thereof may *teach* and *Propheſie* (and it may be frequently and excellently, but yet for) an *hire* and for *money*; And that yet their *conſciences* may lean upon *Jehovah*, and they may ſay with *confidence*, is not the *Lord* amongſt us? None evil ſhall come unto us; &c. O remember that your *Gifts* are rare, your Profeſſions of *Religion* (in ſuch way) rare, your Perſecutions and hidings from the ſtorms abroad, rare and wonderfull: So in proportion your Tranſgreſſions, eſtate and publick ſins cannot but be of a rare and extraordinary *Guilt*: Nor will *New England's* ſorrowes (when ſins are *ripe* and *full*) be other then the *Dregs* of *Germanie's*, of *Ireland's*, of *England's*, and of *Scotland's* Tears and Calamities.

The wonderfull deceitfulneſſe of the hearts of Gods only people.

Mic. 3. [11.]

N. England muſt be ſingular as in Mercies, ſo in Judgments.

Amongſt the crying ſins of our own or other ſinfull Nations: thoſe two are ever amongſt the lowdeſt, to wit, *Invented Devotions* to the *God* of *Heaven*. Secondly, *Violence* and *Oppreſſion* on the Sons of men

[1] "For lo, I raiſe up the Chaldeans, that bitter and haſty nation." *Habakkuk*, i: 6.

2 of the loudeſt State-crying ſins.

(eſpecially (if his ſons) for diſſenting, and againſt both theſe, and that the *impartial* and *dreadfull hand* of the moſt holy and *Jealous God* (a *conſuming fire*) tear and burn not up at laſt the Roots of theſe Plantations, but graciouſly diſcovering the Plants which are not his, he may graciouſly fructifie and cauſe to flouriſh what his *Right hand* will own: I ſay this is the humble and and unfeigned deſire and cry (at the *Throne* of *Grace*) of your ſo long deſpiſed Out-caſt:

ROGER WILLIAMS.

To the Merciful and Compaſsinate READÆR.

WHile the unmercifull *Prieſts* and *Levits* turn away their cruel *Eyes* and *Feet* from their poor wounded *neighbours* (the oppreſſed for matters of *Religion* and *Worſhip*) it will be no ingratefull act to preſent thy tender *heart* and *Ear* (*Compaſſionate Samaritane*) with the dolefull cry of the *Souls* under the *Altar* [How long *Lord* before thou avenge our bloud on them that dwell upon the Earth][1] and to pray thy mournfull view of the *Akeldemae's* and *fields* of *Blood*, where thouſands and ten thouſand times ten thouſands of the pretious *Saints* (*Servants* and *Witneſſes* of *Jeſus*) lie ſlaughtered in their bloudie Gore, in all *Ages* and in all *Nations*, where the *Trumpet* of the *Son* of *God* hath ſounded: *Soul wounds, the deepeſt.*

Here and there among theſe ſlaughtered heaps of *Saints* lie (thin and rare) the ſlaughtered Carkaſſes of ſome poor *Arrians* or *Papiſts*, or other poor *delud-*

1 "I ſaw under the altar the ſouls of them that were ſlain for the word of God, and for the teſtimony which they held: and they cried with a loud voice, ſaying, How long, O Lord, holy and true, doſt thou not judge and avenge our blood on them that dwell on the earth?" *Revelation*, vi: 9, 10.

The Akeldamaes, or fields of Bloud, caused by the Bloudy Tenent of Persecution.

ing and *deluded ſouls*: This ſeeming colour of Impartiall *Juſtice* ſerves (wofully) that *murtherous enemy* of all *Mankind* for a *Stale*[1] or *Covert* under which his *bloudie Game* goes on, of perſecuting (or hunting) the harmleſs *Deer*, the children of the living God.

For the ſake then of the dear *Saints* and *Followers* of *Jeſus*, for his holy ſake and *Truth*, for the holy name and *Truth* of the moſt holy *Father* of *Lights*, the *God* of it, thy compaſſionate eye is here preſented with a Second *Conference* and *view* of Mr. *Cottons Reply*, and artificial bloudie waſhing of the *Bloudie Tenent*.

Michael, the ſon of God, and Sathan the red Dragon, the two great Generals.

The *Battel* about any *Truth* of *God* in *Chriſt*, is fought and managed by that moſt high and glorious *Michael* the *Arch-Angel* and *Son* of *God*, attended with all his *Holy Angels*, the *Meſſengers* and *Witneſſes* of his Truth on the one ſide: On the other ſide by that great red *Dragon*,[2] whoſe bloudie *Followers*, Devils and men of all ſorts and Nations, but eſpecially the *Roman* bloudie *Emperor*, and *Roman Popes* (with *Lyon*-like *Furie*, and *Fox*-like craft) have ſuck'd the *Bloud* and broke the *Bones*, and devoured the *Fleſh* of ſo many hundred thouſand, thouſands of the *King* of *Kings* his ſpiritual *Hinds* and R*oes*[3] in this their bloudie hunting: So that *aptly* (I had almoſt ſaid *Prophetically*) wrote one of their own R*oman Poets* of the lamentable condition of the *harmleſſe Deer* above other Creatures: *Dente tuetur Aper*,

[1] A decoy.
"Still as he went, he craftie *ſtales* did lay,
With cunning traynes him to entrap unwares."—Spenſer, *Færie Queene*, B. II., C. I., § 4.

[2] "There was war in heaven: Michael and his angels fought againſt the dragon; and the dragon fought and his angels and prevailed not." *Revelation*, xii: 7.

[3] *Song of Solomon*, ii: 7.

defendunt, Cornua Taurum, Imbelles Damæ quid nisi Præda sumus?[1]

'Tis a lamentable and cruell sight to see the sons of one poor man and woman, (all the Globe of the world over (like *Babels* builders) so vastly disagreeing about a *God* and his *Worship.*

'Tis lamentable to see these one *Mans* sons *Murthered* and *Massacred* (in mutual slaughters) as for other pretended *Causes*: So this especially of *Conscience* and *Religion.*

'Tis yet more *lamentable* and never enough to be lamented, that while the *Sons* of *Men* do but their *kind*! the *Sons* of *God*, the *sons* of the *God* of *Peace*, the *Lillies*, *Doves* and *Spouses* of *Jesus* should thus discord and jarr about this *Christ* their *hope*! that (like the very *Turks* and *Persians* contending about their *Mahomet* his *Successors*) the Children of *God* should tear out each others Throats about the last *Will* and *Testament* of the *Son* of God their elder brother: That *Ephraim* should be against *Manasseh*, and *Manasseh* against *Ephraim*, and both against *Judah*;[2] yet all sons of one, and professors of one *God* of *Israel.*

Lamentable discords about Religion, even among the servants of the true and living God.

But oh the low and shallow comprehensions of the sons of men, who as a *Rotten thing* (saith *Job*) [xiii. 28.] consumeth: Oh the *depths* of the *Councels* and

[1] Dente timentur apri; defendunt cornua cervos:
Imbelles damæ quid, nisi præda, sumus?—Martial, *Epigr.* Lib. xiii: 94.

"The tusk, the Boar: Harts, horns defend, to all
We naked Does, prey undefended, fall."
Wright, *Bohn's Martial*, p. 600.

[2] "They shall eat every man the flesh of his own arm: Manasseh, Ephraim; and Ephraim, Manasseh; and they together shall be against Judah." *Isaiah*, ix: 20, 21.

The Israelites divided. *workings* of the most *High*, most *Holy*, and only *wise*, outshooting all the *Generations* of men, who hear and know no more then *Jonathans* Lad, Is not the Arrow beyond thee? &c. [1 *Samuel*, xx: 37.]

His holy *Wisdom* hath an heavenly *Reason* (to touch a little upon this *sorrowfull string*) of that bloudie D*evice* and *Sale* of innocent *Joseph* by his own *Brethren*, the sons of one *Israel* and *God*. [*Genesis*, xxxvii: 18–28.] *Joseph sold by his brethren.*

He knowes why so holy a *Leader* of such a *miraculous People* (as I may truly call them) why *Aaron* (I say) was so left to the horrible, ungratefull, and outragious importunities of this (then the only) People of *God*, as to frame a *Beastly worship*, and to turn the most glorious and dreadfull *Godhead* into the similitude of a *Beast* that eateth grasse. [*Exodus*, xxxii: 1–6.] *Israel force Aaron to make them Gods.*

He knowes why the *Israel* of *God*) *Rebels*, as *Moses* passionately called them) should so often grieve the holy *Spirit* of *God* with their *murmurings*, and be so near to dash out the brains of their most faithfull *Leaders*. [*Numbers*, xiv: 1–5; xvi: 41.] *Israels murmurings.*

He knowes why two Parts or *Angles* of that Heavenly *Triangle* (*Moses*, *Aaron*, and *Miriam* so neer in *Earthly* and *Heavenly Relations*) I say why that rare Pair, *Aaron* and M*iriam* should yet envie and mutiny against their so dear a *Brother*, and so meek and heavenly a *Ruler*, M*oses*. [*Numbers*, xii.] *Aaron and Miriam against Moses.*

His heavenly wisdom hath a reason of that wonderfull Shrinking of an *Army* of 32 thousand *Israelits*, into one poor 300 left behind, and found only fit for *Gods battels* against the M*idianits*. [*Judges*, vi.–vii.] *An Armie of 32000 Israelites shrunk into 300.*

Samſon and David diſcouraged by their own brethren.

A reaſon why thoſe two famous *Champions, Samſon* and D*avid* ſhould find ſo great diſcouragement to their fighting of *Gods Battels,* the men of *Judah* baſely binding *Samſon,* and the chief of D*avids* own *Brethren* flying in his face with open Railings. [*Judges* xv : 9–13 ; 1 *Samuel,* xvii : 28.]

Benjamin almoſt deſtroyed by the 11 *Tribes.*

A reaſon of that all moſt utter conſumption of one whole *Tribe* of *Iſraels* 12. by the furious flames of the *Zeal* and *Indignation* of the eleven. [*Judges,* xx.]

Iſraels rejecting of Samuel & the Lord himſelf.

Theſe things happened not by *chance,* but as the *Apoſtle* ſpeaks in *Types* (in curious and wonderfull *figures*) ſo that his holy wiſdom knowes : why *Iſrael* muſt be ſo weary of *Samuel* and himſelf, and (like the *Nations* of the *World*) muſt have a *King* to be their C*hampion* and fight their *Battels* : [1 *Samuel,* viii.]

Saul perſecuting David.

Why *Saul* this deſired *King,* the *King* of *Gods* own *choice* and *Iſraels,* why yet he muſt hunt an innocent D*avid,* as a *Flea* in the boſom, or a *Partridg* on the mountains, until he hath ſlain himſelf to ſet the *Crown* on D*avids* head. [1 *Samuel,* xxvi : 20.]

Iſhboſheth and Iſrael againſt David and Judah.

A reaſon of that long continued *Faction* of ſo many *Tribes* againſt this D*avids* Crown, and that *Iſrael* (ſo importunate, ſo impatient for a *King*) ſhould now powre out each others blood about a *Succeſſor,* whether a D*avid,* or (the ſon of *Perſecution, Saul*) *Iſhboſheth.* [2 *Samuel,* ii.–iv.]

David ſtabbing Uriah with his Pen.

A reaſon (when D*avid* wears both Crowns in one, and hath all that a moſt *gracious God* could eſpie out fit for D*avid* to receive, that yet he wants a wife that had ſo many, and rather then a D*avids* ſinfull Deſires and Whoredomes ſhall want a Covering, the blood of *Uriah* (that is *fire* or *zeal* of *God*) ſhall die and make up one to cover them. [2 *Samuel*, xi: 15.]

The diviſ-ions & diſ-perſions of the Tribes.

O the D*epths* of the *Councels* of the holy one of *Iſrael* why (there being but 12 *Tribes* in all) 10 *Tribes* of his own people ſhould tear away from 2, and after many *Captivities* of the one and the other, both the one and the other now are ſcattered from each other upon the face of the Earth, and as yet no certain *Tidings* what's befaln to the 10 Tribes of the *Iſrael* of God. [1 *Kings*, xii: 16–20; 2 *Kings*, xviii: 9–12.]

Aſa impriſ-oning the Prophet.

He knowes why to leave an upright perfect *Aſae's heart* to ſuch *folly* and *wrath*, as to lay a Faithfull *Prophet* (admoniſhing him from God) by the heels. [2 *Chronicles*, xvi: 7–10.]

Chriſts Diſciples deſirous of fire from heaven, &c.

Yea, why the *Followers* of the meek *Lamb* of *God*, ſhould burn in ſuch *Unchriſtian Flames*, as to call for fire from *Heaven* to conſume the *contemners* and *deſpiſers* of their *Lord* and *Maſter*, who quencheth the fire of their raſh *zeal* with this mild *Check*, You know not of what *Spirit* you are of. [*Luke*, ix: 54–55.]

Bitterneſs between Saul and Barnabas.

Why ſuch πιχρια (*Bitterneſſe* as the Word is) ſhould riſe between two *Turtle* D*oves*, *Paul* and *Barnabas*, and that about their moſt laborious and moſt dangerous *Miniſteries*. [*Acts*, xvi: 39.]

Why one cries *Paul*, another *Apollo*, another *Cephas*, another C*hriſt*, even in the firſt eſtabliſhed *Churches*. [1 *Cor.*, i: 12.]

This holy *Plot*, this heavenly *deſigne* of the moſt holy and only wiſe G*od*, thus to permit the *contentions* and *diviſions* of his own *Servants*, as it diſplaies

Himſelf only Perfect and *Excellent*, and all (the beſt of) men in all *Ages*, but *farthing-candles*, yea *ſmoaking Firebrands:* As it brightly proves the admirable conſent and *Angelical Harmony* of the holy *Scripture*, relating *Hiſtories*, and in thoſe *Hiſtories* infolding *Propheſies*, fulfill'd before mens daily view thouſands of years after: As it makes us ſee our ſpiritual *Povertie* and *Beggary*, and infinit need of *Mercy* and *Grace*, and *Peace* from *Heaven*, and drives us to continual *Prayers* and *cries*, for mercifull ſupplies from thence! As it diſreliſheth this preſent ſweeteſt life, yea the very life of *Spiritual Love*, in the Communion of the Saints of *God* themſelves, if compared with the moſt pure and ſpiritual and abſolute *Joyes* and *Life* approaching.

Gods mercy drawes out many ſweet fruits from the bitter contentions of his ſervants.

So doth this heavenly *Councel* of the moſt *High*, aboundantly ſtop the mouths of all *malicious*, who (although they delight to ſcratch their *Athenian Itch* of hearing *Novelties*,[1] *new things*, *Newes*, yet) ſtumble they at this ſtumbling-block of *Novelties*, *new Churches*, *new Miniſters*, *new Diſcipline*, *new Baptiſm*, *new Light:* The ancient of days (ſay they) the *God* of *Peace* and *Love* cannot be in ſuch *Diviſions*: The old Biſhops were better, the old Popes themſelves more tolerable.

But this is but the barking of *malice* againſt *Gods* holyneſs which his true ſervants deſire to partake of! Againſt *Gods Truth*, which his ſervants muſt contend for, (yea though it be one againſt another) againſt *Gods Councels* who hath ſo laid his holy *pro-*

[1] "Having itching ears." 2 *Tim.* iv: 3. "For all the Athenians ſpent their time in nothing elſe, but either to tell or to hear ſome new thing." *Acts*, xvii: 21.

ject, that what he now ſets out in a clear *Light* and fairer *Print*, is the very ſame (had we inlightned eyes to ſee it (with the old *edition* of former times, more dark and rude in *Ceremonies*, *Types*, and figures.

Various affections of Readers expected.

I cannot but foreſee *variety* of divers *Paſſions* and *Affections*, in a *Variety* of *Beholders* of this preſent *Controverſie*: Some will pleaſe themſelves and their *curioſities* in the *Noveltie* of ſuch diſcourſes: ſome will rejoice to ſee the light appear, and yet mourn in the lamentable differences of ſuch who profeſs the ſame *God* and *Chriſt* about it: Some will be angry and cry out of *Blaſphemy* againſt their *Gods*, their *Bellies*, and their *Titles*, &c. Some will fear diſturbances of the *Civil*, and ſome of the *Spiritual peace* and *Chriſtianity*: Yet ſome will truely deſire to ſearch and know the will of *God*, humbly deſirous to do it on earth, as the Angels doe it in heaven.

The Model of N. Engliſh Church and Civil Power.

The *Courteous Reader* may pleaſe to ſee, that in the firſt Conference of Peace and Truth, there was Diſcuſt, a Modell of *New Engliſh* Church and Civill Power, which Mr. *Cotton* in his Reply waved and referred to others of the *New Engliſh* Elders to Reply unto, which whether they have ſo done as yet I have not heard:

Of Mr. Cottons Reply to the Anſwer to his Letter.

Together with Mr. C*ottons* Reply to the *Bloudy Tenent*, there was alſo added a Reply of Mr. C*otton* to an Anſwer of his Letter: The Examination of this Reply I deſired, and intended ſhould have been here preſented; But the ſtreights of time (being conſtantly drunk up by neceſſary Labours for bread for many depending on me, the diſcharge of Engagements, and wanting helps of tranſcribing) I ſay the ſtreights of time were ſuch, that the Examination of that Reply could not together with this, be fitted for Publick view, though with the Lords aſſiſtance will not delay to follow.[1]

Touching Mr. *Cotton* I preſent two words: Firſt for his Perſon, Secondly for his Work.

For his Perſon, although I rejoyce that ſince it pleaſed *God* to lay a *Command* on my *Conſcience* to come in as his poor Witneſſe in this great Cauſe: I ſay I rejoice it hath pleaſed him to appoint ſo able, and excellent, and Conſcionable an Inſtrument to bolt out the Truth to the bran: So I can humbly ſay it in his holy preſence, it is my conſtant heavineſs and ſouls grief as to differ from any fearing *God*; ſo much more ten thouſand times from Mr. *Cotton*, whom I have ever deſired and ſtill deſire highly to eſteem, and dearly to reſpect, for ſo great a portion of mercy and grace vouchſafed unto him, and ſo many Truths of *Chriſt Ieſus* maintained by him. And therefore (notwithſtanding that ſome (of no common Judgement and reſpect to him, have ſaid, that he wrote his waſhing of the *Bloudie Tenent* in *Bloud* againſt *Chriſt Ieſus*, and Gall againſt me, yet) if upon ſo ſlippery and narrow a paſſage I have ſlpit [ſlipt] (notwithſtanding my conſtant reſolution to the contrary) into any *Tearm* or *Expreſſion* unbeſeeming his Perſon, or the Matter (the cauſe of the moſt high in

Gods wiſdom adored in the Diſcuſſing of the Bloudie Tenent.

[1] The *Reply to Mr. Williams his Examination, &c.*, was printed in the ſame volume with *The Bloudy Tenent Waſhed*, with ſeparate paging. It is reprinted in *Pub. Narr. Club*, ii. Williams's intention to publiſh an "Examination of that Reply" was probably never carried out. It may have been arreſted by Cotton's death, which took place Dec. 23, 1652, not long after the iſſue of this book.

The error in the title at the top of this page will be noticed.

hand confidered) I humbly crave pardon of G*od*, and Mr. C*otton* alfo.

A memorable Speech touching Mr. Cotton.

Secondly concerning his Work, I call to mind a fpeech of one of eminent Note in *N. England* (obferving a difpofition in men for one man to deifie another, and that fome of no fmall note had faid they could hardly believe that G*od* would fuffer Mr. *Cotton* to err) the Speech was this [I fear that G*od* may leave Mr. C*otton* to fome great error, that men may fee he is a man] &c.

But concerning his Work, the obfervant Reader will foon difcover, that whatever Mr. C*ottons* Stand is, yet he moft weakly provides himfelf of very ftrange Referves, and Retreats*:* to point with the finger at 2 or 3 moft frequent and remarkable.

The ftrange retreats Mr. Cotton makes in this controverfie.

Firft when he feems to be overwhelmed with the lamentable and doleful cries of the Souls under the *Altar*, crying out for *Vengeance* on their *Perfecutors* that dwell upon Earth! He often retreats, and profeffeth to hold no fuch Doctrin of perfecuting the *Saints*, no nor of any for caufe of Confcience, nor that the Magiftrate fhould draw forth his Sword in matters of R*eligion*.

The roaring of Lyon like perfecution, pag.

When it is urged that through this whole Book he Perfecutes or Hunts (by name) the *Idolater*, the *Blafphemer*, the *Heretick*, the *Seducer*, and that to Death or Banifhment: and amongft other Expreffions ufeth this for one [If there be ftones in the ftreets, the Magiftrate need not run for a Sword to the Smiths fhop, nor to the Ropier for an Halter to punifh *Hereticks,*[1] &c.] Mr. C*otton* retreats into the

[1] *Bloudy Tenent Wafhed,* Chapter 68, p. 156.

Land of *Iſrael,* and calls up M*oſes* and his Laws againſt *Idolaters, Blaſphemers, Seducers,* &c.

When he is Challenged (and that by his own frequent confeſſion in his Book) for producing the Pattern of a *National* C*hurch* when he ſtands only for a Congregationall! for producing that national church of *Iſrael,* ſo miraculous, ſo typical, as a Copie or Samplar for the Nations and Peoples of the World (who have no ſuch miraculous and Typicall reſpect upon them) Mr. C*otton* retreats to M*oral Equity,* that the *Seducer* and he that kills a Soul ſhould die.

When it is urged that C*hriſt Ieſus* at his ſo long typed out coming, aboliſhed thoſe *National ſhadowes,* and erected his *Spiritual Kingdom* of I*ſrael,* appinted Spiritual Officers, Puniſhments, &c. and that thoſe Scriptures, *Tit.* 3. [10.] againſt the *Hereticks*; and *Rev.* 2. [14. 20.] againſt *Baalam* and *Iezabel* prove only a ſpiritual death and cutting off from Chriſt Jeſus his holy land of life and peace, his church & kingdom.

The ſtrange reluctancies of the Lamb like ſpirit of Mr. Cotton forced to againſt the Perſecuting Lyon.

Mr. C*otton* retreats and confeſſeth Chriſts Kingdon is ſpiritual, not national, but congregational, and that thoſe Scriptures hold forth a Spiritual cutting off, and he ſo produceth them to prove the *heretick* ſo to be cut off, alledging that the queſtion was put in general tearms, that he knew not what Perſecutution ſhould be intended, and that an unjuſt excommunication is as ſore a perſecution as an unjuſt baniſhment. When he is urged with the nature of the conſciences (even of all men to God or Gods in their worſhips, he profeſſeth that he is wronged, & that he doth not hold that any man ſhould be perſecuted for his conſcience, but for ſinning againſt his conſcience. When al the conſciences in the world cry out againſt him for ſetting up the *civil power* & *officers*, and Courts of *civill Iuſtice*, to judg of the *conviction* of mens *ſouls* and *conſciences*! Mr. Cotton retreats to his laſt refuge, and ſaith that although this be the duty of all the Magiſtrates in the *world*, yet not any of them muſt meddle to puniſh in *Religion*, untill they be informed which is (upon the point) untill he is ſure they will draw their ſwords for his Conſcience, Church, &c. againſt all other as heretical, blaſphemous.[1]

Monſtrous partiality, as touching the Magiſtracy.

The monſtrous *Partiality* of ſuch *ſuſpending*, &c. of *hanging* up all the Magiſtrates in the world, (except a few of his own *perſwaſion*) and that from ſo *principall* and *main* a part of their *Office*, and that ſo many *thouſands* in the *Nations* of the *world* all the *world* over, and that *conſtantly* and *perpetually* all their dayes. If it pleaſe the moſt *jealous* and righteous God to hide it (I ſay the *monſtrouſneſſe* of ſuch a *Suſpenſion*) from Mr. *Cottons* eyes, yet *thouſand* and *ten thouſands* will behold and wonder at it.

But (fearing to exceed in diſcourſe at [the] *dore*) let every mercifull and compaſſionate *Reader* freely enter in, and ſearch the inmoſt *Rooms* and *Cloſets*.

The ſlaughter of the Witneſſes, Revel. 2. 10. [13. 5]

If thou truly love the *Truth* and *Peace*, thou art too neer of kin to the *Prince* of *Peace* and *Truth* it ſelf, long to eſcape the *Hunters*. If the *fourty two moneths* of the *Beaſts reign*, and the *two hundred and threeſcore dayes* of the *propheſie* of the *Witneſſes* of *Jeſus* in *Sackcloth* be expired: yet I fear the three dayes and a halfe of the greateſt *ſlaughter* of the *Wit-*

[1] *The Bloudy Tenent Waſhed,* Chaps. xiii. lv.

neſſes is not over: Yet fear not what muſt be ſuffered, although the Devill caſt (not onely ſome, but) all *Chriſts Witneſſes* into *Priſon*: yea, although he murther and fling out the *Karkaſſes* of the Saints to *ſhame* and *injury*, yet the mighty *Spirit* of *God* will raiſe them on their feet again, and into heavenly *glory*, out of this ſhame ſhall they aſcend in the ſight of their bloody enemies.

How many and how various are the *Diſputings*, *&c.* about what ſhould be this *three dayes* and a *halfes calamity*? How many hope this ſtorm is over? how many fear it is now a breeding? Yet why ſhould we fear ſo ſhort a draught (though) of a bitter *Cup*, when tempered by the gracious hand of an Heavenly Father, begun by ſo dear an *Elder Brother*, ſo ſweet a *Saviour*? The *Revelations* of *John*, and the *Revelations* of *Gods* wonderfull *Providences*, ſeem to proclaim wonderfull and dreadfull *Diſcoveries* of the Son of God approaching. And it is as ſure as that there is a Lord *Jeſus Chriſt*, that God will ſubdue all his enemies, that he will ſhortly break (and make all his *followers* tread on) the proudeſt *Necks* born up this day in the world, even the grandeſt *Seigniories* of the *Turkiſh* and *Popiſh* Empires, the two ſo mighty oppoſers of the Son of *God*. And it is not improbable, both their *ruines* and *downfall* muſt be from ſome *top* and *pinacle* of glorious *proſperity* and furious outrage againſt their (Antichriſtian and Chriſtian) enemies.

Chriſt Jeſus ſhortly ruining the two dreadfull Empires of the bloody Turk and Pope.

The chiefeſt *European enemies* of the All devouring *Turk* (though all that bear the name of *Chriſt* are his enemies) are more eſpecially the *Pope*, the *Emperour*, the King of *Spain* and the *Venetians*, by

The Turks foreſt enemies in Euope.

whom *Christ Jesus* (probably) will dash that mighty *Empire* into pieces, as he seems to have prophesied of old by his servant *Daniel*: yet probably, as I said before, this *downfall* must be from some more eminent height of *Turkish* bloody *pride* and *glory*, which that blasphemous and bloody Monarchy shall immediately before attain unto.

The Popes forest enemies.

The forest enemies of the *Roman Popes*, are the *witnesses* of the *Truths* of *Jesus*, whom he hath not left himself without, during the 42 *moneths* of the *reign* of this mighty and dreadfull *Beast*. Against these blessed *followers* of the *Lamb* must (probably) the rage of this bloody *Beast* rise high in that his great *slaughter* of them and *triumph* three days and an half over them, (*Rev.* 11.) [9. 11.] and this not long before his own *eternall downfall.*

Many have been the *Interpretations* of that prophesie, and some late *Applications* of the *witnesses* and Time to particular *persons* and *Times* of late. But (with all due respect to the *Apprehensions* of any studious of the truth of *Jesus*) I conceive the matter is of a more *generall consideration.*

For in all that *world* over that wondred after the *Beast*, hath *Christ Jesus* raised up a *Generation* or kind of *Witnesses* bearing *testimony* against him. This *witnesse* (more or lesse) to the severall *Truths* of *Jesus*, he hath been pleased to maintain, before and since *Luthers* time, especially: The *finishing* of the *Testimony* must (probably) be *generall*, not only in *England*, but in the rest of the *Protestant Nations*; which *finishing* of the *witnesse* (probably) wil consist in the matters of the *purity* of his *worship*, and the *Govern-*

ment of the *Lord Jesus* in his own holy Appointments and Institutions. The *slaughter* of these *witnesses* must also (probably) be *generall,* and in the three dayes and half *triumph* over them *generall*: upon which follows that most glorious and *generall* rising of the *witnesses* unto their *glory* promised, *Rev.* 11. [11. 12.]

I confess in this plea for *freedom* to all *Consciences* in *matters* (meerly) of *worship,* I have impartially pleaded for the *freedom* of the *consciences* of the *Papists* themselves, the greatest *enemies* and *persecutors* (in *Europe*) of the *Saints* and *Truths* of *Jesus*: Yet I have pleaded for no more then is their *due* and *right,* and (what ever else shall be the *Consequent*) it shall stand for a *monument* and *testimony* against them, and be an *aggravation* of their former, present, or future *cruelties* against *Christ Jesus* the *Head,* and all that uprightly love him, his true *Disciples* and *Followers.*

Freedome of Conscience in worship due even to the Papists themselvs. See Chap.

It is true, I have not *satisfaction* in the clear discovery of those holy *Prophesies* & *Periods* set down and prefixed by the holy *Spirit* in *Daniel, John, &c.* concerning the *Kingdom* of *Christ Jesus*: Yet two things I professe in the holy presence of *God, Angels* and *Men.*

First, my humble *Desires* and *Resolution* (the Lord assisting) to *contend* for the true and *visible worship* of the true and living *God,* according to the *Institution* and *Appointment* of the last will and *Testament* of *Christ Jesus.*

2. I beleeve and profess, that such *persons,* such *Churches* are got neerest to *Christ Jesus,* on whose *forehead* are written these blessed characters of the

true *Lord Jesus Christ*; First, *content* with a poor and low condition in worldly things. 2. An holy *cleansing* from the *filthines* of *false worships* and *worldly conversations*. 3. An humble and constant *endeavour* to attain (in their *simplicity* & *purity*) to the *Ordinances* and *appointments* of *Christ Iesus*. 4. Are so far from smiting, killing, and wounding the *Opposites* of their *profession* and *worship*, that they resolve themselves patiently to bear and carry the *Cross* and *Gallows* of their *Lord* and *Master*, and patiently to suffer with him. In the number of such his poor servants who as unfeignedly desire (notwithstanding my plea against *Persecutors* and *Persecution*) I say as unfeignedly desire to suffer as *cheerfully* with *Christ Iesus*, as *gloriously* to *reign* with him, desires to be,

Thine unfeigned, though unworthiest of all the Followers *of* JESUS.

Roger Williams.

The Bloody Tenent yet more Bloody, By Maſter *Cottons* attempting to waſh it with the Blood of the Lambe.

Examination of CHAP. I.

Truth.

BLeſt be the *God* of *truth* and *peace* (*ſweet peace*) that once againe, we finde a *corner* and a few *hours* to entertaine our ſweet *embraces* and *diſcourſes* about that *Bloody Tenent* of *Perſecution* for *cauſe* of *conſcience.*

Peace.

It is indeed *Jehovah's* work, and it is marvellous in our eyes, that 'midſt this worlds *combuſtions*, ſuch a *corner* and ſuch *hours* are found.

Truth & *peace* rarely meet in this vale of tears.

Truth. Dear *friends*, the longer abſent, meet the *ſweeter*; and have cauſe to ſpend each minute to his praiſe, who wonders works, and this not the leaſt, that we *two* ſee each others face at all in theſe tempeſtuous dayes and *vale* of *tears.*

2] How harſhly were our laſt *conferrings* entertained by ſome? How were our ſelves ſuſpected, and traduced for *counterfeits*; and our pious and peaceable *Meditations*, cruelly condemned to the devouring *flames*?[1]

Truth. That ever was our *portion*, ever ſince the *earthen pots* aroſe againſt their glorious *Potter*; and no better *lot* we muſt expect, while the *time* doth laſt that is determined.

Many dear Saints of God plead for perſecution: Oh how righteous is it with God to ſend them perſecution!

Peace. Mean while tis yet our *lamentation*, that ſo many of our *darlings*, whom we have tendred as our *eyes*, have both in *Print* and *Pulpit*, cried out againſt us; and amongſt the reſt, one of thy deareſt eldeſt *children*, (too too worthy to be) the *defender* of the *Bloody Tenent* of Perſecution.

Truth. Our *love* ſhall cover his ſhame and *nakedneſs*; and our *wiſdoms* pity his heavy labour, Blackamore-waſhings, and ſo great expence of precious *time* and *ſpirit*, in labouring to waſh this ſo deeply bloody, and Blackamore-*Tenent*, in the blood of the *Lamb* of *God*.

Peace. So *parents* and true friends love and pity theirs, though ſick, though froward and diſtracted; and let our *Bowels* yearne over him, who teares out *ours*: who knows but once before he ſleep his laſt, in the pit of rottenneſs, he may awake and give *glory* to the *God* of *peace* and *truth*, of *patience* and *long ſuffering*; whoſe *thoughts*, whoſe *wayes*, whoſe *love*, whoſe *pity* hath no *bounds*, nor *limits*, toward them whom he hath loved before the *worlds foundation*.

[1] His previous work had been burned, as he ſays, "by the Preſbyterian party (then prevailing.)" Letter to John Cotton, Jr. *Maſs. Hiſt. Soc. Proceedings*, March, 1858. See alſo *Neceſſity of Toleration, &c.*, in *Tracts on Liberty of Conſcience*, p. 270. *Pub. Narr. Club*, iii: xiii.

O let theſe bleſſed *buds*, of *hope* and ſweet *deſires* (dear Truth) put forth in pious fruits of renewed endeavors, and let me once againe prefer my ſuit for your impartial weighing of what *replies*, *objections*, *pleadings*, he hath brought againſt us.

Truth. For the *God* of *Peace*, for the *Prince* of *Peace* his ſake, yea for his *ſervants* ſake, for *Zions* ſake, I will not be ſilent, and know (at laſt) I ſhall prevaile to ſcatter and diſpell the *miſts* and *fogs*, that for a while ariſe to cloud and choak us.

Peace. Firſt, then, what cauſe ſhould move this ſo able a *defendant* to leap over all our firſt *addreſſes* both to the high Court of *Parliament*, and to every *Reader*? and what may be conjectured, why himſelf directs a word to neither in this *controverſie*?

Quere why Maſter Cotton leaps over the Epiſtles to the Parliament and Reader.

Truth. I deſire my *Rejoynder* may be as full of *love* as *truth*; [3] yet ſome ſay Maſter *Cotton* is wiſe, and knows in what *door* the wind blows of late; he is not ignorant what ſad *complaints* in *letters*, *printings*, *conferences*, ſo many of Gods *people* (and of his own *conſcience* and *judgement* of Independency) have poured forth againſt *New Englands* perſecuting, &c. He knows what *Bars New Englands* bloody *Tenent* and *practice* may put to his *brethrens* juſt *deſires* and *ſuits* for *moderation* and *toleration*, to *non-conforming conſciences*.

N.E. *Perſecution guilty of the perſecution in old, eſpecially (ſince this Rejoynder) by their Law for Baniſhing ſuch as hold not childrens Baptiſme, and their late fourſcore and ten bloody*

Tis true, his *conſcience*, and the *credit* of his *way*, compels his *reply*, but the *times* adviſe him, with as little noiſe as may be, and it ſeems with no great willingneſs, that that high and *ſearching houſe* of *Englands Parliament* ſhould ſearch and ſcan his *Meditations*.

lashes to the body of the Lord Jesus in the sufferings of his faithful witness, Obadiah Holmes *at* Boston, *meerly about that point of Baptisme.*[1]

Peace. Well, if the name of *God* were truely called upon them and (as his *title* intimateth) the great *controversies* of these present *times* are herein handled; If all that is here presented be truly *practised*; and he desire to buy and sell by one *measure*, and to be no otherwaies *measured* unto, then he *measureth* unto others: why should not that renowned *Court* be more particularly and expresly attended with so high and needful examinations? But now enough of that, I long to see that weighed, which is presented, take up those holy *weights* of thine, which may faithfully

[1] November 13, 1644, a law had been passed by the General Court of Massachusetts in the following terms: "It is ordered and agreed that if any person or persons within the jurisdiction shall either openly condemne or oppose the baptising of infants, or go about secretly to seduce others from the approbation or the use thereof, or shall purposely depart the congregation at the administration of the ordinance, or shall deny the ordinance of magistracy or their lawful right or authority to make war, or to punish the outward breaches of the first table, and shall appear to the Court wilfully and obstinately to continue therein after due time and means of conviction, every such person or persons shall be sentenced to banishment." *Mass. Col. Records*, ii: 85.

The case of Obadiah Holmes had been fully made known in England by John Clarke, Williams's colleague, who published his *Ill Newes from New England*, according to Mr. Savage's notes (3 *Mass. Hist. Coll.* viii: 287), May 13, 1652. That work contains a letter from Holmes to Baptists in London giving his account of his offence and its punishment. 4 *Mass. Hist. Coll.*, ii: 45–52. Holmes was a man of character and importance. He was probably of good family, as he states himself that three of the sons were "brought up at the university in Oxford." Backus, *Hist. of Baptists*, i: 208. He was for six or seven years a member of the Church in Salem, and in 1645 went to Rehoboth. Here he withdrew from the Congregational church and became a Baptist, and was presented to the General Court at Plymouth, June 4, 1650, for "continuing a meeting upon the Lord's-day from house to house" with eight others. *Plymouth Records*, ii: 162. He immediately took refuge in Newport. In July of the next year, he with two others, one of whom was Clarke, was sent to Lynn to visit an aged member of their church. While there on Sunday Clarke preached. The three were arrested and brought to Boston for trial. Holmes was sentenced to pay a fine of thirty pounds, "or else to be well whipt." He refused to pay the fine, and in default suffered the alternative. It was not lightly done, "the man striking with all his strength (yea spitting on his

difcover how *light* or *ponderous* each parcel is in *Gods* moft holy prefence. Mafter *Cotton* firft complaines againft the *publifhing* of his *private letter,* with an *Anfwer* thereunto: he faulteth the *difcuffer* for *punifhing* his *confcience,* againft the *difcuffers* own *Tenent* of *liberty* of *confcience,* for breach of *rule,* in firft *publifhing* to the world before *private admonition,* and telling the *Church.*

Truth. How juftly may I begin with the *defenders* own *conclufion* of this firft *Chapter*! He that fetteth forth of his *way* in the firft *entrance* of his *journey,* no marvel if he *wander* all the day after. For,

Firft, the *difcuffer* never wrote any fuch *letter* to Mafter *Cotton,* as Mafter *Cotton* fo often affirms, and mentioneth throughout his *Book.*

hand three times many affirmed) with a three-coarded whip, giving me therewith thirty ftroaks." Gov. Jencks teftifies that he was whipt "in fuch an unmerciful manner, that in many days, if not fome weeks, he could take no reft but as he lay upon his knees and elbows, not being able to fuffer any part of his body to touch the bed whereon he lay." Backus, *Hift.*, I: 237. Mr. Palfrey makes light of it and "ventures to hope that the executioner had been directed by his fuperiors to vindicate what they thought the majefty of the law at little coft to the delinquent," becaufe the poor fufferer had fuch inward peace that "in a manner he felt it not." *Hift. of N. E.*, ii: 353.

The Appendix to this work contains a letter from Williams to Gov. Endicott in reference to this cafe of perfecution, Cotton had been a party to it. "Mr. Cotton in his Sermon immediately before the Court gave their Sentence affirmed, that denying Infants Baptifm would overthrow all: and this was a capitall offence: and therefore they were foul-murtherers." *Ill Newes*, 56.

His part in fo infamous a tranfaction provoked Sir Richard Saltonftall, who was then in England, to write to him and Mr. Wilfon in remonftrance. He fays "Thefe rigid wayes have lay'd you very lowe in the hearts of the faynts." 2 *Mafs. Hift. Coll.*, iv: 171. Sir Henry Vane wrote to Winthrop (June 10, 1645,) expreffing his apprehenfions "left while the Congregational way among you is in its freedom, and is backed with power, it teach its oppugners here to extirpate it and root it out, from its own principles and practice." *Hutch. Coll.*, 131. Such intimations may have induced the caution which Williams alleges againft Cotton in the text.

The like miſtake he fals into, in ſome other *paſſages*, which ſhall be gently toucht at, and paſſed by, as the failing of *memory*.

Peace. It is often ſeen, that ſmall *matters* in the firſt *ſteps* and [4] *entrance* of a *buſineſs*, prove *ominous*; and although *love* bids us lay the *blame* on *memory*: yet ſince *Nil ſine providentia & Deus eſt maximus in minimis*, and not a *Sparow* nor a *Haire* fals without him; methinks ſuch a *ſtumble* in the *threſhold* ſhould have one ſad *conſideration* in Maſter *Cottons breſt*, ſo long as he reſides in the *chamber* of this *diſcourſe*.

The occaſion of publiſhing the bloody Tenent.

Truth. To my *knowledge* there was no ſuch letter or *intercourſe* paſſed between Maſter *Cotton* and the diſcuſſer; but what I have heard, is this: One Maſter *Hall* of *Roxbury*,[1] preſented the priſoners Arguments againſt perſecution to Maſter *Cotton*, who gave this preſent controverted *Anſwer*; with the which Maſter *Hall* not being ſatisfied, he ſends them unto the *diſcuſſer*, who never ſaw the ſaid *Hall*, nor thoſe *Arguments* in writing; (though he well remember that he ſaw them in print ſome yeers ſince) and apprehending no other, but that Maſter *Cottons Anſwer* was as publike, as Maſter *Cottons profeſſion* and *practice* of the ſame *Tenent* was and is, what *breach* of rule can Maſter *Cotton* ſay it was, to anſwer that in the *ſtreets* which Maſter *Cotton* proclaimeth on the *Houſe top?*

Peace. But grant it had been a *private letter*, and the *diſcourſe* and the *opinion* private: yet why doth

[1] John Hall, of Roxbury, arrived in Boſton in 1633, and was probably admitted freeman May 14, 1634. He afterwards removed to Connecticut, and died at Middletown, May 26, 1673. Cf. Preface to *Bloody Tenent, Pub. Narr. Club*, iii: v.–vi.

he charge the *diſcuſſer* with breach of *rule,* in not uſing orderly wayes of *Admonition,* and telling the *Church,* when Maſter *Cotton* himſelf in this *Book* blames the *diſcuſſer* for diſclaiming *Communion* with their *Church,* and they alſo (after he was driven by *baniſhment* from civil *habitation* amongſt them) had ſent forth a bull of *excommunication* againſt him in his abſence.[1]

Maſter Cotton blames the diſcuſſer for not walking in contradictions.

Such *practiſe* the *Lord Jeſus* and his firſt *Apoſtles* or *Meſſengers* never taught, nor any that are truely their *ſucceſſors* ever will. But to end this Chapter, in the laſt place, why doth Maſter *Cotton* complaine of the *loſs* of the *liberty* of his *conſcience,* and of the *puniſhing* of his *conſcience,* by the publiſhing of his *letter*; aggravating it, becauſe the *diſcuſſer* pleads for *liberty* of *conſcience*? Is he indeed on the Lord Jeſus mind for the ſparing mens *bodies,* and preſent *life,* for their *ſouls* and eternal *lives* ſake? Doth he indeed plead for *liberty of conſcience*? Let the following *diſcourſe,* and this preſent *paſſage* manifeſt how tender he is of his own *conſcience,* and of the *liberty* of it; But how *cenſo-* [5] *rious* and ſenſeleſs of the *pangs* and *agonies* of other mens *conſcience* and *ſpirits,* and *ſorrows*? As if his alone were the *Apple* of his *eye,* but Theirs like the *brawny* hoofs of the roaring *Bulls* of *Baſhan.*

Unchriſtian partiality.

Peace. Complaines Maſter *Cotton* of *perſecution* for ſuch dealing againſt him? I never heard that *diſput-*

[1] Hugh Peters writes in the name of the church in Salem to the church in Dorcheſter, under date "1ſt 5th mo. 39. We thought it our bounden duty to acquaint you with the names of ſuch perſons as have had the great cenſure paſſed upon them in this our church, with the reaſons thereof. Roger Williams and his wife, &c. Theſe wholly refuſed to hear the church, denying it, and all the churches in the Bay, to be true churches, and (except two) are all re-baptized." Knowles, *Life,* 176.

Master Cotton complaining of being persecuted by the discusser.

ing, discoursing and *examining* mens *Tenents* or *Doctrines* by the word of *God,* was (in proper *English acceptation* of the word) *persecution* for *conscience*: well had it been for *New England,* that no servant of *God,* nor *witness* of *Christ Jesus,* could justly take up no other *complaint* against *New England* for other kinds of *persecution*: surely the voice of *Christ Jesus* to *Paul*; S*aul, Saul,* why *persecutest thou me?* was for another kind of *persecution.*

Truth. Deare Peace, if the *Bishops* of *Old England* or *new* had never stirred up the *Civil Magistrate* to any other suppressing of mens *consciences,* nor no other *persecuting,* then *discussing, disputing* &c. they should never have needed to have been charged so publikely in the face of the world, with the *bloody Tenent* of *persecution* for *cause* of *conscience.*

Examination of CHAP. II.

Peace.

IN this *Chapter* Master *Cotton* much complaines, that he is charged in the *Title* to maintaine *persecution* for *cause* of *conscience,* and professeth, That he would have none be punished for *conscience,* unless his errour be *fundamental,* or *seditiously*; or *turbulenly* promoted, and that after due *conviction* of *conscience,* and that it may appear he is not punished for his *conscience,* but for sinning against his *conscience.*

Persecution in plaine Eng-

Truth. Persecution for *conscience,* is in *plaine English, hunting* for *conscience*; and Master *Cotton* being a son of *wine* (as the *Jews* speak in their *Proverb*) is loth to be counted a ſon of *vinegar*, and therefore would avoid the word *perſecuting* or *hunting* (as ſomething too wilde and fierce an *expreſſion*, more ſutable to the bloody ſons of *vinegar* and *gall* the *Roman Emperors*, *Popes* and *Biſhops*) and he much deſires to have the word *perſe-* [6] *cuting* changed for the word *puniſhing*, a tearm more proper to true *Juſtice*.

liſh is hunting.

Maſter Cottons tender conſcience, can hardly digeſt to be a perſecutor, but a puniſher.

But is not this the *guiſe* and *profeſſion* of all that ever *perſecuted* or *hunted* men for their *Religion* and *conſcience*? are not all *hiſtories* and *experiences* full of the *pathetical* ſpeeches of *perſecutors* to this purpoſe? You will ſay you are perſecuted for your *conſcience*, you plead *conſcience*; Thou art a *heretick* the *devil* hath deceived thee, thy *conſcience* is deluded, *&c.* And

2. Whether ſuch *puniſhing* as Maſter *Cotton* aſſigneth to that threefold degree of *heretical* wickedneſs, *chap.* 5. to wit, To hold a *fundamental error*, To *perſiſt* therein after *conviction*, and laſtly, To *ſeduce* others thereuntó, Or theſe five ſummed up (*page* 186 of his book) *ſubverters* of the *Chriſtian Faith*, *perſiſters* therein after *conviction*, *blaſphemers*, *idolaters*, *ſeducers*; I ſay, ſuch a puniſhing which he affirmes to be *death* and *killing* will not amount to make up a *perſecution* for *cauſe* of *conſcience* let the *Spaniſh Inquiſitions* be an inſtance, who when they torture and rack, and kill and burn for ſuch *crimes*, yet varniſh they and guild all over with the painted *Title* of *Gods Glory*, holy *zeal*, juſt *puniſhment* of *hereticks*, *blaſphemers*, &c.

Peace. But Maſter *Cotton* blameth, that he ſhould be charged with the *Doctrine* of *perſecution* by *conſequence*.

Truth. Let his whole *book*, and the *proſecuting* of this *controverſie* be *judge*, whether it be only drawn from *conſequences*, and not expreſs *Tearms*. And for the waſhing of this *bloody Tenent* in the *blood* of the *Lambe*, *Time* hath and will diſcover that ſuch a *Black-amore* cannot be waſhed in the *blood* of *Chriſt* himſelf, without *Repentance*; for they that waſhed their *robes* in the *blood* of the *Lamb* (*Revelations the* 7. [14.]) were true *penitents*: untill therefore that *perſecutors* repent of this bloody *Doctrine* and *practice*, they muſt hear (as the men of *Judah* did) the prophet *Iſaiahs thunder*, Iſa. 1. [15. 16.] *Your hands are defiled with blood*; *waſh you, make you clean*, &c.

7] *Examination of* CHAP. III.

Peace.

BUt what *knot* in a *Bulruſh* is that, which Maſter *Cotton* obſerves the *diſcuſſer* findes in his firſt *diſtinction* of *perſecution* for *cauſe* of *conſcience?*

Truth. For the matter upon the point, they both agree, as Maſter *Cotton* hath penned himſelf, that *perſecution* for *cauſe* of *conſcience*, is not onely when a man is puniſhed for *profeſsing* ſuch *Doctrines* and *Worſhips*, as he believes to be of *God*, but alſo when he is puniſhed for renouncing ſuch *Doctrine*, and not practiſing ſuch *Worſhips*, which he believes are not of *God*, &c.

All the *difference* is this, that the *diſcuſſer* ſaith, This ſhould have been expreſſed in the *diſtinction*; Maſter *Cotton* ſaith, it was implied, and therefore the obſerving of the not expreſſing of it, was but a *knot* in a *Bulruſh.*

Peace. Tis wofully true, that the *peace* of the *Saints,* and the *peace* of the *world,* hath been lamentably, broake and diſtracted, in *puniſhing* or *perſecuting* of men, but eſpecially the *Saints,* upon both theſe grounds: but yet the *records* of *time* and *experience* will tell us, that ſince the *Apoſtaſie* from the *truth* of *Jeſus,* the riſing of *Antichriſt,* and the ſetting up of many State-*Religions,* the ſoreſt and frequenteſt *puniſhing* or *hunting* of the children of *God* hath been (as in the caſe of *Nebuchadnezzars Image*) for not bowing *down* to the *State-Images,* for not coming to *Church,* for not obeying the *Laws,* for withſtanding the *Kings,* or *Queens,* or *Parliaments proceedings.*

Gods children commonly perſecuted for not yeelding to State worſhips.

Truth. Your *obſervation* is moſt *ſerious* and *ſeaſonable,* and your *complaint* as *true* as *lamentable*: for ſince all *States* and *Governments* of the world (which lies in wickedneſs) ſet up their *State* or *Commonweal-Religions, Nebuchadnezzars* golden *Images* and *Jeroboams* golden *Calves* (the *types* of the *State-Worſhips* of after *Ages*) whereby others are made to ſin and bow down to their ſeeming glorious *worſhips*; and ſince the *diſſenters, refuſers, non-conformers, non-covenanters* (the *witneſſes* of *God* againſt ſuch *abominations*) are but few; and what *poſitive worſhip* they
8] hold or practice (commonly) is moſt *retired,* and flying into *private corners,* by reaſon of the *violence* of the *perſecution*; they are hence, ſooneſt in all *places* of their abode, and more *ſpeedily* and *immediately* called for and ſought out, in the ſeveral *Pariſh-towns* where they live to bow down to the *common-Image,*

the *beaſtly* and *Calviſh* inventions of the *Ieroboams* of this periſhing *world*; and for refuſing to *ſubſcribe*, to *conforme*, to come to *Church*, to do as their *neighbours*, for being wiſer then their *Teachers*, their *Fathers*, their *Magiſtrates*, the *Country*, the *Parliament*, the *Kingdome* (and ſometimes the whole *world*, in their *Oecumenical*, or *worldly Councels*) they are thus puniſhed and hunted for their *conſcience*, for *Gods*, for *Jeſus* ſake; which is a point Maſter *Cotton* will ſay (if the *blood* of his *dear Redeemer* ſpilt in the *blood* of his ſervants, kindly affect him) of greater weight then *knots* in *bulruſhes*.

Examination of CHAP. IV.

Peace.

IN the ſecond *diſtinction* (to wit, of *fundamentals*, without right *belief* whereof, a man cannot be ſaved) Maſter *Cotton* upon the point confeſſeth it was a juſt reproof, and ſaith, that he meant only of the firſt ſort of *foundations*, that concern *ſalvation*, and not of thoſe that concerne the *foundation* of the *Church*, and *Chriſtian Religion*.

Truth. It is ſtrange that Maſter *Cotton* ſhould ſo
Act. 2. [1.] diſtinguiſh of *foundations*, when the holy *Scripture*
2 [1.] Pet. 3. [21.] attributes *ſalvation* to thoſe *foundations* of the *Church*, and the *order* of it: The Lord added to the *Church* ſuch as ſhould be *ſaved*, and the like *figure* whereunto *Baptiſme* now *ſaveth* us; and concerning the *reſurrection* that we are ſaved by *hope*, *Rom.* 8. [24.]

Befides, are not thofe firft *foundations*, which he faith concerne *falvation*, *foundations* alfo of the *Chriftion Religion*? If not of the *Chriftian*, then I demand of what *Religion* are they *foundations*?

Peace. It cannot therefore be denyed, but that his *diftinction* of *fundamentals*, was moft dangerous, tending directly to con- [9] demne the *generation* of the *righteous*, who have been generally for many *generations* ignorant of the *Chriftian* way of *worfhip*. But what fay you to this *reply*, touching how far the *New Englifh* (implicite) *Parifhes* compare and partake with thofe of *old*?

Truth. How far thofe *Churches* cannot be cleered from not *comming out* from the *Parifh-worfhip*, from being themfelves (implicitely) *Parifh-Churches* (notwithftanding their *Fig-leaves*, &c.) and from being *perfecutors* of fuch as endeavour to cover their *nakedne∫s* with better clothing, will appear, with Chrifts affiftance, in the *examination* of his reply to the *Anfwer* of his *Letter*.[1]

Examination of CHAP. V.

Peace.

THe difcourfe of this *chapter* is *larger* and more *controverfial*, and therefore (*dear Truth*) requires your moft *ferious* and deeper *examination* of it. Mafter *Cotton* here diftinguifheth *worfhip* into *true* and *falfe*, and infers, that if *true worfhip*, *fellowfhip* with

[1] This "examination," which was promifed in the addrefs to the Reader, p. 40 *fupra*, was probably never publifhed.

God is held; but if *falſe*, *fellowſhip* with *God* is loſt. And whereas he was thereupon minded by the *diſcuſſer* to have lived in a falſe *Miniſtery* in *England*, and to have practiſed the falſe *worſhip* of the *Common Prayer*, he labours to clear both, and in particular he ſaith, It is not truly ſaid, that the *Spirit* of *God* maketh the *Miniſtery* one of the *foundations* of the *Chriſtian religion*, (*Heb.* 6. [1. 2.]) For it is (ſaith he) only a *foundation* of *Chriſtian order*, not of *faith* or *religion*: and he adds, The *Apoſtle* puts an expreſs *difference* between *faith and order*, *Col.* 2. 5. What can be ſaid thereunto?

Truth. 1. Alas, what buildings can weak ſouls expect from ſuch Maſter-builders, when Maſter C*otton* is ſo confounded about the very *foundations?* In the former *Chapter*, he diſtinguiſheth between *foundations* that concern *ſalvation*, and thoſe that concern the the *Church* and *Chriſtian religion*: here he diſtinguiſheth between thoſe of Chriſtian *order*, and thoſe of *Faith*, or *Chriſtian religion.* In the former, he oppoſeth *faith* againſt *religion* and [10] *order*; here he oppoſeth *faith* and *religion* to *order*. Grant his *memory* (in ſo ſhort a turn) failed him, yet doubtleſs his *miſtakes* about the *foundation* of *Chriſtian religion*, are moſt groſs and inexcuſable.

Truth. 2. I finde no ſuch *diſtinction* in the *Teſtament* of *Chriſt Jeſus*, between the *Chriſtian order*, and the *Chriſtian religion*; as if the *order* of the *Church* of *God* (I might ſay, the *Church* it ſelf, and the *Miniſtery* of it) were no part of the *Chriſtian religion.*

It is true, *Coloſſ.* 2. [5.] ſpeaks of *faith* and *order*, but yet denies not the *Chriſtian Church*, and the *order* of it, to be any part of the *Chriſtian religion.* It is true, that ſometimes *faith* implies the particular *grace* of *believing*, and yet ſometimes it is put for the whole *Chriſtian religion* (as *Jude* 1[3]. contend for the *faith* once delivered) ſo that if Maſter *Cotton* confeſſeth the *Miniſtery* of the *Word* (*Heb.* 6.) to be a *foundation* of *Chriſtian* or *Church-order*, he cannot deny it to be a *foundation* of the *Chriſtian religion* or *worſhip* reduced to thoſe two, of *Faith* and *Order.*

Peace. What anſwer you to his ſaying, It is not a *true* and a *ſafe ſpeech*, to call the *fellowſhip* and *bleſſing* of *God* vouchſafed to corrupt *Churches* or *Miniſters*, or *miniſtrations* unpromiſed, or beyond a word of *promiſe*, of *God?* Againſt which he alleadgeth (*Ier.* 13.[33.8.]) That *God* will be *merciful* to his peoples iniquities, and 2 *Chron.* 30. [19.] *Gods* mercy to every one that prepareth his *heart*, &c. although he be not cleanſed after the *preparation*, &c.

Truth. The *promiſes* hold forth no *bleſſing* or *fellowſhip* of *God* to *falſe worſhips*; againſt which all the holy *Scripture* denounceth *curſings*, both in the old and new *Teſtament*; nor in particular doth that of *Ieremy* promiſe any *pardon* of ſin, but to the *repentant*, though moſt true alſo is that *diſtinction* of *particular* repentance for known ſins, and *general* for ſins unknown. Such was the ſin (it may be) of the *Iſraelites*, 2 *Chron.* 30. in their want of ſuch their legal cleanſing.

But I add, how can that one act of covering or conniving at *ceremoniall* uncleanneſs (about a true *worſhip*) be brought to prove a promiſe of *Gods* bleſſing and fellowſhip, to a conſtant courſe of a *falſe* and invented way of prayer by the *Latine* or *English Masse-book*, as some have rightly called it?

11] *Peace.* Concerning *Ordination*, Master *Cotton* saith, that it is no *essential* part of a call to the *Ministery*; no more then *Coronation* is *essential* to the Office of a *King*: And *Jehoshua* the *high priest* did not lose *fellowship* with *God*, though he was clothed with *filthy* garments, *Zech.* 3. [3. 5.]

Truth. I answer, *Ordination* or laying on of hands, comprizeth the whole *Ministery*, *Heb.* 6. [2] wherein if *Election* or *Ordination* be false, I see not how the *Ministery* is true, any more then a *marriage* can be true, where either *consent* or *solemnity* by a true power is wanting: or a *King* rightly instituted in his *Kingly* office, when either *election* or *coronation* is given or made by a false power.

Ordination of Christs Ministry undfily compared to the coronatien of Kings.

2. But further, *Ordination* is not well represented by a *Kings coronation* (to say nothing of the statelines of the simile) for a *King* may administer by *successive election* and *consent* (in some States) before *coronation*, and *coronation* is but for publike *state* and *ceremony*; but a *Minister* cannot administer before *ordination* (no more then a *husband* enjoy his *spouse* before marriage) which is the puting of him into, and the investing of him with his Authority, as we see both in the *priests* of the *law*, and the *Ministers* of the *Gospel*.

Concerning *Jehoshua* his garments; This kind of *confession* is not after the *patterne* of *Ezra*, *Nehemiah*, *David*, *Daniel*, &c. but with mincing and excusing. Moreover, in this place of *Zechary*, *God* only comforts his people with the promise of *better times*, and more new and coſtly garments: for the *High prieſt* now returning from *captivity*, his garments were torne, foule and filthy.

Laſtly, Theſe were the *garments* of the *Lords* appointing, though in a poor and afflicted condition: what is this to a *fools cap* or *coate* (the *cap* or *ſurplice*) what is this to the office of *Ieroboams prieſts*, which never were of *God*, though happily ſome of them might ſtudiouſly give themſelves to attaine and teach the knowledge of *God*, and might (in a kind) ſeparate from the falſe, 2 *Chron.* 13. [9.] and ſome good thing might be found in ſome, as in *Ieroboams* child, and happily many others as in theſe our times?

Maſter Cotton pleads for Common prayer.

Peace. Concerning *common prayer*, he pleades the time of their *ignorance*; as alſo that the *high places* were removed, 2 *Chron.* [12] 14. [5.] and knows not of any ſuch faithful *admonition* as was mentioned.

Truth. God winketh at ſome *ignorance*, but is not blind to paſs by all: The *high places* were an high ſin, and in *Gods* time diſcovered, repented of, and removed; but ever by God diſclaimed, &c. And although the *diſcuſſer* acknowledgeth himſelf unworthy to ſpeak for *God* to Maſter *Cotton* or any, yet poſſibly Maſter *Cotton* may call to minde, that the *diſcuſſer* (riding with himſelf and one other of precious memorie (Maſter *Hooker*) to and from *Sempringham*) preſented his *Arguments* from *Scripture*, why he durſt not joyn with them in their uſe of *Common prayer*; and all the *Anſwer* that yet can be remembred the *diſcuſſer* received from Maſter *Cotton*, was, that he ſelected the good and beſt prayers in his uſe of that *Book*, as the *Author* of the *Councel* of *Trent* was uſed to do, in his uſing of the *Maſſe-book*.[1]

Peace. Yea but further (ſaith Maſter *Cotton*) *Numbers* 20. [1–11.] *Moſes* uſed an unwarrantable way of *propheſying*, and yet *God* gave water; therefore ſet *formes* of *prayer* may bring a bleſſing down.

Examination of Num. 6. 20.

Truth. *Moſes* his calling was true in a true *Church*; his failing was in point of *paſſion* and *unbeliefe*. What is this to the *Common prayer*, where all were *Idols*, both the *ſociety* or *communion*; in which the *prieſt* himſelf, and the *worſhip* were but inventions? *&c.*

Peace. But, ſaith he, *Common prayer* is not ſuch a *fundamentall errour*.

Acts 6. [4.]

Truth. The *word* and *prayer* are thoſe two great *ſervices* of *God*, which even the *Apoſtles* themſelves gave themſelves unto: And if Maſter *Cotton* intend not that his *Argument* ſhall ſtand good againſt Maſter *Ball*,[2] to prove the falſeneſs of ſuch a maine *worſhip* of *God*, let him ſhew what that *worſhip* of *God* is, which he intendeth, when he ſo diſtinguiſheth of ſome *falſe worſhip* wherein *fellowſhip* with *God* is loſt.

Peace. To end this Chapter, Maſter *Cotton*, to clear

[1] Sempringham is a ſmall pariſh in Lincolnſhire, about eighteen miles from Boſton where Cotton was rector. Hooker was miniſter at Chelmsford from 1626 to 1630. Whence they rode "to and from Sempringham" is nowhere indicated, or we might have ſome clue to Williams's own reſidence at that time. The liberality of Father Paul Sarpi, the hiſtorian of the Council of Trent, is familiar to all who know his hiſtory. See Rev. James Martineau's article on his life and his biographies, *Weſtminſter Review*, April, 1838. Cf. *Pub. Narr. Club*, iii: 69.

[2] Rev. John Ball, of Braſenoſe College, Oxford, publiſhed in 1640 a defence of ſet forms of Prayer. To this Cotton publiſhed a reply entitled "A Modeſt and Cleare Anſwer to Mr. Balls Diſcourſe of Set formes of Prayer, &c. Written by the Reverend and Learned John Cotton B. D. and Teacher of the Church of Chriſt at Boſton in New England. London, 1642." Cf. *Pub. Narr. Club*, i: 324; ii: 38, 162.

himſelf from *partiality*, and that he never uſeth to *meaſure* that to any, which he would not have meaſured to himſelf, He propoſeth a threefold *wickedneſs*, which he ſaith *God* never left him to fall into.
13] Firſt, Any *fundamental errour*. Secondly, perſiſting therein after *admonition* and *conviction*. Thirdly, *ſeducing* of others. And laſtly, he profeſſeth, that if he ſhould ſo fall, it were better for him to be cut off by *death* or *baniſhment*, then the *flocke* of *Chriſt* to be *ſeduced* by his *heretical* wickedneſs.

Truth. I here firſt obſerve (as alſo in other places) Maſter *Cottons* acknowledgement and *profeſſion* of what a man may be puniſhed for: to wit, a *fundamental errour*, *perſiſting* in it, and *ſeducing* others; all which are *ſpiritual* matters, of *religion* and *worſhip*, for which he decrees from the *Magiſtrate*, *death* or *baniſhment*; and yet elſewhere in many other paſſages, he profeſſeth againſt all *perſecution* for *conſcience*.

Three cauſes for which Maſter Cotton maintaines perſecution

Secondly, If Maſter *Cotton* ſhould ſo fall, and be ſo dealt withall by the *civil ſtate*,

Firſt, would not Maſter *Cotton* conſcientiouſly be perſwaded of the *Truth* of what he held, though accounted by others *fundamental error*, *obſtinacy*, *hereſie?* &c.

Secondly, Will Maſter *Cotton* think that *death* or *baniſhment* would be wholeſome and *Chriſtian* meanes and *remedies* to change and heal his *conſcience*.?

Thirdly, He (to prevent the *infection* of others) granting the *civil Magiſtrate* muſt puniſh him with *death* or *baniſhment*, doth he not make the *Magiſtrate*, yea the *Civil State* (what State ſoever he live in) the *Judge* of his *conſcience* and *errors?*

Fourthly, Confessing it now, that to worship *God* with a *Common prayer*, was his sin, and yet it was his *conscience*, that he might so do: If the *Magistrate* had judged it to be a *fundamental error*, he grants he might then have put him to *death* or *banishment*, if persisting, &c. though yet he hath a *proviso*, and a *retreat* against this *assault*, professing, that if the *Magistrate* be not rightly informed, he must stay his *proceedings*: of which afterward.

Peace. What is this, but, in plaine *English*, to profess that all the *Magistrates* and *Civil powers*, throughout the whole world, although they have command and power from *Christ Jesus*, to judge in matters of *conscience*, *religion*, and *worship*, and live in daily sin, that they do not cut off the *heretick*, *blasphemer*, *seducer*, &c. yet except they be of Master *Cottons* minde and *conscience*, to [14] account and judge to be, they must *suspend* their *duty* and *office* in this case, until they be better informed, that is, untill they be of his mind?

Examination of CHAP. VI.

Peace.

BUt to proceed to the sixth Chapter, in which is handled that which more especially concerns my *self*. It is too lamentably known, how the furious *troopes* of *persecutors* in all *States*, *Cities*, *Towns*, &c. have ever marched under my name, the white colours of *peace*, *civil peace*, *publike peace*.

Truth. Yet Maſter *Cotton* confeſſeth, that the *Cities* peace is an *humane* an *civil peace*, as was further explained in many *inſtances* from *Babylon*, *Epheſus*, *Smyrna*, &c. againſt which Maſter *Cotton* excepts not.

Peace. The difference or controverſie in this Chapter lies in two things. Firſt, In the *ſimilitudes* uſed from *companies* and *ſocieties*, voluntarily entering into *combinations*, which are diſtinct from the City.

2. In the nature of the *Church*, which he maintaines to be a *ſociety*, whoſe *order* the City is bound to preſerve, as well as any of their civil *orders* or *ſocieties*.

Truth. To begin with the firſt, Maſter *Cotton* " replies, " That although ſuch *ſocieties* be not of the " *eſſence* of the *City*, yet they are of the *integral* and " *conſervant* cauſes of the City, and ſo the *diſturbance* " of any of thoſe *orders* or *ſocieties* in the City, diſ- " turbes the *City* it ſelf.

Chriſts Church may be gathered and diſſolved without diſturbance of civil Peace.

But I anſwer, The *ſimilitude* was uſed more eſpecially from a *colledge* of *Phyſitians*, or a *ſociety* of *Merchants*, *Turkiſh*, *Eaſt-Endies*, &c. and conſequently any other of that kinde, voluntarily combining together for the better inriching of themſelves in the improvement of their *faculties* for publike good (at leaſt ſo pretended.) It was never intended, that if ſuch neceſſary Trades, Callings, *&c.* as he mentioneth, be diſſolved and ruined, that there would be no *diſturbance* of the *peace* of the City: But that if ſuch or ſuch a way and *order* of men of thoſe faculties I mentioned, [15] voluntarily *combine*, and voluntarily alſo *diſſolve*; yet all this may may be, without any breach of *civil* and *publike peace.*

Peace. If ſo, much more the *church* of *Chriſt*, which is a *ſpiritual ſociety* voluntarily uniting, may diſſolve; I ſay, much more, without the breach of the *peace* of the *city*, which is of a *civil* and humane nature, as is confeſſed, and was urged in the inſtances of *Epheſus*, &c.

Truth. 2. We are wont when we ſpeak of keeping or breaking the *Peace*, to ſpeak of *Words* or *Actions* of *Violence*, *Sedition*, *Uproare*, &c. for, *Actions* of the *Caſes*, *Pleas*, and *Traverſes* may be, and yet no peace broken, when men ſubmit to the *Rule* of *State*, for the compoſing of ſuch *differences*, &c. Therefore it is that I affirme, that if any of *Chriſts Church* have difference with any other man in *civill* and *humane* things, he ought to be judged by the *Law*: But if the *Church* have *ſpiritual controverſies* among themſelves or with any other, or if *God* take away the *Candleſtick* as he threatned the Church in *Epheſus*, all this may be, and yet no civil peace broken: Yea, amongſt thoſe that profeſs the ſame *God* and *Chriſt*, as the *Papiſts* and *Proteſtants*, or the ſame *Mahomet*, as the *Turks* and *Perſians*, there would no civil *Peace* be broken, notwithſtanding their *differences* in *Religion*, were it not for the bloody *Doctrine* of *Perſecution*, which alone breaks the bounds of *civil* peace, and makes *Spiritual* cauſes the cauſes of their bloodie *diſſentions*.

The doctrine and practiſe of Perſecution, breaks the peace wherever it comes.

I obſerve therefore, a twofold *Fallacie* in Maſter *Cottons reply*. Firſt, he fallaciouſly mingles *Peace* and *Proſperity* together: for though it be true, that under the terme *Peace* all good things are ſometimes concluded, yet when we ſpeak of *Hereticks* or *Schiſ-*

The civil peace of a place or people is one thing,

maticks breaking the *civil* peace, or ſtrowing *Doctrines* tending to break the *civill peace*, we muſt underſtand ſome ſuch words or acts of *violence*, wherein the *bounds* and *orders* of the *City*, *Laws*, and *Courts* are violated; taking it for granted (for this is the *Suppoſition*) that the *Lawes* of the *City* be meerely civil and humane. Hence then I affirme, that there is no *Doctrine*, no *Tenent* ſo directly tending to break the *Cities peace*, as this *Doctrine* of *perſecuting* or *puniſhing* each other for the cauſe of *conſcience* or *Religion*.

and the welfare or proſperity in health wealth, &c. another.

Againe, it is a ſecond Fallacie to urge your order of the *Church*, [16] and the *Excellency* thereof, and that therefore it is a Breach of the *civil peace*, when the *Order* of the *church* is not preſerved: For although it is moſt true, that ſooner or later the *God* of heaven puniſheth the *nations* of the world, for their *Idolatries*, *Superſtitions*, &c. yet Maſter *Cotton* himſelf acknowledgeth (as was affirmed) that many glorious flouriſhing *cities* there are all the world over, wherein no *church* of *Chriſt* is extant: Yea, that the *Commonweale of Rome* flouriſhed five hundred years together, before ever the name of *Chriſt* was heard in it; which ſo great a *Glory* of ſo great a *continuance*, mightily evinceth the diſtinction of the *civill peace* of a *State* from that which is *Chriſtian Religion*.

The Cities of the world enjoy peace and proſperity, where Chriſt is not heara of.

It is true (as Maſter *Cotton* tells us) that the Turks have plagued the *Antichriſtian* world, for their *Idolatries*: Yet *Hiſtory* tels us, that one of their *Emperours* (*Mahomet*) was the man that firſt broke up and deſolated two moſt glorious ancient *cities*, *Conſtantinople* (which had flouriſhed 1120 yeares (ſince its firſt building by *Conſtantine*) and *Athens*, which from

Solons giving of it *Laws*, had flouriſhed two thouſand yeares, notwithſtanding their Idolatries, &c.[1]

Truth. It is apparent that then the *Chriſtian Religion* glorioully flouriſhed (contrary to Maſter *Cottons* obſervation) when the *Roman Emperours* took not power to themſelves to reform the *abuſes* in the *Chriſtian* Church, but perſecuted it; and then the *church* was ruined and overwhelmed with *Apoſtacy* and *Antichriſtianiſm*, when the *Emperours* took that power unto themſelves: And then it was (as Maſter *Cotton* elſewhere confeſſeth) that *Chriſtianitie* loſt more, even in *Conſtantines* time, then under bloody *Nero*, *Domitian*, &c.[2]

Chriſtianity loſt moſt under ſuch Emperours as claimed Chriſts power to reform the Church, &c.

Peace. It cannot be denied (dear Truth) but that the *Peace* of a *civil State* (of all States, excepting that of typical *Iſrael*) was and is meerly and *eſſentially civil.* But Maſter *Cotton* ſaith further, Although the *Inward Peace* of a *church* is *Spiritual*, yet the *outward* Peace of it, *Magiſtrates* muſt keep in a way of *Godlineſs* and *Honeſtie*, 1 Tim. 2. 1.

Truth. The *Peace* of a *church* of *Chriſt* (the onely true *Chriſtian State*, *Nation*, *Kingdom*, or *city*) is *Spiritual*, whether *internal* in the *Soul*, or *external* in the *adminiſtration* of it; as the peace of a *civil State* is

[1] The ſiege of Conſtantinople under Mahomet II., begun on the 6th of April, 1453, and the city was taken the 29th of May. Conſtantine XI., the Byzantine Emperor, fell, exclaiming "I would rather die than live." The city had ſuffered twenty-nine ſieges in the courſe of a thouſand years. This was the laſt. With it fell the Roman power in the Eaſt, and the Ottoman Turks eſtabliſhed their empire in Europe. Gibbon, *Decline and Fall*, 1230–1238; Creaſy, *Hiſt. of Ottoman Turks*, i: 123–141. Athens was taken poſſeſſion of by Mahomet II., in 1456. Finlay, *Hiſt. of Greece*, 1204 to 1461, p. 191.

[2] See *Bloudy Tenent*, 211; *Pub. Narr. Club*, iii: 368. The reference is to Cotton's application of the Song of Solomon to the hiſtory of the Chriſtian church, in his *Expoſition of the Canticles*, p. 141.

civil, internal in the mindes of men, and [17] *external* in the adminiſtration and converſation of it; and for that place of *Timothy*, it hath been fully ſpoken to in this *diſcourſe*, and the Diſcuſſer hath as yet ſeen no *exception* againſt what hath been ſpoken.

Peace. But further, ſaith Maſter *Cotton*, although the *peace* of a Country be *civil*, yet it is diſtracted by diſturbing the peace of the *Church* for God cut ſhort the Coaſts of the *civil State* when *Jehu* ſhortned his *Reformation*, 2 King. 10. 31, 32.

Truth. Maſter *Cotton* denies not (but confeſſed in his diſcourſe concerning *Baptiſm*)[1] that *Canaan* was *Typical*, and to be caſt out of that *Land*, was to be caſt out of *Gods ſight:* which proves thus much, That the *church* of *Chriſt*, the *Iſrael* now, neglecting to reform, *God* will cut this *Iſrael* ſhort. But what is this to a meerly *civil State*, which may flouriſh many hundreds, yea ſome thouſands of yeers together (as I before inſtanced) when the Name of the true Lord *Jeſus Chriſt* is not ſo much as heard of within it?

Peace. Laſtly, (ſaith he) the *church* is a *Society*, as

[1] This work was entitled "The grounds and ends of the Baptiſme of the Children of the faithfull. By the Learned and Faithfull Miniſter of Chriſt, John Cotton, Teacher of the Church of Boſton in New England. London, 1647." The reference is to page 40. "*Canaan* itſelfe was not given as a meere temporal bleſſing: but as a pledge of a ſpiritual inheritance, a Seale of the Church, a type of Heaven. Hence it was that *Jacob* gave ſuch a ſolemne charge by oath unto *Joſeph*, and *Joſeph* to his brethren, the one to bury his dead body in *Canaan*, the other for the tranſportation of his bones to *Canaan:* which they would never have done for an earthly inheritance, but to nouriſh in the hearts of their poſterity, faith and deſire of their communion in the Church, and of their reſt in heaven, whereof the reſt in *Canaan* was a type, whereunto not *Moſes* but *Joſhua* muſt bring them, that is, not the law, but Jeſus, *Heb.* 3. 11. with Chap. 4. 5, 8. And their caſting out of that Country by captivity was their caſting out of Gods ſight. 2 *Kings*, 17. 28. Whereby their church Eſtate was diſſolved, the Communion of Saints ſcattered, &c."

well as the *Societies* of *Merchants, Drapers,* &c. and it is juſt to preſerve the *Society* of the *church,* as well as any other *Society.*

Truth. When we ſpeak of the *balances* of *Juſtice,* we muſt diſtinguiſh between the *Balances* of the *Sanctuary,* and the *Balances* of the *World* or *civil States.* It is *ſpiritual juſtice* to preſerve *ſpiritual right*; and for that end, the *ſpiritual King* thereof hath taken *care.* It is *civil Juſtice* to preſerve the *civil rights*; and the *Rights* of a *civil ſociety* ought juſtly to be *preſerved* by a *civil State*: (and yet if a *company* of men combine themſelves into a *civil ſociety* by voluntary agreement, and voluntarily diſſolve it, it is not *juſtice* to force them to continue together.)

The Societies or Churches of the Saints are meerly voluntary in combining or diſſolving.

Peace. The *church* can leaſt of all be forced: for as it is a *ſpiritual ſociety,* and not ſubject to any *civil Judicature*; (though ſome ſay that a *church* in *New England* was cited to appear before a *civil Court*:) ſo is the *combination* of it *voluntary,* and the *diſſolution* of it in part or whole is voluntary, and endures no Civil violence, but as a *virgin* (in point of *marriage*) *nec cogit, nec cogitur,* ſhe forceth not, nor can be forced by any *civil power.*

Chriſts Church is called out of the world.

Truth. But laſtly, if it be *juſtice* to preſerve the Society of the *church,* is it not partiality in a meer *civil State* to preſerve one [18] onely *ſociety,* and not the perſons of other Religious ſocieties and *conſciences* alſo? But the Truth is, this mingling of the *church* and the *world* together, and their *orders* and *ſocieties* together, doth plainly diſcover, that ſuch *churches* were never called out from the *world,* and that this is only a ſecret *policy* of *fleſh* and *blood,* to get *protec-*

tion from the *world*, and ſo to keep (with ſome little ſtilling of *conſcience*) from the *Croſs* or *Gallowes* of *Jeſus Chriſt*.

Truth. Yea, but hear (ſaith Maſter *Cotton*) thoſe *excellent penmen* of the *Spirit* (both the *Father* and the *Son*) *David* and *Solomon*. Firſt *David* (Pſalme 122 [6.]) They ſhall proſper that love the peace of *Jeruſalem*: and Solomon, Where the *righteous* rejoyce, there is great *glory*, *Prov*.28.[12.] Now(ſaith he) what is the *church* but a *congregation* of *righteous* men? If the *rejoycing* of the *Church* be the *glory* of a *Nation*, ſurely the *diſturbing*, and deſtroying, and diſſolving the *church* is the *ſhame* and *confuſion* of a *Nation*.

Truth. The outward *proſperity* of a *Nation*, was a typical figurative *bleſſing*, of that *national* and figurative *church* of *Iſrael* in *Canaan*. It is now made good ſpiritually to them that love the *ſpiritual Jeruſalem*: for though *godlineſs* hath a promiſe of things of this life convenient; yet *perſecution* is the common and ordinary portion of the *Saints* under the *Goſpel*, though that *cup* be infinitely ſweetned alſo to them that drink of it with *Chriſt Jeſus*, by the meaſure and increaſe of a hundred fold for one, even with perſecution in this life.

The flouriſhing of civil ſtates.

2. It is true, the *rejoycing* of a *Church* of *Chriſt*, is the *glory* of any *Nation*, and the contrary a ſhame: yet this proveth not that *God* vouchſafeth to no *ſtate*, *civil peace*, and temporal *glory*, except it eſtabliſh and keep up a Church of *Chriſt* by force of armes; for the contrary we have mentioned, and Maſter *Cotton* confeſſeth the flouriſhing of *States* ignorant of *Chriſt*, from *Age* to *Age*, yea, and as I have mentioned, even

to two thouſand yeers in *Athens*; ſix *generations* before it heard of *Chriſt*, and fourteen *generations* ſince, with the ſprinking (for ſome time) of the knowledge of *Chriſt Jeſus* in it.

Peace. 2. But conſider (ſaith Maſter *Cotton*) the *excellency* and *preheminence* of the *church*, that the *world* is for it, and would not ſubſiſt but for it, *&c.*

No Civil ſtate can either by Chriſts Teſtimony, or true reaſon, be judge of the Eccleſiaſtical and ſpiritual.

19] *Truth.* Tis true, *glorious* things are ſpoken of the *City* of *God*, &c. yet for many *Ages* together Maſter *Cotton* confeſſeth the *Nations* of the *world* may ſubſiſt & *flouriſh* without it; and though it be the *duty* of the *Nations* of the *world* to *countenance* and cheriſh the *church* of *Chriſt*; yet where is there any *commiſſion*, either in the *New* or *Old Teſtament*, that the *Nations* of the *world* ſhould be the *judges*, *governors*, and *defenders* of *Chriſt Ieſus* his *ſpiritual kingdome*, and ſo bound to take up *Armes* and ſmite with the *civil ſword* (among ſo many pretenders) for that which they believe to be the *church* of *Chriſt*?

Peace. 3. (ſaith he) It is matter of juſt diſpleaſure to *God*, and ſad grief of *heart* to the *church*, when *civil ſtates* looke at the *ſtate* of the *church*, as of little or no concernment to themſelves, *Zech*. 1. 19. *Lam*. 1. 13.

Truth. Grant this, and that the moſt jealous *God* will awake in his ſeaſon, for theſe *ſins*, and for the *perſecutions*, *idolatries*, and *blaſphemies*; which the *Nations* live in: yet what is this for warrant to the *Nations* (as before) to judge and rule the *church* of *Chriſt*, yea, and under the colour of defending *Chriſts* faith, and preſerving *Chriſts church* pure, to tear *Chriſt* out of *heaven*, by *perſecuting* of his *Saints* on *earth*; and to fire the *world* with devouring *flames* of bloody *wars*, and this onely for the *ſweet ſake* of the *prince* of *peace*?

Peace. Dear *Truth*, we are now upon an high point, and that which neerly concerns my ſelf, the *peace* of the *world*, and the *Nations* of it. Maſter *Cotton* ſaith further, *God* winketh at the *Nations* in the time of their *ignorance*, and ſuffers the *Nation* to flouriſh many hundred yeers together, as did the *Empire* of *Rome*; yet when the *church* of *Chriſt* comes to be planted amongſt them, then, as he brought the *Turkes* upon the *Romans*, for their *perſecuting* the *church*, and not preſerving it in *purity*; ſo conſequently will he do unto the *Nations* of the *world*.

Truth. I anſwer, the moſt righteous *Judge* of the whole world hath plauged the *Nations* of the *world*, both before *Chriſts coming*, and ſince, for their *pride* and *cruelty* againſt his people, for their *idolatries*, *blaſphemies*, &c. Yet Maſter *Cotton* acknowledgeth that many *ſtates* have flouriſhed many hundred yeers together, when no true *church* of *Chriſt* hath been found in them: [20] and Maſter *Cotton* will never prove, that *God* ever commanded the *Nations* and *governments* of the world, to gather or conſtitute his *churches*, and to preſerve them in *purity*: For *God* gave his *ordinances*, both before and ſince *Chriſt*, to his *people* onely, whom he *chuſeth* and calleth out of the *World*, and the *Nations* of it: and he hath puniſhed and diſſolved them for their obſtinate *neglect* thereof. And for the *Roman Empire*, and the *Emperors* thereof, the *Chriſtian Religion*, and the *purity* thereof, never loſt ſo much, as when the *Emperors* were perſwaded of Maſter *Cottons bloody Tenent*, as Maſter *Cotton* and all men ſeen in *Hiſtory* and *Chriſtianity* muſt confeſs.

Peace. But further, although (ſaith Maſter *Cotton*) the peace of the *church* be a *ſpiritual inward* peace, yet there is an *outward peace* of the *church* due to them from *Princes* and *Magiſtrates*, in a way of *godlineſs* and *honeſty*, 1 *Tim.* 2.[2.] But in a way of *ungodlineſs* and *idolatry*, it is an wholeſome *faithfulneſs* to the *church*, if *Princes* trouble the *outward peace* of the *church*, that ſo the *church* finding themſelves wounded, and pricked in the houſe of their *friends*, they may repent, and return to their firſt *husband*, *Zech.* 13. [6.] *Hoſ.* 2. [7.]

Difference of ſpiritual and civil peace.

Truth. The peace of the Church is not only *inward*, between *God* and *themſelves*; but as the *Argument* importeth, to which Maſter *Cotton* anſwereth, the peace of the Church *external* and *outward*, is *ſpiritual*, eſſentially differing from the *peace* of the *civil ſtate*, which is meerly *civil* and humane. When the *peace* of the *churches*, *Antioch*, *Corinth*, *Galatia*, was diſturbed by *ſpiritual oppoſitions*, the *Lord* never ſent his *Saints* for *civil* help to maintaine their *ſpirituall* peace, though the *Lord* did ſend *Paul* to the higher *civill powers*, to preſerve his *civill* peace, when he was moleſted and oppreſſed by the *Jews* and *Romans*.

2. For that place of *Timothy*, though I have fully ſpoken to it in this diſcourſe elſwhere, yet this now: It proves not, becauſe the *church* muſt pray for *civil Rulers*, that ſo they may live a quiet and peaceable life in all *godlineſs* and *honeſty*, that therefore *civil*

rulers are *ſupream rulers* and *judges Eccleſiaſtical*, next unto *Chriſt Jeſus*, of what is *godlineſs*, *holineſs*, &c. ſince God hath choſen few *wiſe* or *noble*, to know *godlineſs*: And although it is true that Gods end of vouchſafing *peace* and *quietneſs*, is, that [21] his *Churches* might walk in his fear, and in the wayes of *godlineſs*; yet it doth not hence follow, that *Magiſtrates* were the *cauſes* of the *Churches* walking in the fear of *God*, and being edified, but only of enjoying *Reſt* from *Perſecution*, *Act*. 9. [31.]

3. Although *Gods chaſtiſement* call to *repentance*, and although the *falſe Prophet* in the *church* of *Iſrael* was to be wounded and ſlaine (as they are now to be cut off *ſpiritually* from the *church* of *ſpiritual Iſrael*) yet was it ſo in all the other *Nations* of the world? Or did *Chriſt Ieſus* appoint it to be ſo in all the *Nations* of the *world*, ſince his coming, which is the great *queſtion* in difference?

4. And indeed, what is this, but to add *coals* to *coals*, and *wood* to *fire*, to teach the *Nations* of the *world*, to be *briars* and *thorns*, *butchers* and *tormentors* to the *Lilies* and *Lambes* of the moſt holy and innocent *Lamb* of *God Chriſt Ieſus?*

Peace. But God (ſaith Maſter *Cotton*) cut *Iſrael* ſhort in their *civil ſtate* or *Nation*, when they cut ſhort their *reformation*, 1 [2] *King*. 10. [32.]

Truth. Maſter *Cotton* elſwhere denying a *National church*, which is bounded with natural and earthly limits, it is a wonder how he can apply that inſtance of *National Iſrael*, to the now *ſpiritual Nation* and *Iſrael* of *God*? May he not as well promiſe earthly *peace* and *proſperity* then moſt to abound to *Gods*

When Gods people flourish most in godlinesse then most persecuted.

people, when they most prosper and flourish in *holinesse*, *zeal*, &c. The contrary whereof, to wit, *persecution*, is most evident in all the New *Testament*, and all mens new and fresh *experience*.

Peace. To end this Chapter, Master *Cotton* affirmes, that *civil* peace (to speak properly) is not only a *peace* in *civil* things for the *object*, but the peace of all the *persons* in the *City* for the *subject*. The *church* is one *society* in the *City*, as well as the *society* of *Merchants*, *Drapers*, &c. And if it be *civil justice* to protect one, then the other also.

Truth. *Civil peace* will never be proved to be the *peace* of all the subjects or *Citizens* of a *City* in *spiritual* Things: The *civil state* may bring into *order*, make *orders*, preserve in *civil order* all her members: But who ordained, that either the *spiritual estate* should bring in and force the *civil state* to keep *civil order*, or that the *civil state* should sit, *judge*, [22] and force any of her *subjects* to keep *spiritual order?*

The true and *living God*, is the *God* of *order*, *spiritual*, *civil* and *natural: Natural* is the same ever and perpetual: *civil* alters according to the *constitutions* of *peoples* and *nations*: *spiritual* he hath changed from the *national* in one figurative land of *Canaan*, to *particular* and *congregational churches* all the world over; which *order spiritual*, *natural* or *civil*, to confound and abrogate, is to exalt mans *folly* against the most holy and incomprehensible *wisdome* of God, *&c.*

Examination of CHAP. VII.

Peace.

IN his defcription of *Arrogancy* and *impetuoufnefs*, Mafter *Cotton* tels us, that he that refufeth to fubject his *Spirit* to the *Spirit* of the *prophets*, that fhall oppofe fuch as diffent with *clubs fwords* and *cenforious reproaches*, or reject *communion* with the *church*, &c. his practife tends to the difturbing of *civil* or *church*-peace, or both.

Truth. It is a fallacious mingling of *clubs*, *fwords*, *reproaches*, &c. with refufing to fubmit to the *Spirit* of *prophecie* in the *Prophets*, and rejecting of *communion*, &c. For a man may out of true and upright *confcience* to *God* (as Mafter *Cotton* will not deny) refufe to fubmit to a whole true *church*, having the *Truth* of *God* on his fide; and may withdraw from *communion* with a *church obftinate* in fin, and this without *breach* of *civil peace*; and therefore the mingling or confounding of thefe *fpiritual refiftances* or *difturbances* with *guns, fwords*, &c. is a mingling and confounding of *heaven* and *earth* together.

A monftrous mingling of fpiritual and civil refiftance or difturbance.

2. In that he faith, thefe wayes tend to the difturbance of either *civil* or *church*-peace, or both; he fpeakes too like the doubtful *oracles* of *Apollo*, which will be true however the event fall out; but yet he toucheth not the *Truth* of the *queftion*, which concernes *civil peace* only; againft the *difturbers* of which, I grant the *civil powers* to be armed with a *civil fword*, not in vaine, and concerning which divers cafes were propounded of feeming *Arrogance* and *impetuoufnefs*

in *Gods* ſervants, and yet they fell not juſtly under any cenſure of *breach* of *civil peace*.

23] *Peace.* Tis true (ſaith Maſter *Cotton*) becauſe they were not wayes of *Arrogance* nor *Impetuouſneſs*.

Truth. But will Maſter *Cotton* give way that any *conſcience* but his own may freely *preach* and *diſpute* againſt the *ſtate-religion*, freely reprove the *higheſt*, in ſharpeſt language, for matter of *religion*, refuſe *conformity* to the *common eſtabliſhed religion* and *worſhip*, diſclaime ſubjection to the *civil powers*, in *ſpiritual caſes*, preach againſt the *common policy* and ſeeming *wiſdom* of the *State*, even to a ſeeming *hazarding* of all, and laſtly occaſion great *tumults* and *uproars* (which were the ſix caſes alleadged?) If Maſter *Cotton* granteth this *freedome* to other *conſciences* beſide his own, why preacheth he *perſecution* againſt ſuch a *liberty*, which other *conſciences* beſide his own, believe they juſtly challenge? If to no other *conſcience* then his own, it is not his ſaying ten thouſand times, that his *conſcience* is true, and others falſe, nor any other *diſtinction* in the world, can clear him from moſt unrighteous and unchriſtian *partiality*.

Six inſtances of holy zeal in Scripture, far from arrogance or impetuouſneſs. Theſe were aleadged from Scripture in the bloody Tenent and acknowledged by Maſter Cotton.

Examination of CHAP. VIII.

Peace.

IN this Chapter (dear Truth) lies a charge concerning thy ſelf. For whereas thou anſwereſt an objection, that this diſtinction concerns not *Truth* or *errour*, but the *manner* of holding or divulging, Maſter *Cotton* affirmes the *diſtinction* to ſpeak expreſſly of things *unlawfull* and *erroneous*, and therefore that it cannot be ſaid with *Truth*, that the *diſtinction* concernes not *truth* and *error*.

Truth. The truth is this, the former *diſtinction* ſpeakes of *matter*, and this *diſtinction* ſeems wholly to intend the *manner* of holding forth. The words were theſe: [Again, in points of *Doctrine* and *Worſhip* leſs principal, either they are held forth in a meek and *peaceable* way (though the things be *erroneous* and *unlawful*) or they are held forth with ſuch *Arrogance* and *Impetuouſneſs* as tendeth to the diſturbance of *civil peace*.][1] In which although things *erroneous* and *unlawful* are mentioned; yet who [24] ſees not but that thoſe words are brought in by the way of *Parentheſis*, which may or may not be left out, and the *diſtinction* be whole and intire? And therefore Maſter *Cotton* doth not well to ſpend precious *time* and *life* upon ſeeming *advantages*.

Peace. Yea, but (ſaith he) why is this *diſtinction* blamed, when the diſcuſſer himſelf acknowledgeth, that there may be a way and manner of holding forth, which may tend to break the *civil peace*.

Truth. That which was excepted most againſt in the *diſtinction*, was the perſecuting *language* of [*arrogance, impetuouſneſs, boiſterouſneſs*,] without declaring what that was: to which Maſter *Cotton* anſwers, that the diſcuſſers requeſt, was not that he ſhould compile a *diſcourſe*, but return an *anſwer* to the *letter* of his *friend*; as alſo that he charged none of *Gods children* with ſuch things.

I reply (as formerly) Maſter *Cotton's* memory (though otherwiſe excellent) herein faileth; for, ſuch

[1] Cotton's *Anſwer, &c.*, in *Bloudy Tenent*, p. 7. *Pub. Narr. Club*, iii: 41.

a *requeſt* the diſcuſſer never made unto him, by letter or otherwiſe. 2. Although he charged not *Gods people* with *arrogance* and *impetuouſneſs,* yet moſtly and commonly *Gods children* (though meek and peaceable) are accuſed to be *arrogant, impetuous* &c. and 'tis the common notorious *language* of *perſecutors* againſt them.

Peace. Concerning thoſe ſix *inſtances* wherein *Gods children* were occaſion of great *oppoſition* and *ſpiritual hoſtility,* yea and of breach of *civil peace,* notwithſtanding the *matter* delivered was holy, and the *manner* peaceable, Maſter *Cotton* anſwers, they nothing concern the *diſtinction* which ſpeaks of holding forth things *erroneous* and *unlawful* for the matter, and for the *manner* in a way of *arrogance* and *impetuouſneſs,* to the *diſturbance* of *civil peace.*

Truth. I reply, firſt, it ſpeaks not only of *erroneous* and *unlawful* things (though *erroneous* and unlawful things be admitted in way of *Parentheſis,* as before.) 2. He deſcribes not what this *arrogance* and *impetuouſneſs* is, but wraps up all in one general dark cloud, wherein the beſt and moſt zealous of *Gods Prophets* and ſervants are eaſily wrapt up as proud, arrogant, and impetuous.

25] *Examination of* CHAP. IX.

Peace.

IN this Chapter I remember you affirmed, that one cauſe of civil *diſſention* and uproar, was the lying of a *State* under *falſe worſhip,* whence it endures not the preaching of *light* and *truth*, &c. Maſter *Cotton* anſwers, This is not to the purpoſe, becauſe this is by *accident*.

Truth. It is as much to the purpoſe to declare (in the examination of the breach of *civil peace* about matters of *Religion*) I ſay, to declare the true cauſe of ſuch *troubles* and *uproares*, as it is in the ſearch after the *leaks* of a *ſhip*, to declare where the *leake* is indeed, when many are ſaid to be where they are not.

2. Whereas he confeſſeth that *vigilant* and *faithful* ones are not ſo troubled at the falſe *Religion* of *Jew* or *Gentile*, as not to tolerate them amongſt them in a civil body, he alleadgeth for *inſtance*, that the *Indians* ſubjected to their *government*, are not compelled to the *confeſſion* or *acknowledgement* of their *Religion*: I reply, firſt, who ſees not herein unchriſtian *partiality*, that *Pagans*, *Barbarians* (who happily might more eaſily be brought from their *natural Religion* to a new forme, then any other) I ſay, that they ſhould be tolerated in their hideous *worſhips* of *creatures* and *devils*, while *civil people* (his *countrymen* yea it may be the precious *ſons* and *daughters* of the moſt *high God*) ſhall be *courted*, *fined*, *whipt*, *baniſhed* &c. for the matters of their *conſcience* and *worſhip* to the true and living *God*?

The Indians profeſsing ſubjection to the Engliſh in New England permited in their deviliſh worſhips, when Engliſh fearing God, perſecuted.

2. Is not this paſſage *contradictory* to all Maſter *Cottons* whole diſcourſe in this book, which pleades for the *purity* of *Religion* to be maintained by all *Magiſtrates* and *civil governments* within their *juriſdictions*, and the ſuppreſſing of the contrary, under the penalty of the *deſtruction* of their *lands* and *countries*, and accordingly hath not the practice of *New*

England anſwered ſuch a *doctrine*? and yet, ſaith he, we tolerate the falſe *Religion* of *Jew* or *Gentile.*

Peace. Poſſibly (Dear Truth) the *diſtinction* between *Jew, Pagan,* and *Chriſtian,* may ſatisfie (for the preſent) Maſter *Cottons* conſcience ſo to write and practiſe: for thus he addeth, But [26] if *Chriſtians* ſhall *apoſtate,* or if *Jews* and *Pagans* be blaſphemous and ſeducing, then, *&c.*

Truth. Who knows not but that the very *Religion* of *Jew* or *Pagan* is a blaſpheming of the true *Religion*? *Revel.* 2. [9.] I know the blaſphemy of them that ſay they are *Jews,* and are not, but are the *Synagogue* or *church* of *Sathan.*

Unchriſtian concluſions.

And whereas Maſter *Cotton* alleadgeth for proof of this, *Pauls* blaming of falſe *teachers,* for being *troublers* to the *churches* of *Galatia, Gal.*5. [12.] and *Acts* 15 [24.] &c. Who, that puts this *inference* into *Chriſts* balance, but will ſee the lightneſs of it, thus? The *churches* of *Chriſt* are to draw forth the *ſword* and *power* of *Chriſt,* and are not to ſuffer ſuch as with falſe *doctrine* trouble their *peace, Ergo*: Therefore the *civil ſtate* muſt not permit ſuch perſons to live in the *world,* &c.

Jonahs caſting over-board a ground of perſecution, &c. *examined.*

Peace. The ſecond cauſe I remember, you alleadged of civil *diſturbances* and *hubbubs* about *Religion,* was the *prepoſterous way* of healing of *corruptions* in *Religion,* as by *whips, ſtocks, impriſonment,* &c. unto this Maſter *Cotton* anſwers, Then the *Mariners* caſting *Jonah* over-boord, for his ſin was the *cauſe* of the *ſtorme.*

Truth. I anſwer, if that *extraordinary* and *miraculous inſtance,* be ſufficient ground for *Magiſtrates* caſting over-boord whomſoever they judge *Hereticks*, then all civil *ſtates* and *ſhips* muſt ſo practiſe in *ſtormes* and troubles on *ſea* or ſhore, to wit, throw over-boord, put to death, not only *Hereticks*, *Blaſphemers*, *Seducers* &c. but the beſt of *Gods Prophets* or *ſervants*, for neglect of their *duty*, *Miniſtery*, &c. which was *Jonahs* caſe.

And if ſo, doth not this ſet up (and all the world over) by *land* or *ſea*, all *Kings* and *Magiſtrates*, all *Maſters* of *ſhips* and *captaines*, to be the *ſpiritual* and *Eccleſiaſtical Judges* of the *religion* and *ſpiritual* neglects of all their *ſubjects* or *Paſſengers?* Such *doctrine* I cannot imagine would have reliſhed with Maſter *Cotton* in his paſſage to *New England*; and I humbly deſire of God, that he may never taſt the bitter fruit of this *Tree*, of which yet ſo many thouſands of *Gods ſervants* have fed, and himſelf not a little (to the *Lords* praiſe and his own) in former times.

27] *Peace*. Whereas you argued it to be *light* alone, that was able to diſpell and ſcatter the *miſts* and *fogs* of *darkneſs* in the ſouls and *conſciences* of men, Maſter *Cotton* anſwers, The judgements of God are as *light* that goeth forth, *Hoſ*. 6. 3. *Iſa*. 26. 9. and the falſe *Prophet* repenting will acknowledge this *Zech*. 13. 6. Thus was I *wounded* in the houſe of my *friends*.

Truth. But doth Maſter *Cotton* indeed believe that not only *publike Magiſtrates*, but alſo each private *father* and *mother* (as that place of *Zechary*, literately, taken carries it) muſt now in the dayes of the *Goſpel* wound and pierce; yea run through and *kill* their *Son* the falſe *Prophet?* would he juſtifie a parent ſo practiſing though it were in the neglect of the pub-

The killing of the falſe Prophet. Zech. 13. 6. *examined.*

like *Magiſtrate*, who happily may be of the ſame *Religion* with the falſe prophet? Will not this *doctrine* reach & extend to the pulling down *depoſing* and *killing* of all ſuch *governors* and *governments*, which *God* in his gracious *providence* hath ſet up amongſt all peoples in all parts and *dominions* of the world, yea and harden the heart of *Pharoah*, the very *Pope* himſelf, in his *King-killing* and *State-killing doctrine*?

Peace. If ever Maſter *Cotton* wake in this point, he will tell all the *world*, that it is more *Goſpel-like* that *Parents*, *Brethren*, *Fathers*, *Friends*, impartially fulfill this of *Zechary* 13. and *Deut*. 13. [6–10.] ſpiritually, in the friendly wounding, yea and zealous ſlaying by the two-edged *ſword* of the *Spirit* of *God*, which is the *word* of *God* comming forth of the *mouth* of *Chriſt Jeſus*, *Epheſ*. 5. [6: 17.] *Revel*. 1. [16.]

Truth. And it is moſt true (as Maſter *Cotton* ſaith) that the *judgements* of *God*, legally executed, or more terribly poured forth in the vials of *ſword*, *plague*, and *famine*, they are as heavenly *lights* ſhining out from the *Father* of *lights*, teaching the inhabitants of the world *righteouſneſs*.

Eſa. 26. & Hoſ. 6. 2. *examined.*

Yea the *creation* it ſelf, or each *creature*, are as *candles* and *glaſſes* to light and ſhew us the *inviſible God* and *creator*: but yet theſe are not the *ordinances* of *Chriſt Jeſus* given to his *church*. Theſe are not the *Preachings* of the *word*, and the opening of the *myſteries* of ſalvation, which give *light* and underſtanding to the ſimple, and convert the ſoul: Theſe are not that marvailous *light* unto which the *call* of *Chriſt Jeſus*, in the [28] *preaching* of the *word*, had brought the S*aints* unto whom *Peter* writes: The weapons of *Pauls* fighting, whereby to batter down the high *thoughts* and *imaginations* of the ſons of men againſt the *ſons* of *God*, were of another nature, 2 *Cor*. 10. and his *directions* to *Timothy* and *Titus*, how to deal with *Hereticks* and *Gainſayers* were never heard of to be ſuch, till the *ſon* of man, and *ſon* of *perdition*, brought forth ſuch bloody *weapons* and bloody *doctrines* in the affaires of *Chriſt Jeſus*. 2 Cor. 10. [4. 5.]

Examination of CHAP. X.

Peace.

IN this paſſage Maſter *Cotton* will ſubſcribe to the whole matter, ſaying, This Chapter may ſtand for us without impeachment, and yet in this Chapter is reported the *perſecution*, which both *rightly informed* and *erroneous conſciences* ſuffer, and the blind *eſtate* of ſuch blinde *guides* and blinded *conſciences* who ſo *preach* and *practice*.

Truth. Theſe firſt words [*We approve no perſecution for conſcience*] fight againſt his whole endeavour in this book, which is to ſet up the *civil throne* and *judgement-ſeat* over the *conſciences* and *ſoules* of men, under the pretence of preſerving the *church* of *Chriſt* pure, and puniſhing the evil of *hereſie, blaſphemy* &c.

2. They fight againſt their *fellows*, which follow, thus [unleſs the *conſcience* be convinced of the *error* and *pernicioiuſneſs* thereof] which is all one, as to ſay, We hold no man is to be *perſecuted* for his *conſcience*, unleſs it be for a *conſcience* which we judge danger-

ous to our *Religion*. No man is to be perſecuted for his *conſcience*, unleſs we judge that we have *convinced* or conquered his *conſcience*.

conviction of conſcience.

Tis true, all *errour* is pernicious many wayes to *Gods glory*, to a mans owne *ſoul*, to other mens *ſouls* and *conſciences:* yet I underſtand Maſter *Cotton* to ſay, Except we judge the *error* to be ſo and ſo miſchievous. Tis true, there is a *ſelf-conviction* which ſome *conſciences* ſmite and wound themſelves with? But to ſub-[29]mit theſe *conſciences* to the *tribunal* of the *civil Magiſtrate*, and *Powers* of the *World*, how can Maſter *Cotton* do this, and yet ſay no man is to be perſecuted for his *conſcience*?

Peace. Alas, how many *thouſands* and *millions* of *conſciences* have been perſecuted in all *Ages* and *Times* in a *judicial way*, and how have their *Judges* pretended *victory* and *triumph*, crying out, We have *convinced* (or conquered) them, and yet are they *obſtinate*.

Truth. Hence came that helliſh *Proverb*, That nothing was more *obſtinate* then a *Chriſtian:* under which *cloud* of *reproach* hath been overwhelmed the moſt faithful, zealous, and conſtant *witneſſes* of *Jeſus Chriſt*.

Peace. But ſaith Maſter *Cotton*, Some blinded *conſciences* are ſo judicially puniſhed by *God*, as his in *Irelond* that burnt his *child* in imitation of *Abraham*.

Truth. In ſuch *caſes* it may be truly ſaid, the *Magiſtrate* beares not the *ſword* in vaine, either for the *puniſhing* or *preventing* of ſuch *ſins*, whether *uncleanneſs*, *theft*, *cruelty*, or *perſecution*.

The violation of civil peace though out

And therefore ſuch *conſciences* as are ſo hardned

by *Gods judgement*, as to ſmite their fellow-ſervants, under the pretence of *zeale* and *conſcience* (as in the inſtance of *Saul* his *zeal* for the children of *Iſrael* againſt the *Gibeonites*) they ought to be *ſuppreſt* and *puniſhed*, to be reſtrained and prevented.

of conſcience, to be puniſhed.

And hence is ſeaſonable the ſaying of *King Iames*, that he deſired to be ſecured of the *Papiſts* concerning *civil obedience*,[1] which *ſecurity*, by wholeſome *Lawes*, and other wayes: according to the *wiſdome* of each *ſtate*, each *ſtate* is to provide for it ſelf even againſt the *deluſions* of hardned *conſciences*, in any *attempt* which meerly concernes the *civil ſtate* and *Commonweale*.

30] *Examination of* CHAP. XI.

Peace.

IN this Chapter Maſter *Cotton* takes himſelf wronged, that he ſhould be thought to lay this down, as a *concluſion*, viz. that it is not lawful to perſecute *Ieſus Chriſt*.

Truth. What difference is there in ſaying, It is not lawful to perſecute a *conſcience rightly* informed, and to ſay, It is not lawful to perſecute *Chriſt Ieſus*; was it not all one in effect for *Chriſt* to ſay, Take up thy *bed* and walk, as to ſay, Thy ſins are *forgiven* thee?

[1] "I gave good proofe that I intended no perſecution againſt them for Conſcience cauſe, but onely denied to be ſecured for civill obedience, which for conſcience cauſe they are bound to performe." *Workes of the Moſt High and Mightie Prince James*, 248. London, 1616. Quoted in *Scriptures and Reaſons*, &c. *Publications Narraganſett Club*, iii: 31.

Peace. He adds, It is no matter of wonder to lay down the *principles* of *Religion* for a *proof*, as *Gamaliel* did.

Truth. Who ſees not a vaſt difference between Maſter *Cottons* and *Gamaliels* ſpeech? *Gamaliel* ſpeaks of that particular *controverſie* concerning *Chriſts perſon* and *profeſſion*, which the *Iews* ſo gainſayed and perſecuted. *Gamaliel* fitly aggravateth their *oppoſition* by the danger of their *courſe*, if poſſibly it might prove to be the *Truth*, which they perſecuted. Maſter *Cotton* is to lay down not a *particular anſwer*, but *general concluſions*; and notwithſtanding that in the *courſe* of his *Book* he maintaines ſuch and ſuch *perſecution*, yet he layes this down as his firſt *concluſion*: "It is not lawful to perſecute a *conſcience* rightly informed, that is, *Chriſt Ieſus* in his *Truths* and *Servants*; and that, I ſay never *perſecutor* profeſſed to do without a *Maske* or covering.

An over-ruling finger of God, ordering Maſter Cotton to alleadge Gamaliel, ſure he had forgotten Maſter John Goodwins excellent labour in his Θεομαχεία or fighting agaiuſt God.[1]

Peace. What of that ſaith Maſter *Cotton*, for although they do not *perſecute Chriſt* as *Chriſt*, yet they do it, and it is no matter of *wonder* to tell them as *Chriſt* tells *Paul*, It is not lawful for them ſo to do.

Truth. Doubtleſs whatever *perſecutors* profeſs, and what *Apologies* ſoever they make in all the particular caſes for which *Gods ſervants* are perſecuted; yet the *Saints* of *God* have dealt faithfully to tell *Perſecuters* that they perſecute *Chriſt* himſelf, and to breath out

[1] John Goodwin, (1593–1655,) of Queen's College, Oxford, was ejected from the living of St. Stephens, Coleman street, London, for refuſing the ſacraments indiſcriminately to his whole pariſh. He was a zealous republican, and a warm Arminian. Lowndes (*Bibliographers Manual*, ii: 805,) gives a liſt of his more important works, not including this. Calamy, *Nonconformiſts Memorial*, i: 151, names it, but no copy is within the Editor's reach.

the *fire* of *Gods judgements* againſt them, even out of their own *mouth*.

But what is this to a *concluſion* laid down? for ſo *Chriſt* laid [31] not down his *expoſtulation* with *Paul* as a *concluſion*, as Maſter *Cotton* doth by way of *teaching*, but as a *conviction*, by way of *reproofe*.

Peace. Yet *perſecutors* (ſaith he) have perſecuted *Chriſt* as *Chriſt*; for the *Scribes* and *Phariſes* ſaid, This the is *heir*, come, let us kill him: and *Iulian* perſecuted *Ieſus* as *Ieſus*: And if a *Chriſtian* in *Turkie* ſhall ſeek to gaine a *Turke* to *Chriſtianity*, they will perſecute ſuch a *Chriſtian*, and in him *Ieſus* as *Ieſus*.

Truth. It is ſaid *Acts* 3. [17] that the *Iews* perſecuted *Chriſt* out of *ignorance*; for though they had ſufficient *knowledge* to convince them, yet did they not perſecute *Chriſt* out of a clearely *convinced conſcience*, for then it could not be out of *ignorance*. And yet it was ſufficient, that ſo great a power of *Gods Spirit* appeared in the *evidence* of *Chriſts works*, as to make their *ſin* to be againſt the *Spirit* of *God*: yet had they their *mask* and *covering* (as is evident:) For, this is not the true *Chriſt* or *Meſſiah*, ſay they, but a *deceiver*, a *witch*, working by the power of the *devil*, a *blaſphemer*, a *ſeducer*, a *Traitor*, &c.

Chriſt Jeſus never perſecuted as Chriſt but as a deceiver, blaſphemer ſednced.

Againe, although wretched *Iulian* perſecuted the very name of *Chriſt* and *Ieſus* (whom formerly he had acknowledged and profeſſed) Yet was it ſtill under a *mask* or *covering*, to wit, that he was not the true *Son* of *God*, nor his *worſhip* the *Truth*, but his *Roman gods* were true *&c.*[1] And the ſame ſay the

[1] The Emperor Julian never had any ſincere faith in Chriſtianity. "The Chriſtianity which he naturally poſſeſſed, a Chriſtianity that turned wholly on ex-

Turkes in perſecuting *Chriſtians*, and in them *Chriſt Ieſus* as a *Prophet* inferiour to their onely great and true *Prophet Mahomet*.

And laſtly, neither *Scribes*, nor *Phariſees*, nor *Iulian*, nor *Turkes*, did or do perſecute *Chriſt Ieſus* otherwiſe then as they were and are bound ſo to do by Maſter *Cottons doctrine*, as ſhall further appear, notwithſtanding his *plea*, that ſuch *Magiſtrates* muſt forbeare to puniſh untill they be better informed.

Peace. But let *tyrants* and *perſecutors* profeſs what they will (ſaith Maſter *Cotton*,) yet this varieth not the *truth*, nor impeacheth the *wiſdome* of the *concluſion*.

Truth. *Sweet peace*, how can I here chuſe, but in
Cant. 5. [2.] *I ſleep yet my heart waketh.* the firſt place obſerve that great *myſtery* of the *waking ſleep* of the moſt precious ſervants of the moſt *high God*, in the affaires of his *worſhip*, and the *Kingdome* of his dear *Son?* Awake; for what fiery
32] *cenſures* juſtly poureth forth this our excellent Adverſarie againſt the oppreſſours of *conſcience*, entituling them with the names of *tyrants* and *perſecutors*, notwithſtanding their vaine *profeſſions*, *pretences*, *apologies* and *pleas* for their *tyranny* and *Bloodſhed*? Againe, how faſt aſleep, in his ſo zealous pleading for the greateſt *tyranny* in the *world* (throughout his whole book) though *painted* and *waſhed* over with faire *pretences* &c?

2. He granteth upon the point the *truth*, which was affirmed, and he denyed, to wit, that no *perſecutor* of *Chriſt* ever perſecuted him as the *Son* of *God*,

ternals, could eaſily make the tranſition to Paganiſm. Julian was converted from being an outward Chriſtian with a ſecret leaning to Paganiſm, of which perhaps he was himſelf unconſcious, into a decided and zealous Pagan." Neander, *Church Hiſtory*, ii: 40.

as *Iesus*, but under ſome *mask* or covering, as thouſands of black and bloody *clouds* of *perſecuting witneſſes* in this caſe moſt lamentably make it evident and apparent.

Peace. Maſter *Cottons* next *charge* is very heavy againſt the *diſcuſſer*, for exalting himſelf above *God* in the diſcerning of Maſter *Cottons* fellowſhip with *perſecutors*, notwithſtanding his *profeſſion* againſt ſuch *perſecution.*

Truth. The Lord Jeſus ſaw in the *Iews* ſuch a *contrariety* between their *profeſſions* and *practiſes* (even in this caſe of *perſecution*) Mat. 23. [29–31.]

2. Himſelf in effect, but even now, ſaid the ſame of all *perſecutors*: [What ever pretences they make, ſaith he] and they will pretend great things of *love* to *Chriſt*, and kiſs him ten thouſand times, when *treaſons* and *ſlaughters* are is [ariſe?] in their courſes. And will Maſter *Cotton* ſay that *Chriſt Ieſus* exalted himſelf above *God*, in ſpying out ſo great a *myſtery*? It is no new-thing, that Maſter *Cotton* ſhould be apt to ſay with *David*, That man that hath done this thing ſhall die, not duely conſidering and pondering that our ſelves are *ſons* of *blood*, and children of *death*, condemned by our own *mouth*, if the righteous *Iudge* of the whole world ſhould deal ſeverely with us.

A deep myſtery in perſecution.

Peace. But Maſter *Cotton* (for a cloſe of this Chapter) complaines of his own ſuffering of bitter perſecution, and the *Lord Ieſus* in him, being unjuſtly ſlandered, except the diſcuſſer can prove, that any *doctrine* of his tendeth to perſecute any of the *ſervants* of *Chriſt.*

Truth. Let a mans *doctrine* and *practiſe* be his *wit-*

neſſes, and let every ſoul judge in the fear of *God*, whether the *doctrine* of [33] this *Book* maintaining ſuch and ſuch a *perſecution* to be an holy *truth waſh'*d *white* in the *blood* of the *Lamb*, agree not lamentably with all their *impriſonings*, *baniſhings*, &c. inflicted upon ſo many ſeveral ſorts of their own *countrimen*, *friends*, and *brethren* in the *wilderneſs*, for matter of *Religion* and *conſcience*; amongſt which the *Lord Jeſus* will be heard at laſt to have ſaid, Why perſecuteſt thou *me*? why baniſheſt and whippeſt thou *me*, &c?

2. Will not all perſecuting prelates, *Popes* &c. take heart from hence (according to their ſeveral *religions* and *conſciences*) to perſecute the *heretick*, *blaſphemer*, *ſeducer*, &c. although they all will ſay with Maſter *Cotton*, It is not lawful to perſecute a *conſcience* rightly informed, that is, *Chriſt Jeſus* in his *truths* or *ſervants*?

Peace. But the diſcuſſer (ſaith Maſter *Cotton*) is a bitter *perſecutor*, in ſlandering him, and *Chriſt Jeſus* in him, for a *perſecutor*.

Wolves complaining that the ſheep perſecute them.

Truth. I ſee not but Maſter *Cotton* (though of *Davids ſpirit*) may be guilty of *Sauls* lamentable *complaint*, that *David* perſecuted him, and that he could finde none to *pity* him? Who knows not that all and our own Popiſh *Biſhops* in *Queen Maries*, yea and of late times our Proteſtant *Biſhops* againſt the *non-conformiſts* have been wont to cry out, what bitter *perſecution* themſelves have ſuffered from the *ſlanderous cenſures* and *reproaches* of the *ſervants* of *Chriſt Jeſus* againſt them? Who yet have ſhot no other *arrowes* at them but the faithful *declarations* and *diſcoveries* of Gods holy truth, and the evil of the *oppoſing* and *perſecuting* of it, and the *profeſſors* of it? And how neer will Maſter *Cotton* be found to cloſe with that late bloody *Woolfe* (ſo far as his *chaine* reached) *Biſhop Laud*, who being an *inſtrument* of the bloody hunting and *worrying* of thoſe three famous *witneſſes* of *Chriſt*, Maſter *Prin*, Maſter *Baſtwick*, and Maſter *Burton*; yet at their publike ſentence in the *Star-chamber*, he lamentably *complained* that thoſe poor *Lambs* did bark and bite him with unjuſt *reproaches*, ſlanders, *&c*,[1]

34] *Examination of* CHAP. XII.

Peace.

MAſter *Cotton* here firſt complaineth that his words are *miſ-reported* concerning the *puniſh-*

[1] William Prynn, a barriſter, who had written againſt theatrical amuſements, John Baſtwick, a phyſician, who had written a book denying the divine right of biſhops above preſbyters, and Henry Burton, a clergyman, who had publiſhed two ſermons reflecting on the proceedings of the hierarchy, were each brought before the High Commiſſion in 1633–4, and ſentenced to very ſevere puniſhment. All were impriſoned and fined, and Prynn ſuffered mutilation. In 1637 they were brought before the Star-chamber, charged with having employed their leiſure in priſon in writing againſt the hierarchy. They were condemned "and the Court proceeded to ſentence and fined each of the defendants Prynn, Baſtwick and Burton, 5000 l. apiece to the King, and adjudged the two latter to ſtand in the Pillory at Weſtminſter, and then to loſe their ears; and that Mr. Prynn having once loſt his ears before by ſentence of this Court, Anno 1633, whereof he was now ſentenced to have the remainder of his ears cut off, and alſo it was decreed that he ſhould be ſtigmatized on both cheeks with S. L., ſignifying a Seditious Libeller. And in June 30 the above named three defendants loſt their ears, the hangman rather ſawing off the remainder of Prynn's ears, than cutting them off." All three were alſo to ſuffer perpetual impriſonment in the remoteſt priſons of the kingdom. Ruſhworth, *Hiſt. Collections*, ii: 382: Neal, *Hiſtory of Puritans*, i: 317, 327; Hallam, *Conſt. Hiſt. of England*, 259.

Archbiſhop Laud in paſſing ſentence made a laboured ſpeech, defending himſelf againſt the accuſations of the Puritans, and complained of "this Malicious Storm, which hath lowred ſo black upon me." Ruſhworth, *Hiſt. Coll.*, ii: 383.

ment of the *heretick* after once or twice *admonition*, *Tit.* 3. 10.

Truth. I desire that others may judge in three *particulars.*

First, whether the *summ* and *pith* of the *words* are not rendred.

2. Whether this *Titus* 3. was brought by Master *Cotton* to prove (as is now pretended) that an *Heretick* might be persecuted with an *excommunication* after once or twice *admonition*: or whether the *question* be not of another kind of *persecution.*

3. Whether that *Tit.* 3. 11. do hold forth, That although a man be a *heretick*, *blasphemer*, *seducer*, he may be punished with a *Civil* or *corporeal punishment*, yea though he sin against his own *conscience.*

I add a fourth, whether indeed (as Master *Cotton* intimates) the *discusser* makes this *Tit.* 3 a *refuge* for *hereticks.* Great *sound* and noise makes this word *heretick*, *heretick.* I dare appeal to Master *Cottons* *conscience* and *memory*, whether the reading of *histories*, and the *experience* of time will not evince and prove, that *hereticks* and *Christians*, *hereticks* and *Martyrs* (or witnesses of *Christ*) have not been the same *men* and *women*: I say againe, that such as have been *ordinarily* and *commonly* accounted and persecuted for *hereticks*, have been the servants of the most *high God*, and the *followers* and *witnesses* of the *Lord Jesus Christ.*

The blood of the souls under the Altar is a sealed mystery, Rev. 6. [9.]

Peace. You know (*dear truth*) the *catalogues* of *heresies* and *hereticks* extant, &c.

Truth. Grant it (sweet peace) that some in all times have suffered for *erroneous conscience.* Yet I dare challenge the father of *lies* himſelf to diſprove this aſſertion, That the moſt of ſuch (beyond all compariſon) that have ever ſuffered in this *world* for *hereticks*, have been the diſciples and followers of *Chriſt Jeſus*. And oh that not only the *Lions*, *Leopards*, the *Bears*, *Woolves*, and *Ty-*[35]*gers* (the bloody *Pharoahs*, *Sauls*, *Herods*, *Neroes*, *Popes*, *Prelates* &c.) ſhould fetch from hence, their perſecuting *arrows* and *commiſſions*, but that even the *Davids*, the men after *Gods* own *heart*, the *Aſa's* (whoſe *hearts* are *perfect* with God) that ſuch as are the *ſheep* and *lambs* of *Chriſt*, ſhould be ſo monſtrouſly changed and transformed into *lyons*, *beares*, &c. yea and ſhould flie to this holy Scripture of *Tit*. 3. for this their *unnatural* and monſtrous change and *transformation*.

A challenge to the devil himſelf.

All Antichriſtian hunters or perſecutors make Tit. 3. *their den and Fortreſs.*

Examination of CHAP. XIII.

Peace.

IN this 13 Chapter, dear truth, you argue the great miſtake of the *world* in their common clamour, an *heretick*, an *heretick*, a perſon *obſtinate* in *fundamentals*; and you prove that this word *heretick* intends no more then a perſon *obſtinate* againſt the *admonitions* of the Lord, although in leſſer *matters*: upon this Maſter *Cotton* concludes in this 13 Chapter, that the diſcuſſer gives a larger *allowance* for proceeding againſt *erroneous* perſons then himſelf did.

Tit. 3. *Diſcuſſed.*

Truth. I muſt deny that the diſcuſſer gives a larger *allowance* then Maſter *Cotton*, or any at all, that the *hereticks* or *obſtinate perſons* ſhould be dealt withall by the Civil *Magiſtrates* of *Crete*, but onely by the ſpiritual power of the *Lord Jeſus*.

1. For firſt, What though I granted that an *obſtinate perſon*, contending about *Genealogies*, ought not to be ſuffered, but after once or twice *admonition* ought to be *rejected*? And,

2. What though I grant that after ſuch faithful *admonitions* once or twice, he cannot but be condemned of himſelf? yet according to his third anſwer, how will it appear that I grant, that an *heretick* is rightly defined to be one *obſtinate* in *fundamentals*, when I maintaine, and Maſter *Cotton* ſeemeth to grant, that the *heretick* may be ſuch an one as is *obſtinate* in *leſſer points* and *practiſes*?

3. Further, let the word ἐξεςραπται imply an overturning, yet will it not follow, that therefore an *heretick* is he, who is wil- [36] fully obſtinate, in holding forth ſuch *errors* as ſubvert the *foundation* of the *Chriſtian religion*: For however that Maſter *Cotton* ſaith, That ſuch *diſputes* may tend to overthrow *Chriſtianity*, yet that is but in remote *poſſibility*, as the prick of a *finger* may kill the *heart*, if it ranckle and feſter, and ſo go on from *member* to *member* without means applyed: yet this cannot be ſaid to be a mortal *wound* at firſt. So is it in the *body* of Chriſt.

Peace. The Apoſtle diſcourſing of meats and drinks, of eating and drinking with *offence*, calls an offenſive eating a *deſtruction* of the *ſoul* for which *Chriſt died*: and yet I ſuppoſe he will not ſay that that *difference* was a *fundamental difference*.

Truth. It hath been a groſs and barbarous miſtake

of the *monopolizers* of *learning*, both *divine* and *humane*, The Clergy both of *Popiſh* and *Proteſtant factions* and *worſhips*: And how many are the thouſands of millions of *abuſes, prophanations* and *blaſphemies* againſt the *God of heaven* in all (the *Antichriſtian*) *Chriſtendome*, in all *preachings, writings, proceedings*, and *proceſſes*, touching this name *heretick, hereſie*, &c? By the impartial *cenſure* of the *Lord*, he is an *heretick*, who wilfully perſiſts in any ſinful *doctrine* againſt the due *admonitions* of the *Lord*; for every *bit* and *parcell* of *leaven* is to be purged out of the houſe of *God*, as well as the greater and *fundamentall* lumps.

The horrible abuſing and profaning of that word Heretick. Great ſins of Gods own children.

Examination of CHAP. XIV.

Peace.

IT is a falſhood (ſaith Maſter *Cotton*) that I call the ſlight *liſtnings* of *Gods* people to the *checks* of their *conſciences*, their ſinning againſt their *conſcience*: for I ſpeak not (ſaith he) of the ſinning of *Gods* people againſt *conſcience*, but of an *heretick* ſubverted, much leſs do I call their *ſlight liſtening* to *conſcience* an *heretical* ſinning againſt *conſcience*, leaſt of all do I ſay, that for *ſlight liſtening* to the *checks* of *conſcience*, he may lawfully be perſecuted as for ſinning againſt his *conſcience*. And he adds this *gall* to the former *vinegar*, Thus men that have time and *leaſure* at will, ſet up *images* of *clouts*, and then ſhoot at them.

37.] *Truth.* Maſter *Cotton*, elſewhere, granteth that *Gods children* may (through paſſion, *&c.*) be carried on to despise *admonition*, and may be *excommunicated*, and if so, how can they refusing of *Christs admonition* in the *church*, be excused from sinning against the self-*condemning* of themselves? For if a *child* of *God* may possibly be *excommunicated* for *obstinacy* in some *passion*, *temptations*, &c. then may he be this *heretick* or *wilfull* man in this *Tit.* 3.

Tis true, that in an houre of great *temptations*, *Gods* people may sin against clear *light* of *conviction*, and *sentence* of *conscience*, as *David* and *Peter*, &c. But (as I conceive) the holy Spirit of God in this 3 of *Titus* intends not such a *clearness* of *self-condemning*, but either that the *admonitions* of the *Lord* are so evident and clear, that either if he in his own *conscience* before *God* improved them seriously and duely, they would clear up the *truth* of *God* unto him: or else the *checks* of *conscience* are such as are recorded to have been (*Cant.* 5.) in the *members* of *Christ*, in the *Church* of the *Jews*; and Master *Cotton* cannot render a sufficient reason, why they may not also be found in the members of the *churches* of the *Christians*.

A child of God may possibly be an Heretick.

Peace. I perceive indeed (dear truth) the wonderful effects of a *strange tongue*, in the *church* of *Christ*: The noise and sound of a *Greek* word *heretick*, in poor *English* eares, hath begot a *conclusion*, that a person refusing once or twice *admonition* for some point of *Doctrine*, is such an *heretick* or *monster*, that he cannot possibly be a child of *God*; whereas Master *Cotton* granting that a child of *God* may possibly refuse once and twice *admonition*, and so come to be *excommunicated*; What doth he then in plaine *English*, but ſay, that a child of *God* may be obſtinate to *excommunication* or *rejection* (that is in Greek) be an *heretick?* And what is this but contrary to his former *Aſſertion*, that a childe of *God* cannot be heretically obſtinate to *rejection*, &c.

Truth. Queſtionleſs no child of *God*, but in temptation, may ſin *heretically*, that is, *obſtinately* upon once or twice *admonition*, againſt the checks and whiſperings of his own *conſcience*, and againſt that evidence of *light*, which (afterward) he wondreth how he could deſpiſe: and this rejecting or caſting forth of the viſible *ſociety* of *Chriſt Jeſus* and his ſervants, is not for *deſtructi*-[38]*on* but *humiliation* and *ſalvation*, in the day of the *Lord Jeſus*.

Peace. I judge, that no ſon of *peace*, in a ſober and peaceable minde, can judge, as Maſter *Cotton* here doth, this to be an *image* of clouts.

Truth. Nor can I learn, that the diſcuſſer ſo abounded in time and *leaſure*, as to make ſuch *images* (as Maſter *Cotton* inſinuates.) It is not unknown to many witneſſes in *Plymmouth*, *Salem*, and *Providence*, that the diſcuſſers time hath not been ſpent (though as much as any others whoſoever) altogether in ſpiritual labours, and publike *exerciſe* of the *word*, but day and night, at home and abroad, on the land and water, at the How, at the Oare, for bread; yea and I can tell, that when theſe *diſcuſſions* were prepared for publike in *London*, his time was eaten up in attendance upon the ſervice of the *Parliament* and *City*, for the ſupply of the poor of the *City* with *wood* (during the ſtop of coale from *Newcaſtle*, and the mutinies of the poor for firing.) Tis true, he might

For which ſervice through the hurry of the times and the neceſſity of his departure, he loſt his recompence to this day. The ſtraights of the diſcuſſers time in compoſing of the Bloody Tenent.

have run the rode of *preferment*, as well in *Old* as *New England*, and have had the leaſure and time of ſuch who eat and drink with the *drunken*, and ſmite with the fiſt of *wickedneſs* their fellow ſervants; But *God* is a moſt holy witneſs, that theſe *meditations* were fitted for publike view in change of *roomes* and *corners*, yea ſometimes (upon occaſion of travel in the *country*, concering that buſineſs of *fuell*) in variety of ſtrange *houſes*, ſometimes in the *fields*, in the midſt of *travel*; where he hath been forced to gather and ſcatter his looſe *thoughts* and *papers*.

Peace. Well (notwithſtanding Maſter *Cottons* bitter cenſure) ſome perſons of no contemptible *note* nor *intelligence*, have by letters from *England*, informed the *diſcuſſer*, that theſe *Images* of *clouts* it hath pleaſed God to make uſe of to ſtop no ſmall *leakes* of *perſecution*, that lately began to flow in upon diſſenting *conſciences*, and (amongſt others) to Maſter *Cottons* own, and to the *peace* and *quietneſs* of the *Independants*, which they have ſo long, and ſo wonderfully enjoyed.

Truth. I will end this Chapter, with that famous *diſtinction* of the Lord *Jeſus*; **Digging*, *Begging*, *Stealing*, are the three wayes by the which all that pretend to be *Chriſts Stewards* are maintained. They that cannot *digg*, can *begg* the glittering pre-[39]ferments of this preſent evil world, and the wages of *Balaam*. They that cannot *dig* can *ſteal*, in the wayes of *fraud*, *oppreſſion*, *extortion*, &c. But by the mercy of the moſt *high*, the *diſcuſſer* hath been inabled to get his bread by as hard *digging*, as moſt *dig-*

* *I prejudice not the free and comfortable ſupplies of temporals, which the Saints ought to make for their Teachers in ſpirituals; only I affirme, that ſuch as will not teach without money, they muſt and do beg or ſteal.*

gers in New or old *England* have been put to: and let all men judge, whether ſuch as can *beg* or *ſteal* and cannot *dig*; or ſuch as chuſe neither to *beg* nor *ſteal*, but *dig*, have moſt time and leaſure to make ſuch *images* of clouts, *&c.* *Chriſt Jeſus his diſtinction of Diggers, Beggers, Stealers.*

Examination of CHAP. XV.

Peace.

IN this paſſage (Dear Truth) we hear a ſound of *Agreement*; Maſter *Cotton* conſenteth, that this third of *Titus* evinceth no *civil rejection*, but *excommunication* out of the *Church* of *Chriſt*; and he ſaith, That no ſillable of his *concluſion* lookes at more.

And whereas it might be objected, That *excommunication* cannot fitly be called *perſecution*: he anſwers yes, and quotes *Luk.* 21. 12. *John* 16. 2.

Truth. Were it not for the fierce hands of angry *Eſaus*, this ſhril ſweet voice might paſs for *Jacobs*. What ever Maſter *Cottons* ends and intentions were (of which I cannot but judge chatitably) the eye of *God* alone diſcerneth, but for Maſter *Cottons words*, ſillables and *arguings*, let all impartial *readers* and *conſciences* judge of theſe four *conſiderations*.

Firſt, Whether the word *perſecution*, do not in all proper and ordinary ſpeech ſignifie *penal* and *corporal* puniſhment and affliction.

2. Whether the point in queſtion agitated between the *priſoner* and Maſter *Cotton* throughout the book, concern not only *penal* and *corporal* afliction: and whether it can be imagined, that the *priſoner*, or the

Perſecution, not properly, nor uſually taken for any ſpiritual puniſhment.

diſcuſſer, or any that plead for the *purity* of *Chriſts ordinances*, could ever plead againſt *excommunicating* an *heretick* or wilful offendor out of the *Church* of *Chriſt:* And although the Scriptures by Maſter *Cotton* quoted, do mention *ex*-[40]*communication*, as an unjuſt oppreſſion; yet they ſpeak alſo of *corporal* afflictions, *impriſonments*, bringing before *judgementſeats*, and killing alſo.

3. It could be told in what *countrey*, at a publike ſentence of *baniſhment* of a certaine perſon, a text of Scripture, *Rom.* 16. 17. (parrallel with this of *Tit.* 3.) was alleadged by the chief *judge* in *court* for a ground (not of *ſpiritual excommunication*, but) of *civil*, out of the *Commonweal.*[1]

4. Were it not more for the name of *God*, for the honour of his *truth*, and the comfort of Maſter *Cotton*, plainely and ingenuouſly to acknowledge his miſapplying of this holy *Scripture* of *Tit.* 3. then to cover it by ſo thin and poor a plea, *viz.* that he intends by *perſecution*, *excommunication* out of the *Church* of *Chriſt*?

[1] This of courſe refers to the ſentence paſſed againſt Williams himſelf in the General Court of Maſſachuſetts, Oct. 8, 1635. The judge was John Haynes, who was Governor that year. *Maſs. Col. Records*, i. 145, 161. The text reads, "Now I beſeech you, brethren, mark them which cauſe diviſions and offences contrary to the doctrine ye have learned: and avoid them."

Examination of CHAP. XVI.

Peace.

MAfter *Cotton* here grants a *toleration* to *Jews, Turkes, Pagans,* yea and *Antichriſtians,* with one exception, to wit, ſo that they continue not to ſeduce, *&c.*

Truth. But it muſt be remembred, that before and after he maintaines *perſecution* againſt *Apoſtates, blaſphemers,* and *idolatours,* and then who knows not how all theſe four ſorts, *Jews, Turkes, Pagans,* and *Antichriſtians,* are full of *blaſphemy* and *idolatry*? Now in caſe rhey ſeduce not, they are to be perſecuted as *idolaters* and *blaſphemers,* how then are they to be tolerated?

Peace. It could not be (had not this holy man been catcht with ſipping at the bloody cup of the great *whore*) that Maſter *Cottons affirmations* and *doctrines* ſhould thus quarrel among themſelves.

But further, I ſee not the equality of his yoaking the *Oxe* and the *Aſſe* together, when he further coupleth *ſeducing* of people into *worſhip* of falſe *Gods, confidence* of a mans own *merit,* &c. (which are *ſpiritual matters*) with *ſeducing* into *ſeditious conſpiracies* againſt the *lives* and *eſtates* of ſuch Princes [41] as will not ſubmit their *conſcience* to the *Biſhop* of *Rome.*

Truth. Your obſervation (*dear peace*) is ſeaſonable; the former are meer *Religious* and *ſpiritual,* the latter are meerly *civil,* againſt which the *civil ſtate* is bound to defend it ſelf with *civil weapons.*

Peace. In the next place Maſter *Cotton* chargeth the *diſcuſſer* with want of *reaſon, truth,* and *candor,* for obſerving how unfitly thoſe Scriptures of *Phil.* 3. [17.] *Rom.* 14. [1–4] are produced to prove a *tolleration* of leſſer *errors*: And he affirmes, that he never intended, that what the *Churches* might not tolerate, the *Cities* might not, &c.

Examination of Phil. 3. and Rom. 14.

Truth. The point is *tolerating* or *perſecuting* by the *civil ſtate*; whatever therefore be Maſter *Cottons* intentions, it is apparant, unleſs the *Cities* and *Churches* of *Rome* and *Philippi* be confounded together (as commonly they are in *caſe* of *perſecution*) I ſay it is then apparent that there is no Scripture brought for the *civil ſtate* its *tolerating* of *points* of leſſer moment, nor are theſe *Scriptures* brought to any purpoſe in hand, but prophaned.

Peace. But obſerve his *Argument*, The *civil ſtate* tollerates petty *theeves* and *lyers*, to live in *Towns*, *Cities* &c.

Very ſevere, but not Chriſtian, more then Judaical puniſhment of Theeves in England.

Truth. No well ordered *State* or *City* can ſuffer petty *Theeves* and *lyers* without ſome *puniſhment*, and we know how ſeverely in the *State* of *England*, even *theeves* have been puniſhed even with *death* it ſelf;[1] but Maſter *Cotton* is againſt ſuch *cruelty*, for he pleades for tollerating of leſſer errors, even in points of *Religion* and *worſhip*.

2. If *tollerating* of leſſer *errours* be granted upon this ground, *viz.* till *God* may be pleaſed to manifeſt

[1] "In this country our antient Saxon laws nominally puniſhed theft with death, if above the value of twelve pence; but the criminal was permitted to redeem his life by a pecuniary ranſom. But in the ninth year of Henry the firſt this power of redemption was taken away, and all perſons guilty of larceny above the value of twelve pence were directed to be hung. So that ſtealing to above this value became a felony abſolutely capital and ſo continued to our own times." Stephen, *Commentaries on Laws of England*, iv. 187.

his *truth*; is not the ſame a ground for *tollerating* of greater, as the holy *ſpirit* of *God* argues 2 *Tim.* 2. trying if *God* may be pleaſed to give *repentance*?

Peace. Yea but (ſaith he) the greater will *infect*, and ſo is more dangerous, and the *tolleration* is the more unmerciful and cruel to the ſouls of many.

Truth. Lyars and *Theeves* infect alſo, even the *Civil ſtate*, and a little *leaven* will leaven the whole lumpe; and therefore as the *Commonweal* ought not upon that ground to tollerate petty [42] *theeves* and *lyars*, ſo hath *Chriſt Jeſus* provided in his holy *kingdom* and City againſt leſſer evils, and upon this ground, that a little *leaven* will leaven the whole lumpe. But yet *Chriſt Jeſus* hath not ſpoken (where he gives command for this thing to the *Corinthians* or *Galatians*, that ſuch perſons ſo leavened, ſhould (together with their being put out of the *Church* for obſtinacy in a little *leaven*) be put out of the *world* or *civil ſtate*: (The one (the *Church* (being his *Garden*, the other, the *Commonweal*, being the high wayes, *Field*, &c. the proper place for men as men to abide in.)

Examination of CHAP. XVII.

Peace.

COncerning the holding forth of errour with an arrogant and boyſterous *ſpirit* to the diſturbance of *civil* peace, Maſter *Cotton* moderates the matter, that he would not have ſuch put to *death*, unleſs the *civil peace* be deſtroyed, to the *deſtruction* of the *lives* and *ſouls* of men.

The civil and ſpiritual life confounded.

Truth. I cannot but here firſt obſerve the confounding of *heaven* and earth together, the *Church* and the *world*, *lives* and *ſouls*, &c. as if all were of *one nature*.

2. Neither bleſſed *Paul*, nor I, need to be accuſed of *cruelty* in that grant of *Paul*, if alleadged (*Acts* 25. [11].) for there will not be found ought but a willingneſs to bear a righteous ſentence of *death* in ſome crimes committed againſt the *civil ſtate*.

3. Maſter *Cotton* may here obſerve, how juſtly (as he ſpeaks of the *heretick*) he condemnes himſelf, for it is too bloody a *Tenent* (ſaith he) that every man that holdeth *errour* in a boyſterous and arrogant way, to the diſturbance of *civil peace*, ought to be puniſhed with *death*. Is not this the whole ſcope of his diſcourſe from *Deut.* 13. and other abrogated repealed *laws*, to prove (what was juſt and righteous in the land of *Iſrael*) ſo bloody a *Tenent* and courſe to be inforced in all *Nations* all the world over?

Peace. Maſter *Cotton* excepteth againſt that ſpeech [But if the [43] matter be of a *ſpiritual* or *divine nature.*] There is no error, ſaith he, can be of *divine nature*, though it may be *ſpiritual*.

Truth. Maſter *Cotton* may hear *Solomon* here ſaying unto him, Be not overwiſe *&c.* [*Ecc.* 7. 16.]

God & Cæſar.

For firſt, the words are not, If the *errour* be of a *divine nature*, but if the *matter* (that is, the *controverſie*, *cauſe* &c.) be of a *ſpiritual* or *divine* nature: which *diſtinction* between *humane* and *divine* things, I conceive is the ſame with that of *wiſdome* it ſelf dividing between *God* and *Cæſar*: Give to *God*, &c. [*Matt.* 22. 21.] And ſo, though no errour be of a *ſpiritual* or *divine* nature (taking the words in their highth) yet the *matter* in queſtion may be of ſome *ſpiritual* or *divine* conſideration, belonging to *God*, and his *worſhip*; and not concerning the *Commonweal* or *Civil ſtate* of *men*, which belong to *Cæſars* care.

2. Taking ſpiritual as it is uſed ſometimes in the holy *Scripture* as oppoſite to *fleſh* and *blood*, I ſee no ground for that diſtinction, between *ſpiritual* and *divine*: *God* is a *ſpirit*, and the *ſpiritual* man diſcerneth All things: In ſuch places and their like (to my underſtanding) *ſpiritual* and *divine* are the ſame thing.

Peace. But I marvel at the next paſſage: how can Maſter *Cotton* with any colour of *reaſon* or *charity* conceive the *diſcuſſer* ſo reaſonleſs and ſenceleſs, as to intend by theſe words, [Such onely break the *Cities* or *Kingdomes peace*, as call for *priſon*, and *ſword* againſt *hereticks*?] as if (as Maſter *Cotton* infers and ſaith) that *murtherers*, *ſeditious* perſons, *rebels*, *traitors*, were none of them ſuch, *viz.* *Peace-breakers.*

Truth. This word [onely] can onely have a faire reſpect to ſuch as are charged by their opinions of *Religion* and *worſhip* to break the *Peace* of the *Commonweale*, who (of what conſcience ſoever they are) may freely enjoy their *conſcience* and *worſhip* (either of many and falſe *Gods*, or of the true *God* in a falſe way) and yet not be guilty of the breach of *civil peace*, but onely they (I ſay they onely in this *conſideration*) who by their *doctrine* and *practice* cry out for *priſon*, and *fire* and *ſword*, againſt *hereticks*, &c.

The great peace breakers.

Peace. As the *devil* appeared an *Angel* of *light* in *Samucls* mantle, So *John Hus* and *Jerome* of *Prage*, are declared for *devils* with the pictured *devils* upon their heads;[1] and under this cloud of *heresie* and black name of *hereticks*, most commonly have [44] suffered in all ages the true *messengers* of *Christ Jesus*. Thus cryed they out, *Acts* 17. [6.] These are they that have turned the *world upside* down, and are come hither also; and thus did they set the *City* all on an uproare. And *Acts* 19. not the *worshippers* of *Christ* fill'd the whole *City* with *confusion*, but the worshipers of *Diana*, who filled the *heavens* with that *Bedlam Outcry* of two houres continuance, Great is *Diana* of the *Ephesians*.

English Diana's.

Truth. With as little *reason* and *peaceablenes* of *spirit* hath our *English Nation* used to cry *Great* is the *Church* of *Rome*, *Great* is our holy *Father* the *Pope*, *Great* the *Mass*, *Great* the *Virgin Mary*, *Great* the *General Councels*, &c. And in later times, Great the *Church* of *England*, *Great* the *Christian Magistrate*, *Great* the *Ministery* and *Bishops* of *England*, *Great* the *swearing* and *covenant* of the people, *&c.* and such as dissent from us in these *points* and *practices*, persecute them as *hereticks*, and *disturbers* of the *common civil peace*.

Peace. In the rest of this Chapter, Master *Cotton* makes three *grants* with his *exceptions* annexed.

Truth. Please you (*dear peace*) to mention them in one, and accordingly I shall weigh them in the *balance* together.

Peace. 1. Saith he, The many *causes* which the *discusser* before wrote of, are all of them allowed, but

[1] This was a part of the degradation of Huss from his office. As Jerome was a layman he had no such ceremony of degradation to undergo, but he went to execution with the same sort of cap with horrid forms of devils painted on it. Gilpin, *Lives, &c.*, 224, 253.

none of them concern holding forth of *errors*, which is the point in hand.

2. Saith he, It is eaſily granted that *they* do break the *Cities* or *kingdoms peace*, who cry out for *priſons* and *ſwords* againſt ſuch who croſs their *judgement* or *practice* in *religion*, to wit, ſaith he, unleſs their *religion* be of *God*, and the croſſing of it be ſuch as deſtroyeth and *ſubverteth* the *Religion* of *God*.

Groſs partiality to private intereſts.

3. It is alſo eaſily granted (ſaith he) that many complaine moſt who are moſt in fault themſelves.

Truth. To theſe three I may anſwer thus in one. The *Myſtery* of *preaching* or holding forth the witneſs of the *Truth* of *Jeſus*, is interpreted by many to be the *Myſtery* of the firſt ſeal, the *white horſe*; and the being *perſecuted* or ſlaughtered for the word of *God* and teſtimony of *Jeſus*, to be the *Myſtery* of the third *ſeal*, where the ſouls under the *Altar* cry to the *Lord* for *vengeance* againſt their *perſecutors*. Theſe *myſteries* are ſealed up, and they are the *Lords letters*, not to be opened and read by every [45] one, but (as ſealed *letters* be) by ſuch to whom they are directed.

Peace. It follows therefore, that in the midſt of all the cries of *Iews*, *Pagans*, *Turkes*, and *Antichriſtians* [Our *Religion* is the *Religion* of *God*: You are an *heretick*, you are a *perſecutor*, We are true *Chriſtians*, we are *perſecuted*, &c.] that the hearts of *Gods* children muſt be comforted and ſtaid up with the ſight of this *Myſtery*. And doubtleſs it is moſt commonly (though not alwayes) true, that the impriſoned, fined, whipt, baniſhed, hanged, burned, *&c.* in point of *Religion*, have been ſo inhumanely oppreſſed for the word of *God* and the *Teſtimony* of *Ieſus*.

Our own *Chronicles*, *Records* of *England*, and bleſſed Maſter *Fox* will in part evidence to us, that ſcarce a *King* or *Queen* of *England* hath paſt ſince *Richard* the ſecond his time, but the *blood* of the *witneſſes* of *Ieſus* more or leſs hath been ſpilt in their *Raignes*, as the blood of *Hereticks*, *Schiſmaticks* &c. and but few drops of the blood of any *Heretick* indeed have faln to the ground.

England in all Ages guilty of much perſecution.

Truth. The *diſcuſſer* therefore humbly (to my knowledge) deſireth according to Maſter *Cottons* wiſh to reflect upon his own way, and humbly to beg of God two things for himſelf, and all in any meaſure *cenſured* and *perſecuted* as *hereticks*.

Two ſeaſonable petitions of any perſecuted.

Firſt, *Ioſephs innocency*, *purity*, *chaſtity*, in all thoſe *points* and *queſtions* wherein they are *charged* and *condemned unclean*.

Secondly, *Ioſephs patience* to bear the *accuſations*, *cenſures*, *impriſonments* &c. from the *tongues* and *hands* of them who are notoriouſly *unclean* and *guilty* before the *zealous* and *revenging eye* and hand of *God*.

46]

Examination of CHAP. XVIII.

Peace.

MAny of the following leaves and Chapters (*dear truth*) are ſpent upon that great and heavenly *parable* of the *Tares*, a *knot* about which ſo many holy fingers, dead and living, have been ſo laboriouſly exerciſed, all profeſſing to unty, yet ſome by ſeeming to *untie*, have tyed the *knot* the faſter.

Truth. It is no wonder (*ſweet peace*) to finde Maſter *Cotton* ſo intangled both in his *anſwers* and *replies* touching this *Parable*; for men of all ſorts in former ages, have been ſo intangled before him: To which purpoſe, with thy patience I ſhall relate a notable paſſage recorded by that excellent *witneſs* (or Martyr) of *God*, Maſter *Fox* in his book of *Acts* and *Monuments*: tis this, In the ſtory of Maſter *George Wiſehart* (that famous *Scotch witneſs* of *Chriſt Ieſus*) in the dayes of King *Henry* the eighth, there preached at the arraignment of the ſaid *Wiſehart*, one *Iohn Winryme*, *ſubprior* of the *Abbey* of Saint *Andrews*, he diſcourſed on the Parable of the *Tares*, he interpreted the *Tares* to be *hereticks*; and yet contrary to this very Scripture (as Maſter *Fox* himſelf obſerveth, though elſwhere himſelf alſo maintaining it the duty of the *civil Magiſtrate* to ſuppreſs *hereticks*) I ſay the ſaid *Winryme* concludeth that *hereticks* ought not to be let alone until the harveſt, but to be *ſuppreſt* by the power of the *civil Magiſtrate*: So that memorable it is that both the *Popiſh Prior*, and that truely *Chriſtian Fox*, were intangled in *contradictions* to their own *writings* about the interpreting of this Heavenly Scripture.[1]

The Parable of the Tares.

[1] George Wiſehart ſuffered martyrdom at St. Andrews, March 26, 1546. At his trial John Winryme, ſub-prior of the Abbey, preached from the 13th chapter of Matthew. "At the laſt he added, That Hereticks ſhould be put down in this preſent life. To which Propoſition the Goſpel appeared to repugn, which he intreated of: *Let them go into the Harveſt;* the Harveſt is the end of the world. Neverthelеſs he affirmed that they ſhould be put down by the Civil Magiſtrate and Law." Fox, *Acts and Monuments*, ii. 522. The inconſiſtency here alleged againſt Winryme is of a piece with his courſe afterward. "He

The Parable of Tares groſly abuſed.

Peace. O what cauſe therefore have all that follow *Ieſus* to beg of *Ieſus* (as the *Diſciples* did) the bleſſed *Key* of *David* to unlooſe this holy *miſtery*? In the entrance therefore of this *diſcourſe*, the *diſcuſſer* obſerving Maſter *Cottons expoſition* to be fallacious, and the *Tares* to be interpreted, either *perſons*, or *doctrines*, or *practices*, he blames that Maſter *Cotton* gives no argument for proof of ſuch an interpretation: Maſter *Cotton* replies.

Firſt, Neither did the *Author* of the letter give *reaſon* for his *in-*[47]*terpretation.* 2. That they both gave *one interpretation.* For the *Author* of the *letter* ſaid, that ſome expounded the *Wheat* and *Tares*, to ſignifie ſuch as walk in *truth*, and ſuch as walk in *lyes:* now are not (ſaith Maſter *Cotton*) *hypocrites* and ſome corrupt *doctrines* and *practices* coincident with ſuch as walk in *lyes*, &c?

Truth. I anſwer, Firſt it might be both their failing, not to ſtrengthen their *interpretations* with ſome *light* and evidence from *Scripture* or *reaſon*, although the *Priſoners* failing the leſs, as being forced to write by *ſhifts* and *difficulties* in *priſon*, and ſo the ſhorter, when Maſter *Cotton* had free *liberty* to inlarge and confirm without control, *&c.*

2. When the *priſoner* interprets the *Tares* to be ſuch as *walk* in *lyes*, it will be found evident upon examination, that he meaneth ſuch as manifeſtly,

was an early convert to the proteſtant doctrines, but he neither abandoned his ſituation nor emoluments in the Catholic church; and when Knox, at the meeting of the Black and Grey Friars, demanded whether he conſcientiouſly conſidered the doctrines then called heretical contrary to God's word, he not only evaded the queſtion, but argued on the popiſh ſide." Chambers, *Biog. Dict. of Scotſmen*, iv. 457.

openly, viſibly walk in the true *profeſſion* of *Chriſtianity*; and ſuch as openly and viſibly walk in the *lyes* of falſe and *Antichriſtian doctrine* and *worſhip*. That diſtinction of ſecret and open Hypocriſie is ſeaſonable: *ſecret*, implies ſuch a *diſſimulation* as may lie hid under the true *outward profeſſion* of *Chriſt Jeſus*, as in *Judas*, *Simon Magus*, *Ananias* and *Sapphira* &c. Open *hypocriſie* implies the profeſſion of the *man* of *ſin*, ſitting in the *Temple* of *God* (or over the *Temple* of *God*) pretending the *Name* of *Chriſt*, and yet apparantly and viſibly, falſe and counterfeit, and but pretending, when ſuch *pretences* and *ſhewes* are brought to the *Touchſtone* of true *Chriſtianity*.

Hypocriſie ſecret and open hypocriſie.

Peace. Your *obſervation* is true, as alſo a ſecond, That theſe hypocritical *doctrines* and *practices* are to be tollerated to the end of the world, this he ſets down in *general*, not inſtancing in particular what *doctrine* and *practiſes* are to be tollerated: and on the other hand, the whole drift of his *Booke* maintaineth, that ſuch *perſons*, *doctrines* or *practices*, that are *idolatrous*, or *blaſphemous*, or *infectious*, are not to be *tollerated* or permitted at all; which *paſſages* to my underſtanding have not *harmony* among themſelves: For what is all the whole *Religion* of every *Antichriſt*, but a *Maſs* or *Chaos* of *Hypocriſie*, *Idolatry*, *Hereſie*, *Blaſphemy*, *Poyſons*? &c.

Beſides, Maſter *Cotton* had dealt more plainly with this holy *Scripture*, if he had explained what he meant by ſuch *doctrines* [48] and *practiſes* [comming neer the *truth*] and ſet down the *bounds* how neer as to make them *Tares*.

Truth. Dear Peace, Who knows not that the *weeds*

of the *wildernefs* come neer the *flowers* of the *Garden*, the *counterfeit* may come neer the *life*, and the falfe *mettal* the true *gold*? And though it be true that fome *doctrines* and practices be not fo *grofs* as other, yet they differ but (as the *Scripture* fpeaks) as *whores* and *whoremongers*, amongft themfelves; fome are more *proper*, and *fine*, and *young*, and *painted*; fome are *old*, *deformed*, &c. And yet the *fineft weeds*, *counterfeits*, and *whores* are unfufferable in the *Garden*, in the *Commonweale*, *houfe*, and *bed* of *Chrift*: Though yet in the *civil Commonweale*, the vileft *fpiritual ftrumpet* may challenge a civil Being, if in *civil* things unreprovable.

Spiritual whoredome in worfhip may and doth in all Nations fubfift with Civil Beings, Relations, &c.

Examination of CHAP. XIX.

Peace.

BUt in this Chapter, Mafter *Cotton* in the iffue granteth, that the *Tares* fignifie *perfons*, by *Chrifts* own interpretation: For [them that do *iniquity*] may feem to be an explanation of πάντα τὰσκάνδαλα, All *fcandals*, that is, *perfons* holding forth of *fcandalous* and corrupt *doctrines* and *practices*, like unto true and found.

Truth. Yet withall he chargeth the difcuffer with *lightnefs* and *inconftancy*, for endeavouring to prove that *corrupt doctrines* and *practices* are not to be tollerated, and yet, faith he, the *difcuffer* pleades that fuch *perfons* ought to be tollerated. Whereas the difcuffer twice in this Chapter exprefly diftinguifheth between *toleration* in the *Church*, and *tolleration* in the *world*, and affirmeth, that although the *Church* of *Chriſt Jeſus* cannot tollerate either *perſons* or *practices* which are falſe and *Antichriſtian*, yet the *civil ſtate*, the *world*, ought to tolerate and permit both.

And therefore Maſter *Cottons* inconſiderate charge of *contradiction* will not ſtick, becauſe of thoſe divers *reſpects* or *States*, the *ſpiritual* and *civil*, as it was no *contradiction* in *Chriſt Ieſus*, to affirme that *Iohn Baptiſt* was *Elias*, when *Iohn* himſelf affirmeth, that he was not *Elias*: For in ſeveral reſpects the [49] Negative of *John*, and the Affirmative of *Jeſus* were both true.

Examination of CHAP. XX.

Peace.

IN this paſſage (to my underſtanding) Maſter *Cotton* after much ſeeming *conteſtation* and *diſagreement*, yet in concluſion he ſhakes hands and agrees with the *diſcuſſer* in the maine point in queſtion.

Truth. Your *obſervation* reacheth home; for let it be granted, that the *Greek* word Ζιζάνια ſhould not ſignifie All *weeds* ſprung up with the *wheat*, but one kind of weed, and that in ſpecial which Maſter *Cotton* ſaith, *Dioſcorides* deſcribeth: Let it be granted to be the ſame with *Lolium*, and that there is a great *ſimilitude* between the *Tares* and the *Wheat*, while they are in the blade (ſome of which particulars are *controverſial*:) yet it no way oppoſeth that which the diſcuſſer maintaineth, to wit, the eaſineſs of diſcerning theſe *tares* to be *tares*, when they are grown up to blade and fruit. And therefore Maſter *Cotton* at the laſt, confeſſeth that even theſe *tares* (*unknown*

Of the Tares.

[*known*] *hypocrites*) (according to his own *expoſition*) ought to be ſuffered in the *church* of *Chriſt* to the *harveſt* or end of the *world*.

Peace. I cannot but wonder how Maſter *Cotton* ſhould once imagine, that it might poſſibly ſtand with the *order*, *piety*, and *ſafety* of the *profeſſion* of *Chriſt Jeſus*, that ſuch a *generation* of known *hypocrites* ſhould be perpetually ſuffered.

Truth. Doubtleſs the *Lord Jeſus* was not of Maſter *Cottons* minde, who ſo vehemently warned his *followers* to take heed of the *leaven* of *hypocriſie*. Beſide, if known *hypocrites* may be ſuffered and not caſt out, Why may not known *hypocrites* be taken in? And what is then become of the true *matter* of the *church*, to wit, true *living ſtones* of a *ſpiritual life* and *nature*, ſo far as outwardly can be diſcerned?

Peace. This *aſſertion* hath ſo foule a *repreſentation*, that Maſter *Cotton* is forced to draw this *vaile* over, and therefore he adds, untill the *fruits* of *hypocrites* grow *notoriouſly ſcandalous*.

50] *Truth.* I cannot fathom how theſe two agree: Firſt, known *hypocrites* may be tolerated untill the *worlds* end; 2. *Tolerated* no longer, then untill the *fruits* of the *hypocriſie* grow *notoriouſly ſcandalous:* For will not all *reaſon* and *experience* ask this *queſtion*: How comes it that this *ſriend*, *ſubject*, and *Spouſe* of *Chriſt* is now a known *diſſembler*, *traitor*, *whore*, unleſs by ſome *ſcandalous fruits* ſo declaring and uncaſing[1] of them? If the ſhameful fruits of the unclean perſon, 1 *Cor.* 5.]13.] were ſufficient to de-

[1] Uncaſe,—to ſtrip off the covering. "Commit ſecurely to true wiſdom the vanquiſhing and *uncaſing* of craft and ſubtlety, &c." Milton, *Of Reformation in England.* lib. ii. Works, ii. 47. (Bohn's edition.)

nominate him a *wicked perſon*, why were they not ſufficient to warrant *Paul* to ſay, *Put away* therefore that *wicked* perſon from amongſt you?

Peace. But let us mind the Scripture quoted: If (ſaith Maſter *Cotton*) fooliſh *Virgins* be caſt out of the *church*, the *wiſe Virgins* may be found ſometimes ſleeping as well as they.

Truth. Neither *good wheate*, nor *wiſe Virgins* are to be caſt out of the *church* of *Chriſt*, while they appear to be ſo: yet ſince Maſter *Cotton* elſewhere grants, that a child of *God* (*good wheat, and a wiſe Virgin*) may ſo ſtand out againſt the *church of Chriſt* (in ſome paſſion) that he may be caſt out &c. How much more then ought the *tares* and *fooliſh Virgins* (while ſo appearing) be excluded?

Of the wiſe and fooliſh Virgins.

2. If the *wiſe Virgins* be received into *heaven*, as the *fooliſh* ſhut out, will it not evidently follow (even the contrary to that for which Maſter *Cotton* alleadgeth this Scripture) to wit, That when *hypocrites* are diſcovered, they are to be *kept* out, and conſequently to be *caſt* out of the *church* of *Chriſt*? except Maſter *Cotton* will ſay, that the *kingdome* of *Chriſt* on *earth*, may receive and keep in her *boſome* ſuch ſtinking *weedes*, declared ſo to be, which the *kingdome* of *Chriſt* in heaven abhors.

Who queſtions, but while the *hypocriſie* of theſe *fooliſh Virgins* lay hid in their empty *veſſels*, that outwardly they appeared as *wiſe* as the *wiſe Virgins*? But when the *fruits* of their *hypocriſie* diſcovered them to be *fools*, how can Maſter *Cotton* (according to the truth as it is in *Jeſus*) affirme, that *fooliſh Virgins* (*known hypocrites*) are to be kept in and not caſt out of the *church* of *Chriſt* unto the end of the *world*?

Peace. O how contrary is this to the very *fundamentals*, *eſſence*, *nature* and *being* of a *church* or *Spouſe* of *Chriſt Jeſus*, [51] which is (by the *confeſſion* of *Papiſts* and *Proteſtants*) a *ſociety* of *wiſe Virgins*, viſibly *Saints* holy and faithful perſons, a *ſociety* of ſuch perſons as outwardly profeſs to love *Chriſt Jeſus* uprightly (*Cant.* 1. [4.]) and to be eſpouſed to him, 1 *Cor.* 11. [3.]

Truth. Yea, and how contrary is this to the nature of *Chriſt Ieſus*, whoſe *heart* is all one *fire* towards the *daughters* of *Ieruſalem* (*Cant.* 4.) and how contrary to the *charge* that great and ſolemn *charge* of the *Lord Ieſus* to all his followers, to take heed of that *leaven* which is *hypocriſie*, which if ſuffered, will leaven the whole *lumpe*, and render the *garden* and *ſpouſe* of *Chriſt* a filthy *dunghill* and *whore-houſe* of rotten and ſtinking *whores* and *hypocrites*.

No true church of Chriſt conſiſting of viſible hypocrites.

Examination of CHAP. XXI.

Peace.

MAſter *Cotton* here endeavors to prove (as many have done before) that the *Field* which the *Lord Ieſus* interprets the *world*, was meant by him to be the *Church*, as he is ſaid to love the *world*, *Iohn* 3. [16.] to be propitiation for the ſins of the *world*, 1 *Ioh.* 2. [2.]

Truth. In theſe and many other places of like nature, it pleaſeth the *Spirit* of *God* to ſet forth his *love* to *mankinde*, diſtinct from all other *creatures*: As alſo the *impartiality* of his *love*, calling his choſen out of all ſorts of *ſinners*, *mankinde* all the world over: and yet it cannot be denyed, but that the Scriptures ſpeak frequently of the *world* and of the *church* in a far diſtinct and contrary *acceptation*. So, as when he nameth the *church*, it cannot ſignifie the *world*; and when the *world*, he cannot be ſaid to intend the *church*, the *reaſons* therefore on either ſide muſt be expended and weighed in the fear of *God*, why the *Field* here called by *Chriſt* the *world*, cannot be intended to be the *church* of *Chriſt*.

The field of the World.

Peace. Your *right diſtinguiſhing* is a *right dividing* of the *word* of *Truth*; but (ſaith Maſter *Cotton*) it cannot be the *world* in proper ſignification; for which he aleadgeth three reaſons.

52] Firſt, Becauſe there had been (ſaith he) no place for the ſervants wonder at the appearing of the *tares* verſe 27. for what wonder that the *world* ſhould be ſo full of *fornicators*, &c? Was it ever otherwiſe?

Truth. It is true, that the *world* lyeth in *wickedneſs*, and is full of *fornicators*, *idolaters*, &c. and yet it was ſome thouſands of yeers when the world was not full of *Chriſtian*, that is, *anointed*, or *holy fornicators*, holy *idolaters*, &c. That is indeed and truth *Antichriſtian*, and that alone is the point in queſtion, about which this anſwer of Maſter *Cotton* hovers, but comes not neer it. This is indeed a moſt dreadful and *wonderful point* of the *wiſdome*, *juſtice*, and *patience* of *God*, ſo to ſuffer ſo many *millions* of men and women, to arrogate to themſelves the *name* and *profeſſion* of the moſt *holy* living *God*, and his holy

The myſtery of Antichriſtians or falſe Chriſtians.

Son *Chriſt Ieſus*, to be called *Chriſtians*, *anointed* or holy, and yet upon the point to hate the *holineſs*, *truth*, and ſpirit of *Chriſt Ieſus*.

Truth. This is doubtleſs to me (what ere Maſter *Cotton* imagines) a wonderful *myſtery* in all *Ages* ſince theſe *tares* were firſt ſown, to ſee, I ſay, ſo many *millions* of holy *idolaters*, holy *murtherers*, holy *whoremongers*, holy *theeves*, &c.

The *blaſphemy* of this is ſo wonderful and dreadful, that I cannot ſufficiently *wonder* at him that *wonders*, not how this comes to paſs.

Truth. The like I anſwer to his ſecond *Reaſon*, that it is true that we read not that ever any of the *Miniſters* or *Prophets* of *Chriſt* ever eſſayed to pluck up all ſuch *vicious* notorious perſons out of the *world*, as they demanded concerning the *tares*, for then indeed as the S*pirit* implies, 1 *Cor*. 5. [10.] the whole ſtate of the *world* would be overthrown ;[1] but yet this hinders not, but there may be a *deſire* in *Gods ſervants* to pluck up this or that ſect or ſort of people, *Jews*, *Turks*, or *Antichriſtians*.

Peace. Dear Truth, you make me call to minde the deſire of *Chriſts diſciples*, that fire might deſcend from *heaven*, not to conſume all *fornicators*, *idolaters*, all *cruel* and *unclean perſons* out of the *world*, yet that *particular*, *unmerciful*, *ſuperſtitious Town* of the *Samaritans*, they deſired that *fire* might come from *heaven* and conſume them.

Truth. Indeed this *deſire* of the *diſciples* is no ſtrange

[1] "I wrote unto you in an epiſtle, not to company with fornicators: yet not altogether with the fornicators of this world: for then muſt ye needs go out of the world." 1 *Corinthians*, v. 9, 10.

deſire, [53] for what elſe do All they deſire, which permit not in the *civil ſtate,* any *Religion, worſhip* or *conſcience* but their own? Nay far beyond that, were the whole *worlds neck* under their imperial *yoake* (the many *millions* of *millions* of *blaſphemers,* and *idolaters* of all ſorts) if they will not be convinced at their *word,* muſt be cut off from all *natural* and *civil* being in the world, by *Fire* and *Sword.*

Maſter Cotton knows not his own deſire.

Peace. His third reaſon is, That the diſcuſſer reckoned up as paralel *goats* and *ſheep, wheate* and *tares* (as generally, ſaid he, others do) and he addeth, that in the pureſt *church* after the *ruine* of *Antichriſt,* there ſhall be *goats* and *ſheep, wiſe* and *fooliſh Virgins,* untill the coming of *Chriſt* to judgement, *Mat.* 25. [32. 33.]

Truth. Although the diſcuſſer ſpake of that eternal *ſeparation* between *wheat* and *tares, ſheep* and *goats* approaching; yet he never ſaid, that the *tares* and *goats* ſignified *hypocrites* in the Church, which is the point in *queſtion:* Nor dare I ſubſcribe to that opinion, that after the *deſtruction* of *Antichriſt,* when pureſt times of the *church* ſhall come, that there ſhall be ſuch a mixt eſtate in the *church* of *Chriſt,* untill the *coming of Chriſt* to judgement.

For firſt, Although *goats* were clean for *food* and *ſacrifice,* yet it is apparant, that as they are for the *left hand,* So they are viſibly known by every child, where *goats* and *ſheep* are kept. And to image that viſible *hypocrites,* ſuch as *tares, goats, unprofitable ſervants, fooliſh Virgins* &c. ſhall in a mixt way make up *Chriſts church,* and that in the pureſt times of the *church,* of which there are ſo many and wonderful *prophecies*, is to me not onely to frame a *church eſtate* point blank croſs to the purity of thoſe *churches*, but even to the firſt *Apoſtolical churches*, yea and againſt that *frame* of *church* eſtate in *New England*, where Maſter *Cotton* hath profeſſed (though now it is ſaid the door is wider) againſt receiving in ſuch members as are viſibly *fooliſh Virgins*, *goats* &c.[1]

Peace. Maſter *Cottons* ſecond anſwer is, that if the Field be the *world*, as the *tares Antichriſtians* and falſe *Chriſtians*, yet they were firſt ſown in the field of the *church*.

The firſt riſe of Antichriſtians argued.

Truth. Not ſo: for although there might be many *infirmities* and *diſtempers*, yea ſome great *corruptions* in the firſt *Chri-*[54]*ſtian body* the *church* of *Chriſt*; notwithſtanding that *Antichriſt* is an *Apoſtate*, yet it will not follow, that the *tares* were firſt ſown in the true *church*, becauſe *Sathan* might eaſily raiſe up ſome *profeſſors* of the name of *Chriſt*, which the true church would never admit. And as *Sathan* might raiſe up *perſons*, *congregations*, *worſhips*, which were not according to *Chriſt*; So might he eaſily raiſe up *churches*, *congregations* and *ſocieties* of ſuch *tares* with whom the *churches* of *Chriſt* might refuſe ſociety. So ſaith *John*, There are many *Antichriſts*, whom yet we cannot well imagine that they were in the *churches* of the *Lord Jeſus*.

1 "It is conſented on both ſides, that it is the duty of all the members of the particular viſible Church, and neceſſarie both by Divine Commandment, and as a neceſſary means of their own ſalvation, to be truly regenerate."

"As for ourſelves, though we neither dare, nor will deny that we doe receive ſome Hypocrites; yet neither alwayes, nor known Hypocrites, nor with allowance of ourſelves therein, if we ſhould ſo do." Cotton, *The Holineſſe of Church Members*, pp. 1, 79. London, 1650.

There came falſe *Apoſtles* to the Church at *Epheſus*, but yet that *church* examined and found them *lyars*. And ſo long as the *churches* were watchful, thoſe *tares* kept in the *world*. But when the *churches* began to be ſleepy, the Tares might undiſcerned creep into the *church*.

This may be as well, as when *Apoſtates* fall off from the *church*, go out from it, becauſe they were never of it: and alſo as well as that the *church* of *Chriſt* may drowzily neglect to purge out the old *leaven* of *perſons* and things, which may ſoon over-ſpread and over-run the whole *lumpe* and *garden* of the *church* of *Chriſt*, untill it be turned againe into one common field of the *world* together.

Peace. Maſter *Cottons* third anſwer is, That *Antichriſtians* muſt not be tolerated unto the end of the *world*, becauſe *God* will put it into the heart of faithful *princes* to hate the *whore*; and after that, we read of a viſible ſtate of *New Jeruſalem* before the end of the world, *Rev.* 20. 21, 22.

Truth. It is not ſaid, that thoſe *princes* that ſhall hate the whore ſhall be *faithful princes*: and ſince Maſter *Cotton* ſeems to hold that by way of *ordinance* (and ſo in *obedience*) the *Kings* of the *earth* ſhall with the ſword deſtroy *Antichriſt*, I deſire his proof for any ſuch prophecy. For,

1. It is not ſaid, that *God* will put it into their hearts, to hate the *whore*. And we finde that they ſhall hate the *lambe*, as well as hate the *whore*. For they ſhall make war with the *lambe*, and the *lamb* ſhall overcome them, as comes to paſs after the ruine of the whore, *Rev.* 19.

The judgement of the great whore.

2. *Judgement* may be executed upon the whore by way of [55] mutual *judgement* each upon others, when in the midſt of their *ſpiritual whoredoms*, and *drunkenneſs* with the S*aints blood*, they ſhall fall out with the *whore* (as uſeth to be in *whoredome*) and turn their *whoriſh loves* into *outragious fury*; and the very deſcription of their fury looks this way, for it is not the property of *ſober* and *faithful* men (though repenting of their whoredom) to make a *woman* naked (though a *whore*) and to eat her *fleſh*, as it is ſaid, thoſe ſhall do.

But grant (as we moſt hopefully do) the *whores conſumption* by the ten hornes of the *Beaſt*, and the flouriſhing of new *Jeruſalem* upon the earth (*Rev.* 20. 21, 22.) before the end of the world (all which are great diſputes among the people of *God*) yet I judge it neceſſary that two or three *queries* be ſatiſfied for the further clearing of the holy minde of the *Lord* in this particular.

1. Whether (as ſome have and do argue) the end of the *world* in this Parable and other Scriptures do expreſly and undeniably ſignifie the end of the world and *judgement*-day literally, and not ſome other myſtical *period* of *time*, ſince the word Αἰὼν (uſually tranſlated *world*) is of various *ſignification*, and ſometimes ſignifies an *Age*.

2. Whether thoſe ten *Kings* which ſhall deſtroy the *whore*, ſhall be abſolutely *Chriſtian*, true *Saints*, *followers of Jeſus* they and their Armies, or elſe remaining *Antichriſtian* hornes of the *Beaſt*, ſhall yet execute the *judgement* of *God* upon the great *whore:* as *Jehu* remaining both hypocritical and idolatrous,

yet daſht out the braines of that great whore *Iezabel*, and executed *judgement* upon *Baals Prieſts*: yea and even as *Henry* the eighth tumbled the *Pope* out of his *chaire* in *England*, and thouſands of his Popelings with him, he ſuppreſt and threw the *whore Iezabel* the *church* of *Rome* out of *Englands* window, and yet continued to burn the *Saints* of *Ieſus* upon his ſix Popiſh and *bloody Articles*.[1]

3. Whether that mighty *Army* of *Gog* and *Magog*, which is muſtered up after the thouſand yeers raigne of *Chriſt*, be not in part made up of the ten hornes, even after the whore of *Romes conſumption* (as before in *Henry* the eighth his caſe) which horns with their peoples *Chriſt* will have yet to be tolerated as *Tares*
56] in the field of the *world*, though not in the Church of *Chriſt*.

Peace. What think you of Maſter *Cottons* grant, that the firſt fruits of *Antichriſtians* may be *tares* ſown in the field of the *church*, which afterwards grow to be Briars and Thornes?

Truth. I obſerve that to be *tares*, of *Antichriſtian worſhippers*, and *briars* and *thornes* (*oppreſſors* and *perſecutors*) are both of them of a falſe and *Antichriſtian* nature, which ought to be far from *imitation* of the *Roſe* of *Sharon*, or the *Lily* of the *vallies*.

1 "The bloody act of the Six Articles," or "the whip with ſix ſtrings," as it was called by the Proteſtants, paſſed through Parliament in June, 1539. It was drawn up by the King and a Commiſſion of the Biſhops, though Mr. Froude charges the extreme ſeverity of the penalties on the biſhops rather than the King. The firſt article eſtabliſhed the doctrine of the Real Preſence, and whoever denied it was to ſuffer death by burning, with no privilege of abjuration, or benefit of clergy. It was oppoſed by Cranmer, and called forth a brave proteſt to the King from Melancthon. Froude, *Hiſt. of England*, iii. 393–400. For Melancthon's proteſt, ſee Fox, *Acts and Monuments*, ii. 413–417.

But 2. Are there no *tares*, that is, hypocrites, but in the *church*; and muſt all the *briars* and *thornes* (*oppreſſors* and *perſecutors*, &c.) have no root from the wilde world, but from the *garden* of *Chriſts church*?

Peace. Now whereas it was urged, that it ſtood not with the *wiſdome* and *love* of *Chriſt*, interpreting this parable, and opening what the field was, to call the *field* the *world*, when he meant the *church*: Maſter *Cotton* anſwers, that *Paul* by the ſame wiſdome uſeth the ſame *word*, 2 *Cor*. 5. [19] God was in *Chriſt* reconciling the *world* unto himſelf.

Truth. *Paul* in uſing that figure of the *world* for all ſorts of men in the *world*, doth not undertake to interpret a *Parable*, which before he had propoſed unto (and at the requeſt of) the *Corinthians*, as the *Lord Ieſus* doth at the requeſt of his *diſciples*.

And where Maſter *Cotton* ſaith, that it is no more an improper ſpeech to call the *church* the *world*, then to ſpeak of *Chriſt* as dying for the *world*, when he dyed for the *church*.

Truth. I finde it not to be ſaid, that *Chriſt* died for the *world*, but grant that it hath pleaſed the *Lord* in his moſt infinite *wiſdome*, to cauſe the tearm of the *world* to be uſed in *various ſignifications*; yet let any inſtance be given of any *Scripture*, wherein the *Lord* oppoſing the *church* to the world, the *wheat* to *tares*, doth not diſtinguiſh between the *church* redeemed out of the world, and the world it ſelf, which is ſaid to lye in *wickedneſs*, and to be ſuch as for which Chriſt Jeſus would not pray, *Iohn* 17. [9.]

57] *Examination of* CHAP. XXII.

Peace.

IN this Chapter was urged the *ſcope* of the *Lord Jeſus*, to wit, to foretell the *Antichriſtian ſtate* oppoſing the true *Chriſtian church* and *worſhip*, as alſo to comfort and ſtrengthen the *hearts* of his *followers*, againſt the *grievances* ariſing therefrom; and where it was urged that the *church* conſiſteth onely of good ground, and that the three ſorts of Bad ground viſibly ſo declared, are properly in the *world*, and not in the *church*, Maſter *Cotton* anſwers,

Chriſts Church by inſtitution, properly conſiſting of good ground.

Firſt, Did not *Chriſt* preach to all theſe ſorts of *hearers* in the *church* of the *Jews*?

Truth. That *national church* of the *Iews*, in its firſt *viſible conſtitution*, conſiſted onely of good ground. Now that the other three ſorts of *hearers* were in the *church* of the *Iews*, it was an *accident* and *corruption*: when they grew incurable, and received not the *admonitions* of the *Lord*, by the *Lord Ieſus* and his *ſervants*, preaching unto them, the Lord *caſt* them out of his ſight, deſtroyed that *nationall church*, and *eſtabliſhed* the *Chriſtian church*.

The natute of Jewiſh Church.

Now what is this to the permitting of known *hypocrites* in the *Chriſtian church* to the worlds end? ſince that the proper ſeat of *known hypocriſie*, and of all other *wickedneſs*, is the world, which indeed properly conſiſteth of the three ſorts of *Bad* ground, as the *church* and *Garden* of *Chriſt*, of the *honeſt* and *good ground*.

Peace. But further, If (ſaith Maſter *Cotton*) the children of the *church*-members be in the *church*, then they growing up to yeers, become ſome of them like the *high-way*, and ſome like the *ſtony*, and ſome like the *thorny* ground.

Truth. Admit the *Chriſtian church* were conſtituted of the *natural ſeed* and *off-ſpring* (which yet Maſter *Cotton* knows will never be granted to him, and I believe will never be proved by him :)[1] yet he knows, that upon the *diſcovery* of any ſuch portion of *ground* in the *church*, the *church* is bound to admoniſh, and [58] upon *impenitency* (after *admonition*) to caſt them into the *world*, the proper place of ſuch kind of hearers and profeſſors.

Peace. Maſter *Cotton* proceeds to a third anſwer, to wit, Though it be not the proper work of the *church* to bring up their own children to become the ſincere people of *God*, And *Chriſt* hath given his Church and his *Goſpel* preached to it, to lye like *leaven* in three pecks of meal, till all be leavened, *Mat.* 13. 31. And he hath given *Paſtors* and *Teachers*, as well for the gathering of the *Saints*, as for the *edification* of the *Body* of *Chriſt*. [*Eph.* 4: 11, 12.]

Truth. I anſwer, the proper work of the *Paſtors* and *Teachers*, is to feed the *ſheep* and *flock*, and not the Heards, the *wild Beaſts* in the world. And

[1] This was Cotton's doctrine, inconſiſtent as it ſeems with his idea of the ſpiritual conſtitution of the Church, although conſiſtent with his views of Infant baptiſm. He ſays: "I have not yet learned, (nor doe I thinke, I ever ſhall) that the children of believing Parents borne in the Church, are all of them Pagans, and no Members of the Church : or that being Members of the Church, (and ſo holy) that they are all of them truly converted." *Bloudy Tenent Waſhed*, 78. "Such as are born of Chriſtian parents, and baptized in their infancy into the fellowſhip of the Church, are initiated members of the ſame Church, though deſtitute of ſpirituall grace, untill they juſtly deprive themſelves of the priviledge of that Fellowſhip." *Holineſſe of Church-members*, 1.

The nature of Chrifts true Apoftles.

although it is the duty of parents to bring up their children in the nurture and *fear* of the *Lord*; yet what if thofe children refufe to frequent the *Affemblies* of the Church, and what if thofe three forts of *bad ground* or hearers will not come within the *bounds* of the *Paftors* and *Teachers* feeding; hath not the *Lord Iefus* appointed other Officers (in the fame *Ephef.* 4. [11. 12.]) for the gathering of the *Saints*, that is, *fending* out of the Church of *Chrift*, *Apoftles*, or Meffengers, to preach *Chrift Iefus* to the three forts of *bad ground*, to labour to turn them into *good* ground?

But alas, to falve up all this, the *civil* fword is commonly run for, to force all *forts* of ground to come to *church*, inftead of the fending forth (*Rom.* 10. [15.]) the *heavenly fowers*, according to the Ordinance of *Chrift Iefus*.

Peace. But what fay you to his fourth anfwer, *viz.* There is no fuch *Refemblance* between the *high-way-ground* and *good* ground, as between the *Tares* and the *wheate*, nor would the fervants wonder at *Tares* in the *high-way*, nor ask about their plucking up.

Truth. I anfwer, Let the *high-way*, *ftony*, and *thorny* ground be confidered in their feveral *qualities* of *prophanenefs*, *ftoninefs*, and *worldlinefs*, and all the *fons* of *men* throughout the whole *world* naturally are fuch; and tis no wonder, nor would the *fervants* of Chrift be fo troubled, as to defire their plucking up out of the *world.* But yet againe confider all thefe forts of men as profeffing the *name* and *anointing* of *Chrift Iefus* in a falfe and [59] counterfeit *Antichriftian* way, and then it may well be wondred,

Antichristians monsters in religion.

whence ſuch monſtrous kind of *Chriſtians* or *anointed ones* aroſe: And *Gods* people may eaſily be tempted rather to deſire their rooting out of the *world*, then the rooting out of any ſuch ſorts of ground or men profeſſing any other *Religion*, *Jewiſh*, *Mahometan* or *Pagan*, *Antichriſtian* and falſe *Chriſtians* being more oppoſite to the *kingdome* of *Chriſt Jeſus*, and more dangerous, by how much more a *counterfeit* and Traytor is worſe then a profeſſed *Fox*, an *Antichriſtian* (whether *Papiſt* or *Proteſtant*) worſe then a *Jew*, a *Pagan*, Whether *Indian*, *Turke* or *Perſian*.

Examination of CHAP. XXIII.

Peace.

Still of the Tares.

THeſe *tares* (ſaith Maſter *Cotton*) are not ſuch ſinners as are oppoſite and contrary, for then none ſhould be oppoſite or contrary but they.

Truth. I acknowledge (as Maſter *Cotton* here obſerveth) two ſorts of perſons *oppoſite* and contrary to *Chriſt Jeſus* and his *Kingdome*.

Two ſorts of ſinners.

Firſt, All ſorts of *ſinners ſcandalous* in their *lives* and *courſes*.

2. More eſpecially oppoſite in point of *Religion* and *worſhip*, as all idolaters, and eſpecially *Antichriſtians*.

Now every man by nature, the beſt and wiſeſt, is oppoſite and contrary to *Chriſt*, his *word* and *kingdome*; but an *idolater* and *Antichriſtian* is more eſpecially oppoſite to his glorious *Name*, *Truth*, and Ordinances.

And therein properly lyes the *myſtery* of *iniquity*, brought in by the *man* of *ſin*, that *lawleſs perſon*, 2 *Theſſ.* 2. moſt oppoſite or contrary to *Chriſt Jeſus*, the Son of *God*, and *Son* of *Righteouſneſs*.

Peace. But this is a begging of the *queſtion* (ſaith Maſter *Cotton*) for the *queſtion* is about *viſible* worſhippers, ſuch as were diſcovered and declared to be what they were, as well by their *fruit* [60] as by their *clads*, and therefore againe (ſaith Maſter *Cotton*) theſe *tares* were the *ſeed* and children of the *Devil*; for why ſhould they be called the *ſeed* of the One, and the children of the Other?

Truth. I anſwer, the *Lord Jeſus* diſtinguiſheth, thus, He that ſoweth the *good ſeed*, is the *Son* of *man*; and the *good ſeed* are the children of the *Kingdome*: he that ſoweth the *tares* is the *devil*, and theſe *tares* are the children of the *evil* or *evil one*; Hence by way of *oppoſition*, theſe children of *evil* or *evil ones* being viſibly ſuch as are *oppoſite* to the children of the *kingdome*, they cannot be *hypocrites* in the *church*, untill they are diſcovered: Theſe children therefore of the *evil one* oppoſite to the *viſible kingdome*, and ſo to *viſible Chriſt Jeſus* in point of his *kingdome*, *church*, and *worſhip* (though they be the *children* of the *devil* in a ſence, yet) can they be no other, but the children of the falſe *Chriſt* or *Antichriſt*, in the *way* of a falſe *church* and *worſhip*.

Peace. Yea, but laſtly (ſaith Maſter *Cotton*) that word τȣ̃ πονηρȣ̃ tranſlated the children of the *wicked one* or *wickedneſs*, will agree to *hypocrites*.

Truth. It will indeed, if we reſpect their *inſide*, which is only *viſible* to the *inviſible King*, as *Judas* in his profeſſion: but it cannot agree to ſuch *hypocrites* as are undiſcovered by their *fruits* in the *church*, but unto ſuch *hypocrites* as are diſcovered in their *blades* and *fruit*, and ſo conſequently are not fit to live with other ſinners in the *world*: I doubt not but Maſter *Cotton* will ſay, That although a member of a Church prove a *theiſe*, *adulterer*, *murtherer*, in the eyes of a Brother, that ſees and knows his ſecret *wickedneſs*, yet that brother is cenſurable as a ſlanderer, if he ſhould report theſe *evils*, though to the Church, untill according to *viſible order* he could produce good proof and *evidence*.

Two ſorts of hypocrites.

61] *Examination of* CHAP. XXIV.

Peace.

Still of the Tares.

MAſter *Cotton* here ſeems to me (with the *Familiſts*[1]) to confound *heaven and earth* together, the matters of *Worſhip*, and *Ordinances* of *Religion*,

[1] The Familiſts were a ſect of German origin, bred in the ferments of the Reformation, ſaid to have been founded by Henry Nicholas, of Münſter, though his tenents are traced back to David Joris, or George, who died in 1556. Nicholas came to England near the cloſe of the reign of Edward VI., and gathered a ſociety called "The Family of Love." They held that the eſſence of religion was in a deep and all-abſorbing feeling of divine love, and that all doctrines and forms were of no conſequence compared with this. That this myſtical doctrine ſhould lead to their confounding the diſtinctions named in the text is not unnatural.

To charge Cotton with any tendency to Familiſm would be a very ſharp thruſt. It was one of the errors which at that time in Maſſachuſetts were regarded with peculiar dread and diſguſt. It was one of the charges againſt Mrs. Hutchinſon,

with the affaires and *bufineffes* of this *life*: for faith he, fuch as ftand for the *kingdome* of *Satan* (as all *evil* men do) they ftand in *oppofition* to the *Kingdome of Chrift.*

Truth. Mafter *Cotton* is not now to be taught the diftinction between the *church* and *Commonweale*; nor that a *national church* is not of *Chrift Jefus* his *inftitution*: yet as this difcourfe ftrongly inclines to erect a *national church*, fo doth this prefent anfwer to the *confufion* both of *Church* and *Commonweale.*

It is true, a *covetous Iew*, that blafphemeth *Chrift Jefus*, ftands for *Satan* againft *Chrift.* But by his *covetoufnefs* in one kinde, as *covetoufnefs* is oppofite to *Righteoufnefs* and *contentation*, &c. and for *Sathan* againft *Chrift* in another fence, that is in a *Religious* and *Spiritual* fence, as he prefers *Mofes* before *Chrift Jefus*, and denies the true *Meffiah* to be yet come in the *flefh.* *Two forts of oppofites to Chrift Jefus.*

A cruel *Turk* ftands for *Satan* againft *Chrift*, by his *cruelty* in one fence, to wit, in *oppofition* to *Chrifts mercy*, *gentlenefs*, *patience*, &c. but by his *belief* in *Mahomet*, preferring him before *Chrift*, he oppofeth him in his *Kingdome* and *Worfhip.*

To come neerer, a *drunken Englifh*, *Dutch* or *Frenchman*, ftands for *Satan* aguinft *Chrift*, as their *drunkennefs* is oppofite to *Chrifts fobriety*, *temperance*, &c. but againft *Chrift* in another fence, as they profefs the wayes of *Antichriftian idolatry* and *fuperfti-*

and Cotton from the firft was implicated with her, and "her adherents were wont to fay, that they held only what Mr. Cotton held." Ellis, *Life of Anne Hutchinfon*, 211. "The name of the no lefs great John Cotton was abufed by thefe bufy fectaries, for the patronage of their whimfies." Mather, *Magnalia*, ii. 440.

tion: And not to obſerve this *diſtinction*, is (with ſome *Familiſts*) to run upon *quick-ſands* of *confounding* the *ſpiritual kingdome* of *Chriſt Jeſus*, his *worſhip* and *ordinances*, with the *kingdomes* of this *world*, and the *common affaires* thereof in *natural* and *civil* conſideration.

Peace. But though *Chriſt* (ſaith Maſter *Cotton*) ſhould com-[62]mand other *offenders* to be let alone beſide *Antichriſtians*, yet he ſhould not contradict any *ordinances* for the puniſhment of *offenders* &c. becauſe, ſaith he, No law of *God*, nor *juſt law* of *man* commands the the rooting out of *hypocrites*, though the *church* be bound to endeavour (as much as in them lies) to heale their *hypocriſie*.

Truth. *Hypocriſie* diſcovered in the *fruit* of it, is not to be let alone in the *church* or *State*: For neither *church* of *Chriſt* nor *civil ſtate* can long continue ſafe, if *hypocrites* or *traitors* (under what pretence ſoever) be permitted to break forth in them, without due puniſhment and rooting out; this *hypocriſie* being eſpecially that great ſin againſt which *Chriſt Ieſus* ſo frequently and ſo vehemently inveighed, and againſt which he denounced the foreſt of *plagues* and *judgements*.

Truth. By whoſe *command*, and by what *meanes* and *ordinances*, by whoſe *power* and *authority*, but by the *command*, *meanes* and *power* of *Chriſt Jeſus*?

And I further aske, If faithful *admonition* be not one good means of *healing*, and if that lye not in the *churches power*; and if the *hypocrite* after faithful *admonition* once or twice, ſubmit not to the *voice* of *Chriſt Ieſus*, I ask where the Lord *Jeſus* commandeth to make a ſtop, and not to caſt forth and reject whomſoever wilfully obſtinate?

Peace. Doubtleſs (dear Truth) many will be apt to ſay Maſter *Cotton* intends *ſecret* and cloſe *hypocriſie.*

Truth. And I doubt not but *himſelf* will ſay, That this is not our *queſtion,* but of known and unmasked *hypocriſie,* as *himſelf* hath formerly declared, and ſuch as here he expreſſeth come under *ordinances* of healing.

Peace. But further (ſaith Maſter *Cotton*) it is not true, that *Antichriſtians* are to be let alone untill the end of the *world,* Why? Becauſe *Chriſt* commanded *excommunication,* &c.

Truth. I am aſtoniſht, and wonder why Maſter *Cotton* here ſpeaketh of *excommunication,* a *ſpiritual ordinance* of *Chriſt Ieſus* in his *ſpiritual kingdome* or *city,* when the *diſpute* onely concerns temporal *excommunication* or cutting off? Let them alone, that is, in *civil State*?

I wonder alſo how he ſhould imagine the *diſcuſſer* in this Chap-[63]ter to affirme, that *Antichriſtians* are to be let alone in the *church* unto the end of the world, when it was the very ſcope of his argument in this Chapter, to prove, that the *ſpeech* of *Chriſt Jeſus,* [let them alone] muſt needs be underſtood of letting *idolaters* and *Antichriſtians* alone in the *civil ſtate,* and in the *world,* becauſe otherwiſe, if he had meant, [Let them alone in the *church*] he ſhould contradict himſelf, who hath appointed meanes for the diſturbing and purging out the corrupt *leaven* both of *perſons* and *practices* out of his *church* and *kingdome.*

Peace. The ſame anſwer indeed will eaſily be

returned to his laſt *ſuppoſition* of any *Popiſh ſpirit* conſpiring againſt the *life* of *King* and *Parliament*: The whole ſcope of this book profeſſeth, and in this Chapter the diſcuſſer profeſſedly argueth, that *Chriſt Jeſus* hath appointed that *civil offenders* againſt the *civil ſtate*, ought not to be let alone.

But Maſter *Cotton* adds, If Popiſh *Prieſts* and *Jeſ*-"*uits* be rightly expounded to be the *Rivers* and "fountaines of water, which drive the dead ſea of "Antichriſtian pollutions up and down all Nations "in Europe, and in ſome caſes are to drink blood; "Then are they not to be let alone, but duely ſup-"preſt and cut off from conveying up and down "idolatrous, heretical and ſeditious wickedneſs, *Rev.* "16. 4, 7.

The rivers and fountaines of blood, Rev. 16.

Truth. The expoſition of this *Scripture* will be further examined in the *ſequel*, and found no true expoſition, That *Rivers* and *fountaines* of *water* drive the *ſea* up and down: For *rivers* and *fountaines* however they come from the *ſalt-water*, yet loſe they the *ſavour* of the *ſalt-ſea*, and yeeld a ſavour of the earth through which they make their paſſages; and again they run into the *ſea*, and are themſelves driven up and down, and ſwallowed up in the ſea: Nor will it be found a true expoſition according to *Godlineſs* and *Chriſtianity*, which commandeth *patience* and *waiting*, not *fire* and *ſword* to *gaineſayers* and *oppoſites*: Nor laſtly, will it be found a true expoſition agreeing with Maſter *Cottons* own profeſſion in ſome paſſage of this book, wherein he holds forth great *toleration* and *gentleneſs* to other *conſciences*, both *Engliſh* and *Barbarians*.

64] *Examination of* CHAP. XXV.

Peace.

IN this Chapter Maſter *Cotton* affirms, that *hypocrites* (even) they that are diſcerned to be ſuch, yet they are not to be purged out, except they break forth into ſuch notorious fruits of *hypocriſie* as tend to the *leavening* of the *whole lumpe*: for otherwiſe (ſaith he) we may roote out the beſt *wheate* in *Gods field*, &c.

Truth. I anſwer, ſince *hypocrites* and all *hypocriſie* is ſo odious in *Gods ſight*, and ſo vehemently inveighed againſt by *Chriſt Jeſus*, what ſhould be the cauſe why the *leaven* of the *Phariſees*, which is *hypocriſie*, ſhould finde greater *favour* and *connivance* in the *church* of *Chriſt*, then the *leaven* of any other *ſin*, ſince all ought to be purged out? 1 *Cor.* 5. [7.]

Of hypocrites in profeſſion of Chriſtianity.

2. Contrary to what Maſter *Cotton* ſaith, [to wit, That no man meerly for *hypocriſie* and want of life and power of Godlineſs ought to be proceeded againſt] the *Spirit* of *God* by *Paul* ſaith, That ſuch kind of profeſſours of the name of *Chriſt* ſhould ariſe, that ſhould pretend a form of *godlineſs*, but not ſhew forth the *power* thereof, from which he commandeth us to turn away, 1 [2] *Tim.* 3. [5.]

Peace. But Maſter *Cotton* excepteth, Except (ſaith he) they break forth into ſome notorious ſcandalous fruits of *hypocriſie*.

Truth. How ſhall an *hypocrite* be diſcovered and known to be an *hypocrite* or *traitor* in *church* or *civil ſtate*, but by ſome ſuch notorious *ſcandalous* fruits as tend to the leavening of the whole *lumpe*? Come to particulars; was *Iudas*, *Ananias* and *Sapphira*, *Simon Magus*, *Demas*, or any other diſcovered to be *Hypocrites*, when they broke forth into *treachery*, *lying*, *covetouſneſs*? and might the *church* proceed againſt ſuch? If it be denied, I ask to what end the *Lord* hath given thoſe holy rules of *admonition*? &c. will it prove ought but prophaning of the name of the *Lord*, to pretend our clear diſcerning of the *Scripture* and *ordinances*, and not to practiſe them? If it be yeelded againſt theſe *fruits* of *hypocriſie*, diſcovering *men* to be *hypocrites*, why do we plead for a *diſpenſation*, and (not for the *wheat* of the *Field*, 65] and *flowers* of the *garden*, but) for the moſt ſtinking and loathſome *tares* and *weeds* to be continued in the holy *garden* of *Chriſt Jeſus*?

Peace. But many *hypocrites* (ſaith Maſter *Cotton*) fall not within the cenſure of that *Scripture*, 2 *Theſſ*. 3. 6. Withdraw from every *brother* that walketh diſorderly; for many *hypocrites* follow their *callings*, and are ſo far from being burthenſome unto others, that they are after choaked with the *cares* and *buſineſſes* of the *world*, and yet are not behind in *liberal contribution* to pious uſes.

Truth. But is not this *halting* between *God* and *Baal*? yea is not this pleading for *Baal*, for *hypocriſie*, *hypocrites* and *diſſemblers*, falſe and *Antichriſtian counterfeits*, to be permitted not onely in the *wilderneſs* of the *world* (which I contend for) but alſo even in the *Garden*, *Houſe*, *Bed*, and *boſome* of *God*? What if men be *civil* and follow their callings? Men that know not God, ſo do. What though they be *liberal* to pious uſes (millions of *Papiſts* are and have been ſo according to their *conſciences*) when as yet they are *choaked* with *cares* and *buſineſſes* of this *world*?

How expreſs is the *charge* of the *Lord Jeſus*, to *with-draw* from ſuch, notwithſtanding their *forme* of *Godlineſs*, and *contribution* to *Godly* uſes, when they declare not the *power* of *godlineſs*, 1 [2] *Tim*. 3. 2. [5.] Not to *eate* with them, and therefore to ſeparate from ſuch a *brother* as is *covetous*, 1 *Cor*. 5. [11.] as well as from an *idolater*, *drunkard*, &c.

The *Church* of *Chriſt* is a *congregation* of *Saints*, a *flock* of *ſheep*, humble, meek, patient, contented, with whom it is *monſtrous* and impoſſible, to couple cruel and perſecuting *lyons*, ſubtle and hypocritical *Foxes*, contentious biting *dogs* or greedy and rooting *ſwine*, ſo viſibly declared and apparant.

Examination of CHAP. XXI. [XXVI.]

Peace.

IN this Chapter four anſwers were given by the diſcuſſer to that great objection of the *miſchief* that the *Tares* will do in the field of the *world*, if let alone and not pluckt up.

66] The firſt was, That if the *tares* offend againſt *Civility* or *civil ſtate*, *God* hath armed the *civil ſtate* with a *civil ſword*, &c.

Maſter *Cotton* replies, what if their *conſcience* incite them to *civil offences*?

I anſwer, the *conſcience* of the *civil Magiſtrate* muſt incite him to *civil puniſhment*, as a Lord Maior of *London* once anſwered, That he was born to be a

Judge, to a Thief that pleaded he was born to be a thief. If the *conſcience* of the *worſhippers* of the *Beaſt* incite them to prejudice *prince* or *ſtate*, Although theſe *conſciences* be not as the *conſcience* of a *thief* (commonly convinced of the *evil* of his *fact*, but) perſwaded of the *lawfulneſs* of their *actions*; yet ſo far as the *civil ſtate* is endammaged or endangered, I ſay the *ſword* of *God* in the hand of *civil Authority* is ſtrong enough to defend it ſelf, either by impriſoning or *diſarming*, or other wholeſome *meanes*, &c. while yet their *conſciences* ought to be permitted in what is meerly point of *worſhip*, as *prayer*, and other *ſervices* and *adminiſtrations*.

Corrupt conſciences diſtinguiſhed.

Hence the wiſdome of *God*, in that 13 *Rom.* (reckoned by Maſter *Cotton* the *Magna Charta* for *civil Magiſtrates* dealing in matters of *Religion*) I ſay, there it pleaſeth *God* expreſly to reckon up the particulars of the *ſecond table*, chalking out (as it were) by his own finger, the civil *ſphear* or *circle*, in which the *civil Magiſtrate* ought to act and execute his *civil power* and *Authority*.

Peace. The ſecond anſwer of the *diſcuſſer* was, that the *church* or *ſpiritual* City hath *laws* and *Armories* to defend it ſelf.

Maſter *Cotton* excepteth, ſaying, That if their *members* be leavened with *Antichriſtian Idolatry* and *Superſtition*, and yet muſt be tolerated in their *idolatry*, and ſuperſtitious *worſhip*, will not a litle *leaven* leaven the whole *lumpe*? and how then is the *church* guarded?

Tolleration of idolaters conſidered.

Truth. The queſtion is, whether *idolatrous* and *Antichriſtian worſhippers* may be tolerated in *civil ſtate*, in the *City*, in the *Kingdome*, &c. under any *civil power*: Maſter *Cotton* anſwers no, they will do miſchief. The reply is, againſt any *civil miſ*-[67]*chief* (though wrought *conſcientiouſly*) *the civil ſtate* is ſtrongly guarded. Secondly, Againſt the *ſpiritual miſchief*, the *church* or *City* of *Chriſt* is guarded with heavenly *Armories*, wherein there hang a thouſand Bucklers, *Cant*. 4.[4] and moſt mighty weapons, 2 *Cor*. 10.[4.] In the *church* of *Chriſt* ſuch *worſhippers* ought not to be tolerated, but *caſt out*, &c.

That is true, ſaith Maſter *Cotton*, but yet their *leaven* will ſpread.

I anſwer, What is this, but to make the moſt powerful appointments of *Chriſt Jeſus*, thoſe mighty *weapons* of God, terrible *cenſures* and ſoul-*puniſhments* in his *kingdome*, but as ſo many *woodden daggers* and *leaden ſwords*, *childrens Bull-beggars*, and *ſcarcrows*, and upon the point ſo baſe and beggarly, that without the help of the *Cutlers ſhop* or *Smiths forge*, the *church* or *kingdome* of *Chriſt* cannot be purged from the *leaven* of *idolatry* and *ſuperſtition*?

Civil weapons in ſpirituals, blur and ſlight the ſpiritual.

Peace. Me thinks the Lord *Jeſus* was of another mind, *Mat*. 18.[17.] when he accounted it ſufficient to cut off the obſtinate, Let him be as a *Gentile* or *publican*: and in the very ſimilitude of *leaven* (here uſed by Maſter *Cotton*) *Paul* counted it ſufficient to purge out the *leaven*, 1 *Cor*. 5.[7.] if that evil perſon were put away from the midſt of them, that is, from their holy and ſpiritual ſociety. *Paul* never asks (as Maſter *Cotton* doth) ſince we have not to our *ſpiritual armes*, *armes* of *fleſh*, and a *civil ſword* to help our *ſpiritual*, how ſhall the *ſafety* of the *church* be guarded?

But let's proceed. The third Anſwer was, That the *elect* cannot be finally deceived: Maſter *Cotton* replies, It is true, but *God* provides meanes of *preſervation*, &c. And *Jezabels* tolerating in *Thiatira* made the *church* guilty.

Truth. This Argument was not uſed in derogation of *Gods* meanes, *ſpiritual* in *ſpiritual* things, *civil* in *civil*, &c. but by way of *ſuppoſition* of the worſt, as *Job* ſpake in another caſe, How helpeſt thou the *Arme* that hath no ſtrength? Not but that in ordinary ſubmiſſion to *means*, man ought to help the *Lord* againſt the mighty. The ſum is this, rather let the *Lord* alone to help himſelf without *meanes*, then to help the *Lord* to ſave his *elect* (who cannot by vertue of his *love* and *decree* finally be deceived) by any ſuch *meanes* as are none of his own appointing.

The tolleration of Jezabel in Thyatira.

68] 2. It is true, that the *church* at *Thyatira*, tolerating *Jezabel* to ſeduce, was guilty, yea and I add the *City* of *Thiatira* was guilty alſo if it tolerated *Iezabel* to *ſeduce* to *fornication*. But what is this to the point of the *iſſue* [to wit, Whether the *City* of *Thiatira* ſhould be guilty or not in tolerating *Iezabel* in that which the *City* judgeth to be *idolatry* and falſe *worſhip?*] *Jezabels corporal whoredoms* (ſinning againſt *civility* or *ſtate* of the *City*) the City by her Officers ought to puniſh, leſt *civil* order be broken, and *civility* be infected &c. but *Iezabels ſpiritual whoredomes*, the *civil ſtate* ought not to deal with but (there being a *church* of *Chriſt* then in *Thiatria*, and the *ſpiritual whoredomes* there taught and practiſed) I ſay the *church* in *Thyatira*, which in the name and *power* of *Chriſt* was armed ſufficiently to paſs and inflict a dreadful *ſpiritual cenſure,* which *God* will confirme and ratifie moſt aſſuredly and undoubtedly in *heaven.*

Peace. Two reaſons more were alleadged out of the Text. The firſt was, that by plucking up the *tares,* the good *wheate* it ſelf by ſuch *hurries* and *perſecutions* about *Religion,* ſhould be indangered to be plucked up: which Maſter *Cotton* ſalveth thus: to wit, If *Gods people* themſelves, for their *idolatry* and *ſuperſtition,* ſhould be cut off, it will be for warning unto others, *&c.*

Truth. Oh *ungodly, unchriſtian,* that is *bloody* and *Antichriſtian doctrin,* by which (under pretence of puniſhing *hereticks, ſchiſmaticks,* and *ſeditious* perſons) the *Son* of *God,* the *Lord* of *Lords,* and *King* of *Kings,* hath ſo many millions of times, in his *ſervants* been *perſecuted, ſlaine,* and *crucified!* As for the world, it lies in *wickedneſs,* is a *wilderneſs* of *ſin* over-grown with *idolatry* and *ſuperſtition.* The *Antichriſtian* (falſly called *Chriſtian* world) in moſt abundant and over-flowing meaſure hath wondred after and magnified the *Beaſt, Rev.* 13. The two *witneſſes propheſie* in ſackcloth againſt this *beaſt,* in all *parts* of his *dominion,* by whom alſo they are perſecuted and ſlaine, and yet we read not that they *judge* or *cenſure,* or fight for themſelves with any other *weapons* then by the *word* of their *prophecie,* the *blood* of the *Lamb,* their patient *ſufferings,* the not loving of their lives unto the *death.*

Chriſt Jeſus under pretence perſecuted.

The weapons of the Saints, Rev. 12.

Peace. The ſecond reaſon out of the *parable* was, That the [69] *Angels* of *God* have in charge to bundle up theſe *tares* for the *burning.* Maſter *Cotton* replies two things. Firſt, ſo theſe *Angels* will gather into bundles for the burning *murtherers*, *robbers*, &c. who are not yet to be tolerated.

Truth. I anſwer, If a man call Maſter *Cotton murtherer*, *witch*, &c. with reſpect to *civil matters*, I ſay the *civil ſtate* muſt judge and puniſh the *offender*, elſe the *civil ſtate* cannot ſtand, but muſt return to *barbariſme.* But if a man call Maſter *Cotton murtherer*, *witch* &c. in *ſpiritual matters*, as *deceiving* and *bewitching* the peoples *ſouls*, if he can prove his *charge*, Maſter *Cotton* ought to give *God* the *glory*, and and repent of ſuch *wickedneſs.* If he cannot prove his *charge*, but ſlander Maſter *Cotton*, yet is the ſlander of no *civil nature*, and ſo not proper to any *civil court*, but is to be caſt. out (as we ſee commonly *ſuits* of *law* are rejected, when brought into *Courts* which take no proper *cognizance* of ſuch caſes.)

The difference between civil and ſpiritual ſlander

Peace. What *relief* then hath Maſter *Cotton* or any ſo charged in this caſe?

Truth. The *court* of *heaven*, the *church* of *Chriſt*, calls ſuch a *ſlanderer* to *repentance* (whether he be within the *church* or without, though orderly proceeding lies only againſt him that is within) If he be *obſtinate*, how dreadful is the *ſentence* againſt ſuch a *ſlanderer*, both in *earth* and in *heaven*? how dreadful the delivering up to *hardneſs* of *heart* (a greater plague on *Pharaoh*, then all the devouring *plagues* of *Egypt*) how dreadful the delivering up to *Satan*, the *paw* and *jaw* of the roaring *Lyon* (infinitely far more terrible, had we eyes to ſee it, then to be thrown with *Daniel* to the devouring *Lyon*:) There is no reaſon in the world therefore, for *theeves* and *mur-*

The dreadful nature of Chriſts ſpiritual puniſhments.

therers to be tolerated unto the laſt day without *ſentence* and *puniſhment*, becauſe *tranſgreſſors* againſt *ſpiritual ſtate* may be tolerated to live in the *world*, yet puniſhed for *ſpiritual tranſgreſſion* with a greater *cenſure* and ſorer puniſhment, then if all their bones and fleſh were rackt and torn in pieces with burning pincers.

Peace. Maſter *Cotton* and others will ſay, The *idolaters* and *ſeducers* were cenſured *ſpiritually* under *Moſes*, and yet were they alſo put to *death.*

70] *Truth.* I deſire Maſter *Cotton* to ſhew me under *Moſes*, ſuch *ſpiritual cenſures* and *puniſhments* beſide the cutting off by the *civil ſword*: which if he cannot do, and that ſince the *Chriſtian Church* antitypes the *Iſraelitiſh*, and the *Chriſtian laws* and *puniſhments* the *laws* and *puniſhments* of *Iſrael* concerning *religion*, I may truely affirme, that that civil ſtate which may not juſtly tolerate civil *offenders*, &c. yet may moſt juſtly tolerate *ſpiritual offenders*, of whoſe *Delinquency* it hath no proper cognizance.

Not ſuch ſpiritual puniſhments in the national church of Iſrael.

Peace. Laſtly, Maſter *Cotton* urgeth, that παρουσία (2 *Theſſ.* 2.[8]) ſhould rather be tranſlated *preſence* then *coming*.

Truth. Admit it (though many able *tranſlators* in divers *languages* rather tranſlate it *coming*) and that *Antichriſt* ſhall not be conſumed by the *breath* of the *mouth* of the *Lord Jeſus* before his laſt coming to *judgement*; yet then Maſter *Cotton* muſt give another *interpretation* of this *end* of the *world*, and the *Angels*, and the *fire*, then is uſually given: however the *tares* ſhall be bundled up for the *everlaſting burnings*, and are at preſent under a dreadful *ſentence* and *puniſh-*

ment, and therefore (not offending in *civil* things) the *civil ſtate* may the better tolerate them in matters of *religion* and *conſcience*; and *Paul* himſelf (if oppoſed by them) might the better wait with patience, if God peradventure will give them *repentance*, &c.

Examination of CHAP. XXVII.

Peace.

IN this Chapter, thoſe three particulars by which the *Miniſters* of *Chriſt* are commanded to let the Tares alone, Maſter *Cotton* evades by calling them ſo many *ſlippery evaſions* &c.

Truth. I believe neither the *interpretations* nor the *intentions* of the *Author* were evaſive: for a faithful *witneſs* will not lye though a falſe *witneſs* will utter *deceit*; however the *fire* ſhall try. The truth is, the greater part, and eſpecially the former of Maſter *Cottons* anſwer in this Chapter, comes not neer the point of the *iſſue*, for that is not whether the *Saints* may pray or prophecy againſt *idolaters* and falſe *worſhippers*, but whether or no for [71] their preſent temporal *deſtruction* and *extirpation*.

Peace. Unto this Maſter *Cotton* ſaith, Yes, for the preſent *deſtruction* of ſome or other *Antichriſtian idolaters* in every age: and he adds, it might as well be ſaid, that a *Miniſter* of *Chriſt* ſhould not denounce preſent or ſpeedy *deſtruction* to any *murtherers*, *whoremongers*, &c. becauſe though ſome of them may fall under grievous plagues, yet there will never want a

Prayer againſt preſent deſtruction of tares.

company of ſuch *evil doers*, untill the great *harveſt* or end of the *world*.

Againe, ſaith he, Though a *Miniſter* denounce not preſent *deſtruction*, yet he cannot let them alone, no more then the *feller* of an *Oake*, that gives many a *ſtroake* before the laſt, *&c.*

2. It is not credible (ſaith he) that ſome of the *Angels* that poure out their *vials* upon the *Antichriſtian ſtate*, ſhall not be *Miniſters*: And, when the ten *horns* ſhall burn the *City* of *Rome*, it is not credible, that they will do it without ſome excitement from the *Angels*.

Truth. The inſtance brought of *murtherers*, *whoremongers* &c. is moſt improper, becauſe we all agree that preſent *corporal* or *civil puniſhment* is due to *murtherers*, *whoremongers*, &c. and other like *tranſgreſſors* againſt the *civil ſtate* of all *Nations* and *peoples* all the *world* over, and this in all *Ages* and *Times*: but Maſter *Cotton* himſelf acknowledgeth, that many *prophecies* and *periods* are ſet for the *continuance* of the *Antichriſtian ſtate*, and the *idolatry* and *deſolations* thereof, and that thoſe *periods* ſhall be accompliſhed before the *judgement* day: nor will it appear that thoſe ten *Kings* that ſhall in the fulfilling of this *prophecy* burn the *whore*, ſhall do it by way of *ordinance* and *obedience* to *Gods* command, otherwiſe then he permitted *Nebuchadnezzar* and *Cyrus*, and other *Tyrants* of the *world* (as the *fiſhes* of the *ſea* one to devoure and ſwallow up another.) And for that inſtance of the *wood-man* felling of the *Oake*, I grant that the *prayers* of the *Saints* haſten the *whores downfal*, and the opening of theſe *prophecies* make way for Gods time; but what is this to a *present downfal* before the time appointed?

Pastors and Teachers not Apostles and messengers.

Againe, That it is not credible but that some of the *Angels* should be *messengers* of the *Gospel*, I answer, Master *Cotton* knows that the *English* word *messengers*, and the Greek word *Apostles*, are the same; but no such *messengers* Master *Cotton* al-[72]lows of: And that the word *messengers* in the *Apostles* sence should imply *Pastors* and *Teachers* (which Master *Cotton* now only allows of) I finde not in the *Testament* of *Christ Jesus*. That those *Angels* should be the *witnesses*, and the *Prophets* in *sackcloth*, seemes more credible.

And I may well affirme the contrary to Master *Cottons credible*, that it is *incredible* that any *servant* or *messenger* of the *King* of *Peace* should stir up the *civil Magistrate* to cut off those by the *civil sword*, whose *repentance* he is bound to wait for with *patience*, bearing in the interim their *oppositions* and *gainsayings*, 2 *Tim*. 2. [24. 25.]

Elijah stirring up Ahab to slay the Baalites.

Peace. Tis most true, according to the *testimony* of *Christ Jesus* (and most contrary to the *tenents* and *practice* of the *Romish* bloody *Popes* and their *followers*) that *Christs Ministers* are *wisdomes Maidens* (*Prov*. 9.[3.]) sent forth in heavenly *Beauty* and *chastity*, with meek and loving, yet vehement *perswasions*, to call in the foolish of the *world* to partake of *wisdomes dainties*: but (dear truth) deliver your minde concerning the last passage, to wit, *Elijahs act* in stirring up *Ahab* to kill all the *Priests* and *prophets* of *Baal*: This *act* (saith Master *Cotton*) was not *figurative*, but *moral*; for (saith he) *Ahab* could not be a *figure* of

Chriſt, nor *Iſrael* after their *Apoſtacie*, a *type* of the true *Church:* Beſide, *blaſphemers* ought to die by the *law*; and *Ahab* forfeited his own *life*, becauſe he did not put *Benhadad* to death for his *blaſphemy*, 1 *Kings* 20. [42.]

Truth. *Chriſt Jeſus* is conſidered two wayes, *Chriſt* in his *perſon*, and *Chriſt myſtical* in his *church*, repreſented by the *Governors* thereof. Some ſay that *Iſrael* was not in *Ahabs* time *excommunicated* and cut off from *Gods* ſight, untill their final carrying out of the land of *Canaan*, 2 *Kings* 17. [6.] and that *Iſrael* remained (though none of *Gods* in reſpect of her *apoſtacy*, yet) *Gods* in reſpect of *covenant*, untill the *execution* of the *ſentence* of *excommunication* or *divorce*: And therefore that *Ahab*, as *King* of *Iſrael*, *Gods people* (untill *Iſrael* ceaſed to be *Iſrael*) was a *figure* of *Chriſt*, that is, *Chriſt* in his preſence, in his *governors*, in his *church*, though faln to *idolatry* under *admonition*, not yet caſt off.

Concerning Iſrael in the Apoſtacy of Jeroboam.

But (2.) grant the *church* falſe, and *Ahab King* of a falſe [73] *church*, how will it appear that *Elijahs Act* was *a moral act*, and ſo *preſidential* to all *Kings* and *Nations?*

Peace. Becauſe (ſaith Maſter *Cotton*) it is moral equity, that *blaſphemers*, and *apoſtate idolaters*, *ſeducing* others to *idolatry*, ſhould be put to death, *Levit*. 24. 16. *Deut*. 13. 5.

Truth. Thoſe Scriptures concern a *ceremonial land* in a *ceremonial time*, before *Chriſt*; and in the ſame *Lev*. 24. the command is equally given for the *lampe* in the *Tabernacle*, and the *ſhew-bread* as well as for the *idolater*.

Peace. But *Benhadad* (ſaith Maſter *Cotton*) was no *Iſraelite*, nor was his *blaſphemy* belched out in the land of *Iſrael.*

Truth. It is moſt true, that *blaſphemers* in *Iſrael*, and *blaſphemers* againſt *Iſrael* and the *God* of it, were put to death. It is alſo true in the *antitype* and *ſubſtance* ſince the coming of C*hriſt*, that *blaſphemers* in *Iſrael*, and *blaſphemers* againſt *Iſrael* (the *church* of *God*) are *ſpiritually* to be put to death by the two-edged ſword coming forth of the mouth of C*hriſt*, *Rev.* 1. [16] and this *Goſpel*-puniſhment is much more dreadful and terrible, then the puniſhment of the firſt *blaſphemers* under *Moſes* or the *prophets.*

** Hence Baalls Prieſts, Monks, Friars, and Biſhops have not been civilly actually ſlaine in England,* &c. *but ſpiritually by Gods word, the ſword of his ſpirit caſhiered and cut off eternally.*

Peace. Methinks alſo, if *Ahab* were now *preſidentiall*, and that which he ſhould have done to *Benhadad* preſidential, then is there now no *ſpiritual* or *myſtical Iſrael*, no ſpiritual *Canaan*, but the *letter*, *ceremony*, and *figure* yet in force, and *Chriſt Jeſus* the *myſtical* and *ſpiritual King* of *Iſrael* is not yet come in the fleſh.

Truth. Yea then not onely a few in a *City* or *Kingdome* (ſuppoſe *hundreths* or *thouſands*) but *millions* of *millions* of *blaſphemers*, *idolaters*, *ſeducers*, throughout the whole wide world, ought corporally to be put to *death.*

Peace. Againſt this methinks Maſter *Cotton* ſhould be and I am ſure againſt this *Chriſt Ieſus* was, who profeſſed in anſwer to the raſh zeal of his *diſciples* (*Luk.* 9.[56.]) That he came not to deſtroy mens lives, but to ſave them: but how reliſh you Maſter *Cottons* interpretation, of Let them alone (which he ſees pleaſeth ſome ſo well) to wit, Let them alone is no *precept*, but *permiſſion*?

74] *Truth.* I anſwer, If let them alone were onely by *permiſſion* in way of *providence*, Why is alſo a word of *prohibition* added, to wit, That ſuch ſhould not be medled with, for theſe and theſe *reaſons*, whereas although *God* permitteth *evil doers* in *ſpiritual* and *civil ſtate* in the *world*, yet there lies a word of *ordinance* to purge them out. Here is no *ordinance* for their plucking up, but for their letting alone, and that in a merciful reſpect of ſparing the *good wheate*, who might be indangered to be pluckt up by the *roots* out of the *world*, by ſuch raſh and furious *zeale* of *plucking up the tares*.

Examination of CHAP. XXIX.

Peace.

MAfter *Cotton* referring the 28 Chapter to former *agitations*, ſeems to invite us to paſs on to Chapter 29.

Truth. Let the 28 Chapter recapitulating the former, and the whole *controverſies*, be referred to the *conſciences* of ſuch to whom theſe paſſages by any *providence* of the moſt holy wiſe ſhall be preſented, and let it graciouſly pleaſe the *Father* of *lights*, to help all his ſons of *light*, to be truely ſtudious of his *truth* in the *love* of it, to caſt up all particulars aright in his fear, by the onely *Arithmetick* of his own moſt holy and unerring *ſpirit*.

Peace. In this Chapter firſt ariſeth a *queſtion* concerning the *Apoſtles privacy*.

Truth. Maſter *Cotton* acknowledgeth them to be called to a *publike Miniſtery*, let others judge then of their *privacy*.

Touching Chriſts Apoſtles or meſſengers.

Peace. But they were not ſent (ſaith Maſter *Cotton*) to the *Scribes* and *Phariſees*, and ſo conſequently were to let them alone.

Truth. I anſwer, Let it be conſidered, how he that grants *men* are ſent to the *ſheep*, can rightly ſay they have nothing to do with the *Wolves* and *Foxes*.

Peace. In this controverſie, Maſter *Cotton* elſewhere, will not onely have *ſheep* fed, but the *Wolves* driven from the *fold*, their *braines* beaten out, *&c.* and that not onely by the *Paſtors* or *ſheapherds ſpiritually*, but alſo by the *civil Magiſtrate*, and [75] to that end, he is to be ſtirred up by the Shepherds and *Miniſters* of *Chriſt*.

Truth. Such exciting and ſtirring up of the *civil Magiſtrate* if it were *Chriſts* will, how can the *Apoſtles* be excuſed, or the *Lord Jeſus* himſelf, for not ſtirring up the *Civil Magiſtrate* to his duty againſt theſe *Scribes* and *Phariſees*, the *Wolves* and *Foxes*, as Maſter *Cotton* here cals them?

Touching fundamentals.

Peace. Neither the *doctrine*, nor their offence at it (ſaith Maſter *Cotton*) was *fundamental*; nor had the *civil Magiſtrate* a *law* eſtabliſhed about *doctrine* or *offences* of this *nature*. Beſides, *Chriſt* gave his *diſciples* a charge to be wiſe as *Serpents*, and himſelf would not meddle with the *Phariſees*, untill the laſt yeer of his *Miniſtery*, leſt their *exaſperation* might have been ſome hinderance to his *Miniſtery* before his hour was come.

Truth. I ſhould deſire Maſter *Cotton* againe to ponder whether the notorious *hypocriſie* of the *Phari-*

ſees (now brought into a *Proverb*) and alſo whether the notorious tranſgreſſing (and upon the point aboliſhing) of the fifth *commandment*, and ſo conſequently of all *civil* obedience (with the *Papiſts*) under pretence of *Gods* ſervice (although indeed but their own *ſuperſtition*) be not of a *fundamental* guilt, both againſt *ſpiritual* and *civil ſtate*.

Peace. I remember Maſter *Cotton* argued againſt *tolleration* of the *Papiſts*, becauſe their *conſcience* excites them againſt the *civil powers*.

Truth. And whither tended theſe principles of the *Phariſees*, but to overthrow all *Family*, yea and (if they be followed home) all *Towne*, or *City*, and *Kingdome*-Government?

Peace. Yea, But the *Romane Magiſtrate* (ſaith he) had no eſtabliſhed *law* about *doctrines* or *offences* of that Nature.

Truth. Maſter *Cotton* in all this *controverſie*, pleades that they ought to have: and though he ſaith, that *Magiſtrates* may ſuſpend their duty, untill they be informed, yet he never ſaith, that the *Miniſters* of *Chriſt* may ſuſpend their *duty* of humble *information*, and ſtirring up them up to ſo high a part of their *Duty*, as concerns the ſouls of their *ſubjects* and the *worſhip* of *God*.

76] *Peace*. I remember, that *Gardiner* and *Boner*, &c. could not make the fire burn to conſume the people of *God*, and *witneſſes* of *Jeſus*, untill *Edwards laws* were *repealed*, and *Maries* bloody *laws* were *eſtabliſhed*; and ſo they were forced to ſuſpend a while untill they had conjured up a *Parliament* to do both the one and the other, as their *ſlaves* and *drudges*, for

Laws for perſecuting of Chriſt Jeſus.

them :[1] And tis true, what the *Spirit* of *God* in *David* pronounceth (*Psal.* 82.) that under the *maske* or *colour* of a *law* (which carries with it the name and sound of *reason* and *righteousness*) the *wickedness* of the *world* is established : And hence the people and *servants*, and *Saints* of the most *high God*, feele the weight of the *violence* of the *Nimrod persecutors* or *hunters*.

But this I wonder at, that Master *Cotton* subjoyneth, that *Christ Jesus* himself, and his *disciples* (under the notion of not *exasperating* the *Pharisees*) should not reprove the *Scribes* and *Pharisees*.

Truth. It cannot sink with me, That the *Spirit* of *God* in *Christ Jesus* himself, and his *messengers*, should so far differ from *himself* in all his former *messengers* and *prophets*, who spared not to reprove the *highest Priests*, *Princes*, *Kings* and *kingdoms*; nor doth the practice of the *Lord Jesus* in so many places of *Matthew* (before his *thunderbolts* shot forth against them, *Mat.* 23.) give any countenance to so loose an *opinion*.

Peace. Master *Cotton*, who argues so much against the permitting of *blasphemers* to live in the *world*, may here call to minde, that if ever *blasphemy* were uttered against the *Son* of *God*, it was uttered by the *Pharisees* in the 12 of *Matthew*, when they imputed the casting out of the *devils* to the power of the *devil*

The Pharisees blaspheming of Christ Jesus.

[1] Mary was proclaimed Queen, July 19, 1553, and Gardiner was released from the Tower and made Chancellor in the following August. In April, 1554, he attempted to carry a Persecution Bill through Parliament, and succeeded in the Commons. But it was not till January, 1555, that Parliament removed all obstacles to the punishment of heresy, and January 28, the first court for heresy was opened, and Hooper and Rogers were tried. Froude, *Hist. of England*, vi. 32, 53, 314.

in *Chriſt Jeſus*, and yet we finde not that *Chriſt Jeſus* ſtirred up the *civil Magiſtrates* to any ſuch duty of his to put the *blaſphemers* to death, not the hereticks the *Sadduces*, who denied that fundamental, the *reſurrection*.

Truth. It is moſt true, that the cauſe needeth no ſuch *weapons*, nor ſpared he the *Phariſees* for fear of their *exaſperations*, but poured forth on their *faces* and *boſoms* the soreſt *vials* of the heavieſt doom and *cenſure* that can be ſuffered by the *children* of men, to wit, an *impoſſibility* of *repentance* and *forgiveneſs* of ſins either in this or the world to come: And for the preſent, at [77] every turn he concludes them *hypocrites*, *blind guides*, which could not eſcape the *judgement* of *Hell.*

So that all other *ſences* of thoſe words [*Let them alone*] that is, of not reprooving them, cannot ſtand: nor if it were the *duty* of the *Miniſters* of *Chriſt* to ſtir up the *civil Magiſtrate* againſt ſuch hypocritical and blaſphemous *Phariſees*, could *Chriſt Jeſus himſelf* or his ſervants the *Apoſtles* be excuſed for not complaining to the *Romane State* againſt them; So leaving the blame upon the *conſcience* of the *governors*, if the land were not purged of ſuch *blaſphemers* and fundamental oppoſers of the *Son* of *God.*

Let me me end (*ſweet peace*) with the *bottome* of all ſuch *perſecutions*, Satan rageth againſt *God* and his *Chriſt*; that *devil* that caſt the *Saints* into *priſon*, *Rev.* 2.[10] (*what inſtruments ſoever he uſeth) would caſt *Chriſt* himſelf into *priſon* againe, and to the *gallows* againe, if he came again in *perſon* into any (the moſt refined) perſecuting *ſtate* in the world.

* *Magiſtrates, kings, high prieſts: Herod, bad kings, good kings,* &c.

Examination of CHAP. XXX.

Peace.

I Doubt not (*dear truth*) in the firſt place, but you caſt an obſervant eye on Maſter *Cottons* collections in this Chapter, from *Pauls* words *Acts* 25. 11. I will mention the two firſt.

1. That a man may be ſuch an *offender* in matters of *Religion* againſt the *law* of *God* (againſt the *church*) as well as in *civil matters* againſt *Cæſar*, as to be worthy of death.

2. That if a *ſervant* of *God* ſhould commit any ſuch *offence*, he would not refuſe *judgement* to the death, *verſ.* 11.

Acts 25. 11. *conſidered.*

Truth. Paul onely ſaith in the general, *If I have committed ought worthy of death, I refuſe not to die:* Now therefore as *Paul* ſaid, *No man* (that is, no man juſtly) may *deliver me to the Jews*; So ſay I, no man from theſe words of *Paul* (without wronging him and his *Maſter* the *God* of *Truth*) can draw ſuch a *concluſion*, as if *Paul* had acknowledged it evil in him to have *preached* againſt the *laws* of the *Jews* or the *temple*, which the *Lord Jeſus* and his *ſervants* after him, ſo abundantly did, [78] although at this time (in point of fact) *Paul* might well ſay, he had not done ought againſt the *law* of the *Jews*, I mean the *ceremonial law* and the *Temple*, for he had now obſerved the ceremonies of the Law, and the holineſs of the Temple: although for this ſome uſe to blame him, not diſcerning that *Paul* knew there was a time to honour thoſe *ceremonies*, even after *Chriſts death*, and a time as much to debaſe, diſhonour, and aboliſh them.

Peace. His third *collection* is, That it is lawfull even in *Eccleſiaſtical cauſes* to appeale to a *Pagan Magiſtrate.*

Truth. As I utterly renounce ſuch a *concluſion* (any otherwiſe then in reſpect of civil *violence* offered for a mans *conſcience*, which *violence Cæſar* ought to ſee revenged and puniſhed) ſo neither will this inſtance of *Paul* prove it: for in appealing to an higher *Judge*, a man alwayes preſuppoſeth (if not skill perfect, yet) competent skill, and a true power committed from *God*, to judge in ſuch caſes, which *Paul* for many reaſons, both in this Chapter, and elſewhere manifeſted, could not ſuppoſe in the *Romane Cæſars*, or any *civil Magiſtrate.*

No appeals to the civil powers in matters meerly ſpiritual.

Peace. Maſter *Cotton* urgeth, that theſe words (*verſe* 9.) [Theſe Things] imply matters of *Religion* as well as *civil things.*

Truth. Thoſe words [Theſe Things] were not the words of *Paul*, but the words of *Feſtus.*

2. Grant them *Pauls* words, yet if for thoſe things the *Jews* ſeek his life, *Paul* well appeals to *Cæſar* againſt them, for *Cæſar* is bound to protect the *bodies*, *goods*, or good *names* of his *ſubjects*, either from falſe *accuſations* in *civil things*, or *perſecution* for matters of *conſcience*, which is a *violence* againſt the *civil ſtate*, of which *Cæſar* was the *ſupreme officer.*

Peace. His fourth *collection* is, that *civil Magiſtrates* may and ought to be acquainted with all matters of *Religion*, eſpecially *capital.*

Truth. In *twenty five* parts of the world of *thirty*,

civil Magiſtrates cannot poſſibly be thus acquainted; for the ſound of *Chriſt Jeſus* is not there to be heard, as the beſt *Hiſtorians* and *Coſmographers* yeeld.[1]

Peace. It ſeemes ſtrange, if *Chriſt Jeſus* had intended any ſuch *delegation* of *ſpiritual power* to *civil Magiſtrates*, that he [79] ſhould keep the very ſound of his name from them.

Few Magiſtrates in the world know Chriſt Jeſus.

Againe, in the other five parts of the world, where his *name* is ſounded, how rarely hath he acquainted any *civil Magiſtrate* with the ſaving *knowledge* of his *will?*

Truth. I add, that ſuch rare ones, that ſavingly know *Chriſt Jeſus* and his *will*, are no *judges* in ſuch caſes over the *conſciences* of their *brethren*, or any, by way of *civil judicature*, this very inſtance of *Pauls* appealing to *Cæſar* hath and ſhall further declare and manifeſt.

Peace. But what ſhould be the reaſon why Maſter *Cotton* affirmeth, That the *civil Magiſtrate* ought to be able to judge of all *capital* offences againſt *Religion*, but not of all *queſtions?*

Truth. The truth is, if the *civil Magiſtrate* were a *Surgeon* appointed of *Chriſt Ieſus* to judge in cauſes that concern cutting of *life* and *limbe*, &c. he would beyond all queſtion be able to judge of *petty cuts, wounds*, &c. But *Satan* that old deceiver, that knew (by *Gods* permiſſion) how to *cozen Adam, David,* Solomon, *Peter* (the moſt perfect, wiſe, and holieſt of *Gods ſervants*) is not now to learn how to cheat Maſter *Cotton* alſo; *Satan* well ſees, if Maſter *Cotton*

Myſtical and cruel Surgery.

1 "The *World* divided (ſay our ableſt *Coſmographers*) into *thirty* parts, as yet but *five* of *thirty* have heard of the ſweet name of *Jeſus* a *Saviour*." *Hireling Miniſtry*, p. 3.

ſhould grant it the *Magiſtrates* duty to judge in leſſer *queſtions*, the hope of *Benefices* and *Livings* were gone, and the trade of *Synods* would down: And if he ſhould not grant it to be the *Magiſtrates* duty to judge in *capitals*, the *Pope*, the *Biſhops*, and all *perſecuting prieſts*, would want the *ſecular* power, the *ſervile executioners* of their moſt wicked and moſt bloody *decrees* and *ſentences*.

P*eace*. In the next place Maſter *Cotton* ſeemes to charge a *contradiction* upon the diſcuſſer, for ſaying, that *civil Magiſtrates* were never appointed by God *defenders* of the *faith* of *Ieſus*, and yet every one is bound to put forth his utmoſt powers in Gods buſineſs.

Truth. Love hath charged the diſcuſſer to ſpare the tearm of *contradiction* in many *paſſages* of Maſter *Cottons* writing, where he hath (to his underſtanding) obſerved them, to prevent exaſperations, &c. contrarily Maſter *Cotton* againſt the diſcuſſer, ſtraines the *text* and *Margin* to ſound out *contradictions*, *contradictions*, to all paſſengers.

80] But let us examine. And firſt, Maſter *Cotton* will not deny, but the *ſon* of *perdition*, the P*ope* of *Rome* (whoſe coming and practice is by the work of the *devil*) was the blaſphemous *author* (he and his *Cardinals* in *Councel* together) of that title *defender of the faith* ſent with great *gratitude* and *ſolemnity* to *Henry* the eighth, as a *kingly popelike reward*, for penning (or bearing the name of) a blaſphemous *writing* againſt *Chriſt Ieſus* in his holy truth proclaimed by *Luther*.[1]

The title of defender of the faith

[1] Henry VIII. wrote *Aſſertio ſeptem ſacramentorum adverſus Martinum Lutherum*, which he dedicated to Leo X., and ſent a copy in elegant Ms. to Rome,

Peace. With what *eyes* and *eares* ſuch *blaſphemous* and *bloody titles* are to be lookt upon and heard by the chaſte *eyes* and *ears* of *Chriſts Doves, Chriſt Ieſus* will one day, and ſhortly make appear.

To ſerve God withal our might, literally taken, horribly abuſed.

Truth. But what *contradiction* will be in the later, to wit, [That every one muſt do his utmoſt in *Gods buſineſs*] when this former (to wit, to be a *defender of the Faith*) is conſtantly denied to be any of the *buſineſſes* of *civil officers*, and the *preſervation* of the *civil ſtate*, which charge and worke by the *civil ſtate* can only lawfully (and therefore poſſibly) be committed to them? For otherwiſe to take theſe *words* in a literal *ſence*, without reſpect to the *rules* and *limits* of *Gods order* and *righteonſneſs*, what is it but to fire the *world* with *wild-fire* of blind *zeale*, and to tumble down all *Gods* beauteous *ſtructures* and *buildings* into a *Chaos* and *confuſion* of *Antichriſtian Babylon*? And this eſpecially by the meanes of ſuch who think and ſay, that they cannot ſerve God with all their might except they puniſh *blaſphemers*, and fight againſt *blaſphemous nations*, and ſubdue (not only the holy land from the *Turk*, but) even all the *world* from their *idolatries* and *blaſphemies*, if it lie in their power; which *ſpirit* whether it be the *ſpirit* of the Son of *God*, and *Prince* of *peace*, or the *ſpirit* of the *world*, the *ſpirit* of the ſon of *perdition*, let every mans own *ſpirit* ſearch and judge in the holy fear and preſence of *God.*

which is ſtill ſhown in the Library of the Vatican. The Pope propoſed in conſiſtory to give Henry the title of *Defender of the Faith*. This gave riſe to conſiderable debate, but the Pope's propoſition finally prevailed, and a bull was iſſued, conferring the title on the King and his poſterity. Roſcoe, *Life of Leo X.* ii. 233.

Peace. But further (ſaith Maſter *Cotton*) it was unneceſſary, yea folly and prepoſterous to have complained to *Herod*, *Pilate*, *Cæſar*, againſt the *Hereſies* of the *Phariſees*: For if a poor *ſheep* ſhould complain to the *Wolves* of the *Wolves hereſies*, would not the whole kennel of *Wolves* riſe up againſt him, *&c*? Would it not have diſturbed the civil ſtate, by putting them into *jealouſies* of a [81] *new kingdome*, and it was neceſſary the *Goſpel* ſhould firſt be known and received, believed and profeſſed, before any could be complained of for *Apoſtacie* from it into *hereſie*.

Truth. Maſter *Cotton* cannot deny, but that moſt of the *Magiſtrates* of the *world* (by far) are ſuch as *Herod*, *Pilate*, *Cæſar* were, without *God*, and *enemies* to him, yea alſo in that little part of the *world* which is called *Proteſtant*. Now if they are but *kennels of Wolves* (compared with *Chriſts ſheep*) as Maſter *Cotton* expreſſeth, I firſt demand how poorely hath *Chriſt Jeſus* in all *ages* provided for and furniſhed his people with ſuch main pillars of their *ſpiritual joyes*, *light* and *confidence*, as *godly* and *Chriſtian Magiſtrates*?

Chriſt Jeſus hath rarely furniſhed his people with godly Magiſtrates.

Peace. It is as cleer as the Sun beams, that if ever *Chriſt Jeſus* had intended ſuch an *ordinance* in and over his *church*, he would never have been ſo miſtaken, as to ſupply his *ſheep* in all *ages*, and in all parts of the *world*, with *kennels* of *Wolves* in ſtead of *godly* and *Chriſtian Shepherds*.

Truth. But ſecondly, Grant them to be *kennels* of *Wolves* in Maſter *Cottons* ſence, yet what *bar* is this to any from *preſenting*, and to them from receiving ſuch *complaints* as are proper to their *cognizance*, to their *duty* and *calling* (were they truely called of *God* and *Chriſt* to ſuch a *ſervice*) to wit, to govern in *ſpiritual*, *Eccleſiaſtical* or *Church cauſes*? what though a *Magiſtrate* be a *drunkard*, *whoremonger*, *opperſſour*, is it not the *duty* of the people to complaim to him of *drunkards*, *thieves*, *whoremongers*, *oppreſſors*? whom if he puniſh not, but countenance, *&c.* yet have ſuch *petitioners* diſcharged their *conſciences*, and left the *guilt* upon the right head, who ſhould be an *head* of *civil righteouſneſs*, but is an *head* of *wickedneſs* and *iniquity*.

Peace. By this *argument* of Maſter *Cottons*, the poor *widow*, that ſued for right to the unjuſt *Judge*, that neither feared *God*, nor regarded man, took a fooliſh and a preſtoperous courſe, though commended by the *Lord Jeſus*, Luk. 18. [2–7.]

Truth. Indeed (as Maſter *Cotton* ſaith) If we look at the probability of any wholeſome fruit from ſuch *trees*, we cannot expect *grapes* from ſuch *briars*, nor *figs* from ſuch *thiſtles*: But looking at the providence of *God*, who ruleth and over-ruleth the hearts of *Kings* and all *Magiſtrates* (as in the caſe of the poor *widow* and [82] thouſand others) as alſo at what is their *Duty* and *profeſſion*, to wit, to invite cheerfully their *ſubjects* to bring their *complaints* to them; as alſo what is the *duty* of the wronged and *oppreſſed* to wit, to deliver and diſcharge their own *ſouls*, I ſee not but it is ſafe, ſeaſonable, and a duty, to cry even to the unjuſt *Judge* for *Juſtice*, as that poor woman did.

Peace. Yea, were *Cæſar*, *Herod*, *Pilate* (by virtue of their *places*, *offices*, and *duties* (*Eccleſiaſtical Judges*, and ought to have ſuppreſſed the *hereſies* and *blaſ-*

phemies of the *Pharisees*? why ſhould it be impoſſible, but they might have removed the *Phariſees offence*, as many *Kings* of *England* and *France* (though evil themſelves) have ſtirred mightily upon complaints of their *ſubjects* againſt the *Popiſh Phariſees* of their times, yea the higheſt of them the *Pope* himſelf? And if Maſter *Cottons* doctrine be true, why muſt not the *Magiſtrate* be ſought unto, that a true *Goſpel* be received and believed? Why may not the *civil power* be a judge in the firſt receiving of the *Goſpel*, as afterward for the *preſerving* and *reſtoring* of it?

Truth. Such is the *brightneſs* of the *Goſpel* of *Chriſt Ieſus*, and the dread and the power of the two-edged *ſword* coming out of his *mouth*, ſubduing and ſlaying the higheſt *oppoſites* and *adverſaries*, that it will prove to be unneceſſary, fooliſh and prepoſterous to run to any other *ſword* or *cenſures*, then thoſe alone of *Chriſts*, ſo mighty, and ſo powerful, were they rightly adminiſred, as the *Popiſh* and *Proteſtant world* pretendeth.

Peace. Laſtly, Maſter *Cotton* profeſſeth he knows not how Magiſtrates can know the *Son*, and kiſs him, and acknowledge his *kingdome*, and ſubmit their *crowns* to it, love his *truth*, be *nurſing Fathers* and *Mothers* to his *church*, and yet not be *defenders* of it.

Truth. If kings muſt ſubmit their *crowns* to this *kingdome* of *Chriſt*, muſt it not undeniablly follow, that the *kingdom* of *Chriſt Ieſus* is far greater and *higher* then their *thrones* and *crowns*? (for none will ſubmit to the *leſſer*, *weaker* &c.) And if ſo, what weakneſs is it yet to expect, that the inferiour *power* and *authority*, to wit, *civil* and earthly, muſt defend the higheſt and moſt *glorious crown* and *throne* of

Defendor of the faith.

Chriſt Ieſus? Like as if a poor *Indian Canow* ſhould ſubmit it ſelf to ſome *Royal Navy*, and yet muſt be 83] this *Navies defender*; or a few naked *Americans* ſubmit to ſome *Army* or *kingdome*, and yet theſe poor naked ones muſt bear (and that ſeriouſly without *Ieſting*) the title of their *defenders*.

Truth. Maſter *Cotton* and thoſe of his bloody *judgement* are not contented that the *civil powers* defend the *bodies* and *goods* of the *Saints* from *oppreſſors*, from *perſecutors*, &c. that *love* and *affection* by all gracious means be expreſt more to the *Saints* then to other people of their *dominions*, that all true Chriſtian meanes be uſed for the ſpreading of the name and *truth* of the *Lord Ieſus*; I ſay, this ſerves not the turn, and gives not content, except alſo the *Magiſtrate* defend by *civil ſword*, the *purity* of the *doctrine*, and the *ordinances* of *Chriſt Ieſus* in his *church*, in *puniſhing* and *ſuppreſſing* the contrary by arme of *fleſh*, whether *within* or *without* the *church*.

A bold, but a true word.

Peace. In this laſt reſpect I muſt ſpeak an high and bold word, to wit, That the pooreſt *youth* or *maid*, who hath more *knowledge* and *grace* of *Chriſt* then a king or Emperour hath (as well ſometimes it hath and may come to paſs) may be a greater *contender* for the truth, and a great *defender* of the *faith* of *Ieſus*, then the *king* or Emperor, and ſo conſequently then all the *kings* of the whole world.

Truth. Paul was ſet for the *defence* of the *Goſpel* and conſequently every *believer* in *Ieſus* (according to his meaſure of *grace* received) and therefore, your word is not more *bold* then *true*. For *ſpiritual defences* are moſt proper to a ſpiritual eſtate, and ſo accordingly moſt potent, prevalent, and mighty.

Examination of CHAP. XXXI.

Peace.

HEre firſt Maſter *Cotton* will not own it, that the *title* of *Iudges* of *ſpiritual cauſes* be given to *Civil Magiſtrate.*

Truth. The P*arliament* of *England* eſtabliſhed King *Henry* the eighth *ſupreame head and Governor* over the *church* of *England*, and what is this but *ſupreme Iudge* in all *Eccleſiaſtical cauſes*? What though the tearme *judge* be ſtumbled at by ſome, [84] and the tearm *head* will not down with others? yet take but what Maſter *Cotton* grants: And (as the *devil* himſelf, lay hid under *Samuels* mantle,[1] ſo) under Maſter *Cottons* tearm of *fathers*, *mothers*, *ſhepherds* (that is, *ſpiritual fathers*, *mothers*, *ſhepherds*) muſt of neceſſity be concluded an *headſhip*, and *power*, and *office* of *judging*, when this *child* doth a miſs, when theſe *ſheep* go aſtray, who are *ſchiſmaticks*, who *hereticks*, who *ſheep*, who *Wolves*, that the *ſheep* may be corrected and reduced, and the *Wolves* braines knockt out.

The title of ſupream head, oath of ſupremacy, &c.

P*eace.* They may judge (ſaith Maſter *Cotton*) but (not with a *church*) but *politick power*, and for want of which, and for giving their *kingdome* to the *Beaſt* (*Revel.* 17. 12, 13.) God (ſaith he) opened a way for the *Turkes* to break in and deſtroy the third part of *Chriſtendome*, Rev. 9. 14. to 21.

Truth. Let it be under what *cloake*, or *colour*, or notion ſoever, let it be *politick* (indeed) and *ſubtle*, or

[1] This aſſumes the apparition of an evil ſpirit under the form of Samuel in Saul's interview with the witch of Endor. "And ſhe ſaid, An old man cometh up: and he is covered with a mantle. And Saul perceived that it was Samuel." 1 *Samuel*, xxviii. 14.

plaine and ſimple, yet it ſeemes it is true, that he muſt *judge*, which will not be owned in *plaine tearmes*, but as a P*rotector*, a *Father* or a *Shepheard*.

Secondly, Thoſe S*criptures* quoted do not lay a *guilt* upon the ten *horns* or *kings* for ſuffering the *beaſt* in their *dominions*, but for giving their power and *authority* unto him.

The plague of the Turkes upon the Antichriſtian world.

Thirdly, the *civil peace* was not diſſolved but preſerved for many hundred yeers before the *Turkes* roſe, to puniſh either the *Eaſtern* or *Weſtern* part of *Antichriſtian Chriſtendome*: So that a falſe *religion* doth not immediately and inſtantly *diſſolve* the *civil peace*, but *kingdomes* and *ſtates* profeſſing falſe *religions* may flouriſh. Tis true, *God* in his deep *councels* and *times* brings *judgements*, *eternal* and *temporal*, upon falſe worſhipping *ſtates*, eſpecially where the *truth* of *Chriſt* is *preſented* and *perſecuted*; Yet divers *ages* of temporal *proſperity* to the *Antichriſtian kingdom*, prove that common *Aſſumption* and *maxime* falſe, to wit, that the *church* and *Commonweale* are like *Hipocrates twins*, weep and laugh, flouriſh and fade, live and die together.[1]

P*eace*. I cannot reach the *bottome* of this next paſſage of Maſter *Cotton*, *viz*. that *Magiſtrates* may be ſubject to the *church* and lick the duſt of her *feet*, and yet be *ſupreme governors of the* [85] *church* alſo: In *ſpiritual matters* (ſaith he) and in a right *adminiſtration* of them, he is ſubject; but in *civil things*,

[1] "Wee may try the waight of that commonly received and not queſtioned *opinion*, *viz*. That the *civill ſtate* and the *ſpirituall*, the *Church* and *Commonweale*, they are like *Hippocrates twinnes*, they are borne together, grow up togetner, laugh together, weepe together, ſicken and die together." *Bloudy Tenent, Pub. Narr. Club*, iii. 333. After ſome ſearch we have failed to verify this reference.

and in the corrupt adminiſtration of *church*-affaires (ſo far corrupt as tendeth to the diſturbance of *civil peace*) there the *Magiſtrates* (ſaith he) are *ſupream governors*, even over the *churches* in their own *dominions*.

The Civil Magiſtrate no govern- or over the ſpiritual kingdome of Chriſt.

Truth. Who ſees not here, but by this Doctrine *Magiſtrates* muſt judge, when the *church* is rightly adminiſtred, and when it is corruptly adminiſtred: And that whatever the *Miniſters* of the *church*, or the whole *church* judge, that is nothing, for the *Magiſtrate* if he be *ſupream governor*, he muſt *judge?* and what is this but even in the very ſame reſpect, I ſay in one and the ſame reſpect, to make them *high* and *low*, *up* and down, *mountaines* and *vallies*? *ſupream governors*, and ſo above the *church*, anon agen to lick the duſt of the *feet* of the *church*; which Maſter *Cotton* will as ſoon make good, as bring the *Eaſt* and the *Weſt* together.

Beſides (as elſewhere I obſerved) what if the people will have no *kings*, *governors* &c. nay no *Parliament*, nor *general courts*, but leave vaſt *interregnums* or *Ruptures* of *government*, yea conclude upon frequent *changes* (as all *nations* of the *world* have had great changes this way) ſhall the *churches* of *Chriſt Jeſus* be without an *head*, a *governor*, *defender*, *protector?* What a ſlavery doth this *bloody doctrine* bring the faire *Spouſe* of *Chriſt* into?

Peace. In the paſſage concerning *Saul*, Maſter *Cotton* obſerveth, that *Saul* was not taken away for exerciſing *civil power* againſt *ſpiritual wickedneſs* in the caſe of *witches*.

Truth. *Saul* was *king* of *Iſrael*, the *church* of *God*, and a typical *king*, the anointed or *Chriſt* of *God*;

Whether Saul a type of Christ.

and Master *Cotton* himself will subscribe to the confession of *Nathaniel* to *Christ Iesus*, Thou art the *king* of *Israel*, which he was and is in his own most holy *person*, as also in his *Ministers* and *governors* during his absence. It was now *Sauls* duty to put literal *witches* to death in his *Christian Israel*, his *church* and *Congregation*.

It is true, *Saul* forsaking the *God* of *Israel*, perished for other wickedness, and among other his sins, for persecuting or hunting righteous *David*, and therein *Saul* is a *type* and warning to all [86] the *apostates* and *persecuting Sauls* of the earth, that *desperation* and desperate self-destruction attend them.

Peace. But whither tends this last passage concerning *David*? We read not (saith Master *Cotton*) that he did exercise any *spiritual power* as a *King*, but as a *prophet*. Will he commend *Sauls* kingly acting in *spiritual* things, as just; and shall not *David* (whose *name* and *throne* were most eminently figurative of *Christ Jesus*) be found a *king* in *Israel*, the house and *church* of *God*?

The kings of Israel and Judah types.

Truth. The patern of *David*, *Solomon*, and the good *kings* of *Israel* and *Judah*, is the common and great *argument* of all that plead for *Magistrates* power in *spiritual* cases: And indeed, what *power* was that but *spiritual*, which he exercised in bringing up the Arke, expresly said to be done by *king David*? 2 *Sam*. 6. [12.] What power was that but *kingly*, put forth in ordering and disposing the *services* of the *Priests* and *Levites*, and *singers*, 1 *Chron*. 16 [4–6?]

Peace. Master *Cotton* not ignorant of this, it may be was not pleased with that *passage*, *viz*. [That *God* will take away ſuch *ſtayes*, upon whom *Gods* people reſt in his wrath, that *king David*, that is, *Chriſt Jeſus* the *Antitype*, in his own *ſpiritual power* in the hands of his *Saints*, may ſpiritually, and for ever be advanced.]

Truth. This *power* the *General Councels*, the P*opes*, the *Prelates*, the *kings* of the earth, the *civil courts* and *Magiſtrates*, lay claime unto, and moſt of them with *bloody hands*, yea and *Gods* ſervants have too long leaned unto, and longed after, ſuch an *arme* of *fleſh*, which proves (moſt commonly) but S*auls arme*, an oppreſſing and *perſecuting*, and a ſelf-*killing* and deſtroying power at the laſt.

Examination of CHAP. XXXII.

Peace.

THis Chapter containes, a twofold denyal: Firſt (ſaith Maſter *Cotton*) we hold it not lawful for a *Chriſtian Magiſtrate* [87] to compell by civil ſword, either *Phariſee*, or *Pagan*, or *Jew*, to profeſs his *religion*.

Truth. He that is deceived himſelf with a *bad commodity*, puts it off as *good* to others: Maſter *Cotton* believes, and would make others believe, that it is no *compulſion*, to make *laws* with *penalties* for all to come to *church*, and to *publike worſhip*; which was ever in our *father dayes*, held a ſufficient *trial* of their *religion*, and of *conſenting* to or *diſſenting* from the *religion* of the times. Hence by ſome is that of *Luk.* 14. [23.] alledged, Compel them to come in, ſufficiently fulfilled, if they be ſo far compelled, as to be conformable to come to *church*, though it be under the pretence and mask of comming only to hear the *word*, whereby they may be *converted*.

But it is needleſs to ſtand *gueſſing* and *gueſſing* at the *weight*, when the *ſcales* are at hand, the holy *word* of *God*, by which we all profeſs to have our *weight*, or to be found too light.

Peace. Maſter *Cotton* therefore (Secondly) denies that a blind *Phariſee* may be a good *ſubject*, and as peaceable and profitable to the *civil ſtate* as any, ſince they deſtroyed the *civil ſtate* by deſtroying *Chriſt*.

Truth. When we ſpeak of *civil ſtate*, and their *adminiſtrations*, it is moſt improper and fallacious to wind or weave in the conſideration of their true or falſe *religions*.

It is true, *idolatry* brings *judgement* in *Gods* time (and ſo do other ſins, for we read not of *idolatry* in *Sodoms puniſhment*, *Ezek*. 16.[49. 50.])notwithſtanding there is a preſent *civil ſtate* of men combined to live together there in a *commonweale*, which Gods people are commanded to pray for (*Jerm*. 29.[7.]) whatever be the *religion* there publikly profeſſed. Beſide, the *Phariſees* deſtroying *Chriſt*, were guilty of blood and perſecution, which is more then idolatry, *&c*. and cries to heaven for vengeance.

Peace. It cannot therefore with any ſhew of *charity* be denyed, but that divers *prieſts* of *Babel*, might be *civil* and *peaceable*, notwithſtanding their *religion* and *conſcience*.

Truth. Yea it is known by experience, that many thouſands of *Mahumetan*, *Popiſh* and *Pagan Prieſts* are in their perſons, both of as *civil* and courteous and peaceable a nature, as any of the *ſubjects* in the ſtate they live in.

88] The truth is, that herein all the *prieſts* in the *world*, *Mahumetan*, *Popiſh*, *Pagan* and *Proteſtant*, are the greateſt *peace-breakers* in the *world*, as they (fearing their own cauſe) never reſt ſtirring up *Princes* and people againſt any (whether *Gods* or the *devils inſtruments*) that ſhall oppoſe their own *religion* and *conſcience*, that is in plaine *Engliſh*, their *profits*, *honours* and *bellies*.

The prieſts and Clergy in all Nations the greateſt peace-breakers.

Examination of CHAP. XXXIII.

Peace.

THe entrance of this Chapter (*dear truth*) looks in mine eye like one of the bloody *fathers* of the *inquiſition*, and breaths (like *Paul* in his mad *zeal* and *frenzy*) *ſlaughters* againſt the Son of *God* himſelf, though under the name or brand of a *ſeducer*, as all *perſecutors* have ever done: For (ſaith Maſter *Cotton*) he that corrupteth a ſoul with a corrupt *religion*, layeth a *ſpreading leaven* which corrupteth a ſtate, as *Michals idolatry* corrupted *Laiſh*, *Judg*. [18.] 19. and that *Apoſtacy* was the *captivity* of the land; and the worſhipping of *images* brought the plague of the *Turkes*, and therefore it is *lex talionis*, that calleth for not only *ſoul* for *ſoul*, but *life* for *life*.

Touching the ſeducer.

Truth. Thy tender *braine* and *heart* cannot let flie an *arrow* ſharpe enough to pierce the *bowels* of ſuch a *Bloody Tenent.*

Peace. The flaming *jealouſie* of that moſt holy and righteous *Judge*, who is a *conſuming fire*, will not ever hear ſuch *Tenents*, and behold ſuch practices in ſilence.

Truth. Sweet peace, long and long may the *Almond*-tree flouriſh on Maſter *Cottons* head in the armes of true *Chriſtianity* and true *Chriſtian* honour, And let New-*Englands Colonies* flouriſh alſo (if Chriſt ſo pleaſe) untill he come againe the ſecond time: But that he who is love it ſelf, would pleaſe to tell Maſter *Cotton* and the *Colonies*, and the *world*, the untrueneſs, uncharitableneſs, unmercifulneſs, and unpeaceableneſs of ſuch *concluſions*: For is not this the plaine *Engliſh* and the bottome, to wit, If the *ſpirit* of *Chriſt Jeſus* in any of his *ſervants*, *ſons* or *daughters*, [89] witneſſing againſt the *abominations* or ſtinks of *Antichriſt*, ſhall perſwade one *ſoul*, man or woman, to fear *God*, to come out of *Babell*, &c. to refuſe to bow down to, and to come out from communion with a *ſtate-golden-image*, and not to touch what it is perſwaded is an unclean thing.

That man or woman who was the *Lambs* and the *Spirits inſtruments* thus to inlighten and perſwade one ſoul, he hath (ſaith this tenent) laid a *leaven*, which corrupteth the *ſtate*, that is, the *land*, *town*, *city*, *kingdome*, or *Empire* of the *world*; that *leaven* ſhall bring the *captivity*, ruine and deſtruction of the *ſtate*, and therefore *Lex Talionis*, not only *ſoul* for *ſoul* in the next, but *life* for *life* alſo in this preſent *world*.

Of ſeducing.

Peace. All thy *witneſſes* (*dear truth*) in all ages

have borne the *brand* and black mark of *ſeducers*, and ſtill ſhall, even *Chriſt Jeſus* himſelf, to the laſt of his holy *army* and followers againſt his enemies.

Truth. How famous, or rather abominably infamous hath been the practice of all *perſecutors* this way? I ſhall pick out one inſtance, a very ſtinking weed out of *Babels* deſart (to let paſs all the bloody, *bulls* and their roarings and *threatning* of *Councels*, *Popes* and *Emperors*, *kings*, *Biſhops*, *Commiſſaries* &c. againſt the *Waldenſians*, *Wicklevians*, the *Huſſites*, *Hugonites*, *Lutherans*, *Calviniſts*, &c.) their infections and ſeducings. To let paſs former and latter *perſecutions* in our own *Engliſh* Nation, which hath been (as *France*, *Spaine*, *Italy*, *Low-countries*, &c. alſo) a *ſlaughter-houſe* of *Chriſts lambs*; one inſtance more pertinent then many, we have (in the raigne of that wiſe and mighty prince *Henry* the eighth) of bloody *Longland*, *Lincolnes Biſhop*, acting to the life Maſter *Cottons Tenent* againſt *ſeducers* throughout his *Dioceſs*. What *oaths* did he exact? what *articles* did he invent, to find out the *meetings* the *conventicles*, the *conferences*, of any poor ſervants of *God*, men and women, day or night; whether the *father* read to the *child*, or the *childe* to the *father*, the *husband* to the *wife*, or the *wife* to the *husband*? Yea, whether they ſpake any thing (though never ſo little) out of any line of holy *Scriptures*, or any of *Wickliffes* books, or any good *Engliſh writings*: By which abhorred *practices*, the *fathers* (caught in this bloody *Biſhops oath*, vehemently forced upon all ſuſpected) [90] the *fathers*, I ſay were forced to accuſe and betray their *children*, the *children* their *fathers*, *husbands* their *wives*, *wives*

Biſhop Longlands ſubtle Oaths of inquiſition.

their *husbands*, for fear of horrible death on the one ſide, or elſe of running upon the rocks of *Perjury* on the other ſide.[1]

Peace. Hold (*dear truth*) and ſtop; my *ſpirit* is wounded with ſuch *relations*.

Truth. O how were the *Saints*, and *Chriſt Jeſus* in them, wounded with ſuch *tenents* and *practices*!

Peace. Maſter *Cotton* will ſalve this up (with what he elſewhere ſaith) thus: *Longlands*, and the *Papiſts religion*, and the *religion* of *England*, was then falſe in that *kings* time.

Truth. What then? No pious and ſober man can hold all men devoid of *conſcience* to *God*, except himſelf. In all *religions*, *ſects*, and *conſciences*, the ſons of men are more or leſs zealous and preciſe, though it be in falſhood.

2. But let it be granted, that the *religion* perſecuted is falſe, and that a falſe *religion* like *leaven*, will ſpread, as did this *idolatry* of *Michal*, *Jeroboam*, and others; and grant that this *idolatry* will bring *judgements* from heaven in the end, yet I deſire Maſter *Cotton*, or any knowing man, to anſwer to theſe two *queſtions*.

1. Where finde we, ſince the comming of *Chriſt Jeſus*, a *land* like *Canaan*, a *ſtate-religion*, a *City*, or *Town-religion*, wherein the *Townes*, or *Cities*, or *kingdomes apoſtacie* may be feared (as Maſter *Cotton* here

[1] John Longland (1473–1547) was confeſſor of Henry VIII., and became Biſhop of Lincoln in 1520. Fox gives a table from the regiſters of the dioceſe of Lincoln, with the proceſs of trial in the caſe of a large number of perſons, who were ſubjected to the inquiſitions deſcribed in the text. There is no doubt that this account given by Fox was Williams's authority for the above ſtatements. *Acts and Monuments*, ii. 23–40.

writes of *Laiſh*) and conſequently the *Townes* or *Cities captivity* for that ſin?

2. Where read we of the deſtruction of a *land* for *idolatry*, or *images*, without a ripeneſs in other ſins, and eſpecially of *violence* and oppreſſion (of which *perſecution* is the greateſt?) And therefore to follow Maſter *Cottons* inſtance of the *Turks*, beſide *idolatry* (which ſaith Maſter *Cotton* brought the plague of the *Turks*, Rev. 9. [14–21.) read we not alſo in that *Scripture*, and in all *hiſtories*, of their deteſtable and wonderful *whoredomes*, *witchcrafts*, *thefts*, *ſlaughters*, and *murthers*, amongſt which this bloody Tenent of *perſecution* was ever in moſt high eſteem? *&c.*

Cauſes of deſtruction to a Nation.

Peace. Indeed *Babel* hath been filled with blood of all ſorts, *Revelations* the 18.[24] but in eſpecial manner hath the *whore* [91] been drunk with the blood of the *Saints*, and *witneſſes* of *Jeſus*, Revel. 17. [6.]

Truth. Hence then not *idolatry* onely, but that bloody *doctrine* of *perſecution* (the great *fire-brand* and *incendiary* of all *Nations* and *Commonweals*) brought in the bloody *Turkes* to revenge Gods *truth* and *witneſſes* ſlaine by the idolatrous and bloody *Antichriſtians*.

Peace. I ſomething queſtion, that it can be proved, that the moſt righteous *Judge* of the whole world ever deſtroyed *ſtate* or *nation* for *idolatry*, but where this bloody *doctrine* of *perſecution* was joyned with it, that is, until he had graciouſly ſent *witneſſes* againſt ſuch *idolatries*, and till ſuch *witneſſes* were deſpiſed and perſecuted, and therefore here comes in ſeaſonably the ſad exprobation of the *Lord Jeſus*, againſt *Jeruſalem*, threatning the ruine and deſolation of it,

Oh *Ieruſalem, Ieruſalem,* which killeſt the *Prophets* ; and ſtoneſt them which were ſent unto thee, *&c !*

Truth. I add laſtly, Let it be granted that a ſoul is corrupted with a falſe *religion,* and that that falſe *Religion,* like a *leaven,* in time hath corrupted the *ſtate*;

All nations Cities, Towns, &c. are part of the world.

Yet firſt, that *ſtate* or *land* is none elſe but a part of the *world,* and if ſo (ſince every part more or leſs in degree follows the nature of the whole) it is but natural, and ſo lieth as the whole *world* doth in *wickedneſs* ; and ſo, as a ſtate or part of the world, cannot but alter from one falſe way or path to another (upon this ſuppoſition (as before) that no *whole ſtate, kingdome, City,* or *Town* is *Chriſtian* in the new *Teſtament.*

Secondly, Grant this ſtate to be ſo corrupted or altered from one corrupt *religion* to another, yet that *ſtate* may many *ages* enjoy civil *peace* and worldly proſperity, as all *hiſtories* and *experience* teſtifies.

Change of Religions.

Thirdly, That *idolatry* may be rooted out, and another *idolatrous religion* of the *conqueror* (as in the *Romane* and other *conqueſts*) brought : in or the *religion* may be changed ſomething to the better, by the coming of new *Princes* to the *crown,* as we ſee in *Henry* the eighth, King *Edward,* and Queen *Elizabeth,* in our own *Nation,* and of late times.

Laſtly, A *ſoul* or *ſouls* thus leavened, may be reduced
92] by *repentance* (as often it pleaſeth *God* ſo to work, why then ſhould there (as Maſter *Cotton* intimates) ſuch a peremptory bloody ſentence be thundred out as *life* for *life,* &c.

Peace. But, ſaith Maſter *Cotton, falſe prophets,* in the old *Teſtament,* were to die, but for attempting ;

and the reaſon was not from any *typical holineſs* of the *land*, but from the dangerous wickedneſs of the attempting to thruſt away a ſoul from *God*, which is a greater injury, then to deprive a man of *bodily life*.

Truth. The reaſon to me appears plainly *typical*, with reſpect to that holy *nation*, and the *ſeducers*, ſeeking to turn the ſoul away from the *Lord their God*, who had brought them forth from the *land* of *Egypt*, by ſuch *ſignes*, *miracles* &c. Let Maſter *Cotton* now produce any ſuch *nation* in the *whole world*, whom *God* in the *New Teſtament* hath literally and miraculouſly brought forth of *Egypt*, or from one *land* into another, to the truth and purity of his *worſhip*, &c. then far be it, but I ſhould acknowledge that the *ſeducer* is fit to be put to death. But draw away the *curtaine* of the *ſhadow*, and let the *ſubſtance* appear, not a whole *Nation*, City, *&c.* but the *Chriſtian church* brought by ſpiritual *ſignes* and *wonders* from the *Egypt* of this *world* in all *nations* of the *world*, where the *Goſpel* comes. Juſtly therefore he that ſeduceth a ſoul from his *God* in *Chriſt*, and ſo endangereth to leaven that only true *Chriſtian ſtate* or *kingdome* the *church* of *Chriſt*, he ought to die (upon his obſtinacy) without mercy, as well under *Chriſt*, as under *Moſes*. Yea, he is worthy of a ſorer *puniſhment* (as ſaith the *Spirit* of *God*) who trampleth under feet the blood of *Chriſt*: ſuch a *deceiver* or *ſeducer* (except he repent) is to be cut from the preſence of the *Lord*, and to loſe an *eternal life*: He that is cut off from *material Iſrael*, might yet repent and live eternally, but he that is cut off from *myſtical Iſrael* under the *Goſpel*, that is, for obſtinacy in ſin

The ſtate of Iſrael unparlleld.

The puniſhments of Chriſt ſorer then the puniſhments of Moſes.

(the proper *hereticke*) he is cut off to all eternity; which puniſhment as it is infinitely tranſcendent and more dreadful in the nature and kind of it, ſo anſwereth it fully and infinitely that clauſe of Maſter *Cotton*, to wit, To thruſt a ſoul from *God* is a greater injury then to deprive a man of his bodily *life*.

Peace. Now whereas the diſcuſſer added, That dead men cannot [93] die, nor be infected with falſe *doctrine*, and ſuch is the *State* of all men, all *nations*, all the *world* over, until the *life* of *Chriſt Jeſus* quicken them; Maſter *Cotton* replies,

" Firſt, Dead men may be made worſe, and more " the children of *hell* then before, *Mat*. 23. [15.] and " therefore ſuch as ſo corrupt them, are worthy in a " way of due proceeding of a twofold death.

" Secondly, Such as profeſs the truth of the *doc*- " *trine* and worſhip of *Chriſt*, they live a kind of " *ſpiritual life*, though not ſuch as accompany *ſalva*- " *tion*, elſe how are falſe *teachers*, and ſuch as are *led* " by them, ſaid to be twice dead, pluckt up by the " *roots*, *Jud*. 12.

Truth. Dead men may be made worſe, that is, more to rot and ſtink; yet this is no taking away of any *life*. And therefore there is no proportionable reaſon, why the *ſeducers* ſhould ſuffer a *temporal death*, having neither taken away *ſpiritual* nor *natural life*; only thus he may be juſtly liable to a *ſpiritual death*, for endeavouring to hinder a *ſpiritual life*, by furthering any in their natural ſtate of *ſpiritual death*.

Of ſeducing.

2. For that place of *Iude*, Maſter *Cotton* knows that *Beza* propounds two ſenſes.

First, Twice dead, that is a certaine number for an uncertaine. *What meant by twice dead.*

Secondly, This fence urged by Mafter *Cotton*, which if it be to be admitted, yet is it but in appearance, as his *life* which in *hypocrifie* he profeffed, was but in fhew and appearance, he being never raifed up from the *fpiritual death* to a *fpiritual life*, and therefore really never fuffered the lofs of a *fpiritual life*, which he never had: And yet as in *typical Ifrael*, it ftood with *Gods juftice* to take away the *life* of the *feducer*, which feduced an *Ifraelite* from the *God* of *Ifrael*, or but attempted to do it: fo ftands it with the holy *juftice* of *God*, to cut him off eternally, who but attempteth to take away or hinders the *fpiritual* and *eternal life* of any.

P*eace*. Mafter *Cotton* in the next place prefumes on advantage that the difcuffer fhould fay, that none are infected with *natural plagues* or *fpiritual*, but fuch [as] are thereto appointed, *&c.*

94] *Truth*. It is plaine that the difcuffer alleadged not that, to diminifh or leffen fin (let it have its due *aggravation*) but as was faid before in cafe of the not final deceiving of the *elect*, fo was it here fpoken not to derogate from *Gods meanes* and *remedies* againft *natural* or *fpiritual infection*, but to abate the needlefs feares of men, who are apt to cry out. Except the *civil fword* be drawn (and fo therewith the *world* fet together by the *eares*) the *world* cannot be preferved from *infection*.

Peace. Whereas the difcuffer had affirmed, that *Chrift Jefus* had not left his people deftitute of *fpiritual means* againft *fpiritual infections*; This is true (ſaith Maſter *Cotton*) but it falleth out ſometimes, that when the *church* hath caſt out an *heretick*, yet he may deſtroy the *faith* of many, as did *Hymeneus* and *Philetus* (2 *Tim.* 2. 17.) and if the *Magiſtrates* ſword do here ruſt, *&c.* ſuch *leaven* may leaven the whole *country* &c. as *Arrianiſme* leavened the *world* by *Conſtantines* indulgence.[1]

Againe, ſaith he, it may be the *heretick* was never a member of the *church*; how then ſhall the *church* do?

Truth. Who can marvel at this, that the *dunghill* of this *world*, worldly men under the power of *Satan*, unto whom the obſtinate perſon the *heretick* is caſt, I ſay, that they, many of them, receive *worldly doctrine*, which the *church* as filth caſts out? *&c.*

2. As *Paul* ſaith concerning the *ſalvation* of *Gods children:* Let the world periſh, yet the foundation of *God* remaineth ſure, he knows who are his, and how to provide meanes to ſave them, though the world ſtill act it ſelf, wallowing and tumbling (like *Swine*) in one puddle of *wickedneſs* after another.

Of infection.

3. Maſter *Cotton* ſhould read a little further in the ſame *Scripture* quoted by him, where he finds not a tittle of *Pauls* directing *Timothy* to ſtir up the *ſecular*

[1] Conſtantine, at firſt indifferent, after the Council of Nice, baniſhed Arius, "But," ſays Gibbon, "as if the conduct of the Emperor had been guided by paſſion inſtead of principle, three years from the council of Nice were ſcarcely elapſed, before he diſcovered ſome ſymptoms of mercy, and even of indulgence, towards the proſcribed ſect. The exiles were recalled. Arius himſelf was treated by the whole court with the reſpect which would have been due to an innocent and oppreſſed man. The Emperor ſeemed impatient to repair his injuſtice, by iſſuing an abſolute command that he ſhould be ſolemnly admitted to the communion in the cathedral of Conſtantinople. On the ſame day, which had been fixed for the triumph of Arius, he expired." Gibbon, *Decline and Fall*, 317; Neander, *Church Hiſtory*, ii. 387; Stanley, *Eaſtern Church*, 311.

power (as the *Pope* ſpeakes) to cut off *Hymeneus* and *Philetus*, to prevent *infection*; but tels him, that the ſervants of *God* muſt not ſtrive, but muſt quiet themſelves with *patience*, waiting if peradventure *God* will pleaſe to give *repentance*.

Peace. Methinks this Anſwer may alſo fully ſatisfie his ſecond *ſuppoſition*, to wit, if that the *heretick* was never of the *church*.

95] *Truth*. Yea what hath the *church* to do (that is, judicially) with him that is without? and what hath the *civil ſtate* to judge him for who in *civil matters* hath not tranſgreſt? In vaine therefore doth Maſter *Cotton* ſuggeſt a perſecuting or hunting after the *ſouls* or lives of ſuch, as being caſt out of the *church*, keep private *conventicles* &c.

Peace. How grievous is this *language* of Maſter *Cotton*, as if he had been nouriſhed in the *chappels* and *cloiſters* of *perſecuting prelates*, and *prieſts*, the *Scribes* and *Phariſees*? As if he never had heard of *Jeſus Chriſt* in truth and meekneſs: For ſurely (as the diſcuſſer obſerved) *Chriſt Jeſus* never appointed the *civil ſword* an *Antidote* or *remedy* in ſuch a caſe, notwithſtanding Maſter *Cotton* replies that the *civil ſword* was appointed a *remedy* in this caſe, by *Moſes*, not *Chriſt*, *Deut*. 13.

Truth. *Moſes* in the *old Teſtament* was *Chriſts* ſervant, yet *Moſes* being but a ſervant, diſpenſed his power by carnal *rites* and *ceremonies*, *laws*, *rewards* and *puniſhments* in that holy *nation*, and that one land of *Canaan*: But when the *Lord Jeſus* the *Son* and *Lord* himſelf was come, to bring the *truth*, and *life*, and *ſubſtance* of all thoſe *ſhadowes*, to break down the *partition-wall* between *Jew* and *Gentile*, and to eſtabliſh the *Chriſtian worſhip* and *kingdome* in all *Nations* of the *world*, Maſter *Cotton* will never prove from any of the *books* and *inſtitutions* of the New *Teſtament*, that unto thoſe *ſpiritual remedies* appointed by *Chriſt Jeſus* againſt *ſpiritual maladies*, he added the help of the *carnall ſword*.

Peace. But Chriſt (ſaith Maſter *Cotton*) never abrogated the *carnal ſword* in the new, which he appointed in the *old Teſtament*, and the reaſon of the *law*, to wit, an offence of thruſting away from the *Lord*, is perpetual.

Truth. If it appear (as evidently it doth) that this king (*Jeſus* the *King of Iſrael*, wears his *ſword* (the *Antitype* of the *Kings* of *Iſrael* their *ſwords*) in his mouth, being a ſharpe two-edged ſword, then the anſwer is as clear as the S*un*, that ſcatters the clouds and darkneſs of the night.

The ſword of typical Iſrael a type of Chriſts ſpiritual ſword.

Beſides, Maſter *Cotton* needs not flie to the *Popes argument* for *childrens baptiſme*, to wit, to ſay that *Chriſt* never abrogated *Deut*. 13. therefore, *&c.* For Maſter *Cotton* knows the *profeſſion* [96] of the *Lord Jeſus, Iohn* 18. [36] that his *kingdome* was not earththly, and therefore his ſword cannot be earthly; Maſter *Cotton* knows that *Chriſt Ieſus* commanded a *ſword* to be put up when it was drawn in the cauſe of *Chriſt*, and addeth a dreadful *threatning*, that all that take the ſword (that is the *carnal ſword* for his *cauſe*) ſhall periſh by it.

Peace. And for the perpetuity of the *reaſon* of the *law*, you formerly fully ſatisfied, that even in the dayes of *grace*, for him that ſhall thruſt away an

Israelite from his *God*, there is upon his *obstinacy* a greater punishment beyond all imagination (to wit, a spiritual cutting off from the *land* of *Canaan*) then under *Moses*, which was but from the *temporall*, the *type* and *shadow*.

But Master *Cotton* proceedeth, alleadging, that the *Minister* of *God* must have in a readiness to execute *vengeance* on him that doth *evil*; and *evil* it is (saith he) to *thrust* away *Gods* people from him.

Truth. Every *lawful Magistrate*, whether succeeding or elected, is not only the *Minister of God*, but the *Minister* or servant of the people also (what *people* or *nation* soever they be all the world over) and that *Minister* or *Magistrate* goes beyond his *commission*, who intermeddles with that which cannot be given him in *commission* from the people, unless Master *Cotton* can prove that all the people and inhabitants of all *nations* in the *world* have *spiritual power*, *Christs power*, *naturally*, *fundamentally* and *originally* residing in them (as they are people and *inhabitants* of this world) to rule *Christs Spouse* the *church*, and to give spiritual power to their officers to exercise their *spiritual laws* and commands; otherwise it is but prophaning the holy name of the most *high*. It is but flattering of *Magistrates*, it is but the accursed trusting to an *arme* of *flesh*, to perswade the *rulers* of the *earth*, that they are *Kings* of the *Israel* or *church* of *God*, who were in their *institutions* and *government* immediately from *God*, the *rulers* and *gavernors* of his holy *church* and people.

Magistrates cannot receive from the people a spiritual power.

Peace. Grant (saith Master *Cotton*) that the *evil* be spiritual, and concern the inner man, and not the *civil ſtate*, yet that evill will be deſtructive to ſuch a *City*, it ſhall not riſe up the ſecond time, *Nahum*. 1. 9.

Truth. Although that it pleaſeth *God* ſometimes to bring a [97] people to utter *deſtruction* for their *idolatry* againſt himſelf, and *cruelty* againſt his people; yet we ſee the Lord doth not preſently and inſtantly do this, but after a long courſe of many *ages* and *generations*, as was ſeen in *Nineve* her ſelf, and ſince in *Athens*, *Conſtantinople*, and *Rome* both *Pagan* and *Antichriſtian*. And therefore the example hereby Maſter *Cotton* produced, gives not the leaſt colour of *warrant* for the *civil ſtate* preſently and immediately to execute vengeance for *idolatry* or *hereſie* upon *perſons* or *Cities* now all the world over, as he gave commandment to that *typical nation* of *Iſrael*, which is now alſo to be fulfilled ſpiritually upon the *ſpiritual Iſraelite*, or *Iſraelitiſh City*, a *particular church* or people falling away from the *living God* in *Chriſt Jeſus*.

The charge of the civil Magiſtrate

Peace. Whereas it was ſaid by the diſcuſſer, that the *civil Magiſtrate* hath the charge of the *bodies* and *goods* of the ſubjects, and the *ſpiritual officers* of the *church* or *kingdome* of *Chriſt*, the charge of their *ſouls* and ſoul ſafety. Maſter *Cotton* anſwers, Firſt, If it were ſo that the *civil Magiſtrate* had the charge of the *bodies* and *goods* onely of the ſubject, yet that might juſtly excite to watchfulneſs againſt ſuch *pollution* of *religion* as tends to *apoſtacy*, for *God* will viſit *city* and *country* with publike *calamity*, if not with *captivity*, for the *churches* ſake. The *idolatry* and *worſhip* of *Chriſtians* (ſaith he) brought the *Turkiſh captivity* upon the *citys* and *countries* of *Aſia*.

Truth. By *ſoul* and *ſoul* ſafety, I think Maſter *Cotton* underſtands the ſame with the *diſcuſſer*, to wit, the *matters* of *religion* and *ſpiritual worſhip*. If the *Magiſtrate* hath received any ſuch *charge* or *commiſſion* from *God* in *ſpiritual* things, doubtleſs (as before) the people have received it *originally* and *fundamentally* as they are a people: But now if neither the *nations* of the *world*, as peoples and *nations*, have received this *power originally*, and *fundamentally*; nor can they derive it *Miniſterially*, to their *civil officers* (by what name or *title*, high or low, ſoever they be diſtinguiſhed) Oh what *preſumption*, what *prophaning* of *Gods* moſt holy name, what *uſurpation* over the *ſouls* and *conſciences* of men, though it come under the *vaile* or *vizard* of ſaving the *City* or *kingdome*, yea of *ſaving* of *ſouls*, and honoring of *God* himſelf?

98] Beſide, *God* is not wont to viſit any *country* or people in general for the ſin of his people, but for their own *idolatries* and *cruelty* toward his people, as all *hiſtories* will prove. And for this inſtance of the *Turkes*, I ſay it was not the *idolatry* and *image-worſhip* alone of the *Antichriſtians*, but joyned with their other ſins, which brought *Gods* vengeance by the *Turks* upon them, as was ſaid above, from *Revel.* 9. and eſpecially their *Antichriſtian* cruelty grounded upon this bloody *doctrine* of *perſecution*.

The plague of the Turkes.

Both theſe *Antichriſtian ſtates*, and ſince alſo the *Turkiſh Monarchy*, have flouriſhed many *generations* in external and outward proſperity and glory, notwithſtanding their *religion* is falſe, and although it is true, that in the time and period appointed, all *nations* ſhall drink of the cup of *Gods* wrath, for their *nationall* ſins, both againſt the firſt and ſecond table, in matters concerning *God* and man.

Peace. How ſatisfie you Maſter *Cottons* ſecond anſwer or queſtion, to wit, Did ever *God* commit the charge of the *body* to any *Governor*, to whom he did not commit in his way the care of their *ſouls* alſo?

Truth. There is a twofold care and charge of *ſouls* manifeſted in holy Scripture.

A twofold care and charge of ſouls.

Firſt, That which in common belongs to all, to love our neighbor as our ſelves, to endeavor the preſent and eternal *welfare* both of *ſuperiors*, *inferiors*, *equals*, *friends* and *enemies*; and this by *prayers*, *exhortations*, *reproofs*, *examples* of *juſtice*, *loving kindneſs*, *ſobriety*, *godlineſs* &c.

Chriſt the true King of Iſrael.

But what is this to the ſecond *charge* by way of *office*, which in the *old Teſtament* was given not only to *Prieſts* and *Levites*, but to the *governors* and *rulers* of the *Iewiſh ſtate*: of which *ſtate* (being mixed of *ſpiritual* and *civil*) they were the *head* and *governors*, as it was *Iſrael*, a *nation* of *worſhippers* of the true *God*: And therein were they the *types* and *forerunners* of *Chriſt Jeſus* the true *King* of *Iſrael*, as he is called, *Joh.* 1. [49.] The cure and charge of ſouls, now (ſaith Maſter *Cotton*) in this Chapter, belongeth by vertue of *office* to the *ſpiritual officers* of *Chriſts kingdom*: I add, and during the *deſolation* of *Zion*, and the time of the *apoſtacy* from *Chriſts viſible kingdome*, belongeth to the two *Prophets* and *witneſſes* of *truth*, Rev. 11. [6.] but not to the *kings*, *rulers*, [99] *nations*, and *civil ſtates* of the *world*, who can be no true *parallel* or *antitype* to the *Iſrael* or people of *God*.

Peace. Maſter *Cotton* objects *Jehoſaphat* ſent abroad *preachers* throughout all the *Cities* of *Judah*; and if that were a *type* of *Chriſt*, it were to act that now, which typed out *Chriſt*, and he fulfilled in his own perſon.

Truth. Chriſt Jeſus ſends out *preachers* three waies.

Chriſts three-fold ſending of preachers.

Firſt, In his own *perſon*, as the twelve and the ſeventy.

Secondly, By his *viſible, kingly power*, left in the hand of his true *churches*, and the *officers* and *governers* thereof: In which ſence that *church* of *Antioch*, and the *governors* thereof, rightly inveſted with the *kingly* power of *Chriſt Jeſus*, ſent forth *Paul* and *Barnabas* with *prayer* and *faſting*, and laying on of *hands*: And *Paul* and others of *Chriſts meſſengers* being furniſhed with this kingly power, not only *planted churches*, but alſo ordained *elders* viſited theſe *churches* or viſible *cities of Judah*; that knowledge and teaching, and the *word* of *God* might dwel plenteouſly among them.

Thirdly, *Chriſt Ieſus* as *king* of his *church*, and *head* of his *body*, during the *diſtractions* of his *houſe* and *kingdome* under *Antichriſts apoſtacy*, immediately by his own holy Spirit, ſtirs up and ſends out thoſe fiery *witneſſes* (*Rev.* 11.) to teſtifie againſt *Antichriſt* and his ſeveral *abominations*: For as for lawful *calling* to a true ordinary *Miniſtery*, neither *Wickliff* in *England*, nor *Waldus* in *France*, nor *Iohn Hus* and *Ierome* of *Prauge* in *Bohemia*, nor *Luther* in *Germany*, nor multitudes more of famous *preachers* and *prophets* of *Chriſt*, both in theſe *countries*, and alſo in *Spaine*, *Italy* &c. I ſay, no true ordinary Miniſterial calling

No other true office of the Miniſtery, ſince the apoſtacie, but that of prophecy

and opening the Testament of Christ against the falshood of Antichrist.

can they ever ſhew; but Chriſt Jeſus by the ſecret motion of his own holy *Spirit* extraordinarily excited, in couraged and ſent them abroad as an *Angel* or *meſſenger* (*Rev.* 14. [6.]) with the *everlaſting Goſpel* &c.

Peace. To apply theſe three wayes, or any of them, to the civil *Magiſtrates* and *rulers* of the *world* (of whom *Iehoſaphat* in that his act ſhould be a *type*) is but to prophane the holy name of *God*, to leane upon and idolize an *arme* of *fleſh*, &c.

Truth. I grant, the *civil Magiſtrate* is bound to countenance the true *Miniſters* of *Chriſt Ieſus*, to incourage, protect, [100] and defend them from injuries, but to ſend them armed (as the *Popes Legats* and *Prieſts*) with a *ſword* of *ſteel*, and to compel people to hear and obey them, this ſavours more of the ſpirit of the *Pope*, his courſes and practiſes, Yea of *Mahomet* his *Muſſel-men*, *Dirgies*, &c. then the *Lambe* of *God* and his *followers*.

Peace. What *Iehoſophat*, *Aſa Hezekiah*, *Ioſiah*, &c. did, they did not only by *perſwaſion*, *countenance*, *example* (by which all are bound to further the *preaching* of *Chriſt Ieſus*) but alſo by force of *armes* and *corporal puniſhments*.

Truth. Yea even to the death it ſelf: and this is not a bare ſending out of *Miniſters* (as Maſter *Cotton* gives the inſtance:) For by his argument, all *rulers*, *kings*, and *Emperors*, and other *ſtates* of the world ought to embrue their hands in the blood of the many *thouſands* and *millions* of the poor people, if they forſake not their *idolatry* and embrace the *religion* which they ſay is *Chriſtian* and the only true.

Peace. No, ſaith Maſter *Cotton*, this ought not to

be, becaufe only *godly* and truly *Chriftian Magiftrates* may fo put forth this power of *Chrift*; others muft ftay until they be informed.

Truth. Can it enter into any *Chriftian* heart, to believe, that *Chrift Jefus* fhould fo loofly provide for his *affaires*, fo flightly for his *name* and *Fathers work* and fo regardleffly for his deareft *Spoufe*, as to leave fo high a *care* and *charge* with fuch as (generally and conftantly throughout the *whole world*) are ignorant of, yea and oppofite to the very name of *Chrift* and true *Chriftianity*?

A foule imputation put upon Chrift Jefus.

Peace. Surely if this *payment* were offered to the *governour* (as *Malachy* faith[1]) to the *world*, or *governments* of it, it would not pafs.

Truth. I never knew a *king* or *captaine councellor* or *conftable*, officers of high or low condition, rightly called according to to *God*, who were not invefted with *ability* more or lefs for the *maine* and *principal* points of their charge and duty.

Peace. It feemes indeed a marvelous, and yet it is Mafter *Cottons*) *conclufion*, that fuch *Magiftrates*, yea all or moft of the *Magiftrates* that ever have been fince *Chrift*, and now extant [101] upon the face of the earth, muft fit down, ftay and fufpend, and that all their life long, from the executing of the maine and principal part of their *office*, to wit, in *matters* concerning the *confcience*, *religion*, and *worfhip*, of the people.

Truth. Yea (Secondly) in a due furvey of the whole *univerfe* and *globe* of this world, will one of a thou-

[1] Offer it now unto thy governor; will he be pleafed with thee, or accept thy perfon? faith the Lord of hofts. *Malachi*, i. 8.

ſand or ten thouſand (according to Maſter *Cottons* diſabling of them from the chief part of their *office*) be found, I will not ſay fit to be, but to be at all lawful *civil Magiſtrates* or *rulers* according to *Gods ordinance* of *Magiſtracy* but meer *ſhadows* or *images* ſet on high with empty *names* or *titles* only of *Magiſtrates* ?

Peace Maſter *Cotton* adds, Although the good of ſouls is the proper or adequate object of the *ſpiritual officers* of *Chriſt*, and the *bodies* and *goods* of the people, the proper or adequate *object* of the *civil Magiſtrate* ; yet in *order* to the *good* of their *ſouls*, he ought to procure *ſpiritual helpes*, and to prevent *ſpiritual evils*.

Pretended order, monſtrous diſorder.

Truth. I reply, If he mean (as it is clear he doth) that the civil *Magiſtrate* ought to do this not only as a *Chriſtian* by *ſpiritual meanes*, but as a *civil Magiſtrate* by *force* of *armes*, It is not in *order*, but monſtrous *diſorder*, for then he (the *civil Magiſtrate*) muſt ſit *Judge* (judicially and formally) in thoſe *ſpiritual cauſes* and caſes, which Maſter *Cotton* grants are proper and adequate *objects* of the *ſpiritual officers* which *Chriſt* hath appointed.

Peace. Yea, why may not (ſaith Maſter *Cotton*) the *Magiſtrate* uſe his power (ſpiritually) in order to the good of *bodies*, as the *officers of Chriſt* dehort from *idleneſs* and *intemperance* of meats and drinks *&c.* in order to the *good* of *ſouls ?*

Truth. The *ſpiritua*l *officers* in dehorting from theſe *evils* or any other of that kind, interfere not, nor take cognizance of that which belongs not to their *ſpiritual court* ; for *holineſs* in all manner of *converſation* is the *circle* wherein they ought to ſee all their *ſpiritual ſubjects* to walk. If the *ſpiritual officers* ſhould cauſe by force of *armes* their people to walk juſtly, temperately, *&c.* as Maſter *Cotton* ſaith the *civil Magiſtrate* in order to the good of *bodies* ought to deal in *ſpiritual* and *ſoul*-matters, I ſay then the *eyes* of the *civil Magiſtrate* would begin to open [201] [102] and to ſee the horrible *diſorder* and *Babyloniſh confuſion* of that which is here masked under the abuſed name of *order*.

Peace. Maſter *Cotton* cloſeth up this *chapter* with very bitter cenſures againſt the diſcuſſer.

Truth. The diſcuſſer may well reply, that although ſince the *apoſtacy* he ſees not the *viſible thrones* and *tribunals* of *Chriſt Jeſus* (according to his firſt *inſtitution*) erected, and although the *civil Magiſtrate* hath not the power of *Chriſt* in *matters* of *religion*, yet they that ſlay the *Lords ſheep* are not exempted from all *judgement*: For, if the *offenders* ſlay them *corporally*, the *Lord* hath armed the *civil Magiſtrate* with the *ſword* of *God* to take vengeance on them. In which reſpect *God* hath crowned the *ſupream court* of P*arliament* with everlaſting honour, in breaking the jaws of the oppreſſing Biſhops, *&c.* Oh that ſuch glorious *Juſtice* may not be blemiſhed, by erecting in their ſtead a more *refined*, but yet as cruel an *Epiſcopacy.*[1]

The Parliaments high juſtice aggainſt oppreſſors.

2. If the offence be of a *ſpiritual nature*, is there

[1] The Parliament aboliſhed the hierarchy by two ordinances dated October 9 and November 16, 1646. The very name of Biſhop was aboliſhed. Neal, *Hiſt. of Puritans*, ii. 35, 36. There is a repetition of this idea on page 108 *infra*, where the reference to the Preſbyterians and Independents as ſeeking the power of the prelates is more definite.

no *ſpiritual way* of *judging*, except the *church* of *Chriſt* be granted *viſible* during *Antichriſts Apoſtacy*? Hath not *Chriſt Jeſus* given *power* to his two prophets (even all the *Raigne* of the *Beaſt*) to ſpeak *fire*, *Revelations* the 11. to ſhut up *heaven*, to turn the *waters* into *blood*, to ſmite the *earth* with all manner of *plagues*, and this untill the time of the finiſhing of their *prophecie* or *Teſtimony*, when their great *ſlaughters* ſhall prepare the way for the downfal of *Antichriſt* and their own moſt glorious *raiſing* and *exaltation*?

There was no Chapter 34 (which probably was Maſter *Cottons* overſight, or the Printers) therefore I paſs to Chapter 35.

103] *Examination of* CHAP. XXXV.

Peace.

HEre, whereas it was ſaid, if it were the *Magiſtrates* duty or office to puniſh *hereticks* &c. then he is both a *temporal* and *Eccleſiaſtical officers*: Maſter *Cotton* anſwers, It follows not: except the *Magiſtrate* were to puniſh with *Eccleſiaſtical* cenſures, his puniſhment is meerly *civil*, whether *impriſonment*, *baniſhment*, or *death*.

Truth. I reply, firſt, the *ſtatutes* of the *Engliſh nation*, and the *oath* of *ſupremacy*, have proved the *Kings* and *Queens* of *England heads* and *governors* of the *church* of *England*:[1] And if to be an *head* or *governor* be not an *office*, let Mafter *Cotton* be againe requefted to ponder the *inftance* given, which he paffeth by in filence; deny it ingenuoufly he cannot, and to juftifie it I hope his *light* from *heaven* will not fuffer him, although yet he would faine excufe it, by faying, they punifh only with *civil punifhment*, *imprifonment*, *banifhment* or *death*. Therefore, *The title head of the church.*

2. Here lies the *myftery* of *iniquity*, and the *Babel* and *confufion* of it, that either according to *Popifh Tenents* the *kings* of the earth muft give their power to the *beaft*, and enflave themfelves under the name and vizard of the *fecular power* to be the Popes *executioners*, or according to P*roteftant Tenents*, to wit, that *Kings* and *Governours* be *heads* of the *church* and yet be furnifhed with no *Church-power* nor *fpirituall* cenfures.

Peace. It would be thought fome *myftical* and *monftrous* thing, that *Kings* and *Governors* fhould be obliged to act in *civil Judicature*, and yet be furnifhed with no *civil power*, but ought to punifh onely with *fpirituall* or *Church-cenfures*.

Truth. The blinde and the lame mans robbing the Orchard is here verified. The Minifter (though a blinde guide) he is the feer, but wanting legs and ftrength of civil power, he is carried upon the civil Magiftrates fhoulders, whofe blindnefs the fubtle Clergy abufeth, *&c*. but both together, rob the Orchard of the moft high and fure-avenging *God*.

[1] "Be it enacted by authority of this prefent Parliament, that the King our Sovereign Lord, his heirs and fucceffors, Kings of this realm, fhall be taken, accepted and reputed the only Supreme Head in earth of the Church of England, &c." Act of Supremacy, given by Froude, *Hift. of England*, ii. 324.

104] *Truth.* I conceive it true, that the *Kings* and *Governors* of the *national church* of *Iſrael* had a *national power*; and had the K*ord Jeſus* been pleaſed to have continued *national churches*, the *Lings* and *governors* of ſuch *ſtates* might well (as they of *Iſrael* were) have been both *Temporal* and *Eccleſiaſtical officers*.

The civil Magiſtrate no ſpiritual officer, now as in Iſrael

Peace. But now the *Lord Jeſus* aboliſhing that *national ſtate*, and inſtituting and appointing his *worſhippers* and *followers* to be the *Iſrael of God*, the holy *nation* and proper *Antitype* of the former *Iſrael*; it ſeems moſt *unchriſtian*, that either the *work* or the *title* ſhould remaine, whether with open or a masked face or vizard.

Truth. Therefore as it pleaſed *God* in wonderful *wiſdome* and inconceiveable depths of councel for a while to continue a *national church*, *national covenant* &c. and to take them away as unſufficient, beggarly, and weak, either for the further advancement of his own *glory*, or *ſalvation* of men: ſo hath he taken away the *adminiſtration* thereof by *carnal weapons*, *armes* of *fleſh* &c. Inſtead of *fire* and *ſword*, and *ſtoning* the *oppoſit;es* in ſtead of *impriſonment*, *baniſhment*, *death*, he hath appointed *exhortations*, *reprehenſions*, *denunciations*, *excommunications*, and together with *preaching*, patient *waiting*, if *God* peradventure will give *repentance*.

Laſtly, If the *civil Magiſtrate* muſt impriſon and baniſh, and put to death in *ſpiritual caſes*; and the *civil Magiſtrate*, is but a *Miniſter* or ſervant of the people (and ſo of *God*) and if the people make the *laws*, and give the *Magiſtrate* his *commiſſion* and

The peoples power.

power; doth it not follow by this *doctrine*, that the people of the *nations* of the *world* are *fundamentally* and *originally* both *Temporal* and *Ecclesiastical*? And then what is become of the *foundations* of the *Christian faith*? And also are not hereby the *people* and *nations* of the *world* (whatever care be had to the contrary to restraine) incouraged, according to their several *consciences*, I say encouraged and hardened in their bloody *wars*, *imprisonings*, *banishings*, and putting to death for cause of *conscience*?

Peace. Whereas it was said to be *Babel* or *confusion*, for the *church* to punish the offences of such as are not within its *jurisdiction* with *spiritual censures*, or the *civil state*, *spiritual offences* [105] with *corporal* or *temporal weapons*, Master *Cotton* answers, No *confusion*, for so *Paul* directs the *church* of *Corinth*.

Truth. That very *Parenthesis* which Master *Cotton* stumbleth at, takes away his answer.[1] For as it would be confusion for the *church* to censure such *matters*, and of such persons as belong not to the *church*: So is it *confusion* for the *state* to punish *spiritual offenders*, for they are not within the *sphear* of a *civil jurisdiction*. The *body* or *Commonweal* is meerly *civil*, the *Magistrate* or *head* is a *civil head*, and each *member* is a *civil member*: and so far forth as any of this *civil body* are spiritual, or act spiritually, they and their actions fall under a *spiritual cognizance* and *judicature*.

All Commonweals that ever have been, are or shal be in the World (excepting that of typical Israel) meerly civil.

[1] "Why the Discusser putteth in that parenthesis (the offender not being a member of it:) I cannot tell: sure I am, it is nothing to the purpose. For as the Church cannot punish any offendor, unlesse he be a member of the Church, so neither may the Civil Magistrate punish an Heretick or other Spiritual offender, unless he be a member of his Commonwealth." Cotton, *Bloudy Tenent Washed*, p. 70.

Peace. The *reaſon* (ſaith Maſter *Cotton*) is the ſame, for there be offences which tend to provoke *wrath* againſt the *civil ſtate, Ezra* 7. [23] Why ſhould there be *wrath* againſt the *king* or his *ſons?*

The Decrees of Pagan kings for Iſrael, and the God of it, conſidered.

Truth. This reaſon indeed Maſter *Cotton* often inculcates and beates upon it, that the P*agan kings* of *Perſia* were of his mind: I believe Maſter *Cotton* out of a *zeal* to *God,* but the *Pagan kings* out of a ſlaviſh *terror,* which never prevailed ſo far (that I know of) as to bring them to a kindly *repentance* of their own *idolatries,* or a true *love* to the *God* of *Iſrael* or his *people.*

Peace. However your former anſwer is to me *ſufficient*; to wit, that thouſands of famous *Townes, Cities* and *Kingdomes* have flouriſhed in *peace* and *tranquillity* for many ages and generations, where *God* hath had no houſe, and not only where it was by the *civil ſtate* neglected, but alſo wholly perſecuted.

Truth. In the time appointed and full *ripeneſs* of their *ſins,* the *vengeance* of *God* (after *patience* many *generations* abuſed) hath ſurely and fearefully viſited, yet in the *interim,* it is clear it is no ground of a neceſſity of preſent puniſhing of falſe *worſhippers* and *idolaters,* leaſt preſent *wrath* fall upon the *King* or his *Son.*

The Miniſters lay heavy loads upon the Magiſtrates back.

Peace. Now whereas it was ſaid [to be] an intollerable *burthen* laid upon the *Magiſtrates* back, together with the care of the *Commonweal* to be charged alſo with the *ſpiritual,* &c. Maſter *Cotton* anſwers, 1. That the *Magiſtrate* ought to ſeek out meanes [106] of *grace* for the people. 2. To remove *idolatry* and *idolatrous Teachers.* 3. It is commonly added, that he ought to preſerve the *church* pure by *reformation.*

Truth. I reply, This *work* charged upon the *kings, governors*, and *Magiſtrates* in the *world*, makes the weight of their *care* and charge far greater, then ever was the charge of the *kings* of *Iſrael* and *Judah*, For their people were miraculouſly brought into *covenant* with *God*, to their hands, like a *bridge*, or *houſe*, or ſhip ready built; and needed only keeping up in *reparation*: yea an heavier *yoak* then either their or our *fathers* were able to bear, conſidering all the ſeveral different *conſciences, religions*, and *worſhips* of all mankind naturally, and the many different *opinions, factions*, and *ſects*, which daily do ariſe, and that conſcientiouſly and zealouſly unto death: All theſe muſt by Maſter *Cottons doctrine*) lie before the *bar*, beſide all *civil caſes*, &c.

Peace. Tis memorable that P*aul* himſelf, that had the care of all the *churches*, would not be intangled with *civil affaires*, further then his own *neceſſities* did call for, and ſometimes the *neceſſities* of his *companions*: but this yoak put upon the necks of *Magiſtrates*, is as full of temporal as ſpiritual care: And as it is impoſſible for them to bear, So the *Lord* in his holy *ſeaſon*, may pleaſe to teach them (as he hath taught ſome already through his grace) to lay that ſpiritual Burthen upon the *ſhoulders* of their only King of *Saints Chriſt Jeſus*, to whom the *ſupream power* and care of *ſouls* and *churches* doth alone belong.

Whereas it was further ſaid, that the *Magiſtrate* is to cheriſh, and to cleave unto the *Saints*, and to defend them from *civil violence*, but the *ſpiritual* care of them belongs to *ſpiritual officers* appointed by *Chriſt Jeſus* to that end, Maſter *Cotton* replies, this is but a pretence, becauſe the diſcuſſer acknowledgeth no *churches* extant, *&c.*[1]

Truth. Although amongſt ſo many pretending *churches*, the diſcuſſer be not able to ſatisfie himſelf in the rightly gathering of the Churches, according to the true *order* of *Chriſt Jeſus*, yet this is far from a pretence, becauſe the *inſtitution* of any *ſtate government*, *order*, &c. is one thing, and the *adminiſtration* 107] and *execution*, which may be interrupted and eclipſed, is another.

A time when no viſible Church of God in the world for the right forme and order, &c.

Peace. Indeed *Ieremy* could not rightly have been judged a pretender, when he mourned for, and lamented the *deſolations* of the *temple*, *prieſts*, *elders*, *altar*, *ſacrifice*, &c. and neither he nor *Daniel*, nor any of *Gods prophets* or *ſervants*, could (during the time of the *deſolation* and *captivity*) acknowledge either *temple*, or *altar*, or *ſacrifice* right, extant upon the face of the *earth*.

Truth. He that ſaith the *Sun* (*Chriſt Jeſus*) is not to be ſeen in our *Horizon* or *Hemiſphere*, in his abſence, or when he ſuffers an *Eclipſe*, cannot be ſaid to deny that the *Lord Jeſus* his holy ordinances ought to be *viſible* in the *worſhip* and *ſervice* of *God:* Although the diſcuſſer be not ſatisfied in the *period* of the *times*, and the manner of his glorious appearing, yet his *ſoul* uprightly deſires to ſee and adore,

[1] "In the poor ſmall ſpace of my life, I deſired to have been a diligent and conſtant obſerver, and have been myſelf many ways engaged, in city, in country, in court, in ſchools, in univerſities, in churches, in Old and New England: and yet cannot, in the holy preſence of God, bring in the reſult of a ſatisfying diſcovery, that either the begetting miniſtry of the apoſtles or meſſengers to the churches, or the feeding and nouriſhing miniſtry of paſtors and teachers, according to the firſt inſtitution of the Lord Jeſus, are yet reſtored and extant." *Hireling Miniſtry*, p. 4.

and to be thankful to Maſter *Cotton,* yea to the leaſt of the *diſciples* of *Chriſt Jeſus,* for any *coal* or *ſparke* of true *light,* amongſt ſo many falſe and pretended *candles* and *candleſticks,* pretending the glorious name of the *Lord Jeſus Chriſt.*

Peace. Next, Maſter *Cotton* demands what *reaſon* can be given, why the *Magiſtrate* ought to break the teeth of *lyons* (ought to ſuppreſs ſuch as offer *civil violence*) and not of the *Wolves,* that make havock of their *ſouls,* who are more miſchievous then the *lyon,* as the *Pope* of *Rome,* then the *Pagan Emperors?* He wonders the diſcuſſer ſhould favor the *Pope* more then the *Emperour,* except it be that he ſymbolizeth rather with *Antichriſt* then with *Cæſar.*

Truth. It may here ſuffice to ſay two things (not to repeat other *paſſages.*)

Firſt, The *civil ſtate* and *Magiſtrate* are meerly and *eſſentially civil*; and therefore cannot reach (without the tranſgreſſing the bounds of *civility*) to judge in matters *ſpiritual,* which are of another *ſphere* and *nature* then *civility* is: Now it is moſt juſt and proper, that if any member of a *civil body* be oppreſt, the *body* ſhould relieve it: As alſo it is juſt and proper, that the ſpirituall *ſtate* or *body* ſhould relieve the ſoul of any in that ſpiritual combination oppreſſed.

108] Therefore (Secondly) for *ſpiritual* and *religious* oppreſſions, the *king* of *kings Chriſt Ieſus* hath ſufficient providedly in his ſpiritual *kingdome*: therefore (*Acts* 20 [29]) *Paul* gives the charge againſt thoſe *ſpiritual Wolves* to the *elders* of the *church* at *Epheſus,* and not to *civil Magiſtrates* of the *city,* which *Paul* ſhould

The wolves at Epheſus, Act. 20.

have done (notwithſtanding they were *worſhippers* of *Diana*) if it had been *their* duty to have broke the *teeth* of thoſe ſpirituall *Wolves* &c.

The duty of civil power in matters of Religion

Peace. It is (indeed) one thing to prohibite the *Pope*, the *prelates*, the *Presbyterians*, the *Independents*, or any from forcing any in the matters of their reſpective *conſciences*, and accordingly to take the *ſword* from ſuch mens hands, or (as their executioners) to refuſe to uſe it for them: It is another thing to leave them freely to their own *conſciences*, to defend themſelves as well as they can, by the two-edged ſword of the *ſpirit*, which is the *word* of *God*, which all the ſeveral ſorts of *pretenders* ſay they have received from *Ieſus Chriſt*.

The changing of perſecutors is one thing, the aboliſhing of perſecution another.

Truth. The renowned *Parliament* of *England* hath juſtly deſerved a *crown* of *honour* to all *poſterity*, for breaking the *teeth* of the *oppreſſing Biſhops* and their *courts*; but to wring the *ſword* out of the hands of a few *prelates*, and to ſuffer it (willingly) to be wrung out of their own hands, by many thouſand *Presbyterians*, or *Independants*, what is it but to change one *wolfe* or *lyon* for another, or in ſtead of *one*, to let looſe the *Dens* of thouſands?

Peace. But why ſhould Maſter *Cotton* inſinuate the *diſcuſſer* to glance a more obſequious eye upon the *Pope*, then upon the *Emperor*?

The perſecuting Cleargy no cordial friends to

Truth. I fear Maſter *Cotton* would create ſome evil opinion in the *heart* of the *civil Magiſtrate*, that the diſcuſſer is (as the *bloody Iews* told *Pilate*) no friend to *Cæſar*: whereas upon a due ſearch it will be found clear as the light, that it is impoſſible that any that ſubſcribe *ex animo* to the bloody Tenent of perſecution, can (*ex animo*) be a *friend* to *Magiſtracy.* The reaſon is, all *perſecutors*, whether *prieſts* or *people*, care onely for ſuch *Magiſtrates* as ſuite the *end*, the great bloody *end* of *perſecution*, of whom they either hope to borrow the *ſword*, or whom they hope to make their *executioners*. Their very principles alſo (*Papiſt* [109] and *Proteſtant*) lead them neceſſarily to diſpoſe [depoſe] and kill their *heretical*, *Apoſtate*, *blaſpheming Magiſtrates*.

Magiſtracie.

Peace. But why ſhould Maſter *Cotton* inſinuate any affection in the diſcuſſer to that *Tyrant* of all earthly *Tyrants*, the *Pope*?

Truth. To my knowledge Maſter *Cotton* and others have thought the diſcuſſer too zealous againſt the bloody *beaſt*: yea, and who knows not this to be the ground of ſo much ſorrowful *difference* between Maſter *Cotton* and the diſcuſſer, to wit, that the diſcuſſer grounds his ſeparation from their *churches* upon their not ſeperating from that man of ſin? For Old *England* having compelled all to *church*, compel'd the P*apiſts* and the *Pope* himſelf in them: The daughter *New England*, ſeparating from her *mother* in *Old England*, yet maintaines and practiſes communion with the *Pariſhes* in *Old*. Who ſees not then, but by the *links* of this *myſtical chaine*, *New England Churches* are ſtill faſtned to the *Pope* himſelf?

Neither Old nor New England ſtate-churches ſeparate from the Pope.

Peace. Maſter *Cottons* third *repiy* is this, that it is not like that ſuch *Chriſtians* will be faithful to their *prince*, who grow falſe and diſloyal to their *God*, and therefore conſequently the *civil Magiſtrate* muſt ſee that the *church degenerate* and apoſtate not, at leaſt ſo far as to provoke *Chriſt* to depart from them.

Maſter Cotton and Bellarmine all one, for thedepoſing heretical princes, &c.

Truth. This is indeed the down right moſt bloody and *Popiſh Tenent* of *perſecuting* the *degenerate*, *heretical* and *Apoſtate* people: of depoſing, yea and killing *Apoſtatical* and *heretical princee* and *rulers*.

The gods of this World.

The truth is, the great *Gods* of this world are *God-belly*, *God-peace*, *God-wealth*, *God-honour*, *God-pleaſure* &c. Theſe *Gods* muſt not be blaſphemed, that is, evil ſpoke of, no not provoked, *&c.* The ſervants of the living *God* being true to their *Lord* and *Maſter*, have oppoſed his *glory*, *greatneſs*, *honour* &c. to theſe *Gods*, and to ſuch *religions*, *worſhips*, and *ſervices*, as commonly are made but as a *mask* or *vaile*, or covering of theſe *Gods*.

Peace. I have long been ſatisfied, that hence proceeds the *mad cry* of every *Demetrius* and *crafts-Maſter* of falſe *worſhip* in the *world*, *Great* is our *Diana* &c. Theſe men blaſpheme our *goddeſs*, diſturbe our *City*, They are falſe to our *Gods*, how will they be true to us?

The Lord Cobham his troubles in Henry the 5. dayes.

The beſt of our late Biſhops, as Biſhop Hall have not ſpared to render

110] Hence that bloody Act of P*arliament* in *Henry* the fifth his dayes made purpoſely againſt that true *ſervant* and *witneſs* of *God* (in thoſe points of *Chriſtianity* which he knew) and other ſervants of *God* with him, the Lord *Cobham*, concluding *Lollardy* not only to be *hereſie*, (that is, indeed true *Chriſtianity*) but alſo *treaſon* againſt the *Kings perſon:* whence it followed, that theſe poor *Lollards* (the *ſervants* of the moſt *high God*) were not only to be burnt as *hereticks*, but hanged as *traitors*.[1]

[1] Sir John Oldcaſtle, Lord Cobham, was accuſed of hereſy in the firſt year of the reign of Henry V., 1413. A ſynod was called by Arundel, Archbiſhop of Canterbury, "to repreſs the growing and ſpreading of the Goſpel, and eſpecially to withſtand this noble and worthy Lord Cobham, who was then noted to be

Truth. Accordingly it pleaſed God to honour that noble Lord *Cobham* both with hanging and burning, as an *heretick* againſt the *church*, as a *traitor* againſt the *king*: And hence thoſe diveliſh accuſations and bloody huntings of the poor ſervants of *God* in the reign of *Francis* the ſecond in *Paris*, becauſe it was ſaid, that their meetings were to conſult and act againſt the *life* of the *king*.

hereticks and Traitors all one.[1]

Peace. If this be the *touchſtone* of all *obedience*, will it not be the *cut-throat* of all *civil relations, unions* and *covenants* between Princes and people, and between the people and people? For may not Maſter *Cotton* alſo ſay, he will not be a faithful *ſervant*, nor ſhe a faithful *wife*, nor he a faithful *husband*, who grow falſe and diſloyal to their *God*? And indeed what doth this, yea, what hath this truly-ranting doctrine (that plucks up all relations) wrought but confuſion and combuſtion all the world over?

Civil ſociety pluckt up by the rootes.

Truth. Concerning *faithfulneſs*, it is moſt true, that *godlineſs* is profitable for all things, all *eſtates*, all *relations*: yet there is a *civil faithfulneſs, obedience, honeſty, chaſtity*, &c. even amongſt ſuch as own not

a principal Favourer, Receiver and Maintainer of them whom the Biſhop miſnamed to be Lollards," and he was excommunicated. He had been a favorite of the king, and appealed to him, but without ſucceſs, for he was ſent to the Tower. He eſcaped, and fled into Wales, where he concealed himſelf for four years. He was finally captured, taken to London and executed in a moſt barbarous manner. Gilpin, *Lives, &c.*, ii. 105–153. The act referred to is given in full by Fox, who goes at length into an account of Lord Cobham's views, and argues fully the point made by Williams, that the Lollards were condemned for treaſon as well as hereſy. *Acts and Monuments*, i. 635–668.

[1] Biſhop Hall diſtinguiſhes between mere and mixed hereſy. "The latter of them hath no reaſon to be exempted from bodily puniſhments; no, not from the utmoſt of all pains, death itſelf. If it be attended with ſchiſm, perturbances, ſeditions, malicious practices, it tends to ſetting whole kingdoms on fire; and therefore may be well worthy of a faggot." *Works*, vii. 95.

Civil honesty may stand with dishonesty against God and Christ in matters of Religion.

God nor *Christ*: else *Abraham* and *Isaac* dealt foolishly to make *leagues* with ungodly *Princes*. Besides, the whole Scripture commands a continuance in all *Relations* of *government*, *marriage*, *service*, notwithstanding that the *grace* of *Christ* had appeared to some, and the rest (it may be an *husband*, a *wife*, a *Magistrate*, a *Master*, a *servant*) were false and disloyal in their several kinds and wayes unto *God*, or wholly ignorant of him.

4. Grant *people* and *Princes* to be like *Iulian*, *Apostate* from the true service of *God*, and consequently to grow less faithful in their places and respective services, yet what ground is there, from the *Testament* of *Christ Jesus*, upon this ground of their *Apostacie*, [111] to prosecute them, as Master *Cotton* saith, The *civil Magistrate* must keep the *church* from *Apostatizing* so, as to cause *Christ* to depart from them.

5. Can the *sword* of *steel* or *arme* of *flesh* make men faithful or loyal to *God*? Or careth *God* for the outward *Loyalty* or *Faithfullness*, when the *inward-man* is *false* and *treacherous*?

A turncoat in Religion more faithless then a resolved Jew, Turk or Papist.

Or is there not more danger (in all *matters* of *trust* in this *world*) from an *hyyocrite*, a *dissembler*, a *turncoat* in his *religion* (from the *fear* or *favour* of men) then from a resolved *Jew*, *Turke* or *Papist*, who holds firme unto his *principles*? &c.

Or lastly, if one *Magistrate*, *King* or *Parliament* call this or that *heresie*, *apostacie*, &c. and make men say so will not a stronger *Magistrate*, *King*, *Parliament*, *Army* (that is, a stronger *arm*, or longer and more prosperous *sword*) call that *heresie* and *Apostacie*

Truth and *Chriſtianity*, and make men call it ſo? and do not all *experiences*, and our own moſt lamentable, in the changes of our *Engliſh Religions*, confirme this?

Hereſie and apoſtacie often change their names to truth, and Chriſtianity,&c.

6. Laſtly, As carnal policy ever fals into the pit, it digs and trips up its own heels, ſo I ſhall end this *paſſage* with two *paradoxes*, and yet (dear *peace*) thou and I have found them moſt lamentably true in all ages.

Peace. God delights to befool the *wiſe* and *high* in their own *conceit* with *paradoxes*, even ſuch as the wiſdome of this world thinks *madneſs*: but I attend to hear them.

Truth. Firſt then, The ſtraining of mens *cinſciences* by *civil power*, is ſo far from making men faithful to *God* or man, that it is the ready way to render a man falſe to both: my ground is this: *civil* and *corporal puniſhment* do uſually cauſe men to play the *hypocrite*, and diſſemble in their *Religion*, to turn and return with the tide, as all *experience* in the *nations* of the *world* doth teſtifie now.

Who knows not that the many turnings of Do. Pearne in Cambridge brought it into a proverb, to wit, to pernifie.[1]

This *binding* and *rebinding* of *conſcience*, contrary or without its own *perſwaſion*, ſo weakens and defiles it, that it (as all other *faculties*) loſeth its ſtrength, and the very nature of a common honeſt *conſcience*:

[1] Andrew Perne (1519–1586) was educated at St. John's College, Cambridge, and was five times Vice Chancellor of the Univerſity. He went through many changes of religious opinion.

"His mutability in religious matters expoſed him to no little ridicule. The ſcholars in merriment tranſlated perno, I turn, I rat, I change often. It became proverbial to ſay of a coat or cloak which had been turned that it had been Perned. On the weathercock of S. Peter's church in Cambridge, were the letters A. P. A. P., which it was ſaid might be taken to mean Andrew Perne A Papiſt, or Andrew Perne A Puritan." *Athenæ Cantabrigienſes*, ii. 48.

Consciences yeelding to be forced or ravished, loosen all conscience. Hence it is, that even our own histories testifie, that where the *civil sword*, and carnal power, hath made a change upon the *consciences* of men, those *consciences* have been given up, [112] not only to spiritual, but even to *corporal filthiness*, and bloody, and mad oppressing each other, as in the *Marian* bloody times *&c.*

Peace. Indeed no people [are] so inforced as the *Papists* and the *Mahumetans*: and no people more filthy in soul and body, and no people in the *world* more *bloody* and *persecuting*: but I listen for your second *paradox.*

Truth. Secondly, This *Tenent* of the *Magistrates* keeping the *church* from *Apostatizing*, by practising *civil force* upon the *consciences* of men, is so far from preserving *Religion* pure, that it is a mighty *Bulwark* or *Barricado* to keep out all true *Religion*, yea and all *godly Magistrates* for ever coming into the *World.* *2 Paradoxes.*

Peace. Doubtless this will seem a hard *riddle*, yet I presume not too hard for the fingers of *time* and *truth* to unty, and render easie.

Truth. Thus I unty it: If the *civil Magistrate* must keep the *church* pure, then all the *people* of the *Cities*, *Nations*, and *kingdomes* of the *world* must do the same much more, for primarily and fundamentally, they are the *civil Magistrate*: Now the world (saith *John*) lyeth or is situated in *wickedness*, and consequently according to its disposition endures not the *light* of *Christ*, nor his golden *candlestick* the true *Church*, nor easily chooseth a true *Christian* to be her *officer* or *Magistrate*, for she accounts such false to her *Gods* and *Religion*, and suspects their faithfulness *&c.*

Peace. Hence indeed is it (as I now conceive) that ſo rarely this *world* admitteth or not long continueth a true ſervant of *God* in any place of *truſt* nnd *credit,* except ſome extraordinary hand of *God* over-power, or elſe his ſervants by ſome baſe *ſtaires* of *Flattery* or worldly *compliance,* aſcend the chaire of *Civil-power.*

But (to proceed) ſaith Maſter *Cotton,* "It was the "duty of *Jehoſaphat, Hezekiah* &c. to reduce the "people of *Iſrael* from their backſlidings becauſe "they were an holy people, and is it not the duty of "godly Princes to reduce their backſliding Churches "to their primitive purity? It is true (ſaith he) *David* "and *Solomon* were types of *Chriſt,* but ſo were not "the other Kings of Iſrael [113] and *Judah,* who "were the one (the kings of *Iſrael*) all Apoſtates, "and the other (the kings of *Judah*) many of them "Apoſtates from Chriſt: And Secondly, If they were "(ſaith he) all types of Chriſt, yet Chriſt being the "Antitype, Chriſt hath aboliſhed them all, and ſo it "were ſacrilege or Antichriſtian uſurpation for any "king to be ſet over Chriſtians: Or if they were "types of Chriſt in reſpect of their kingly office over "the Church alone was it typical in *Solomon* to put "*Joab* a murtherer to death, or *Adonijah* a traitor? "and ſo conſequently unlawful for Chriſtian Princes "to put murtherers and traitors to death? Further, "ſaith he, What thoſe kings might do in type, Chriſt "Jeſus might much more do in his own perſon, "as the Antitype: but he put no man to death in "his own perſon, and therefore they were not types "but ſervants of Chriſt, and paterns and examples to

How the kings of Israel and Judah were types and figures of Christ to come.

"Christian Magistrates, yea, *Ahab*, who should have "put *Benhadad* to death for his blasphemy.

Truth. I understand those *kings* of *Israel* and *Judah*, untill their *cutting* off or *excommunicating* out of the land of *Canaan*, to be yet *visible members* of the *church* of *Israel* and *Judah*, and as *kings* of *Israel* and *Judah* *types* of *Christ Jesus*, partly in his own *person*, who did that (being the true *spiritual king* of *Israel*) which they did or should have done, in that typical *national church* or land of *Israel*, and (2) partly in the *officers* of his *kingly power* and *government* of his *church* which *officers* and *church* falling away, untill an absolute cutting off, are the *Antitypes* (in respect of visible government) of those former kings of *Israel* and *Judah*.

Peace. Can it be imagined that those wicked *Kings Jeroboam*, *Baasha*, *Ahab* &c. were figures of *Christ Jesus*?

Truth. Master *Cotton* himself grants *David* and *Solomon types* of *Christ Jesus*, and yet, how abominable and monstrous some of their practices? we must therefore distinguish between their *persons*, and *sins*, and *frailties*.

As kings of *Israel* (*Gods* Church and *people*) doubtless they were the *figures of* (the *K.* of *Israel*) *Christ Iesus*: yea it is probable that the land of *Canaan*, with the *officers* and *governors* thereof, before *Christ* time, was but a figure of the *spiritual land* or *Christian church*, with the *officers*, *governors*, & *administrations* therof good [114] and evil: Although the applying of the *times* and *persons* each to other requires a more then ordinary *guidance* of the finger or holy *Spirit* of *God*.

The types of the old Testament many and deep.

Peace. I remember that ſome of eminent note for *knowledge* and *godlineſs* have not ſtuck to affirme, that the *Gentile* Prince *Cyrus* as he was called *Gods ſervant, anointed,* or *Chriſt* (*Iſa.* 44) [45: 1.] I ſay, that he in a reſpect, as a *reſtorer* of *Gods* people was a *figure of Chriſt Ieſus.*

Cyrus called Chriſt, a figure of Chriſt.

Truth. It is not improbable, but that the moſt holy and only wiſe (whoſe works are known unto *himſelf* from the beginning of the *world*) did by ſuch famous *inſtruments* of *mercy* to the literal *Iew,* type out *Chriſt Ieſus* and his heavenly *inſtruments,* mercy and goodneſs to the *myſtical* and *ſpiritual, Chriſtian Iews,* &c.

Examination of CHAP. XXXVI, and XXXVII.

Peace.

IN theſe paſſages Maſter *Cotton* firſt queſtions (having not his copy by him) the truth of ſome *expreſſions* printed as his.

Truth. It is at hand for Maſter *Cotton* or any to ſee that *copy* which he gave forth and corrected in ſome places with his own hand, and every word *verbatim* here publiſhed.

2. To the *anſwer* it ſelf, or reproof of the *Lord Ieſus* given to his *diſciples* for their *bloody* and raſh *zeal* deſiring fire to come down from heaven, *&c.* we both agree that *Chriſts* rebuking of his *diſciples* did not hinder the *Miniſters* of the *Goſpel* from proceeding in a *Church-way* &c. 2. That falſe *perſecution* in a *church*-way is as odious and dreadful a *perſecu-*

tien, as any *proſecution* in a *court* of *civil juſtice*, as alſo that this is not the point intended, though it be reckoned up with the reſt.

Peace. I marvel at that which follows, where Maſter *Cotton* ſaith that it never fell from his pen in any writing of his, *viz.* that it is lawful for a *civil Magiſtrate* to inflict *corporal puniſhment* upon ſuch as are contrary indeed in *matters of Religion*: and therefore he paſſeth by the *diſcuſſers reaſons* as which might well have been ſpared, being brought but againſt a *ſhadow* of his own *fancy*.

115] *Truth.* I am not able to imagine what Maſter *Cotton* meanes by ſuch as are *contrary minded*, againſt whom he will not (in this Chapter) maintaine any *corporal puniſhment* to be inflicted, when in ſo many of his *writings* and throughout his whole *book* he maintaines *corporal puniſhment*, and that to death it ſelf in many caſes, againſt the *idolatrous*, the *blaſphemous*, the *heretical*, the ſeducing, yea the *degenerate* and *Apoſtate*.

The fire from heaven, Rev. 13. [13.]

Peace. Love bids us take this paſſage as a pang of *reluctancy* (in his otherwiſe-holy and peaceable breaſt) againſt ſuch unholy *bloody Tenents*.

But what ſay you to the paſſage about the *ſecond beaſt*, bringing *fire* from *heaven*? (*Rev.* 13.) This was no wonder (ſaith Maſter *Cotton*) for *Conſtantine* had done the like before to *hereticks*, the *Arrian Biſhops* againſt the *Orthodox Saints*. Alſo, it is related as a different matter from the former (*verſ.* 15.) that he had power to cauſe, that as many as would not worſhip the *image* of the *beaſt* ſhould be killed. And this fire comes not down upon the *Saints*, but the *earth*.

Truth. Maſter *Cotton* I think knows that the diſcuſſer is not alone in this *interpretation:* If he propoſe any other more ſuitable to *Chriſt Ieſus*, I hope the diſucſſer deſires thankfully to embrace it. But this *fire* being not *literal*, but *myſtical*, in *imitation* of the true prophet *Elijah*, and alſo as the true *witneſſes* cauſe *fiery judgements* [to] deſcend from *heaven* upon the *enemies* of the *truth:* ſo the falſe *witneſſes* cauſe *fire* to deſcend againſt the *faithful*: and ſure it is (as the diſcuſſer related) that the P*opiſh Biſhops* in *France*, and *England* and other places have ever conſtantly cryed out, that the *juſt judgements* of *God* are brought down by them upon the *hereticks*, which is no ſmal wonder that the *hearts* of the *ſons* of *men* ſhould be ſo hardened againſt the *light* of *truth* in *truths witneſſes*, notwithſtanding the acts of *Conſtantine* and the *Arrian* Biſhops long before.

Peace. But this fire (ſaith Maſter *Cotton*) comes down from *heaven* upon the *earth.*

Truth. True, but it may well imply no more, then in the open view and *face* of all men in this world.

Peace. And laſtly (ſaith he) it is ſaid, that he cauſeth that as [116] many as would not worſhip the *Image* of the *Beaſt* ſhould be killed, which is a different effect.

Truth. Becauſe it comes from a different *cauſe*, with reſpect, not to the firſt *Beaſt* himſelf, but only to his *picture* or *image*, and implies, that *fiery judgements* deſcend not onely upon ſuch as refuſe to worſhip the *firſt* or ſecond *beaſt*, but the very picture of the *beaſt* likewiſe.

Examination of CHAP. XXXVIII.

Peace.

MAfter *Cotton* here firſt obſerving the diſcuſſers agreement with him, that this inſtruction (2 *Tim.* 2. [24. 25.]) to be meek and patient to all men, is properly directive to the *Miniſters* of the *Goſpel*, he concludes that therefore hitherto his anſwer was not perplext and ravelled.

Truth. Many plaine threads may be drawn forth of a perplext and ravelled ſtring, as it ſeemes to me the many *particulars* of *different natures* here wrapt up together were.

Peace. Yea, but he ſeems to diſown thoſe words [*unconverted Chriſtians in Crete*) and more then once in the *Chapter* toucheth the diſcuſſers credit, *&c.*

Truth. I know the diſcuſſer deſires unfainedly (with the *Lords aſſiſtance*) rather to die a thouſand deaths, then willingly to impeach the leaſt of *holy* or *civil truths*; and therefore affirmeth in this caſe, that at his pleaſure the copy (not which he received from Maſter *Cotton* for there never paſſed ſuch writings between them as Maſter *Cotton* often affirmeth, but) which he received from another, with the correction of Maſter *Cottons* own hand to it, ſhall be ready for himſelf or any to view.

All truth, heavenly, moral, civil &c. precious.

Peace. However, Maſter *Cotton* maintaining the tearms of *unconverted converts* from *Ier.* 3. 10. (*Iudah* turned unto me, but not with all her heart, but fainedly:) ſo *Iudas*, *Ananias*, and *Sapphira*, *Balaam*, the *Nicolaitans*, *Iezabel* in *Thyatira*, as alſo the children of believing *parents* born in the *Church*, who though holy, yet cannot be conceived to be truely holy.

Truth. Were the *queſtion* about *hypocrites*, *counterfeits* and [117] *trayters* in the *church* and *kingdome* of *Chriſt*, theſe words might here rightly be alleadged; but Maſter *Cottons* words being theſe [*unconverted Chriſtians* in *Crete*, whom *Titus* as an *Evangeliſt* was to ſeek and to convert] I conceive that Maſter *Cotton* will not affirm that the office of an *Evangeliſt* was to ſeek to convert the *church* (though poſſibly an *hypocrite* may be turned from his *hypocriſie* by an *Evangeliſt* or private man in the *church*.)

Vnconverted Chriſtians viſibly a paradox.

2. He makes in the very words a *diſtinction* between theſe *unconverted Chriſtians*, and thoſe *Iews* and *Gentiles* in the Church, who (ſaith he) though *carnal*, yet were not convinced of the *error* of their *way*.

And to conclude this Chapter, the diſcuſſer readily with thanks acknowledgeth Maſter *Cottons* words, that it is not probable that *Timothy* was now at *Epheſus*, and that the *ſubſcription* added to the ſecond Epiſtle of *Timothy* in the *Engliſh tranſlation*, is juſtly to be ſuſpected.[1]

[1] Cotton adduces the argument that Timothy could not have been at Epheſus or St. Paul would not have written as he did, 2 *Tim.* 4: 12, "And Tychicus have I ſent to Epheſus." *Bloudy Tenent Waſhed*, p. 80. To this Williams aſſents. But this argument is not deciſive. Biſhop Ellicott thinks that the arguments on one ſide and the other "render it ſlightly more probable that at the time when the Second Epiſtle was written, Timothy was conceived by the Apoſtle to be at the ſcene of his appointed labors, and as either actually at Epheſus or viſiting ſome of the dependent churches in its immediate neighborhood." *Paſtoral Epiſtles*, 119, Cf. Conybeare and Howſon, *St. Paul*, ii. 474, note. The ſubſcription to this Epiſtle in the Engliſh verſion ſays nothing about the direction of the letter, and is not open to ſuſpicion on that or any other account, though of courſe it is no part of the original Epiſtle.

Examination of CHAP. XXXIX.

Peace.

Many excellent Magistrates of the Parliament, of the Councel, of the Army, of the City, of the Country, are also excellent prophets or iuterpreters of Scripture, & yet may not use a civil but a spiritual sword in spirituals.

MAster *Cotton* here argues, That if the *Magistrate* be a *Prophet*, and oppoſed in his *doctrine*, he ought (from this Scripture, 2 *Tim.* 2. [25.]) meekly to bear the *oppoſition*, waiting if *God* peradventure will give *repentance*; yet withal by the way he obſerveth, that if the *Magiſtrate* be a *prophet*, he may do ſome things as a *Magiſtrate*, which he may not do as a *Prophet*.

Truth. Of this no *queſtion?* but what is this to a coercive *Magiſterial power* in *ſpiritual* things, which is the *queſtion*?

Magiſrates may be prophets in Chriſts Church.

2. Since that Maſter *Cotton* acknowledgeth that *Magiſtrates* may be *prophets*, and that divers *Magiſtrates* of *New Engliſh churches* have ſpoken as *prophets* (eminently able in their *churches*) what ſhould be the reaſon (I ask by the way) that their *Churches* hear no more of ſuch their *propheticall* gifts, but that their *talent's* wrapt up? *&c.*[1]

[1] The exerciſe of propheſying as it was called, grounded on the practice of the primitive church as deſcribed in 1 Cor. xii., xiv., in which laymen taught and exhorted in public worſhip, was early practiſed in New England, and ſeems to have been ſuſtained by Cotton. Winthrop ſtates that when Mr. Wilſon, paſtor of the church in Boſton was about to embark for England in 1631, he met his congregation and "commended to them the exerciſe of prophecy in his abſence, and deſigned thoſe whom he thought moſt fit for it, viz. the Governour, Mr. Dudley, and Mr. Nowell the elder." *New England*, i. 60. In October, 1632, Gov. Winthrop and Mr. Wilſon viſited Plymouth. "On the Lord's day there was a ſacrament, which they did partake in; and in the afternoon Mr. Roger Williams (according to their cuſtom) propounded a queſtion, to which the Paſtor, Mr. Smith, ſpake briefly; then Mr. Williams propheſied; and after the governour of Plimouth ſpake to the queſtion; after him the elder; then ſome two or three more of the congregation. Then the elder deſired the governour of

118] *Peace.* Of this let their *consciences* give account to *Jesus Christ*, whom they call the *King* of their *churches*, and the *fountaine* of such heavenly *abilities*: But to proceed, Master *Cotton* grants that *Magistrates* ought to bear in the *church oppositions* against their *prophecyings*, but not *continued* opposings, nor sedu-ings &c.

Truth. What is then the waiting here commanded, until *God* peradventure will give *repentance*?

Peace. It is true (saith Master *Cotton*) it is not in the power of *man* to give *repentance*, but *God* alone: Neither is it in mans power (saith he) to give *repentance* to *scandalous* persons against the *civil state*; and yet the discusser acknowledgeth that the *civil Magistrate* ought to punish these.

Truth. It is not the *Magistrates* work and office in the *civil state*, to convert the *heart* in true *repentance* unto *God* and *Christ*: The *civil state* respecteth conformity and obedience to *civil laws*, though indeed the works and *office* of the *Ministers* of *Christ Jesus* are commonly laid upon the *Magistrates* shoulders, and they pretending themselves the *Ministers* of

More confidence commonly put in the civil sword then the spiritual.

Massachusetts and Mr. Wilson to speak to it, which they did." *Winthrop*, i. 109.

Gov. Bradford in his *Brief Dialogue*, defends it as an ancient practice, and adds: "The chief of our ministers in New England agree therein. See Mr. Cotton's Answer to Baylie, page the 27th, 2d part. "Though neither all" saith he "nor most of the brethren of a church have ordinarily received a gift of public prophesying, or preaching, yet in defect of public ministry, it is not an unheard of novelty that God should enlarge private men with public gifts and [that they who have received such gifts, should take liberty] to dispense them to edification."" Young, *Chron. of Pilgrims*, 421; Cotton, *Way of Churches cleared*, 27.

Lechford, however, writing in 1641, says: "It is generally held in the *Bay* by some of the most grave and learned men amongst them, that none should undertake to prophesie in publique, unlesse he intend the worke of the Ministery, &c." *Plain Dealing*, 16.

Chriſt Jeſus, armed with the two-edged ſword of the *Spirit* of *God* (the *Word* of *God*) do commonly flye unto and put more confidence in the *ſword* of *ſteel* in the hand of their *civil Miniſters*, the *Magiſtrates*.

Engl. changes in Religion excuſed by thoſe of Judah, bnt not juſtly.

Peace. The *ſword* of ſteel hath done *wonderful* things throughout the whole *world* in *matters* of *Religion*, and *woful* and *wonderful* (as was formerly obſerved) hath *Religious changes* been the *Engliſh nation*, and that by the power of the *civil ſword*, backward and forward, and that in the ſpace of a few yeers, in the *reigne* of four or five *Princes:* But this (ſaith Maſter *Cotton*) is no more then befell the *church* of *Iudah* in the dayes of *Ahaz*, *Hezekiah*, *Manaſſeh*, and *Ioſiah*.

Truth. *Englands* changes will be found upon examination incomparably *greater*, and wrought in the eighth part of the time that the *changes* of the *church* of *Iudah* were. And yet this *inſtance* will not infringe that the *civil ſword* of the *Magiſtrate*, in a *national way*, is ordinarily able to turn about a *Nation* to and againe, to and from a *truth* of *God*, in *national hypocriſie*, and [119] therefore moſt wiſely hath the moſt holy and only wiſe, by the moſt golrious brightneſs of his *perſon* and *wiſdom* of the *Father* (*Chriſt Jeſus*) aboliſhed his own *national* and ſtate-*church*, whether *explicit* or *implicit*, that the two-edged ſword of the *word* of the *Lord* in the mouths of his true *meſſengers*, might alone be brandiſhed and magnified.

Peace. Maſter *Cotton* concludeth this Chapter with the obſervation, that the *revolt* of *England* againe to Popery wanteth *Scripture*-light.

Truth. He that loves *Chriſt Ieſus* in ſincerity, cannot but long, that *Chriſt Ieſus* would ſpeedily be pleaſed with the breath of his mouth to conſume that man of ſin: But yet that worthy ſervant of *God* (according to his *conſcience*) Maſter *Archer*, doth not barely propoſe his *opinion*, but alſo his *Scripture-grounds*, which I believe, compared with all former *experiences*, will ſeem to be of great and weighty *conſideration*, and call all that wait for *Chriſt Ieſus* to beg his *Spirit* deeply to weigh and ponder them.[1]

Whether England may not receive the Pope againe.

Examination of CHAP. XL.

Peace.

TO the ſeveral *allegations* concerning the woful *ſlavery* of all *oppoſites* of *Chriſt Ieſus*, and the mighty power of *free grace*, only able to releaſe them; Maſter *Cotton* replies, So is it with *ſcandalous* offenders againſt the *Civil ſtate*, and yet this doth not reſtraine *Magiſtrates* from executing juſt *judgements* upon them *&c.* And he adds, that better a *dead ſoul* in a *dead body*, and that *ſeducers* die without *faith*, then *murther* and *ſeduce* many *precious ſouls* from the *faith.*

[1] Henry Archer was a non-conformiſt preacher in London, who fled to Holland and became paſtor of the Engliſh Church in Arnheim. He was a Millenarian, and wrote a work entitled, "The Perſonal Reign of Chriſt upon Earth. In a Treatiſe wherein is fully and largely laid open and proved, that Jeſus Chriſt, together with his Saints, ſhall viſibly poſſeſs a Monarchicall State and Kingdom in the World. 1642." Brook, *Lives of the Puritans*, ii. 455. Williams expreſſes the ſame apprehenſions in regard to the Pope's recovering his power in *The Bloudy Tenent*, 64. 185. *Pub. Narr. Club*, iii. 137, 326.

Things of God and Cæsar.

Truth. The *Lord Iesus* commanding to give *God* the *things* that be *Gods*, and to *Cæsar* the things that be *Cæsars*, gives all his *followers* a clear and glorious *torch* of light to distinguish between *offenders* against *God* in a *spiritual* way, and *offenders* against *Cæsar*, his *Lawes*, *state* and *government* in a *civil* way.

Religions of the world politick inventions to maintaine a civil state.

Tis true, *flatterers* and *time-servers* use to make *Religion* and [120] *justice*, the two *pillars* of a *State*, and so indeed do all such *states* in the world as maintaine a *state-Religion*, invented and maintained in *civil policy* to maintaine a *civil state*. But all men that have tasted of *history* or *travel*, are witnesses sufficient of these two particulars.

The absolute necessity of some order of government all the world over.

First concerning *justice*, that if the *sword* and *balances* of *justice* (in a sort or measure) be not drawn and held forth, against *scandalous* offenders against *civil state*, that *civil state* must dissolve by little and little from *civility* to *barbarisme*, which is a *wildernes* of *life* and *manners*.

Peace. Yea the very *barbarians* and Pagans of the *world* themselves are forced for their *holding* and hanging together in barbarous *compaines*, to use the *ties* and *knots*, and *bands* of a kind of *civil justice* against scandalous offenders against their Commonweale and profit.

Truth. But too many thousands of *Cities* and *states* in the *world* have and do flourish for many *generations* and *ages* of men, wherein (whatever *Cæsar* gets) *God* cannot get one penny of his due in any bare *permission* or *toleration* of his *religion* and *worship*.

Peace. *Dear Truth*, these two points being so constantly proved, I can but wonder that Master *Cotton* or any ſervant of *Chriſt Ieſus*, ſhould cry out to the *Cæſars* of this *world* to help the eternal *God* to get his due, becauſe *Chriſt Ieſus* grants them a *civil ſword* in *civil caſes*, to preſerve their *civil ſtates* from *barbariſme* and *confuſion*.

Truth. That worthy *Emperor, Antoninus Pius*, in his letters for the *Chriſtians*, plainly tels the *governors* of his *provinces*, that the *gods* were able to puniſh thoſe that ſinned againſt their *worſhip*; evidently declaring, by that light of *conſcience* and *knowledge* which *God* had lighted up in his ſoul, the vaſt *difference* between *offenders* in the *civil ſtate*, and *offendors* againſt the true and only *religion* and worſhip, about which the whole world diſagreeth, and is hiſt together (by this bloody tenent) I ſay hiſt together by the *ears* and *throat*, in *blood* and *fire*, as the tide of *times, major vote, armies* and armes of *fleſh* prevaile.

Antoninus Pius his diſtinction.

Peace. Ah (Dear *truth*) is there is no *Balme* in *Gilead*, no *balances*, no ſword of *ſpiritual juſtice* in the *City*, and *kingdome* of *Chriſt Jeſus*, but that the *officers* thereof muſt run to borrow [121] *Cæſars*? Are the *Armories* of the true *king Solomon Chriſt Jeſus* diſarmed? Are there no *ſpiritual ſwords* girt upon the thighs of thoſe valiant ones, that ſhould guard his heavenly bed, except the *ſword* of *ſteel* be run for from the *cutlers* ſhop? Is the *Religion* of *Chriſt Jeſus* ſo poor and ſo weak and feeble grown, ſo cowardly and baſe (ſince *Paul* ſpake ſo glorioully of it, and the weapons of it (2 *Cor*. 10.[4.]) that neither the *ſouldiers* nor *Commanders* in *Chriſts Army* have any *courage* or *skill* to withſtand ſufficiently in all points a falſe *teacher*, a falſe *prophet*, a *ſpiritual cheater* or *deceiver*?

The degeneracy of Chriſtianity now profeſſed.

Truth. This muſt all that follow *Jeſus* bitterly lament, that not a ſpiritual *ſword* or *ſpear* is to be found in the ſpiritual *Iſrael* of *God*, but that his poor *Iſraelites* are forced down to the P*hiliſtins* of this *worlds Smiths*, &c. And that the princes of *Zion* are become feeble like *harts* without paſture, as *Jeremy* complaineth in his *Lamentations.* [1 : 6.]

Peace. Now whereas it was added, that a *civil ſword* hardens the *followers* of falſe *teachers* in the ſuffering of their *leaders*, and begets an impreſſion of the *falſhood* of that *religion*, which cannot uphold it ſelf all the *world over*, but with ſuch *inſtruments* of *violence*, &c. Maſter *Cotton* replies, that the *Magiſtrate* ought not to draw out his *ſword* againſt *ſeducers*, untill he hath uſed all good means for *conviction*, &c. and then (ſaith he) he ſhould be cruel to *Chriſts Lambs* in ſparing the *Foxes*, &c.

The loathing hypocriſie of perſecutors.

Truth. Who knows not this to be the plea and practiſe of all *Popiſh perſecutors* in all *ages*, to compaſs *ſea* and *land* to reduce the *heretick* to the *union* and *boſome* of the *church*, not only with *promiſes*, *threatnings*, &c. but oftimes with ſolemn *diſputations*, and ſometimes *writings* and *waitings*, before they come to the *definitive ſentence*, and deliver him to the *ſecular power*, and ſo to the uſe of thoſe deſperate *remedies* of *hanging*, *burning*, &c. How do the bloody *Popes* and the bloody *Bonners* in their *hypocritical letters* and *bloody ſentences*, profeſs their lamentable *grief* at *errors* and *hereſies*; their *clemency* and *mercy*, and *great pains* taken to reduce that *wandring*, to return the *loſt childe*, to heal the ſcabbed *ſheep*? yea and when they are forced (as they ſay) for the ſaving of the *flock* from *infection* to deliver ſuch *ſheep* to the *ſecular* power, as their *butchers* and *executioners*; yet beſeech they [122] that power, and that (moſt hypocritically without ſhame) in the bowels of *Chriſt Jeſus*, to Miniſter *juſtice* with ſuch *moderation*, that if it be poſſible the *hereticks* ſoul may be ſaved, but however the *flock* may be preſerved from ſuch damnable *Doctrine*.

In their bloody ſentence, and proceedings with the perſecuted.

Peace. Maſter *Cotton* will here blame the alleadging of this: for the *Popiſh Religion* is falſe, but theirs true, *&c.*

Truth. Tis true, the P*apiſts Religion* is falſe, yet Maſter *Cotton* cannot paſs without ſuſpition to be too neer of kin to the bloody *Papiſt*, to whom they are ſo neer in *practice*: The *Lord Jeſus* gave an everlaſting *rule* to his poor ſervants, to diſcern all falſe *prophets* by, to wit, their *fruits* and bloody *practices*. But,

Secondly, The holy *Spirit of God* in this 2 to *Tim.* now inſiſted on, not only commands *Timothy* to exhort the *oppoſite*, but patiently to wait and attend *Gods* will, if peradventure *God* will give *repentance*, and that they may recover themſelves *&c.*

Peace. Maſter *Cotton* will not deny, together with meek exhortation, *patient waiting*, *&c.*

Truth. Why then doth he limit the holy one of *Iſrael* to *dayes* or *moneths*? Three months was by the *law* (in *Maſſachuſets* in *New England*) the time of *patience* to the *excommunicate*, before the *ſecular power* was to deal with him:[1] But we finde no time limi-

[1] "It is therefore ordered, that whoever ſhall ſtand excommunicate for the ſpace of 6 months, without labouring what in him or her lyeth to bee reſtored, ſuch perſon ſhall be preſented to the Court of Aſſiſtants, and then proceeded with by fine, impriſonment, or further, &c." *Maſs. Col. Records*, i. 242, Sept.

Too ſhort a time ſet for repentance in New England.

ted, nor no *direction* given to *Timothy* or his *ſucceſſors* to proſecute the *oppoſite* before *Cæſar's* bar, in caſe *God* vouchſafed not *repentance* upon their means and waiting.

3. *Chriſt Jeſus* hath not been without *bowels* of *compaſſion* in all his gracious *care* and *proviſion* he hath made for his *ſheep* and *lambs*, againſt the ſpiritual *Wolves* and *Foxes*; although we read not a word of the *arme* of *fleſh* and *ſword* of *ſteel* appointed by himſelf for their *defence* in his moſt bleſſed laſt Will and Teſtament.

Falſe teachers commonly hardned by perſecution.

4. Laſtly, to that inſtance of the *Donatiſts* and Papiſts ſuppreſſed by the *civil ſword*, no queſtion but (as before) a *civil ſword* is able, among *civil* people, to make a whole *nation*, or *world* of *hypocrites*: and yet experience alſo teſtifies (however Maſter *Cotton* makes it but *accidental*) that it is the common and ordinary *effect* of the *civil ſword* drawn forth (as they ſpeak) [123] againſt *hereticks*, *ſeducers* &c. to harden the *ſeducers* and *ſeduced*, by their *ſufferings*, and to beget no other *opinion* in their hearts, then of the *cruelty* and *weakneſs* of the *heart* and *cauſe* of their *perſecutors*.

The great ſufferings of Maſter Gorton and his friends

Peace. There hath been no ſmall noiſe of Maſter *Gortons* and his friends being *diſciplined* (or as the *Papiſts* call it, *diſcipled* in the Schoole of the *New Engliſh churches*: It is worth the inquiry to ask what *conviction* and *converſion* hath all their *hoſtilities*, cap-

6, 1638. In *The Bloudy Tenent*, 222, *Pub. Narr. Club*, iii. 386, Williams refers to this law, and with the ſame unimportant error as to the time, intimating that he only knew the law by hearſay. It continued in force but one year, having been repealed Sept. 9, 1639, ſometime before the preſent work was written. *Maſſachuſetts Colonial Records* i. 271.

tivatings, courtings, imprisonings, chainings, banishings, &c. wrought upon them?[1] *in New England.*

[1] Samuel Gorton and his associates had been taken at Warwick and brought to Boston, where they were placed on trial, and received sentence Nov. 3, 1643. "They were charged to be blasphemous enemies of the true religion of our Lord Jesus Christ, and of all his holy ordinances, and likewise of all civil government among his people, and particularly in this jurisdiction." Winthrop, *New England,* ii. 176; *Mass. Col. Rec.,* ii. 51. Gorton himself states that "they rehearsed in the ears of the people, divers gross opinions, which they had compiled together out of our writing, which we abhorred: that we denied all the Churches of Jesus Christ, because we could not join with them in that way of Church order which they had established among them: again, that we denied all the holy ordinances of Christ, because we could not join with them in their way of administration; as also that we denied all civil Magistracy, because we could not yield to their authority, to be exercised in those parts where we lived, (that place being above four and twenty miles out of their bound) which we would not once have questioned, if we had been within the compass of their jurisdiction." *Simplicitie's Defence, R. I. Hist. Coll.,* ii. 120.

The attempt on the part of Massachusetts to exercise territorial jurisdiction over Shawomet, which Gorton and his company had purchased of Miantinomi on purpose to escape from it, was mixed with the hatred for his opinions. But heresy and blasphemy were the charges which occupied the chief attention of the Court. After a long process, conviction came, and "the Court proceeded to consider of their sentence, in which the Court was much divided. All the Magistrates, save three, were of opinion that Gorton ought to die, but the greatest number of the deputies dissenting, that vote did not pass." Winthrop, *New England,* ii. 177. Gorton was sentenced "to be confined to Charlestown, there to be set on work, and to wear such bolts or irons as may hinder his escape," and "if he shall break his said confinement, or publish, declare, or maintain any of the blasphemous or abominable heresies wherewith he hath been charged," "upon conviction thereof shall be condemned to death and executed." *Mass. Col. Rec.* ii. 52. *Simplicitie's Defence,* 134.

Cotton had taken his share in these atrocious proceedings. While the Court was deliberating upon the sentence, "the judgment of the elders also had been demanded about their blasphemous speeches and opinions, what punishment was due by the Word of God. Their answer was their offence deserved death by the law of God." Winthrop, *New England,* ii. 176. On the forenoon of the day in which sentence was passed upon them Cotton preached. Gorton says that he urged that if they had dissented not out of ignorance, but "out of tenderness of conscience, and able to render reason for what we did (and other things of like nature) then were we ripened for death." *Simplicitie's Defence,* 133. Gorton also accuses Cotton of having advised in a sermon on Zephaniah, ii. 10, 11, that all necessaries be witheld from him and that he be

Truth. Shall I ſpeak my thoughts without *partiality?* I am no more of Maſter *Gortons Religion* then of Maſter *Cottons:* and yet if Maſter *Cotton* complaine of their *obſtinacy* in their way, I cannot but impute it to this *bloody tenent* and *practice*, which ordinarily doth give ſtrength and *vigour*, *ſpirit* and *reſolution* to the moſt erroneous, when ſuch *unrighteous* and moſt *unchriſtian* proceedings are exerciſed againſt them.

Antoninus Pius his Edict againſt perſecution.

Peace. Touching the *Edict* of *Antoninus* Pius concerning *perſecution* of *Chriſtians*, and the opinion it begat in their hearts of the cruelty of their *perſecutors*, Maſter *Cotton* anſwers, firſt, the *Pagan Religion* is not of *God* but the *Religion* of *Chriſtians* came down from Heaven in the *Goſpel-truth.*

Truth. This is moſt true, to him that believeth that there is but one *God*, one *Lord*, one *Spirit*, one *baptiſm*, one *body* &c. according to *Chriſt Jeſus* his *inſtitution*; and that from that bleſſed *eſtate* the *Apoſtacy* hath been made; and that all other *Gods*,

ſtarved to death. *Simplicitie's Defence*, 138.

That Williams was not only not "of Maſter Gorton's religion," but even held him in conſiderable diſlike at an earlier period, is ſeen in a letter to Winthrop, publiſhed in Winſlow's *Hypocriſie Unmaſked*, 55, 56. "Providence, 8th 1ſt, 1640. Maſter Gorton having abuſed high and low at Aquidnick, is now bewitching and bemadding poor Providence, both with his uncleane and foul cenſures of all the miniſters of this country (for which myſelf have in Chriſt's name withſtood him), and alſo denying all viſible and externall ordinances in depth of Familiſme, againſt which I have a little diſputed and written, and ſhall (the moſt High aſſenting) to death. As Paul ſaid of Aſia, I of Providence (almoſt) all ſuck in his poyſon, as at firſt they did at Aquidnick. Some few and myſelf withſtood his inhabitation, and town privileges, without confeſſion to reformation of his uncivil and inhuman practiſes at Portſmouth: Yet the tide is too ſtrong againſt us, and I feare (if the framer of hearts helpe not) it will force me to little Patience, a little iſle next to your Prudence." Arnold, *Hiſt. R. I.*, i. 172.

Lords, Spirits, Faiths, Baptiſms or *churches*, are falſe: But what is this to many *millions* of men and women, in ſo many *kingdomes* and *nations, Cities* and parts of the *world*, who believe as confidently their lies of many *Gods* and *Chriſts*, all which they believe (as the *Epheſians* of their *Diana*, and of the *image* of *Jupiter*, and (as Maſter C*otton* of the way of his *Religion*) that they come down from *heaven?*

Peace. Doubtleſs, according to their belief, all the *peoples* of thoſe *nations, kingdoms* and *countries*, wherein the name of *Chriſt* is ſounded, whether of the *greek church* or the *latine*, whether of *Popiſh* or *Proteſtant* profeſſion will ſay as Maſter *Cotton*, my *religion* came down from *heaven* in the *Goſpel* of *Truth*, &c.

124] *Truth*. Now then either the *ſword* of *ſteel* muſt decide this *controverſie* (according to the bloody *tenent* of *perſecution*) in the ſuppreſſing of *hereticks, blaſphemers, idolaters* and *ſeducers*, by the ſtrength of an arme of *fleſh*: or elſe the two-edged ſword of the Spirit of *God*, the *word* of *God* coming out of the mouth of *Chriſt Jeſus* in the *mouths* of his *ſervants*, which will either *humble* and *ſubdue* the *Rebels*, or cut moſt deep, and kill with an *eternal vengeance*.

Peace. But (ſaith Maſter *Cotton*) it will beget an *opinion* of *cruelty* to murther *innocents*, but not to put to *death murtherers* of *ſouls*.

The difference between ſpiritual and corporal murther.

Truth. I anſwer, beſide that great and common *difference* of *civil murther*, and *ſpiritual*, there is a ſecond, to wit, that in the *murther* of an *innocent*, the conſcience of a *murtherer* is opened, and commonly the mouth confeſſeth I am a *murtherer*, I have killed an *innocent*: but run through all the *coaſts* and *quar-*

ters of the whole *world*, and the very *conſciences* of ſo many thouſands of ſoul-*murtherers* are rootedly ſatisfied and perſwaded, that they are ſo far from being *murtherers* as that they are ſo many *ſaviours* of the *ſouls* of *men*, and *Prieſts* and *Miniſters* of the moſt high *God* or *Gods*, &c.

Peace. For inſtance, if a man ſay Maſter *Cotton* is a *ſubject* of the ſtate of *England*, and a *Miniſter* of that *worſhip*, which he believeth to be true, confirmed by *argument* and *light* ſufficient to his *underſtanding ſoul* and conſcience: How many thouſand are there fellow-*ſubjects* with Maſter *Cotton* to the *Engliſh ſtate*, yet of a contrary mind to Maſter *Cotton* in matter of *Gods worſhip*? yea how many are there (it may be thouſands) profeſſing a *Miniſtery* contrary to Maſter *Cottons?* and the like may be found in other *nations* and *parts* of the *world*.

Civil juſtice ought impartially to permit one conſcience as well as another.

Truth. What true *reaſon* of *juſtice*, *peace*, or *common* ſafety of the whole, can be rendred to the *world* why Maſter *Cottons* conſcience and *Miniſtry* muſt be maintained by the *ſword*, more then the *conſciences* and *Miniſteries* of his other fellow-ſubjects? Why ſhould he be accounted (I mean at the bar of *civil juſtice*) I ſay accounted a ſoul *Saviour*, and all other *Miniſters* of other *Religions* and *conſciences*, *ſoul-murtherers*, and ſo be executed as *murtherers*, or forced to temporize or turn from their *Religion*, [125] which is but *hypocriſie* in *Religion* againſt their *conſcience*, which is ten thouſand times worſe, and renders men, when they ſin againſt their *conſcience*, not only *hypocrites*, but *Atheiſts*, and ſo fit for the practiſe of any *evil murthers*, *adulteries*, *treaſons*, &c?

Peace. Master *Cottons* second Answer is, that the persecuting *Emperors* and *governors* of *Provinces* under them, attended not to the conviction of *christians*, nor did they endeavour to make it appear that the *Christians* sinned against the light of their *consciences*, and therefore no marvel if it bred in the people a just opinion of the *cruelty* of *persecutors*, and of the *innocency* of *christians*.

The difference of the persecution of the Roman Emperors and the Roman Popes.

Truth. Let it be granted that the *Roman Emperors* did not attend to, nor endeavour this, yet the *Roman Popes*, and all the *Antichrist* governors of their mystical *Provinces*, *Bishops* and *Priests*, have professedly compassed *Sea* and *Land* to make a *Proselyte*.

Peace. Tis true, the *history* of the death of the *Saints*, slaughtered by such persecutors abundantly testifie this, and yet their *persecution* will be found no other then *cruelty* and *murther*, and the opinion of it will never be razed out of the heart of *Gods* people, whatever the whole *world* (which wonders after and *worships the beast*) think to the contrary.

Truth. And I add, that herein Master *Cottons* former position, to wit [that *hereticks* must be punished by the *civil sword*, for sinning against the light of their own *conscience*] accords fully with the Popish clamors, [the *hereticks* mouths are stopped, they are *convinced*, they have not a word to say, and yet they are *obstinate*; away with them, hang them, burn them.]

Peace. Master *Cotton* saith, It is an untrue intimation of the *discusser*, that *Antoninus* forbod the persecuting of *christians* upon any such ground.

Truth. That it may not rest upon the discussers

credit or *diſcredit*, I think it not unſeaſonable if I preſent to *Engliſh* eyes the *Engliſh* teſtimony of the diligent and praiſe worthy-Chronicler *John Speede*, who alſo ingageth *Euſebius* his credit, and thus relateth the effect of *Antoninus* his mind in theſe words.[1]

The Emperor *Cæſar*, *Marcus*, *Aurelius*, *Antonius*, &c. Unto the Commons of *Aſia*,

Sendeth Greeting.

Antoninus Pius his famous Edict for liberty to the Chriſtians related by that praiſe-worthy Maſter John Speede out of Euſebius.

I Doudt not, but the Gods themſelves have a care that wicked perſons ſhall be brought to light; for it doth much more appertaine to them, then it doth to you, to puniſh ſuch as refuſe to yeeld them worſhip: but this courſe which you take, doth confirme them whom you perſecute in this their opinion of you, That you are impious men, and meer Atheiſts; whereby it commeth to paſs, that they deſire in the quarrel of their GOD, rather to die then to yeeld to the will of ſuch as you are, and to embrace your form of Religion: Let it not ſeem unſeaſonable to call to your remembrance the Earthquakes which lately have happened, and which are yet, to your great terrour and grief; becauſe I underſtand, that in ſuch like Accidents, you caſt the Envy of ſuch common miſfortune, upon their Shoulders; whereby their confidence, and truſt in their GOD is much the more increaſed: Whereas, you being ignorant of the true cauſes of ſuch things, do

[1] *The Hiſtorie of Great Britaine under the Conqueſts of the Romans, Saxons, Danes and Normans, &c.*, by John Speed. Lond. 1632. p. 100. John Speed (1552–1629) was a tailor by trade, but Sir Fulk Greville diſcovering his love for the antiquities of Great Britain, gave him an allowance to enable him to proſecute his ſtudies.. The book named above, from which Williams quotes the tranſlation of the reſcript, is his great work, on which he ſpent fourteen years labor, and appeared in 1614. It is conſidered ſuperior to any of the preceding chronicles, and entitles him to the praiſe beſtowed in the text. Roſe, *Biog. Dict.*, xii. 84.

both neglect the worſhip of the other Gods, and alſo baniſh and perſecute the ſervants of the immortal GOD, whom the Chriſtians do worſhip; and you perſecute to the death all the embracers of that profeſſion. In the behalf of theſe men, many of the Provinces Preſident have written before to my Father of famous memory, to whom he anſwered, That they ſhould not be moleſted, unleſs they were proved to have practiſed Treaſon againſt the Imperial State; and concerning the ſame matter, ſome have given notice to me, to whom I anſwered with like moderation as my Father did before me: And by our Edict, do ordaine, That if any hereafter be found thus buſie in moleſting theſe kind of men, without any their offence, We command that he that is accuſed upon this point, be abſolved; albeit he be proved to be ſuch an one as he is charged to be, that is, a Chriſtian; and he that is his accuſer, ſhall ſuffer the ſame Puniſhment which he ſought to procure unto the other.[1]

127] In this paſſage the *wiſe* and *experienced Emperor* obſerveth many *reaſons* for the toleration of *Chriſtians*, and inſinuates that the perſecuting of the Chriſtians, confirmed them in their opinion, that their *perſecutors* were not only *cruel* (for that is the leaſt that can be implied in *perſecution*) but alſo as the words run, impious men and meer *Atheiſts*.

[1] This reſcript is given by Euſebius, *Ecc. Hiſt.*, Lib. iv., Cap. 13, Cantabrigiæ, 1720; alſo by Juſtin Martyr, *Opera*, tom. i., p. 100, Pariſiis, 1636. But its authenticity is generally doubted by ſcholars. "It is now generally given up as ſpurious." Milman, *Hiſt. of Chriſtianity*, ii. 158. "Any man moderately acquainted with Roman hiſtory will ſee at once from the ſtyle and tenor that it is a clumſy forgery." George Long, *Thoughts of M. Aurelius*, 24. "The author of this reſcript ſpeaks rather the language of a Chriſtian than of a pagan emperor. The ſucceeding hiſtory, moreover, does not notice the exiſtence of ſuch an edict." Neander, *Church Hiſtory*, i. 104. "That it is not genuine has been ſhown moſt convincingly by *Is. Haffner, &c.*" Gieſeler, *Ecc. Hiſt.* i. 79, note 4.

The persecuted ever nourish an hard conceit of cruelty and Tyranny in their persecutors, whereas Malefactors confess frequently the justice of their condemners.

Peace. Dear Truth, your *observation* forceth from my peaceable mind, this *Testimony*, which oft to my grief and horror, mine eares have heard many *persons* (I hope in their *persons* chosen of the *Lord*) having as they conceived, suffered *persecution* from the hands, and by the means of many worthy men both of *Magistracy* and *Ministry* of *New England*: I say, they have been by such *persecution* so far from being wrought on *&c.* that they have been moulded into a strong *apprehension*, that it was impossible that such their *persecutors* should be men of any *fear* of *God*, but meer *dissemblers*, *time-servers*, *Jehues reformers*, for their own ends of *honor*, *ease*, and *liberty* from the *cross* of *Christ*: which apprehension although the *discusser* (to my knowledge) hath often labored to root out of many, yet could he hardly prevaile to stir it, so grossly, *odious*, *unchristian*, or *antichristian*, appears the ugly face of *persecution* &c.

Examination of CHAP. XLI.

Peace.

IN the discussing of the prophecy of *Isaiah* and *Micah*, concerning the breaking of *swords* into *plowshares*, and *speares* into *pruning-hooks*, truely interpreted to foretell the meek temper of *Christians* in bringing others to *Christ Jesus*, Master *Cotton* excepts against the discussers observation upon Master *Cottons* similitude from *Wolves* which he would have driven out from the *sheepfold:* The observation was this, or to this effect, [That if *civil power* might force the *wolves* out, it might force the *ſheep* in.]

Truth. The diſcuſſer denied not the uſe of *Chriſts ſpiritual power* for the life of his *ſheep*, and *deſtruction* of the *Wolves*: but *heaven* and *earth* ſhall fall before this truth, to wit, [That *power* that driveth *Wolves* out, may drive ſheep in.] If *ſpiritual* [128] *power* drive out the *wolfe ſpiritual*, alſo drives in the *ſheep*, but if *civil power* (to wit, by *ſwords, whips, priſons, burnings*, &c.) drives out the *ſpiritual* or *myſtical Wolfe*, the ſame undeniably muſt drive in the *ſheep*.

If Civil power may force out of the church, it may alſo force in.

Peace. Yea, but Maſter *Cotton* (too too weakly) would pleaſe himſelf upon the word [*ſame*:] a *father*, ſaith he, with a *ſtaffe* or *ſword* may drive away *dogs* that might by the way worry or bite his *children* going to *School*, may he therefore with a *ſtaffe* or *ſword* drive his *children* to School? and are *wolves* to be driven away, and *ſheep* brought into the *fold* by the ſame *inſtruments*? The *dog* that teares a *wolfe*, if he tear the *ſheep* alſo, will finde an *halter*, &c.

Truth. Maſter *Cotton* hath had a name for a man of *Moſes ſpirit*, of a meek and gentle temper; he cannot but know he hath loſt that name with thouſands fearing *God*, by not putting that difference, between the *Wolves* and the *ſheep*, the *Egyptians* and the *Iſraelites*, as *Moſes* did: *Moſes* killed the *Egyptian*, he reproves the *Iſraelite*: All that contradict Maſter *Cottons church* way (though before dear *brethren*, familiar and intimate) he not only drives them out, as *wolves blaſphemers, ſeducers* &c. by his pretended *ſpiritual weapons* of *Chriſt Jeſus*, but alſo by *civil ſword*, impriſoning, baniſhing, whipping, *&c.*

Every true Moſes will make a difference between Iſraelites and Egyptians.

But more particularly, The discusser indeed useth this word the *same power*, but not as Master *Cotton* seemeth to understand it, for the *same weapon*. He hath in this very place printed the discussers words, that a *staff* is for the *wolfe*, and a *rod* or *hook* for the *sheep*. The *dog* that teares the *wolf*, is but to affright the sheep and consequently the *father* that hath a stick a *rod* for the *child*; But yet these *swords*, *staves*, *sticks*, and *rods*, are all of the same *nature* in general, that is of a *material*, temporal and *civil nature*, which may be used about natural *wolves*, *sheep*, *children*, &c. And if they may be used also about spiritual or mystical *wolves*, to force them out; it is as cleare as the *Sun-Beames*, that they may be used, that is such *civil weapons* as are fit for *mystical wolves* to force them into the *sheepfold*: And thus have all *Popish* persecutors practised in our own and other countries, to wit, by *civil power* (as well as by their own pretended *spiritual*) in forcing their supposed *sheep* to *church*, and to *conformity*, as well as by *whips*, and *Prisons*, *Ropes* and *Fires*, driving out the supposed *wolves* or *hereticks*.

129] *Peace*. In the close of this, Master *Cotton* adds that (*Rev.* 6. 6.) the *Antichristian wolves* shall drink *blood*, for they are worthy.

Truth. I have in former passages declared the misconceit of Master *Cotton* and others, as touching that *Scripture*, and that, although they shall drink *blood* filled out of the *cups* of *Gods* righteous *vengeance* yet not by judicial prosecution in *civil courts* for *spiritual offences*, although yet it is most righteous for the *kings* and *powers* of the earth, meerly with respect to these *wolves* their *oppreſſions* and *bloodſheddings*, to repay them again with the like ſmart and paine, and kinds of *puniſhment*.

Peace. Yea and tis for ever memorable, that while the *kings* of the *earth* have given their power to the *beaſt*, againſt the *bodies* of the *Saints*, what *cups* of *blood* hath the righteous hand of the moſt *high* filled to *Antichriſtian kings* and *kingdomes*, by the bloody *Turkes*, and by their own more bloody *wars*, ſome-times for the empty *puffs* of their *titles* and *honors*, but as frequently for *God* (as they pretend) and for his *Religion*.

Cups of Blood given into the hand of perſecuting nations.

Examination of CHAP. XLII.

Peace.

IN this Chapter Maſter *Cotton* chargeth the diſcuſ-ſer for making work, to wit, for examining more particularly the ſimilitude of *wolves* brought in by Maſter *Cotton* himſelf: yet he conſenteth with him in the firſt *quæry*, that thoſe *Wolves* of which *Paul* warns the *elders* at *Epheſus*, were *myſtical* and *ſpiritual wolves*; yet he adds that ſuch cannot be good *ſubjects*, loving *neighbors*, faire *dealers*, becauſe they ſpiritually are not ſuch; and he argues, that then it will be no advantage to *civil ſtates*, when the *king-domes* of the earth ſhall become the *kingdomes* oft he *Lord*: and that then they may do as good *ſervice* to the *civil ſtate*, who bring the wrath of *God* upon them by their *apoſtacy*, as they that bring down *bleſſ-ings* from heaven by *profeſſion* and *practiſe* of the true *religion* in *purity*.

Whether a common-weal proſper in divers religions permitted.

Truth. I desire that this *reply* be well pondred, for it will be found dangerously destructive to the very *roots* of all civil *relations*, [130] converse and dealing; yea, and any *civil being* of the *world it self.*

Men may be very faire and peaceable, though not of the only one religion.

For, if none be peaceable *subjects*, loving *neighbors*, faire *dealers*, but such [as are] of Master *Cottons conscience* and *religion* (which he conceives to be the only true *religion*) what will become of all other *states*, *governments*, *cities*, *towns*, *peoples*, *families*, *neighbors*, upon the *face* of the earth? I say, what will become of them (especially if power were in Master *Cottons* hand to deal with them as *Wolves*?)

Peace. Alas, too too frequent *experience* tels us in all parts of the *world*, that many thousands are far more peaceable *subjects*, more loving and helpful *neighbors*, and more true and fair *dealers* in *civil conversation*, then many who account themselves to be the only *religious* people in the *world.*

Truth. But againe, What the state of things shall be, and what the manner of the *administration* of *Christs kingdome*, when the *kingdomes* of the *earth* shall become the *kingdomes* of the *Lord*, Master *Cotton* doth not express: and for wrath brought upon *civil states* for their *apostacy*, I desire Master *Cotton* to shew, where ever *God* destroyed any Nation in the world (one only excepted) for *Apostacy* from his *truth* and *worship*? Yea and where was ever *Israel* (the only true *national church* that Master *Cotton* will acknowledge) meerly for apostasie destroyed, without general ripeness in other sins also, and especially for their persecuting of such, as declared their *apostasie*, *superstition*, and will-worship from *God* unto them.

Peace. In the next place Maſter *Cotton* granting that the charge given to watch againſt theſe *Wolves*, was not given to the *Magiſtrates* of the City of *Epheſus*, but to the *elders* of the *church* of *Chriſt* in *Epheſus*, he yet chargeth the diſcuſſer with a palpable and notorious ſlander, for ſaying, that many of thoſe *charges* and *exhortations* given by the *Lord Jeſus* to the *ſhepherds* and *Miniſters* of the *churches*, are commonly attributed by the anſwerer in this diſcourſe to the civil *Magiſtrate*.

Truth. This heavy charge of Maſter *Cottons* againſt the diſcuſſer, will be found to be a fruit of *Anger* and paſſion, and not of *reaſon* and *moderation*; as alſo his denyal that one of thoſe charges given to *Miniſters*, were directed by him to *Magiſtrates*.

131] For if Maſter *Cotton*, or any pleaſe to view over Maſter *Cottons allegations* from the New *Teſtament* in this diſcourſe, he ſhall finde that (*Tit.* 3. [10.]) *reject the heretick* a charge given by the *Lord Jeſus* to *Titus*, and the *church* at *Crete*, is brought for the proof of the *Magiſtrates* puniſhing, impriſoning, baniſhing, killing the *heretick*, *idolater* &c.

Scriptures perverted from the church to the civil ſtate.

The like charges of *Chriſt Jeſus* ſent to the *Miniſters* and *churches* of *Aſia*, for tolerating amongſt them *Balaam* and *Jezabel*, are produced to prove proſecutions againſt falſe *Prophets* and profeſſors in the *City* and *Commonweal*.

Yea although Maſter *Cotton* name not *Act*. 20. [29.] yet in that Maſter *Cotton* affirmeth that *Magiſtrates* with the *civil ſword* muſt drive away *Wolves*, from the ſheepfold of *Chriſt* the *church*, meaning ſpiritual *wolves*, falſe *teachers*, he may be truly ſaid to quote all ſuch *Scriptures* as give charge againſt ſuch *Wolves*.

Peace. Indeed Master *Cotton* more then once pleaseth himself with this similitude of *Wolves*, to prove the *Magistrates* piety and pity to the *sheep*, in slaying and driving away the *wolves*, *false teachers*, &c.

The Magistrate usually the Cleargies Cane, &c.

Truth. Hence was it (for commonly where *state-Religions* are set up, the *Magistrate* is but the *Ministers Cane* through whom the *Clergy* speaks) I say probably hence from such misapplyed *Scriptures* in their *churches*, that in their solemn *civil* general *court*, at the banishment of one poor man amongst them, hunted out as a *wolf* or *heretick*, the *governor* who then was, standing up alleadged for a ground of their duty to drive away such by *banishment*, that famous charge of *Christ Jesus* to his *Ministers* and *Church* at *Rome* (*Rom.* 16. [17.]) Marke them that cause *divisions* contrary to the *doctrine* which you have received, and avoid, that is, by *banishment*:[1] By all which and more it may be found, how *Sathan* hath abused their godly minds and apprehensions in causing them so to abuse the holy *writings* of *truth* and *Testament* of *Christ Jesus*, and that how ever they deny it in express tearms, yet by most impregnable *consequence* and implication they make up a kind of *national church*, and (as the phrase is) a *Christian state* and *government* of *church* and *Commonweale*, that is, of *Christ* and the *world* together.

Rom. 16. 17. *grosly abused by a governor in New England.*

[1] See page 106, *supra*. This refers to Williams's own banishment. The ministers were invited to meet with the magistrates, and give their advice in his case. Which was worse, for the ministers to declare such opinions as they did, or for the court to ask their advice, is not easy to say. How completely they acted together, and united Church and State, is seen in Winthrop's account of the trial. *New England*, i. 194. John Haynes was Governor. Six months after, when Winthrop was called in question for his administration, Haynes accused him of too great lenity, which he seems to have determined should be no fault of his. *Winthrop*, i. 212.

Peace. To proceed, it being further inquired into, whether in [132] all the *New Teſtament* of *Chriſt Jeſus* there be any ſuch word of *Chriſt*, either by way of *command, Promiſe*, or example countenancing the *civil ſtate* to meddle with theſe *myſtical Wolves*, if in *civil* things peaceable and obedient. Maſter *Cotton* replieth, that this *condition* of *peaceable* and *obedient*, implies a *contradiction* to the *nature* and practiſe of *wolves.* How can, ſaith he, *wolves* be peaceable and obedient, unleſs *reſtrained*? Can there be peace, *Jehu*, ſo long as the *whoredomes* of *Jezabel* and her *witchcrafts* are ſo many? And when it might be objected that *ſpiritual whoredomes* and *witchcrafts* might ſtand with *civil* peace, He anſwers, No verily, for the *whoredomes* and *witchcrafts* of the *Jezabel* of *Rome* took away *civil* peace from the *earth*, and brought the *Turks* to oppreſs both the peace of *Chriſtian churches* and *Commonweals*, Rev. 9. 15, 21.

Truth. I wonder ſince Maſter *Cotton* in this very paſſage mentioneth the *ſpiritual wolves, whores*, and *witches*, as well as *natural* and *moral.* How he can imagine that a *ſpiritual wolf* or *witch* (to wit, ſo or ſo in matters of *ſpiritual* worſhip and *religion*) might not poſſibly be peaceable and *obedient* in *civil* things.

Peace. Yea but he alleadgeth the *whoredomes* of the *Jezabel* of *Rome.*

Truth. Why, was not the State of *England*, the *Kings* and *Queens*, and *Parliaments* thereof, lawful as *kings* and *ſtates*, though overwhelmed and overſpread univerſally with the *Romiſh abominations*? If ſuch *wolves, whores*, and *witches* could yeeld no *civil* obedience, could they then exerciſe (by the ſame *argu-*

The bloody Tenent plucks up the nations and all civil being, &c.

ment) any *civil authority*? And ſhall we then conclude all the former Popiſh *kings* and *Parliaments* (and conſequently *lawes*) unlawful, becauſe in *ſpiritual* things they were as *Wolves*, &c. tearing and burning the poor ſheep of *Chriſt*? will it not then be unlawful for any man, that is perſwaded the whole *nation* where he lives is *idolatrous*, *ſpiritually whoriſh*, &c. I ſay unlawful for him to live in ſuch a *ſtate*, although he might with freedome to his own *conſcience*? whither will ſuch kind of arguing drive at laſt, but to pluck up the *roots* of all *ſtates* and peoples in the *world*, as not capable to yeeld *civil* obedience, or exerciſe civil *authority*, except ſuch people, *Magiſtrates*, &c. as are of Maſter *Cottons church* and *religion*.

133] *Peace.* Methinks *experience* (were there no S*cripture* nor *reaſon*) might tell us how peaceable and juſt neighbors and dealers many thouſands and millions of *Jews*, *Turks*, *Antichriſtians*, and *Pagans* are to be found, notwithſtanding their ſpiritual *whoredoms*, *witchcrafts*, &c.

The plague of the Turkes.

Truth. Yea, and why doth Maſter *Cotton* alleadge the *Jezabel* of R*ome*, and the comming in of the *Turks*? It is true, *God* brought in the *Armies* of the *Turkes* upon the *Eaſtern* Empire, which yet flouriſhed many ages (even in their *apoſtacies*) before their *deſtruction* by the *Turkes*. And how many *ages* and *generations* hath *Iezabel* of R*ome* ſitten as a *Queen* in triumphant *peace* and *glory*, even ſince the riſing of the *Turks* (and ſo ſhall ſit probably in greater and greater, untill the time of her appointed *judgement* and downfal? If *Chriſt Jeſus* were a true Prophet

Romes glory and downfal.

(*Iohn* 16.) outward peace, prosperity, *riches*, *honor*, is the portion of this *world*, notwithstanding their *idolatries*, *apostacies*, *blasphemies:* But the portion of *Christs* followers (like his own, and both like a woman in travel) paine and *sorrow*, yea *poverty* and *persecution*, untill the great day of *refreshing*, neer approaching.

P*eace*. Master *Cotton* againe sends us to R*evelations* the 16. 4, 5, 6, 7.

Truth. And I must also send Master *Cotton* and the Reader to our disproving of that proof above said.

Further, whereas he calls R*om*. 13. [4.] the great *Charter* for all *Magistrates* to deal in *spiritual matters*, I have and shall manifest in the *examinations* upon that place, how weak a *warrant* it is for the civil *state*, and the *officers* thereof, to conceive themselves *spiritual Physitians*, by vertue of their office, appointed by God, in spiritual and *soul-evils*.

Peace. Whereas it was urged, that *Magistrates* beside their skil in *civil laws* and *government*, must be able (if Master *Cottons bloody tenent* be true) as *judges* and *heads* to determine *spiritual causes* and *controversies*, and that by the sight of his own eyes, and not other mens; Master *Cotton* replies, that *Magistrates* ought to be skilled in the *fundamentals* of *religion*, and that their *ignorance* excuseth not.

The civil state and officers thereof cannot be spiritual judges.

Truth. In this passage Master *Cotton* waveth that *inference* [134] [That then *Magistrates* must be *heads* and *judges* in *spiritual causes*:] That *inference* cannot possibly be avoided, if we grant it their *duty* (as Master *Cotton* seemes to do) to pass sentence in the *fun-*

damentals of *religion*, and in thoſe points which have been and are ſo greatly controverted among all ſorts of men that name the *name* of *Chriſt*.

2. If *Magiſtrates* muſt thus judge, reforme, *&c.* where hath been the care of *Chriſt Ieſus* to appoint in all parts of the world, ſuch *Magiſtrates*, as might take care of his *religion* and *worſhip?* why hath he not furniſhed them with ſome *capacity* and *ability* to the work?

Foul neglects caſt upon Chriſt Jeſus.

Peace. It is lamentable to think that moſt of the *Magiſtrates* in the world (beyond compare) know not ſo much as whether there be a *Chriſt* or no.

Truth. If *Chriſt Ieſus* had forgotten himſelf for three hundred yeers together, furniſhing his *church* with no other *heads* but of *Wolves*, *Bear*, *Lyons*, and *Tygers*, the R*omane Emperors* yet (after a little refreſhing by *Conſtantine*, *Theodoſius* &c.) why ſhould he ſtill forget himſelf (even a thouſand yeers together, providing no other *heads*, but bloody and *Popiſh kings* and *Emperors*?

The caſe of Gallio.

Peace. What think you (*dear truth*) of Maſter *Cottons* grant of *Gallios* not being bound to judge in matters of *religion*, becauſe he had no Law from *Cæſar* whoſe *deputy* he was?

Truth. I anſwer what if he had not a law from *Cæſar*, if yet he had a law from *Chriſt Ieſus*, as Maſter *Cotton* implies? Or will Maſter *Cotton* ſuſpend the *execution* of *Chriſts will*, upon the *kings*, *ſtates*, or *peoples* minds that chooſe ſuch *Magiſtrates* to be their *deputies* in the *Commonweale*? But the truth is, concerning *Gallio*, whatever he was in his perſon, and however he did evil in ſuffering the peace to be broken; yet will Maſter *Cotton* never prove, that he had calling from either *God* or *man*, to go beyond his *civil Magiſtracy* and *office* to intermeddle with *matters* of a *ſpiritual nature*, and that *Gallio* knew well enough, and other *Magiſtrates* of the *world* ſhall know in the *Lords* moſt gracious appointed ſeaſon.

Peace. The diſcuſſer ending this Chapter with the infallible ſafety of *Gods* choſen, notwithſtanding all ravenous *wolves*, &c. [135] Maſter *Cotton* replies from *Deut* 13. that *God* was able to keep his ſheep in *Iſrael*, yet they that ſeduced them were to be put to *death*.

Truth. That *argument* was not alleadged with the derogation to any of *Gods* holy *ordinances*, which concern the *calling* or *preſerving* of ſuch whom *God* hath choſen to *ſalvation*, but only to diſcover the over-buſie fear of *Gods* looſing any of his choſen to *ſalvation*, by the jaws of ſpiritual *wolves*, &c. For *Deut*. 13. [5. 10.] Let Maſter *Cotton* produce ſuch a *miraculous nation* or *people* (as I may call it) ſo brought out of the land of *Egypt* into *covenant* with *God &c.* and I ſhall readily grant that *ſeducers* of ſuch a people from ſuch a *God*, are worthy to die a thouſand *deaths*: But if Maſter *Cotton* will now tell me that the *Chriſtian congregational church* is the *Iſrael* of *God*, and the coming forth of *Egypt* is now *myſtical* and *ſpiritual*, why will he not content himſelf with a *myſtical* and *ſpiritual death* to be inflicted upon him that ſhall ſeduce an *Iſraelite* from the *Lord* his *God*?

Examination of CHAP. XLIII.

Peace.

Shameful weaknes cast upon the spiritual Artillery of Christ Jesus.

UPon the fifth query to wit, whether the elders of the *church* at *Ephesus* were not sufficiently furnished by the *Lord Jesus* to drive away these *spiritual* and *mystical wolves*, Master *Cotton* replies, by granting, that they were furnished with sufficient power to cast them out of the *church*; but being cast out, they had not sufficient power to drive them away from *conferring* and *corrupting* the members of the *church*, or other *godly* ones out of the *church*; and he adds, that it is no dishonour to *Christ*, nor *impeachment* to the *sufficiency* of his *ordinances* left by *Christ*, that in such a case the *minister* of *justice* in the *civil state*, should assist the Ministers of the *Gospel* in the *church state*.

The spiritual liberties of Christs people in spiritual causes.

Truth. This grant and this *addition* do as ill agree, as *light* and *darkeness*, *Christ* and *Belial* together. For, is the *church* or *kingdome* of *Christ Jesus* sufficiently furnished (that is, in it [136] self without the help of the *civil Magistrate*) to *excommunicate*, to cast these *wolves* out of the Fold: Oh let M. *Cotton* then, and all that love *Christ Jesus* in truth, observe what evidently follows, then is this *church* of *Christ* sufficiently furnished to receive such persons in againe upon *repentance*, then sufficiently furnished at first to be congregated together by *Christs meanes* to *ordaine* their *officers*, to judge of *doctrines* and *persons*, and all this (necessarily upon Master *Cottons* grant) without the help of the *civil Magistrates*.

Peace. Yea, and it ſeemes to me incredible, and unreaſonable, that *Chriſt Jeſus* ſhould have left *power* and *authority* ſufficient to take and bind a *rebel* againſt his *kingdome*, to *arraigne* him and paſs *ſentence* upon him, yea and *execute* him in the *cutting* off ſuch an *offendor* from the *land* of the *living*, delivering him over into the power of that roaring *Lyon* the *devil*; And yet that *Chriſt Ieſus* ſhould not have left *power ſufficient* (in ſuch *publick*, high and ſolmne *actions* of his *kingdome*) to declare ſufficient cauſe of ſuch *proceedings*, by which all men may ſee, the goings of the *Son* of *God* in his *church* and *kingdome*, or if willfully blind may juſtly be further hardned.

The mighty power of ſpiritual weapons.

Truth. The place from *Titus* alleadged (unto which many other *Scriptures* teſtifie) I ſay that place doth evidently ſhew, that the power of *Chriſt Ieſus* left in the hand of his *churches* and *elders*, was not only ſufficient to caſt out ſuch *wolves*, but even to ſtop or *muzzle* their *mouthes* (whatever their *gainſaying* be, whether by *conferring*, *preaching*, *printing* &c.) which takes off the plea of the great need of the *civil ſword*, to correct the *conference* of ſuch perſons &c. when by the words of *Paul* it is here plaine, that they can perform ſuch conferences, no otherwiſe, but with a ſtopt or *muzled mouth*.

A vaine fear of falſe teachers.

Let it be produced where *Chriſt Ieſus* in ſuch caſes writes to the *Magiſtrates* (either of *Crete*, or *Epheſus*, or any other *civil juriſdiction* where the *churches* were reſident) to help the Miniſters and *churches* with their *civil powers*, after they had caſt forth any perſon obſtinate: Doubtleſs *Chriſt Ieſus* in *Paul* and other of his ſervants would have written to ſome of *ſuch Magiſ-*

Chriſt Jeſus nor Paul adreſt themſelves to the civil ſtate.

trates in ſome place or other, having occaſion to write to ſo many *churches* about ſuch caſes.

137] *Peace.* It will (poſſibly) be ſaid, it had been in vaine, for they were *idolaters* and *perſecutors.*

Truth. The Lord is pleaſed throughout the whole Scripture in the mouths of his *ſervants* and *prophets* to call for duties at the hands of all *men,* notwithſtanding their natural *hardneſs* and *inability,* that ſo he might drive them to ſee their *duty* and *miſery,* and *remedy* alone in *God* by *Chriſt Jeſus.*

Turk and Pope and all Proteſtants againſt free conference.

Peace. I ſee now, that this hindring of *conference* &c. by the *civil ſword* is nothing elſe but a *conformity* with the *Pope* in defending his *Canons,* and with the *Turk* in guarding his *Alcoran* by *fire* and *ſword*; with whom, and their ways *Chriſt Jeſus* hath no *conformity* nor *communion,* nor with their *carnal ſword,* his two-edged *ſword* that proceedeth out of his *mouth Rev.* 1. [16] Beſide *Chriſt Jeſus* hath not onely furniſhed his *church* with *power* ſufficient to *excommunicate,* but every one of his *followers* with a *compleat armour* from *head* to *foot* (*helmet, breaſt-plate ſword* and *Target,* and and ſpiritual ſhoes (*Epheſ.* 6. [14. 15.]) in which reſpect the leaſt of *Chriſts ſervants* are inabled to ſtop the mouth of *Papiſts, Pope, Turks* and *devils.*

The ammunition of Chriſts ſouldiers.

David and Goliah types.

Peace. Yea all *experience* ſhews how *Chriſt Jeſus* (little *David*) in the leaſt of his *ſervants,* hath been able with thoſe plaine *ſmooth ſtones* out of the brook of holy *Scripture,* to lay groveling in their *ſpiritual gore,* the *ſtouteſt Champions* (*Popes, Cardinals, Biſhops, Doctors*) of the *Antichriſtian* Philiſtins.

Truth. I add, if the *elders,* and *churches,* and *ordinances* of *Chriſt* have ſuch need of the *civil ſword* for their *maintenance* and *protection* (I mean in *ſpiritual things*) ſure the *Lord Jeſus Chriſt* cannot be excuſed for not being careful either to expreſs this great *ordinance* in his *will* and *Teſtament*, or elſe to have furniſhed the *civil ſtate* and *officers* thereof with *ability* and *hearts* for this their great *duty* and *employment*, to which he hath called them; the contrary whereof in all *Ages*, in all *nations*, and in all *experience*, hath ever been moſt lamentably true.

Peace. I am not clear (*dear truth*) in the *diſtinction*, Maſter *Cotton* makes of *Chriſts Miniſters* in the *Goſpel*, and *Chriſts Miniſters* in the *civil ſtate*.

Truth. There is a miſtake in it, for although *Chriſt* hath all power delivered to him in *heave* and *earth*, yet as touching his [138] *ſpiritual church* or *kingdome* he diſclaimes it to be of the *world*, or *worldly*. Hence cannot the *civil ſtate* or *officers* thereof be called *Chriſts*, as if they were of *Chriſts inſtitution* and *appointment*, himſelf being their *ſpiritual head*. And therefore it is that the *Spirit* of *God* cals him the *head* of the *body*, which is the *church*, and the *Miniſters* and *officers* of this his *kingdome* and body *Chriſts Miniſters* or *ſervants*. Beſide, Maſter *Cotton* will not ſay that the *kingdomes* of the *world* are yet become the *Lord Chriſts*: In what manner alſo thoſe *kingdomes* ſhall become his, we have need of the holy Spirit to evidence and demonſtrate to us.

Difference between ſpiritual and civil Miniſters.

Peace. To the fifth *query*, whether (as *men* deal with *wolves*) theſe *wolves* at *Epheſus* were intended by *Paul* to be *killed*, their *braines* daſht out with *ſtones*, *ſtaves*, *halberts*, *guns*, &c. in the hands of the *elders* of *Epheſus*: Maſter *Cotton* replies, *Elders* muſt keep within the *bounds* of their *calling* : But ſuch courſes were commanded the people of *God* by order from the *Judges*, *Deut.* 13. [10.] And where it was added, that comparing Things *ſpiritual* with *ſpiritual*, ſpiritual and myſtical *wolves* ſhould be *ſpiritually* and *myſtically* ſlaine. Maſter C*otton* replies, True, but in deſtroying *religion* they alſo diſturbe the *civil ſtate*, and accordingly are to be dealt withal by *civil Juſtice*, as *Achan* was for troubling *Iſrael*, *Ioſh.* 7. 25.

Truth. This acknowledgement of Maſter C*otton*, that theſe *wolves* muſt *ſpiritually* be killed, their *braines* daſht out by the *elders* and *Saints* might (if the *Lord* ſhould graciouſly ſo pleaſe) eaſily ſatisfie himſelf and all men, that the type of *Iſrael ſtoning* and *killing corporally*, is here fulfilled in all dreadful abundance *ſpiritually*.

Iſraels corporal killing types of ſpiritual.

Peace. Yea, but ſaith Maſter C*otton*, they diſturbe the civil ſtate as *Achan* did.

Achans troubling of Iſrael a figure of troubling the Iſrael or Church of Chriſt now.

Truth. I anſwer, *Achan* troubling of *Iſrael*, the people of the *Lord*, muſt figure out any ſuch like troubling *Gods Iſrael*, the *church* of C*hriſt*, for which he is accordingly to be ſpiritually ſtoned or executed: For, as touching the *civil ſtate* of the *nations* of the *world*, who can prove (and Maſter *Cotton* will not affirme) that they are as the *national church* of the *Iews* was? but being meerly *civil*, are armed with *civil power* and *weapons* for their *civil defence* againſt all *diſturbers* [139] of their *civil ſtate*, as alſo Maſter C*otton* confeſſeth the *ſpiritual ſtate* is furniſhed with *ſpiritual power* againſt all the *diſturbers* of its *ſpiritual* peace and ſafety.

Peace. Now whereas it was further added, that

under pretence of driving away the wolves, and preſerving the ſheep, that ſtreams of the blood of Saints have been ſpilt, *&c.* Maſter *Cotton* replies, belike it is a milky, and peaceable, and Goſpel-like Doctrine, that the wolves (*hereticks*) are to be tolerated, not an haire ſtrook from their heads; but for the poor ſheep, for whom Chriſt died, let them periſh, unleſs Chriſt mean to preſerve them alone with his immediate hand, and no care of them belongs to the civil *Magiſtrate.*

The duty of the civil ſtate in matters of worſhip.

Truth. I have here in this *diſcourſe* ſhewed with what honorable and tender *reſpect* every *civil Magiſtrate* is bound to honor and tender *Chriſt Ieſus* in his *chriſtian ſheep* and *ſhepherds,* but withall, that it is againſt *chriſtianity* for the civil *Magiſtrate* or *civil ſtate,* to imagine that all a whole *nation* was or ever will be called to the *union* of *Gods Spirit* in *communion* with *God* in *Chriſt*: Alſo, that it is againſt *civil juſtice* for the *civil ſtate* or *officers* thereof to deal ſo partially in matters of *God,* as to permit to ſome the freedome of their *conſciences* and *worſhips,* but to curbe and ſuppreſs the *conſciences* and *ſouls* of all others of their *free-born* people &c.

Peace. To end this Chapter: whereas it was ſaid, is not this to take *Chriſt* and to make him a *temporal king* by force? Is not this to make his *kingdom* of this *world,* and to ſet up a *civil* and *temporal Iſrael?* To bound out a new *holy land* of *Canaan*? yea and to ſet up a *Spaniſh inquiſition* in all parts of the *world,* to the ſpeedy deſtruction of *millions* of *ſouls,* and to the fruſtrating of the ſweet end of the coming of the *Lord Ieſus,* which was to ſave mens ſouls (and to that end not to deſtroy mens bodies) by his own blood.

To this Maſter C*otton* replies, when the *kingdomes* of the *earth* ſhall become the *kingdomes* of the *Lord* (*Rev.* 11. [15.]) it is not by making C*hriſt* a *temporal king*, but by making *temporal kings* nurſing fathers to the Church.

Concerning the kingdomes of the world becoming the kingdoms of Chriſt Rev. 11.

Truth. If the *Scripture* [At the ſound of the ſeventh *trumpet*] which is the laſt of the great *woes*, when the time of *Gods* wrath ſhall be come, be to be underſtood of the *removing* of the *kingdomes* of the *world* unto C*hriſt*, Maſter C*otton* cannot excuſe [140] C*hriſt Ieſus* from being a *temporal king*, and the kings of the earth to be but as inferior and *ſubordinate officers*: For if they adminſter C*hriſts kingdome* temporally, as *deputies*, *officers* or *Miniſters temporally*, he is much more then himſelf a *temporal king* and *Monarch*.

Peace. Methink salſo, if that committing of all *judgment* to the *Son* (*Iohn* 5. [22.]) be meant of *Temporal judgement* in *ſpiritual things*, then can he not be ſaid, not to be a *temporal king*, then can he not be ſaid (when thoſe words were ſpoken and ever ſince) not to have exerciſed a *temporal government*. The contrary whereof is moſt true, both at his firſt coming, and ever ſince, in all *generations*, it having been his *portion*, and the *portion* of his *followers* to be judged by this *world*, although *himſelf* and his judge the *world ſpiritually*, and will ſhortly paſs an *eternal ſentence* upon all the children of men.

Chriſt no temporal King.

Peace. Maſter C*otton* addeth, this will not ſet up a *civil* or *temporal Iſrael*, unleſs all the *members* of the *Commonwealth* be compelled to be *members* of the *church*.

Truth. If that will do it then *Chriſt* muſt be a *temporal king*, I ſay then, when the *kingdomes* of the earth ſhall become the kingkoms of the *Lord*, for ſhall not the *kings* of the *earth* compel all *Chriſts ſheep* to ſubmit unto *Chriſt Ieſus* their heavenly *ſhepherd?*

Peace. Yea ſecondly, will it not prove that all thoſe *commonweals*, where *men* are compelled *explicitly* or *implicitly* to be *members* of the *church*, are holy lands of *Canaan*, and if ſo, Oh that Maſter C*otton* and other worthy ſervants of *God*, may timely conſider, whether an explicit forcing of all men to come to *church*, becauſe men cannot be denied to be *members* (at leaſt by implication) with ſuch *members* and *congregations*, with whom they do ordinarily aſſemble and congregate, although they be injuriouſly (indeed but injuriouſly) kept off from *communion* and *participation* of all *ordinances*, which is indeed their *right* and *due* if they be (though but implicity) conſtrained and forced to partake of any.

Touching forcing men to church,

Againe (ſaith Maſter C*otton*) it is no S*paniſh Inquiſition* to preſerve the *ſheep* of *Chriſt* from the ravening of the *wolves*, but this rather (which is the practice of the diſcuſſer) to promote the principal end of the *Spaniſh inquiſition*, to advance the *Romiſh tyranny*, 141] *idolatry* and *apoſtacie*, by proclaiming *impunity* to their whoriſh and wolviſh *emiſſaries*.

Truth. If the Nations of the world muſt judge (as they muſt by Maſter *Cottons* doctrine) who are *Chriſts ſheep*, and who are *wolves*, which is a *whore* (ſpiritually) and which the true S*pouſe* of *Chriſt*, and accordingly perſecute the *whores* and *wolves*, this then

A Spanish Inquisition all the world.

they must do according to their *conscience*, or else (as Master *Cotton* elsewhere) they must suspend. What is this but either to set up a *Spanish inquisition* in all *territories*, or else to hang up all matters of *religion* (by this *suspension* he speakes of) untill the *civil states* of the *world* become *christian*, and godly, and able to judge, *&c.* and what is this in effect, but to practise the very thing which he chargeth on the discusser, to wit, a proclaiming an *impunity*, all the world over, except only in some very few and rare places, where some few *godly Magistrates* may be found rightly informed, that is according to his own *conscience* and *religion.*

A twofold fire kindled.

Peace. Yea further (which I cannot without great horror observe) what is this but to give a woful occasion at least to all *Magistrates* in the world (who will not suspend their bloody hands from *persecuting*, until Master *Cotton* shall absolve them from their *suspension*, and declare them *godly*, and informed, and fit to draw their swords in matters of *religion*) I say occasion (at least) to all the *civil powers* in the *world*, to persecute (as most commonly they have ever done and do) *Christ* himself, the *Son* of *God* in his poor *Saints* and *servants.*

That may consume the kindlers.

Truth. Yea, if Master *Cotton* and his *friends* of his *conscience* should be cast by *Gods providence* (whose *wheels* turn about continually in the depth of his *councels* wonderfully) I say should they be cast under the reach of opposite *swords*, will they not produce Master *Cottons* own bloody *tenent* and *doctrine* to warrant them (according to their *consciences*) to deal with him as a *wolfe*, an *idolater*, an *heretick*, and as dangerous an *emiſſary* and *ſeducer* as any whom Maſter *Cotton* ſo accounteth?

But laſtly, Maſter *Cotton* hath no reaſon to charge the diſcuſſer with an *indulgence* or *partiality* toward *Romiſh* and wolviſh *emiſſaries*, his judgement and practiſe is known ſo far different, that for departing too far from them (as is pretended) he ſuffers the
142] *brands* and bears the marks of one of *Chriſts* poor perſecuted *hereticks* to this day: All that he pleaded for, is an impartial *liberty* to their *conſciences* in *worſhipping God* as well as to the *conſciences* and *worſhips* of other their fellow-ſubjects.

Peace. When *Mathias* the ſecond king of *Hungary, Bohemia* &c. (afterward *Emperor*) granted to his Proteſtant *ſubjects* the *liberty* of their *conſciences*, doubtleſs it had been neither *prudence* nor juſtice, to have denyed equal *liberty* to all of them impartially.[1] But to finiſh this Chapter, Maſter *Cotton* laſtly affirmeth, that it is not fruſtrating of the ſweet end of *Chriſts coming* which was to ſave *ſouls*, but rather a direct advancing of it, to deſtroy (if need be) the *bodies* of thoſe *wolves*, who ſeek to deſtroy the *ſouls* of thoſe for whom *Chriſt* died, and whom he bought with his own blood.

Mathias the ſecond Emperor granting liberty of conſcience.

Truth. The place referred to, was *Luk.* 9. [56.] where the *Lord Jeſus* profeſſeth unto the raſh zeal of his *Diſciples* (deſiring that *fire* might come down from heaven upon the *refuſers* of *Chriſt*) that he came not

Chriſt came not to deſtroy

[1] Matthias, third ſon of Maximilian II, (1557–1619) in carrying out his policy of wreſting the crown from his incapable brother, Rodolph II., was obliged to promiſe the Proteſtants equal civil privileges. He was obliged to make conceſſions which were not altogether agreeable to him. Coxe, *Auſtria*, ii. 95–108; Schiller, *Thirty Years War*, 24.

mens bodies, though to ſave their ſouls. to deſtroy mens lives but to ſave them: from whence it appears that *Chriſt Jeſus* had no ſuch intent (as Maſter *Cotton* ſeems to make him to have had) to wit, to ſave *ſouls* by deſtroying of *bodies*: but to ſave *ſoul* and *body*, and that for *ſoul* ſake, for *religion ſake*, for his ſake, the *bodies* of none ſhould be deſtroyed, but permitted to enjoy a temporal being, which alſo might prove a means of their *eternal life* and *ſalvation*, as it may be was the very caſe of ſome of thoſe *Samaritans*.

Examination of CHAP. XLIV.

Peace.

Chriſtian weapons conſidered. THe next Scripture produced by the priſoner againſt *perſecution* for cauſe of *conſcience* was 2 *Cor.* 10. The weapons of our *warfare* are not *carnal*, but mighty through *God*, &c. unto which Maſter *Cotton* anſwers, that he ſpeaks not there of *civil Magiſtrates*.

It was replied, True, for in ſpiritual things the *civil weapons* were improper, though in *civil* things moſt proper and ſuitable.

Maſter *Cotton* now replying grants, that it is indeed improper [143] for a *Magiſtrate* to draw his *ſword* in matters *ſpiritual*, yet ſaith he, about matters ſpiritual they may, as to *protect* in peace, and to *ſtave* of *diſturbers* and *deſtroyers* of them: And he adds, if it were unfitting for *carpenters* to bring *axes* and *hammers* to build up the ſpiritual *kingdome* of the *church* of *Chriſt*, yet their tooles are fit to build *Scaffolds* for *hearing*.

Truth. It is ſtrange, and in my underſtanding ſuits not with the reſt of Maſter *Cottons* diſcurſe, to wit, that which Maſter *Cotton* here acknowledgeth, that a *Magiſtrate* is not to draw his ſword in ſpiritual things, but only about them: when throughout the *diſcourſe* he maintaines, that the *Magiſtrate* muſt ſuppreſs the *heretick*, *blaſphemer*, *idolater*, *ſeducer*, that he muſt reforme the *church*, puniſh the *apoſtate*, and keep the *church* in her *purity*; which whether they be *ſpiritual matters* or no, let ſuch as be ſpiritual judge.

Peace. He is (ſaith Maſter *Cotton*) to draw his *ſword about* ſpiritual matters, to protect in peace, as a *carpenter* may build *Scaffolds*, &c.

A fallacious diſtinction of uſing the civil ſword not in, but about ſpiritual matters.

Truth. If Maſter *Cotton* mean *civil* peace, he knows we agree, for all the *officers* of peace and juſtice ought to attend that *work*. But if he mean *ſpiritual*, to wit, that by his *ſword* he is to provide, that no man diſpute againſt his *religion*, that no man *preach* nor *write* againſt it, let it be well weighed, whether the *ſword* be not now uſed in ſpiritual matters: As alſo whether in ſuch caſes and others before mentioned, the *civil Magiſtrate* be not bound by Maſter *Cottons doctrine* to interpoſe as *Judge* in theſe *controverſies*, to paſs *ſentence* and to puniſh whom he judgeth *delinquent*, notwithſtanding that both *parties* and both *religions* are *right*, and *righteous* and holy in their own *perſwaſions* and *conſciences*.

Peace. Beſide, I know you deny not *civil conveniences* in *Gods worſhip*, and (therefore when there is need upon occaſion) the help of a *carpenter* to build *Scaffolds*.

Truth. True, but ſince Maſter *Cotton* compares the work of the *Magiſtrate* to the building of a *carpenters* Scaffold, let us in the fear of *God* conſider, if this *ſimilitude* (like ſome S*caffolds*) be not all too weak, whereon to hazard ſo mighty a *weight* and *burthen:* For what ſhould we think of ſuch a *carpenter*, that 144] after he hath built his *Scaffold* for people more conveniently to hear the word of *God*, ſuffers no man to *preach* in the whole *country* (where his *Scaffolds* are ſet up) but whom he pleaſeth, nor no *doctrine* to be taught but what he liketh; no *church* to be gathered, no perſons to make up this *church*, no perſons to receive the *Sacrament* but what he approves of: yea and further, with broad *axes* and *hammers*, and other tooles of *violence*, ſhould compel all perſons (directly or indirectly) to come to *church*, to make uſe of his *Scaffold* &c. Whether this be not the true *ſtate* of the *buſineſs*, the *Carpenters Son Chriſt Jeſus* will ſhortly more and more diſcover, and break, and tumble down thoſe painted S*caffolds* and faireſt *houſes*, which are not built and framed according to the firſt moſt bleſſed *line* and *rule* of his holy *inſtitution* and *appointments*.

Strange Carpenters

Examination of CHAP. XLV.

Peace.

UPon the unfitneſs (alleadged) of *ſpiritual weapons* to batter a *natural* or *artificial* hold, and conſequently the unfitneſs of *natural* and *carnal* weapons to batter the *ſpiritual* ſtrong holds in the heart, Maſter *Cotton* replies, that he allows not the *civil ſtate* to make uſe of their civil weapons to batter down *idolatry* and *hereſie* in the ſouls of men: But if (ſaith he) the *idolater* or *heretick* grow obſtinate, worſe and worſe, deceiving himſelf, *&c.* Now, he maketh not uſe of *ſtocks* and *whips* (which will but exaſperate the *malady*) but of *death* and *baniſhment*, that may cut him off from the opportunity of ſpreading his *leaven*, &c.

Truth. Methinks in this paſſage, Maſter *Cotton* reſembleth an armed man, who being almoſt convinced, or overcome by the *Spirit* of *God* in the former part of this paſſage (granting how unproper and unfit *carnal weapons* be in *ſpiritual* matters) yet being loath to yeeld, and holding up the goodneſs of his cauſe, he recovers again, and grows more fierce and violent: for bearing more gentle ſtroaks of *ſtocks* and *whips*, he cuts deeper with no leſs then quick and dreadful gaſhings of *death* or *Baniſhment*, that the world (were he one of the *worlds Monarchs*) may be rid of ſuch *idolaters*, *hereticks*, &c.

The bloody tenent in plaine Engliſh.

145] *Peace.* Oh, How can Maſter *Cotton* waſh this *Tenent* from *blood!*

Truth. Yea whether this *tenent* be not invented (as once that learned *chancellor* of *England* ſaid of all *violence* againſt *conſcience*) for an *end* or *intereſt*:[1] or as (that incarnate *devil*) the *Pope* ſaid more plainly of

All civil violence in ſpirituals, is for intereſt.

[1] "It was a notable obſervation of a wiſe father, and no leſs ingenuouſly confeſſed, that thoſe which held and perſuaded preſſure of conſciences, were commonly intereſted therein themſelves for their own ends." Bacon, *Of Unity in Religion*, *Works*, i. 13, Montague's edition.

the *fable* of *Chriſt*, for *honor* and *profit*, ſhall further be examined.

Peace. But who can read the *bloody colour* in this *book*, and yet believe what Maſter *Cotton* elſewhere ſaith, that he holds not *perſecution* for *cauſe* of *conſcience?*

Truth. Laſtly I aske, whether is it not the ſame skill and *power* of *Phyſick* and Surgery, that preſerves the *body* and each member in *health* and *welfare*, with that which cuts off (as Maſter *Cotton* ſpeaks) the *Gangrene* &c? and (ſince alſo tis in vaine to go about when the next way is as good or better) what means then Maſter *Cotton* to bring in the *Magiſtrate* uſing *ſpiritual* means in all lenity and *wiſdome* againſt *hereſie* and *idolatry* in the ſouls of men, ſince *death* or *baniſhment* will effect the *cure* ſo quickly.

Peace. To proceed, whereas it was urged, that although *civil weapons* were proper in *ſpiritual* matters, yet they were not *neceſſary* &c. Maſter *Cotton* replies, this is but a meer *pretence*, becauſe the diſcuſſer (ſaith he) denies all Church officers and Church *weapons*.

Chriſts ſpiritual weapons never wanting.

Truth. This formerly was cleered from all appearance of *pretence* becauſe during all the *reign* of the *beaſt* the diſcuſſer granteth the impregnable *power* of the *ſpiritual weapons* of *Chriſts witneſſes*, *Rev.* 11. although he ſee not extant the true form and order of the *kingdome* of *Chriſt Jeſus* which at firſt he was pleaſed to eſtabliſh.[1]

Peace. Maſter *Cotton* adds, Although *ſpiritual weapons* are mighty to purge out *leaven*, and to mortifie the *fleſh* of offenders, yet that is not a *ſuperſedeas*

[1] See 202d page, *ſupra*.

to *civil Magiſtrates* to neglect to puniſh thoſe ſins, which the *church* hath cenſured, if the perſon cenſured do proceed to ſubvert the *truth* of the *Goſpel*, or the *peace* of the *church*, or the *ſouls* of the *people*.

Truth. Why muſt the *Magiſtrate* ſtay until the party cenſured do proceed ſo and ſo? Why could not he have ſpared the drawing [146] forth of any ſpiritual *weapons*, ſince they are ſo effectual to do that which was not in the power and reach of the *ſpiritual?* Why was not the firſt *obſtinacy* (which merited the ſpiritual *ſtroaks* and *cenſures*) worthy of the *exerciſe* of the *civil Magiſtrates* power and zeale?

The civil ſword eſteemed more powerful then the ſpiritual.

Peace. Me thinks this is an evident *demonſtration* that men repoſe more *confidence* (however they deceive themſelves to the contrary) in the *ſword* of *ſteel* that hangs by the ſide of the *civil officer*, then in the two-edged ſword proceeding out of the mouth of *Chriſt Jeſus*, Rev. 1. [16.]

Truth. The truth is, ſuch doctrine makes *Chriſts ſpiritual ſword* but *ſerviceable* and *ſubordinate* unto the *temporal* or worldly *powers:* and preſents the *church* but making *eſſayes* and *trials* of that *cure* which *death* and *baniſhment* (gilded over with pretence of Gods glory, *&c.*) they think will not faile to effect, *&c.*

Peace. More plainly therefore writes another *Author* (of Maſter *Cottons* mind) thus*:* It is known by *experience* that one *reproof* or *threatning* from the *Magiſtrate*, hath been known to do more then an hundred *admonitions* from the *Miniſter*.

Truth. Yea no queſtion, to force a *nation* or a *world* of men to play the *idolaters*, *hypocrites*, &c. but

Gods true *ſervants* (of whom theſe three famous *Jews* are type, *Dan.* 3. [17.]) know that *God* whom they ſerve is able to deliver them from ſuch fiery *threatnings* and executions. But if he pleaſe to try them (as his *gold*) in ſuch *fiery tryals*, they will not bow down to invented *gods* or *worſhips*.

Peace. Methinks (dear truth) ſuch *Miniſters* deal upon the point and in effect with the *civil Magiſtrate*, juſt as that *ambitious Pope* with the *Emperors*, to wit, make them hold the *ſtirrop* while they mount, *&c.*[1] But I grieve, *&c.* What think you therefore of Maſter *Cottons* cenſure of the reſt of the diſcourſe in this Chapter, to wit, that it is but (as *Jude* ſpeaks) *clouds* without *waters*, *words* without *matter*, &c.

Truth. I will ſay no more, but this, Happily (through *Gods* mercy) Maſter *Cottons* cenſure may occaſion ſome to view what he deſpiſeth, yea and happily to finde ſome heavenly *drops* out of thoſe contemned empty *clouds*.

147] *Examination of* CHAP. XLVI.

Peace.

Rom. 13. *Conſidered*

THe 13 to the *Rom.* which the *anſwerer* quotes, is a *fort* of of ſuch importance, in ſo many *controverſies* depending between the Papiſt and *Proteſtant*, and between many *Proteſtants* among themſelves,

[1] Alexander III. and Frederick Barbaroſſa, met at Venice July 24th, 1177, to cloſe the ſtrife of the Popes with the imperial houſe of Hohenſtaufen. When the Pope left St. Marks the Emperor held his ſtirrup as he mounted. Milman, *Latin Chriſtianity*, iii. 537.

that all ſeek to gaine and win it: In this preſent controverſive I finde a wonderful *wreſting* of this holy Scripture even by many holy and peaceable (though herein violent and ſinful) hands: and let the charge be examined in the fear of *God*, whether ſlanderous (as Maſter *Cotton* intimates) or true and righteous.

Maſter *Cotton* freely grants, that this 13 to the *Rom.* exhorteth unto *ſubjection* to *Magiſtrates*, and *love* to all men, which are *duties* of the ſecond *table*: But yet withal he anſwers, that it will not follow that *Magiſtrates* have nothing to do with the *violation* of the *firſt table*; and further ſaith, that it is a plaine caſe that amongſt the *duties* of the *ſecond table*, people may be exhorted to honor their *Magiſtrates*, and *children* may be exhorted to honour their *Parents*; but will it (ſaith he) thence follow, that *Magiſtrates* have nothing to do with matters of *religion* in the *church*, or parents in the *family*?

The great fort of The civil Magiſtrate not charged with the keeping of the ſecond tables.

Truth. I anſwer, the *ſcope* of the *diſcourſe* was to prove, that it pleaſeth the *Spirit* of *God* in *Paul* here only to treat of the duties of the *ſecond table*, unto which *limitation* or *reſtriction* Maſter *Cotton* ſpeaks not at all, but only granteth in general, that it ſpeaketh of the *duties* of the *ſecond table*: And I ſtill urge and argue, that the *ſpirit* of *God* diſcourſing ſo largely in this *Scripture* of the *duties* of *Magiſtrates* and people, and treating only of *civil* things, in that *civil relation* between *Magiſtrates* and people, points as with a finger of *God* at their *error*, that wreſt this Scripture to maintaine the power of *Magiſtrates* and *civil ſtates* in the *ſpiritual* and *church eſtate* of the *kingdome* of *Chriſt*.

Peace. But what may be ſaid to Maſter *Cottons* argument?

Truth. I anſwer If people are bound to yeeld *obedience* in *civil* things to *civil officers* of the *ſtate*, *Chriſtians* are much more bound to yeeld *obedience* (according to *God*, to the *ſpiritual officers* [148] of *Chriſts kingdome*: But how weak is this argument to prove that therefore the *civil officers* of the *ſtate* are conſtituted *rulers* or *governors*, *preſervers* and *reformers* of the *Chriſtian* and *ſpiritual ſtate*, which differs as much from the *civil*, as the *heavens* are out of the reach of this earthly *Globe* and *Element*?

Examination of CHAP. XLVII.

Peace.

Calvin and Beza's judgement on Rom. 13.

AGainſt the Judgement of thoſe bleſſed *worthies* alleadged, (*Calvin* and *Beza*) confining this paſſage of *Rom.* 13. to the *ſecond table*, Maſter *Cotton* here oppoſeth their *judgement* for the *Magiſtrates* power in matters of *religion* in other writings of theirs, yea and from this very *Scripture*.

Truth. This their *judgement* for the *Magiſtrates* power was granted and premiſed before; yet let the *expreſſions* of thoſe *worthy* men (produced by the *diſcuſſer* on this Chapter) be faithfully weighed, and it will cleerly appear, that (as *James* ſpeaks) thoſe excellent men endeavoured to bring from the ſame *fountaines ſweet* water and *bitter*, which is monſtrous and contradictory.[1]

Peace. The pith of what Maſter *Cotton* further ſaith in this Chapter, I conceive is couched in theſe demands: Are not (ſaith he) all *duties* of *righteouſneſs* to man commanded in the *ſecond table*, as well as all *duties* of *holineſs* to *God* are commanded in the *firſt table*? Is it not a *duty* of *righteouſneſs* belonging to the people of *God*, to enjoy the free paſſage of *religion*? &c. Is it not an injurious dealing to the people of *God*, to diſturbe the truth of *religion* with *hereſie*, the *holineſs* of *worſhip* with *idolatry*, the *purity* of *government* with *tyranny*? and he concludes, If ſo, then theſe wayes of *unrighteouſneſs* are juſtly puniſhable by the *ſecond table*.

[1] Williams quoted from the Commentaries of Calvin and Beza to ſuſtain his view of Romans xiii. See *Bloudy Tenent*, 75–76, *Pub. Narr. Club*, iii. 153–155. Cotton replies, "how farre off Calvin's Judgement was to reſtraine Civill Magiſtrates from meddling in matters of Religion, let him interpret himſelfe in his own words (in his *opuſcula*) in his Anſwer to Servetus, who was put to death for his Hereſies at Geneva by his procurement. This one thing (ſaith he) ſufficeth me, that by the coming of Chriſt neither was the State of Civill Government changed: nor anything taken away from the Magiſtrate's office. Goe to then, that which Paul teacheth (Rom. 13. 4.) that he beareth not the Sword in vaine, ought it to be reſtrained to one kind onely? they themſelves confeſſe with whom I have to deale, the Magiſtrates are armed of God to puniſh open crimes, ſo that they abſtaine from matter of religion, that ſo ungodlineſſe may run riot by their connivance. But the Holy Ghoſt crieth out againſt this in many places, &c." "Heare now how Beza interpreteth the ſame Text in his Booke entitled *De Hæreticis, à Magiſtratu puniendis*. Paul witneſſeth ſaith he, that the Magiſtrate is God's Miniſter, who beareth the Sword to take vengeance on them that doe evill, Rom. 13. 4. wherefore one of theſe two muſt needs be, If Magiſtrates ſhould have no juſt power over Hereticks, either that Hereticks are not evill doers (which is ſo groſſe, that I thinke, it needs no Refutation) or elſe that Pauls ſpeech is to be reſtrained to a certaine ſort of evill deeds, to wit, ſuch as they call corporall ſinnes: of which diſtinction of evil deeds, I ſhall diſpute more largely hereafter." *Bloudy Tenent Waſhed*, 97–100. Cotton makes reference to both theſe works in his *Anſwer* to the Priſoner's Arguments. *Pub. Narr. Club*, iii. 52.

Unrighteouſneſs civil and ſpiritual.

Spiritual wars without civil diſturbance.

Truth. I anſwer, It hath pleaſed the *Father* of *lights* to open the eyes of thouſands of his ſervants in theſe later times to diſcerne a fine ſpun fallacy in the tearm of *unrighteouſneſs* and injury which being twofold *ſpiritual* againſt *religion* or *ſpiritual ſtate,* and 149] civil againſt the *worldly* or *civil ſtate*: It is no *civil injury* (which he grants is the buſineſs of this 13 to the R*omanes* in matters of the *ſecond table*) for any man to diſturbe or oppoſe a *doctrine, worſhip* or *government ſpiritual*: *Chriſt Jeſus* and his *meſſengers* and ſervants did, and do profeſs a *ſpiritual war* againſt the *doctrine, worſhip* and *government* of the *Jewiſh* the *Turkiſh* and other *Pagan* and *Antichriſtian religions* of all *ſorts* and *ſects, churches* and *ſocieties*: Theſe all againe oppoſe and fight againſt his *doctrine, worſhip, government*: And yet this war may be ſo managed (were men but humane *civil* and peaceable) that no *civil* injury may be commieted on either ſide.

Peace. We may then well take up (as Maſter C*otton* doth) *Beza's* own words on *Rom.* 13. 4. The *civil ſword* muſt take vengeance on them that do *evil*: It muſt therefore follow that *hereticks* are not *evil doers* (which is groſs, *&c.*) Or elſe that *Pauls* ſpeech is to be reſtrained to a certaine ſort of evil deeds, to wit, ſuch as they call *corporal ſins,* of which he ſaith, he diſputeth largely, elſewhere.

Truth. And ſo (through the help of the moſt *high*) ſhall I, in proving, that the ſecond ſort, to wit, *external, corporal, civil evils* between *man* and *man, city* and *city, kingdomes* and Nations (in this faln eſtate of mankind, wherein all *civility,* and *humanity* it ſelf are violated) are alone, and only intended in this *Scripture* by the holy Spirit of *God* and *Paul* his penman.

Examination of CHAP. XLVIII.

Peace.

TO the ſecond argument, to wit, the *incompetency* of thoſe *higher powers* to which *Paul* requires *ſubjection*, which in his time were the ignorant and Pagan *perſecuting Emperors*, and their ſubordinate *governors* under them, Maſter *Cotton* replies.

Firſt, It is one thing to yeeld ſubjection to the *righteous decrees* of *ignorant* and Pagan *Magiſtrates*: And another thing to obey their *ordinances* in matters of *faith* and worſhip, and *government* of the *church*: The former of theſe, *Chriſtians* did [150] yeeld unto the *Romane Magiſtrates*, even *ſubjection* unto the *death*; the other they did not, nor ought to yeeld, as knowing *God* was rather to be obeyed then *man*.

Truth. Subjection may be either to lawful *governors*, or but *pretenders* and *uſurpers*: Again *ſubjection* to *lawful rulers* may be in caſes pertaining to their *cognizance*, or in caſes which belong not to their, but another *court* or *tribunal*; which undue proceeding is not tolerable in all well-ordered *ſtates*.

The nature of twice ſubjection to civil powers.

We uſe alſo to ſay, that *ſubjection* is either *active* or *paſſive*: Now although we finde the *Lord* requiring and his *ſervants* yeelding, all *active* or *paſſive obedience* to the *Romane Emperors*, and their *deputies*, yet finde we not a tittle of the *Lords* requiring, or his people yeelding any kind of *ſubjection* to thoſe *Ro-*

mane Emperors or their *deputies* in the *matters* of *Chriſtian religion* except it be of ſo many hundred thouſand of their *bodies*, as the bodies of *Lambs* to the devouring jaws of thoſe *bloody lyons* and *devilliſh Monſters*, of more then barbarous cruelty.

Of the Roman Emperors power in ſpirituals.

Peace. But (Secondly, ſaith Maſter *Cotton*) although the *Roman Emperors* were incompetent *Judges*, yet the *Word* of *Chriſt* which commandeth a duty, commandeth alſo the neceſſary means which tend to that duty, and therefore giving them a power and charge to execute vengeance on evil doers, and that in matters of ſpiritual unrighteouſneſs againſt the Church, as in matters of civil unrighteouſneſs againſt the Commonweal, it behooved them to try and liſten after the true Religion, to heare and try all.

Truth. Maſter *Cotton* may here be intreated to take notice of his own *diſtinction* of *unrighteouſneſs* (which a little before he ſeemed to me to forget) for here he rightly diſtinguiſheth between *ſpiritual matters* of *unrighteousneſs* againſt the *church*, and *civil unrighteouſneſs* againſt the *Commonweal*: I therefore urge (as before) that the *civil Magiſtrate*, although he puniſh (according to his *civil place* and calling) *civil unrighteouſneſs* againſt the *ſtate*, yet he hath no *warrant* from Maſter *Cottons* argument, nor any from the *Lord Jeſus Chriſt*, to puniſh *ſpiritual unrighteouſneſs* againſt the *church*, and why then ſhould that tearm of *unrighteouſneſs* ſo generally and fallaciouſly go undiſtinguiſhed, and Maſter *Cotton* thus promiſcuouſly proclaime *idolatry* is *unrighteouſneſs*, *hereſie* is *unrighteouſneſs*, and therefore the *civil Magiſtrate* is bound to puniſh, *&c?*

151] 2. But oh that this *maxime* alleadged by Maſter *Cotton* might receive its due *weight* and *conſideration*! hath *Chriſt* commanded all means, as well as the *duty*? what then is the *reaſon* that ſince (as Maſter *Cotton* argues) that *Chriſt* hath commanded all the *civil powers* of the *world* ſuch a *ſpiritual duty*, and yet (I ſay) that all or moſt of the *civil ſtates* of the *world*, (beyond compariſon) are not furniſhed by *Chriſt* with thoſe chief *means*, of *grace* and *light*, whereby to *try* and *ſearch*, as Maſter *Cotton* exhorteth? Or (in ſome few places, where means of *light* are vouchſafed) with *hearts* and *ſpirits* unto ſuch a duty? May we not here ſay, that men make *Chriſt Jeſus* (in appointing ſuch officers, ſuch a duty, without furniſhing them accordingly) to forget that maxime of his Type *Solomon* (*Prov.* 26. [6.]) He that ſendeth a *meſſage* by the hand of a *fool*, cutteth off the *leg*, and drinketh *dammage*? Did not *Chriſt* know (as well as *John*) that all the *world* lay in *wickedneſs*, that all the *world* (in a reſpect) was then *Roman Paganiſh*, and that all the *world* in after ages would wonder after the *beaſt*, and become *Roman Popiſh*? Or can we imagine that *Chriſt Jeſus* did not foreſee the cutting off of *legs*, and the cup of *dammage* and loſs which he muſt drink, in ſending his minde and will into the world by ſuch fooliſh *inſtruments*?

Foule imputations againſt Chriſt Jeſus.

Peace. Surely Maſter *Cotton* would never adviſe the *civil ſtate* ty [to] ſend a weighty *cauſe*, and the *lives* of *ſouldiers* with ſuch *captaines*: Nor will he ſet an unruly *childe* under the *rod* of ſuch *teachers* or *reformers*:' He will not ſet forth his *Farme* or betruſt his *cattel*, no not his very *hogs* to ſuch keepers.

Chriſt permitteth Tyrants over his churches Saints, but appointeth none but his true ſpiritual Miniſters.

Christ Jesus his careful and most wise provision for his kingdome.

Truth. On the other hand, let the *government* of *Christs kingdome* be laid upon the right *shoulders*, and we shall finde the admirable *wisdome* and *care* of *Christ*, in the *affaires* of his *kingdom*, in appointing such *messengers* or *Apostles* to gather and found his *churches*, as also ordinary *Pastors*, *Shepherds*, or *teachers*, for their feeding and building up, *&c.*

The qualification of these the *Spirit* of *God* hath expresly and exactly recorded, wherein (according to the *principle* mentioned by Master *Cotton*) *Christ Jesus* his highest *care* and *wisdome* shines most gloriously in appointing the *means* as well as the *duty* it self.

Peace. But Master *Cotton* addeth, that the *causes* of *religion*, [152] wherein we allow the *civil Magistrate* to be *Judges*, are so *fundamental* and palpable, that no Magistrate studious of Religion in the fear of God, cannot but judge: such as cannot, they ought to forbear, *&c.* the exercise of their power, either in protecting or punishing matters of Religion till they learn so much knowledge of the truth, as may inable them to discerne of things that differ. This forbearance of theirs (saith he) is not for want of authority in their callings, nor for want of duty in their consciences, but want of evidence to them in the cause: In which case Magistrates are wont to forbear their exercise of power and judgement even in civil cases.

Truth. O the miserable *allowance* which Master *Cotton* hath brought the *kings* and *governors* of the *world* unto! *We allow them* (saith he) *to judge in such fundamentals and palpable causes*, &c. Oh with what *proud* and domineering feet do all *Popes* tread upon the *necks* even of the higheſt *kings* and *Emperors*! The *Magiſtrate* muſt wait at their *gates* for their poor *allowance:* They ſhall *judge*, and they ſhall not *judge*: They ſhall judge that which is *groſs* and *palpable*, and enough to hold the people in *ſlavery*, and to force them to ſacrifice to the *Prieſts belly*; but the more ſublime and nicer *myſteries* they muſt not *judge* or touch, but attend upon the tables of the *Prieſts infallibility*.

The Cleargies civil dealing with the civil Magiſtrate

Peace. Concerning *fundamentals* (*dear truth*) you have well obſerved, that ſince the *apoſtacy*, and the *worlds* wondring after the *beaſt*, even *Gods* ſervants themſelves (untill *yeſterday*) have not ſo much as heard of ſuch a kind of *church* (and ſo conſequently of ſuch a *Chriſt* the *head* of it) as Maſter *Cotton* now profeſſeth: For, no other *matter* and *forme* of a *church* (about which Maſter *Cotton* juſtly contends) was known I ſay among *Gods* people themſelves, (till yeſterday) then the *matter* and form of the ſtone or *woodden Pariſh-church*.

The nature of a church but lately diſcovered ſince the apoſtaſie.

Truth. Yea an happy man were Mr. *Cotton* could he rectifie and ſettle thoſe *foundations* which are yet ſo controverted amongſt *Gods* ſervants, to wit, the *Doctrine* of *Baptiſmes*, and laying on of *hands*.

Peace. You may alſo mention other *foundations*, which want not their great diſputes among the *ſervants* of *Chriſt*.

Truth. But further, that *Chriſt Jeſus* the *wiſdome* of the [153] *Father*, ſhould commit his *wife*, his *church*, to be governed in his abſence by ſuch who generally know not the *church* and *Saints* but cruelly and blaſphemouſly *perſecute* them with *fire* and *ſword*,

Monſtrous Suſpentions

and this with *charge* to ſuſpend moſt *Magiſtrates* of the *world*, and that all their dayes from *generation* to *generation*, as appeareth in all parts of the *world* which is ſuch a *monſtrous* and *blaſphemous Paradox*, that *common reaſon* cannot digeſt, nor ſuffer.

Peace. If *Merchants* and *owners* of *ſhips* ſhould commit their *veſſels* to ſuch men as wanted *ability* to *ſteer* their *courſes*, nay could not tell what a *ſhip* was, yea were never like to know all their dayes, ſurely it were not only matter of *admiration*, but even of *laughter* and *deriſion*, among all the ſons of men.

Truth. But further, How weak is that *diſtinction* which Maſter *Cotton* makes between *authority* of *calling*, and *duty* and *evidence* in the *cauſe*, when in all *judicatures* in the whole world, even amongſt the *Pagans*, there is neceſſarily ſuppoſed beſide theſe three, a fourth, to wit, *ability* or skill of *diſcerning* or judging in ſuch *caſes*: Now *cognizance* of the *cauſe* or *evidence* of the *cauſe* may be wanting in moſt able *judges*, where matters are not *proper* or not *ripe* for *hearing* and *trials*; whereas our diſpute is of the very *ability* or *skil* of judging, which Maſter *Cotton* himſelf confeſſeth is wanting, except in ſuch *Magiſtrates* as *fear God*, which will be found to be but a little *flock*, eſpecially compared with the many thouſands and ten thouſands of thoſe who neither know *God* nor *Chriſt*, nor care to know them, and this in all the *ſtates*, *regions* and *civil governments* of the *world*.

Spiritual courts and Judges.

154] *Examination of* CHAP. XLIX.

Peace.

COncerning *Pauls* appeale to *Cæſar*, it was argued that *Paul* appealed to *Cæſar* even in *ſpiritual* things; which that *Paul* did not nor could not do without the committing of five great *evils*, was pleaded in this Chapter, Maſter *Cotton* replies no more but this, The *reaſons* are but *Bulruſhes.*

Truth. Whether they are ſo or no, or rather the *Bulruſhes* and weak things of *God*, which the gates of hell ſhall never be able to ſhake, let the *Saints* judge in the fear of *God.*

Peace. Maſter *Cotton* adds further in this Chapter, that *Paul* pleadeth he was not guilty in any of thoſe things whereof the *Jews* accuſed him: thoſe things (ſaith he) concerned the *Law* of the *Jews* and the *Temple*, which were matters of *religion*; and for trial thereof, he appealed to *Cæſar.*

Truth. Lyſias the chief captaine in his letter to *Felix* the Governor (Chap. 24.) diſtinguiſheth (verſ. 29.) into *queſtions* of the *Jews*, *Law*, and (ſecondly) matters worthy of *death* or *bonds:* Now tis true the *Jews* charged *Paul* with offences againſt *religion*, their Law and the Temple: Secondly, againſt the *civil ſtate*, and with *ſedition.* For the firſt, although it is apparent that all the ſcope of *Pauls* preaching, was to exalt *Chriſt Jeſus*, and to preach down *Moſes* Law; yet at this preſent time of his apprehenſion, he had ſeen cauſe to honour *Moſes* his *inſtitution* at *Jeruſalem* (which was the wiſdome of *God* in him for a ſeaſon, for the Jews ſake, and his own *glory-*

Touching Paul appealing to Cæſar.

ſake:) And he had not at this preſent ſo much as diſputed with any in the *temple* (which was not ſo hainous a matter in P*auls* eye, as it is well known by his conſtant practice.) Secondly, for *matters* of *civil crime*, he pleadeth that he ſtirred up no man, not in the *Synagogue* nor *City*, and profeſſeth (Chap. 25.) that if he had committed ought worthy of *death*, he would not *wave* death: Tis true that *Paul* was charged by the *Iews* with both theſe kinds of offence, *religious* and *civil* (according to *Lyſius* his *diſtinction*) but that *Paul* appealed to *Cæſar* for *tryal*, that is, for *trial* of his *perſon* and *cauſe* in any *religious* reſpect, as it cannot be collected from the *Scripture* or 155] *Pauls* own words: ſo thoſe five reaſons againſt it, will evidently diſprove it, if they be well and throughly weighed in the *balance* of the S*anctuary* in the ſight and fear of *God.*

Pauls appeal to Cæſar.

Peace. I cannot in my underſtanding clear Maſter *Cottons* own words from deſtroying one another. Tis true (ſaith he) thoſe five ſins might have been charged upon P*aul* with ſome colour, if he had appealed to *Cæſar* whether his *religion* or *Miniſtery*, or *Miniſtration* were of God or no? But yet (ſaith he) he might appeal whether his *religion*, *Miniſtry* or *Miniſtration* were guilty of any *capital crime* againſt the *Law* of the *Iews*, or the *temple*, or againſt *Cæſar*.

Truth. Indeed what difference is there between the judging whether this *Miniſtery* deſerve death (ſuppoſing a falſe *Miniſtery* is worthy of *death*) or judging whether it be of *God*, or *falſe* and *idolatrous?* muſt not he that ſits judge of the *deſert* and *puniſhment*, judge alſo of the *crime* and fact, whether ſo or no?

P*eace.* When Maſter *Cotton* ſhall affirme (and truly) that the *Magiſtrates* of *Iſrael* were to judge a falſe *prophet* to *death,* will he not alſo grant that they were to judge whether ſuch perſons ſo charged were falſe *prophets* or no?

Truth. Yea, and when Maſter *Cotton* ſhall affirme (as unjuſtly) that *civil Magiſtrates* in all *nations* of the *world* ought to kill or baniſh *hereticks, blaſphemers, ſeducers,* out of their *dominions* and *juriſdictions,* doth he intend that they ſhall try and examine, whether they be ſuch and ſuch or no? But bleſſed be the *Father* of *lights,* who hath now opened the eyes of ſo many thouſands of his people to diſcern the *difference* between the *Forts* and *Bulwarks* of *God,* here called *Bulruſhes,* and thoſe *ſtrong holds* and high *imaginations* of men (erected againſt the *crown* and *kingdome* of the *Lord Ieſus*) which in Gods holy ſeaſon ſhall more and more be found to be but *ſtraws* and *Bulruſhes.*

156] *Examination of* CHAP. L.

Peace.

TO the arguing againſt the *Magiſtrates civil* power in *Spiritual* cauſes taken from the *nature* of the *Magiſtrates* weapons (a *material* earthly and worldly *ſword,* diſtinguiſhed from the two-edged ſword of *Chriſts ſpiritual* power in the mouth of *Chriſt*) Maſter *Cotton* replies,

Firſt, the *Magiſtrate* muſt governe his people in *Righteouſneſs,* and it is *Righteous* to defend his people in their *Spiritual* Rights, as well as in their *civil* Rights.

Spiritual rights and civil.

This *distinction* of *spiritual* and *civil Righteousness* doth truely anatomize the cause; It is righteous for the *Magistrates* to defend their *jubjects* in their *civil Rights*, for it is within the compass of his *calling*, being essentially *civil*: And unless we also grant him a *spiritual calling* and *office* (which is the Point denied) 'tis beyond his *calling* and compass to judge of what is *spiritual Right* and *wrong*, and accordingly to pass a *spiritual* sentence, and and execute and inflict *spiritual* punishment.

The civil Magistrate not bound to defend spiritual rights.

Peace. Methinks I may add, if the *Magistrate* be bound to defend his *Subjects* in their *spiritual* rights, then as he is bound impartially to defend all his *subjects* in their several and respective *civil Rights*, so is he bound as impartially to defend all his *subjects* in their several and respective *spiritual Rights*; and so accordingly to defend the *Iews*, the *Papists*, and all several sorts of *Protestants* in their severall and respective *consciences*; or else, he must sit down in *Christs* stead, and produce a *Royal* charter from the *New Testament* of *Christ Iesus* to judge dinifitively which is the onely right, to pass *sentence*, and execute *spiritual* punishment on all offenders, &c.

Peace. But Master *Cotton* adds a second, the sword was *Material* and civil in the *Old Testament*.

I answer, If Master *Cotton* granted a *national church* under the Gospel, his Argument were good; but when he grants that *national church* under the *Jews* (as afterward in this chapter he doth) did type out the *Christian church* or *churches* in the *Gospel*, why muſt he not grant that material Sword of the *Church of Iſrael* [157] types out the *ſpiritual ſword* of *Chriſt Ieſus*, proceeding out of his mouth, and cutting off offenders *ſpiritually* with *ſpiritual* and ſoul-*puniſhments?* And I add, As the ſword was *material*, ſo alſo was the *Tabernacle* and *Temple* worldly and *material*; which he denies not to be typical of the *ſpiritual Temple* of *Chriſt* and his *Church* in the New Teſtament.

Iſrael a type of the Chrriſtian Church.

Peace. Maſter *Cotton* adds (Thirdly) that the *Magiſtrates Sword* may well be call'd the *Sword* of *God*, as the Sword of War, *Iudg.* 7. [18.]

Truth. As it was call'd *Iehovahs* Sword in that typical Land; So muſt it needs be typical as well as the Land it ſelf, which is alſo called by the Prophets, *Iehovah's Land, Emanuels land*; which *names* and *titles* I think Maſter *Cotton* will not ſay are competent and appliable to any other *Lands* or *Countries* under the *Goſpel*, but onely to the Spiritual *Canaan* or *Iſrael*, the Church and people of God, the true and onely *Chriſtendome*.

The trme and odely Chriſtendome.

Peace. But (Fourthly) ſaith he, they are called Gods, and ſhall they not attend *Gods* work?

Truth. In the ſtate of *Iſrael* they were *Gods* deputies to attend the cauſes of *Iſrael*, the then onely *Church* of *God*: But Maſter *Cotton* can produce no parallel to that, but the *Chriſtian* Churches and people of God, not *national* but *Congregational*, &c.

2. Grant the *Magiſtrates* to be as *Gods*, or ſtrong *ones* in a *Reſemblance* to *God* in all *Nations* of the *world*, yet that is ſtill within the compaſs of their calling, which being confeſſed to be *eſſentially civil*,

the *civil work* of theſe ſervants of the *Commonweal* is Gods work, as well as *Paul* calls (in a ſence) the work of the ſervants of the *Family*, *Gods* work, for which he pays the wages, *Eph.* 5. [vi: 5, 6.]

Laſtly, for *ſpiritual* cauſes we know the *Lord Ieſus* is call'd *God*, *Pſal.* 45. [6.] *Heb.* 1. [8.] whoſe *Scepter* and *Kingdome* being eſſentially *ſpiritual*, the *adminiſtrations* which he hath appointed are alſo *ſpiritual*, and of an heavenly and ſoul *Nature*.

Peace. Maſter *Cotton* (Fifthly) adds, *Revel.* 17. [xi: 15.] The *Kingdoms* of the *World* are become the *Kingdoms* of the *Lord*, and of his *Chriſt*.

Truth. How the *Kingdomes* of the *World* ſhall become the *Kingdomes* of *Chriſt*, is no ſmal *myſtery* and *controverſie*; but [158] grant it to be true, that either *Chriſt Ieſus* perſonally, or by his *Deputies* the Saints, ſhall rule all the *Nations* of the *world* in hearing and determining all *civil Controverſies*: Yet why doth Maſter *Cotton* draw an Argument from this *Prophecie,* of what ſhall be in one *Age* or *Time* of the World, and to come, to prove an *Univerſal power* and *Exerciſe* of ſuch power in all *Ages* and *times* ſince *Chriſt Ieſus* his firſt comming to this day?

Peace. Me thinks Maſter *Cotton* may as well argue, that becauſe it was propheſied that a *Virgin* ſhould conceive, and bring forth a child in *Gods* appointed ſeaſon, that therefore all *Virgins* muſt ſo conceive and ſo bring in forth all *ages* of the *world*.

But, (Laſtly) ſaith Maſter *Cotton*, although the *nations* have not that typical *holineſs* which the nation of Iſrael had; Yet all the Churches of the Saints have as much truth and realty of *holineſs* as *Iſrael* had: And therefore, what holy care of *Religion* lay upon the *Kings* of *Iſrael* in the *Old Teſtament*, the ſame lyeth now upon Chriſtian *Kings* in the *New Teſtament*, to protect the ſame in their Churches.

Chriſt Jeſus in himſelf and his ſpiritual officers the onely Key of Iſrael.

Truth. Oh how neer the precious *Iewels*, and *Bargains* of *Truth*, come ſometimes Gods Saints, and yet miſs of the finding and going through with it! The *churches* of the New *Teſtament*, Maſter *Cotton* grants ſucceed the *Church* of *Iſrael*; The *Kings* and *Governours* therefore of the *churches* of *Chriſt* muſt ſucceed thoſe *Kings*. What King and Governours of *Iſrael* are now to be found in the *Goſpel*, but *Chriſt Ieſus* and his Servants, deputed in his abſence, which are all of a *ſpiritual* conſideration? What is this to the *Nations*, *Kings*, and *Governours* of the world; where few *Kings*, few *Nobles*, few Wiſe, are cald to profeſs *Chriſt*? Is not Chriſt *Ieſus* the onely King of *Iſrael*; and are not all his holy ones made *Kings* and *Prieſts* unto *God*? And unto his *Saints*, and his *ſpiritual* officers *Adminiſtration* in the midſt of them, is his *Kingdomes* power committed in his abſence. This *ſpiritual* power, however the *Pope* and *prelates*, *Kings* and *Princes*, *Parliaments* and *General Courts*, and their reſpective *Officers* of *Juſtice* (to be honoured and obeyed in *civil things*,) I ſay however they have challenged and aſſumed this *Kingly* Power of the Son of *God*, yet the *King* of *Kings*, *Chriſt* Jeſus hath begun to diſcover, and will never leave until he hath made it clear as [159] the Sun Beames, that he is robd of his *crown*, and will ſhake, and break, all the *nations* and *Powers* of the world until his Heavenly *crown* be again reſtored.

Chriſt Jeſus robd of his crown.

Examination of CHAP. LI.

Peace.

TO the fourth *Argument* (Rom. 13. [6. 7.]) from the *civil rewards* due to *Magiſtrates*; to wit, *cuſtom, Tribute*, &c. Maſter *Cotton* replies, That even the *contributions* of the *Saints*, are called *carnal* things; ſhall therefore their work be called *carnal?* It is true (ſaith he) the *contributions* of the *Saints* are called *holy*, becauſe they are given to God for his ſervice about holy things; So the *reward* given to *Magiſtrates*, is for their ſervice about *Righteous* things: And it is righteous (ſaith he) to preſerve the purity of *Doctrine, VVorſhip*, and *Government*, which if *Magiſtrates* do not, they do not deſerve all their *wages*.

Of cuſtome tribute, &c.

Truth. It is true that *money* or *monies-worth* is the ſame for value in the *contribution* of the *Saints*, and in that of *cuſtome, tribute*, &c; and yet Maſter *Cotton* grants a *Holineſs* of the *Saints contribution*, which he doth not affirme of *cuſtome, tribute*, &c.

Spiritual defence for ſpiritual right, &c.

There is alſo a two fold way diſputed, of preſerving of the purity of *Doctrine, worſhip*, &c.

Firſt, That which I plead for, by *ſpiritual weapons* appointed by *Chriſt Ieſus*.

Secondly, that of Civil *weapons, Force* of *Armes*, &c. which Maſter *Cotton* affirmes, and I deny to be ever appointed by *Chriſt Ieſus*, or able to accompliſh a *ſpiritual* end, but the Contrary.

Peace. Me thinks Maſter *Cottons addition*, not a little concernes my ſelf in the peace of all Citties and *Kingdomes*: for if (as Maſter *Cotton* ſaith) *Magiſtrates* ſhall not deſerve all their *wages* except they preſerve the *purity* of *Doctrine*, *worſhip*, &c. (which upon the point is that *Doctrine* Worſhip and *Government* Maſter *Cotton* approves of) what is this (in effect) but to deny *tribute*, *cuſtome*, *ſubſidies*, &c. to *Cæſar*, the *Kings* and *Governours* of the Earth, if they prove *Hereticks*, *Idolaters*? &c. I cannot ſee, but [160] this in plaine *Engliſh* tendeth to little leſs then the *Popiſh bloudy Doctrine* of depoſing *heretical Kings*, *&c.*

But Maſter *Cotton* further adds, that *ſpiritual wages* are to be paid to *Magiſtrates*, 1 *Tim*. 2. [1. 2.] to wit, *Prayers*, *Interceſſions*, &c. If therefore (ſaith he) the *Magiſtrates* ſuffer their Subjects to live a quiet life in *ungodlineſs* and *Diſhoneſty*, the *Magiſtrate* fals ſhort of returning *ſpiritual* recompence for the *ſpiritual Duties* and *ſervices* performed for them.

Touching prayer for all authority. 1 Tim. 2.

Truth. Thoſe prayers are not the proper *wages* paid to *Magiſtrates* for their work; for then ſhould they not be paid (as the *Spirit* of *God* there exhorteth) to all men, whether Magiſtrates or not.

Peace. And I may add, nor paid to thoſe *Magiſtrates* that are *Idolatrous*, *Blaſphemous*, *Perſecutors*: But thoſe *prayers* were to be poured forth for ſuch *Magiſtrates* (ſuch as moſt of the *Magiſtrates* in the *world* then were and are.) Thoſe prayers then were a general *Duty* to be paid to all men, and eſpecially to the *chiefe* and *principal*, *Kings* and all that are in *Authority*.

Truth. Now further, wherein it is ſaid, that ſuch Magiſtrates as ſuffer the people to live in ungodlineſs, fall ſhort in returning ſpiritual Recompence: I anſwer, By this *Doctrine*, moſt of the free Inhabitants of the *world*, who live in ignorance of *God*, and

Groſs Slavery.

in abominable *Religions* without him, muſt yet be ſuppoſed to chooſe and ſet up ſuch *Miniſters* or Servants of *civil Juſtice* amongſt them, who during their *termes* of *adminiſtration* or ſervice, ſhould not ſuffer their *Chooſers* and *Makers* to enjoy their owne *Conſcience*, but force them to that, which their *Officers* ſhall judge to be *Godlineſs*; but the *neck* of no free people can bow to ſuch a *Yoak* and *Tyrany*.

Civil Miniſters and Spirital.

Peace. But (laſtly) to that Argument of *Rom.* 13. from the *title* which God gives to *Magiſtrates*, to wit, Gods *Miniſters*, and to the *Diſtinction* of Spiritual Miniſters for *ſpiritual*, and *civil Miniſters* for civil matters; Maſter *Cotton* replies. If *Magiſtrates* be Gods Miniſters or *Servants*, then muſt they do his work, and be for *God* in matters of *Religion*: And further, ſaith he, *Magiſtracy* is of God, for *light* of Nature, and not onely for *civil* things, but alſo in matters of *Religion*; and he produceth divers inſtantces of *Pagans zeal* for their Religion, and worſhip.

The God of heaven hath ſeveral ſorts of Miniſters.

Truth. Becauſe *Magiſtrates* are Gods Servants, or Miniſters [161] *civil*, and receive *civil* wages for their *civil* ſervice; will it therefore follow that they muſt attend, and that chiefly and principally a *ſpiritual* work? That *noble-man* or *Lord*, that ſets one to keep his *children*, and another to keep his *ſheep*, expects not of him appointed to keep his ſheep (though a *Miniſter* or *Servant*) to attend upon the keeping of his *children*, nor expects he of the *waiter* on his *children*, to attend the keeping of his *ſheep*.

Tis true, that *Magiſtraſie* is of God, but yet no otherwiſe then *Mariage* is, being an *eſtate* meerly *civil* and humane, and lawfull to all *Nations* of the World, that know not God.

Tis true that *Magiſtrates* be of God from the *light* of nature; but yet, as the *Religions* of the World, and the *worlds* zealous contending for them, with perſecuting of others, are from the *Father* of lies and murther from the beginning; ſo ſeldome is it ſeen, that the *nations* of the world have perſecuted or *puniſhed* any for error, but for the *truth*, condemned for error.

Ordinarily the Truth is perſecuted.

Peace. Alas, who ſees not that all *nations* and people bow down to *Idols* and *Images* (as all the world did to *Nebuchadnezzars* Image.) If any amongſt them differ from them, it is commonly in ſome *truths*, which God hath ſent amongſt them, for witneſſing of which they are perſecuted.

Truth. Your obſervation (deare *peace*) is evident from the *caſes* of thoſe *Philoſophers*, by Maſter *Cotton* alledged; how weak and poor therefore is that *Argument* from the zeal of *Pagans*, *&c.* It is evident that ſuch *Builders*, frame by no other then that of *nature* depraved and rotten, and not by the *Goulden* reed of the glorious goſpel of *Chriſt Jeſus*.

162] *Examination of* CHAP. LI. [LII.]

Peace.

IN the diſcourſe concerning that terme, *Evil*, Maſter *Cotton* produceth *Pareus*, who makes that *Evil* puniſhable by the *Magiſtrate*, fourfold, *natural*, civil, *moral*, and *ſpiritual*.

Truth. That excellent and holy *witneſs* of Chriſt Jeſus (in many of his precious *truths*) *Pareus* being here produced without Scripture or *Argument*, for the *Magiſtrates* puniſhing of the fourth ſort of *evil*; to wit *ſpiritual*: nor anſwering my *Arguments* brought againſt ſuch an *Interpretation*, gives me occaſion of no further anſwer to Maſter *Cotton* or him in this place.

Touching the tearms Evil, Rom. 13.

Peace. Whereas it was alleadged, that the *Elders* of the *New Engliſh Churches*, in the model prohibite (*expreſly*) the *Magiſtrates* from the puniſhing or taking notice of ſome *Evils*, and that therefore as they aſcribe to the *Civil Magiſtrates*, more then God gives, ſo they take away and diſrobe him of that *Authority*, which God hath cloathed him with: Maſter *Cotton* replies, when we ſay that the Magiſtrate is an avenger of *evil*, we mean of all ſorts or kindes of *evil*, and not every particular of each kind; and further he ſaith, that *domeſtick evils* may be healed in a domeſtick way.

The civil Magiſtrate robbed of his civil power.

Truth. I readily concur with him, that the *Magiſtrate* may not puniſh *evils* that he knowes not of in a due and orderly *way* ſufficiently proved before him; as alſo, that many *domeſtick* evils are beſt healed in a *domeſtick* way; but yet that *Limitation* added, to wit, without acquainting the *Church* firſt) ſeems to bind the *Magiſtrates* hand, where no true *Church* of Chriſt is, to acquaint with ſuch things) yea and further where it is, why ſhould the *Magiſtrate* be denied, to exerciſe his power in caſes meerly *civil* (the old practice of the *Popiſh* Church?) And to whom ſhould the *Servant* or *Child*, or *Wife*, petition and complaine againſt *oppreſſion*, unleſs to the publike *Father*, *Maſter*, and *Husband* of the *Commonweal*? And therefore from their own Interpretation, they may well *ſpare* that ſtrict and literal *aception* of the word *evil*, and ceaſe to cry *Hereſie* is *evil*, *Idolatrie evil*, *Blaſphemie evill*, &c.

163] *Examination of* CHAP. LIII,

Anſwering to

Chap. LIII, LIV, LV.

Peace.

IN theſe three Chapters, the laſt Reaſon which the Author of the *Arguments* againſt *perſecution* produced, was diſcuſſed; to wit, that the *diſciples* of *Chriſt* ſhould be ſo far from perſecuting, that contrariwiſe they ought to bleſs ſuch as curſe them, *&c.* and that becauſe of the freeneſs of *Gods grace*, and the deepneſs of his *counſels*, calling home them that be enemies, *perſecutors*, *no people*, yea ſome at the laſt hour. In anſwer to which, Maſter *Cotton* complaineth that two of his *Anſwers* were omitted; and ſuſpecteth that as *children* skip over hard places, ſo they were skipt over, *&c.*

Truth. It is true, thoſe two *anſwers* were omitted, not becauſe the chapter was too hard, *&c.* but becauſe the Diſcuſſer ſaw (nor ſees) not any *controverſie* or *difference* between Maſter *Cotton* and himſelf in thoſe paſſages; and alſo ſtudying *brevity* and *contraction*, as Maſter *Cotton* himſelf hath done, omitting far more, and contracting three Chapters in one, in this very paſſage.

Upon the ſame ground, I ſee no need of mentioning his Reply in theſe three Chapters, wherein Maſter *Cotton* concurs in the point of the *neceſſity* of tolerating even notorious offenders in the *State* in ſome caſes.

Of tolleration which Maſter Cotton in caſes makes large enough.

P*eace.* The reſult of all *agitations* in this paſſage is this: Maſter *Cotton* denies not but that in ſome caſes a notorious *malefactor* may be tolerated, and conſequently (as I underſtand him) an *heretick*, *ſeducer*, *&c.* But that ordinarily it is not lawful to tolerate a *ſeducing teacher*, and that from the clearneſs of *Gods* command, *Deut.* 13. and from the reaſon of it verſ. 10, *Becauſe he hath ſought to turn thee away from the Lord thy God.* Withal he concludes, that all *Moſes capital* P*oliticks* are *eternal.*

Truth. Thus far is gained, that it wa. no vain exception againſt Maſter C*otton*'s general *propoſition*, to wit, that it is evil to tolerate [164] notorious *evil doers*, *ſeducing teachers*, *ſcandalous livers*, becauſe he ſees cauſe of toleration in ſome caſes.

P*eace.* Yea but, ſaith he, In ordinary caſes it is not lawful to tolerate, from *Deut.* 13.

The land of Iſrael a type.

Truth. I am of Maſter C*otton*'s minde: It is not lawful for *Iſrael*, that is, the Church of God, to tolerate: and the *reaſon* it pleaſeth the *Lord* to alleadge, is *eternal.* But what is this to the *nations* of the *world*, the *ſtates*, *cities*, and *kingdoms* thereof? Let Maſter C*otton* finde out any ſuch *land* or *ſtate* that is the C*hurch* and *Iſrael* of God. Yea Maſter C*otton* confeſſeth in a fore-going paſſage, that the Church is the *Iſrael* of God: Then muſt he with me acknowledge that this *Deut.* 13. only concerns the

Iſrael or *Church* of God, whom *Chriſt Jeſus* furniſhed with ſpiritual *weapons* againſt ſuch ſpiritual *offenders*.

Peace. But I wonder that Maſter *Cotton* ſhould ſay that *Moſes capitals* are *eternal*.

Truth. I wonder not, becauſe I have ſeen in print ſixteen or ſeventeen *capital* evils (a great part of them of a *ſpiritual* nature) cenſured with death in *New England*.[1]

And yet again, me thinks it is wonderful, ſince Maſter *Cotton* knows how many of *Moſes capitals* were of a *ceremonial* nature. The breach of the *ſabbath*, the not coming to keep the *paſſover*, (for neglect whereof the *Iſraelites* were to be put to death)

[1] In the *Body of Liberties*, the code of laws eſtabliſhed in Maſſachuſetts in 1641, the 94th Section contains the Capital Laws. This ſpecified twelve caſes in which the penalty of death is to be inflicted. 3 *Maſs. Hiſt. Coll.*, viii. 232.

In 1641 a pamphlet was publiſhed in London, entitled "An Abſtract of the Laws of New England as they are now eſtabliſhed." In 1655, the ſame work in a more complete form, with ſome changes in the title, was publiſhed by William Aſpinwall, who ſtates that this Abſtract was collected out of the Scriptures by Mr. John Cotton and preſented to the General Court of Maſſachuſetts. Winthrop, (*Journal*, i. 240,) under date of October, 1636, ſays: "Mr. Cotton did this court preſent a Model of Moſes his Judicials, compiled in an exact method, which were taken into further conſideration, &c." The Abſtract was probably this "Model" of Cotton's, by ſome error printed as if the code was actually adopted. It has been ſuppoſed to be the baſis of the Body of Liberties. But they have very little reſemblance, and we know that the Body of Liberties was compoſed, not by Cotton, but by Ward of Ipſwich. Winthrop, *Journal*, 2. 66.

The Abſtract is printed in 1 *Maſs. Hiſt. Coll.*, v. 173–187. Chapter VII. is of Capital crimes, and enumerates twenty-four caſes which are to be puniſhable with death or baniſhment. Of theſe, "ſixteen or ſeventeen" are "cenſured with death." It was this "Abſtract" of Cotton's, without doubt, which Williams had "ſeen in print." Blackſtone ſays that in England, in his time, no leſs than 160 crimes were declared by act of Parliament worthy of inſtant death. *Commentaries*, iv. 18. The Plymouth code, adopted in 1636, recognized eight capital offences. Brigham, *Compact, Laws, &c.*

how can Master *Cotton* make these *eternal* in all nations?

Peace. How many *millions* of *millions* of Heads (and not a few of the highest) in our own and other *Nations*, would soon feel the *capital calamity* of such a *capital bloody* Tenent, if Master *Cotton* swayed the *Scepter* of some of the worlds former or present *Cæsars?*

Truth. And yet I readily affirm, that *spiritually* and *mystically* in the *Church* and *Kingdom* of *Christ*, such evils are to be spiritually (and so eternally) punished.

165] CHAP. LIV, Replying to Chap. LIV. *Examined.*

Peace.

IN this 56 Chap. were observed two *evils* in Mr. *Cottons* conjoyning of *seducing teachers, and scandalous livers*, as the proper and adequate object of the *Magistrates* care and work to suppress and punish: Unto which Master *Cotton* replies, First, That he no where makes it the proper and adequate object of the *Magistrates* care and work to suppress seducing teachers, and scandalous *livers*, saying, that it ought to be the care of the *church* to suppress and punish seducing teachers, and scandalous livers in a *church*-way, as well as the *Magistrates* in a *civil* way.

Truth. By this Doctrine, Master *Cotton* will seem to deny it, to be the *Magistrates* proper and adequate object to puniſh ſcandalous livers, becauſe the *church* alſo (ſaith he) is to make it her work alſo.

Touching falſe and ſeducing Teachers.

It is true, if a ſcandalous liver be of the *church*, and fall into any ſcandal, ſhe by the *ruls* and *power* of *Chriſt* ought to recover him in the *ſpirit* of *meekneſs*: but yet the puniſhing of him with temporal puniſhment, who will deny it to be the proper work of the *civil ſtate*?

But (Secondly) what if the *ſeducing teacher*, or *ſcandalous* liver, be neither of them members of the Church (and the *church* hath nought to do to judge them without) will not Maſter *Cotton* then affirm the ſeducing Teacher, or ſcandalous liver to be the proper and adequate object of the *Magiſtrates* care and work?

Peace. When it was excepted againſt that things of ſuch a different *nature* and kind, as *ſeducing* Teachers, and ſcandalous livers, ſhould be coupled together at the *civil* Bar? Maſter *Cotton* replies, that both theſe agree in one common kind, to wit, they are *evil* and deſtructive to the common good of *Gods* people, which ought to be preſerved both in *church* and *Commonweal*: If a man ſhall ſay (ſaith he) that the *work* of *creation* on the ſixth day, was either of *man* or of *Beaſt*, is here any ſuch commixture.

Truth. Were Maſter *Cotton* the *worlds* Monarch, what [166] bloody *reformations* or deſtructions rather, would he fill the world withal, if he walk by ſuch rules and principles? for, what *religions* or almoſt men (all the world over) would he finde not oppoſite and deſtructive to *Gods* people.

Monſtrous Mixture.

2. But (Secondly) an hiſtorical narration of *Gods*

The great difference of evil and sin, as against the civil or spiritual estate.

works on man or *Beast*, Birds, *Fishes*, and all creatures *Cœlestial*, and *Terrestial* is one thing: But to mix them together in *doings* or *sufferings inconsistent* with, and improper to their kinds is another thing, far different and insufferable: As for a man to affirme that a man and a beast sin'd against their *Maker*, and therefore were justly punished with spiritual *blindness* and *hardness* of heart, loss of *Gods Image* &c. The same difference and no less is between transgressors against the *heavenly state* and *kingdome* of *Christ*, and the *earthly state* or *Commonweal* of *Cities, kingdomes*, &c.

Peace. Master *Cotton* adds, that it is more tolerable for seducing Teachers to *seduce* those who are in the same gall of *bitterness*, as for *Pagans* to seduce *Pagans* &c.

Truth. That is but in the degree, and so (according to his supposition) must be punished gradually; but what is this to prove *seducing* Teachers as well as *scandalous* livers, the joynt object of the *civil sword?*

Peace. Why doth Master [*Cotton*] say it is more tolerable for *Pagans* to seduce Pagans, Antichristians Antichristians? What Scripture doth he produce for this toleration, this *indulgence*, this *partiality*? All that is here said, is this, We look at it as more tolerable?

Gross partiality the bloody doctrine of persecution.

Truth. One thing is shroudly to be suspect in this matter, and that is a most *unchristian partiality*, in directing the sword of the *Magistrate* to fall heaviest on such seducers only, as trouble *his* conscience, his Doctrine, Worship, and Government: suppose in some of the Cities of *Holland*, *Poland*, or *Turkie* (where ſome freedome is) that *Jews*, P*agans*, *Anti-chriſtians* and *Chriſtians* (that is Chriſtians of Maſter *Cottons conſcience*) together with *Turkes* were com-mingled in civil cohabitation and commerce together: Why now ſhall that *Turke* that hath ſeduced one of Maſter *Cottons* conſcience to *Mahumetaniſme* be more puniſhed for that crime, then for turning a *Jew*, P*agan*, or Papiſt to his *Belief* and worſhip? What warrant ſhall the *Magiſtrate* of ſuch a *city* or place 167] finde to their *ſouls*, either for ſtriking at all with the *civil* ſword in ſuch a caſe? or elſe in deal-ing ſuch partial blows among the people?

Peace. I fear that *Gods* own people (of this opin-ion) ſee not the deceitfulneſs of their own heart, crying up the *Chriſtian Magiſtrate*, the C*hriſtian Magiſtrate*, Nurſing fathers, Nurſing mothers, &c. when all is but to eſcape the bitter ſweeting of C*hriſts* croſs, ſo daſhing in pieces the moſt wiſe *councels* of the *father*, concerning his bleſſed Son and his follow-ers, to whom he hath (ordinarily) alotted in this *world*, the *portion* of *ſorrow* and *ſuffering*, and of *raigning* and *triumphing*, after the *battel* fought and *victory* obtained in the world approaching.

Great ſhifting to eſcape Chriſts croſs.

Peace. But Maſter *Cotton* will ſay, that in ſuch fore-mentioned caſes, ſuch *Magiſtrates* muſt ſuſpend puniſhments for *religion*, &c.

Truth. I ſay, conſequently all or moſt of the *Mag-iſtrates* in the world muſt ſuſpend and none but ſome few of his *conſcience* (by his *doctrine*) ſhall be found fit, to uſe the *civil ſword*, in matter of *Religion*, and that is (in plaine *Engliſh*) to fight only for *his con-ſcience*.

Peace. But to proceed, it will be hard (ſaith Maſter C*otton*) for the diſcuſſer to finde *Antichriſtian ſeducers* clear from *diſobedience* to the *civil laws* of the *ſtate*, in caſe that *Antichriſt* (to whom they are ſworn) ſhall excommunicate the *civil magiſtrate*, and preſcribe the *civil ſtate* to the invaſion of his *followers*.

Truth. Moſt properly *ſeducing teachers* ſin againſt the *church* and *ſpiritual kingdome* of C*hriſt Jeſus*, which if erected and governed according to C*hriſt Jeſus*, ſhe is a Caſtel or Fort ſufficiently provided with all ſorts of heavenly *ammunition* againſt all ſorts of her *ſpiritual* adverſaries: yea and in the deſolation of the *churches* (during the *Apoſtacy*) C*hriſt Jeſus* (as I have elſewhere obſerved) hath not left his *witneſſes* deſtitute of terrible *defence* againſt all gaineſayers: But grant (what Maſter C*otton* ſuppoſeth) ſuch ſeducers from *obedience* to the *civil ſtate*, &c. Such as the Seminaries and bringers over of Pope *Pius* the 5 his Bul againſt Queen *Elizabeth* &c.[1] The anſwer is ſhort and plain, civil officers bear not the ſword in vain, when the *civil ſtate* is aſſaulted as the *ſpiritual officers* and *governors* of the church bear not in vain 168] the *ſpiritual* and *two-edged ſword* coming out of the *mouth* of Chriſt.

Chriſtien weapons.

Peace. Whereas now (ſecondly) there was obſerved by the Diſcuſſer in ſuch coupling of [*ſeducing teachers*

[1] Pius V. iſſued his Bull of excommunication againſt Elizabeth, February 25, 1570. It was not publiſhed in London till the 15th of May. Froude, *Hiſtory of England*, x. 59. It was then affixed to the gates of the Biſhop of London's palace by John Felton, who was executed for the offence. Hume, *Hiſtory*, v. 179.

A *Seminary* is "an Engliſh popiſh prieſt educated abroad." Halliwell, *Dictionary*, ii. 721.

& *ſcandalous livers*] a ſilent and implicite *juſtification* of the Jews and Gentiles their coupling *Chriſt Jeſus* and his *followers*, as *ſeducing teachers* with *ſcandalous livers*, *Chriſt* between *two thieves*, &c. The ſum of what Maſter *Cotton* replies, is, that the *Lord Jeſus* and his *followers* ſuffering under thoſe names, weakens not the hand of *Authority* to puniſh ſuch who are *ſeducing teachers* & *ſcandalous livers*.

Truth. It hath ever been the portion of the Lord Jeſus and his followers (for the moſt part theirs onely) to be accounted *ſeducing teachers*, *deceivers* and *cheaters* of the people, *blaſphemous* againſt God, *ſeditious* againſt the State; and accordingly to be numbred (as *Chriſt Jeſus* between *two thieves*) both in *eſteem* and *puniſhment* with ſcandalous and notorious *malefactors*; and this for no other cauſe, but cauſe of *conſcience* in ſpiritual matters, and moſt commonly for differing from and witneſſing againſt the ſeveral *State* and *City-Religions* and *Worſhips* wherein they lived.

Chriſt Jeſus between two Thieves.

Peace. If the *Jews* (notwithſtanding their fair *colours* to the contrary) walking in the doctrine of *Perſecution* for *conſcience*, juſtified their *fathers* for murthering the *Prophets*, &c. I cannot (*dear Truth*) but ſubſcribe to your ſorrowful obſervation that Maſter *Cotton* and others (otherwiſe excellent ſervants of God) in coupling *ſeducing teachers* and *ſcandalous livers*, as the proper object for the *civil ſword* to ſtrike at, they do no other but act the *Jews* true *Antitype*, coupling *Chriſt Jeſus* the *ſeducing teacher* with *Barabbas* the *ſcandalous liver* and *murtherer*.

Truth. Yea, and who ſees not how often *Barab-*

bas the *ſcandalous liver* is cried out of the *Magiſtrates* hands by the ſcandalous people, while *Chriſt Jeſus* in his ſervants is cried to the *Croſs*, to the *Gallows*, to the *Stake*, to *Baniſhment*, &c. Their Perſecutors alſo are applauded, for (not perſecuting men for their *Conſciences*, but) *righteouſly*, *legally* (and with great ſorrow) puniſhing them for ſinning againſt their own *conſcience*, for diſturbing of the *civil State* and *peace*, for contemning of *Magiſtrates*, *Kings Queens*, and *Parliaments*, for blaſpheming *God*, and for ſeducing and deſtroying the ſouls of the people.

The horible Hypocriſie of all perſecutors.

169] CHAP. 55. *Replying to* CHAP. 66. *Exam:*

Chriſts charge to Pergamus *and* Thiatira *againſt Tolleration examined.*

Peace. THe Diſcuſſer admired in this Chap: how Mr. *Cotton* ſhould alledge (*Revel.* 2. [14.]) *Chriſts* charge againſt the *Church* of *Pergamus* for tollerating them that hould the *Doctrine* of *Balaam*, and againſt the *Church* of *Thiatira* for tollerating *Jezabell* to teach and ſeduce: Mr *Cotton* here replies, that he meant not in alledging thoſe Scriptures to prove it unlawfull for *Magiſtrates* to tollerate ſeducing *Teachers*, but unlawfull for *Churches:* adding that the Letter of the *Priſoner* was ſo ſtated, in *generall tearmes* that he knew not (upon the point) what *Tolleration* or *Perſecution* ſhould be meant or intended, otherwiſe then *generall* againſt all *Perſecution* for *Conſcience*, withall affirming that an unjuſt *Excommunication* is as true Perſecution as unjuſt *Baniſhment*.

Truth. It is true what Mr *Cotton* ſaith, An unjuſt *Excommunication* is as true *Perſecution* as an unjuſt *Baniſhment*, and therefore ſome may juſtly complaine againſt Mr *Cotton* and others, for practicing ſuch *perſecution* in both kindes, being not onely *baniſhed* from their *civill State*, but unjuſtly (and after the Popes way) *Excommuuicated* alſo, from their *Churches*, but of that more elſewhere.

Falſe Excommunication one kinde of perſecution.

2. We doe not in ordinarie *Engliſh* read, but that the word *Perſecution* is taken for *civill corporall violence* and puniſhment inflicted on the *body* for ſome ſpirituall and religious matter ; according to the Lord *Chriſt* his words to *Paul*, Acts 9. [4.] *Saul, Saul*, why *perſecuteſt* thou me?

The word Perſecution *how ordinarily it is taken.*

3. The paſſages in the *Letter* ſhew that the whole *ſcope* of the *Letter* was to contend againſt outward *violence* and *corporall affliction* in *matters* of *Conſcience.*

Peace. It may not be a loſt Labour (Deare *Truth*) to draw a taſte of ſome paſſages in the *Letter.*

Truth. For further ſatisfaction, my *paines* ſhall be a *pleaſure* ; and firſt

From the *Arguments* from holy *Scripture*, obſerve *Luc.* 9. [55.] the *Lord Chriſt* reproving his two *zealous Diſciples*, You know not of what *Spirit* you are of: The Son of Man is not come to deſtroy mens *lives*, but to ſave them.

170] Againe, That of the *Prophets*, *Iſaiah* [2. 4.] and *Micah*, [4. 3.] They ſhall breake their *Swords* into *Mattocks*, and their *Speares* into *Sithes*.

Againe, *Chriſts* charge unto his *Diſciples*, that they ſhould be ſo farre from *perſecuting* thoſe that would

Perſecution ordinarily implies corporall violence.

not be of their *Religion*, that when they were *perſecuted*, they ſhould *pray* and *bleſſe*, &c. [Luke 6. 28.]

Peace. Theſe holy *Paſſages* (Me thinks) are not unlike the Stones in *Davids* ſling, ſmooth and plaine enough, yet powerfull and dreadfull, both againſt this *Goliah Tenent* of *perſecution*, and alſo prove a corporall *perſecution* intended.

Truth. Now a taſte of the ſpeeches of ſeverall *Kings* produced by the *priſoner*.[1]

1. That of King *James*; *God* never loves to plant his *Church* by *Violence* and *Bloudſhed*.

Speeches of Princes againſt Perſecution.

2 That of *Stephen* King of *Poland*; I am King of *Men*, not of *Conſciences*, of *Bodies*, not of *Soules*.

3. Of the King of *Bohemia*; When ever Men have attempted any thing in this *violent courſe*, the iſſue hath been ever pernicious, and the cauſe of great and wonderfull *Innovations*.

4. Another of King *James*; That he was reſolved not to *perſecute* or *moleſt*, or ſuffer to be *perſecuted* or *moleſted* any Perſon whatſoever, for matter *Religion*.

In the third place, a taſte of the *Speeches* of the ancient Writers produced by the *Priſoner*.[1]

1. That of *Hilarius*: That *Church* which formerly by enduring *miſery* and *impriſonment*, was knowne to be the true *Church*, doth now terrifie others by *impriſonment*, *baniſhment*, and *miſerie*.

2. Of *Jerome*; *Hereſie* muſt be cut off with the *Sword* of the *Spirit*, Let us ſtrike through with the Arrowes of the *Spirit*; implying, not with other weapons.

3. Of *Luther* in his Booke of the *Civill Magiſtrate*;

[1] *Bloudy Tenent, Pub. Narr. Club,* iii. 31. 37.

The *Lawes* of the *Civill Magiſtrate* extend no further, then over the *Bodies* and *Goods*. And againe upon *Luk.* 22. It is not the true *Catholike church* which is defended by the *Secular Arme* or humane *Power*.

Laſtly, The *Papiſts* in their Booke for *Tolleration*; When *Chriſt* bids his *Diſciples* to ſay, *peace* to this houſe, he doth not ſend *Purſevants* to ransack or ſpoyle the houſe.

171] Laſtly, The *Priſoner* in anſwering ſome *Objections*, concludeth; It is no *prejudice* to the *Commonwealth*, if *Libertie* of *Conſcience* were granted to ſuch as feare *God* indeed: He alſo alledged that many *Sects* lived under the *Government* of *Cæſar*, being nothing hurtfull unto the *Common-weale*.

Peace. From these severall Taſts (Deare *Truth*) I cannot imagine how the *Priſoner* can be underſtood to caſt the leaſt glance unto ſpirituall *perſecution* or *proſecution*, as Mr *Cotton* in this Chap: calls it: But to end this Chapter: When as the *Power* of *Chriſt Jeſus* in his *Church* was argued ſufficient for *ſpirituall* ends, Mr *Cotton* grants both for the *healing* of ſinners, and for keeping of the *Church* from *Guilt*, but not for the preventing of the *ſpreading* of *falſe Doctrine*, among thoſe out of the *Church*, and in private among *Church*-Members: nor ſufficient to cleare the *Magiſtrates* of a *Christian State* from the Guilt of *Apoſtaſie* in ſuffering ſuch *Apoſtates* amongſt them, &c.

Truth. I have in other Paſſages of this Diſcourſe proved;

1. That *Chriſt Jeſus* (whiles his *Churches* and

Ordinances flouriſhed, and ſince the *Apoſtaſie* of *Antichriſt* in the hands of his *Witneſſes*) hath gloriouſly and ſufficiently furniſhed his Servants for all *ſpirituall* caſes of all ſorts, *defending*, *offending*, &c.

No Civill Chriſtian State. 2. That there is no other *Chriſtian State* acknowledged in the *New Testament*, but that of the Chriſtian Church or Kingdome, and that not Nationall but Congregationall.

Chriſts Sword. 3. That the *Apoſtles* or *Meſſengers* of *Chriſt Jeſus* never addreſſed themſelves by Word or Writing to any of the *Civill States* wherein they lived and taught, and were mightily oppoſed and blaſphemed. I ſay they never ran to borrow the *Civill Sword*, to helpe the two edged Sword of *Chriſt Jeſus*, againſt *Oppoſers*, *Schiſmaticks*, *Hereticks*. The *Lord Jeſus* was a wiſer *King* then *Solomon*, even *Wiſdome it ſelfe*, and cannot without great *Diſhonour* and *Derogation* to his *Wisdome* and *Love*, be imagined to leave open ſuch *Gaps*, ſuch *Leakes*, ſuch *Breaches* in the *Ship* and *Garden* of his *Church* and *Kingdome*.

172] *The Exam: of* Chap. 56. *replying to* 58. *&* 59.

Peace. TO the firſt obſervation, that Mr *Cotton* urgeth that *Princes* are nurcing *Fathers* to *feede* and *correct* (and conſequently muſt judge of *feeding* and *correction*, and all men are bound to ſubmit to ſuch their *feeding* and *correction*:) Mr *Cotton* ſayth, This is falſe and fraudulent ſo to collect, and theſe are *deviſed Calumnies*.

Truth. It will evidently appeare, how greatly Mr *Cotton* forgets the *Matter* and *Himſelfe*, when he ſo deeply chargeth, for all this he granteth in this his *Reply*, onely with this *Limitation*, that *Subjects* are bound to ſubmit to them herein when they judge according to the *Word.* This *Limitation* takes not away the *obſervation*, for it is alway implyed in *ſubjection* to all *Civill Rulers, Fathers, Huſbands, Maſters*, that it be according to the *Word.*

Peace. Yea but ſayth he, it is a Notorious *Calumnie* ſo to repreſent Mr *Cottons* dealing with Princes, as if he made his owne *Judgment* and *practice* the *Rule* of the proceeding of *Princes.*

Truth. Let it be laid in the *Ballance*, and ſeene "where the *Calumnie* or *ſlander* lies: *Princes* or "*Civill Rulers*, ſaith Mr *Cotton*, are *Fathers* to *feed* "and *correct*, and their *Judgment* ought therein to be obeyed according to the *Word.* Now ſome *Princes* and *Rulers* declare themſelves againſt Mr *Cottons Tenent* of *perſecution* for *conſcience.* Mr *Cotton* will anſwer; The *profeſſion* and *practice* of *Princes* is no *rule* to *Conſcience.* I reply, and ask, who ſhall judge of *Princes profeſſion* and *practice*, when they thus *feed* and *judge* in *ſpirituall* matters? whether their *profeſſion* and *practice* be according to the *Word* or no? Mr *Cotton* (when *Princes* are alleadged againſt his *judgment* and *conſcience*) pleads, that *Princes profeſſion* and *practice* is no rule: Let all men judge whether his *judgment* and *conſcience* be not made the *Rule* to the *conſciences* and *practices* of *Princes*, whom yet he makes the nurcing Fathers.

Nurcing Fathers dealt withall as children.

Peace. When it was further demanded, whether

M[r] *Cotton* and others of his minde could ſubmit in *ſpirituall* caſes to any *Magiſtrates* in the *world*, but onely to thoſe juſt of his *own Conſcience?* [173] He anſwers, they will ſubmit to any in *Active* or *Paſſive* obedience.

Active obedience cannot be given but to a competent Judge.

Truth. But how can M[r] *Cotton* ſuppoſe *Active obedience* in *ſpirituall* things to ſuch *Magiſtrates*, who are *Pagans*, *Turkiſh*, *Antichriſtian*, and unable to judge, and bound (by his *Doctrine*) to ſuſpend their Dealings upon *matter* of *Religion*, untill they be better informed? What *Active obedience* can I be ſuppoſed to give to him that hath no *Activitie* nor *Abilitie* to command and rule me? And muſt it not evidently follow, that *Active obedience* in theſe caſes (according to his *judgment*) muſt onely be yeelded to ſuch *Magiſtrates* as are able to judge the true *Religion* and way of *Worſhip*; That is, the *Religion* and *Worſhip* which he takes to be of *God*.

Peace. Whereas it was ſaid, will it not follow that all other *Conſciences* in the *world*, beſides their owne muſt be perſecuted by ſuch their *Magiſtrates* (were power in their hand)? M[r] *Cotton* replyes, no; except all Mens *conſciences* in the *world* did erre *fundamentally* againſt the *Principles* of *Chriſtian Religion*, or *fundamentally* againſt *Church-Order*, and *Civill Order*, and that in a *tumultuous* and *factious* manner; for in theſe caſes onely (ſayth he) we allow *Magistrates* to puniſh in matters of *Religion*.

Truth. I have and muſt obſerve the Evill of that *Diſtinction* between *Chriſtian Religion* and *Chriſtian Order*, as not finding any ſuch in the *Teſtament* of the Sonne of *God*, but finding *Church-Order* a *prin-*

cipall part of the *Chriſtian Religion,* as well as *Repentance* and *Faith,* Heb. 6. [1. 2.]

But (2.) grant once Mr *Cottons Religion* and way of *Worſhip* to be the onely true *Religion* and way of *Gods Worſhip,* and all other *Religions* and wayes of *Worſhip* falſe, how can that *Errour* be otherwiſe then *fundamentall?* And if other mens *Conſciences* attend not to Mr *Cottons convictions,* but obſtinately maintaine their blaſphemous *Religions,* how can the *Magiſtrates* of his *conſcience* be diſpenced with and abſolved from perſecuting ſuch *obſtinate Conſciences* throughout the whole *World* beſide?

Perſecutors, if it were in their power, would, and are bound to perſecute all Conſciences and Religions in the World.

Peace. When it was further demanded, if this were not to make Magiſtrates *Staires* and *Stirrops* for *themſelves* (the Clergie) to mount up in the ſeats and ſadles of their great and ſettled *Maintenance?* Mr *Cotton* replyes, this is rather to make them [174
Swords and *Staves* to puniſh them (if need be) *Hereticall Delinquencie:* 2. Their *Magiſtrates* themſelves fall ſhort of great and ſettled *Maintenance:* And laſtly, Himſelfe liveth upon no *great* and *ſetled Maintenance.*

Truth. It is true Mr *Cotton* allowes the ſame *Power* to *Magiſtrates* to puniſh all *Hereticks, Blaſphemers, Seducers,* one as well as another: But what if it ſhould fall out that his *Magiſtrates* ſhould declare themſelves for the *Pope,* or for the *Prelates,* or for the *Presbyters,* yea, or for ſome other way then is profeſſed: and left it free for each mans *conſcience* to *worſhip* as he believed, and to pay or not pay toward this or that *Worſhip* or *Miniſtrie,* according to his owne *perſwaſion* more or leſſe, *any thing* or *noth-*

All perſecutors hould the Popes tray-

terous Doctrine of depoſing hereticall Princes.

ing, will not Mr *Cotton* then plead that ſuch *Magiſtrates* themſelves (Apoſtatizing from the *Truth* of *God*, and turning *Enemies* (as the *Pope* clamours) to the holy *Church*) I ſay, that ſuch ought not onely to be accurſed with the leſſer and greater Cenſures of *Suſpention* and *Excommunication*, but alſo puniſhed with *Impriſonment*, *Baniſhment*, and *Death:* Or if they finde the mercy of *Life* and *Favour* of an *Office* (by ſome over-ruling *Providence*) will not Mr *Cotton* then pleade that ſuch *Magiſtrates* ought to ſuſpend their Power to hould their hands, and not to medle untill they be better informed, &c. Into ſuch poore withered *Strawes* and *Reedes* will the *Allowance* of *Swords* and *Staves*, Mr *Cotton* here ſpeakes of come to? Concerning the ſeats and ſadles of great and ſetled *maintenance* of *Magiſtrates*, the Diſcuſſer ſpake not, but heartily wiſheth their *Maintenance* as *great* and *ſetled*, as he knowes their *Labours* and *Travells* and *Dangers* be: He ſpake onely of *Miniſters* great and ſetled *maintenance*.

Peace. O *Truth*, this is the *Apple* of the *Eye*, the true cauſe of ſo much *combuſtion* all the *World over*, eſpecially *Popiſh* and *Proteſtants*.

The Popiſh and Proteſtant

Truth. Indeed this was the cauſe (as *Eraſmus* told the *Duke* of *Saxonie*, that *Luther* was ſo ſtormed at) becauſe he medled with the *Popes Crowne* and the *Monkes Bellies*.[1] To obtaine theſe warme and ſoft

[1] "Eraſmus met the elector of Saxony at Cologne, Dec. 5, 1520. 'What is your opinion of Luther?' immediately demanded Frederick. The prudent Eraſmus, ſurpriſed at ſo direct a queſtion, ſought at firſt to elude replying. He ſcrewed up his mouth, bit his lips and ſaid not a word. Upon this, the elector, raiſing his eyebrows, as was his cuſtom when he ſpoke to people, from whom he deſired to have a preciſe anſwer, ſays Spalatin, fixed his piercing glance

and rich *ſeats* and *ſadles* (who ever ſtand or goe on foote, or creepe, or beg, or Starve) the *Prelates* practices all Ages know. Yea and other *practices* of ſome of late, who (with the Evill *Steward* providing wiſely) firſt made ſure of [175] an Ordinace of *Parliament* for *Tithes* and *Maintenance*, before any *Ordinance* for *God* Himſelfe.

Clergie set the Popiſh and Proteſtant World on fire for their Maintenance.

Peace. This is that indeed which the *Politick State* of *Holland* well foreſaw, when they were lamentably whipt by the King of *Spaines* (and *Gods*) Scourge, *Duke D'alva*, into a Toleration of other mens *Conſciences:* The *Politick States-men*, I ſay, ſaw a neceſſitie of ſtopping their *Dominies* Mouths with ſure and ſetled *Maintenance* out of the *States* purſe. Hence it is the *Dutch Miniſters zeale* is not ſo hot againſt the *Toleration* of *Hereticks* in the *Civill State*, as the *Engliſh* hath been.

The Dutch *device to winne their Clergie to Tolleration of other Religions.*

Truth. To this purpoſe (ſweet *Peace*) how fitly did that learned *Prideaux*[1] once tell his Sons the *Oxford Doctors*, at one of their Superſtitious *Creations*, that ſince they could not *dig*, and were aſhamed to *beg*, they had great need (therefore) of ſetled *Maintenance*, This was but the Evil *Stewards* device, and (I adde) little better then ſtealing.

All that profeſſe to be Chriſts Miniſters, muſt Dig, or Beg, or Steale.

Peace. Yea but ſayth Mr *Cotton*, I live not ſo, &c.

Truth. One *Swallow* makes not a *Summer:* what

on Eraſmus. The latter not knowing how to eſcape from his confuſion, ſaid at laſt, in a half jocular tone: 'Luther has committed two great faults: he has attacked the crown of the pope and the bellies of the monks.'" D'Aubignè, *Hiſt. of Reformation*, iii: 166.

[1] John Prideaux (1578–1650) profeſſor and vice-chancellor at Oxford, was made biſhop of Worceſter in 1641. He adhered to Charles I., and was reduced to poverty. Wood, *Athenæ Oxonienses*, iii: 265–273. Fuller, *Worthies*, i: 279.

others have done and doe, and what *practices* have been and are for a forced ſetled maintenance (as firme and *ſetled* as ever was the *Pariſh maintenance* of *Old England*) hath been, to the ſhame of *Chriſtianitie*, too apparent: For Mr *Cotton* himſelfe, as I envie not the *fatnes* of his *morſells*, nor the *ſweetnes* of his *Cups*, but wiſh him as large a *purſe*, as I beleeve he hath an *Heart*, and a deſire to doe good with it: Yet it hath been ſaid, that his caſe is no *Preſident*, becauſe what he looſeth in the *Shire*, he gets in the *Hundredth*, and ſits in as ſoft and rich a *ſadle* as any throughout the whole *Countrey*, through the *greatnes* and *Richnes* of the *Marchandize* of the *Towne* of *Boſton*, above other parts of the Land.[1] The truth is, there is no Tryall of the good or Evill Servant in this caſe, untill it comes to *Digging* or *Begging*, or the third way, viz: of *couzening* of the great *Lord* & *Maſter Chriſt Jeſus*; by running to *carnall meanes* and *carnall weapons*, to force mens *purſes* for a rich and ſetled *Maintenance*.

[1] In 1633, William Wood ſaid of Boſton, "This town, although it be neither the greateſt nor the richeſt, yet it is the moſt noted and frequented." *New England Proſpect*, 38. In the ſame year a tax was laid upon the towns for public purpoſes, and Roxbury, Newton, Watertown and Charleſtown, were aſſeſſed as much as Boſton, namely, £48, while Dorcheſter paid £80. *Maſſ. Col. Rec.*, i: 110.

Edward Johnſon, writing about the ſame time with Williams, deſcribes the larger towns, and ſpeaks of Boſton as "being the centre town and metropolis of this wilderneſſe worke." He ſpeaks of it as "this city-like towne," "the buildings beautiful and large, and orderly placed with comly ſtreets, whose continuall inlargement preſages ſome ſumptuous city." "This town is the very mark of the land. French, Portugalls and Dutch come hither for traffic." *Wonder working Providence*, 42. 43. "Boſton, being the chiefeſt place of reſort of ſhipping, carries all the trade." *Do.*, 66. 208. 209.

Chap. 57. (*replying to* Chap. 60.) *Examined.*

Peace. COncerning *Princes* Mr *Cotton* addeth, that *Princes* out of *State policie*, doe ſometimes tollerate what [176] ſuits not with *Chriſtianitie* (as *David* did *Joab*) againſt their wills.

Unto this it was anſwered, that this agrees not with his former generall *Propoſition*, to wit, that it was evill to Tollerate *ſeducing Teachers*, and *ſcandalous livers*; Mr *Cotton* replyes; Yes, for *Moſes* laid downe in generall, Who ſo ſheddeth mans *blood*, by man ſhall his *blood* be ſhed; yet *Joab* was tollerated to live, &c.

Truth. If *Moſes* had ſaid; It is not lawfull to tollerate a *Murtherer*; and yet afterward had tollerated a *Murtherer*, his later *practice* would not have ſeemed harmonious to his former ſpeech, but *Moſes* did not ſo, and therefore I conceive is not rightly alledged.

Peace. Whereas it was further alledged, that that *State policie*, and *State neceſſitie*, which permitted the *conſciences* of *Men*, will be found to agree moſt punctually with the *Rules* of the beſt *politician* that ever the world ſaw (the L*ord Jeſus* himſelfe) who commanded the permitting of the Tares.

Mr *Cotton* replyes, that he is not againſt the permitting of ſome *Antichriſtians*, or falſe *Chriſtians*, unleſſe they maintaine *fundamentall* Hereſie againſt the *Foundation* of *Religion*, and that *obſtinately* after *conviction*, and withall *ſeduce* others: But for ſuch

Hereticks and *seducing Teachers*, they are none of those *Tares*, of which *Christ* sayth, Let them alone.

Besides, sayth he, If by *Tares* are meant grosse *offenders:* then the *speech* of *Christ*, *Let them alone*, is not a *word* of *command*, but a word of *permission* and *prediction*; like that *Luc.* 22. 36. He that hath no *Sword*, let him sell his *Garment* and buy a *Sword*.

All Antichristians are fundamentally opposite to Christ Jesus.

Truth. I answer, that there should be *Antichristians*, or false *Christians*, which maintaine not *fundamentall* Heresie against *Foundation* of *Religion*, I thinke is new to the *New Testament* of *Christ Jesus*, and to the *Tryalls* the holy *Spirit* proposeth by *John* in his *Epistles*, discovering such to be the *Hereticks* and *Apostates*, as deny the *Lord Jesus* (as all *Antichristians* or false *Christians* doe more or lesse) to be come in the Flesh the true *Messiah*, and anointed *King*, *Priest*, and *Teacher* to his *Church*.

Peace. If Mr *Cotton* will make good his word, to wit, that he will permit some *Antichristians* or false *Christians*, methinks [177] the whole *Tryall* of this *matter* might well turne upon this *Hinge*, so that the *true* or *false Christian* be tryed by the *Rules* of the *New Testament*.

Truth. If so, he must undeniably subscribe to this great and *Christian policie* of *permission* or *Tolleration:* " As for the *Exceptions* following [Unlesse they main-" taine Fundamentall Heresie, and unlesse they sin " actually] These pull backe againe with the Left hand what merciful *Freedome* he had given before with the Right.

Touching the Tares.

3. But lastly, by this *Interpretation* of, Let them alone, by way of *permission* and *prediction*, it appeares

that Mʳ *Cottons* Thoughts are not without *checks* and *doubtings* what theſe *Tares* might be: For (ſayth he) [if by *Tares* are meant groſſe *offendours*] whereas before he ſpent much precious time to prove the *Tares* to be a kinde of *cloſer Hypocrite.*

Moreover, all permiſſion is of *Evill*, for ſome *Good*, ſo he, the permiſſion of *Tares* for the *Wheate* ſake: In which reſpect (as I conceive) the good *Wheate* is not ſo tendred, nor the *Word* of *Chriſt* ſo attended to by ſuch, as preſume (in pretence for the good wheate ſake) to pluck up thoſe *Tares*, unto whom *Chriſt Jeſus* for the good *Wheate* ſake, hath for a Time granted a *permiſſion.*

Exam: of Chap. 58. *replying to* Chap. 61.

Peace. WHereas the Diſcuſſer profeſſedly waved any *Argument* from the *number* of *Princes* witneſſing in *profeſſion* or *practice* againſt *perſecution* for cauſe of *Conſcience*, Mʳ *Cotton* replyes, that this is a yeelding of the *Invaliditie* of the Argument: But 2. that he urgeth not the *number*, but the greater *pietie* and *preſence* of *God* with thoſe *Princes* who have profeſſed and practiced againſt *Tolleration.*

Truth. As I would not uſe an Argument from the number of *Princes* about an heavenly matter (as knowing that the *Kings* and *Rulers* of the Earth commonly minde their owne *Crownes*, *Honours*, and *Dominions*, more then *Gods*; and ſuch *Princes* as are

Policie ſtore, but

Pietie rare in Princes. called *Chriſtian,* uſe *Gods* Name, *Crowne,* and *Ordinances,* [178] as *Jeroboam* uſed *Gods Name,* and *Jezabell* uſed *Faſting* and *prayer,* for the advancement of their owne *Crownes,* and perſecuting of the *Innocent* and *Righteous*) So neither would I reſt in the *Qualitie, Greatnes* or *Goodnes* of any. That which I attend in this Argument is the *Ground* and *Reaſons* of their *Speeches*; which may alſo have this *Conſideration* to boote, that they are the *Speeches* of ſuch who ſit at the helme of great *States,* and were not ignorant of the *Affaires* of *States,* and what might conduce to the *peace* or *diſturbance,* to the *wealth* or *woe* of a *Common weale.* To their *Ground* and *Reaſons* therefore I attend in the next Chapter.

Exam: of Chap. 59. *replying to* Chap. 62.

Peace. IN this Chap. the *Conſideration* of the *Speeches* themſelves, Mr *Cotton* ſayth, he paſſed by, becauſe, either the *Reaſons* wanted waight, or did not impugne the cauſe in hand, as

A Speech of King James *conſidered.* Firſt, That *Speech* of King *James*; *God never loved to plant his Church by blood:* It is farre from us (ſayth Mr *Cotton*) to compell men to yeeld to the *Fellowſhip* of the *Church* by bloudie *Lawes* or *Penalties:* Neverthteleſſe, this hindreth not but that his *Blood* may juſtly fall upon his owne head that ſhall goe about to *ſupplant* and *deſtroy* the *Church* of *Chriſt.*

Truth. How light or how impertinent ſoever theſe *Speeches* may ſeeme to Mr *Cotton,* yet to others (fearing *God* alſo) they are moſt *ſollid* and *waighty.*

This Speech of King *James* ſeemes impertinent in this cauſe, becauſe (ſayth Mr *Cotton*) we compell no man by *bloudy Lawes* and *Penalties* to yeeld themſelves to the Fellowſhip of the *Church*.

I anſwer, as *Saul* by perſecuting of *David* in the Land of *Canaan*, and thruſting him forth of *Gods Heritage*, did as it were bid him goe ſerve other *Gods* in other *Countries*: So he that ſhall by bloudie *Lawes* and *Penalties* force any man from his owne *Conſcience* and *Worſhip*, doth upon the point, ſay unto him, in a language of *bloud*, Come be of my *Religion*, &c.

No Man to be forced from his owne Worſhip, &c.

179.] 2. *Peace*. Why ſhould not *Men* as well be forced to the *Truth*, as forced from their *Errours* and *Erroneous practices?* Since (to keepe to the Similitude) it is the ſame *Power* that ſets a *plant*, and plucks up *weedes*, which is true (myſtically) in the *ſpirituall worke* of *Chriſt Jeſus*, in his heavenly planting by his *Word* and *Spirit*.

3. *Truth*. I adde, if men be compelled to come to *Church* under ſuch a *penaltie*, for *Abſence* (as hath been practiced in *Old* and *New England*)[1] How can Mr *Cotton* ſay, there is no forcing to the *Fellowſhip* of the *church*; when (howſoever with the *Papiſts*) he makes ſo great difference, which *Chriſt* never made, between the *Lords Supper*, and the *Word* and *Prayer*, and ſay, that men may be forced to the hearing of the *Word*, but not to the *Supper*. Yet the *conſciences* of *thouſands* will teſtifie, that it is as truely grievous to them to be forced to the one as to the other, and that they had as lief be forced to

Touching compelling to come to Church and to heare.

[1] See note, *Bloudy Tenent*, 101, *Pub. Narr. Club*, iii. 194.

the *meat* as to the *Broth*, to the more inward and retired *chambers* and *closets*, as into the *Hall* or *Parlor*, being but parts of the same house, &c.

Peace. And I may adde (Deare *Truth*) that the bloudie *Imprisonments*, *Whippings* and *Banishments*, that have cryed, and will cry in *New England*, will not be stild untill the cry of *Repentance*, and the *bloud* of the *Lambe Christ Jesus*, put that cry to *silence.* But to the second Speech of King *James*, No marvell (sayth M[r] *Cotton*) that I past by that Speech, to wit, [that *Civill obedience* may be performed by the *Papists*,] for I found it not in the *Letter*; and beside, how can Civill *obedience* be performed by *Papists*, when the *Bishop* of *Rome* shall *Excommunicate* a *Protestant Prince*, dissolve the *Subjects Oath*, &c.

A second Speech of King James.

Truth. I answer; King *James* professing concerning the *Oath* of *Allegiance* (which he tendred to the *Papists*, and which so many *Papists* tooke,) that he desired onely to be secured for *Civill Obedience*, to my understanding did as much as say, that he beleeved that a *Papist* might yeeld *Civill obedience*, as they did in taking this *Oath*, as quiet and peaceable *Subjects*, some of them being employed in places of *Trust*, both in his and in Queene *Elizabeths* dayes.

Papists *may yeeld Civill obedience.*

What though it be a *Popish Tenent*, that the *Pope* may so doe, and what though *Bellarmine*, and others, have maintained such [180] bloudie *Tenents*, yet it is no *Generall Tenent* of all *Papists*, and it is well knowne that a famous *Popish Kingdome*, the whole *Kingdome of France* assembled *in Parliament* in the yeare (so calld) 1610. condemned to the *Fire* the

The Parliament at Paris, *although Popish, yet condemned*

booke of *Johannes Marianus* for mainteining that very *Tenent.*[1] And two moneths after *Bellarmines* booke it ſelfe was condemned to the Fire alſo, by the *ſame Parliament* for the ſame deteſtable *Doctrine*, as the *Parliament* calld it, as tending to deſtroy the *higher Powers*, which *God* hath ordained, ſtirring up the *Subjects* againſt their *Princes*, abſolving them from their *Obedience*, ſtirring them up to attempt againſt their Perſons, and to diſturbe the common *peace* and *quiet:* Therefore all Perſons who ever under Paine of High Treaſon, were forbidden to *print*, *ſell*, or *keepe* that booke, &c.

Bookes and Tenents againſt Civill obedience.

Peace. This *paſſage* being ſo late, and ſo famous in ſo neere *a Popiſh Countrie*, I wonder how Mr *Cotton* could chaine up all P*apiſts* in an *Impoſſibilitie* of yeelding *Civill obedience*, when a whole Popiſh Kingdome breakes and abhorres the *chaines* of ſuch bloudy and unpeaceable *Doctrines* and Pr*actices*.

2. *Experience* hath proved it poſſible for Men to hould other *maine* and *fundamentall Doctrines* of that *Religion*, and yet renounce the *Authoritie* of the P*ope*, as all *England* did under King *Henry* 8. when the ſix bloudie *Articles* were maintained and prac-

All England *Papiſts, and yet the Pope renounced.*

[1] John Mariana, (1537–1624,) a Jeſuit, publiſhed at Toledo, a work entitled *De Rege et Regis Inſtitutione.* In the ſixth chapter he conſiders the queſtion whether it is lawful to kill a tyrant, and approves the aſſaſſination of Henry III. It is ſaid to have excited Ravaillac to the aſſaſſination of Henry IV. As ſtated in the text, it was burned by decree of the Parliament at Paris, in 1610. Bayle, *Dict*, IV. 127.

The treatise of Bellarmine, was entitled *Tractatus de poteſtate ſummi Pontificis in Temporalibus adverſus Gulielmum Barclaium*, and was printed at Rome, in 1610. Bayle quotes Mayer as ſaying: "The executioner already began to light the fire to puniſh the book and its author, had not the diſpoſition of the Queen, influenced by the repeated and inceſſant intreaties of the Jeſuits extinguished it." *Dictionary*, 1: 732.

ticed, and in them the *Subſtance* of that *Idolatrous Religion*, although the Power of the P*ope* of *Rome* was generally acknowledged no other, then of a forreigne *Biſhop* in his owne *Dioceſſe*.[1]

A twofold holding the Pope as Head.

3. But grant the *Engliſh Catholicks* maintaine the Supreame *Authoritie* of the *Pope*, even in *England*, it muſt be conſidered and declared how farre: If ſo farre, as to owne his Power of abſolving from *obedience* (againſt which the aforeſaid P*arliament* of *Paris* declared) the *wiſdome* of the *State* knowes how to ſecure it ſelfe againſt ſuch Perſons. But if onely as *Head* of the *Church* in ſpirituall *matters*, & they give *Aſſurance* for *Civill obedience*, why ſhould their *Conſciences* more then others be oppreſſed?

P*eace*. M[r] *Cotton*, (as all men and too juſtly in this *Controverſie*) alledgeth the P*apiſts practices*, what ever *profeſſions* otherwiſe have been: So long as they hould the P*ope*, they are [181] ſure of a *Diſpenſation* to take any *Oath*, ſubſcribe to any *Engagement*, and of *Abſolution* for the *Acting* of any *Crime* of *Treaſon* or *Murther* againſt the chiefeſt *States-men*, and the *State* it ſelfe.

Truth. What is it that hath rendered the P*apiſts* ſo inraged and deſperate in *England*, *Ireland*, &c? What is it that hath ſo *imbittered* and *exaſperatea* their minds, but the *Lawes* againſt their *Conſciences* and *Worſhips?*

The two Siſters Lawes con-

Peace. The two *Siſters Lawes* compared, *Maries* and *Elizabeths*, concerning mens *Conſciences*, while *Maries* were certainly written with *bloud* againſt the

[1] See page 129, *Supra*.

Proteſtants, *Elizabeths* may ſeeme to be written with *milke* againſt the *Papiſts*.

cerning conſcience.

Truth. Deare *Peace*, *Chaines* of *Gold* and *Diamonds* are chaines, and may pinch and gall as ſore and deepe, as thoſe of *Braſſe* and *Iron*, &c. All Lawes to force even the groſſeſt *Conſcience* (of the moſt beſotted *Idolaters* in the world, *Jew* or *Turke*, *Papiſt* or *Pagan*) I ſay, all ſuch *Lawes*, *reſtraining* from or *conſtraining* to *Worſhip*, and in matters meerly *Spirituall*, and of no *Civill* nature, ſuch *Lawes*, ſuch *Acts*, are *chaines*, are *yoakes*, not poſſibly to be fitted to the *Soules neck*, without *oppreſſion*, and *exaſperation*.

Peace. It is no wonder indeed that the Brains of thoſe of the *Popiſh Faith* are ſo diſtempered and enraged by *yoakes* clapt on the neck of their *Conſciences*, when *Solomon* the wiſeſt obſerves it common: that Civill *oppreſſion* (how much more *Soule-oppreſſion*, the moſt *grievous* and *intollerable*) doth uſe to render the *Braines* of men (otherwayes moſt *ſober* and *judicious*) *madde* and *deſperate*. [Ecc. 7. 7.]

2. *Truth.* I anſwer (ſecondly) grant the *Practices* of the *Papiſts* againſt the *Civill State*, fowle, dangerous, &c. yet why ſhould there not be hope (according to the rules of *pietie* in *Scripture*, and *policie* in *Experience*) that the *coales* of *mercy* and *moderation* may melt the *Head* of an *Enemie*, as hard as any *ſtone* or *mettall*, and render *imbittered Enemies*, *loving Friends*, combined and reſolved for their common *ſafetie* and *Liberties*.

Coales of moderation and kindneſſe, may melt an Enemie, as David *melted* Saul, *&c.*

Thirdly, Againſt the feare of Evill *practices* the *Wiſdome* of the *State* may ſecurely provide, by juſt *cautions* and *proviſoes*, as of *Subſcribing* the *Civill*

Cautions for pre-

venting of diſturbance by Papiſts, *&c.*

Engagement; of *yeelding* up their *Armes*, the *Inſtruments* of *miſchiefe* and *diſturbance*; of being noted [182] (as the *Jewes* are in ſome parts) by ſome *diſtinction* of or on their *Garments*, or otherwiſe, according to the *Wiſdome* of the *State*. And without ſuch or the like ſufficient *cautions* given, it is not *Civill Juſtice* to permit juſtly ſuſpected *perſons*, dangerous to the *civill peace*, to abide out of places of *Securitie* and ſafe *Reſtraint*.

Peace. If ſuch a *courſe* were ſteered with the *Conſciences* of that *Religion*, yet are there ſome *Objections* waighty concerning the Body of the *People*.

Firſt, There will be alwayes danger of *tumults* and *uproares* between the *Papiſts* and the *Proteſtants*.

Sufficient proviſions are made in other Nations, againſt Diſtractions and Tumults from oppoſite Conſciences and Worſhips.

1. *Truth*. Sweet *Peace*, thou mayſt juſtly be tender of the quiet *repoſe* and ſecure *Tranquilitie* of all men, and with *All men* (if it be poſſible, as the *Scripture* ſpeakes) as thou art an heavenly daughter of the *God* of *peace* and *love*. But yet thou knoweſt the *Wiſdome* of the *Engliſh State* needs not be taught from abroad (where *Libertie* abroad is granted to the *Popiſh* or *Proteſtant Conſciences*) of making ſafe and ſufficient proviſion againſt all *Tumults*, and feare of *uproares*.

2. But ſecondly, it is too too fully and lamentably true, that the *Congregations* or *Churches* of the ſeverall ſorts of ſuch as in whole or in part ſeperate from the *Pariſh worſhip* and *worſhippers*, are farre more odious to, and doe more exaſperate a thouſand times, the *Pariſh Aſſemblies*, then the *Papiſts* or *Catholiques* themſelves are or doe: So that if the *People* were let looſe to take their choice of exerciſing *violence*

and *furie*, either upon a *Popiſh* or a *Proteſtant Seperate Aſſembly*, it is cleare from the greater *corrivation* [corrivalry] and *competition* (made by the *Proteſtants that ſeperate*,) to the true *Church*, true *Government*, true *Worſhip*, true *Miniſtrie*, true *Seales*, &c. the rage of the People would mount up incomparably fiercer againſt the one then the other. Hence it was the *Papiſts* ever found more favour with the laſt two *Kings* and their *Biſhops*, then the *Puritants* (ſo called) did, and the ſeperate *Aſſemblies* were not ſo maligned by them as the *Nonconformiſts*, nor they ſo much as the very conforming *Puritants*. And therefore ſuitably it was belcht out from a fowle mouth *Rabſhekeh*, a *Chaplaine* to one of the late *Biſhops*; A *plague* (ſaid he) on all Conforming *Puritants*, they doe us moſt miſchiefe. Notwithſtanding all this, and the bitter *Indignation* [183] of *People* againſt theſe *Sectaries* (ſo called) and their *Aſſemblies*, yet the moſt holy *wiſdome* of the *Father* of *Lights* hath taught the *Parliament* of *England* that wonderfull skill (in the midſt of ſo many *Spirituall oppoſitions*) to preſerve the *Civill peace* from the *dangers* and *occaſions* of *civill Tumults* and *Diſtractions*.

Neerer Competition & home-bred oppoſitions moſt of all exaſperate, &c.

The admired Prudence of the Parliament in preſerving Civill Peace.

Peace. Admit the *civill peace* be kept inviolate, yet how ſatisfie we the *feares* and *jealouſies* of many who cry out of danger of *Infection*, and that *Jezabels Doctrine* will leaven and ſeduce the Land &c. [?]

Truth. I will not here repeate what in other parts of this booke I have preſented touching that Point of *Infection*. At preſent, I anſwer;

Firſt, It is to me moſt improbable, that (except the *Body* of the *Nation* face about from *Proteſtaniſme*

Increaſe of Papiſts *unlikely in* England.

to *Poperie*) (as in Queene *Maries* dayes) that the number of *Proteſtants* turning *Papiſts*, will be great in a *Proteſtant Nation*, eſpecially if ſuch *ſecuritie* be taken, as was above-mentioned, and otherwiſe, as the *State* ſhall order, &c. together with ſuch publick *notes* and *markes* (before mentioned) on the People of that *Way*, becauſe of their former *practices*.

Secondly, Yea, why ſhould not rather the glorious *Beames* of the *Sunne* of *Righteouſneſſe* in the free *Conferrings*, *Diſputings* and *Preachings* of the *Goſpel* of *Truth*, be more hopefully like to expell thoſe *Miſts* and *Fogs* out of the *minds* of *Men*, and that *Papiſts*, *Jewes*, *Turkes*, *Pagans*, be brought home, not onely into the *common roade* and *way* of *Proteſtaniſme*, but to the grace of true *Repentance* and *Life* in *Chriſt*. [?] I ſay, why not this more likely, by farre, then that the *miſts* and *fogs* of *Poperie* ſhould over-cloud and conquer that moſt *glorious Light*. [?]

Peace. 'Tis true, the holy Hiſtorie tells us of one *Sampſon* laying heapes upon heapes of the proudeſt *Philiſtims*; of one *David*, and of his *Worthies*, encountring with and ſlaying their ſtouteſt *Gyants* and *Champions*, yet it is feared ſuch is the depraved *nature* of all *mankinde* (and not of the *Engliſh* onely) that like a *corrupted* full *Body*, it ſooner ſucks in a *poyſoned breath* of *Infection*, then the *pureſt Ayre* of *Truth*, &c.

Truth. Grant this, I anſwer therefore (thirdly) If any of many conſcientiouſly turne *Papiſts*: I alledge the *Experience* [184] of a holy, wiſe, and learned man, experienced in our owne and other *States affaires*, who affirmes that he knew but few *Papiſts*

Mr John Robinſon (*deceaſed*) *his Teſti-*

increaſe, where much *Libertie* to *Papiſts* was granted, yea fewer then where they were reſtrained: Yet further, that in his *Conſcience* and *Judgement* he believed and obſerved that ſuch Perſons as *conſcientiouſly* turned *Papiſts*, (as believing *Poperie* the truer way to *Heaven* and *Salvation*) I ſay, ſuch Perſons were ordinarily more conſcionable, loving, and peaceable in their dealings, and neerer to Heaven then thouſands that follow a bare common *trade* and *roade* and *name* of *Proteſtant Religion*, and yet live without all *Life* of *Conſcience* and *Devotion* to *God*, and conſequently with as little *love* and *faithfulneſſe* unto *Men*.

monie in a Manuſ: from Holland.[1]

Peace. But now to proceed; a third Speech of King *James* was, [*Perſecution* is the note of a *falſe*

A third Speech of

[1] John Robinſon died at Leyden, March 1, 1625. His firſt work was publiſhed in 1609. The only one iſſued after his death was a Catechiſm which he had prepared as an appendix to a work by Rev. W. Perkins, (1558–1602,) entitled The Foundation of the Chriſtian Religion gathered into Six Principles; which, by the way, probably anticipated Williams's doctrine in regard to the Six Principles of the Chriſtian Religion. See page 21 *Supra*. The firſt edition of this which has ever been found was printed in 1642, ſeventeen years after Robinſon's deceaſe. But the edition of 1655 has a preface written by him, and which would ſeem to have been taken from an edition publiſhed at Leyden during his life. The manuſcript from which Williams quotes in the text, was probably never publiſhed as Robinſon's, and we may reaſonably ſuppoſe it to be ſome letter of his, ſent to ſome of his Plymouth friends, which had come into Williams's hands. His works were republiſhed in London by the Congregational Union in 1851, in three volumes. Among his Eſſays written in the latter part of his life, when he was more liberal than in his earlier days, is one Of Religion and Differences and Diſputations thereabout. In it he ſays, "Men are for the moſt part minded for or againſt toleration of diverſity of religions, according to the conformity which they themſelves hold, or hold not, with the country or kingdom where they live. Proteſtants living in the countries of Papiſts commonly plead for toleration of religion: ſo do Papiſts that live where Proteſtants bear ſway: though few of either, ſpecially of the clergy, as they are called, would have the other tolerated, where the world goes on their ſide." *Works*, I. 40.

King James *conſidered.*

Church, the wicked are *Beſiegers*, the *Faithfull* are beſieged, upon *Revel.* 20.] Mr *Cotton* here grants, that it is indeed a Note of a falſe *Church*, but not a certaine One; for, ſayth he, which of all the *Prophets* did not the *Church* of the *Old Teſtament* perſecute?

Perſecution ordinarily the marke of a Falſe Church.

Truth. Mr *Cotton* granting *perſecution* to be a degree of *Falſehood* and *Apoſtacie*, as he doth in his following words, he muſt alſo grant, that where ſuch a *Doctrine* and *practice* prevailes, and the *Church* growes obſtinate after all the *Lords* meanes uſed to reclaime, ſuch a *Church* will proceede to further degrees, untill the whole be leavened with *Falſhood* and *Apoſtacie*, and the *Lord* divorceth her, and caſts her out of his *Heart* and *Sight*; as he dealt with *Iſrael* and *Judah*: And it will be found no falſe, but a dutifull part of a faithful childe to abhorre the *whoredomes* of ſuch an one, though his own *Mother*, who for her *obſtinacie* in *whoredomes* is juſtly put away by his heavenly *Father*, but of that (the *Lord* aſſiſting) more in its place.

Peace. Further, Whereas it was ſaid, that Mr *Cotton* had paſſed by King *Stephen* of *Poland* his *Speech*, to wit, the true *Difference* between the *Civill* and *Spirituall Government*, Mr *Cotton* anſwers, that it is true, that the *Magiſtrate* cannot command their *Soules*, nor binde their *Conſciences*, nor puniſh their *Spirits*: All that he can doe is to puniſh the *Bodies* of Men for deſtroying or diſturbing *Religion*.

Stephen *King of* Poland *his Speech.*

185] *Truth.* It is true, the *Lord* alone reacheth the *Soules* or *Spirits* of Men, but he doth it two wayes.

Firſt, Immediately ſtirring up the *Spirits* of the *Prophets*, by *Viſions*, *Dreames*, &c.

Secondly, By inſtituted *Meanes* and *Ordinances:* of which is the Queſtion: Now *Stephen* King of *Poland* profeſſed that he was *King* of *bodies*, and not of *Conſciences:* It being moſt true, that the *Lord Jeſus* hath appointed *ſpirituall Rulers* and *Governours*, to binde and looſe *Soules* and *Conſciences*, to wound and kill, Comfort and ſave alive the *Spirits* and *Conſciences* of Men. This power *Chriſt Jeſus* committed to his true *Meſſengers*; but oh, how many are there that pretend to this *Apoſtleſhip* or *Miniſtrie*, who yet have ſold away this *ſpirituall* Power to the *Earthly* or *worldly powers*, upon an (implyed ſecret) *Condition* or *Proviſo*, to receive a broken *Reed* an *Arme* of *Fleſh*, (inſtead of the *Everlaſting Armes* of *Mercy*,) to protect them.

The Spirituall Power of Chriſt Jeſus betruſted not with Civill but ſpirituall Miniſters.

Peace. With your leave (Deare *Truth*) let me adde a ſecond: If the *Magiſtrate* (as M[r] *Cotton* ſayth) puniſh the *body* for a *ſpirituall* offence, why doth he not puniſh by a *ſpirituall* power as a *ſpirituall Officer*, with a *ſpirituall Cenſure* and *puniſhment*?

Truth. M[r] *Cotton* will tell us that the *bodies* of the *Iſraelites* were puniſhed for *ſpirituall offences:* And we may againe truely affirme, that the very cutting off by the materiall *Sword* out of the *typicall* Land of *Canaan*, was in the type, a *ſpirituall puniſhment.*

Peace. M[r] *Cotton* is not ignorant of this, and hath often taught of theſe *Types* from *Paſſages* on *Geneſis* and other bookes of *Moſes*, &c.

Truth. The *Father* of *Lights* graciouſly be pleaſed to ſet home the *light* he hath vouchſafed him, & fix and imprint the beames thereof in his *heart* and *affections* alſo.

An Argument used in Parliament against the Persecuting Bishops.

Peace. This Argument (of puniſhing the *body* for the *ſoules* good) I remember was feelingly reſented by an honourable *Gentleman* in the *Parliament* againſt the *Biſhops*, urging how contrary unto *Chriſt Jeſus* thoſe *Prelates* were; for *Chriſt Jeſus* did make way for his working upon Mens *ſoules*, by ſhewing kindneſſe to their *bodies*, &c. but *Prelates* contrarily, &c.

Truth. All the *Angells* of *God* will one day witneſſe, that *Chriſt Jeſus* was never *Captain* to *Pope*, nor *Prelate*, *Presbyter*, no [186] nor *Independent*, *Emperour*, nor *King*, *Parliament*, nor *Generall Court*, who puniſh and afflict, perſecute and torture the *bodies* of *Men* under pretence of a *ſpirituall* and *religious* medicine.

Peace. Yea, but ſayth Mr *Cotton*, *Religion* is diſturbed and deſtroyed, what ſhall be done?

Of diſturbance of Religion.

Truth. *Religion* is diſturbed and deſtroyed two wayes.

Firſt, When the *Profeſſors* or *Aſſemblies* thereof are perſecuted, that is hunted and driven up and downe out of the *world:* Againſt ſuch *Deſtroyers* or *Diſturbers* (being Tyrants and Oppreſſours,) the *Civill Sword* ought to be drawen.

The Biſhops as Tyrants juſtly ſuppreſſed, and the Parliament therein proſpered from Heaven.

Peace. The drawing of the Sword of *Juſtice* againſt ſuch *Tyrants*, I believe hath prevailed in *Heaven*, for the *Parliaments ſucceſſes* and *proſperitie:* The turning from the *violence* that was in the hands of thoſe Men of *Bloud* the *Biſhops*, (as in the Men of *Ninivies* caſe) hath laid the long and violent ſtorme of *Fire* and *Bloud*, &c.

Truth. Yea let the moſt renowned *Parliament* of *England*, and all *England* know, that when they ceaſe to liſten to *Daniells counſell* to *Belſhazzar*, to wit, to ſhew *Mercy* to the *poore*, (even the pooreſt and moſt afflicted in the *World*) the *Conſciences* of Men, then is their *Parliamentarie Glory* and *Tranquillitie* eclipſed: Till then I confidently believe, their *Government* (which hath now ſo many yeares with ſo many *Wonders* continued) ſhall not be numbred, nor another fatall change ſurprize them.

Daniells *Counſel to* Bel-ſhazzar *preſerveth Parliaments & Kingdomes.*

But now (2) the *Diſturbance* or *Deſtruction* of *Religion* is *ſpirituall*, by falſe *Teachers*, falſe *Prophets*, by ſpirituall *Rebells* and *Trayters* againſt the *Worſhip* and *Kingdome* of *Chriſt Jeſus:* Againſt which *Diſturbers* or *Deſtroyers*, if *Chriſt Jeſus* have not provided ſufficient *ſpirituall Defence*, let *Moſes* (his ancient Type,) be ſaid to exceede him in *Faithfulneſſe*, *David* in holy *zeale* and *affection* to the houſe of *God*, and *Solomon* in *wiſdome* and heavenly *prudence*, in *ordering* the *Affaires* of the holy *Worſhip* of *God*.

Peace. But further, whereas it was ſaid, that to confound theſe (to wit, a *Civill* and *Spirituall Government*) was *Babell* and *Jewiſh:* M[r] *Cotton* replyes, *That* is *Babell* to tollerate and advance *Idolatrie*. 2. (Sayth he) though *Chriſt* hath aboliſhed a *Nationall Church-State*, which *Moſes* ſet up in the Land of *Canaan*, [187] yet *Chriſt* never aboliſhed a *Nationall Civill State*, nor the *Judiciall Lawes* of *Moſes*, which were of *Morall Equitie*, and therefore (ſayth he) If the true *Chriſts* bloud goe for the planting of the *Church*, let the falſe *Chriſts* goe for ſupplanting it.

Truth. I anſwer; *Babell* was infamous for *Pride*,

for *Confuſion* or *Diſorder*, for *Idolatrie*, for *Tyrannie:* Now let all perſecuting *Cities* and *Kingdomes* be examined and ſee if they have been cleare from any of theſe: and eſpecially from *Babells confuſion* and *diſorder*, from monſtrous mingling of *Spirituall* and *Civill*, the *Devills Worſhip* with *Gods veſſels:* It was no *Confuſion* in the *Nationall Church* of *Iſrael* for the Power of that *Nation*, in the hands of *Kings* and Civill *Rulers*, to purge that *Nationall Church* by *Nationall* force of *weapons* and *Death:* But ſince M[r] *Cotton* acknowledgeth that *Chriſt* hath aboliſhed that *Nationall Church*, and eſtabliſhed *Congregationall Churches*, (in ſome of which poſſibly may be no *Civill Magiſtrate* fearing *God*, for few *wiſe* or *noble* are called, and conſequently few *godly* or *Chriſtian Magiſtrates* profeſſing *Chriſt Jeſus*) What is this but *Babell* or a *Babyloniſh* mixture of the *Old* and *New Teſtament*, *Nationall* and *Congregationall Churches power* and *practices* together?

Touching the Nationall Church of Iſrael.

Peace. 2. What if *Chriſt Jeſus* have not aboliſhed a *Nationall Church State*, it is ſufficient that he hath aboliſhed a *Nationall Church.* And if ſo, then in *Church matters* thoſe *Nationall Judicialls*, and the uſe of thoſe *Nationall Weapons* and *Puniſhments*, in attending upon ſuch a *Nationall Church:* Yea what colour of *Morall Equitie* is there that all the *Nations* of the *World* (moſt of which never heard of *Chriſt*) ſhould be ruled by ſuch *Lawes* and *Puniſhments* as were *peculiarly* and *miraculouſly* given and appointed to one ſelected and culd out *Nation*, conceived, borne, and brought up (as I may ſo ſpeake) from firſt to laſt, by extraordinarie, and *miraculous diſpenſation?*

Iſrael *a miraculous Nation.*

Peace. There may be (ſayth Mr *Cotton*) *difference* between the *Nations* profeſſing *Chriſtianitie*, and other *Nations*.

Truth. There is indeed great *Difference:* There are two ſorts of *Nations* or *Peoples* of the *World*, which ſhall be *Fewell* for the devouring flames of the Lord *Jeſus*, 2 Theſſ. 1. [8.] Firſt, ſuch as know not *Chriſt Jeſus*, of which ſort the greateſt part of the *Nations* of the *World* (beyond all colour of compariſon) conſiſt. 2. Such as have heard a ſound, and make ſome profeſſion [188] of the Name of *Chriſt Jeſus*, and yet obey him not as *Lord* and *King*, &c. *Two ſorts of the Nations of the World.*

Now it is true at the *Tribunall* of this dreadfull *Judge*, *Tyre* and *Sidon*, *Sodome* and *Gomorra*, ſhall ſinde an eaſier doome, then ſhall *Bethſaida*, *Chorazin*, *Capernaum*, *Jeruſalem*, &c. And Mr *Cotton* need not feare the eſcaping of a falſe *Chriſt*, when all *Nations* profeſſing *Chriſtianitie* (*Papiſt* or *Proteſtant*) (if yet found diſobedient to the true *Chriſt*) ſhall paſſe under a more fierie Sentence then all *Mahumetane* and *Pagan* Countries.

Peace. Mr *Cotton* will not ſtick to ſubſcribe to this; But, the falſe *Chriſts* bloud (ſayth he) ought *now*, to be ſpilt.

Truth. Since there are ſo many falſe *Chriſts* (as the true *Chriſt* Propheſied) Mr *Cotton* muſt unavoydably name and detect and convict thoſe falſe *Chriſts*, *Popiſh* and *Proteſtant*, &c. upon whom he paſſeth ſuch a preſent Sentence. He muſt alſo direct the way how the true *Chriſt* may ſhed the bloud of the falſe *Chriſts*. When Mr *Cotton* hath done this faith- *Touching the true and falſe Chriſts.*

fully and impartially (according to his *Conſcience* and preſent *Judgement*) what Reader will not at firſt view ſee riſing up from ſuch Premiſes theſe foure *Concluſions?*

Firſt, Amongſt ſo many *Chriſts* extant (that is viſible *Chriſts Head* and *Body*) in the *Chriſtian Antichriſtian* World, there can but One *Chriſt* be found to be true.

Secondly, That *Chriſt* which M[r] *Cotton* profeſſeth (according to his *Conſcience*) will be *He.*

Thirdly, All ſuch *Chriſts* as are extant, beſide M[r] *Cottons, Head* and *Body*, ought impartially to be put to *Death*, as *falſe, counterfeit, blaſphemous*, &c.

Fourthly, Such as embrace his *Chriſt*, that is, be of his *Church* and *Conſcience*, are bound (if they once get *power* in their hands) to purſue with *fire* and *ſword*, and to ſhed the bloud of all the falſe *Chriſts*, that is, the ſeverall ſorts of *falſe* or *Antichriſtian Worſhippers.*

Peace. Oh how *wiſe* and *Righteous* is the *Lord*, in letting looſe the *Wolfe* and *Lyon* (*perſecutors* and *Hunters*) upon his *Sheepe* and *People*, that by their owne painfull ſence of ſuch bloudie *violence* and *crueltie*, he may graciouſly purge out the *Malignant venemous Humours* of ſuch fowle *Antichriſtian* and bloudie *Doctrines?* But to the next, the King of *Bohemia* his ſaying. [189] Whereas it was ſaid that

King of Bohemia *his Speech.*

in this *Kings Speech* M[r] *Cotton* had paſſed by that *Foundation* in *Grace* and *Nature*, to wit, that *Conſcience* ought not to be violated or forced, and that ſuch *forcing* is no other then a *Spirituall Rape.*

M[r] *Cotton* replyes, It was not paſſed by, but pre-

" vented in ſtating the *Queſtion*, where it was ſaid, It " is not lawfull to Cenſure any, no not for *Errour* in " *Fundamentall* Points of *Doctrine* or *Worſhip*, till the " *Conſcience* of the *offendour* be firſt convinced (out of " the *Word* of *God*) of the dangerous Errour of his " way, and then if he will perſiſt, it is not out of " *Conſcience*, but againſt his *Conſcience*, as the Apoſtle " ſayth, (*Tit*. 3. 11.) and ſo he is not perſecuted for " cauſe of Conſcience, but for ſinning againſt his " Conſcience.

Truth. I anſwer, the forcing of a *Woman*, that is, the violent Acting of *uncleanneſſe* upon her *bodie* againſt her will, we count a Rape: By Proportion that is a *Spirituall* or *Soule-rape*, which is a forcing of the *Conſcience* of any Perſon, to Acts of *Worſhip*, which the Scripture entitles by the name of the Marriage bed, *Cant*. 1.

Spirituall Rapes.

This forcing of *Conſcience* was in an high meaſure the branded ſinne of that great typicall *Machiavel Jeroboam*, who made *Iſrael* to *Worſhip* before the *Golden Calves:* And this is the abominable *practice* of the Second Beaſt, who compells all to take the Marke of the firſt *Beaſt*, and this is the ſinne of (the myſticall *Ammon*) the Princes of *Europe*, and of the *Antichriſtian* World, thoſe myſticall effeminate *Ahabs*, who give their power to the *Beaſt*, themſelves (together with that Man of *Sinne* and *Filthineſſe* (the *Pope*) Practicing moſt odious ſpirituall *uncleanneſſe* upon the *Conſciences* of the *Nations* of the *Earth*.

2. *Peace*. Deare *Truth*, who knowes not whoſe voyce and Song this is, but that, of all the bloudie

All persecutours contumeliously object against Conscience. *Bonners*, *Gardiners*, and most devouring *persecutors* that ever have or shall legally in way and pretence of *Justice*, *persecute.* [You pretend *Conscience* that you dare not come to *Church* because of *Conscience*, that so to *sweare*, *submit*, *subscribe*, or *conforme*, is against your *Conscience*, that you are persecuted for your *Conscience*, and forced against your *Conscience*.

Truth. Indeed, what is this before the flaming eyes of *Christ*, but as (*Amnon*-like in the type) some lustfull *Ravisher* deales [190] with a beautifull *Woman*, first using all subtle *Arguments* and gentle *perswasions*, to allure unto their spirituall *Lust* and *Filthinesse*, and where the *Conscience* freely cannot yeeld to such *Lust* and *Folly* (as *Tamar* said to *Amnon*) then a forcing it by *Penalties*, *Penall Lawes* and *Statutes*? Yea, what is this but more filthy and abominable then is commonly practiced against *ravished Women*, to wit, a perswading *Conscience* that it is *obstinate*, obstinate against its knowledge, that a man might lawfully have yeelded, that he is convinced of the *lawfulnesse* of the *Act*, and therefore may justly be punished for repelling such *Arguments*, and resisting such *perswasions* against the *Conviction* of his owne *Conscience*.

Amnon *his ravishing of* Tamar, *a Type.*

3. *Peace.* It is a common *Question*, made by most, who shall be Judge of this *Convicted Conscience*; shall the lustfull *Ravisher* (the *Persecutor*) be Judge? Will the burning Rage of his *Spirituall Filthinesse* and *Antichristian Beastialitie* cause no shaking of the scales of *Justice*? And will M[r] *Cotton* indeed (except he suspend them) have all the *Civill Magistrates*, or *Civill States*, or *Generall Assemblies*, or *Courts* of

A Query, who shall judge, whether Conscience be convict.

People in the *World* (according to their *ſeverall Conſtitutions*) ſit *Judges* o're *Conſcience*, to wit, when the poore *raviſhed Conſciences* of Men are *convinced.*

Truth. What is this, but (in truth) to ſubmit the *Soules* and *Conſciences* of the *Saints* (yea the *Conſcience* of the *Lord Jeſus* in them,) unto the *World* that lyes in wickedneſſe (and to the *Devill* in it) out of which *God* hath choſen; but few, that are *wiſe*, or that are *Great*, *Rich*, or *Noble*.

4. And to end this Paſſage, what is this, but to deſtroy that diſtinction of a true and falſe *Conſcience*, which the holy *Spirit* expreſſely maketh, telling (2 *Theſſal.* 2. [11. 12.]) of *Antichriſtians* that make *Conſcience* of *Lyes*, believing them *conſcientiouſly* for *Truths*. What is it now to force a *Papiſt* to *Church*, but a *Rape*, a *Soule-Rape?* he comes to *Church*, that is, comes to that *Worſhip*, which his *Conſcience* tells him is falſe, and this to ſave his *Eſtate*, *Credit*, &c. What is this in a *Papiſt*, but a yeelding unwillingly to be *forced* and *raviſhed?* Take an inſtance of holy *Cranmer*, and many other faithfull *Witneſſes* of the *truth* of *Jeſus*, who being *forced* or *raviſhed* by *terrour* of Death, *ſubſcribed, abjured*, went to *Maſſe*, but yet againſt their *Wills* and *Conſciences*. In both theſe *Inſtances* of *Papiſt* and *Proteſtant*, Mr *Cotton* muſt confeſſe [191] a *Soule-Raviſhment*; for, the *Conſcience* of a *Papiſt* is not *convinced* that it is his *Dutie* to worſhip *God* by the *Engliſh common Prayer-Booke*, or *Directorie*, &c. And the *Conſciences* of many are not convinced but that it is their ſinne to come at either the *Papiſts* or common *Proteſtants Worſhip*. So both *Papiſt* and *Proteſtant* are forced and raviſhed

Church-Papiſts and Proteſtants alſo raviſhed.

by *force* of *Armes*, (as a Woman by a Luſtfull *Raviſher*) againſt their *Soules* and *Conſciences*.

Peace. Againe, in that *King* of *Bohemia's Speech* Mr *Cotton* paſſed by that moſt true and lamentable *experience* of all *Ages*, to wit, that *perſecution*, for cauſe of *Conſcience*, hath ever proved pernicious, and hath been the cauſe of great *Alterations* and *changes* in *States* and *Kingdomes*. To this Mr *Cotton* replyes, No *experience* in any *Age* did ever prove it *pernicious* to puniſh *Seducing Apoſtates*, after due *Conviction* of the *Errour* of their way: And he asks, wherein did the burning of *Servetus* prove *pernicious* to *Geneva*, or the juſt Execution of many *Popiſh Prieſts* to Queene *Elizabeth*, or the *Engliſh State* ?

Truth. I anſwer, though no *Hiſtorie* did expreſſe what horrible and pernicious *miſchiefes* the perſecuting of the *Arians* and others cauſed in the *World*: yet is it lamentably ſufficient to the Point, that all *Ages* teſtifie (and I had almoſt ſaid all *Nations*) how pernicious this Doctrine hath been in raiſing the devouring flames of *Fire* and *Sword*, about *Hereticks*, *Apoſtates*, *Idolaters*, *Blaſphemers*, &c.

Wars for Religion.

Peace. Later Times have rendred the obſervation of that *King* moſt lamentably true, in the many great *Deſolations*, in *Germany*, *Poland*, *Hungaria*, *Tranſilvania*, *Bohemia*, *France*, *England*, *Scotland*, *Ireland*, *Low Countries* (not to ſpeake of the mighty warres between thoſe dreadfull *Monarchies* of the *Turkes* and *Perſians*, and other *Nations*) to the *Flames* whereof although other cauſes have intermingled, the *Matters* of *Hereſie*, *Blaſphemie*, *Idolatrie*, &c. have been the chiefeſt ſparkes and *Bellowes*.

Truth. It is true (as Mr *Cotton* ſayth,) it hath pleaſed the *God* of *Heaven* to ſpare ſome particular places, and to preſerve wonderfully for his Name and Mercy ſake, *Geneva, England,* &c. &c. When they have been *beſieged* and *invaded:* Yet Mr *Cotton* confeſſeth, that Queene *Elizabeth* by that courſe had like to have fired the *Chriſtian World* in *Combuſtion,* which though it [192] pleaſed God to prevent, yet later times have ſhewen how pernicious this *Doctrine* hath proved unto *England, Scotland, Ireland,* &c. in the ſlaughter of ſo many hundreth thouſand *Papiſts* and *Proteſtants,* upon the very point (principally) of *Hereſie, Idolatrie,* &c.

The bloudie Tenent Guiltie of all the bloud of Papiſts *and* Proteſt-ants *lately ſpilt.*

Peace. To end this Chapter: To that obſervation that *Perſecution* for cauſe of *Conſcience* was practiced moſt in *England,* and ſuch places where *Poperie* reignes, implying that ſuch practices proceed from the great *Whore,* and her *Daughters:* Mr *Cotton* replyes, it is no marvaile he paſſed by this *obſervation* in the *Kings* ſpeech, for it was not the Speech of the *King,* but of the *Priſoner,* and it was not the perſecuting of *Antichriſtians,* but of *Nicknamed Puritants,* and of them too without *Conviction* of the *Errour* of their way: He addeth that he could never ſee "Warrant to call that *Church* an *Whore,* that wor- "ſhipped the true *God* onely in the name of *Jeſus,* "and depended on him alone for *Righteouſneſſe* and "*Salvation,* and that it is (at leaſt) a baſe part of a "*childe* to call his Mother *whore,* who bred him and "bred him to know no other *Father,* but her lawfull "*Huſband* the *Lord Jeſus Chriſt*

[1] *The Powring out of the Seven Vials, &c.* p. 7. See *Pub. Narr. Club,* iii. 189.

Truth. Whether the *Obſervation* was the *Kings*, or the *Priſoners*, yet it was paſſed by: And if thoſe *Puritants* or *Proteſtants* perſecuted, were not *convinced*, Himſelfe (as he here ſayth) never ſaw Warrant, that is, was *convinced*, for to call ſuch a *Church* as he here deſcribeth, an *Whore*, yet not a few of his *oppoſites* will ſay, and that aloud, that *He* and *they* were or might have been convinced, what ever *He* or *they* themſelves thought. The truth is, the *carnall Sword* is commonly the *Judge* of the *conviction* or *obſtinacie* of all *ſuppoſed Hereticks*. Hence the faithfull *Witneſſes* of *Chriſt*, *Cranmer*, *Ridley*, *Latimer*, had not a word to ſay in the *Diſputations* at *Oxford:*[1] Hence the *Non-conformiſts* were cryed out as obſtinate Men, abundantly convinced by the Writings of *Whitgift* and others: And ſo in the Conference before King *James* at *Hampton Court*, &c.[2]

The ſtrongeſt Arme & ſword the ordinarie Judge of the Conviction of Conſcience.

But concerning the *Church* of *England*, whether a *daughter* or no of the *Great Whore* of *Rome*, It is

[1] A Diſputation was held at Oxford, April 16, 18, 1554, and Cranmer, Ridley and Latimer, were by warrant of Queen Mary removed from the Tower to Oxford to defend the doctrine of the Reformers. Fox reports it in full. *Book of Martyrs*, iii. 36–70.

[2] The Conference was held at Hampton Court, January 14, 16, 18, 1604. Only four Puritan miniſters appeared againſt the King, nine biſhops and as many more dignitaries of the church. The King cloſed it, ſaying, "I will have none of this arguing. Therefore let them conform, and that quickly too, or they ſhall hear of it. The biſhops will give them ſome time, but if they are of an obſtinate and turbulent ſpirit, I will have them enforced into conformity." Neal, *Hiſt. of Puritans*, i. 233.

Says Mr. Hallam, "In the accounts that we read of this meeting we are alternately ſtruck with wonder at the indecent and partial behaviour of the King, and at the abject baſeness of the biſhops, mixed, according to the cuſtom of ſervile natures, with inſolence toward their opponents. It was eaſy for a monarch and eighteen churchmen to claim the victory, be the merits of their diſpute what they might, over four abaſhed and intimidated adverſaries." *Conſt. Hiſtory*, 173.

not here ſeaſonable to repeate what the *Witneſſes* of *Chriſt* to *Bonds*, *Baniſhments*, and *Death* (whom Mr *Cotton* here calls the rigid *Seperation*) have alledged in this caſe. I thinke it here ſufficient to ſay two [193] things. Firſt, Mr *Cotton* himſelfe is thought to believe that it is not a *profeſſion* of *words* containing many *fundamentall Doctrines* that makes a people a true *Church*, who profeſſing to know *God*, yet in *workes* deny him; notwithſtanding that amongſt them by *Gods* gracious *Diſpenſation* much good may be wrought by many.

Touching the Nationall Church of England.

Reall denying, the greateſt denying of Chriſt Jeſus.

2. Mr *Cotton* himſelfe will not ſay that ever *Chriſt Jeſus* was married to a *Nationall Church*, which all men know the *Church* of *England* ever was, and Mr *Cotton* elſewhere acknowledgeth (as *Nationall*) to be none of *Chriſts*, but onely *Churches Congregationall.*

Exam: of Chap. 60. *Concerning the* Romane Emperours, *which did or did not* perſecute.

Peace. WHereas it was anſwered, that *Godly Perſons* (as ſome *Godly Emperours*) might doe evill, to wit, in *perſecuting:* And *ungodly Emperours* in not perſecuting, might doe well, &c. Mr *Cotton* replyes, This begs the *Queſtion*, to ſay that *Kings* alledged by the *Priſoner* did that which was good, but *Kings* alledged by Mr *Cotton* (though better perſons) did that which was *Evill.*

Truth. I think Mr *Cotton* miſtakes the *poore Priſoner* if he conceives him to have argued from the

Number, or (by way of *comparison*) the *Qualitie* or *Goodnesse* of the *Kings*. I am sure he mistaketh the Discusser, who argues neither from their *Persons*, nor *Number*, nor *Practices*, but from the *waight* of their *Speeches*, *qualified* onely with the *consideration* of their *State:* Their *Speeches* M[r] *Cotton* passed by, but now hath waighed, though not so fully as it may please *God* to cause *Himselfe*, or *others* to doe hereafter.

Peace. I conceive it to be a further mistake, to thinke the Discusser accounted the *Persons* alledged by M[r] *Cotton* better *Persons* then those alledged by the *Prisoner*.

Truth. The Discusser compared them not, but desired that their *Speeches* and *Arguments* might have their just and due *waight*, and then I believe it will be found, not a *begging*, but a *winning* of the *Question*, even from the *Testimonie* of some *Kings* themselves.

194] Chap. 61. *replying to* Chap. 64. *Examined.*

Peace. IN this Chapter *God* is pleased to leave M[r] *Cotton* to fall into two *Evills*, then which (ordinarily) *greater* cannot be among the *sonnes* of *Men:* I speake not of the *Aggravations* of *malice* and *obstinacie*, which I hope the most gracious *Lord* will keepe him from, but of the *sinnes* themselves in *themselves:* The One is monstrous *Blasphemie* and abominable profanation of the most holy Name of his most *High* and holy *Maker*, &c. The second extreameſt *Crueltie* and *Tyrannie* againſt *Men* his fellow *Creatures.*

For the firſt, after a new *refined faſhion* and dreſs, he projects how to turne this whole *Dunghill* of the corrupt and *rotten World,* into a moſt ſweet and fragrant *Garden* of the *Church,* or *Dove* of *Chriſt.*

Two high Tranſgreſſions objected againſt Mr Cotton.

For the ſecond, he contents not Himſelfe with the *Severitie* and *Crueltie* of former times exerciſed by the *Emperours* profeſſing the Name of *Chriſt,* againſt ſuch, whom they reputed *Hereticks,* but blames them for applying too favourable and gentle *Medicines* of *Exile* and *Baniſhment,* and in *plaine tearmes* he ſayth, It had been better they had put them to death.

Truth. Your obſervation (ſweet *Peace*) is full of *pietie* and *Mercy:* It is moſt true, that a private *opinion,* or an *Act* of *Antichriſtianiſme* and *Idolatrie,* like a dead flie, may cauſe a ſweet pot of *Chriſtian Oyntment,* to yeeld a *ſtincking favour,* but ſuch a *Doctrine,* of ſuch a *generall Nature* and extent, as reaches to *all men,* to all the *World* (in my apprehenſion) ſhould cauſe Men to feare and tremble at ſuch *Rocks,* againſt which ſuch *Gallant veſſels* may *ſtrike,* and *ſplit,* if the moſt *holy* and *jealous God,* be pleaſed a little to withdraw his holy hand from the *ſteering* of them.

Peace. Let me (Deare *Truth*) ſumme up the *Heads,* to which I ſhall requeſt your *Conſideration.*

It is true (ſayth Mr *Cotton*) when *God* advanced *Conſtantine* and other *Chriſtian Emperours* to ſit on the *Throne,* the *Church* ſoone became a *Wilderneſſe,* " and he alſo ſeemeth to conſent that the *unknowing*

Touching the Romane Emperours

practices in Religious Affaires.

“*zeale* of *Conſtantine* and other good *Emperours* did “more hurt to *Chriſtianitie*, then the raging fury of 195] “bloudie *Neroes*: But withall he addeth that “their *unknowing zeale* did not lye in puniſhing noto-“rious *Hereticks*, *Seducers*, &c. And he ſayth, that “the *Church* never had hurt by ſuch *puniſhments*. He “affirmeth that it is no *Sollecīſme* in *Religion* for the “whole *World* to become *Chriſtian*: that the *World* “became *Antichriſtian* by the *tolleration* of *Princes*, “and their advancing of *Church affaires*, together “with the *unwatchfullneſſe* of ſuch being advanced: “that if the *World* had renounced *Paganiſme*, and “profeſſed *Chriſt* to be the Sonne of *God*, but yet “had been kept from the *Fellowſhip* of the *Church* “till they had approved their *profeſſion* by a ſincere “*converſation*, it had been no *Solleciſme*, &c.

Further, He ſayth, the *Chriſtian Emperours* did “permit *Hereticks* to live in the field of the *World*, “that they ſeldome or never put them to Death ſor “*hereticall pravitie* (though it had been *better* (ſayth “he) they had ſo done with *ſome* of them, but onely “*expelled* them from *populous Cities* and *Countries*, “where the *Gangrene* might ſpread, &c.

Chriſts Garden gaines by violent Stormes, and looſeth by ſweete Sunſhines.

Truth. You have well ſummd up (*Sweet Peace*) I ſhall briefly touch theſe *Heads*, with *Gods* aſſiſtance; and firſt concerning the *zeale* of the *Romane Emperours*. It is confeſt by Mr *Cotton*, that upon the good *Emperours* coming to the *Throne*, the *Church* ſoone became a *Wilderneſſe*, and that was a greater hurt and miſchiefe then ever befell the *Saints* and *Churches* under the fierie *perſecution* of the moſt *bloudie Neroes*; ſurely ſuch *zeale* that brought forth ſuch *fruit* to *Chriſ-*

tianitie might ſeeme juſtly to be ſuſpected not to be kindled from *Heaven*, but from *Men*.

2. It ſeemes not *reaſonable* to the weakeſt underſtanding, nor ſuitable to the *wiſdome* and conſtant *care* and *love* of *Chriſt Jeſus* to his *Wife* and *Spouſe* in his *abſence*, that the *Romane Emperours* ſhould be ſuch *Godly Perſons*, and that alſo neither by *Chriſt Jeſus* nor his *Apoſtles* or *Meſſengers* the leaſt *word* ſhould be directed to them, when, as yet, they were *extant*, in *Chriſts* and his *Meſſengers* times; and (by the *bloudie Tenent*) muſt be ſuppoſed *inveſted* with ſo high a *calling* too, ſo high a *worke* and *dutie*, as higher is not to be performed in the whole *World* (and that *Ex Officio*) to wit, the *Eſtabliſhing*, *Governing*, *Reforming*, &c. the *Church*, the *Spouſe*, and *Kingdome* of *Chriſt Jeſus*.

The Romane Emperours.

196] *Peace.* 2. The *Church* and *Servants* of *Chriſt* had great hurt (notwithſtanding Mr *Cottons* contrary beliefe) by the *Emperours* perſecuting, of whom they judged *hereticall*, partly in that the *Arrians* were hardned by their *ſufferings*, and *Arrianiſme* increaſed by the *ſufferings* of the *profeſſours* of it; as alſo that the *Chriſtians* were more ſeverely perſecuted (as hath often alſo come to paſſe (in the *Interchanges* between the *Papiſt* and the *Proteſtant*) when the *Arrians* came to weare the *Sword*, and the *Orthodox Chriſtians* were under *Hatches*.

The Arrians *perſecuted and perſecuting.*

Truth. 3. But that the *whole World* that wonders after and worſhippeth the *Beaſt*, ſhould yet poſſibly be of the ſmall *Number*, that follow the *Lambe*, and ſtand oppoſite to the *Beaſt*, on *her*, that follow the *Lambe*, and ſtand oppoſite to the *Beaſt*, on Mount

Zion: That the *World* upon whom the *vialls* of *plagues* and *vengeance* are to be powred according to the infallible *Prophecies* (not to ſpeak of the *World* from other *Scriptures*) that this whole *World* (I ſay) ſhould be brought into ſuch an *Onenes* with *Chriſt Jeſus*, ſeemes ſo croſſe to the *fundamentall Enmitie* between *Chriſts Seede* and the *Serpents*, to the *priviledges* of the *Saints*, to the *puritie* of *Chriſt*, to the *ſtreame* of *Scripture*, and in particular to the ſweete laſt *Will* and *Teſtament* of the *Lord Jeſus*, and the *nature* of his particular *Flocks*, &c. That I cannot wonder ſufficiently, how any man profeſſing but a ſmall *Knowledge* of the *Myſteries* and *Kingdome* of *Chriſt Jeſus*, ſhould be ſo vailed, ſo obſcured, ſo to write of the ſtate of *Chriſts Church* and the *World*, as Mr *Cotton* doth?

The great Difference between this World and Chriſt.

Peace. Chriſt Jeſus (Bleſſed *Truth*) gave not thankes to his moſt holy, moſt wiſe *Father* in vaine, for hiding from *Wiſe and Prudent*, and opening to *Babes* and *Sucklings*.

Truth. 4. But further, Such a Converſion of *People* from *Idolatrie* to *Chriſtianitie*, as fits them to be *profeſſours* of the *Sonne* of *God*, but yet not fits them for the *Fellowſhip* of *Chriſtians* in *Church State*, I finde not in the *Teſtament* of *Chriſt Jeſus*. Surely the *Converſion* of the *Theſſalonians* was not ſuch, 2 [1] *Theſſ.* 1. [9.] Who turned not onely from *Idolls*, but to ſerve the living and *true God*, which ſervice of *God* in *Chriſt* no Soule uprightly in love with *Chriſt Jeſus*, but (in its meaſure) longs after, as vehemently and cordially as ever *chaſt Spouſe* after her deareſt earthly *Huſbands* preſence and Enjoyment, *Cant.* 1. & 3. & 5.

A Chriſtianitie ſtrange from Chriſt.

Peace. *Gods Spirit* (in *John*) defcribes one Difference, &c. [197] between the true *Spirit* and *Profeſſours,* and the *falſe,* to wit, that fuch as acknowledge (that is truely as I conceive) *Chriſt Jeſus* to become in the flefh, are borne of *God.*

Truth. Yea therefore confequently fuch a *Spirit* cannot be of *Jeſus,* that makes fuch a profeffion of *Chriſt Jeſus* as the *Devills* themfelves may make, and (even for want of *Regeneration* and *Perſonall Grace,*) the *profeſſours* are not fit for the *Fellowſhip* of the true *Chriſtian Worſhip,* and *Worſhippers.* *Antichriſtian Chriſtianitie.*

5. But laftly, if M[r] *Cotton,* or any of his bloudie *Judgement* woare the *Imperiall Crowne* of the *Worlds Majeſtie,* what *ſlaughters* fhall we imagine the *World* fhould heare and feele? Whether would fuch *fierie zeale* tranfport Men? Yea what an *Earthly Dunghill Religion* and *Worſhip* fhould the moft *High God* be ferved with, fit onely for the *Dunghill Gods* and *Goddeſſes,* whom all *Aſia* (as the *Towne-clarke* fpeakes) and the *World* worfhippeth. [Acts 19. 27.]

Peace. If the Report of M[r] *Cottons* interpreting that *Scripture* of *Serving God* with all our *Might,* &c. be true, to wit, of employing our *Civill Armes* and *Forces* to the utmoft, and that againft other *Peoples* profeffing *Idolatrie* and *Antichriſtianiſme:* His *Conſcience* (as I conceive) muft needs force on and preffe after, an *univerſall Conqueſt* of all *Conſciences,* and under that (like thofe bloudie *Spaniards, Turkes* and *Popes*) lay under that *faire cloake,* the *Rule* and *Dominion* over all the *Nations* of the *Earth.* *The bloudie Tenent tends to an univerſall Conqueſt of the whole World.*

Truth. But may not M[r] *Cotton* better liften to the voyce of the *Lord Jeſus,* faying to him and fuch of *The bloudie Tenent in its colours.*

his *bloudie Tenent,* You know not of what *Spirit* you are of: Were the *Emperours* too favourable (as Mr *Cotton* ſayth) in but *Baniſhing?* How *keene* a *Sword* would Mr *Cotton* draw againſt ſo many *Millions* of *Gangreene Soules* throughout the *Turkiſh* and the *Popiſh World?*

Peace. Oh, how farre different would Mr *Cottons* Sword be from the *Sword* of the *Spirit* of *God,* proceeding from the *Mouth* of *Chriſt Jeſus,* yet ſharpe enough with *two edges,* piercing between *Soule* and *Spirit,* &c.

Truth. Yea how farre different from the *Meeke Spirit* of the L*ambe* of *God,* who came not to deſtroy *Mens lives,* but to ſave them, yea how different from the former *meeke* and noted gentle [198] *Temper* of Mr *Cottons* own *Spirit,* now over-heat and enflamed by his *unmercifull* and *bloudie Tenent?*

Exam: of Chap. 62. *replying to* Chap. 65.

Peace. WHen Mr *Cotton* was juſtly obſerved to uſe the *Language* of *Lyon*-like *perſecution* in theſe words, "[More and greater Princes "then theſe you mention have not tollerated *Here-* "*ticks* and *Schiſmaticks,* notwithſtanding their pre- "tence of *Conſcience,* and arrogating the Crowne of "Martyrdome to their ſuffrings] He defendeth ſuch *Language* by the *Scripture Freedome* in ſuch *Tearmes* againſt *Sinners,* which ſayth he, the Diſcuſſer acknowledgeth.

Truth. In holy Scripture are many *Expreſſions* full of *Holineſſe, Gravitie, Love, Meekneſſe,* &c. which yet are wreſted by us poore Men to *unholy* and *unchriſtian Ends* and *purpoſes.* How many wofully pervert many *grave* and heavenly *Paſſages* and *Expreſſions* of holy *Scripture* to baſe and filthy *Jeaſting?* How many from ſome *ſharp Expreſſions* of *Chriſt Jeſus* and *Paul* (in *caſes*) take licence to *raile* and call Men all to naught, in *Wrath, Revenge,* and *Paſſion?* And how many out of *pride* and *falſe zeale* trampling upon the *Heads* and *Conſciences* of all *Men,* are ready (not in an holy Meeke and *Chriſtian* way but) in a *Phariſaicall, Biſhop-like* and *Pope-like* way, to roare and thunder out againſt *Gods meekeſt Servants* the odious *tearmes* of *Hereticks, Schiſmaticks, Blaſphemers, Seducers,* &c. Which *tearmes* though uſed in holy *Scripture,* yet never in ſuch a *way,* as *commonly* and *conſtantly* the *bloudie* and *perſecuting* expreſſe themſelves in.

No Booke or Writing ever ſo abuſed as the holy Writing & Scripture of God is.

The Language of perſecutours.

Peace. But what or whom meanes Mr *Cotton* in this *paſſage,* what *Language* have they learned, who in point of *worſhip* have left *Zion,* but not the *Gates* and *Suburbes* of *Babylon,* for they ſet up *Bull-warkes* of *Impunitie* to ſecure them.

Truth. Surely Mr *Cotton* knowes that none that plead againſt the *Civill Power* and *Weapons* in *Spirituall Matters,* but they alſo maintaine, that, there ought to be in vigorous uſe the *Spirituall* and *two edged Sword* that comes forth of *Chriſts Mouth* (not for the *Impunitie* but) for the *Ruine* and *Deſtruction* of all *Babells Brats* and *Abominations.*

199] *Peace.* Mr *Cotton* ſpends many lines, and quotes

Auſtin to prove, that *Julians* End of tollerating *Hereſie* to grow, was to choake *Chriſtianitie.*

Julian *his Tolleration.*

Truth. What ever were *Julians* End, yet I deny that *Tolleration* of the weedes of *Hereſie* and blaſphemous *Religion* (*Paganiſh, Turkiſh, Jewiſh, Popiſh*) in the field of the *Civill State* and *World*, hath power to choake the *vitalls* of *Chriſtianitie* in the *Garden* or *Bodie* the *Church* of *Chriſt Jeſus.*

Touching Infection of falſe Doctrine, &c.

And concerning *Infection*, It is to be obſerved that when the holy Scriptures ſpeakes by the *Similitudes* of *Leaven, Gangrene*, or *Poyſonfull weedes*, of *Wolves*, or *ſcabbed ſheepe*, &c. it is commonly with reſpect to ſuch Evills got in among the *Saints* and *Churches*, the *Flocks* and *Gardens* of *Chriſt*, where ſuch *Leaven, weedes*, &c. tollerated may ſpread and infect: But what is this to the *Lyons, Beares*, or *Wolves*, not to be ſuffered in the *Wilderneſſe*, or *Swine*, or *Dogs*, in the common *high wayes*; or *weedes* in the *Common* or *Foreſt*, which all may be, and yet the *Garden, Body*, and *Flock* of *Chriſt* be pure and ſafe from ſuch *Infection.*

Peace. One *paſſage* more is very Conſiderable. In former *Diſcourſe* about the *Tares* M[r] *Cotton* was large in proving the *permiſſion* of *weedes*, even in the *Church* of *Chriſt*, and that untill *Chriſts Comming*, and that after they be diſcovered to be *Hypocrites.*

Hypocrites tollerated in the Church, but not in the World.

Truth. O what a *Diſtance* is between that *Doctrine* and this here? There the *Tares* muſt not be touched in the *Garden* of the *Church*, here they muſt not be ſuffred abroad in the field of the *World*, for feare of *choaking* the *good plants* in the *Garden* of *Chriſt.* Who can finde out how theſe *Doctrines* ſuit with *Godlineſſe*, with *Reaſon*, or *Themſelves*?

Peace. But now you ſpeake of *ſuiting:* It is (ſayth Mr *Cotton*) (for a cloſe) a plaine *Contradiction* of the Diſcuſſers former Speech to ſay, that *perſecuting* of others was a meanes of *choaking Chriſtianitie,* whereas he had ſaid, that *Conſtantines unknowing zeale* did more hurt to *Chriſts Kingdome,* then the raging furie of the moſt bloudie *Neroes.*

Truth. Let the words be well weighed, and no ſuch *Affirmation* will be found: The words are; "[It was not when *Chriſtians* lodged in cold *Priſons,* "but in *Downe Beds* of *Eaſe,* and [200] *perſecuted* "others.] The Diſcuſſer made not *perſecution* to be a *meanes* of *choaking Chriſtianitie,* but attributes the *Loſſe* of *Chriſtians Life* and *Love,* to thoſe *Beds* of their abuſed *Sweete proſperitie.*

2. If he had made *perſecution* a meanes to *choake Chriſtianitie,* it had been the *perſecution* of *Chriſtians* among *Themſelves,* and not the *perſecution* of bloudie *Neroes*: Which yet if it had been ſo, it might yet be no *Contradiction,* for *Neroes perſecution* might doe hurt, although *Conſtantines* unknowing zeale might doe much more.

Exam: of Chap. 63. *replying to* Chap. 66.

Peace. MAfter *Cotton* here being underſtood to *ſmile* on Q: *Elizabeth* for perſecuting the *Papiſts,* and to *frowne* on K: *James* for *perſecuting* the (ſo named) *Puritans,* he denies neither, but inſiſts onely upon the *Number,* that as *many* and as *great Princes* are againſt *Tolleration* as for it, and in particular Q: *Elizabeth* and K: *James.*

Truth. I ſay (as before) I ſhould never uſe an *Argument* from the *Number* of *Princes* (no more then from the *Number* of any other men) for any truth of *Chriſt Jeſus:* Who as he was not pleaſed himſelfe to be borne of the *ſons* of *Nobles,* ſo hath he not choſen many *Nobles* and *Wiſe men* of this *World* to be borne of him: Yet 2. If that be his *Argument,* he hath not ſatisfied, in naming theſe two, for more were named by the *Priſoner,* and beſides one of theſe *Witneſſes,* K: *James* abundantly declared himſelſe, not onely againſt *perſecuting* of *Papiſts,* but againſt all *perſecution* in generall, what ever otherwiſe or afterwards his practices were againſt ſome Perſons, as Mr *Cotton* too truely alledgeth.

Touching the Perſecution of K: James *and Q:* Elizabeth.

Truth. In the next *Paſſage* the Diſcuſſer having objected that both Q: *Elizabeth* and K: *James* did perſecute according to their *Conſciences,* and arguing why ſhould the one (namely) K: *James* be more blamed for *perſecuting* according to his *Conſcience,* then Q: *Elizabeth* for *perſecuting* according to hers: Mr *Cotton* diſtinguiſheth of *Conſciences:* The *Queenes* ſayth he, was rightly informed, but the *Kings* was not. When it was replyed, [201] that either K: *James,* and ſuch *Princes,* whoſe *Conſciences* (according to Mr *Cottons Conſcience*) are ill informed, muſt act according to their *Conſciences,* or elſe they want the *Qualification* and *Fitnes* for ſuch *places:* Mr *Cotton* anſwers two Things.

Firſt, that ſuch *Qualifications* are not *Eſſentiall,* but *Integrall.*

Secondly, That ſuch *Princes* muſt forbeare all *Civill Cenſures* in *matters* of *Religion* untill they be better informed.

Truth. It is moſt true as Mr *Cotton* ſayth, if we ſpeake of the right of *Succeſſion*, a *childe* may be a *Lawfull King* (as K. *James* himſelfe was being but a yeare old)[1] But if we ſpeake of the *Qualifications* of the *minde*, by which a *King* is enabled to rule his *State* (as is ſuppoſed *Eccleſiaſticall* and *Civill*, and to judge under *Chriſt Jeſus* in all *Cauſes Eccleſiaſticall* as well as *Civill:* Surely, he that knowes not which is the true *Church*, true *Miniſtrie*, true *Ordinances*; yea and *perſecutes* the true *Church*, *Miniſtrie*, and *Worſhip*, what ever his *Qualifications* be for the *Government* of the *Civill State*, yet can it never be made good that he is furniſhed with any *Eſſentiall Qualification* for the *Spirituall Adminiſtration*, any more then He that undertakes to be a *Guide*, and yet is *blinde*, and never ſet foote in the *way*, and knowes not the *true* from the *falſe:* Or to be a *Captaine Generall*, yea or but a *Shepheard*, &c. 2. Beſide, *Chriſt Jeſus* never calld any perſon to any *Employment* of his, to any *Worke*, whom he inables not in a *Meaſure* proportionably, &c.

Touching the Qualification of Princes.

Peace. In ſuch caſes (ſayth Mr *Cotton*) *Princes* are *called* to *ſuſpend* and *forbeare* all *Execution* of *Civill Cenſures* in the *matters* of *Religion*, till they be better informed, leaſt they doe *perſecute* the *Son* of *God* in ſtead of the *Son* of *Perdition*.

[1] James was born June 19, 1566. His mother having been taken captive June 16, 1567, was forced to reſign her crown in favor of her ſon, July 24; and he was crowned at Sterling, July 29, as James VI., of Scotland, being but little more than a year old. Hume, *Hiſtory*, v. 127. Froude, *Hiſtory of England*, ix. 142.

Truth. I anſwer: Firſt, Then Mr *Cotton* hath cut off K: *James* from acting, though ſo long eſteemed and ſworne Supreame in all Cauſes Eccleſiaſticall.

Touching Magiſtrates ſuſpending from acting in matters of Religion.

Secondly, I aske, how *many* ſhall forbeare, and *how long*, for evident then it is that moſt (beyond all compariſon) of all the *Princes* and *Magiſtrates* in the *World*, muſt not meddle with this *pretended chiefe part* of their *Dutie* and *Office*, and that (if they convert not) for the whole *Courſe* and *Race* of their *Life*: In particular, that no *Pagan Magiſtrate* (of all the ten thouſands [202] in the *World*, no *Perſian*, *Turkiſh*, *Popiſh*, nor *Proteſtant* (if *Prelaticall* or *Presbyterian*,) ought to exerciſe any of this *High* and *Glorious Power*, but onely ſuch *Princes* and *Magiſtrates* as are of Mr *Cottons Conſcience*; for otherwiſe what Prince in the world more learned King in his time then King *James*, yet was not he of Mr *Cottons Conſcience*.

Monſtrous partialitie.

Peace. Deare *Truth*: The *fall* of this *partialitie* is ſo *apparent*, and withall ſo *fowle*, that I thinke it impoſſible, but ere long it muſt needs be *condemned* by *Men* on Earth, as doubtleſs it is abhord by the moſt *holy* and *impartiall God*, and his holy *Angells* in *Heaven*: Upon this occaſion I call to minde that famous *Act* of the ſo greatly renowned *Conſtantine*, who in his firſt wearing of the *Diademe*, put forth (his *Colleauge Licinius* concurring alſo) a famous and moſt ſolemne *Charter* and *Edict*, that no man throughout the whole *Empire* ſhould be conſtrained in his *Religion*.

Conſtantines *Edict*.

Truth. Mr *Cotton* (according to his *proviſo* of *ſuſpenſion*) muſt doubtles applaud *Conſtantine* for this his *Forbearance* untill he were better informed, whereas afterward his *Edicts* againſt *Arrius* and *Arrianiſme*, teſtifie his practice to the contrary. But he that ſhall reade ſeriouſly in *Gods preſence* that firſt *Edict* of *Conſtantine* and *Licinius*, will there finde *Conſtantine* to uſe ſuch *Arguments*, as might for ever have cauſed him to have ſorbore *perſecution*, to have ſtill ſuſpended, to have gratified the *Subjects* of all his *Empire* with *Liberitie* and *Freedome* in the Point of *Worſhip* and *Religion*.[1]

But I will End this Paſſage with this *Querie*; If *Chriſt Jeſus* have left ſuch Power with the *Civill Rulers* of the *World*, *Kingdomes*, and *Countries*, of or for the *Eſtabliſhing*, *Governing*, and *Reforming* his *Church*, what is become of his *Care* and *Love*, *Wiſdome* and *Faithfulneſſe*, ſince in all *Ages* (ſince he left the *Earth*) for the *generall*, beyond all *exception*, he hath left her deſtitute of ſuch *qualified Princes* and *Governours*, and in the Courſe of his *Providence* furniſhed her with ſuch, whom he knew would be, and all men finde as fit, as *Wolves* to protect and feede his *Sheepe* and *People*.

Foule imputations caſt on Chriſt Jeſus.

[1] Reference is made in note p. 6. *supra*, to the edict of toleration iſſued by Conſtantine and Licinius in 312. This recognized "univerſal and unconditional freedom and liberty of conſcience." But a dozen years later, after the council of Nice, he iſſued an edict "in which he places Arius in the ſame claſs with Porphyry, the antagoniſt of Chriſtianity, orders their writings to be burned, no penalty of death even being threatened againſt thoſe who ſhould be detected in any clandeſtine attempt to preſerve theſe writings." Neander, *Church Hiſt.*, ii. 13. 378.

203] *Exam: of* Chap. 64. *replying to* Chap. 67.

Peace. WHen it was queſtioned, what good to the *Soules* or *Bodies* of their *Subjects* did thoſe *Princes* bring in perſecuting! Mr *Cotton* produceth a good fivefold that is brought to *Princes* and *Subjects* by the due *puniſhment* of *Apoſtates*, *Seducers*, *Idolaters*, and *Blaſphemers*.

Truth. Let all that feare God and Mr *Cotton* himſelfe be perſwaded to obſerve, whether under this *faire cloake* of puniſhing theſe and theſe *ſpirituall ſinners*, he maintaine not ſtrongly (what elſewhere he denies) to wit, *Perſecution* for *cauſe* of *Conſcience*. But we know the *Evaſion*. It is not for *Apoſtatizing*, *ſeducing* out of *Conſcience*, but after *Conviction*, againſt their *Conſcience*, &c.

Unchriſtian Tribunals.

Peace. You have before ſatisfied me (beſides other *Paſſages*) with this one, that to this End of diſcerning the poore *Hereticks* ſinning againſt his *Conſcience*, the *Civill State*, the *Earth*, the *World* muſt neceſſarily Erect its *Tribunall*, to judge not onely *Civill Things*, but even the *Heart* and *Conſcience* alſo; but now to Mr *Cottons* five-fold good.

Firſt (ſayth he) it puts away *Evill* from the *People*, by cutting off a *Gangrene* which would ſpread to further *ungodlineſſe*, *Deut.* 13. 5. 2 *Tim.* 2. 1. 6. 7. 13.

Dent. 13. 5. & 2 Tim. 2. 16. *Unchriſtianly conjoyned.*

Truth. I anſwer, theſe Scriptures (though pure and holy in their places, yet) are here coupled together as *Linſey*, *Wollſey*, contrary to the Law. *Deut.* 13. which concerns the typicall *Nationall Church*, uſing *Nationall* & *temporall Weapons*: The

2 *Tim.* 2. concernes the *Particular Congregations* or *Churches* of *Chriſtians*, uſing onely the *Sword* of Gods *Spirit*, the *Word* of *God*, &c.

Beſide, *Deut.* 13. concerned ſuch a *People* whom the *Lord* brought forth of *Ægypt* with *Miracles*, into *Canaan*, &c. Let any ſuch People be now produced, excepting the *Chriſtian* (particular) *Churches*. Why doth Mr *Cotton* then alledge this Scripture ſo frequently, and in theſe five *Reaſons* brings two from hence; This the *firſt*; and the *Third*, to wit, that all the *People* may *heare* and *feare*, &c. which is alone made good in the *Antitype* or *Chriſtian Church*; according to that 1 *Tim.* 5. 20. *Rebuke* them that ſinne openly, that others may learne to *feare*.

204] 2. *Peace.* Mr *Cotton* mentioneth a ſecond good, which is driving away *Wolves* from *worrying* and *ſcattering* the *Sheepe* of *Chriſt*.

Truth. This was largely anſwered in diſcourſing the nature of *myſticall* or *ſpirituall Wolves*, upon that very place which he quotes, *Acts* 20.[1] From whence it may evidently appeare that from the *literall* urging of ſuch *myſticall Scriptures*, all *Peoples* and *Nations* are enforced (and that *Conſcientiouſly*) like *Wolves* and *Lyons* to teare and devoure each other.

3. *Peace.* Mr *Cotton* addes, that *Puniſhments* are *wholeſome Medicines* to ſuch as are curable of ſuch *Evills*, *Zach.* 13. 4, 5, 6.

Truth. I anſwer; All the holy *Appointments* of *God* are moſt *powerfull* (in their ſeverall reſpective *ſeaſons*, and *manner* of *Diſpenſations*, to his owne moſt holy *Ends* and *purpoſes*, &c. The *Materiall*

[1] *Bloudy Tenent*, 67, *Pub. Narr. Club*, iii. 141.

Nationall Sword in the *Nationall Church* of *Israel* before *Christ:* and the *Spirituall Sword,* in the *spirituall* and *Christian Church* since his comming to abolish those *shadowes.*

Touching Excommunication in Israel.

As it was therefore in vaine to have cut off or *Excommunicated spiritually* in that *Nationall State:* So is it in vaine to use the materiall or carnall Sword in the *spirituall.* Wherefore (according to this place of *Zach.*) a true penitent will blesse *God* for the *Wounds* of *Friends* and *Lovers* (faithfull and sharpe dealing) and for *Deliverance* from the *Kisse* of deceitful flatterie: But what is this to prove (that which is so much denied) to wit, *Corporall Death* or *Wounds* now to be inflicted upon *false Teachers* in these times of the *Gospel,* and that in all *parts* and *Nations* of the *World.*

4. *Peace.* The *punishment,* sayth M[r] *Cotton,* executed upon *false Prophets* and *seducing Teachers,* doe bring downe *Showres* of *Gods* blessing upon the *Civill State,* 1 King. 18. 40, 41.

Ans: *Truth.* If that *Nationall State* of *Israel,* and that *Nationall* or *Corporeall killing* of so many hundreth *false Prophets,* and that *literall drouth* and *literall showres* of *Raine* and *plentie* were *figures* of no other *Prophets* and *slaughters, drouth and showers,* but *literall, materiall,* and *corporeall,* (now since the *Body* and *Substance Christ Jesus* is come): What should hinder but that those *Priests* of *Israel,* and *Sacrifices,* and *Temple,* and *Nationall Church* should all be in force, for our *Imitation, literally,* the one as well as the other?

205] *Peace.* I cannot possibly conceive but that (all

being of the ſame *Nature,*) the one is *Typicall* as well as the other, and that they muſt flouriſh and be glorious (as *Gods Ordinances,*) or *vaniſh* and *diſappeare* (giving place to brighter *diſpenſations*) at the ariſing of *Chriſt Jeſus* the *Son* of *Righteouſneſſe.*

Spirituall Bleſſings and Curſes the Anti-types of Corporall before Chriſt.

Truth. Hence *falſe Apoſtles, falſe Teachers, falſe Prophets,* are *Spiritually cut off,* Revel. 2. [2.] 2 Pet. 2. [1.] Gal. 4. [1. 9.] And *ſpirituall ſhowres* of *Bleſſings* deſcend upon the *Iſrael* of *God*; for although *corporeall Bleſſings* of *Food* and *Raiment* and *plentie,* are Gods bleſſings, yet *principally* under the *Goſpel God* bleſſeth his *Iſrael,* the *Antitype* with *ſpirituall Bleſſings,* Eph. 1. [3.] *Houſes, Lands, Fathers, Mothers, Children,* &c. with perſecution, *Mark.* 10. [29. 30.]

Great overſight imputed to Chriſt Jeſus.

Peace. Me thinks (Deare *Truth*) If *Chriſt Jeſus* had appointed ſuch *puniſhments,* ſuch *executions,* literall, in the *Chriſtian Church,* he would alſo have appointed *Offices* and *Officers* ſuitable and proper for ſuch *Ends* and *purpoſes,* ſuch *puniſhments,* ſuch *executions.*

If civill puniſhments for ſpirituall offences: they muſt be inflicted by holy and Chriſtian Inſtruments and Officers.

Truth. It cannot otherwiſe with *Reaſon* and *common prudence* be ſuppoſed, but that, if *Chriſt Jeſus* had appointed (which we finde not in his holy *Teſtament*) *holy* and *Chriſtian Magiſtrates* for thoſe great *decrees* and *ſentences,* wee ſhould alſo have read of his holy *Conſtables,* holy *Sergeants,* holy *Priſons,* holy *Stocks,* holy *Whipping Poſts,* holy *Gibbets,* and holy *Tyburnes*; together alſo with holy *Hangmen,* the *ſpirituall Inſtruments* and *Officers* of *Chriſt Jeſus,* for the *Executions* of his holy *puniſhments* upon *Apoſtates, Hereticks, Blaſphemers, Idolaters, Seducers,* &c.

5. *Peace. Gods Juſtice* (ſayth M[r] *Cotton*) is hon-

oured in the *Execution* of ſuch *Judgements*, Revel. 16. 5, 6.

1. *Truth.* I have (to my underſtanding) formerly ſhewed Mr *Cottons* miſtake in his expounding of this third *Violl*, and have preſented an *Expoſition* more agreeable with the *ſcope* of this *Prophecie.*

Peace. 2. *God* was honoured in all his *Judgements* which the *Tyrants* of the World have executed, (the *Babylonian, Perſian, Grecian, Romane*) yet not by way of *Law* and *Ordinance*, but in the way of his holy *providence* and juſt *permiſſion.*

3. *Truth.* Yea the Witneſſes of *Jeſus*, by the *two-edged Sword* of *God* in their Mouths, execute Gods *Judgments*, to the vindicating [206] of *Gods Glory*, and their *Innocencie*, (Revel. 11.) although they uſed no *carnall Weapons.*

A true Chriſt, a true Sword; a falſe Chriſt, a falſe Sword.

4. The holy Name of *God* is much *diſhonourea* and *prophaned*, when the *Inventions* of *Men* are ſet up, againſt his holy *Appointments*, and when the *Sword* of *Steele* (in *ſpirituall caſes*) is drawen in ſtead of the *ſpirituall Sword*, proceeding out of the Mouth of *Chriſt Jeſus* in his *ſervants Teſtimonie.* All ſuch worſhip, is but vaine or idle worſhip (*Mark* 7. [7.]) and ſuch is the *carnall Sword* and *Executions* of it.

Peace. Whereas it was obſerved, that Mr *Cotton* acknowledged that Queene *Elizabeth* had well neere fired all *Europe*, by ſuch *Executions*, Mr *Cotton* anſwers, *God* bore witneſſe to his *Truth* in *Deliverance:* And when it was replyed, that *Succeſſe* doth not prove *cauſes* true, Mr *Cotton* anſwers, yes; *Pſal.* 1. 3, 4. *Jer.* 22. 15, 16, 17.

Truth. I reply, *Temporall proſperitie, ſucceſſe*, &c.

were proper in that *Temporall* and *Civill State*, of that *Nationall Church*, and *ſpirituall Bleſſing* and *proſperitie* proper in the Goſpel now, *Epheſ.* 1. [3.]

Peace. 2. It was anſwered that *God* had given *victorie* to the *Papiſts*, eſpecially againſt the *Waldenſes* (and the *Beaſt* makes warre againſt the *Witneſſes*, Revel. 11. [3.] and *overcomes* them, &c.) Mr *Cotton* herein firſt obſerveth a *Contradiction*, in the words, to wit, that the *Papiſts* ever had the *victorie*, and yet their *ſucceſſe* hath been *various*.

Truth. I reply; the words are not that the *Papiſts* had *ever* the *Victory*, but that they ever had both *Victory* and *Dominion*; which words may be true, although that the *Event* were ſometimes *various*.

2. *Peace.* Againe (ſayth Mr *Cotton*) Queene *Elizabeth* ever had the *Victorie* againſt the *Papiſts*.

*Q: Eliza*beth *her wars againſt the Papiſts.*

Truth. I anſwer; Many gracious *Deliverances God* vouchſafed to Q: *Elizabeth*, yet ſometimes her *Armies* proſpered not againſt the *Papiſts*, as in that famous *Expedition* of *Eſſex*, *Drake* and *Norris* (though in a moſt righteous cauſe,) againſt the *Papiſts* of *Spaine* and *Portugall*, as alſo againſt the *Papiſts* in *Ireland* and the *Low Countries*, at ſometimes.[1]

2. Grant not onely *Deliverances*, but *Victories* and

[1] In 1589 an expedition ſtarted from England under the command of Sir Francis Drake and Sir John Norris, to help Don Antonio to the throne of Portugal. They firſt made an aſſault upon Groine in order to break up a Spaniſh armament which was preparing there. Here they were joined by the Earl of Eſſex, then only twenty-two years old, and proceeded to the coaſt of Portugal. The expedition was unſucceſsful and returned to England, half of the adventurers having periſhed.

In 1599, Eſſex was appointed Lord Lieutenant of Ireland, and proceeded thither to reduce the rebels. But his expenſive expedition came to a miſerable iſſue and he returned to England. Hume, *Hiſt. of Eng.*, v: 362. 420.

Succeſſe, Her *cauſe* (how ever intermingled) was civill *Defence* of her [207] *Kingdome*, againſt *Invation* and *Ambition*, *Dominion* and *Conqueſt*, by *practices* of *Tyrannie* and *oppreſſion*, both againſt the *Engliſh* and the *Hollanders* (eſpecially) as appeared by the horrible *Exactions*, *Outrages*, *Murthers* and *Slaughters* committed upon them by *D'Alva* the King of *Spaines Generall*.

Peace. But although the *Papiſts* (ſayth Mr *Cotton*) fought with *various* ſucceſſe, yet it is *Gods manner* to nurture his *People* with ſome *croſſes*, to teach them not to fight in their owne *ſtrength*, &c.

Truth. Yea and it might alſo teach them not to fight but with *Chriſts Weapons* in *Chriſts Cauſe*; who hath ſaid, That all that take the *Sword*, that is, (as I conceive) in *Chriſts cauſe*, ſhall periſh by it, *Matth*. 26. 52.

The Warres of the Wal-denſes.

3. *Peace*. Concerning the *Walldenſes* Mr *Cotton* ſayth, They never loſt *Victorie*, but when they complied with the *Papiſts*, and truſted more to their *falſe pretences*, then to the *Lord*. And he adds, that it is not true, that the *finall ſucceſſe* of *Victorie* fell to the *Papiſts*, to the *utter extirpation* of thoſe *Walldenſes*; for ſayth he, thoſe *Witneſſes* were not *extirpated* but *diſperſed*.

Truth. For their Complying with *Papiſts*, alas, what can *Gods* little flock, his two *Witneſſes* doe with *carnall weapons*, unleſſe aſſiſted by *carnall Men*, to whom this *carnall courſe* cauſeth them to *bow downe*, *diſſemble*, *lye*, &c. as holy *David* with *Achiſh* and his *Philiſtims*.

2. For the *Succeſſe* it is evident that the *Waldenſes*

and their *Adherents*, were ſo defeated by the *Popes Armies*, that in reſpect of any *power* to reſiſt, the *Armies* of the *Waldenſes* were wholly *extirpated*, although it is true (through *Gods* o're-powring hand) the *Truths* of *Chriſt* (which the holy *Waldenſian Witneſſes* teſtified) were more and more propagated by their *Diſperſions*, *Chriſt Jeſus* gaines more by *preaching* his *Truth* in a flying *perſecuted diſperſion*, then by *fighting* on *Horſbacke* with *carnall weapons* in *carnall companies*, &c. Acts 8. & 11.

4. *Peace*. But, whereas it was obſerved from *Daniell* and *John* their *Prophecies*, that *Antichriſt* was foretold to obtaine great ſucceſſe againſt *Chriſt Jeſus*, for a time determined: Mr *Cotton* ſayth, Not againſt *Chriſt Jeſus*, but his *Servants*, and that either in *Suffring* for his *Truth*, or when they ill handled his *Cauſe*.

208] *Truth*. Be it ſo, yet the *Propheſies* were true, and truely were fulfilled, and it is *Gods Counſell* that for the time appointed, *Chriſt Jeſus* in his *Truths* and *Servants* is *deſpiſed*, Pſal. 89. &c. How can then *temporall victorie* and *proſperitie* be expected by *Chriſts followers* for *Chriſts Cauſe*, or the *temporall Sword* be an *Ordinance* for *Chriſts ſpirituall Kingdome* and *Worſhip*?

5. *Peace*. Now laſtly, when the *weapons* of the *Saints Victories* were mentioned three; (*Revel.* 12.) 1. *Chriſts Bloud*. 2. The *Word* of their *Teſtimonie*. 3. Their *owne Bloud*: Mr *Cotton* anſwers; this is true in *private Chriſtians*: But (ſayth he) the *Sword* of *Gideon*, the *publike Magiſtrate* is the *Lords Sword*, &c. when drawen out for *Gods cauſe* and *Worſhip*, *Chriſtian weapons.*

according to *God*, is *Victorious*, Revel. 17. with Revel. 19. 14. 19, 20.

Chrifts Sword.

Truth. I anfwer; *Gideons Sword* (if well examined) will be found a *Figure* of that *fharpe Sword* of that great *Captaine* and *Generall Chrift Jefus*. This *Sword* comes forth of his *Mouth* in the *Preachings* and *Writings* of his *Servants:* other fword we never finde he ufed in all his *Battells* againft all his *Adverfaries:* yea even againft the *Devill* himfelfe and his *Inftruments*.

Chrifts Warres and Victories, Revel. 17.

Peace. Yea, thofe very *Victories* of the Saints, *Revel.* 19. are expreffely won with that *Sword* which comes forth of his *Mouth:* And his owne *white Horfe*, and the *Horfes* of his *Followers*, and the *white Linnen* with which they are clothed, cannot with any fhew of *Chriftian Reafon* hould forth the *carnall preparation* of *white Horfes*, (literally) *Guns, Swords*, &c. But of the *Word* of *Meekneffe, Innocencie* and *Righteoufneffe* (which is interpreted the *Fine Linnen*, verf. 8.

Gideons *Army typicall.*

Truth. To fhut up this Chapter, *Gideons Armie* and *Artillerie* and *Victorie*, cannot be *type* of fuch *Materiall Armies, Artillerie*, and *Victories*, but of a *Spirituall Armie*, fighting with the *Light* and *Teftimonie* of *Gods Truth* openly *proclaimed*, and the chearefull breaking of the *earthen Veffells* of their *Bodies* for *Chrifts Caufe*, when in *conclufion*, the *Antichriftian Midianites* (by their *Divifions* and *Combuftions*) run their *Swords* in each others *Bowells*, with *mutuall flaughters* and *Deftructions*; as woefull experiences hath declared.

209] *Exam: of* Chap. 65. *replying to* Chap. 68.

Peace. FRom the *Argument* of the *Teſtimonie* of *Kings* and *Princes* concerning *perſecution* for *matters* of *Religion* in their *Kingdomes* and *Dominions*, the *Priſoner* deſcended to the Argument from *ancient Writers:* unto ſome of which ſayth the Diſcuſſer, the Anſwerer pleaſeth to make Anſwer: Unto this M[r] *Cotton* replyes; As if any of them were *omitted*, or as if all of them were not *anſwered*: Compare the *Priſoners Letter* and mine together, and ſee if I have balked any one of them.

Truth. M[r] *Cotton* would here inſinuate a *falſe Charge:* I have compared the *Priſoners Letter*, and the *Anſwer*, and although M[r] *Cotton* hath ſaid *ſome-thing* to *ſome-thing*, which every one of them ſpake: Yet he that impartially will view the *Paſſages* ſhall finde, that although in ſtrictneſſe of *Gammar Rules*, he may not be ſaid to omit to ſay ſome thing to each of them, yet in reſpect of *Matter* and *Argument*, he hath toucht but ſome, and that but lightly, as the *Candle* of *Examination* will make it appeare.

Peace. Hilarius words in the Letter are theſe: "The *Chriſtian Church* doth not *perſecute*, but is "*perſecuted:* and lamentable it is to ſee the great "*folly* of theſe *Times*, and to ſigh at the fooliſh "opinion of this *World*, in that Men thinke by "humane ayde to helpe *God*, and with *worldly pompe* "and *power* to undertake to defend the *Chriſtian* "*Church:* I aske you *Biſhops*, what *helpe* uſed the "*Apoſtles* in the *publiſhing* of the *Goſpel?* With the

The Chriſtian Church doth not perſecute, but is perſecuted.

“ayde of what *power* did they *Preach Chriſt*, and
“*convert* the *Heathen* from their *Idolatrie* to *God?*
“When they were in *priſons*, and lay in *chaines*, did
“they praiſe or give thankes to *God* for any *Digni-*
“*ties* or *Graces* and *Favours* received from the *Court?*
“Or doe you thinke that *Paul* went about with *Re-*
“*gall Mandates* or *Kingly Authoritie*, to *gather* and
“and *eſtabliſh* the *Church* of *Chriſt?* Sought he *pro-*
“*tection* from *Nero*, *Veſpatian*, &c? The *Apoſtles*
“wrought with their own hands for their *Mainten-*
“*ance*, travelled by Land, and wandred from *Towne*
“to *Citie* to preach *Chriſt:* Yea the more they were
“forbidden, the more they taught and preached
“*Chriſt:* But now alas *Humane helpe* muſt *aſſiſt* and
“and *protect* the *Faith*, and give *countenance* to it,
210] “and by vaine and *worldly Honours* doe men
“ſeeke to defend the *Church* of *Chriſt*, as if he by
“his *power* were unable to performe it.

Truth. How many goulden heavenly *Sentences* (like ſo many precious *Jewells*) are treaſured up, in the *Cabinet* of this holy *Teſtimonie* of *Hilarius?* And yet, but ſome of them, nay onely one of them doth M[r] *Cotton* chooſe to anſwer, to wit, this, The *Chriſtian Church* doth not *perſecute*, but is *perſecuted.*

Truth. Deare *Peace*, Each *inch* and *ſhread* of *heavenly Gold* is *precious*, forget not therefore the *Addition* in the *Letter*, *Hilarie* againſt the *Arrians*

Worldly glory and perſecution characters of the falſe Church.

“thus: The *Church* which formerly by enduring
“*miſerie* and *Impriſonment*, was knowne to be the
“true *Church*, doth now *terriſie* others by *Impriſon-*
“*ment*, *Baniſhment*, and *Miſerie*, and boaſteth that
“ſhee is *highly eſteemed* of the *World*, whereas the

" *true Church* cannot but be *hated* of the ſame. In which and other *Paſſages* of *Hilarius* M[r] *Cotton* might ſee as in a *Glaſſe*, the foule *ſpots* of his *owne* and *New Englands face*, in a moſt lively *Teſtimonie* againſt both *bloudie Tenents* and *practices*.

Peace. To cloſe upon the Point: M[r] *Cotton* ſayth, He cannot make it a *marke* of a *Chriſtian Church* to be *perſecuted*, for (*Acts* 9 31.) the *Churches* had reſt, &c. Nor a *marke* of a *falſe Church* to *perſecute*; for, *Aſa* perſecuted the *Prophet* (2 Chron. 16. 10.) *Acts* 7. 51. the true *Church perſecuted* the *Prophets*.

Truth. When the *Scripture* or *common* Reaſon ſpeakes of a *common marke* or *Character*, proper to one they deny not; but in an *Act*, or unuſuall caſes that *Marke* or *Character* may be worne by the *Contraries*. *Noah* was *drunk*; *Abraham* lyes; *David* commits *Adulterie*: yet *lying*, *drunkenneſſe* and *whoredome* were not their ordinarie *Characters*, but the *Markes* of the *common Lyars*, *Drunkards* and *Adulterers* of this *World*: *David* ſtobd *Uriah* with his Pen, and *Aſa* impriſoned the *Prophet*; yet theſe *Acts* were not their ordinarie *Badges*, but rather *Spots* or *Blemiſhes*, *Warts*, or *Scabs*, which grew on and were caſt off (like *Pauls Viper*) without the note of a *conſtant marke* or *character*.

The ſins of Gods children.

It is the propertie of *Fire* to aſcend, and *Water* to deſcend, yet the *Scripture* relates of the *deſcending* of *Fire*, and the *aſcending* of *Water*, which takes not away the *ordinarie Nature* of the [211] *marke* and *character* of *Fires aſcending*, and *Waters deſcending* the *Hills* and *Mountaines*.

An arrant *Whore* is not alwayes in actuall *Whore-*

dome and *Bloud*, though both are her *Markes* and *Diſpoſitions:* A *chaſt* wife or *Virgin* abhorres both, and yet by force or great *Temptation*, may be *vanquiſhed* (as *Bathſheba*) which afterwards the *Teares* of godly *Sorrow* and *Repentance* waſh away.

Peace. Yea but, the *Queſtion* is (ſayth Mr *Cotton*) whether *Magiſtrates* may not puniſh arrogant *Hereticks* and *Seducers?*

Christs Witneſſes.

Truth. In all ages *God* hath permitted, *Goulden Images* (like *Nebuchadnezzars*) to be ſet up, I ſay *State Worſhips* and *Religions!* And he hath alſo provided his *Witneſſes* to teſtifie his *Truth* againſt ſuch *Abominations:* Such *Witneſſes diſſenting*, *Non-conforming*, and refuſing to come to the *Common Aſſemblies* of ſuch *Worſhippers* (to come to *Church* in plaine *Engliſh*) to yeeld *Conformitie*, to *Subſcribe*, to *Sweare*, &c. are commonly cryed downe for *Hereticks*, *Schiſmaticks*, &c. And if they open their Lips in defence of their owne *Conſcience*, and profeſſion of *Gods Truth! Seducers*, *Seducers*, *Blaſphemers*, *Blaſphemers*.

2. *Peace*. But 2. ſayth Mr *Cotton*) it is another begging of the *Queſtion*, to take it for granted, that it is a *marke* of no true *Church* to procure the *Civill puniſhment* of incorrigible, obſtinate *Hereticks* and *Seducers*.

A true Wife of Chriſt no perſecutour.

Truth. I intend by a *marke* or *character*, an inbred conſtant *diſpoſition*, put forth in a *conſtant* and *ordinarie practice:* And then I dare challenge Mr *Cotton* to produce any true *Church* of *Chriſt*, eyther in *Scripture* or *Hiſtorie*, that did *ordinarily* and *conſtantly profeſſe* and *practice* to ſtirre up the *Civill Magiſtrate* againſt ſuch whom they judged incorrigible *obſtinate Hereticks* and *Seducers*.

Peace. That which follows is full of *Wonder* and *Aſtoniſhment*, for M[r] *Cotton* confeſſing the *Chriſtian Church* doth not *perſecute*, that is (ſayth he) *perſecute* in *Excommunicating* the *Heretick*) it was replyed; this is but an Evaſion, for who denies Power to *Chriſts Church* to *Excommunicate?* or who underſtands by *Excommunication, perſecution* for *Conſcience?* M[r] *Cotton* anſwers; the *Priſoner* did not expreſſe himſelfe, what *perſecution* he meant, and alſo ſince *falſe Excommunication* is a great *perſecution*, and ſo *Chriſt Jeſus* himſelfe eſteemes of it, *Luk.* 21. 22.

Touching perſecution what it is.

212] *Truth.* I have formerly and muſt againe appeale to the *nature* of the *word*, commonly uſed and taken, and aske, if *perſecution* properly ſo taken be not a *corporeall violence*, or *hunting* for *Religion* and *Conſcience* ſake! And then halfe an eye will ſee through this poore and thin *excuſe* and *covering*, notwithſtanding that falſe *excommunication* be a *ſpirituall perſecution*, and the abuſe of the *ſpirituall Sword* be alſo *deeper* and *fouler* then the *abuſe* of the *civill* and *materiall.*

Peace. To this (upon the Point) M[r] *Cotton* conſented, to wit, that *Hilarius* complaint, ſpeaketh not to *Excommunication*, but *civill cenſures*, and therefore anſwers, firſt by *proportion* that *excommunication* of an *Heretick* is no *perſecution*, and therefore by *proportion* neither is the *civill puniſhment* of an *Heretick, perſecution.* By *conceſſion* of *Hilaries* words, that the *Apoſtles* did not, and we may not propagate *Religion* by the *Sword.*

Truth. The Queſtion with *Hilarie* was not whether a true *Church* did *perſecute* an *Heretick, Idolater, Blaſ-*

Difference between a civill and ſpirituall State.

phemer, &c. but whether a true *Church* perſecuted at all by *civill cenſures:* Now there being *two States*, the *Civill* or *Corporeall* and the *Eccleſiaſticall* or *ſpirituall:* There are conſequently two ſorts of *Lawes*, two ſorts of *Tranſgreſſions*, two ſorts of *puniſhments*, to wit, *Civill* and *Spirituall*, and there muſt of neceſſitie be two ſorts of *falſe* or *corrupt puniſhments*, which are not *juſt puniſhments*, but *oppreſſions*, *perſecutions* or *huntings*, to wit, the *Civill perſecution* and the *ſpirituall:* Now M[r] *Cotton* (confounding *Heaven* and *Earth* together) deceives himſelfe and others by a notion of *ſpirituall perſecution*, to wit, by *Excommunication*, contrary to *Hilaries ſcope*, and the *ſcope* of this whole *Diſpute* and *Controverſie*.

The nature of ſpirituall puniſhments.

I may illuſtrate it thus: Some *Tutours* of *Kings Children*, not being authorized to correct the *Bodies* of ſuch *young Princes*, are ſaid ſometimes (not without ſome deſert) to correct the *Bodies* of *Inferiours* (the young *Princes Favourites*,) by which the minds of ſuch young *Princes* ſmarted *ſufficiently*, if not *exceedingly*. I parallell not the *ſimilitude* in all reſpects, but to illuſtrate the *difference* and *diſtinction*, between a *ſpirituall puniſhment* of the *minde*, and *ſpirit*, *ſoule* and *affections*, with which *Chriſt Jeſus* hath furniſhed his *Churches:* and that *Civill* or *corporall puniſhment*, which he never gave them power to inflict (unleſſe in *miraculous diſpenſation*) over the *Bodies* of any, *directly* or *indirectly* by *Themſelves* or *others*.

213] *Peace*. It is an everlaſting Truth; *Rightly diſtinguiſh*, *rightly Teach:* but let us view M[r] *Cottons* Second Anſwer, He grants that the *Chriſtian Religion* was not, nor is not to be *propagated* by the *Sword*.

Truth. Then let *Heaven* and *Earth* judge, if Mr *Cotton* may not (in this caſe) out of his owne *mouth* be judged, ſince in this whole *Diſcourſe* he ſets the viſible *Headſhip* of *Chriſt Jeſus* (that golden *Head*, Cant. 5. [11.]) over the *Church* and all her *Officers*, *Doctrines* and *Practices*, (in the power of *Correcting*, *Reforming*, &c.) on the *ſhoulders* of the *Civill State*, the *Miniſters* and *Officers* thereof: provided that they execute not this *Headſhip* or *Government*, except they be able to judge, that is, (in *Engliſh*) provided they be of his *Conſcience* and *Judgement*, and ſo conſequently will *judge* and *execute*, according to the *Clergies* (though implicite) *decree* and *ſentence*.

The nature of Chriſts ſpirituall Government.

Peace. It is not much unlike that Mr *Cotton* affirmeth in the words following: for although he confeſſeth it is not proper for *Chriſtian Churches* to inflict *Civill puniſhments* by *Themſelves*, yet makes he (as all *Popes* and *Popiſh perſecutours* have done) the *Magiſtrates* and *Civill powers*, their *ſervants* and *ſlaves* for execution, &c.

The Civill Powers and Officers the Clergies Executioners.

Truth. This Mr *Cotton* covers over with this *Similitude*, ſaying that although it is not proper for *Lambes* to teare *Wolves*, yet if they were reaſonable they would run to their *Shepheards* to ſend out their *Dogs* after them.

Now under this fine *Paint* and *vizard* of *Lambelike diſpoſitions* of *Shepheards*, the *Biſhops*, *Presbyterians*, and *Independents*, may render the *Civill Magiſtrates* not as *Shepheards*, but no other, upon the point and in *plaine Engliſh*, then their *ſervants* and *Executioners*, to puniſh ſuch on whom the *Clergie* firſt have paſt their Sentence. The bloudie *Papiſts* have commonly uſed to perſecute *Chriſt Jeſus formally* and *judicially*, delivering over *Chriſt Jeſus* (in his Servants,) orderly to *Pontius Pilate*, the *Secular Power*. The *Proteſtant perſecutors* uſe a *finer vaile* (every ugly *vizard* will not ſo deceive) for though they practice not ſo *above boord*, in reſpect of a formall and judiciall delivering of *Chriſt* (the *Heretick*) unto their *Shepheard Pontius Pilate* the *Secular power*, yet they doe it, and doe it as ſubſtantially and fully by *preaching* and *chalking* out to their *ſervants* the *Magiſtrates*, [214] their task, I ſay, as fully as ever the bloudie *Popes*, the *Biſhops*, or their *Chancellours* did.

Peace. But why (ſayth Mr *Cotton*) ſhould a *Chriſtian Church* ſpare an *Idolater*, tempting of her now, any more then the eye of an holy *Iſraelite* was to ſpare the like *Tempters* in the dayes of old, *Deut.* 13. 3?

Spirituall Judgements more terrible ſince Chriſt, then corporall before his coming.

Truth. Mr *Cotton* cannot get over this *block*, though it be but a *ſhadow*, yea the *ſhadow* of a *ſhadow*, aboliſhed by *Chriſt Jeſus:* Mr *Cotton* a little before grants that the *power* of *ſpirituall chaines* far exceeds the power of *materiall*, and if ſo how cleere is it, that the *ſpirituall impartialitie* and *ſeveritie* of a *Virgin Iſraelite* now, is incomparablie *ſharper* and more *dreadfull*, by putting *ſpiritually* to Death ſuch as *Tempt* them from the *Lord* their *God*, who hath brought them forth of *Ægypt* into *ſpirituall Canaan*, then the *impartialitie* and *ſeveritie* of any literall *Iſraelite*, againſt ſuch as tempted them from the *Lord*, who in a Type had brought them forth of materiall *Ægypt* into *materiall Canaan*?

I adde (ſweete *Peace*) to end this Chapter, If the *Father* of *Lights* graciouſly pleaſe to open a *crevis* of *Light* to that (otherwiſe) *excellent* and *piercing* eye of Mr *Cotton* in this *Controverſie*, he will confeſſe concerning this cutting off in *Iſrael* theſe two things.

Firſt, that the cutting off in *materiall Iſrael,* was by *Swords, Stones,* &c. a cutting off from the *holy Land,* and a caſting out of *Gods ſight,* which *cutting* off *God* executed either by legall *Judgement* and *Sentence* among Themſelves, or by furious hand of *perſecutours* and *oppreſſours, ſlaughtering* or *captivating* that People.

Secondly, That there is no other cutting off in the *Goſpel,* but by the *ſpirituall Sword* of the *Word* & *Ordinances* of *Chriſt,* or the violent hand of *Oppreſſours, Antichriſtians,* &c. carrying Gods *Iſrael* captive into *myſticall Babylon,* or *Ægypt* of falſe *Worſhip,* or *worldly corruption,* which is ten thouſand-fold more *terrible* and *dreadfull,* then the literall and materiall *Captivitie* of *Iſrael.*

The cutting off or Excommunicating from the holy Land of Iſrael *figurative and typicall.*

215] *Exam: of* Chap. 66. *replying to* Chap. 69.

Peace. Here Mr *Cotton* complaines of wrong, in that the Diſcuſſer chargeth him to plead for *perſecution,* and yet confeſſeth that he agrees with *Hilarie.*

Truth. Mr *Cotton* indeed agrees with *Hilarie* in *generall profeſſion,* that the *Goſpel* is not to be propagated by *Sword,* but in particulars he affirmes, the *Blaſphemer,* the *Idolater,* the *Heretick,* the *Seducer* is to be *perſecuted.* In the *generall* he ſaith, the *Magiſtrate* may not *conſtraine* any to *believe* & *profeſſe* the *Truth*, yet in particulars; thus far ſaith he, a man may be *conſtrained* by the *Magiſtrates* withdrawing *Countenance* and *Favour*, *Incouragement* and *Employment* from him, which affirming, what doth he elſe but affirme that he may be *conſtrained*, depoſed, puniſhed, that is, *perſecuted.*

A twofold way of conſtraint.

Peace. Indeed ſuch kinde of *puniſhment*, as to diſplace men, to keepe them out from all *offices*, or *places* of *Truſt* and *Credit* (becauſe of *difference* of *Conſcience*) may prove in the particular a *greater affliction* and *puniſhment*, then a *Cenſure*, a *Fine*, *Impriſonment*, yea ſometimes more bitter to ſome *Spirits* then *Death* it ſelfe.

Truth. Yea and Mr *Cottons* ground is both *unſafe* and *darke*, and needs a *candle* of Light to diſcover the *bottome* and *compaſſe* of it: Such, ſaith he, as walke not according to their *Light*, are neither true *ſervants* to *God* nor *Man*, but

What it is to walke according to a mans Light.

First, what meanes here Mr *Cotton* by *Light?* Light in this ſence is commonly taken two wayes.

Firſt, For that is *Light* indeed, to wit, the precious Light of *Gods* revealed will.

Secondly, That which ſo appeares to be, to a mans minde and *Conſcience*, but may be a *falſhood*, a *lye*, a *miſtake*, and *darkneſſe*. Mr *Cotton* had done well to have diſtinguiſhed, for (before) he blamed King *James* for walking according to his *Light*: and although (upon the point) he makes the *Civill Magiſtrates* in all parts of the *World*, the *Heads*, *Protectours*, and *Governours* of *Chriſts Church*; yet if the *eyes* of theſe *Heads* ſee not by his *Light*, he *cuts* off theſe *Heads*, ſorbidding them to act as *Heads*, and to walke according to their *Light*, they muſt (as [216] often he tells us) ſuſpend, untill they have *Light*, &c.

2. *Peace.* Beſide, it comes oft to paſſe, that the *Light* which ſhines by *preaching* or *practice* of others, although it be a meane ſufficient to *convince*, if *God* pleaſe to bleſſe it, yet untill the *Conſciences* of men be *convinced* of the *Light* of it, I judge it cannot properly be ſaid to be the *Light* of their *Conſciences*, nor they to ſin againſt the *Light* of their *Conſciences*.

Conviction two-fold: Sufficient in it ſelfe: or to the partie efficacious.

3. *Truth.* Yea, and there is a *morall vertue*, a *morall fidelitie*, *abilitie* and *honeſtie*, which other men (beſide *Church-members*) are, by good *nature* and *education*, by good *Lawes* and good *examples* nouriſhed and trained up in, that Civill places of *Truſt* and *Credit* need not to be *Monopolized* into the hands of *Church-Members* (who ſometimes are not fitted for them) and all others deprived and deſpoiled of their *naturall* & *Civill Rights* and *Liberties*.

Peace. But what ſay you (Deare *Truth*) to Mr *Cottons Apologie* for *New England* (for as for *conſtraint* in *old* he is ſilent) he ſayth he knowes not of any *conſtraint* upon any to come to *Church*, to pay *Church Duties*, and ſayth it is not ſo in his *Towne*.

Truth. If Mr *Cotton* be *forgetfull*, ſure he can hardly be *ignorant* of the *Lawes* and *Penalties* extant in *New England* that are (or if *repealed* have been) againſt ſuch as abſent Themſelves from *Church Morning* and *Evening*, and for *Non-payment* of *Church-Duties*, although no Members.

Touching the Maintenance of the new English Ministers.

For a *Freedome* of *Not paying* in his *Towne*, it is to their *commendation* and *Gods praise*, who hath shewed him and others more of his holy *Truth:* Yet who can be ignorant of the *Sessments* upon all in other Townes, of the many *Suits* and *Sentences* in *Courts* (for Non-payment of *Church-Duties*) even against such as are no *Church Members?* Of the *Motions* and *pleadings* of some (not the meanest of their *Ministers*) for *Tithes?* And how ever for my part I beleeve M[r] *Cotton* ingeniously willing, that none be forced expressly to pay to his *Maintenance*, yet I question whether he would work if he were not well payd: And I could relate also what is commonly reported abroad, to wit, that the rich *Merchants* and *people* of *Boston* would never give so *freely*, if they were *forced*, yet now they are forced to give for shame (I take it) in the *Publike Congregation.*[1]

[1] "Whereas complainte hath bene made to this Court that dyvers persons within this jurisdiction doe usually absent themselves from church meetings upon the Lords day, power is therefore given to any two Assistants to heare and sensure, either by ffyne or imprisonment (at their discrecõn) all misdemeanors of that kinde committed by any inhabitant within this jurisdiction." March, 1634–5. *Mass. Col. Records*, i. 140.

"And withall it is also ordered, that every such inhabitant who shall not voluntarily contribute, proportionably to his ability, with other freemen of the same towne, to all common charges, as well for upholding the ordinances in the churches as otherwise, shall be compelled thereto by assessment and distress to be levied by the cunstable &c." Sept. 6, 1638. *Mass. Col. Records*, i. 240.

Nov. 4, 1646, a similar order was passed by the General Court requiring attendance upon "ye ministery of the word upon ye Lords dayes and upon such publike fasts dayes and dayes of thanksgiving as are to be generally held by ye appointment of authority" and for every absence the offender was to forfeit five shillings. *Mass. Col. Rec.*, ii. 178.

We have Winthrop's testimony that Cotton promoted "a freedome of not paying in his towne." He says under date of May 2, 1639, "Mr. Cotton preaching out of the 8 of Kings, 8, taught, that when magistrates are forced to provide for the maintenance of min-

217] The *Indians* of this *Countrie* have a Way calld *Nanówwe*, or *Giving* their Commodities *freely*, by which they get better *bargaines*, then if they ſtood ſtiffly on their *Tearmes* of *Anaqúſhento*, or *Trading:* And when not *ſatisfied* to the *utmoſt*, they *grudge*, *revile*, &c.[1] It cannot be, but that to ſuch *Deceitfulneſſe* of *Heart* Mr Cotton is ſubject as well as others, though *Love* bids me, and others, to hope the beſt.

Peace. The cloſe of this Chapter ſeemes *ſtrange* and *wonderfull*, for Mr *Cotton* acknowledged that *Propagation* of *Religion* ought not to be by the " *Sword*, and yet inſtantly againe maintaines he the " uſe of the *Sword* when perſons (which then muſt " be judged by the *Civill State*) blaſpheme the true " *God* and the true *Religion*, and alſo ſeduce others to " damnable *Hereſie* and *Idolatrie:* But this (ſayth he) " is not the Propagation of *Religion*, but the preſerv- " ing of it, and if it doe conduce to Propagation, it is onely *Removendo prohibens*. *Of propagating Religion by the Sword.*

Truth. What is this *Removendo prohibens*, but as

iſters, etc., then the churches are in a declining condition. Then he ſhowed that the miniſter's maintenance ſhould be by voluntary contribution, not by lands, or revenues, or tithes, etc.; for theſe have always been accompanied with pride, contention and ſloth, etc." *New England*, i. 355.

But Winthrop makes another ſtatement which does not agree altogether with Cotton's unqualified aſſertion, "leaſt of all do I know that any are conſtrayned to pay church-duties in New England." He ſays in 1642, "The churches held a different courſe in raiſing the miniſters' maintenance. Some did it by way of taxation, which was very offenſive to ſome." *New England*, ii. 112. Cf. Lechford, *Plain Dealing*, 19.

1 "They are marvellous ſubtle in their Bargaines to ſave a penny. They will often confeſs for their own ends, that the Engliſh are richer and wiſer and valianter them themſelves; yet it is for their owne ends, and therefore they add *Nanoüe*, give me this or that, a diſeaſe which they are generally infected with." Williams, *Key, &c.*, 156. *Pub. Narr. Club*, i. 243.

the *weeding* of a *Field* or *Garden?* And every *Husbandman* will ſay, that the end of ſuch his *work*, is the *propagation* and *increaſe* of his *graine* and *fruit*, as well as the making of his *fence*, and *planting* and *ſowing* of his *Field* or *Garden:* What therefore is this *Confeſſion*, (though with this *Diſtinction*) but in truth an acknowledgement of what in *Words* and *Tearmes*, he yet denies (with *Hilaire*) to wit, a propagating of *Chriſtian Religion* and *Truth* by the *Civill Sword?*

2. Beſides it is the ſame *hand* and *power* that plucks up the *weedes*, and *plants* the *Corne*, and conſequently, that ſame *hand* and *Sword* that *deſtroyes* the *Heretick*, may *make* the *Chriſtian*, &c.

Exam: of Chap. 67. *replying to* Chap. 70.

Peace. COncerning *Tertullians* ſpeech, and eſpecially that Branch, to wit, that [By the Law of *naturall equitie*, Men are not to be compelled to any *Religion*, but permitted to *believe* or not *believe* at all] M[r] *Cotton* anſwers, that they doe permit the *Indians*, but it will not therefore be ſafe to tollerate the *publicke Worſhip* of *Devills* or *Idolls*. The Diſcuſſer replied, [218] that they doe permit the *Indians* in their *Paganiſh Worſhip*, and therefore were partiall to their *Countrymen* and *others:* M[r] *Cotton* anſwers; that it is not true, that they doe ſo permit the *Indians*, what ever they may doe privately: That the *Indians* ſubmit to the ten *Commandments*, and that ſome of their *Miniſters* have preached to them in *Engliſh*, which hath been *interpreted:* That one now

Touching the Indians *of* New-England.

preacheth in their owne *Language:* Further, That they permit *ſtrangers* in their *Worſhip.* And for their *Countrymen,* for the moſt part that they worſhip *God* with them: They which are diſtant have *Libertie* of *publike prayer* and *preaching,* by ſuch as themſelves chooſe without *diſturbance.*

Truth. Concerning the *Indians,* it is moſt true, that the *Monahigganéucks, Miſhawomêucks, Pawtuckséucks,* and *Cawſumſéucks* (who profeſſe to ſubmit to the *Engliſh*) continue in their publike *Paganiſh Worſhip* of *Devills,* I ſay *openly* and *conſtantly.*[1]

Peace. Yea but (ſaith Mr *Cotton*) they have ſubmitted to the ten *Commandments.*

Truth. I anſwer; the ten *Commandments* containe a *Renunciation* of all falſe *Gods* and *Worſhips,* and a *Worſhipping* of the true *God,* according to his owne *Inſtitutions* and *Appointments,* which their practice is as farre from, as *Mid-night* is from *Mid-day.*

Worſhipping of God and Chriſt before the foundation of Repentance, is nothing but Antichriſtian diſorder.

2. To put men upon *obſervations* of *Gods Worſhip,* as *Prayer,* &c. before the *Foundations* of *Repentance* from *dead workes* (their *worſhipping* of *Idolls,* &c.) is as farre from the *Order* of *Chriſt Jeſus,* and his *Chriſtian principles* (whereof *Repentance* from *dead workes* is the firſt) as the building of an *Houſe* or *Palace,* without the firſt *Groundſell* or *Foundation* laid.[2]

[1] The *Monahigganéucks* are the Narraganſetts, which elſewhere he calls the *Nanhigganēucks.* The *Miſhawomêucks* are probably what he calls in the *Key* the *Maſſachuſêucks,* or Maſſachuſetts. The *Pawtuſuckéucks* are the Pawtuckets. The *Cawſumſéucks* are "probably the Wampanoags or Pokanokets." *Key, &c.,* 22. *Pub. Narr. Club,* i. 82. For Williams's derivation of the name Narraganſett, ſee his depoſition, June 18, 1682. *R. I. Col. Rec.,* i. 26.

[2] Williams ſays in his *Key,* that he "could eaſily have brought the countrey

Peace. Mr *Cotton* therefore ſaith, they *preach* unto them.

Truth. I from my ſoule wiſh that all the *Lords* people in *New England* were *Prophets*, yea true *Apoſtolicall Miniſters* or *Preachers*, truely furniſhed with *Chriſts Abilities*, and *Chriſts Commiſſion*, to goe forth to convert and baptize the *Nations*, even theſe *Wildeſt* of the *Nations* of *Adams* Children: But *Converſion* of *Nations* Mr *Cotton* ſayth (upon *Revel.* 15.) untill the *ſeaven plagues* of the *ſeaven Angells* be fullfilled, will not be great.[1]

to "keeping the Engliſhman's day of worſhip," but that I was perſwaded, and am, that Gods way is firſt to turne a ſoule from its Idolls, both of heart, worſhip, and converſation, before it is capable of worſhip, to the true and living God. As alſo, that the two firſt Principles and Foundations of true Religion or Worſhip of the true God in Chriſt, are Repentance from dead workes, and Faith towards God, before the Doctrine of Baptiſme or waſhing and the laying on of handes, which containe the Ordinances and Practiſes of worſhip." *Key, &c.*, 130. *Pub. Narr. Club*, i. 160, 161.

[1] *Bloody Tenent Waſhed*, 148. "Mr Cotton out of that in Revelations 15. none could enter into the temple until, etc., delivered, that neither Jews nor any more of the Gentiles ſhould be called until Antichriſt were deſtroyed, viz. to a church eſtate, though here and there a proſelyte." *Winthrop*, ii. 36.

This is one of the reaſons Lechford gives in 1641 why "there hath not been any ſent forth by any Church to learne the native's language, or to inſtruct them in the Religion." "Some ſay out of *Rev.* 15. laſt [verſe], it is not probable that any nation more can be converted, til the calling of the Jews; till the seven plagues finiſhed none was able to enter into the Temple, that is, the Chriſtian Church, and the ſeventh viall is not yet poured forth." *Plain Dealing*, 21.

"Three things have made us thinke it is not yet time for God to worke. 1. Becauſe till the Jewes come in, there is a ſeale ſet upon the hearts of thoſe people, as they thinke from ſome Apocalypticall places." *The Day-Breaking, if not the Sun-Riſing of the Goſpell with the Indians in New England.* (1647,) p. 15. 16. 3 *Maſſ. Hiſt. Coll.*, iv. 15. This tract is aſcribed to Eliot in this reprint of the Maſſ. Hiſt. Society. But there is internal evidence that it is not his. It is with more reaſon aſcribed to Rev. John Wilſon, of Boſton. See Francis's *Life of Eliot*, 346.

Williams in the next paragraph acknowledges this interpretation "to be very probable." In this ſame year, 1652, he writes: "We may ſee a great miſtake as touching that great point of *Converſion:* There is a great breathing

219] This *Interpretation* I acknowledge to be very *probable*, ſo far as concernes any great *Converſion* of the *Nations* before the downfall of *Antichriſt*, and in the meane ſeaſon I commend the pious *Endeavors* of any (profeſſing *Miniſtery* or not) to doe good to the *Soules* of all Men as We have *opportunitie*. But that any of the *Miniſters* ſpoken of are furniſhed with true *Apoſtolicall Commiſſion* (Matth. 28. [19. 20.]) I ſee not for theſe Reaſons.

Touching preaching to the Indians *in* New-England.

Firſt, The *Miniſter* or *Miniſters*, whom Mr *Cotton* I conceive intends, profeſſe an ordinarie *Office* in the *Church* of *Chriſt*, which is cleerely diſtinct, yea and another thing from the office of an *Apoſtle*, or one ſent forth to *preach* and *baptize*, Epheſ. 4. [11.] & 1 *Cor.* 12. [28.]

Secondly, Such *Churches* as are inveſted with the power of *Chriſt*, and ſo authoriz'd to ſend forth, are ſeperate from the *World*, which many thouſands of *Gods* people (dead and living) have ſeene juſt Reaſons to deny thoſe *Churches* ſo to be.

Thirdly, Were the *Church* true, and the *Meſſenger* or *Apoſtle* rightly ſent forth with *prayer* and *faſting*, according to *Act.* 13. [3.] yet I believe that none of the *Miniſters* of *New England*, nor any perſon in the whole *Countrey* is able to open the *Myſteries* of *Chriſt Jeſus* in any proprietie of their *ſpeech* or

in the *ſouls* of *Gods* people after the *Converſion* of the *Engliſh*, *Iriſh*, *Jewes*, *Indians*, and bleſſed be God for thoſe Breathings. Yet doubtleſſe the firſt great *worke* is the bringing of the *Saints* out of *Babel*, or *confuſed worſhips*, and the *downefall* of the *Papacie*, after the *witneſſes* *ſlaughtered*. Hence it is probably conceived by ſome upon *Revel.* 15. that untill the *vyals* be powred forth upon Antichriſt, the ſmoak ſo filleth the Temple, that no man, that is (Jew' of the *Jewes* or *Gentiles*) ſhall by converſion enter in." *Hireling Miniſtry*, p. 12.

Language, without which *proprietie*[1] it cannot be imagined that *Chriſt Jeſus* ſent forth his firſt *Apoſtles* or *Meſſengers*, and without which no people in the World are long willing to heare of *difficult* and heavenly matters. That none is ſo fitted;

Firſt, The *Natives* themſelves affirme, as I could inſtance in many particulars.

Secondly, The *Experience* of the Diſcuſſer and of many others teſtifie how hard it is for any man to attaine a little *proprietie* of their *Language* in common things (ſo as to eſcape *Deriſion* amongſt them) in many yeares, without abundance of *converſing* with them, in *Eating*, *travelling* and *lodging* with them, &c. which none of their *Miniſters* (other affaires not permitting) ever could doe.[2]

[1] Property, poſſeſſion.

[2] The "experience" of Williams in the ſtudy of the Indian language begun very early, even before his baniſhment. He ſays in 1677, ſpeaking of his negociations with Canonicus and Miantinomi in 1634–5: "God was pleaſed to give me a painful, patient ſpirit to lodge with them in their filthy, ſmokey holes, (even while I lived at Plymouth and Salem) to gain their tongue. I could debate with them (in a great meaſure) in their own language." Knowles, *Memoir*, 109. Of his experience in preaching to them, he ſays, in 1643, "of later times (out of deſire to attaine their Language) I have run through varieties of *Intercourſes* with them Day and Night, &c. Many ſolemn diſcourſes I have had with all *ſorts of Nations* of them, from one end of the Countrey to another (ſo farre as opportunity, and the little Language I have could reach.)" Of their ſpiritual condition "from my ſelfe many hundreths of times, great numbers of them have heard with great delight, and great convictions." *Key, &c.* Introduction and p. 123. *Pub. Narr. Club*, i. 85. 215.

In his *Key* he ſpeaks of a "little additional diſcourſe" which he had written on "that great point of their converſion" "becauſe this is the great inquiry of all men what Indians have been converted? What have the Engliſh done in thoſe parts? What hopes of the Indians receiving the knowledge of Chriſt?" *Key*, Introduction and Table. *Pub. Narr. Club*, i. 87. 281. This Diſcourſe has not been diſcovered. This is to be regretted, as it would bring from his "experience" ſome anſwer to "the great inquiry" which at that time had been awakened in England through the repreſentations of Winſlow, the reports

Peace. There being no helpes of *Art* and *learning* amongſt them, I ſee not how without conſtant *uſe* or a *Miracle,* any man is able to attaine to any *proprietie* of *ſpeech* amongſt them, even in common things. And without *proprietie* (as before) who knowes not how hardly all men (eſpecially *Barbarians*) [220] are brought to heare *matters* of *Heaven* (ſo *ſtrange* and contrary to *Nature*) yea, even *matters* of the *Earth,* except profit and other *worldly ends* compell them to ſpell out Mens *minds* and *meaning?*

Proprietie of Language neceſſary to the true preaching of Chriſt Jeſus to any people.

Truth. 3. I may truely adde a third, an *Inſtance* in the booke of their *Converſion,* written by Mr *Tho: Shepheard,* there Mr *Eliot* (the ableſt amongſt them in the *Indian Speech*) promiſing an old *Indian* a ſuit of Cloths, the man (ſayth the relation) not well underſtanding Mr *Eliots* ſpeech, asked another *Indian* what Mr *Eliot* ſaid.[1]

of Eliot's labors made by Wilſon, (*The Day-Breaking*), and Shepard, (*The Clear Sun-ſhine*), as well as by the organization of The Society for the Promoting and Propagating of the Goſpel of Jeſus Chriſt in New England. Quotations are made from it in Baylies' *Diſſuaſive* (1645). See Mr. Trumbull's note, *Pub. Narr. Club,* i. 220. In theſe he declares that he could have eaſily converted all the natives to an outward obſervance of Chriſtianity. But this, as he ſays above, is "farre from the Order of Chriſt Jeſus and his Chriſtian principles (whereof Repentance from dead workes is the firſt)." This may ſubtract a little from the force of the imputation caſt upon him by one of Shepard's ſtories. He ſays Eliot aſked a Narraganſett Sachem "why they did not learn of Mr. Williams who had lived among them divers years? and he ſoberly anſwered that they did not care to learn of him, becauſe hee is no good man but goes and workes upon the Sabbath day." *Clear Sun-ſhine,* p. 31.

1 "Mr. Eliot told him that becauſe he brought his wife and all his children conſtantly to the lecture, that he would therefore beſtow ſome clothes upon him, (it being now winter and the old man naked:) which promiſe he not certainly underſtanding the meaning of, aſked therefore of another Indian (who is Mr. Eliot's ſervant and very hopefull) what it was that Mr. Eliot promiſed him." Shepard, *Clear Sun-ſhine,* 12. 3 *Maſſ. Hiſt. Coll.,* iv. 46.

Peace. Me thinks, the *Native* not underſtanding ſuch a *common* and *wellcome* promiſe of cloths upon *Gift,* would farre more hardly underſtand M[r] *Eliots* preaching of the *garment* of *Righteouſneſſe Chriſt Jeſus,* unto which Men mutually turne the deafe Eare, &c.

Truth. Neither you (ſweet *Peace*) nor I Expreſſe thus much to dampe M[r] *Eliot* or any from doing all the good they can, whiles opportunitie laſts in any truely *Chriſtian* way, but to ſhew how great that miſtake is, that pretends ſuch a true *preaching* of *Chriſt Jeſus* to them in their owne *Language.*

Peace. But to proceed, in the next *Paſſage* M[r] *Cotton* affirmes their *Impartialitie* in permitting others as well as the *Indians.*

Truth. I anſwer; it is one thing to connive at a *ſtrange Papiſt* in private *devotions* on ſhoare, or in their *veſſells* at Anchor, &c. Another thing to permit *Papiſts, Jewes, Turkes,* &c. the free and conſtant *Exerciſe* of their *Religion* and *Worſhip,* in their reſpective Orders and Aſſemblies, were ſuch Inhabitants amongſt them.

Peace. Doubtleſſe the *bloudie Tenent* cannot permit this *Libertie,* neither to the *Papiſts, Jewes, Turkes,* &c. nor to the *Indians,* nor doth their *practice* toward their *Countrymen* hould forth a ſhew of ſuch a *freedome* or *permiſſion.*

Truth. I wonder why M[r] *Cotton* writes, that the moſt part of the *Engliſh* worſhip *God* with them, and the reſt abſent have *Libertie* to chooſe their *Preachers!* Since M[r] *Cotton* knowes the *Petition* and *Petitions* that have been preſented for *Libertie* of

Conſcience in *New England*, and he cannot but alſo know the *Impriſoning* and *Fining* of ſome of the *Petitioners*, &c.

221] *Peace.* It may be Mr *Cotton* will uſe the *common objection*, that ſome part of their *Petition* tended to *Diſturbance* in Civill Things.

Truth. Some of their *Petitions* were purely for *Libertie* of *Conſcience*, which ſome in *Office*, both in *Church* and *State* favoured, as is reported, if not promoted. If others or ſome part of them might be judged *offenſive* againſt *Lawes* made, yet why then hath not the *Libertie* of their *Conſcience* (in point of *Worſhip*) been granted to them? When they have complained (amongſt other Paſſages) that they have been forced to ſtay the *baptizing* of other Mens *children*, while their owne might not be admitted, and therefore earneſtly ſued for *Miniſters* and *Congregations* after their owne free *choice* and *Conſciences*, which have ever been denyed to them.

Conſcience to God in Worſhip a cloſe Priſoner in New-England, *and no Petitioner could obtaine its Libertie.*

Peace. It is ſaid, that their *Miniſters* being conſulted with, utterly denied to yeeld to any ſuch *Libertie.*

Truth. They might juſtly feare, that if ſuch a *window* were opened (as once Biſhop *Gardiner* ſpake in another caſe) that the *New Engliſh Congregations* and *Churches* would be as thin, as the *Presbyterians* complained theirs to have been, when the people once began to taſte the *Freedome* and *Libertie* of their *Conſciences*, from the ſlaves whip, &c.

Peace. In the next *Paſſage*, the Diſcuſſer having excepted againſt Mr *Cottons* diſtinguiſhing betweene Members of the *Church*, and ſuch as have given their names to *Chriſt*; Mr *Cotton* replies; they are not all one, and quotes, *Eſa.* 65. 5, 6.

Publike marriage, or giving ones ſelfe to Chriſt.

Truth. Let the place be viewed, and that place will be found to ſpeake of no ſuch *Difference:* It ſpeaks of the *Lords* promiſe to *Eunuches* and *Strangers*, laying hould on the *Lords Covenant*, and joyning themſelves to the *Lord*, which I conceive Mr *Cotton* will not deny to be in a *Church way*; in which *condition* the *Lord* gives the *Eunuches* a name better then of *Sonnes* and *Daughters*.

Peace. In the next *Paſſage* Mr *Cotton* upon *Tertullians* ſpeech, affirmes, that a falſe *Religion* will hurt, becauſe the *Red Horſe* followes the *White*, &c. [Rev. 6. 2–8.]

Truth. I anſwer; *Gods Judgements* (by *Warre, Famine, Peſtilence*) plagueing falſe *Religions* in his time (though after many hundreth yeares *patience*, as hath formerly been opened) is [222] one thing: and the preſent *hurting* or *profiting* of *others*, is another.

Peace. In the next place Mr *Cotton* takes *offence* that the Diſcuſſer ſhould inſinuate Mr *Cotton* to have a hand in the *Modell* of *Church Government*.

Truth. I anſwer; Mr *Cottons* words in the End of his *Anſwer* to the *Priſoner*, (where he ſpeakes of this *Treatiſe* or *Modell*, ſent to ſome of the *Brethren* of *Salem*) ſeemed to hould out the *probabilitie* of it.[1] How ever Mr *Cotton* ſubſcribeth to the reſt of the *Elders*, (as he here ſayth) their *words* being rightly underſtood.

Peace. Further, Mr *Cotton* here affirmes, that the

[1] *Pub. Narr. Club*, iii. 53. See alſo Editor's Preface, p. 8.

want of a *Law* for *Religion* in any *State* provokes the *Wrath* of *God*, as the want of a *King* in *Israel*, Judg. 21. 25.

Judges 21. 25 Considered.

Truth. This *Scripture* proves no more, but that the want of a *King*, *Magistrate*, *Governour*, or *Civill Officer* of *Justice*, provokes the *Wrath* of *God*, and endangereth the people, against which the Discusser never affirmed, but against their *Kingly* or *Civill Authoritie* in *spirituall* cases, since *Christ Jesus* abolished that *Nationall Church*.

Peace. But sayth M[r] *Cotton*, the *best Good* of a *Citie* is *Religion*, and therefore there should be a *Law* for it.

Truth. To this I have spoken largely in discussing of that *Modell*, unto which I know not of any *Reply* yet made by *Himselfe*, or any of those worthy men whom he makes the *Authours* of it.

Peace. But further, whereas the Discusser had said that the *weedes* of the *Wildernesse* will not hurt the *Garden*, nor *poyson* the *Body*, if not suffred to grow in the *Garden*, nor taken into the *Body*, M[r] *Cotton* grants that *Christ* hath ordained *Gardiners* for his *Garden*, and *Physick* and *Physicians* for his *Body*: Yet withall he makes the *Civill Officers*, to be as *Supervisors*, *Superintendents*, and consequently, *Bishops*, *Governours*, and *Heads* of the *Church* or *Churches*, and over the *spirituall Officers* of *Christ Jesus*.

Supreame Authoritie in Spiritualls.

Truth. What is this but to establish *Henry* the 8. a *Spirituall Civill Magistrate*, and *Head* of the *Church*, in the roome of the *Pope?* Contrary to which I have discoursed in the discussing of the *Modell* in the bloudie *Tenent*.[1]

[1] *Bloudy Tenent,* 196. *Pub. Narr. Club,* iii. 344.

223] *Peace.* But what thinke you of Mr *Cottons* interpretation of *Tertullians* minde, to wit, that *Tertullian* ſhould meane, that the *Chriſtian Religion* would not hurt nor diſturbe the *Romane Civill State?*

Tertullians *Speech of one Religion, not hurting or profiting another Conſidered.*

Truth. I conceive it cannot ſtand, for although it be true that the *Chriſtian Religion* hurts no *Civill State* (but infinitly the contrary) yet Mr *Cotton* will not deny that the *Chriſtian Religion* (not of it ſelfe, but through the corruption of the *Civill State*) may provoke a *Civill State* many wayes, and therefore *Tertullian* muſt meane other wayes, to wit, every Man muſt ſtand or fall in his owne *Religion*, and the *Religion* of one man will neither *hurt* nor *ſave* another: Therefore (to end this *Paſſage*) *Tertullians* words may not unfitly be thus applied: The *Religion* of the *Proteſtants*, if permitted by the *Papiſts*, will neither hurt nor profit the *Presbyterians*, if they permitted it: And the *Religion* and *Worſhip* of other *Conſciences* in *old* or *New England*, will neither hurt nor profit the *Independents*, where the power of tollerating or not tollerating lies in the *hands* and *power* of the *Independents*.

Exam: of Chap. 68. *replying to* Chap. 71.

Peace. HEre Mr *Cotton* urgeth two miſtakes: Firſt in the quoting of *Jerome:* ſecondly, in naming *Tertullian* for *Jerome.*

Truth. Poſſible it is, they are neither the miſtakes of the *Priſoner*, nor Diſcuſſer, but either the *Scribe* or *Printers* may ſhare with them; or if they were their owne *miſtakes* (although the *Priſoner* wrote in cloſe priſon in *Newgate*, and the Diſcuſſer in multitude of *Diſtractions*, yet) they are juſtly to be blamed for their leaſt *ſleepines* in the handling of the *matters* of the *moſt High*.

Peace. But, *Jeromes* words (ſaith Mr *Cotton*) imply more then a *ſpirituall* cutting off; *Arius* was but a *ſparke*, but becauſe he was not ſpeedily ſuppreſt, his *Flame depopulated* all the World, which [224] cannot be meant (ſayth he) of cutting off by *Excommunication*, which proceeded againſt him once and twice.

Truth. I cannot be eaſily induced to believe that *Jerome* intended to complaine of *Conſtantine*, who was not ſparing at the firſt to put forth his temporall *Arme* and *power* againſt *Arius*: But this is certaine, his words are theſe, [*Hereſie* muſt be cut off with the Sword of the *Spirit*: and the *Scriptures* quoted by him (1 *Cor.* 5. *Gal.* 5.) as Mr *Cotton* yeeldeth] prove onely a *ſpirituall* cutting off: So that it ſeemes not *rationall* for *Jerome* to run from the *Spirituall Sword*, about which he is now converſant, to the *carnall* and *temporall Sword*, of which thoſe *Scriptures* (as Mr *Cotton* acknowledgeth) diſcourſe not.

Peace. But let no man ſay (ſayth Mr *Cotton*) that this "grant of his [That *Hereſie* muſt be cut off by "the Sword of the *Spirit*] doth imply an abſolute "*ſufficiencie* in the Sword of the *Spirit*, to cut it downe "according to 2 *Cor.* 10. 4, 5. For though *ſpirituall* "*Weapons* be *abſolutely ſufficient* to the *End* for which "*God* hath appointed them, as hath been opened "above, to wit, for the *conviction*, and (if he belong "to *God*) for the *converſion* of the *offendour*, for the "*mortifying* of his *flesh*, and for the *saving* of his *Soule*, "and for the *cleansing* of the *Church* from the *Fel*-"*lowship* of that *Guilt*: Yet if an *Heretick* will still continue obstinate, and persist in *seducing*, creepe into *Houses*, leade captive sillie Soules, and *destroy* the *Faith* of some, it may be of many, such **Gangrenes* would be cut off by another *Sword*, which in the hand of the *Magistrate* is not borne in vaine.

**Mr* Cottons *and Mr* Edwards *Gangrenes have little differd.*[1]

Truth. This answer of Mr *Cotton* lookes too too like that *Distinction* of the bloudie *Bishop* against the poore *Martyr* or *Witnes* of *Jesus* (which Mr *Fox* mentioneth) The *Scripture* is sufficient for *Salvation*, but not for *Instruction*: There is need of *Tradition*, &c.[2] The Sword of the *Spirit* (sayth Mr *Cotton*) is absolutely sufficient, for these foure, to wit, the *Conviction*, *Mortification*, and *Salvation* of the *offendour*, the *Heretick*, yea, and for a fifth, for *Expiation*, and *cleansing* of the *Church* from the *Fellowship* of that *Guilt*, but there is a sixth, to wit, *Infection*, and there the *Sword* of the *Spirit* is too weake, and the Sword of the *Magistrate* must helpe.

Blasphemie against the holy Scripture.

Peace. What sound and modest Reason can be (almost) [225] pretended, why the holy *Ordinances*, *Appointments* and *provisions* of the Lord *Jesus* (who

1 Thomas Edwards, Trinity College, Cambridge (1605), was first a clergyman of the Church of England. He became a Presbyterian in 1642. His *Gangræna* was published in three parts in 1645. It was extremely bitter against all toleration. Some account of it is given by Neal, *Hist. of Puritans*, ii. 37, 38. Milton stings him in his Sonnet "On the new Forcers of Conscience under the Long Parliament," as "shallow Edwards." He retired to Holland soon after publishing this work, where he died. Wood, *Fasti Oxonienses*, ii. 413.

2 This is among the questions put to John Lambert in his examination before Archbishop Warham in 1538. Fox, *Acts and Monuments*, ii. 331.

is the *Wiſdome* of the *Father*, whoſe is all *power* in *Heaven* and in *Earth*, and whoſe *Heart* is all on *Fire* with *Love* to his people) ſhould be ſo weake in ſuppreſſing the *Enemies* of his *Kingdome*, that, all the *Counſell*, *Order*, and *Power* he hath left in his Abſedce, are not able to reſiſt the *Infection* of falſe Doctrine, without the helpe of the *Powers* of the *World* his profeſſed *Enemie*, unto whom who ſo is a *Friend* (ſayth *John*) [*James* iv: 4.] he cannot but be an *Enemie* unto *God*. Oh what ſhould be the *myſterie* that the two-edged *Sword* of *Gods* mighty *Spirit*, is ſufficient for *Conviction*, for *Converſion*, *Mortification*, *Expiation*, *Salvation*, but yet not powerfull enough againſt *Infection*?

Myſteries of falſe Chriſts.

Truth. There is written evidently, on the *Forehead* of this *plea*, as on the forehead of the great *Whore* (Revel. 17.) [5.] *Myſterie*. The *Ægyptian Onions* (as I may ſo ſpeake) are full of *Spirituall Infoldings*, or *Myſteries:* One or two I ſhall briefly unfold or peele.

The true Chriſt deſpiſed for his povertie.

Firſt, the *Clergie* (*ſacrilegiouſly* ſo called) in all *Ages* ſince the *Apoſtaſie*, have (like ſome *proud* and *daintie Servants*) diſdain'd to ſerve a poore deſpiſed *Chriſt*, a *Carpenter*, one that came at laſt to the *Gallowes*, &c. And therefore have they ever framed to Themſelves *rich* and *Lordly*, *pompous* and *Princely*, *temporall* and *Worldly Chriſts*, inſtead of the true *Lord Jeſus Chriſt*, the *ſpirituall King* of his *Saints* and *people*. And however it ſuits well the common End to retaine the Name of *Chriſt* (as the *Lord Jeſus* prophesied many falſe *Chriſts* ſhould ariſe, and many ſhould come in his Name, &c.) yet moſt ſure it will be found, that a temporall *Crowne* and *Dignitie*, *Sword* and *Authoritie*, *Wealth* and *Proſperitie*, is the *White* that moſt of thoſe called *Scholars*, *Miniſters*, *Biſhops*, aime and levell at:[1] How many thouſand of them will readily ſubſcribe to the pleas of the *French Biſhops* againſt the Lord *Peter*, diſputing before *Philip* the *French King* for temporall *Juriſdiction*, and *Peters* two *Swords* in the hands of *Chriſts Miniſters*.[2]

A baſe eſteeme of the Spirituall Sword.

Peace. Mr *Cotton* is not far off, for howſoever He and ſome will ſay with him, one *Sword* is enough for a *Presbyter* or *Elder*, enough for *Conviction*, *Converſion*, *Mortification*, *Expiation*, and *Salvation*, yet one *Sword* is not enough againſt *Infection*, and therefore it is needfull (though we are not of the opinion
226] of thoſe French *Prelates* and others, that challenged to themſelves the *Sword* of *temporall juriſdiction* into their owne hands, yet) it is needfull that it be at our *call* in the hands of our *Executioners* the *Civill Magiſtrates*.

Earthly Chriſts need earthly ſupports.

Truth. It is impoſſible that *temporal* and *worldly Chriſts* ſhould walke with the legs of a *ſpirituall ſupportment*, but as (in reſpect of outward *Government*) they ſpring from the *Earth* and the *World*, it is impoſſible I ſay but their *Feeding* and *Aliment*, *Defence* and *Protection* ſhould be of the nature of the *Root* and *Eliment* from whence they ariſe.

Peace. It is objected, was the *Church* of the *Jewes*

[1] The centre of the target in archery was painted white. Shakeſpeare, *Taming of the Shrew*, v. 5.

[2] A Parliament was called by Philip the Fair at Paris, Dec. 15, 1309. Peter de Cugneriis opened the diſcuſſion on the part of the King, diſtinguiſhing between the temporal and eccleſiaſtical juriſdictions. The prelates made a long reply, which is to be found in Fox, *Acts and Monuments*, 1: 402–414.

temporall that was aſſiſted and protected with a *temporall Sword?*

Truth. The *Spirit* of *God* tels us (*Heb.* 8. & 10.) of a worldly *Sanctuary*, of a *weake* and *old vaniſhing Covenant*, to wit, a *Nationall Covenant*, and *Ordinances* of a *Jewiſh Church.*

Peace. It is againe ſaid how can the Diſcuſſer extoll the *Sword* of the *Spirit* only, and acknowledge no *Churches.*

The ſtate of Chriſtianity during the reigne of Antichriſt

Truth. Although the Diſcuſſer cannot to his *Souls ſatisfaction* conclude any of the various and ſeverall ſorts of *Churches* extant to be thoſe pure *golden Candleſticks* framed after the firſt patterne, *Rev.* 1. [12. 20.] Yet doth he acknowledge *golden Candleſticks* of *Chriſt Jeſus* extant; thoſe golden *Olive trees* and *candleſticks*, his *Martyrs* or *Witneſſes*, ſtanding before the *Lord*, and teſtifying his holy *Truth* during all the *Reign* of the *Beaſt*, *Rev.* 11. [4.] Hence, although we have not *ſatisfaction* that *Luther* or *Calvin*, or other precious *Witneſſes* of *Chriſt Jeſus*, erected *Churches* or *Miniſteries*, after the firſt patterne (as they conceived they did) yet doth he affirm them to have been *Prophets* and *witneſſes* againſt the *Beaſt*, and furniſhed ſufficiently with *ſpirituall Fire* in their *mouthes*, mightily able to conſume or humble their *Eenemies*, as *Eliah* did with the Captains ſent out againſt him. [2 Kings 1: 10.][1]

[1] He ſays in *The Hireling Miniſtry*, p. 4, that he "cannot yet in the holy preſence of God bring in the reſult of a ſatisfying diſcovery, that either the begetting miniſtry of the Apoſtles or Meſſengers to the Nations, or the Feeding and Nouriſhing Miniſtry of Paſtors and Teachers, according to the firſt Inſtitu-

Peace. I will object no more, pleaſe you (*Dear Truth*) to paſſe on to the 2nd. *viz.* the *Miniſtry* of the *Spirits* pretended *inſufficiency* againſt *Infection*: why ſhould not the ſpiritual power of the *Lord Jeſus* be powerful enough againſt *creepers* into *Houſes*, againſt ſuch as lead *captive* ſilly ſouls, againſt ſuch as *deſtroy* the *faith* of ſome, &c. as well as in the firſt *Churches* and *Aſſemblies*, profeſſing his holy *name* and *worſhip*?

Truth. Search his *Will* and *Teſtament*, and we find no other [227] but *ſpiritual* means preſcribed and bequeathed by the *Lord Jeſus*, to *Paul* to *Peter*, or any of the holy *Apoſtles* or *Meſſengers*.

Conſtantines peace a greater tryal and danger to Chriſtians then 300 years perſecutions.

Peace. I muſt needs acknowledge that the poor ſervants of *Chriſt*, for ſome hundereth of years after the departure of the *Lord* enjoyed no other power, no other *Sword* nor *Shield* but *ſpirituall*, until it pleaſed the *Lord* to try his *children* with *Liberty* and *eaſe* under *Conſtantine* (a ſoarer *Tryall* then befell them in 300 years perſecution) under which *temporall protection*, *munificence* and *bounty* of *Conſtantine*, together with his *temporall Sword*, drawne out againſt her *ſpirituall enemies*, the *Church of Chriſt* ſoon ſurfeited of the too much *honey* of worldly eaſe, *authority*, *profit*, *pleaſure*, *&c.*

Truth. Deare Peace, the ſecond *miſtery* is this. In all ages, the world hath been o'reſpread with the

tion of the Lord Jeſus, are yet reſtored and extant. It may then be ſaid, what is that Miniſtry that hath been extant ſince Luther and Calvin's time (eſpecially what is that Miniſtry that hath been Inſtrumental in the hand of the Lord, to the converſion of thouſands?) I anſwer, The Miniſtry of Prophets or Witneſſes, ſtanding with Chriſt Jeſus, againſt his great corrivall and competitour Antichriſt. Revel. 10. 11."

deluſions and *abominations* of *falſe worſhip*, invented by *Sathan* and his *Inſtruments* in oppoſition to the pure *worſhip* of the *God* of *Heaven:* Againſt theſe the *Lord Jeſus* hath not been wanting to ſtir up his *witneſſes*, *ſervants* and *ſouldiers*, fighting for their *Lord* and *Maſter* ſpiritually, &c.

Sathans two wayes of quenching the Candle of Chriſtianity.

Theſe *witneſſes*, when *Sathan* hath not been able to vanquiſh and overcome them by *diſputing*, *writing*, *&c.* (but hath ever loſt that way) he hath been forced to run to the fleſhly *Armories* of temporall *weapons* and *puniſhments*, and to fetch in the powers of the world; So hoping to daſh out the Candle of *Truth* and break the *candleſticks* thereof the *witneſſes* of *Chriſt Jeſus:* This *Sathan* hath ever practiced one of theſe two wayes, ſometimes by (pretended) legall tryals and *executions* of *Juſtice*, ſometimes by moſt horrid and dreadfull *murthers* and *maſſacres*

Peace. Thus hath *Chriſt Jeſus* indeed been vanquiſhed, and driven out of this world by the powers of *Cæſars*, *Kings* and other earthly *Governours* and *Rulers*.

Truth. 'Tis a freſh and bleeding *Hiſtory* of that famous *diſputation* between the *Cardinal* and *Prelates* of *France* and *Beza* with his *proteſtant aſſiſtants* under *Charles* the 9th. And not long after that of that moſt barbarous and horrible *murther* and *maſſacre* of about 30000 Innocents, to finiſh and compleat that *victory* which the pretended *Diſputation* and ſpirituall arme could never effect.[1]

The French Maſſacre muſt doe what their pretended diſputation could not effect.

[1] The Colloquy or Conference of Poiſſy was held in 1561, at the beginning of the reign of Charles IX. The chiefs of the Catholic and Proteſtant parties were invited. Theodore Beza appeared at the requeſt of Calvin, and as his repreſenta-

Pretended diſputes in *Q. Maries* days, ending in fiery flames.

228] *Peace.* Yea in the bloody *Marian* dayes, there muſt be *Convocations* cald at *London*, and downe muſt theſe famous *witneſſes* of *Jeſus*, *Cranmer*, *Ridley*, *Latimer* to diſpute at *Oxford* [:] but faithful *Philpot* for his free diſputing in the *Convocation* at *London*, and *Cranmer*, *Latimer* and *Ridley* for not yeelding away the truth at *Oxford*, they muſt all feel the rage of the *fiery furnace*, who bow not downe to the *golden Image*.[1]

The late Synodicall diſputes.

And (without offence of *civill Authority*, or diſreſpect againſt any mans perſon be it ſpoken) in the late great *diſputes* between the *Presbyterians* and *Independents* at *VVeſtminſter*; what a *Tempeſt* raiſed, what *Earthquakes* and *Thunders* cal'd for, from *Earth* and *Heaven*, ihat the ſecond *ſword* of the *magiſtrate* (herein the *Presbiteriaus Servant* and *Executioner*) might effect that which all the *power* of the *pretended ſword* of *Gods Spirit* was never able to reach to.[2]

Pea. To proceed, M *Cot.* is greatly offended at

tive. The firſt public conference was held September 9, and the laſt October 9. The diſputation was carried on chiefly between Cardinal de Tournon and Beza. Its reſult was not altogether adverſe to the Proteſtants. In January, 1562, an edict of toleration was iſſued, which gave them a protection before denied. The Maſſacre of St. Bartholomew's Day begun Auguſt 23d, 1572. "Le calcul le plus modérè, celui fait par de Thou, éléve le nombre des victims á près de trente mille." H. Martin, *Hiſtoire de France*, xi. 278. *Thuani Hiſt.*, iii. 145. For an account of the Colloquy of Poiſſy, ſee Martin, *Hiſtoir, &c.*, xi. 74–79. *Thuani Hiſt.*, ii. 117–127.

[1] Cranmer, Ridley and Latimer, were ſent to a diſputation at Oxford, April 10, 1554. John Philpot, of New College, Oxford, was Archdeacon of Wincheſter. October 18, 1553, a Diſputation was held at Convocation-Houſe, in London, in which Philpot took part. He was called to account by Gardiner, and was burned at Smithfield, December 18, 1555. He was of Williams's opinion in regard to "the baptizing of infants." Fox, *Acts and Monuments*, iii. 36–74, 16–24, 459–512.

[2] The Preſbyterian party in the Weſtminſter Aſſembly, which was in an overwhelming majority, was againſt toleration, and called upon the magiſtrate to

this *word:* to wit [the *Eye* of the *Anſwerer* could never be ſo obſcured, as to run to the *Smiths-ſhop* for a *ſword* of *Iron*, and *ſteel* to help the *Sword*, of the *Spirit*; if the *Sun* of *Ryghteouſnes* had pleaſed to ſhew him that a *Nationall Church, &c.*] And his anger breaths forth, firſt againſt all *Hereticks* thus: If there be *ſtones* of the *ſtreets*, the *Magiſtrate* need not run for a *Sword* from the *Smiths ſhop*, nor an *Halter* from the *Ropiers* to puniſh an *Heretick*.

A bloody and moſt unchriſtian ſpeech.

Truth. It is true, the *warehouſe* of *perſecution* is ſo abundantly filled with all ſorts of bloody *Inſtruments*, beſides *Swords* and *Ropes*, that the *Primitive* and *Latter* times have told us how many ſeverall ſorts of *ſorrows*, *pains* and *torments* the ſervants of the living *God*, have felt by ſeverall *Inſtruments* of *Blood* and *Death*, beſides *Ropes* and *Swords*, *&c.* and all to puniſh (as *Maſter Cotton* ſayth) the *Heretick*, the *Heretick*, *Blaſphemer*, *Seducer &c.*

Peace. What is this Anger but Fury, *Ira furor brevis eſt?* And what weapons can be wanting to *Fury*, not the *ſtones* in the *ſtreets* (ſaith Maſter *Cotton*) *Furor armor miniſtrat*, for the *magiſtrate* needs not (ſaith he) ſtay ſo long as to run to a *Smiths-ſhop* for a *ſword*, or to the *Ropiers* for a *halter*, &c.

draw his ſword againſt what were called "ſectaries." At a later period the Preſbyterians having a temporary majority in Parliament, ſhowed their intolerant temper in paſſing an "Ordinance againſt Blaſphemy and Hereſy," which went ſo far as to inflict the penalty of death on thoſe who would not abjure certain proſcribed errors of opinion. This act was paſſed May 2, 1648. Neal gives the ſubſtance of the Act, with a liſt of the hereſies, and ſays it was "one of the moſt ſhocking laws I have met with in reſtraint of religious liberty, and ſhows that the governing Preſbyterians would have made a terrible uſe of their power, had they been ſupported by the ſword of the civil magiſtrate." *Hiſt. of Puritans*, ii. 79 Croſby, *Hiſt. of Baptiſts*, i. 199.

Peace. O the *myſteries* of *iniquitie* and *cozenage* of ſin, that a *Lambe* of *Chriſt* ſhould thus roar out like a *Lyon*, and (as the ſpeech may be conſtrued by ſome) ſo far as in him lies to provoke [229] the *civill powers*, yea the people in the ſtreets to furious outrage, and not ſo much as to attend proceedings in pretended legal Trials and executions, but in the madneſſe of *Barbarous murthers* and *maſſacres*, and that even upon himſelfe and the Independants in their meetings, &c.

The raſh fury and madneſſe of perſecutors even againſt themſelves.

Peace. But 2dly. he finds fault with the Diſcuſſers wit, for bringing ſuch light *conceits* into grave *diſcourſes* and *diſputes* about the holy things of *God.*

Truth. If there be anything favouring of wit in the Diſcuſſors ſpeech, let all men judge whether there be not a *double*, yea a *treble* portion in this of Maſter *Cottons*; I acknowledge, *Non eſt major confuſio quam ſerij & Joci.* The Diſcuſſer dares not willingly to prophane the holy name of the *moſt high* with *lightnes*, no not with thoſe fine turnings of wit which the *word* forbids, (ἐυτραπελία, *Epheſ.* 5. [4.] which becomes not *Chriſts ſchollars*, but rather the *giving* of *thanks*: And yet there is an holy wit and pleaſantnes in *Samſons Riddle*, in *Jothams* and *Jeſus* his *Parables*, yea, and in *Eliah* his ſharpe and cutting *language*, which cut as deep to their deluding conſciences, as the *Knives* and *Lances* of their *Idolatrous backs* and *bodies*; Yet none of theſe were (as Maſt. *Cotton* inſinuates againſt the Diſcuſſer) for naming of *Smiths-ſhop*) playings with *feathers, &c.*

Pleaſantneſſe of wit ſanctified, glorifies the giver.

Peace. But what thinke you of his confidence, touching his *New-England Diana*, to wit, that the

Diſcuſſer will never be able to make it good: that the Church in *New-England* is implicitly, a *Nationall* and *State Church?*

Truth. His own words ſeem to prove it, for if it be a *Church* and not *Churches* of *N. England*, as elſewhere he ſpeaks (and as the Scripture ordinarily ſpeaks, the Churches of *Judea*, *Galatia*, *&c.*) it cannot be no other but a *Nationall*, as the *Engliſh-Church*, *Scotch-Church*, *French-Church*, *&c.* But poſſibly it being a miſtake, I anſwer, A *Nation* in the common and large extent, I dare not call *New-England*, but thus, the ſeverall *Plantations* or *Colonies* of one *Religion*, or way of *worſhip* make up one *Colonie* or *Province* of *Engliſh-men* in this part or tract of *America*. I cannot thererefore call the *Church* of *New-England* (properly) a *Nationall Church*, but a *Provincial Church*, a *State Church*; caſt into the mould of a *Nationall Church*, diſtinct into ſo many *Pariſhes*, I ſay not expreſly and explicitly, but implicitly and ſecretly, [230] which the *ſon* of *righteouſneſſe* will at laſt reveal, as clearly and brightly in the eyes of all men, as the *ſun* that ſhines at *Noonday*.

The pretended particular Churches of *N. E.* indeed but a Nationall Church.

At preſent, I affirm (what ever are the *pretences*, *pleas* and *coverings* to the contrary) that that *Church eſtate*, that *religion* and *worſhip* wch is *commanded* or *permitted* to be but one in a *country*, *nation* or *province* (as was the *Jews religion* in that typical land of *Canan*) that *Church* is not in the *nature* of the particular *Churches* of *Chriſt*, but in the *nature* of a *Nationall* or *ſtate Church:* the nature of a particular *Church* of *Chriſt*, is to be one, 2 or 3 (more or leſſe) in *Townes*

No permiſſion of

any Religion or worſhip but one in *N. E.* therefore are the Churches, but a Nationall Church in the mould of them, &c.

or *Cities* (as in all the inſtances of the *New-Teſtament,* but the nature of the State *Church* is when the whole State is turn'd into a State *Church* in ſo many *Pariſhes* or *Diviſions* of *worſhippers*: and it is made odious & intolerable for any part of this *City, ſtate, &ce.* not to attend the *common worſhip* of the *City*, ſanctifie the holy *times*, and contribute to the holy *Officers*, and to walke in another way, which is the generall ſtate and practiſe of *New-England.*

Where the Supream Authority in a Church is Civill, the Body cannot but be like the head, and all make up but one Civil or National mixt Church, like the Jewiſh Nationall Church, The purging a Countrey of Hereticks' declares that Countrey is explicitly or implicitly a National Church.

2. That is a *nationall* and *ſtate Church* where the *Civill power* is conſtitued the *Head* thereof, to ſee to the *conforming* or *reforming* of the *Church*, the *truth* or *falſehood* of the *Churches, Miniſtries* or *miniſtrations, ordinances, Doctrine, &c.*

In the particular *Churches* of *Chriſt Jeſus*, wee finde not a tittle of the power of the *civill magiſtrate* or *civill ſword* in *ſpirituall caſes.* It is impoſſible but a *Nationall* and *Civill head* muſt be *head* of a *Nationall* or *State Church*, which (upon the point is but a *civill* or *temporall Church* (like the *head* thereof) and not a *heavenly* and *ſpirituall*: I ſay, a *Civil* or *temporall Church*, ſubject to the *changes* of a *changeable Court* or *Countrey*, and the *interpretings* and *expoundings* of *Scripture*, to what the *Court* or *Countrey* is ſubject to approve or diſprove of.

3. It is a *Nationall* or *State Church*, where the oppoſite or *gain-ſayer*, the pretended *Heretick, Blaſphemer, Seducer, &c.* is ſome way or other puniſhed, put forth of the *State* or *Countrey* it ſelfe by *death* or *baniſhment:* whereas *particular Churches* put forth no further then from their *particular ſocieties*, and the *Hereticks, &c.* may ſtill live in the *Countrey* or *Countreys* unmoleſted by them.

4. That Church cannot be otherwise than a *Nationall* or [231] *State Church*, where the maintenance of the *Worship, Priests* and *Officers*, is a *State maintenance*, provided by the care and power of the *State*, who (upon the point) payes their *Ministers* or *Servants* their *wages*; whereas the *maintenance* of the *Worship* and *Officers* of a *particular Church*, we finde by *Christs Testament* to be cared for sufficiently by *Christs power*, and meanes in his *Church*.

A State Maintenance proveth a State Church.

5. That *Church* is a *Nationall* or *State Church*, whose whole Assemblies, in *Synods, Councells, Provinciall, Nationall*, &c. If Mr *Cotton* can disprove the truth and substance of these and other *particulars* alledged, so farre as concernes the *generall* and *Body* of the *Countrey* combined (whatsoever little *variation* some particular Townes may make) the Discusser must acknowledge his *Errour*, but if Mr *Cotton* cannot doe it, as I believe he cannot (what ever flourish a wit may pretend) the *God* of *mercy* pardon what by Mr *Cotton* is done in Ignorance, and awaken *him* and *others*, who cause his people to goe astray; according to that of the Prophet; Their *Shepheards* cause this people to goe astray. [Jer.50:6.]

Synods assembled by Civill Power, prove the Churches of the same Nature with the Head that acts and calls them.

Peace. O that all *Gods sheepe* in *New England*, and such as judge themselves their *Shepheards*, may truely judge themselves at the *tribunall* of their *owne Conscience* in the *presence* of the *Lord*, in the *upright Examination* of these *particulars:* But to leave *New England*, and to returne to the *Land* of *Israel:* I "should thinke (sayth Mr *Cotton*) not onely mine "eye obscured, but the sight of it utterly put out, if "I should conceive (as the Discusser doth) that the

"*Nationall Church State* of the *Jewes* did neceſſarily "call for ſuch *weapons* to puniſh *Heretiques* more then "the *Congregationall State* of *particular Churches* doth "call for the ſame now in the dayes of the *New* "*Teſtament*.

Truth. It is a *ſtrange Speech* to proceede from ſo *knowing* a Man, but let us ponder his *Reaſons* in the feare of *God*.

Peace. Was not (ſayth M[r] *Cotton*) the *Nationall Church* of the *Jewes* compleatly furniſhed with *Spirituall Armour* to defend it ſelfe, and oppoſe *Men* and *Devills*, as well as *particular Churches* of the *New Teſtament?* Had they not power to convince falſe *Prophets*, as *Elijah* did the Prophets of *Baal?* had they not power to ſeparate *Evill Doers* from the *Fellowſhip* of [232] their *Congregations?* And he addeth, an *uncleane Perſon*, although he might not Enter into the *Temple*, with the reſt of the *Iſraelites* to *worſhip* the *Lord*, yet he was permitted to live in the *Common-weale* of *Iſrael*, Men *uncircumciſed* both in *Heart* and *Fleſh*.

Touching the difference between the Church of the Jewes *and the Chriſtian Churches.*

He addeth further, that the *Nationall Church* of *Iſrael* was powerfully able by the *Sword* of the *Spirit* to defend it ſelfe, and to offend *Men* and *Devills*, for which he quoteth, *Zach*. 4. 6. And he asketh, doth not the Diſcuſſer himſelfe obſerve that time was, in the *Nationall Church* of the *Land* of *Canaan*, when there was neither *Carnall Sword* nor *Speare* to be found, 1 *Sam*. 13. [19.]? And was not then the *Nationall Church* powerfully able by the *Spirit* of *God* to defend it ſelfe, and to offend *Men* and *Devills* as well as particular *Churches* now?

Truth. I anſwer: Firſt, As much as the *ſhadow* of a Man falls ſhort of a *Man* himſelfe, ſo did all their *Ordinances* (which were but *ſhadowes* of *ſpirituall things* to come) fall ſhort of that bright enjoyment of *Chriſt Jeſus*, and *ſpirituall* and *heavenly things* in him, now brought to Light by *Chriſt Jeſus* in the *Goſpel* or *New Teſtament.*

2. Mr *Cotton* will never demonſtrate that the putting forth, or Excommunicating of a perſon from the *Church* of *God* amongſt them, was other then *cutting* off from the Land by *Death*, and the *Civill Sword*, the ſame being *ſpiritually* executed now in the *Iſrael* of *God*, 1 Cor. 5. Gal. 5. 12.

Thirdly, Although the *Stranger* uncircumciſed might live amongſt them, yet none of the *Native Iſraelites* might ſo live, nor yet might the *Stranger prophane* the *holineſſe* of the *Lord* by *labour* on the *Sabbath*, which Mr *Cotton* will never prove ought now to be kept by all *Countries* of the *world*, and that under ſuch *Penalties*, as was in the Land of *Canaan*, the *holy Land:* Nor that they had *ſpirituall power* ſufficient to puniſh the willfull breach of any *Morall* or *Ceremoniall* dutie, without the helpe of the *Carnall Sword*, the contrary to which is plaine in the *New Teſtament*, 1 Cor. 5. 2 Cor. 10.

The holy Land of Canaan *a* Noneſuch.

A Figure of the Chriſtian.

Fourthly, For the Scripture, *Zach.* 4. 6. Not by *might* nor *Power*, &c. The *Prophet* doth not here oppoſe the *Spirit* to *might* or *power*, ſo as to deny the uſe of *Carnall weapons, might* or *power*, which God had vouchſafed to them againſt all *Enemies*
233] within and without, but ſheweth it to be the
work of *Gods* own *finger* or *Spirit* in the uſe of *car-*

The weapons of the *Jewes* and

Christians compared. *nall meanes* which they uſed for the raiſing of the *Materiall Temple* and *Civill defence* of Themſelves againſt all *Oppoſers, Hinderers,* &c. Whereas 2 *Cor.* 10. [4.] the *Apoſtle* flatly oppoſeth *Spirituall Weapons* againſt *Carnall*, and Mr *Cotton* will never prove that the *Corinthians* or any of the *Saints of Chriſt*, did enjoy other *Weapons*, in that *firſt* or the *Ages* next after, but onely the *Spirituall Weapons* and *Artillery* which the *Apoſtle* mentioneth.

No Speare nor Sword in *Iſrael.* Laſtly, To that of 1 *Sam.* 13. [19.] I anſwer, That when there was no *Speare* nor *Sword* in *Iſraell*, the *Iſraelites* were not powerfully able to defend Themſelves againſt their *Enemies*, except that *God* was pleaſed *extraordinarily* to ſtirre up meanes of their *preſervation*, as wee ſee in the caſe of *Jonathan* and his *Armour-bearer* againſt the *Philiſtims*. In like manner I believe that where the ordinary power of *Gods* hand in his holy *Ordinances* is withdrawen, it is his *extraordinarie* and immediate *power* that preſerveth and ſupporteth his people againſt *Men* and *Devills*; as in particular, during the *reigne* of *Antichriſt* in ſtirring up and ſupporting the two *Witneſſes*.

Exam: of Chap. 69. *replying to* Chap. 72.

Touching the Teſtimony of *Brentius*.

Peace. IT is untrue, ſayth Mr *Cotton*, that we *reſtraine* Men from *Worſhip* according to *Conſcience*, or *conſtraine* them to *Worſhip* againſt *Conſcience*, or that ſuch is my *Tenent* or *practice*.

Truth. Notwithſtanding Mr *Cottons* cloake, to wit, that they will not meddle with the *Heretick* before he hath ſinned againſt his owne *Conſcience*, and ſo perſecute him onely for ſinning againſt his *owne Conſcience*, yet I earneſtly beſeech every Reader ſeriouſly to ponder the whole *ſtreame* and *ſeries* of Mr *Cottons Diſcourſe*, *Propoſitions*, *Affirmations*, &c. through the whole booke, and he ſhall then be able to judge whether it be untrue that his *Doctrine* tends not to *conſtraine*, nor *reſtraine Conſcience*.

234] 2. For the matter of fact, how can he with any *Humilitie* before the *flaming eyes* of the moſt *High*, cry out, no ſuch *practice*, when

New-England loath to be accounted perſecutours.

Firſt, Their *Lawes* cry out a *Command* under *Penaltie* for all to come to *Church*, though not to be *Members*, which in truth (as hath been opened) is but a *colour* and *viſard*, deceiving himſelfe and others: And a *cruell Law* is yet extant againſt *Chriſt Jeſus*, muffled up under the *hood* or *vaile* of a Law againſt *Anabaptiſtrie*, &c.[1]

Secondly, Their *practice* cryes, their *Impriſonments*, *Finings*, *Whippings*, *Bahiſhments* cry in the Eares of

[1] "It is therefore ordered and decreed that whereſoever the miniſtry of the word is eſtabliſhed according to the order of the Goſpell through out this Juriſdiction, every perſon ſhall duely reſort and attend thereunto reſpectively upon the Lords dayes &c; and if any perſon within this juriſdiction ſhall without juſt and neceſſary cauſe withdraw himſelf from hearing the publick miniſtry of the word, after due meanes of conviction uſed, he ſhall forfeit for his abſence from every ſuch publick meeting 5 ſhillings." *Maſs. Col. Records*, iii. 78.

"It is ordered and agreed that if any perſon or perſons within the juriſdiction ſhall either openly condemne or oppoſe the baptizing of infants, or go about ſecretly to induce others from the approbation or the uſe thereof, or ſhall appear to the Court wilfully and obſtinately to continue therein after due time and means of conviction, every ſuch perſon or perſons ſhall be ſentenced to baniſhment." *Maſs. Col. Records*, ii. 85.

the *Lord* of *Hoſts*, and the louder becauſe of ſuch *unchriſtian figleave, cloakes, &c.*

Peace. Let it be granted (ſayth Mr *Cotton*) that we did both, yet this did not make *Lawes* to binde *Conſcience*, but the *outward* man onely! Nor would we (ſayth he) think it fit to binde the *outward* man againſt *Conſcience.*

Truth. I cannot diſcerne the *Coherence* of theſe three Affirmations: 1. We *reſtraine* no man from *Worſhip* according to *Conſcience.* 2. We make *Lawes* but to binde the *outward* man onely. And yet againe (3) we thinke not meete to binde the *outward* man againſt *Conſcience.* Mr *Cotton* lived once under a *Popiſh Law*, to weare a *fooles Coat* or *Surplice* on his back, and to make *Conjuring Croſſe* with his Fingers, why ſhould he ſay, that this Law went beyond his *back* and his *fingers*, and came even to his *Conſcience?* If theſe pettie *bonds* did binde his *Conſcience*, as well as his *back* and his *fingers*; Oh let not Mr *Cotton* ſo farre put off the Bowells of *Compaſſion* toward *Chriſt Jeſus* and his *Followers*, yea toward all men, as to binde their *backs*, and their *Necks*, their *Knees* and *Hands backward* and *forward*, to or from *Worſhip*, and yet ſay he binds but the *outward man*, &c.

Lawes concerning Gods Worſhip.

Dangerous diſtinctions.

Yea and oh let not ſuch *uprightnes*, *candor*, and *Integritie*, as Mr *Cotton* hath been noted for, be blemiſhed with ſuch an *Evaſion* as this, to wit, when it comes to ſelfe, that *Conſcience* his owne or his *Friends* be offred to be bound, &c. then he ſhall flie to his third *Evaſion*, ſaying, We think it not meete to binde the *outward* man againſt *Conſcience*, that is, againſt our *Conſciences*, &c. What ever becomes (ſinck or ſwim) of other Mens.

235] *Peace.* In the next Paſſage, *God* needs not (ſayth Mr *Cotton*) the helpe of the *Magiſtrate* more in the *Second*, then in the firſt *Table*.

Truth. *God* needeth not *abſolutely* for the matters of the *Second Table*, though *reſpectively*, becauſe he hath appointed *Ordinances*, unto which he hath graciouſly referd himſelfe. But for the *firſt Table*, he hath no neede at all, of *carnall weapons*, no not *reſpectively*, becauſe he hath appointed *Ordinances* to thouſand-fold more *potent*, *ſuitable* and *ſufficient*.

Touching keeping of both Tables.

Peace. Whereas it was urged, that if *Magiſtrates* muſt uſe their *materiall Sword* in keeping of both *Tables*, they muſt be able to judge of both: Mr *Cotton* replies, that it is enough, that they be able to judge in *Principles* and *Foundations*, and of the *Arrogancie* of a *tumultuous Spirit*; for ſuch want not *Judgement* to cenſure *Apoſtaſie* or *Hereſie*, *Idolatrie*, &c.

Of Magiſtrates Judgement in Spirituals, &c.

Truth. It is not like that a *Carpenter* who hath skill ſufficient to judge the *Principles* and *Foundations* of a *houſe* or *Building*, ſhould be unable to judge about the *Beames*, *Poſts*, &c.

2. With what great darknes, have the beſt of *Gods children* themſelves been covered theſe many hundreth yeares, touching the very *Fundamentalls* of *Gods Worſhip*!

Peace. Whereas it was ſaid further, that either they are not fitly qualified *Magiſtrates* and *Commonweales*, that want this *abilitie* to *judge*, &c. Or elſe they muſt judge according to their *Conſcience*! Mr *Cotton* replyes; *Many Qualifications* are required in *Husbands*, *Wives*, *Children*, *Servants*, *Miniſters*, *Churches*, the want whereof may make them *ſinfull*, but not *unlawfull*.

Of Qualifications of Magiſtrates.

Truth. I anſwer; ſome *Relations* are *Paſſive*, as that of children, who may be true and lawfull *children*, although they know not that they are *children.* But, ſuch *Relations* as are *active* in their *choice* and *conſent*, as of *Husband, Wife, Magiſtrate*, &c. theſe cannot be *lawfull*, unles they be fitted and *qualified* to performe the *maine* and *eſſentiall* duties of *Husbands, Wives, Servants, Magiſtrates.* That *Husband, Wife, Servant* cannot be lawfull, that are engaged to other *Husbands, Wives, Maſters:* Nor can that *Magiſtrate* be *lawfull*, who is a *mad-man* or *Ideot*, not able to diſcerne between *Right* and *Wrong:* and truely (were *Magiſtrates* bound, as to the *chiefe part* of their *Dutie* and *Office*) to eſtabliſh the true *Religion*, &c. he were no more then [236] a mad-man (as to the firſt Table) that were not ſpiritually indued with ability of diſcerning the true *Church, Miniſtry, Worſhip, &c.*

Peace. Now whereas it was further urged that then the *Common-weale*, the Civil, Naturall ſtate, hath more Light concerning the *Church* of *Chriſt* then the *Church* it ſelf, *&c.* Maſter *Cotton* replies, it followes not, becauſe that is a weak *Church* that knowes no more light then that of the Principles; and beſide; what light the *Common-wealth* hath it may have received from the *Church.*

Of Magiſtrates Abilities.

Truth. I anſwer, If *Kings* and *Queens, &c.* be nurcing *Fathers* and *Mothers* (in a ſpirituall reſpect) over the *Church*, as is uſually alleadged; can it be expected but that the *Nurſe, Father* or *Phyſician* ſhould know more of the *Childs ſtate* then the Child or Patient himſelfe, who oftentimes knows not his ſickneſſe, nor that he is ſick, (as oft may be the caſe of a *Church* of *Chriſt*) It is impoſſible, but they muſt have more light then the Child, yea and much more impoſſible that they ſhould receive their Light and direction from the Child, &c.

Peace. We ſee, ſaith Maſter *Cotton*, that *Magiſtrates* ſometimes have more *Light* in *matters* of *Religion* then the *Church* it ſelf, as *David* and *Hezekiah*.

Truth. This (1) confirmes what I ſaid, that theſe *Kings* being appointed by *God*, *Formers* and *Reformers* of the *Church* of *Judah*, they muſt needs have more *light* in the matter of *Reformation* then the *Church* it ſelfe to be reformed.

David and *Hezekiah* figurative Kings, &c.

2 I muſt deny that *David* and *Hezekiah* were other then types of *Chriſt* *Jeſus*, both in his owne perſon and in ſuch, who in his abſence are by him deputed to manage the *ſpirituall* power and ſword of his holy and ſpirituall Kingdome.

Peace. Yea, but alas, ſaith Maſter *Cotton*, there is no colour, that becauſe *Magiſtrates* are bound to diſcerne and ſerve *Chriſt* with their power, that therefore they may puniſh *Chriſt* and *Chriſtians*.

Truth. True, therefore, Maſter *Cotton* elſewhere ſaith, they muſt ſuſpend to deal in *Church matters* untill they can judge, &c.

And this, Firſt implies their *light* and *judgement* (abſolutely neceſſary) in all ſuch matters of the *Church*, about which they are to Judge and act as often I affirme.

237] 2 I aske what kind of *ſpirituall Phyſicians* will Maſter *Cotton* have, who ſhall be bound to ſuſpend their *power*, all their lives long, unleſſe they have

Magiſtrates ſuſpending in matters of Religion.

skill to judge of *Diſeaſes?* will not the ſimilitude hold againſt ſuch ſpirituall *Fathers, Nurces, Phyſicians,* who all their life long (yea the greateſt number beyond compare of all their ſpirituall *Fathers* upon the face of the Earth) muſt wholly ſuſpend from acting in ſpirituall diſeaſes or caſes, to wit, in reforming, eſtabliſhing, &c.

3. Although it excuſeth not ('tis true) ſuch *Magiſtrates, Princes Common-wealths,* for making this *Doctrine* their ground of perſecuting *Chriſt* and *Chriſtians,* yet doubtleſſe it makes their ſin the greater who feed them with ſuch bloody *Doctrines,* and ſo conſequently occaſion them upon the rocks of ſuch falſ and dangerous and *bloudy practices.*

Exam: of Chap. 70. *replying to* Chap. 73.

Peace. IN this Chap. (*Dear Truth*) lye many *ſtones* of *offence,* at which the feet of the unwary moſt eaſily may ſtumble; I hope your carefull and ſteady hand may be a bleſſed *Inſtrument* of their *Removall*: As Firſt, although Maſter *Cotton* ſubſcribe unto *Luther* that the *Government* of the *Civill Magiſtrate* doth extend no further, then over the *Bodies* and *Goods* of the ſubject, yet (ſaith he) he may and ought to improve that power over their *Bodies* and *Goods* to the good of their *Souls.*

Truth. Sweet *Peace* my hand (the hand of *Chriſt* aſſiſting) ſhall not be wanting: but what offence can be taken at the propoſitions?

Pea. The propoſition like an aple of *Sodom,* is fair

and ſpecious untill you cruſh it by examination: For, by maintaining the *Magiſtrates* power over the *Bodies* and *Goods* of the ſubject, for the good of his *Soul*, it is clear in this Chapter and others foregoing and following, that Maſter *Cottons* words drive at no leſſe then a ſeizing upon, and *plundering* of the goods, the *Impriſoning*, *whipping*, *Baniſhing* and *killing* the *Bodies*, of the poor people, and this under the Cloak and colour of ſaving their *Souls* in the day of the *Lord Jeſus*.

Wofull *Soul-ſaving*.

Truth. The *Civil State*, and *Common-weal* may be compared to [238] a piece of Tapiſty, or rich Arras, made up of the ſeverall parts and parcels of the Families thereof. Now by the *Law* of *God*, *Nature* and *Nations*. a Father hath a power over his Child, the Husband over the Wife, the Maſter over, &c. and doubtleſſe they are to improve that power and *Authority* for the good of the *ſouls* of their Children, Yoak-fellows, &c. But ſhall we therefore ſay that the Father and the Husband hath power under *Chriſt* over the *conſcienies* and *religion* of the Child or Wife, as a Father or Husband had under *Moſes Numb.* 30. Parents are commanded in the *Goſpel* to bring up their *Children* in the inſtruction and fear of the *Lord*; the *Husband* is commanded to labour to win and ſave his *Wife* (with other power then the Wife also her Husband) whether *Turke* or *Jew*, *Antichriſtian* or *Pagan*: but ſuch a *power* and *ſword* to be improved (as Mr *Cotton* here pretends) for *ſoul-good*, Maſter *Cotton* will never finde in the Teſtament of *Chriſt Jeſus*.

The power of Parents, Huſbands, Magiſtrates in ſpirituals.

1 *Cor.*7. [16.]

The *Plain Engliſh* is (what ever be the Cloak or

The tearme [*Souls-good*] commonly but a paint &c.

cover which the *States, Kings* and *Rulers* of this world uſe in this caſe) this terme [for *ſouls good*] is no more then the old Popiſh *Jeſabels* painting, *pro ſalute animæ, pro redemptione animæ,* or as that noble St. *John* obſerved in a ſpeech at *Guild-hall*, that the *Kings* party made uſe of the name of *Peace*, as the *Papiſts* uſed the name of *God, In nomine Domini, &c.*[1]

Peace. It is moſt lamentable to ſee how the *Kings* of the Earth are groſly flattered by their *Clergy*, into as groſſe a belief that they are moſt *Catholick Kings* as in *Spain*, moſt *Chriſtian Kings* as in *France, Defendors* of the *Faith* in *England.* Hence thoſe two bloody *Perſecutors* of *Luther, Charles* the *Fiſth*, and *Henry* the Eighth, were celebrated even upon the poſts of the doors in *Guild-Hall* : *Carolus, Henricus vivant, defenſor uturque, Henricus Fidei, Carolus Eccleſiæ.*

Peace. And yet to what other end have or doe (ordinarily) the *Kings* of the *Earth* uſe their *power* and *authority* over the *Bodies* and *Goods* of their Subjects, but for the filling of their *paunches* like *Wolves* or *Lions*, never pacified unleſſe the peoples *bodies, goods* and *Souls* be ſacrificed to their *God-belly* and their owne *Gods* of *profit, honour, pleasure, &c.*

[1] Oliver St. John of Catherine Hall, Cambridge, and afterwards of Lincoln's Inn, argued in behalf of John Hampden, in the caſe of ſhip-money. He was in Parliament for Totness, and was made attorney-general, and afterwards chief-juſtice of Common-pleas. In 1652, the year of this publication, he was sent ambaſſador to the Netherlands. He died in 1673, aged about ſeventy-five. He was connected with Cromwell by marriage. Mr. Carlyle ſpeaks of him as "duſky, tough St. John, whoſe abſtruse fanaticiſms, crabbed logics, and dark ambitions, iſſue all as was very natural in "decided avarice" at laſt." *Life of Cromwell*, ii. 6. Wood. *Athenæ Oxonienſes*, ii. 453.

Peace. But in the ſecond place Maſter *Cotton* affirmes, that by procuring the good of sheir *ſouls*, they may much advance [239] the good of their *bodies* and outward man alſo.

Truth. This *Propoſition* is as fair as the former, but in the *ſearching* and *cruſhing* is as *rotten*, for however it is moſt true (as he quoteth 1 *Tim.* 4, [8.]) that *Godlineſſe* hath the promiſe of this *Life*, and of a *better*, and alſo that ſuch as ſeek firſt the *Kingdome* of *God*, may expect outward mercies to be caſt upon them, yet theſe promiſes can never by any rule of *Chriſt*, be ſtretched to proue outward proſperity and flouriſhing to the followers of *Chriſt Jeſus* in this preſent evill world.

The promiſes of temporall mercies conſidered.

Peace. He that is in a pleaſant *Bed* and *Dreame*, though he talke idly and inſenſibly, yet is loath to be awaked.

Truth. Thoſe ſweet promiſes ſupply *Gods ſervants* with what outward bleſſings his holy Wiſdome ſeeth they have need of for his ſervice: But when wil Maſter *Cotton* indeed witneſſe againſt a *Nationall Church*, and ceaſe to mingle *Heaven* and *Earth*, the *Church* and *worldly ſtate* together? when will he ceaſe to propoſe the rich and peaceable, victorious and flouriſhing Nationall State of the *Jewes* as the Type of the Carnall peace and worldly wealth and honour of the ſpirituall Nation and Kingdome of *Chriſt Jeſus?* when will he more plainely and ſimply conforme the members to the head *Chriſt Jeſus* in the *Holineſſe*, *Glory* of his *ſpirituall poverty*, *ſhame* and *ſufferings?*

Peace. I have in the experience of many Ages

obſerved the flouriſhing proſperity of many *Cities, Common wealths* and *Nations*, where no ſound of *Chriſt* hath come, and that for hundreths, yea, ſome thouſands of years together, as hath former-[ly] in this diſcourſe been inſtanced.[1]

Truth. You have found that when the *Red* and *Black* and *Pale* horſe of *War, Famine* and *Death* have thundered upon the *Nations*, it hath not been upon the decay of a *State Religion*, but most commonly upon the *rejecting* and *perſecuting* of the *Preachers* and *Witneſſes* against it.

Peace. Yea Maſter *Cotton* himselfe observeth that ſuch of *Gods ſervants* as grow fatteſt in *Godlineſſe*, grow not outwardly in *wealth*, but *God* keepeth them low in *outward eſtate*.

Worldly proſperity ever dangerous to Gods children.

Truth. I conclude this paſſage with an obſervation of conſtant *experience*, ever ſince the *Son* of *God* aſcended the *Heauens*. The neerer *Chriſts* followers have approached to worldly wealth, eaſe, liberty, honour, pleaſure, &c. the neerer they [240] have approached to *Impatience, Pride, Anger* and *Violence* against ſuch as are oppoſite to their *Doctrine* and *Profeſſion* of *Religion:* And (2) The further and further have they departed from *God*, ſrom his *Truth*, from the *Simplicitie, Power* and *Puritie* of *Chriſt Jeſus* and true *Chriſtianitie*.

Peace. In the next Paſſage Mr *Cotton* (though with another heart, yet) in the *Language* and *Tongue* of the *Phariſees*, ſeemes to take part with the *Prophets* against the perſecuting *Fathers*, and amongſt many things he prohibites *Magiſtrates* this one, to wit, that he must not make *Lawes* to binde *Conſcience*.

1 Page 16, *ſupra*.

Truth. What is a *Law*, but a *binding Word*, a Commandement? What is a *Law* to binde *Conſcience*, but a *Commandement* that calls for *Obedience?* And muſt wee raiſe up ſuch *Tumults*, ſuch *Tragedies*, and fill the *face* of the *World* with *ſtreames* of *bloud*, about the *Chriſtian Magiſtrates reforming Religion, eſtabliſhing Religion*, killing the *Heretick, Blaſphemer, Idolater, Seducer*, and yet all this without a *Law*, that may in the name of *Chriſt* exact obedience?

Of Lawes binding Conſcience.

Peace. I wonder what we ſhall thinke of thoſe *Lawes* and *Statutes* of *Parliament*, in *old* or *New England* that have bound the peoples *Conſciences*, at leaſt ſo farre, as to come to the *Pariſh Church*, improving (as Mr *Cotton* sayth) the *power* and *Authoritie* over their *Bodies* for their *Souls good?* What ſhall wee call all thoſe *Lawes, Commandements, Statutes, Injunctions, Directions*, and *Orders*, that concerne *Religion* and *Conſcience?*

Truth. The plaine truth is, Mr *Cottons* former *reforming zeale*, cannot be ſo utterly extinguiſhed, as to forget the *name* and *Notion* of *Chriſtian Libertie*, although in this bloudie *Diſcourse*, he hath well nigh, if not wholly) *ſold away* the Thing! The *Conſcience* (ſayth he) muſt not be bound to a *Ceremonie* (to a pretended *indifferent Ceremonie*): And yet loe, throughout this Diſcouſe, he pleades for the binding of it from theſe and theſe *Doctrines*, from theſe and theſe *Worſhips*, and binding to this or that *Worſhip*, I meane, to come to the publike *Towne* or *Countrey Worſhip!* Juſt for all the world, as if a Woman ſhould not be bound to make a *Curtſie*, or *Salutation* to ſuch a Man, but yet ſhee ſhould be bound (will ſhe nill ſhe) to come to his *bed* at his pleaſure. *Worſhip* is a true or falſe *Bed, Cant.* 1. 16.

Peace. It is obſervable in the next place, what Mr *Cotton* [241] obſerveth, concerning the *Principles* of *ſaving Truth*, to wit, that no good *Chriſtian*, much leſſe good *Magiſtrate* can be ignorant of them.

Truth. In the Conſideration of the *Modell*, this *Goodneſſe* or *Badnes* of the *Magiſtrate* is Examined, and eaſily it is proved (to my underſtanding) that this Aſſertion confounding the nature of *Civill* and *Morall goodneſſe* with *Religious*, is as farre from *Goodnes* as *Darknes* is from *Light.*[1]

Peace. To this Iſſue tends Mr *Cottons* Concluſion of this paſſage [verily the *Lord* will build up and eſtabliſh the *Houſe* and *Kingdome* of ſuch *Princes*, as doe thus build up his.]

Truth. The promiſe of *God* to *David* concerning his *Houſe* and *Kingdome* in the *Letter*, is moſt true in the *Myſtery* and *Antitype*, as to the *Spirituall Houſe* and *Kingdome* of King *David*, King *Jeſus*, in ſuch *Princes* or *Propheticall* Kingly *Spirits*, who *Spiritually*, in the Word of *Propheſie* (the *Sword* of *Gods Spirit*) contend, for the *Spirituall Kingdome* of *Chriſt Jeſus: God* will eſtabliſh them in *Spirituall Dignitie* and *Authoritie:* But take this literally (as Mr *Cotton* carries it) and as he never will finde any ſuch Dutie lying upon *Princes* in the *Goſpell*, nor any ſuch *promiſe* of *temporall proſperitie*, but holy *predictions* and *foretellings* of the *croſſe* and *perſecution* ordinarily to all that will live *Godly* in *Chriſt Jeſus*, and the greater *perſecution* to the moſt zealous and faithfull Servants

Perſecution the ordinarie Portion of Chriſts Followers

[1] *Bloudy Tenent*, 134, 135. *Pub. Narr. Club, III.*, 245, 246.

of *Chriſt Jeſus:* So neither can he give any true Inſtance (truely proper and parallell) to this purpoſe.

Peace. Me thinks although ſucceſſe be no conſtant rule to walke by, yet *Gods providence* in *ſucceſſe* of *Journies, Victories,* &c. are with great *care* and *feare* to be attended to and pondered, and the *Hand* and *Eye* of *God* to be obſerved in them, of what ſort or Nature ſo ever they be.

Truth. Two inſtances of greateſt *ſucceſſe* and *temporall proſperitie* we have preſented to us on the *publike ſtage* of this world, before our owne *Dores,* crowning the *Heads* of ſuch *States* and *States-men,* as have attended to *mercy* and *freedome* toward oppreſſed *Conſciences.*

Two States wonderfully favoured by God, upon mercy ſhewed to oppreſſed Conſciences, formerly *Holland* and now the State of *England.*

The firſt is that of the *State* of *Holland:* The ſecond of our owne Native *England,* whoſe renowned *Parliament* and *victorious Armie* never ſo proſpered, as ſince their *Declaration* and *practice* [242] of *pitie* and *mercy* to *Conſciences* oppreſſed by Mr *Cottons* bloudie *Tenent.*

Peace. In the next Paſſage, it being a *Grievance* that Mr *Cotton* ſhould grant with *Luther* the *Magiſtrates* power to extend no further then the *Bodies* and *Goods* of the Subject, and yet withall maintaineth, that they muſt puniſh *Chriſtians* for ſinning againſt the Light of *Faith* and *Conſcience:* Mr *Cotton* anſwers:

Bodies and Goods the Magiſtrates object.

Firſt; He ſuppoſeth the *chiefe good* to be that of *Chriſtian Faith* and *Good Conſcience.*

Seeondly; Suppoſe (ſayth he) by *Goods* were meant outward *Goods,* yet the *Magiſtrate* may puniſh ſuch in their *Bodies* and *Goods,* as ſeduce, &c. for (ſayth he) in ſeeking *Gods Kingdome* and the *Righteouſneſſe* thereof, Men proſper in their outward *Eſtates*, Matth. 6. 23. Otherwiſe they decay.

Laſtly, He remembers not the propoſition to be his, [The *Magiſtrates power* extendeth no further, then the *Bodies* and *Goods* of the *Subject*] He anſwereth it is true in reſpect of the *Object*, though not in reſpect of the *End*, which (ſayth he) is ἐυπολιτέυειν, *Bene adminiſtrare Rempublicam.* And he asketh if it be well with a *Common-weale*, enjoying bodily *health* and worldly *wealth*, without a *Church*, without *Chriſt!* And he concludes with the Inſtance of the *Romane Empire*, which had it not caſt away Idolatrie (ſayth he) had been ruined.

Truth. For anſwer; Firſt, the *diſtinction* is famous among all Men of the *Bona* or *Goods* of *Animi*, *Corporis*, *Fortunæ:* and againe, that of the *Minde*, *Soule*, and *Conſcience* within, and that of the *Body* and *Goods* without, that it can be no leſſe then a *Civill* as well as a *Spirituall Babell* to conſound them.

Oppreſſion in Bodies Goods and Minde.

Secondly, To his *Suppoſition*, ſuppoſe (ſayth he) by *Goods* were meant outward *Goods*, yet the *Magiſtrate* may puniſh ſuch in their *Bodies* and *Goods*, as doe *Seduce*, &c. I ſee not how theſe Cohere any better then the grant of ſome *Papiſts*, that the *Churches* power extends no further then the matters of *Faith* and *Conſcience:* But yet (ſay they) they may puniſh ſuch in their *Bodies* and *Goods* as *ſeduce*, &c. Mr *Cottons Suppoſitions* and the *Papiſts* come both out of the ſame *Babylonian* Quiver.

But thirdly, let us minde his *Reaſon* from *Matth.* 6. [33.] In ſeeking *Gods Kingdome* men proſper in *out-*

ward eſtate, otherwiſe not: [243] I anſwer, this *Propoſition* would better befit the pen of a *Jew* then a *Chriſtian,* a follower of *Moſes,* then of *Jeſus Chriſt,* who although he will not fayle to take care for his in *Earthly Providences,* that make it their chiefe *worke* to ſeeke his *Kingdome,* yet he maketh (as I may ſay) *Chriſts Croſſe* the firſt *Figure* in his *Alphabet,* taking up his *Croſſe* and *Gallowes* (in moſt ordinarie perſecution,) which with ſelfe-deniall, are the aſſured *Tearmes* his *Servants* muſt reſolve to looke for.

'Tis true, he promiſeth and makes good, an *hundreth Fathers, Mothers, Brothers, Siſters, Wives, Children, Houſes* and *Lands:* But Mr *Cotton* well knowes, it is [with *perſecution*]. And how this outward *prosperitie,* agrees with *Impriſonments, Baniſhments, hanging, burning,* for *Chriſts ſake:* the *Martyrs* or *Witnes* of *Jesus* in all *Ages,* and the *cry* of the *Soules* under the *Altar,* may bring againe to his *Remembrance,* if *New Englands peace, profit, pleasure* and *Honour,* have lulled him into a *Forgetſulneſſe* of the *principles* of the true Lord *Jeſus Chriſt.*

Wealth, Honour, and Proſperitie ſeldome attending Chriſts true Followers.

Peace. But Mr *Cotton* remembreth not the *Propoſition* to be his, to wit, that the *Magiſtrates* power extendeth no further then the *Bodies* and *Goods* of the Subject.

Truth. Mr *Cotton* hinted not his leaſt diſſent from *Luther* (as he otherwayes uſeth to doe if he diſowne,) &c.

Secondly, He grants it true in the *object,* to wit, that the object of the *Magiſtrates power* is the *Body* and *Goods* of the *Subject,* though not in the *End* which he ſaith is εὐπολιτεύειν, well to adminiſter the *Common weale:* Now I aske what is this *Common weale?*

What is the Comon weal of *Iſrael.*

Peace. The *Spirit* of *God* diſtinguiſheth in the *New Teſtament* between the *Common weale* of the *Nations* of the *World*, and the *Common-weale* of *Iſrael.* The *Common-weale* of *Iſrael*, Mr *Cotton* will not affirme now to be a *Church Provinciall, Nationall, Oecumenicall*, but *Particular* and *Congregationall.*

Truth. If ſo, then the *finall cauſe* of both theſe *Common weales* or *States* cannot be the ſame. But although the *End* of the *Civill Magiſtrate* be excellent, to wit, well to adminiſter the *Common-weale*, yet the end of the *Spirituall Common-weale* of *Iſrael* and the *Officers* thereof, is as *different* and *tranſcendent* as the *Heaven* is from the *Earth.*

Peace. But how (ſayth Mr *Cotton*) can it be well with the [244] Common-wealth that injoyes bodily health, and wordly wealth, if there be no *Chriſt*, no *Church* there? and how was it with the *Romane Empire* which the *Red-horſe* of *War*, and *Black horſe* of *Famine*, and *Pale horſe* of *Peſtilence* would have ruined, if ſhe had not caſt away her *Idols.*

The *Roman* Empire flouriſheth in worldly glory without *Chriſt.*

Truth. Concerning this inſtance of *Rome* Maſter *Cotton* here acknowledgeth it abounded in *worldly bleſſings*, till the *Lord Jeſus* came riding forth upon the *White Horſe* of the *Goſpel.* And Maſter *Cotton* may remember that from the Foundation of her riſing and Glory, laid by *Romulus* until *Chriſts* time, it flouriſhed about 750 years in a long chaine of *generations* ſucceeding each other in *worldly* proſperity, and yet no *Church* nor *Chriſt* to uphold it, ſo far is Maſter *Cottons Romiſh inſtance* from countenancing Mr. *Cottons Roman Doctrine.*

Peace. But when *Chriſt* came (ſaith Maſter *Cotton*) and was neglected, then the *Red* and *Black* and *Pale* horſe had almoſt deſtroyed her, if ſhe had not caſt away her *Idols*.

Truth. I anſwer, *Rome* the head of the *Empire* cannot be ſaid to neglect *Chriſt* (until the bloody Tenent of perſecution aroſe among them) I say, not to neglect *Chriſt* more, nor ſo much as other *States*, for there were ſo many of the *Romanes*, and ſo glorious profeſſors of *Chriſt Jeſus*, that all the world over the Faith and *Chriſtian* obedience of the *Romanes* was renowned.

The Citie of *Rome* famous for profeſſing *Chriſt Jeſus*.

2 The *Roman Impire* cannot be ſaid to caſt away her *Idols*, but to change (as the *Portugals* did in the Eaſt-Indies) her *Idols* her more groſſe and *Pagan Idols*, for more refined & beautified *Idols*, painted over with the name of *Chriſt*, the true *God*, *holines*, *&c*. and this in the glorious dayes of *Conſtantine*, or not long after. The *Church* of *Chriſt Jeſus* which under perſecution remained a *wife* and *ſpouſe* of *Chriſt Jesus*, now degenerates and apoſtates into an *Whore*, in the times of her eaſe, ſecurity and proſperity. (Whole Cities, Nations, and the whole world forced and raviſhed into a *whore* or Antichriſtian Chriſtian.)

Chriſts Spouſe moſt chaſt under perſecution.

3 As far as the *Eaſt* is from the *Weſt*, ſo far is the world and nations and Empire of it from the holineſſe of *Chriſt Jeſus*, holy Spirit, Truth and Saints: With what appearance then of *Chriſts holineſſe*, *glory*, *&c*. can Master *Cotton* advance the world, (the *Roman Empire*) to be (as he here ſpeaks) the Advancer of the *ſcepter* of *Chriſt Jeſus*?

245] *Peace.* If this *Roman Empire* be that dreadful *Beaſt*, (in *Daniels* prophecy) more ſtrange and terrible then the reſt, yea, and more terrible to *Chriſt Jeſus* and his ſervants, then was the former *Babilonian Lion*, or *Perſian Beare*, or *Grecian Leopard*, what truth of *Jeſus* is this, that advanceth this dreadfull bloody *Beaſt* to be the *Advancer* of the *Scepter*, that is, the *Church* and Government, the *Truth* and *Saints* of *Chriſt Jeſus.*[1]

The *Roman* Monarchy bloody to the Saints.

Peace. Glorious things (Dear Truth) are recorded of *Conſtan*tine and other glorious Emperors.

Truth. The *Beaſt* was (ſweet Peace) the *Beaſt* ſtill, although it pleaſed *God* to give ſome refreſhing and reviving to his perſecuted ſervants, by *Conſtantine* and other bleſſed Inſtruments yet *Conſtantines* favour was a bitter *ſweeting*, his *ſuperſtitious zeal* laying the *Foundation* for after *Uſurpations* and *Abominations.*

Conſtantine a friend and enemy to *Chriſts Spouſe.*

4 But further, for neer 1000 years together, both before and after *Chriſts time*, *Rome* grew and flouriſhed (with little alterations of her *glory* in compariſon) untill this very time that Maſter *Cotton* cals ths *caſting away* of her *Idols:* For not before, but after *Conſtantines* advancing of *Chriſtians* to wealth and honour, &c. I ſay neer about 300 years together (interchangably) after his time, untill *Pipinus*, and *Charles* the Great, the City and ſtate of *Rome* was almoſt ruined and deſtroyed, by the often dreadfull

The ſtate of the *Romane* Empire before and after Chriſt.

1 After this I ſaw in the night viſions, and behold a fourth beaſt, dreadful and terrible, and ſtrong exceedingly; and it had great iron teeth: it devoured and brake in pieces, and ſtamped the reſidue with the feet of it: and it *was* diverſe from all the beaſts that *were* before it; and it had ten horns. *Daniel* vii: 7.

incurſions of the *Goths* and *Vandals, Huns, Longobards,* and other furious Nations: So contrary to the truth of *Jeſus* is this fleſhly doctrine of worldly wealth and proſperity, and alſo this very inſtance of *Rome* and her glory here diſcuſſed.[1]

Peace. Maſter *Cotton ends* with *prayer* and *bleſſing* to God (as *James* ſpeakes) and bitter and cutting *curſings* and *cenſures* to man, the poor Diſcuſſer, who (ſaith Maſter *Cotton*) *ſeduceth* himſelfe and others and delights to doe it, and againſt the *light* of *grace* and *conſcience*, againſt *reaſon* and *experience.*[2]

Truth. The Diſcuſſor is as humbly confident of *Grace* and *Conſcience, Reaſon* and *Experience*, yea, the *God* of all *Grace, Chriſt Jeſus,* his holy *Spirit, Angels, Truth* and *Saints* to be on his ſide, as Maſter *Cotton* otherwiſe can be: But the day ſhall try, the *Fire* and *Time* ſhall try which is the *Gold* of *Truth* and [246] and *Faithfulneſſe*, and which the *Droſſe* and *Stubble* of *Lyes* and *Errour.*

In the meane time I dare pronounce from the *Teſtimony* of *Chriſt Jeſus*, that in all Controverſies of *Religion*: That *Soul* that moſt poſſeſſeth it ſelfe in patient ſuffering, and dependeth not on the *arme* of *flesh*, but upon the arme of *God, Chriſt Jeſus*, for his comfort and protection, that Soul is moſt likely (in my obſervation) to ſee and ſtand for the *Truth* of *Chriſt Jesus.*

Peace. In the next place Master *Cotton* denyes

[1] For an elaborate account of the deſtruction of Rome and its cauſes, ſee Gibbon, *Decline and Fall,* chap. lxxi.

[2] Therewith bleſs we God, even the Father: and therewith curſe we men, which are made after the ſimilitude of God. *James,* iii: 9.

to compell to the *Truth* by *penalties*, but onely by withdrawing ſuch favours as are comely and ſafe for ſuch perſons.

Truth. I have formerly anſwered, and doe, that a great Load may be made up by Parcels and particulars, as well as by one *maſſe* or *bulke*; and that the backs of ſome men, eſpecially Merchants may be broke, by a withdrawing from them ſome Civill priviledges and rights (which are their due) as well as by afflicting them in their Purſes, or Fleſh upon their backs.

God will notwrong, nor have *Cæſar* wronged.

2 *Chriſt Jeſus* was of another opinion (who diſtinguiſheth between *Gods* due and *Cæſars* due: and therefore (with reſpect to *God* his cauſe and Religion) it is not lawfull to deprive *Cæſar* the Civil Magiſteate, nor any that belong to him of their Civil and Earthly rights. I ſay in this reſpect, although that a man is not *Godly*, a *Chriſtian*, ſincere, a *Chuch member*, yet to deprive him of any *Civill right* or *Priviledge*, due to him as a Man, a Subject, a Citizen, is to take from *Cæſar*, that which is *Cæſars*, which *God* endures not though it be given to himſelfe.

Peace. *Experience* oft-times tell us, that however the ſtream of juſt *Priviledges* and *Rights* hath (out of *Carnal Policy*) been ſtopt by *Gods people*, when they have got the *Staffe* into their hands (in divers *Lands* and *Countreys*) yet hath that *ſtreame* ever returned, to the greater *calamity* and *tryal* of *Gods* people.

Truth. But (thirdly) it hath been noted that even in *New-England*, penalties by *Law* have been ſet to force all to come to *Church*, which will appear upon a due ſearch to be nothing else but an outward profeſſion of *force* and *violence*, for that *Doctrine* which they ſupppoſe is the *Truth*.

247] *Peace.* Concerning coming to *Church*: wee tolerate (ſaith Maſter *Cotton*) *Indians*, *Preſbyterians*, *Antinomians*, and *Anabaptiſts*: and compell none to come to *Church* againſt their *conſcience*, and none are reſtrained from hearing even in *England*.

Truth. Compelling to come to Church is apparant whether with or againſt their Conſcience, let every man look to it. The toleration of *Indians* is againſt profeſſed *principles*, and againſt the *ſtream* of all his preſent diſpute as before I proved.[1]

Concerning toleration in *New-England.*

Touching the *Magiſtrates* duty of ſuppreſſing *Idolatry*, *Witchcraft*, *Blaſphemy*, *&c.* ſuch *Indians* as are (poſeſſedly ſubject to *Engliſh*) in *N. England*, notoriouſly continue and abound in the ſame which if they ſhould not permit, it as apparant, their *ſubjection* is hazarded.

Tis true, this *Toleration* is a *Duty* from *God*, but a ſin in them becauſe they profeſſe it their Duty to ſuppreſſe *Idolatry*, *Blaſphemy*; I adde, Maſter *Cotton* may ſay, we not onely tolerate the *Indians* in their abominable and barbarous *worſhips*, but (which may ſeem moſt incredible) we tolerate the *Indians* alſo in that which by our *civil principles* we ought to tolerate no ſubject in, that is, in abominable *lying*, *whoring*, *curſing*, *thieving*, without any active course of reſtraint, *&c.*

Tis true, Thoſe *Indians* ſubmitting to their Gov-

[1] See pp. 232, 233, *ſupra*.

ernment (as it may be Master *Cotton* will ſay to the ten Commandments) yet living in all kind of *Barbariſme*, live ſome miles more remote: how ever they are (they ſay) their ſubjects) were every miles diſtance an hundreth.

Peace. But is there any ſuch and profeſſed tolleration of *Antinomians*, *Preſbyterians*, *Anabaptiſts*, as is here inſinuated?

Witneſſe the bloody whipping of *Obadiah Holmes* for the point of *Baptiſme* lately at *Boſton*.[1]

Truth. I know of no toleration of *Preſbyterian*, *Antinomians*, *Anabaptiſts* worſhipping God in any meetings, ſeparate from the *common Aſſemblies*.[2] If any ſuch perſons be amongſt them (like Church-Papiſts) it is their ſin, that they separate not from ſuch oppoſite *Aſſemblies* and *Worſhips*, and it is the ſin of ſuch *aſſemblies* to tolerate ſuch persons after due admonitions in the name of *Chriſt* rejected.

But further Master *Cotton* grants a *Communion* in

[1] pp. 52, 53, *ſupra.*

[2] There was from the beginning more or leſs latent diſſent existing in the Maſſachuſetts and Plymouth Colonies, beſides that which found its outlet into Rhode Iſland. Cotton ſays, "There be Anabaptiſts and Antimonians tolerated to live not only in our jurisdiction, but even in ſome of our churches." *Bloudy Tenent Waſhed*, 165. Winſlow in his *Briefe Narration* (1646) alleges not only that Preſbyterians were allowed amongſt them, but ſpeaking of the Anabaptiſts and the law againſt them in Maſſachuſetts, says "certain men deſiring ſome mitigation of it, it was anſwered in my hearing, 'Tis true we have a ſevere law, but we never did or will execute the rigor of it upon any; and have men living amongſt us, nay, ſome in our churches, of that judgment.'" Young. *Chron. of Pilgrims*, 404. Winſlow alſo ſays of Mr. Chauncy of Scituate, who was afterwards Preſident of Harvard College, "In the Government of Plymouth, to our great grief, not only the paſtor of a congregation waiveth the adminiſtration of baptiſm to infants, but divers of his congregation have fallen with him." *Chron. of Pilgrims*, 405. The exact fact however ſeems to have been that he held "that the children ought to be dipped and not ſprinkled." *Winthrop*, 1: 398. ii: 86. He immediately ſucceeded Mr. Dunſter in the Preſidency of Harvard College, who was removed for diſowning the baptiſm of infants altogether. Mather, *Magnalia*, i: 367. Quincy, *Hiſt. Harv. Coll.* i: 18. To theſe inſtances may be added the later teſtimony

hearing in a *Church-Eſtate* by *Church members* but not in any as are no *Church-members*, but come in as the *Pagan*, *Infidell*, 1 *Cor.* 14. [23.]

Truth. Communion is twofold, Firſt, open and profeſſed [248] among *Church Members:* Secondly, *Secret* and *implicite* in all ſuch as give their *preſence* to ſuch *Worſhips* without *witneſſing* againſt them. For otherwiſe, how can a *Church-Papiſt* ſatisfie the *Law*, compelling him to come to *Church*, or a *Proteſtant* ſatisfie a *Popiſh Law* in *Popiſh Countries*, but by this *Cloake* or *Covering*, hiding and ſaving of themſelves by bodily *preſence* at *Worſhip*, though their *Heart* be farre from it.

Communion Spirituall two-fold.

Peace. Whereas it was ſaid, that *Conſcionable Papiſts*, and all *Proteſtants* have ſuffered upon this ground, eſpecially of refuſing to come to each others *Church* or *meeting*. Mr *Cotton* replies; They have ſuffered upon other *points*, and ſuch as have refuſed to come to *Church*, have not refuſed becauſe such hearing implanted them into *Church-Eſtate*, but out of *feare* to be leavened.

The great Triall among *Papiſts* & *Proteſtants* concerning coming to Church

Truth. 'Tis true, many have ſuffered upon other *points*, but upon due *Examination* it will appeare that the great and moſt *univerſall Tryall* hath been, amongſt both *Papiſts* and *Proteſtants* about coming to *Church*, and that not out of *feare* of being *leavened* (for what *Religion* is ordinarily ſo diſtruſtfull of its owne ſtrength?) as of Countenancing what they believe *falſe*, by their *preſence* and *appearance*.

of Cotton Mather. "Infant baptiſm hath been ſcrupled by multitudes in our days, who have been in other points moſt worthy Chriſtians, and as holy, watchful, faithful, heavenly people, as perhaps any in the world. Some few of theſe people have been among the planters of New England from the beginning.' *Magnalia*, ii. 459. But all this does not impugn the allegation of Williams in the text that they were not tolerated "ſeparate from the common aſſemblies."

Exam: of Chap. 71. *replying to* Chap. 74.

Peace. Concerning the *Papists testimonie* against *persecution*; Mr *Cotton* replyes: First, why may not their *Testimonie* be *wicked*, as well as their *Booke*, confest so to be? Secondly, He grants, that *Conversion* of *Soules* ought not to be but by *Spirituall* meanes.

Truth. It is true, the Authour of the *Letter* calls their *booke wicked*, and themselves the *Authours* of *persecution*, yet their *Testimonie* is in part acknowledged by Mr *Cotton* to be true, and will further appeare so to be upon *Examination:* But whether Mr *Cotton* allow of no other *Armes*, then *Spirituall* to be used about *Spirituall conversion*, it hath and will be further examined.

Peace. Whereas the *Papists* alledge (*Matth.* 10. [16]) that *Christ* [249] *Jesus* sent his *Ministers* as *sheepe* among *Wolves*, not as *Wolves* among *sheepe*, to *kill*, *imprison*, &c. Mr *Cotton* grants this true, yet adds that this hindreth not *Excommunication*, Tit. 3. [10.] nor *miraculous Vengeance* against *Spirituall Wolves* (Acts 13. [11.]) where there is a *gift:* nor their *Prayers* against such, 2 *Tim.*4. 4. nor their *stirring up* of the *Civill power* against them, as *Elijah* did *Ahab* and the people against the Prophets of *Baal*, 1 Kings 18. 40.

Touching prayers for Vengeance upon Gods Enemies.

Truth. Concerning the two first we agree, for the third, the *Prayers* of *Gods people* against *Gods Enemies* we finde two-fold: First, *Generall* against all; secondly, *Particular* against some; and that two-fold; First for *Gods Vengeance* in *Gods time*, leaving it to his holy *Wisdome*; as *Paul* prayd againſt *Alexander*. Secondly, For *preſent Vengeance*; as the *Diſciples* deſired in the caſe of *Chriſt*, Luke 9. [54.] And againſt ſuch *Prayers* the Diſcuſſer did and doth contend.

For the fourth, in *Stirring up* of the *Civill State* against *falſe Prophets*, I muſt anſwer as before, Let Mr *Cotton* produce any ſuch *Civill State* in the *World*, as that *Extraordinarie* and *miraculous State* of *Iſrael* was, and I yeeld it: otherwiſe, if the *paſſage* be *extraordinarie* and *typing*, why doth Mr *Cotton* adde fuell to *Nebuchadnezzars fierie furnace*, which hath been ſo dreadfully hot already, and hath devoured ſo many *millions of Gods people?* Stirring up of the Civill State to perſecute.

Peace. Further out of *Matth*. 10. [17. 18.] Where the *Ppaiſts* booke ſays, *Chriſts Miniſters* ſhould be delivered, but ſhould not deliver up, thoſe whom they are ſent unto to *convert*, unto *Councells* or *Priſons*, or to make their *Religion Felonie* or *Treaſon*; Mr *Cotton* anſwers; What is this to *Apoſtates*, who ſeeke to *ſubvert* the Faith they have profeſt? What is this to them that ſeeke to *ſubvert States*, and kill *Kings*; which *Doctrine*, in downeright tearmes, he at laſt chargeth upon the *Authour* of the *Letter*, and the Diſcuſſer.

Truth. But how falls an *Antichriſtian* or *Apoſtate* more directly under the ſtroake of the *Civill Sword*, then a *Jew* or *Turke* or *Pagan?* By what rule of *God* or *Chriſt* hath a *Magiſtrate* of this *World Authoritie*, ſo to puniſh the one above the other? And where hath Mr *Cotton* found one Title, either in the *Letter* or in the *Diſcuſſer*, which forbids the *Magiſtrate* to puniſh *Felonie* [250] or *Treaſon*, whether

The *bloudie Tenent* of persecution is alone the King killing and State-killing Doctrine.

it be in *practice* or in *Doctrine*, leading to it? Doth not every *Leafe* and *Line* breath the contrary to what Mr *Cotton* here insinuateth? The *Truth* is, as *Potiphars* wife accusing *Joseph* was not cleare her *selfe*, so let this charge be well examined, and this will be the *Result* of it; The *Papists* and the *Discusser* agree together in asserting one *Truth* in this Chapter, to wit, that *Gods Messengers* ought not to deliver any to *Prisons* or *Councells*. But in the *Doctrine* of *killing hereticall Kings* or *Magistrates*, who sees not but such *Papists* as hould that *Doctrine*, and Mr *Cotton* meete in the end? For if the *Magistrate* prove an *Apostate*, *Blasphemer*, *Idolater*, *Heretick*, *Seducer*, (according to Mr *Cottons Doctrine*, as well as the *Papists*) such *Kings* and *Magistrates* ought (as well as thousands of his *Subjects* in like case) be put to Death.

Peace. Againe, where the *Papists* booke argued from *Matth.* 10 [12.] that *Christ* bids his *Ministers* to salute an house with *peace*, he sends no *Pursevant* to *ransack* and *spoile* it: Mr *Cotton* answers: True, but if *Seducers* be there, or *Rebells* or *Conspiratours* be there, *God* hath armed the *Magistrate*, Rom. 13. [4.]

Truth. Mr *Cotton* (too too like the bloudie *persecutours* of *Christ Jesus*, in all Ages) still couples the *Seducer* and the *Rebells* together, as the *Jewes* coupled *Christ* and *Barrabbas*, though *Barrabbas* finds more favor then the *Son* of *God*, for *Christ* as a *seducer*, a *Deceiver*, &c. is commonly executed, & *Barrabas* released.

'Tis true the *Magistrates Commission* is from *God*, even in the time of the *Gospel*, but *Christ Jesus* never gave *Commiſſion* to *Magiſtrates* to ſend *Purſevants* to ranſack an houſe, to ſearch for *Seducers* and *Idolaters*, who tranſgreſſe onely againſt the *Spirituall Kingdome* of *Chriſt Jeſus*, but not againſt *Civilitie* and the *Civill State*.

Peace. This *Diſtinction* of *Evills* I remember it pleaſed *God* to open ſome of the *Romane Emperours* eyes to ſee, upon the occaſion of his poore ſervants *Apologies* preſented unto them.

Truth. You ſeaſonably remember this (Deare *Peace*) for although we finde not *Antoninus Pius* or *Aurelius Antoninus* to have been Believers in *Chriſt Jeſus*, yet they gave forth their *Edicts*, that no *Chriſtian* ſhould be puniſhed meerely for that he was a *Chriſtian*, except ſome other crime againſt the *Civill State* were proved againſt him: And the later of theſe gave in Ex- [251] preſſe *charge*, that ſuch as were their accuſers ſhould be burnt alive.[1]

Antonius Pius his Edict for the Chriſtians.

Peace. If ſuch an *Edict* or any farre more moderate ſhould come forth in our Time, againſt the great troublers of all *Civill States*, to wit, *Informers*, *Accuſers* and *Maintainers* of the bloudie *Doctrine* of *perſecution*: Doubtles thouſands and ten thouſands of Men, yea not a few of the moſt *zealous Hunters* or *perſecutors* would eaſily ſubmit to the Truth of the *Diſtinction* between the *crime* of a *Religion* contrary to a *State Religion*, and a *crime* againſt the *Civill State* thereof.

Tranſgreſſion againſt the Spirituall or Civill Peace.

But to the *Papiſts* againe, they (laſtly) alledged *John* 10. [10.] that the true *Shepheard* comes not to kill the *ſheepe*, &c. Upon this Maſter *Cotton* queries.

[1] See pp. 232, 233, *ſupra*.

But what if the *Wolse*, the *Thiefe* come, ſhall the *Shepheard* uſe *Spirituall Cenſures*, when they are not capable of ſuch *ſtroakes*, or ſhall he not ſeeke helpe from the *Magiſtrate*, who is to ſee *Gods* people live a quiet and peaceable *Life* in all *Godlines* and *Honeſtie*, 1 Tim. 2. [2.]?

Perſecutours of Chriſts Sheepe pretend to ſave them and kill none but Wolves.

Truth. I anſwer, and cry out, how long, how long *Lord*, beſore thou avenge the bloud of thy *holy ones*, againſt them that dwell on the *Earth*, both *bloudie Papiſts* and *bloudie Proteſtants?* Out of their owne Mouthes ſhall *Papiſts* and *Proteſtants* be condemned for ſlaughtering *Chriſt Jeſus* (the *Shepheard*) in his poore *Sheepe* and *Servants*, and eſpecially the bloudie *Papiſt*, for alledging that *Scripture*, for the *Popes bloudie Butcherie*, [Ariſe *Peter*, kill and Eate:] yet all pretending to ſave the *ſheepe*, and onely to reſiſt *Wolves*, *Thieves*, &c.

Antichrſtian Miniſters great Thieves.

But more punctually Maſter *Cotton* well knowes, that in the *Myſterie* of *Antichriſtianiſme*, many thouſand *Antichriſtian Wolves* pretend ſtrongly to be the harmles *ſheepe* of *Chriſt Jeſus*, yea his tender and carefull *Shepheards*, yet are but *Antichriſtian Thieves* and *Robbers*, who cannot *dig* and to *beg* are aſhamed, and therefore finde it beſt to *ſteale* and *rob*, whole *Pariſhes* and *Provinces*, whole *Nations*, &c. for *Livings*, for *Benefices*, for *Biſhopricks*, *Cardinalſhips*, *Popedomes*, &c.

Hireling Miniſters.

Peace. What kinde of *Sheepe* and *Shepheards* (Chriſt Jeſus will finde out ſhortly) are thoſe *Hirelings*, *Papiſt* or *Proteſtant*, who no longer *peny*, no longer *paternoſter*, no longer *pay*, no longer *pray*, nor *preach*, nor *faſt*, nor *convert*, &c.

Truth. Theſe *Babylonian Rivers* ſhall at laſt be ſtopt: *God* and [253] *Man* ſhall agree to ſtop them: The truth of that holy *Myſterie* of that great *Exchange* ſhall be opened, *Revel.* 10. [Rev. 18.] And Peoples eyes ſhall be opened to ſee, how theſe *myſticall Marchants* of the *Earth* (pretending to be the great *Sellers* of *Truth*) have been the greateſt *Deceivers*, and *Cheators*, the greateſt *Thieves* and *Robbers* in the *World*.

Peace. But Mr *Cotton* will ſay, *Gods people* would live at *peace* in *Godlineſſe* and *Honeſtie*, 1 Tim. 2. 1. as *Paul* profeſſeth, *Acts* 25. 8.

Fryars in *Chaucers* time and the *Clergie* in our time conſidered

Truth. I remember when old *Chaucer* puts this *Querie* to the foure chiefe ſorts of *Fryers* in his Time [which of the *foure ſorts* is the beſt] he finds every sort applauding it ſelfe, and concluding the other three ſorts of *Fryers* to be *Liars:* whence in concluſion he finds them all guilty of *Lying* (in a round) before *God*, for all profeſt themſelves to be the only *godly* men.[1]

[1] The reference in the text is clearly not to any poem of Chaucer's, but to the *Crede of Piers Ploughman.* In that the writer goes through the experience which Williams here relates. Seeking for a creed, he says,

> "Firſt I frayned the freres,
> And they me fulle tolden,
> That all the fruyt of the ſayth
> Was in her foure orders."

He queſtions the Minorites, the Carmelites, the Dominicans, and the Auſtins, and they abuſe each other and furniſh him no ſatisfaction.

> "For I have fonded the freres
> Of the foure ordres;
> But thei ben fulli faithles,
> And the fend sueth."

Williams may have been led to aſcribe this poem to Chaucer from the fact that another poem of the ſame period, and with the ſame ſpirit towards the clergy of the time, called *Piers Ploughman's Tale,* was inſerted, though without reaſon, among the works of Chaucer. Wright, *Viſion and Creed of P. P.* Introduction, i: xxvi.

I may now ask, who among all the ſorts of *Churches* and *Miniſters* applaud not themſelves (like the *Fryars* in *Chaucers* dayes) to be *Chriſts* onely *Churches, Chriſts Miniſters,* &c. And who among the ſeverall ſorts of ſuch as are *Gods people* indeed, believe not their own *Godlines* (or worſhipping of *God*) to be onely right and *Chriſtian?*

Peace. What now if each ſort ſhould enjoy *Magiſtrates* of their own *profeſſion* and *Way?*

Truth. The *bloudie Tenent* will unavoydably ſet them altogether by the Eares, to try out by the *longeſt Sword,* and *ſtrongeſt Arme,* which *Godlines* muſt live in *peace* and *quietnes:* But as for that Scripture, 1 *Tim.* 2. [1. 2.] I have (as I believe) fully debated it, in the *Examination* of the *Modell,* and made it evident how farre from all *Godlines* and *Honeſtie* that holy *Scripture* is perverted.

Peace. Mr *Cotton* in the next paſſage being charged with partiall dealing, and a double *waight* and *meaſure,* one for himſelfe and another for others; Mr *Cotton* in effect answereth, that it is a true and juſt Complaint againſt *perſecution* and *perſecutours,* but not againſt them, for they are *Righteous* and not *Apoſtates, Seducers, Hereticks, Idolaters, Blaſphemers,* &c.

Peace. What doth Maſter *Cotton* anſwer, but what all *religions, ſects,* and ſeverall ſorts of *worſhippers* in the world: all religious *Prieſts* and *Church-men* plead, We are Righteous?

The Turkes

253] *Peace.* Yea, the very *Turkes* and *Mahumetans* challenge to themſelves true *Faith* in God, yea, whether *Jews*, *Antichriſtians* or *Chriſtians*, they all call themſelves *Muſelmanni* that is the *right beleevers.*[1]

themſelves will be *Muſlemanni*, or right beleevers.

Truth. It is not so great wonder then if the *popiſh* and *proteſtant* ſects, and *miniſters* of *worſhip* cry out (as men use to doe in *ſuits* of *Law* and pretences to the *Crowne*) We are *righteous*, my title is good, and the *beſt*. We are *holy*, we are *Orthodox* and *godly*: You muſt ſpare *us*, beleeve *us*, honour *us*, feed *us*, protect and defend *us* in peace and quietneſſe. Others are *Hereticks*, *Apoſtates*, *Seducers*, *Idolators*, *Blaſphemers*, ſtarve *them*, impriſon *them*, baniſh *them*, yea hang *them*, burne *them* with fire and ſword purſue them.

The horrible partialite of perſecutors.

Peace. When it was urged (by way of prevention) that perſons truly profeſſing *Chriſt Jesus* be the ſheep, and they cannot perſecute;

Firſt, Becauſe it is againſt the nature of *Sheep* to hunt, no not the *Wolves*, that have hunted themſelves, &c. Master *Cotton* anſwers, Firſt if the ſimilitude be ſo ſtretched, then if a *Magiſtrate* be a *ſheep*, he ought not to puniſh *robbers*, *adulterers*, *murtherers*, *&c.*

[1] "The term ſignifies 'reſigned to God' and is the dual number of the ſingular *moſlem*, of which *muslimim* is the plural." Brande, *Cyclopædia.*

"Iſlam or Iſlamiſm is ſaid by Prideaux, to ſignify the Saving religion; by Sale, reſigning one's ſelf to God; by Pocock, obedience to God and his prophet; Moſlem or Muſſulman is a derivation from Eſlam or Iſlam, and is the common name of Mohammedans." Mills, *Hiſt. of Mohammedaniſm, quoted in* Ockley, *Hiſt. of Saracens, note, p.* 13.

In a learned article by Mr. Deutſch, of the Britiſh Muſeum, in *Lond. Qy. Rev.* Oct. 1869, the derivation of the word Muſlim is traced. He ſays, "The word thus implies abſolute ſubmiſſion to God's will—as generally aſſumed—neither in the firſt inſtance, nor excluſively, but means on the contrary, one who ſtrives after righteouſness in his own ſtrength."

2 "*Paul* was a *sheep*, and yet he ſtrook *Elimas* with blindneſſe, *Acts* 13. [11.]

3 "(Saith he) when the *Wolfe* runs upon the "*ſheep*, it is not againſt the nature of the true *ſheep* "to run to the true *ſheepherd*, and is it againſt the "nature of the true *Sheepherd* to ſend forth his "Dogs, to worrie ſuch a *VVolfe*, without incurring "the reproach of a *perſecutour*.

Truth. To the firſt, the finger of true *Diſtinction* will eaſily untie theſe ſeeming knots.

Miſticall ſheep.

Sheep therefore are two-fold, *naturall* and *miſticall*.

Againe, *miſticall* are two-fold, Firſt, *Civill*, and ſo all *Magiſtrates* have rightly been called *Sheepherds* and the people *ſheep*.

2 Spirituall, and ſo *Chriſt Jeſus* gave *paſtors*, that is *Sheepheards* and *Teachers*, and all *Believers* and *followers* of *Jeſus* are *ſheep*.

On the contrary there are *naturall* and *miſticall wolves*: of *miſticall* ſome oppoſe the *ſpirituall*, and ſome the *Civill State*, and ſome both, who muſt be reſiſted by the proper *ſheepheads*, and [254] proper *weapons* in each kind, and to confound theſe is to *deceive* and to be *deceived*.

Peace. Upon the ground of this *Diſtinction* we may eaſily perceive, that a *Shepheard* in *Civill ſtate*, of what Religion ſoever he be, as a *Shepheard* of the people he ought to defend them by force of *Civill arms*, from all oppreſſions of *body*, *goods*, *chaſtity*, *name*, &c. This doth the *Magiſtrate* as a *Shepheard* of the *Civill ſtate* and people, conſidered in a Civil reſpect and capacity, and this ought all the *Magiſtrates* in the world to doe, whether they be *ſheep* or no themſelves in another reſpect, that is in a ſpirituall and *Chriſtian.*

Truth. Yea, and if a *Magiſtrate* be a *ſheep* or a true *Chriſtian*, who ſeeth not that he puniſheth not the *robber*, *adulterer*, *murtherer* as a ſpirituall *ſhepheard* with ſpirituall weapons, but as a *Civill Shepheard* with a *Civill ſtaffe*, *ſword*, *&c?*

Tis true, *Paul* was a *ſheep*, that is a ſpirituall *ſheep*; he alſo was a *ſpirituall Shepheard*, and *Elimas* was a *wolfe* oppoſing ſpiritually, and *Paul* in his oppoſition ſtrook him blind. *Striking* is two-ſold, *ſpirituall* and *corporall*: And all the *ſheep* of *Chriſt* as *ſpirituall*, are alſo *Lyons* and armed *men*, and ſo doe ſtrike *ſpiritually.*

Paul his ſtriking *Elimas* blind conſidered.

Peace. It will be ſaid that *Paul* ſtrook both *ſpiritually* and *corporally.*

Truth. *Corporal ſtroaks* may be conſidered either ordinary or mediate, by force of *armes*, *fire* and *ſword*, *&c.* or extraordinary and immediate, ſuch as it pleaſed *God* to uſe himſelfe, and his holy *Prophets* and *Apoſtles* by his power: Now 'tis true, in this ſecond way, (even in ſpirituall caſes) *Gods ſheep* which hath been indued with power above nature, that is of miracles, have plagued *Egypt*, have burnt up Captaines and their Fifties, yea pluckt up *Nations* and *Kingdomes* as *Jeremie: Peter* kild *Ananias* and his wife, *Paul* ſtrook *Elima's* blind, and the two witneſſes conſume their *Enemies* with fire out of their mouths.

If either of theſe ſhould doe this ordinarily, that is, by ordinary means (for inſtance, if *Peter* had

Of the power of miracles.

killed *Ananias* with a *Sword*, or *Paul* beat out *Elimas* his eyes with a *Fiſt* or ſtone) they ought to have been puniſhed by the *Civill ſtate*, as oppreſſors of the people, and tranſgreſſors againſt *Civill peace*, *&c.* But performing [255] theſe executions, by a ſpirituall, divine and miraculous power, above humane reach: all that heard were to acknowledge, and feare and tremble at the holy *Spirits* might: of this giſt of miracles, I ſay as the Lord *Jeſus* ſpake touching the gift of *Continency*, he that can receive it, let him receive it.

Peace. By what hath been ſaid, I ſee Maſter *Cottons* laſt anſwer will be more eaſily satisfied: when the *VVolfe* runneth ravenouſly (ſaith he) upon the *ſheep*, is it againſt the nature oſ the true *ſheep* to run to their *Shepheards?* and it is not againſt the nature of the true *Sheepherd* to ſend forth his Doggs to worrie ſuch a *VVolfe, &c?*

Truth. Maſter Cotton (doubtleſſe) here intends *miſticall ſheep*, and *Shepheards*, and *VVolves* and *Doggs*, and preſſeth the ſimilitude from the naturall ſheep in Civill reſpect, he cannot here mean (for that is not the *Queſtion*) whether *Wolviſh-men* oppreſſing the *Civill ſtate* are to be reſiſted and ſuppreſſed by *civill weapons, &c.*

Spirituall ſheep and wolves conſidered

Concerning *Spirituall ſheep* then: the firſt *queſtion* is: If the *wolfe* runs ravenouſly upon the *Sheep*, is it againſt the nature of the true *Sheep* to run to their *Shepheard?* I anſwer, a ſpiritual *Wolfe* (a falſe *Teacher, &c.*) may be ſaid to run ravenouſly upon a *ſpirituall ſheep*, by *ſpirituall aſſault* of Argument, Diſpute, Reproach, &c. The ſame man as a *civil wolfe* (for so we muſt ſpeake to ſpeake properly) may alſo run upon a *sheep* of *Chriſt* by *Civill Armes*, that is in a *Civill reſpect*, upon *Body* and *Goods*, &c,

If now the *Wolfe* ravin the firſt way, the *ſheep* of *Chriſt* may and ought to run, to the *Lord Jeſus* (the great Mr *Shepheard*) and to ſuch under and in inferiour *Shepheards* as he hath appointed (if he can attain to them.)

If the ſecond way, the *ſheep* (beſide running to *Chriſt Jeſus* by *prayer*, and to his *Ordinances* and *Officers* for advice and comfort) may run to the Civill *Magiſtrate* (appealing to *Cæſar*, &c.) againſt ſuch uncivill violence and oppreſſion.

Peace. Mine heart joyfully acknowledgeth the *Light* mine eye ſeeth, in that true and neceſſary *diſtinction*: Now to the Second *Queſtion*, is it againſt the nature of the true *Shepheard* (ſaith Mr *Cotton*) to ſend forth his *Doggs* to worrie ſuch a *wolfe*, &c.

256] *Truth.* Mr *Cotton* here diſcourſing of *Chriſts ſheepe*, and *Chriſts Shepheards*, *Reaſon* would perſwade, that the *Shepheards* or *Paſtours* here intended ſhould be the *Shepheards* or *Paſtours* appointed by *Chriſt Jeſus*, Epheſ. 4. [11.]

Peace. If ſo he ſhould attend, it well ſuits with the *ſpirit* of ſome *proud* and ſcornfull (pretended) *Shepheards* of *Chriſt Jeſus* in the World, who have uſed to call their *Clarkes*, *Sumners*, *Proctors*, and *Purſevants*, their *hunting Dogs*, &c.

Truth. But ſuch *Dogs*, (as yet) the *Independent Paſtours* or *Shepheards*, keepe not.

Peace. Yea but the *Pope* (to ſpeake in Mr *Cottons* phraſe, yet with all humble reſpect to *Civill Authori-*

The Pope and all

proud Popish Priests and Cleargie use the Civill Powers but as Dogs.

tie, the blessed *Ordinance* of *God* and *Man*) I say the *Pope* keeps such *Dogs* good store, yea *Dogs* of all sorts, not onely of those lesser kindes, but whom he useth as his *Dogs*, the *Emperours*, *Kings*, and *Magistrates* of the *World*, whom he teacheth and forceth to *crouch*, to lie *downe*, to *creepe*, and kisse his *foote*, and from thence at his beck to flie upon such greedie *Wolves*, as the *Waldenses*, *Wicklevists*, *Hussites*, *Hugonites*, *Lutherans*, *Calvinists*, *Protestants*, *Puritans*, *Sectaries*, &c. to *imprison*, to *whip*, to *banish*, to *hang*, to *head*, to *burne*, to *blow up* such vile *Hereticks*, *Apostates*, *Seducers*, *Blasphemers*, &c.

But I forget, it will be said, the *Protestants Grounds* and *practices* differ from the *Popes* as far as *Light* from *Darknes*, and how ever the *Pope* useth the *secular power* and *Magistrates* thereof, but as *Dogs* and *Hangmen*, yet the *Reformed Churches* teach and practice better.

The Protestant Cleargie their dealing with Magistrates.

Truth. 'Tis true (sweet *Peace*) the *Protestants* professe greater *honour* and *subjection* to the *Civill Magistrate:* But let *plaine English* be spoken and it will be found that the *Protestant cleargie* (as they will be calld) ride the *backs* and *necks* of *Civill Magistrates*, as *fully* and as *heavily* (though not so *pompously*) as ever the great *Whore* sat the *backs* of *Popish Princes*.

Peace. The *Protestant Cleargie* hath yeelded up the *temporall sword* into the hand of the *temporall State*, *Kings*, *Governours*, &c. They proclaime the *Magistrates*, *Head* of the *Church*, *Defenders* of their *Faith*, the *Supreame Judges* in all *causes* as well *Ecclesiasticall* as *Civill*.

Truth. 'Tis true, they make the *Magiſtrate* Head of the [257] *Church*, but yet of what *Church* they pleaſe to make and faſhion.

They make him *Defendour* of the *Faith*, but of what *Faith*, what *Doctrine*, what *Diſcipline*, what *Members*, they pleaſe to admit and account of: And this under the *penaltie* of being accounted either *hereticall* (and ſo *Magiſtrates* worthy themſelves to be put to *Death*) or *ignorant*, and ſo not fit to *act* (as Mr *Cotton* ſayth) but muſt ſuſpend their *power*, untill they ſubmit to the *Cleargies* pretended *Light*, and ſo be learnd to ſee and read with the *Cleargies Spectacles*.

A ſuſpending or hanging up of Magiſtrates.

Peace. To this purpoſe (indeed) agrees the next *paſſage*, wherein Mr. *Cotton* affirmeth, that although all the *Magiſtrates* in the *World* ought to puniſh *Blaſphemers*, *Idolaters*, *Seducers*, yet this muſt they not doe while their *Conſciences* are *blinde* and *ignorant* of the *Truth*, and yet they ceaſe not to be *Magiſtrates* (ſayth he) although they cannot performe all the duties of *Magiſtrates*.

Truth. Concerning this *ſtated Dutie* of all *Magiſtrates*, and yet *ſuſpending* of all *ignorant Magiſtrates* from *acting*, according to this their *Dutie* I have ſpoken to before and often, I now add, according to Mr *Cottons ſimilitude*, if the *Errours* of others be as *motes* in compariſon of the *beames* of this *ignorance* and *blindneſſe* in *Magiſtrates*, which he calleth *Beames*, it will be found that he renders thouſands of the *Magiſtrates* of the *World* as uncapable to be true *Magiſtrates*, as an heape of *Timber* to be an *Houſe*, which wants the *beames* and *principalls*.

Peace. The *ſumme* of the *Difference* in the laſt *paſſage* is not great, nor any in *words*, for ſayth Mr *Cottons Concluſion*, If the *Difference* be onely in the *way* and *manner* of the *Adminiſtration* of *Chriſt*, and the *Difference* be held forth in a *peaceable* and *Chriſtian* way, *God* forbid a *Staffe* ſhould be ſhaken againſt ſuch, or a *Sword* unſheathed.

The great ſpirituall differences of theſe late Times

Truth. Alas, where hath lien the great *Difference* between the *Prelates* and *Preſbyterians*, the *Preſbyterians* and *Independants*, but about the *way* and *Adminiſtration* of *Chriſts Kingdome* (for as for matter of *Doctrine*, according to the 39 *Articles* of the *Church* of *England*, they have little differd)? Yea wherein for matter of *Doctrine*, of *Faith*, *Repentance* and *Holineſſe*) have the *Churches* which make whole *ſeperation*, or ſuch [258] as goe further to a new *Baptiſme*, wherein have they differd from the former? and yet we know what *Lawes* have been and are extant in *Old* and *New England* againſt them, and what *practices* have been felt, and may juſtly be expected both from the *Mother* and the *Daughter*, if a jealous *God* and heavenly *Father* (for our *unthankfullneſſe*) ſhould once be pleaſed to finiſh this late and *wonderfull calme* and *moderation:* Which yet may juſtly be feard to prove, (as Sea-men uſe to obſerve) but a *Winters calme*, and they ſay, a *Winters calme* (for then *ſtormes* are breeding) is as bad as a *Summers ſtorme*.

Of reſt from perſecution.

Exam: of Chap. 72. *replying to* Chap. 75. Concerning the *Testimonie* of *Austin.*

Peace. MAster *Cotton* finds two *faults* in the first entrance. First, that *Antichrist* should be said to be too hard for *Christ* at *voting:* 2. That *Austins Testimonie* should be put off as a *Rhetoricall Evasion.*

Truth. To the first, it will shortly appeare as the *Light* at *Noone day*, what packing of *Votes*, and *listing*, and *mustring* up of *Numbers* have been in all *Ages*, in all *Councells*, in all *Synods*, in all *Parliaments*, and (falsely so called) *Christian Countries*, against the *Lord*, his *Christ* and *Servants.*

Peace. But Mr *Cotton* marvailes that when the *case* concernes *tolleration* of *Hereticks* and *Antichristians*, that *Antichrist* should procure more *Votes* against *Antichristians*, and that *Christ* should procure any *Vote*, though fewer, for them.

Truth. To expound this ridle; It was never affirmed, that *Christ* hath any *Votes* for the tollerating of *Hereticks* or *Antichristians* in the *Religious State* or *Church* of *Christ*, but in the *Civill State* or *Common-weale*, that is, in the common field of the world together.

Secondly, Not onely *Antichrist* may oppose some *Antichristians*, but the *Israel* of *God* may oppose *Israel: Ephraim* may be against *Manasseh*, and *Manasseh* against *Ephraim*, and both against *Judah* in severall respects. Have not the *Presbyterians* been against the *Independents*, and the *Independents* against the *Presbyterians*, and both against such as *seperate* from the *uncleannesses* of them both?

Gods children may possibly fight each against the other.

Antichriſtians againſt Antichriſtians, but principally againſt Chriſt.

259] No wonder then when one *Antichriſtian Faction* prevailes to cruſh another, (and therein wraps up *Chriſt Jeſus* himſelfe as an *Antichriſtian,*) that *Chriſt Jeſus* ſhould finde ſome *Friends* and *Votes* againſt the *Oppreſſing Faction*, though the *number* of the *oppreſſours* doe farre excede, and caſt the cauſe (moſt commonly) againſt *Chriſt Jeſus*, as a *Malefactor*, a *Drunkard*, a *Glutton*, a *Deceiver*, a *mad-man* poſſeſt with a *Devill*, a *Seducer*, a *Blaſphemer*, &c.

Peace. But to the ſecond, let us Examine the *Reaſons* againſt *Auſtins Argument* with Mr *Cottons* defence of them.

Couching ſpirituall murther.

The firſt anſwer was, that *ſoule-killing* was of a large *extent* in *Scripture*, which may reach to many *ſins* that are not *capitall*; Mr *Cotton* replyes; the Anſwer reaches not the *point*; for as every *killing* of the *Body* is not a *capitall crime*, ſo neither is every *killing* of the *ſoule*, but ſuch as is more *voluntary* and *preſumptuous*, and joined with ſome *groſſe* and *murtherous* intent.

Truth. Auſtin and Mr *Cotton* ſpake in generall, without diſtinction of *ſoule-murther* and *killing:* the *Title* and *ſound* of *ſoule-murther* and *ſoule-killing*, ſhould not be caſt abroad like *Thunder* and *Lightning*, with a late excuſe that we intend not every *ſoule-murther* and *killing*.

Peace. Your ſecond *Argument* was from the *Diſſimilitude* of *bodily* and *ſpirituall Death: Body-killing* is but once and for ever, but a *ſoule* killed may recover, &c. Mr *Cotton* replyes, that the very attempt of *ſoule-killing* is *capitall*, Deut. 13. 10.

Truth. Firſt, then the *Diſſimilitude* or *Difference*

remaines good, between the *murthering* of the *body*, and the *killing* of the *ſoule* or *inner man*; contrary to his Anſwer foregoing.

Touching Seducers.

Secondly, Concerning this *attempting* I have ſpoken elſewhere,[1] and proved that *ſpiritually* it may be made good, againſt a *Chriſtian Iſraelite*, falling away from *Chriſt*, and *ſeducing* others; but literally, againſt ſuch *attempting* againſt any mans preſent *Religion* or *Worſhip*, (in any *Civill State* all the *World* over) it cannot be taken, becauſe the *whole world*, the *Nations* and *peoples* of it cannot parallell this *State* of *Iſrael*, whence this plea is taken.

Peace. I preſume (Deare *Truth*) you would not *excuſe* and *extenuate* the *puniſhment* of a *Soule-Traitour* and *ſeducer*, now under the *Goſpel*.

The hainouſness of ſpirituall ſtumbling blocks.

260] *Truth*. No; I aggravate the leaſt attempt of *ſoule-murther*, and the leaſt *prejudice* or *hindrance* to *Eternall Life*, infinitly above what is *temporall* and *corporall murther*, when either *Huſband* or *Wiſe*, *Brother* or *Siſter*, *King* or *Queene*, *Synod* or *Parliament* ſhall lay a *ſtumbling block* in the *heavenly* way, or *grieve* or *offend* the leaſt of the littles ones of *Chriſt Jeſus*, and ſuch *dreadfull puniſhment* ſhall all even the *higheſt* and *greateſt* finde, who now ſeeme to forget the *Millſtone*.

Puniſhing of Seducers.

Peace. The third argument was from the different puniſhment which *Chriſt Jeſus* hath appointed for *Soul-killing*, to wit, by the two edged *ſword*, which comes out of *Chriſts* mouth, which is able to cut downe *Hereſie*, and to ſlay the ſoul of *Hereticks* everlaſtingly.

Maſter *Cotton* replies, *this anſwer hath been*

[1] p. 181, *supra*.

removed above: Church cenſures are ſufficient to heal the Heretick, if he belong to God, and to remove the guilt of his wickedneſſe from the Church, but not to prevent ſpreading, &c. nor to clenſe the Common-wealth from ſuch rebellion as hath been taught by him againſt the Lord.

Common-weale two-fold, and Rebellion two-fold.

Truth. Above hath alſo been ſhewen the ſoveraigne *excellency* and *power* of *Chriſts* ſpirituall meanes againſt ſpirituall infection: Above hath alſo been ſhewen the two-fold *Common-wealth*; Firſt, the *Civill* and *naturall*; Secondly, the *ſpirituall*, *religious* and *Chriſtian.*

Rebellion alſo againſt the Lord hath been proved, two-fold, Firſt, *ſpirituall*, againſt himſelfe in point of his more immediate *worſhip* and *ſervice*, for which he hath provided not onely the *vengeance* of *eternall fire* approaching (according to the degrees and hainouſneſſe of ſuch *rebellion*) but alſo preſent *ſpirituall puniſhment*, far exceeding all *corporall puniſhment* and *torment* in the *world.*

2 Rebellion againſt God is *temporall* and more *mediate*, as it is a *reſiſtance*, *oppoſition* or *violation* of any Civill ſtate or order appointed by *God* or *Men.* Now to confound theſe together, (and to hover in generall tearms of *Rebellion* againſt the *Lord*) is to blow out the *Candle* or *Light*, and to make a noiſe in the dark, with a ſound and cry of a *guilty Land*, a *guilty State*, *ſoul-murtherers*, *ſoul-killers*, *hereticks*, *blaſphemers*, *ſeducers*, *rebels* againſt the *Lord*, kill them, kill them, &c.

Suppoſe theſe *ſoul-murthering Hereticks*, *Seducers*, *&c.* be as [261] full of vexation and miſchief as the

Muſketoes or *Wolves* in *New England* or other Countries; It were to be wiſhed, (but never can be hoped in this world) that every *Civill ſtate, City* and *Towne* in the world, were free from ſuch *myſticall* and *ſoul-vermin*: The poor *Planter* and *Farmer* is glad, if his houſe and chamber, if his yard and field, his family and cattel, may be tolerably clear from ſuch annoyances, however the *Woods* and *Wildernes* abound with them: They that are of ſuch *fierie pragmaticall* reſtles *ſpirits*, that they content not themſelves to keep the *Farme* and *Houſe* of the *Church* of *Chriſt* free from ſuch *Infection* & *annoyance*, but rage that ſuch *vermin* are ſuffered in the worlds *Wood*, &c. It is pity but they had their ful *employment* and *taſke*, to catch and kill even all the *ſwarmes* and *Heards* of all the *Muſkeetoes* and *Wolves*, which either the Wildernes of *America*, or the *whole World* can afford them.

Myſticall Wolves and Muſkeetoes.

4. *Peace.* Accordingly the Fourth Argument was from *Chriſts* tolerating of *ſoule-killers* to live in the *field* of the *World*, though not in the *Garden* of the *Church:* Mr *Cotton* replyes, this hath been largely and fully refeld[1] above.

Truth. It is true, the Diſcuſſer alledged, and Mr *Cotton* refuted the *Expoſition* of this *Parable*, but whether of them according to the minde of *Chriſt Jeſus*, let every reader uprightly judge with feare and trembling at the word of the *Lord.*

Peace. The Fifth Argument was from the *Impoſſibilitie* of *killing* any *ſoule* by a *Heretick:* Mr *Cotton* anſwers, this is againſt *Paul* himſelfe, 1 *Cor.* 8. 11.

Of Soule-killing.

Truth. As I ſpake unto the *Argument* of the *Im-*

[1] Refelled—refuted.

poſſibilitie of the periſhing of any of *Gods Elect*, ſo here, the uſing of ſuch an *Argument* is far from *undervaluing* or *neglecting* of any of the *meanes* or *Ordinances*, *naturall* or *ſpirituall*, which *God* hath graciouſly appointed, but to condemne the *over-wiſe* and *over-buſie Heads* and *Hands* of Men, adding their *Inventions* to *Gods Appointments*, as if *weake* and *inſufficient:* whereas *Gods* number of *living* and *dead* are certaine, and through the meanes which he hath appointed for *life* ſhould faile, and notwithſtanding all other *meanes* in the *World* uſed by men as *helps* and *hindrances*, yet his holy End ſhall not be diſappointed, but fulfilled.

Beſide the Difference between *ſoule-killing* and *body-killing*, is but (as Mr *Cotton* here uſeth the word) *ſo much as in us lieth*, [262] that is by *attempt* or *endeavour*, which may be many wayes fruſtrated, and diſappointed by the holy hand of *God*, and the *ſoule* yet ſaved and live in the day of the *Lord Jeſus*.

Touching State Religions.

Peace. Whereas you ſaid, that the *impriſoning* of Men in a *Nationall* or *State Religion* is *guiltie* of their *Deſtruction*, together with the *monſtrous ſword* of *Civill Warres*, which cuts off Men from all meanes of *Repentance*.

Mr *Cotton* anſwers; If the *Religion* be good, it is no *Impriſonment:* If it be naught, then there ſhould be no *Impriſonment*.

To the ſecond (ſayth he) this *Feare* is *cauſeles*, for if Men belong to *God*, he will give *Repentance*, and how ever (ſayth he) *Gods* revealed *Will* is fullfilled in their juſt *Executions*.

Truth. I could here ask Mr *Cotton* where (amongſt

all the *Religions* and *Worſhips* of the *ſonnes* of men) he ever met in the *whole World*, with above *one Nation*, which *Nationally* profeſt a true *Religion*; and where ever, ſince *Chriſt Jeſus*, ending of the *ſhadowes*, any *State*, *Religion*, or *Nationall Worſhip* can be found true; notwithſtanding Mr *Cotton* knowes I grant *Gods people*, in *Kingdomes*, *Nations*, *Cities*, *Townes*, &c. to be *Gods Kingdome*, *Nation*, *Citie*, &c.

Gods children Gods Citie, Nation and Kingdome.

Peace. And ſince Mr *Cotton* ſpeakes thus of *Impriſonment*, me-thinkes that every *peaceable man* and *woman* may bring in here againſt him, at the *Tribunall* of *Chriſt Jeſus*, an *Action* of falſe *Impriſonment* (indeed falſe every way) not onely of the ſenſible and *outward* man, but of the moſt noble and *inner part*, the *minde*, the *spirit*, and *Conſcience*; for who knowes not that *Jeruſalem* it ſelfe may be a priſon to falſe-hearted *Shimei?* Who hath not found a *pallace* a *priſon*, when forc't to keepe within it? yea *confine* a man to his own *houſe* and *home*, though deare and ſamiliar, and moſt intimate to him, his owne *houſe* during that *force* and *reſtraint*, is a *priſon* to him.

A State Religion a priſon.

Truth. Yea it is moſt wofully found evident, that the beſt *Religion* (like the *faireſt Whores*, and the moſt *golden* and *coſtlie Images*) yea the moſt holy and pure and onely true *Religion* and *Worſhip*, appointed by *God* himſelfe, is a *Torment* to that *Soule* and *Conſcience*, that is forc't againſt its owne *free love* and *choice*, to embrace and obſerve it: And therefore whether the *Religion* be good or naught (as Mr *Cotton* here diſtinguiſheth) there ought to

A forc't Religion.

be no forcing, but the *ſoule* and *minde* and [263] *conſcience* of *man*, that is indeed the *man*, ought to be left free, as in his *Earthly marriage-choice*, ſo here ten thouſand times rather in his *heavenly* and *ſpirituall*.

Of the late Warres.

Peace. But what ſay you to his unmercifull *concluſion*, in the bloudſhed and *deſtruction* of ſo many *thouſands* and *millions*, formerly and lately *ſlaine* and *murthered* by this *bloudie Tenent* of *perſecution?* Yea the *late* and *lamentable ſtreames* of *Engliſh* bloud, and the bloud of our *neighbours*, *friends*, *Brethren*, *Parents*, powred forth by theſe late *Epiſcopall* or *Biſhops Warres?* Mr *Cottons* concluſion is, The revealed will of *God* (ſayth he) is fullfilled in their juſt *Execution*, whether they belong to *God* or no.

The bloudie Tenent guilty of the rivers of Bloud, &c.

Truth. I wiſh Mr *Cotton* more mercy from *God*, and a more mercifull minde towards the afflicted, and I ſay as the *Lord Jeſus* ſaid in the caſe of *offence:* Great *offences*, *Nationall offences* will come for *Religions ſake*, for *Nationall Religion* ſake, but woe unto thoſe that beare the guilt of ſo many thouſand *ſlaughters*, *murders*, *raviſhings*, *plunderings*, &c. The *Pope*, the *Biſhops*, the *Preſbyterians*, the *Independants*, ſo farre as they have been *Authours* or *Actors* in theſe *horrible Calamities*, out of the *perſwaſion* of the *bloudie Tenent* of *perſecution* for *Religion* and *Conſcience*; the voyce of ſo many *Rivers* of *bloud* cry to *Heaven* for vengeance againſt them.

Warres for Religion.

Peace. But may not (bleſſed *Truth*) the *ſword* of *Civill power* which is from *God* (*Rom*. 13. [4.]) be drawne and drunke with *bloud* for *Chriſt* his ſake.

What ſay you (among the many *examples* of *Religious Warres*) to the moſt famous *Battles* of *Conſtantine* againſt the bloudie perſecutor *Maxentius?* Was not *Conſtantine Chriſts Champion*, as once that valiant *Scanderbeg* cald himſelfe againſt the bloudie *Turks?*[1]

Truth. Sweet *Peace*, the *sword* of *Civill power* was *Gods sword* committed by *Gods* moſt wiſe *Providence* into the hands of that famous *Conſtantine:* Doubtles his warre was righteous and pious, ſo farre as he broke the *Jawes* of the *oppreſſing perſecuting Lyons* that devoured *Chriſts* tender *Lambes* and *ſheepe:* And famous was his Chriſtian *Edict*, (wherein *Licinius* joyned with him) when he put forth that imperiall *Chriſtian* Decree, that no mans *Conſcience* ſhould be forced, and for his *Religion* (whether to the *Romane Gods*, or the *Chriſtian*) no man ſhould be perſecuted or hunted:[2]

Conſtantines warres for the Chriſtians.

Conſtantines Edict againſt forcing in Religion.

[1] Maxentius was defeated by Conſtantine, Oct. 28, 312, at the Milvian Bridge, near Rome. Gibbon, *Decline and Fall*, chap. xiv. p. 168. Euſebius in his Life of Conſtantine preſerves the tradition of his becoming a Chriſtian through this victory, and the viſion of the cross which preceded. Neander ſifts the ſtory critically. He ſays, "It was not until after his victory over the tyrant Maxentius, that Conſtantine publicly declared in favor of the Chriſtians." *Church Hiſtory*, ii. 7–12.

George Caſtriot, Prince of Albania, born in 1404, was given as a hoſtage by his father to Sultan Amurath II. when nine years old. On account of his valor the Turks gave him the name Iſcander Beg, or Prince Alexander. In 1443 by ſtratagem he regained the throne of his father and renounced the Mahometan faith. For twenty-three years, with unequal arms, but with unſurpaſſed valor, he reſiſted the powers of the Ottoman Empire. Marvellous tales are told of his ſuperhuman ſize and ſtrength, and of three thouſand Turks ſlain by his ſingle hand. As Gibbon ſays, they "muſt be weighed in the ſcales of ſuſpicious criticiſm." *Decline and Fall*, chap. lxvii, p. 1221. Fox, of whoſe work Williams ſeems to have made conſiderable uſe, gives many of theſe ſtories. *Acts and Monuments*, i. 840.

[2] See pp. 6, 7, *ſupra*.

When *Constantine* broke the bounds [264] of this his owne and *Gods Edict*, and drawes the *sword* of *Civill power* in the suppressing of other *Consciences* for the establishing of the *Christian*, then began the great *Mysterie* of the *Churches* sleepe, the *Gardens* of *Christs Churches* turned into the *Wildernesse* of *Nationall Religion*, and the *World* (under *Constantines* Dominion) to the most *unchristian Christendome*.

Never any true Nationall Religion in the World but one.

Peace. I am unquestionably satisfied, that there was never any *Nationall Religion* good in this *world* but one, and since the *Desolation* of that *Nation*, there was never, there shall be never any *Nationall Religion* good againe: and this will be most evident to such as hould the *Truth* of the *continuance* of *Christs visible Church* in the way of *particular Congregations*.

Touching *Pauls* blasphemy before his Conversion.

6. But now to the Sixt *Argument*, which Mr *Cotton* thus repeats from the *possibilitie* of a false *Teacher*, & a *spirituall Wolves* recoverie from the *estate* of a *soule-killer* to become a *soule-Saviour*, as it was in the case of *Paul:* And thus he answers; If men be such *Blasphemers* and such *Wolves*, as *Paul* was before his *Conversion*, neither the *Law* of *God* nor *man* would put such a Man to death, who sinned of *Ignorance*, and walked (as himselfe professed) in all good *Conscience*, even in his former evill times, *Acts*, 23. [1.] But as for such as *apostate* from the knowne truth of *Religion*, and seeke to *subvert* the *foundation* of it, and to draw away others from it, to plead for their *Tolleration* in hope of their *Conversion*, is as much as to proclaime a *generall pardon* to all *malefactours* (save onely such as sin against

the *Holy Spirit*) *for he that is a willfull murtherer and adulterer now, may come to be converted, and die a martyr hereafter.*

Truth. I ſee not why Mr. *Cotton* ſhould paſſe a more charitable cenſure on *Pauls Conſcience*, then on other Mens profeſſing *Conſcience* alſo and the feare of God: nor an harder *cenſure* upon other Men (to wit, that they are *convinced*, and ſinne againſt their owne *Conſcience*) more then upon *Paul* himſelfe: Heard he not that famous powerfull *Sermon* of *Stephen?* Saw he not his glorious and moſt heavenly *Death?* and having ſo much to doe with the *Saints*, could he otherwiſe chooſe, but heare and ſee many heavenly *paſſages* tending to his ſoules *conviction?*

Peace. Yea why ſhould Mr *Cotton* pinch upon *Apoſtates* from the truth of *Religion* and *Seducers?* he cannot chooſe but know [265] how many thouſands and *millions* of men and women in the world, are *Hereticall*, *Blaſphemers*, *Seducers*, that never yet made profeſſion of that which he accounteth *True Religion?*

Of Apoſtates.

True. Yea and (to plead thy caſe Deare *Peace*) why ſhould Mr *Cotton* couple *Murtherers* and *Adulterers* with *Apoſtates* and *Seducers?* Doth not even the naturall *Conſcience* and *Reaſon* of all men put a *Difference?* Doe not even the moſt bloudie *Popes* and *Cardinalls*, *Gardiners* and *Bonners*, put a difference between the *crimes* of *Murther*, *Treaſon*, *Adulterie* (for which although the offendour repent, &c. yet he ſuffers *puniſhment*) and the *crimes* of *Hereſie*, *Blaſphemie*, &c. which upon *Recantation* and *Confeſſion*, are frequently remitted?

Fallacious mixture and confuſion.

Peace. I remember it was high *Treaſon* in *H.* 8. his dayes to deny the *Kings ſpirituall Supremacie,* as well as to *kill* his *perſon,* and yet upon *Confeſſion* and *Recantation* we finde, that the very *Conſcience* of thoſe bloudy men could diſtinguiſh between theſe *Treaſons.*

Spirituall Treaſon recanted, forgiven: but not ſo (by way of courſe) the Civill.

An Inſtance *Jo: Haywood* and the Lord *Cromwell* in King *Henry* the S. his dayes.

Truth. 'Tis true this *bloudie Tenent* of *perſecution* was lamentably *drunke* with *bloud* in the dayes of that *Henry,* as well as afterwards in the dayes of his *bloudie daughter Marie,* and yet in *Henry* his dayes we finde *John Haywood* recanting his (so cald) *Treaſon* againſt the *Kings Supreamacie* in *ſpirituall* things, and is cleared. When famous and faithfull *Cromwell,* for words pretended to be ſpoken by him againſt the *Kings perſon,* muſt pay his *noble Head.*[1] But to End this Chapter, moſt true it is, that *multitudes* of people in all parts of *bloudie Chriſtendome,* and not a few in *England* in *Henry* the 7. and *Henry* the 8. his dayes, have eſcaped with a *Recantation* and *Abjuration,* for *ſpirituall Treaſons,* when *principles* of *Reaſon* and *Civill Government* have taught men, for their common ſafetie, to thinke of other *puniſhments* for M*urtherers, Adulterers, Traytours.*

[1] John Heywood was one of the earlieſt Engliſh dramatiſts, and a noted jeſter. He was a friend of Sir Thomas More, and through him came into favor with Henry VIII. He was alſo a favourite of Queen Mary. After her deceaſe he was alarmed for his ſafety, as he had been a zealous papiſt. Under Edward VI. he had been in danger of his life. Wood ſays "he left the nation for religion ſake, and settled at Mechlin," where he died in 1565. *Athenæ Oxonienſes,* i. 349. Warton, *Hiſt. of Eng. Poetry* iii. 84–94.

Thomas Cromwell was arreſted in June, 1540, for high treason, and was at once condemned by an act of attainder. For the cauſes of Cromwell's fall and the charges againſt him, ſee Froude, *Hiſt. of Eng.* iii: 488–500.

Exam: of Chap. 73. *replying to* Chap. 76.

Diſcuſſing *the Teſtimonie* of *Optatus.*

Peace. MAfter *Cotton* having alledged *Optatus*, juſtifying *Macarius* his putting *Hereticks* to Death, from the Example of *Moſes*, *Phinehas*, and *Elijah*; it was anſwered, that [266] theſe ſhafts were drawen not out of *Chriſts*, but *Moſes* Quiver: Mr *Cotton* replyes; did ever any *Apoſtle* or *Evangeliſt* make the *Judiciall Lawes* of *Moſes* concerning *Life* and *Death ceremoniall* and *typicall?*

Truth. What ever the Apoſtles of Chriſt did in this matter, yet ſure it is Evident, that Mr *Cotton* himſelfe makes ſome of *Moſes Lawes*, which he calls *Judiciall*, to be but *ceremoniall* and *typicall.* Of *Moſes* Judicialls.

Peace. Me thinks Mr *Cotton* ſhould never grant that, who layes ſo much waight upon *Moſes practices*, and the *morall* and *the perpetuall ground* of them.

Truth. Well take for an Inſtance this very caſe of putting to Death, *Idolaters* and falſe *Prophets*, he grants this in this very "Chapter to be *typicall* in "the State of the *Jewes*; for *Iſraell* (ſayth he) "being the *Church* of *God*, and in Covenant with "*God*, their *Example* will onely extend to the like "*Execution* of all the falſe *Prophets* in the *Church* "of *God.*

Peace. Such a *Candle* lighted up in the *Conſcience* and *Judgement* and *Confeſſion* of Mr *Cotton*, may (if the *Father* of *Lights* ſo pleaſe,) light up many *Candles* more, to Mr *Cottons* owne and the eyes of others.

Truth. Yea if the *Father* of *Lights* ſo pleaſe,

Mr *Cotton* will looke back and ſee, that if the *Example* of *Iſrael* extend no further than to the *Church* of *God*, then thoſe *Lawes* of *Moſes* concerning *Religion*, cannot but be *typicall* and *ceremoniall*; for, what is *morall* and *perpetuall*, none can deny to concerne all Men in all *Nations*, where no *Church* or Houſe of *God* was ever erected.

2. *Peace.* If Mr *Cotton* ſay it extends but to the *Church* of *God*, what *Church* of *God* can Mr *Cotton* meane, but a *particular Congregation* (for he profeſſeth againſt *Nationall*, *Provinciall*, &c.) And yet how can he meane a *particular Church*, ſince he grants the *Church* of *Chriſt* armed with no other *weapons* than *ſpirituall*, like unto the *Head* and *King* thereof *Chriſt Jeſus*?

The firſt three hundred years after Chriſt.

3. *Truth.* If Mr *Cotton* will grant the *Church* of *Chriſt* to have been extant upon the Earth during the firſt *three hundred yeares* of her *fiery tryalls*, he muſt grant that then the *Church* of *Chriſt* was furniſhed by *Chriſt Jesus* with no other *weapons* but *ſpirituall*, for all the *Civill powers* of the World ſeemed to be againſt them. [267] All which time by Mr *Cottons Doctrine*, the *Church* of *Chriſt* his heavenly *Garden* muſt needs be over-growne with *Hereticks*, *Idolaters*, ſalſe *Prophets*, for want of a *Civill Sword*, &c. Or if they were not (as ſure it is, the *Spouſe* and *Garden* of *Chriſt* was never fairer ſince): As Mr *Cotton* grants the *Example typicall*, and extending onely to the *Church* of *God*, ſo muſt he then alſo grant theſe falſe *Prophets* and *Idolaters* to be put to Death by the *Churches power*, which is onely *ſpirituall*, and *Iſraels materiall Sword* will

The Primitive Church the pureſt, and yet without a Civill Sword.

then appeare to be a *type* of the two-edged *ſword* of *Chriſt Jeſus* in the *Goſpel.*

Peace. It is true (ſayth Maſter *Cotton*) what the Diſcuſſer ſayth, that *Chriſt Jeſus* gave no *Ordinance*, *Precept* or *Preſident* in the *Goſpel* for killing men for *Religion*, and no more (ſayth he) for the *breach* of *Civill Juſtice: Civill Magiſtrates* therefore muſt either walke without *Rule*, or fetch their *Rules* of *Righteouſneſſe* from *Moſes* and the *Prophets*, who hath expounded him in the *Old Teſtament.*

Chriſt no Author of Civill violence for Religion.

Truth. If Mr *Cotton* pleaſe more awfully to obſerve & weigh the minde of *Chriſt Jeſus* his *New Teſtament* in this point, he will not onely heare himſelfe ſubſcribing to *Cæſars Right* in *Civill matters*, but alſo by his ſervant *Peter* eſtabliſhing all other formes of *Civill Government*, which the *peoples* or *Nations* of the *World* ſhall invent or *create* for their *civill being*, *Common-weale* or *wellfare*. Yea he may remember that *Chriſt Jeſus* by his Servant *Paul* commandeth the *Magiſtrate*, to puniſh *Murther*, *Theft*, *Adulterie*, &c. for he expreſly nameth theſe *Civill Tranſgreſſions* together with the *civill Sword* the *Avenger* of them, *Rom.* 13. [4.]

Peace. I cannot well conceive what M[r] *Cotton* meanes by ſaying, that *Moſes* and the *Prophets* expounded *Chriſt Jeſus* in the *Old Testament.*

Truth. Nor I: They did ſpeake or *prophecie* of *Chriſt*, they did *type* or *figure* him to come, with his *ſufferings* and *Glory*, but (as *John* ſayth) *Grace* and *Truth* came by *Jeſus Chriſt*, that is, the fullfilling, opening, and *expounding* came by *Jeſus Chriſt.*

Peace. Hence indeed I remember that *Chriſt*

Jeſus (Luc. 24. [27.]) expounded to his *Diſciples*, out of *Moſes* and the *Prophets*, the things written of him. But more particularly touching *Moſes:* [268] *Macarius* did well (ſayth M[r] *Cotton*) in putting *Hereticks* to Death, from the *Example* of *Moſes* putting *Idolaters* to Death, *Exod* 32. [26–28.] and the *Idolater* to Death, *Levit*. 24. [23.]

The Levites killing 3000. *Exoa* 32. typicall.

Truth. Theſe *Inſtances* (by M[r] *Cottons* Confeſſion) extend no further then the *Church* of *God*, and then I deſire my aboveſaid *Anſwer* may be uprightly weighed. And I adde the former *Inſtance* of putting Death the three thouſand *Iſraelites* about the *Goulden Calfe* by the hand of the *Levites*, may moſt lively ſeeme to *typifie*, the zealous *Execution* of *ſpirituall Juſtice* in (the *Iſrael* of *God*) the *Church* of *Chriſt*, by the true *Miniſters of Chriſt Jeſus*, the true *Antitype* of that zealous *Tribe* of *Levi.*

Phineas his Act.

Peace. Concerning *Phineas*, whereas it was ſaid that the ſlaying of the *Iſraelitiſh Prince* and Daughter of *Midian*, was not for *ſpirituall* but for *corporall filthineſſe*, Maſter *Cotton* anſwereth and urgeth the *Iſraelites* eating of their *Sacrifices*, and joyning to *Baal-peor:* Alſo that *ſingle Fornication* was no *capitall crime.*

Truth. It is moſt true, the people committed both *ſpirituall* and *corporall Filthines* (as very often they goe together) but the *Juſtice* of *God* reckoned with theſe two ſinners, for and in the midſt of their *corporall Filthines*, which although it were not *capitall* in *Iſraell*, yet the committing of it with ſo high an hand of *preſumption* (and *ſmall ſinnes* committed *preſumptuouſly* in *Iſrael* were Death) was enough to make it worthy of ſo ſharpe and ſudden a *Deſtruction*.

Peace. Concerning *Phineas* his act Mr *Cotton* acknowledgeth that it is no *preſident* for M*iniſters* of the *Goſpel* ſo to act, but withall ſayth it is *præſidentiall* for *Magiſtrates*.

Truth. Phineas his Act (whether of ordinarie or extraordinary *Juſtice*) how can it be *præſidentiall* to the *Civill Magiſtrate* in a *particular Church*, where the *weapons* are onely *ſpirituall?* And Mr *Cotton* grants theſe *Examples* extend no further than the *Church:* Such as maintaine a *Nationall Church* (which Mr *Cotton* doth not) hath ſome colour to urge this *Example* for a *preſident:* for in a *Civill State, Civill Officers, civill Lawes, civill Weapons, civill puniſhments* and *rewards* are proper, as are alſo (and onely) *Spirituall Officers, ſpirituall Lawes, ſpirituall puniſhments* and *Rewards* in a *ſpirituall State*.

The ſpirituall & CivillState vaſtly different in their frame, Lawes, Officers, &c.

269] *Peace.* Concerning *Eliah*, M[r] *Cotton* excepteth againſt the number eight hundred and fiftie, as too many by halfe.

Truth. It is true, the number of *Baals Prophets* were foure hundred and fiftie (*falſe Prophets* enough to *one* poore *true*) but yet *Eliah* numbers *Jezabells* foure hundred trencher *Chaplins* with them; for, ſayth he, Now therefore ſend and gather unto me all *Iſrael* unto Mount *Carmel*, and the *Prophets* of *Baal* foure hundred and fiftie, and the *Prophets* of the *Grove* foure hundred, which eate at *Jezabells* Table.

Elijah and the *Baalites.*

Peace. But how ever (ſayth Mr *Cotton*) here was no *type* nor *Figure* for *Actions* of *morall Juſtice*, (though ſometimes *extraordinary*) yet they are never *figurative*, but with ſuch as turne all the *Scripture* into an *Allegorie*.

The types and figures of the old Teſtament.

Truth. To make the *ſhadowes* of the *old Teſtament* and the *Subſtance* or *Body* of the *New*, all one, is but to confound and mingle *Heaven* and *Earth* together, for the *ſtate* of the *Law* was *ceremoniall* and *figurative*, having a *worldly Tabernacle* with *vaniſhing* and *beggarly Rudiments:* And I believe it might not onely be ſaid, that *Abrahams* lying with his handmaid *Hagar*, was an *Allegorie*, but that the whole *Church* of *Iſraell*, *Roote* and *Branch*, from firſt to laſt included *figurative* and *Allegoricall Kernells*, were the *Huſks* and *Shells* diſcloſed with more humbly diligent and *ſpirituall teeth* and *fingers*.

Peace. I cannot but aſſent unto you, that to render the *Old Teſtament Allgoricall* in an humble ſobrietie, your *Inſtance* with many more give ſufficient warrant.

Truth. Yet I adde (in anſwer to Mr *Cottons* charge of turning all *Scripture* into an *Allegorie*) that to deny the *Hiſtorie* of either *Old* or *New Teſtament*, or to render the *New Teſtament* (which expounds and fulfills the ancient *figures*) *Allegoricalls* are both *abſurd and impious*.

Peace. But how (ſayth Mr *Cotton*) can an *Act* of *morall righteouſneſſe* be *figurative?*

Righteouſnes two fold.

Truth. There is a *Fallacie* in this tearme [*morall Righteouſneſſe*] for Mr *Cotton* himſelfe hath ackowledged a *Righteouſneſſe* two-fold; A *Spirituall Right-*

eousnesse of the *Church*, and a *civill* of the *Commonweale:* Mr *Cotton* also acknowledgeth *Israel* to be a *Typicall* people, their land a *typicall Land*, their *Ministry* and *Worship typicall!* How can Mr *Cotton* then deny, but [270] that the *weapons* of this people, their *punishments* and *rewards*, &c. (so far as concerned this their mixed *figurative* and *typicall state*) were *figurative* and *ceremoniall* also? And so not parts of *morall civill Righteousnesse*, or common to all other Nations and peoples in the World.

The state of *Israel* typicall.

Peace. I cannot readily assent to Mr *Cotton* that *morall Actions* of *Civill Righteousnesse* could not be *figurative* with this *ceremoniall*, *typicall*, *aud figurative* people; for their *warre* it selfe (which if lawfull, is an *Act* of *civill morall Righteousnesse*) *Paul* seemes to make *figurative* of the *spirituall Warres* of the *Christian Israel* and *Church* of *God.*

Truth. Yea and it is easie to observe that not onely their *spirituall Worship*, &c. not onely *Acts* of *morall* and *civill Righteousnesse* in *peace* and *warre*, &c. but even their very *naturall Actions* and *Excrements* (in *warres* against their *Enemies*) were *figurative* and *typicall*, full of *heavenly* and *spirituall Instruction*, which the *unbelieving Jewes* then saw not, but the *believing* saw, as they saw *Christ Jesus* in the *Sacrifices*, and all their *observations* leading to the blessed *Son* of *God*, the *Messiah*, the *Annointed*, or *Christ* to come, and his *Eternall Kingdome.*

Not only morall but naturall Actions of the *Israelites* typicall.

Peace. Mr *Cotton* in the next place takes offence that the *Fact* of *Elijah* should be called *miraculous*, and askes if it be a *miracle* for *Elijah* with the aide of so many thousand *Israelites* to put to Death *foure hundred and fiftie men.?*

Whether *Elijahs* procuring the slaugh-ter of the *Baalites* was Typi-icall or Morall.

Truth. Mr *Cotton* miſtakes the word, for the word is not *fact* but *paſſage*, which compriſeth not onely the *ſlaughter* of theſe their *Prieſts*, but the whole *matter* and *buſines*, as the putting of the *Worship* of the true *God*, to the *Tryall* of *Fire* from *Heaven*, the deſcending of *Fire* from *Heaven*, the *devouring* of the *Sacrifice*, and *licking* up of ſo much *water*, and upon this ſo great a *number* of their *Prieſts* (the *Fathers*, *Shepheards*, and *Gods* of the people) ſo thunder-ſmitten as from *Heaven*, with ſo ſudden and dreadfull a *ſlaughter*, what can theſe be but an *extraordinary inſpiration* in the *Prophet*, a *ſupernaturall deſcent* and *operation* of *Fire*, yea and an *extraordinary* and wonderfull *change* in the heart of the *People?* And I doubt not but Mr *Cotton* doth ſometimes give an *heavenly* and *ſpirituall ſignification*, to all theſe *figurative* and *miraculous Myſteries*.

Peace. But I wonder at the next words; Though *Chriſt* [271] (ſayth he) gave no ſuch *Commiſſions* to *Miniſters* of the *Goſpel* to put *falſe Prophets* to Death, as *Elijah* did, yet the *Act* of *Dutie* was an *ordinary* dutie of *morall Righteouſneſſe*, belonging to ſuch as bear the *Sword*. Anon againe he writes; This *Example* will not extend to the *Idolaters* of the *World*.

" Firſt, Becauſe many thouſand thouſand of them " are exempt from the *civill Magiſtracie* of *Chriſ-* " *tians*.

" Secondly, They were never in *Covenant* with *God*, " to whom onely the *Law* of *Moſes* concerning the " *puniſhment* of *Idolaters* extended.

" Thirdly, Though the *Israelites* were *Idolaters*, yet " *Elijah* ſpared them, because of their *ſimplicitie* and " *Ignorance.*

Truth. I anſwer, firſt, if *Chriſt Jeſus* gave no ſuch *Commiſſion* (as is confeſſed) then woe to all thoſe *Popiſh* and *Proteſtant Prieſts*, who have (by *theft*, or *flatterie*, or other evill *meanes*) got *Commiſſions* from the *Civill powers* of the *World*, whereby (to maintaine their own *honours*, and *profits* of *Biſhopricks* and *Benefices*, &c.) they ſmite with the *fiſt* and *ſword*, of *wickednes*: or under a *pretence* of *holy Orders* in themſelves, put over the *drudgery* of *Execution* to their enſlaved *Seculars!*

No Commiſſion from *Chriſt* for corporall puniſhment in religious matters.

Secondly, If theſe need no *Commiſſion*, becauſe to put to Death the *falſe Prophets* and *Idolaters*, is an *Act* of *morall Righteouſneſſe*, how agrees that *Poſition* and theſe three together,

Firſt, onely *Chriſtian Magiſtrates* (ſaid Mr *Cotton*) muſt act in theſe caſes.

Secondly, They muſt act againſt ſuch onely as are *Church-members.*

Thirdly, They muſt not act againſt ſuch *Church-members* as commit *Idolatrie* out of *ſimplicitie* or *Ignorance.*

Peace. Deare *Truth*, if it paſſe your *capacitie* to reconcile theſe in point of *Truth*, it muſt needs paſſe mine to ſee how such *Doctrines* can ſtand with any *civill peace* or *order* in the world.

Truth. To affirme ſuch *Actions* to be ordinarie duties of *morall Righteouſneſſe*, belonging to ſuch as beare the *Sword*, and yet not to be practiced but by ſuch *Magiſtrates* as are moſt rarely found in the

Strange and monſtrous duties of Morall Righteouſneſſe.

World, and on ſuch a *people* in ſuch an *Order* as is moſt rare in the *Nations* of the *World*, is to me all one, as to call all *Fathers* and *Maſters* in the *World* to ſuch *ordinarie Duties* as belong to every *Father* and *Maſter* of a *Familie:* Or to call [272] *Maſters* and *Commanders* of *Ships* to ſuch ordinarie duties as belong to all *Maſters* of *Ships* in the *World:* Or *Captaines* and *Commanders* in *Warre* to ſuch *ordinarie Duties* as belong to all *Captaines* and *Commanders* in *World*, and then at laſt to tell them: It is true, the *Duties* are *ordinary* and *common*, to all *Fathers*, *Maſters*, *Commanders*, *Captaines*, but thoſe *Duties* are to be performed onely by ſuch *Fathers*, *Maſters*, *Captaines* and *Commanders*, and in ſuch *Families*, *Ships*, and *Armies* as are not ordinarie to be found in the *World*.

Gods children are wonders and monſters accounted.

Peace. I ſee not but the *Similitude* doth fully reach, for indeed although ſuch a people ſo and ſo in *Covenant* with *God*, according to Mr *Cotton*, were true *viſible Churches* according to *Chriſts Inſtitution*, and ſo conſequently their *Magiſtrates* truely *Chriſtian*, yet compare ſuch *Magiſtrates* with the reſt of the *Magiſtrates* of the *World*, who as lawfully beare the *Sword* as Themſelves, and compare ſuch a people ſo and ſo in *Church-Covenant*, with the reſt of the people and *Nations* of the *World*, and we ſhall not finde them ordinary and *common*, but rather as ſix fingers, *wonders* and *monſters* to all other parts of the *World*, yea even to the very *Popiſh* and *Proteſtant* parts of the *World* alſo.

But to end this Chapter; The other fact of *Elijah* in ſlaying the *Captaines* with their fifties, Mr

Cotton acknowledgeth not to be alledged by any other *Authour* in this *Controverſie*, but onely by the Diſcuſſer, to make himſelfe work in ſuch *Cobweb-Evaſions.*

Truth. Mr *Cotton* forgetteth for *Elijah* his *Act* (from *Luc.* 9. [54.]) hath been mentioned by others, and anſwered too by Maſter *Cotton* in this preſent Booke and *Controverſie.* And for the *Cob-webs,* let the poore *Witneſſes* of *Chriſt* be eſteemed as *Spiders*, and their *Teſtimonie* and *Witnes* but as *Cob-webs,* yet let them not be diſcouraged, but lay hould (like *Solomons Spider*) with the hand of *ſpirituall Diligence,* and let all ſuch their *heavenly Cob-webs* be in *Kings Pallaces.* And let them know their *Cob-webs* be of ſuch a *ſtrength,* that how ever the *cruell Beezome* of *perſecution* may ſweep them downe, out of this *World,* yet in point of *Truth* and true *Chriſtian power* and *worth,* neither *Pope* nor *Prelate,* neither *Preſbyterian,* nor *Independent perſecutour,* nor *Baalzebub* himſelfe (the *God* of *Flies*) ſhall ever be able to ſweepe them downe, or breake through them.

Elijah his ſlaying the Captaines and their fifties.

Wonderfull Spiders and Cobwebs. *Prov.* 30.

273] *Exam: of* Chap. 74. *and* 75. *replying to* Chap. 77. *and* 78.

Peace. IN Chap. 74. One paſſage cannot be paſt by, to wit, [God hath laid this charge upon *Magiſtrates* in the *Old Teſtament* to puniſh *Seducers,* and the *Lord Jeſus,* never tooke off this *Charge* in the *New Teſtament*: *Who is this Diſcuſſer, that he*

Touching Seducers, and their puniſhments.

ſhould account Paul himſelf, or an Angel from Heaven accurſed, that ſhould leave this Charge upon Magiſtrates, which God laid on and Chriſt never tooke off?]

Truth. This is but a *Repetition* of what hath formerly been examined: unto which therefore I briefly ſay, It will never be found true, that *God* hath laid this charge upon all *Magiſtrates* in the *World*, as he did upon the *Magiſtrates* in *Iſrael*, to puniſh *Seducers.*

Chriſt Jeſus aboliſhed former figures, though he name not each of them in particular.

Secondly, *God* laying this charge upon the *Governours* and *Magiſtrates* in *Iſrael*, the *Church* of *God* (in the *type*) lays it ſtill upon *Chriſt Jeſus* and his *Governours ſpirituall* under him in his *ſpirituall Iſrael*, which *Kingdome* he adminiſtreth, with *Lawes, Puniſhments* and *Weapons Spirituall.* All this Mr *Cotton* in his Controverſie hath acknowledged.

Thirdly, When he ſaith, *Chriſt Jeſus* never tooke off this Charge.

Firſt, I anſwer, let that *Parable* which he mentioneth be the *Tryall* of it in the feare of *God.*

Secondly, *God* having now in theſe laſt times declared his will by his *Sonne:* Where hath his *bleſſed Sonne* ſpoken to us, to build no more *Temples*, to erect no more *Altars*, to offer no more *Sacrifices?* And yet theſe and the whole *frame* of that *typicall State* we juſtly *abrogate*, both from the words of *Chriſt* and his firſt *Meſſengers*, which are plaine and eaſie enough to ſuch whoſe eyes it pleaſeth *God* to open, although (in expreſſe Tearmes) *Chriſt Jeſus* hath not given an expreſſe *Catalogue* of all ſuch *particulars* to be aboliſhed.

Peace. In the next paſſage Mr *Cotton* deeply chargeth the poore Diſcuſſer with *partialitie* & *falſhood*; upon which *Grounds* he turnes off all the *Conſequences*, which the Diſcuſſer obſerved to follow upon Mr *Cottons Concluſions.*

Truth. It is true, the *Authour* of the *Letter* expreſſeth *Libertie* [274] of *Conſcience* to ſuch as feare *God* indeed: Mr *Cotton* ſubſcribes, but preſently razeth out his *Subſcription* in theſe words following, which he hath againe now reprinted, to wit, "But "the Queſtion is whether an *Heretick*, after once or "twice *Admonition* (and ſo after *Conviction*) and any "other *ſcandalous* and hainous *offendour*, may be "tollerated, either in the *Church* without *Excom-* "*munication*, or in the *Common-weale* without ſuch "*puniſhment*, as may preſerve others from dangerous "and damnable *Infection*.

Peace. Who ſees not but this *bloudie Tenent* (I meane theſe words now recited) doth not onely reſtraine *Libertie* of *Conſcience* to ſuch as feare *God* indeed, and ſpeakes *fire* and *fagot* to all the *world* beſide: But alſo (under the name of *Heretick* and *Seducer*) throwes into the *Furnace* (moſt commonly and ordinarily) all ſuch as feare *God* (*Chriſt Jeſus* and his *Meſſengers* and *Miniſters* not excepted) who have alwayes been and are accounted, the chiefeſt *Hereticks*, *Blaſphemers*, *Deceivers* and *Seducers* in this World? The Myſterie of Bloudy Tenent.

Truth. I adde the *Conſequences* therefore remaine good, that either All the *Inhabitants* of the World muſt come into the *eſtate* of men *fearing God:* Or elſe *diſſemble Religion*, and fearing *God*, in *hypocriſie*: The bloudie conſequences of the bloudy Tenent.

Or elſe, be driven out of the World. Then alſo the *Civill State* muſt judge of the *Spirituall*, and of *Magiſtrates* fearing or not fearing God: The *People* muſt judge (I ſay) who feare *God indeed*, and are by them to be *permitted*, and who are the *Hereticks*, and to be *puniſhed*, which who may not ſee to be the driving of the *world* out of it ſelfe, and the bloudie routing up of all Societies of Men?

Peace. This charge of *partialitie* and *falſhood*, you have (Deare *Truth*) to my underſtanding ſhielded the poore Diſcuſſer from, Can you now helpe his *Forehead*, and his *Heart*, which Mr *Cotton* in the next paſſage chargeth with another *notorious* and *impudent falſhood*, in relating out of a printed booke an *Anſwer* of the *New Engliſh Miniſters* to *Queſtions* ſent unto them from their *Brethren* in *old*, which anſwer Mr *Cotton* ſaith he cannot finde.

The ſad Effects of the bloudie Tenent on Mr *Cottons* owne Spirit.

Truth. So much *Gall* and *Vinegar* hath Mr *Cotton* powred forth in this whole paſſage from the firſt to the laſt of it, that no ſober minded man fearing *God*, and knowing Mr *Cottons* [275] former temper of *Spirit*, but will confeſſe two things:

A lamentable Character of the change of Mr *Cottons* Spirit.

Firſt, that this *bloudie Tenent* of *perſecution* hath infected and inflamed his very *naturall Temper* and and former ſweet peaceable diſpoſition.

Secondly, his *Eye* (being thus *bloudſhot*) is ſo weakened in its former (and otherwiſe excellent ſight) that it now queſtions no *Difference* between the *Mountaines* and the *Molehills*, for at the *worſt*, in *common probabilite of Reaſon*, there can be but a miſtake in the Diſcuſſer concerning this paſſage.

Peace. If the Diſcuſſer have no ſparke of the

feare of *God,* yet if but *common civilitie* and *honeſtie,* or leaſt reſpect of *common credit* among men, it were impoſſible for him to forge ſo groſſely in *matters* lately *printed,* publike and obvious to every eye.

Truth. The truth is, whether there be different *Editions* or different *Copies* printed, let Mr *Cotton* and whom it concerns take care of it, for the Diſcuſſer is confidently reſolved that if this paſſage (for the *ſubſtance* of it) be not *printed* and to be read in *print* of all men, in their *names,* he will then willingly beare and lye under the charge of a falſe *forehead* and *heart,* which Mr *Cotton* in ſuch heate and anger imputes unto him.[1]

Exam: of Chap. 76. *replying to* Chap. 79.

Peace. IN this ſhort Chapter the Diſcuſſer is charged with *Ignorance* and *uncharitablenes,* for thinking amiſſe of the *Penmen* of the *Anſwer* to the *Queſtions,* to wit, that he ſhould conceive that

1 Cotton charges Williams with "notorious impudent falſehood in matter of fact" becauſe he interpreted the answer to the thirty-firſt queſtion as againſt allowing the Preſbyterians "civill cohabitation" here. This anſwer is quoted in a note to the firſt reference to this matter in *The Bloudy Tenent,* p. 114. *Pub. Narr. Club,* iii. 215. Robert Baillie made a ſimilar charge with Williams, and perhaps took his impreſſion from him. "In all New England no liberty of living for a Preſbyterian. Whoever there, were they angels for life and doctrine, will eſſay to ſet up a different way from them, ſhall be ſure of preſent baniſhment." Quoted by Hallam, *Const. Hiſt. of Eng.* 359.

The movement of Child and others, called by Mr Palfrey a "cabal of Preſbyterians," for more liberal treatment of diſſenters, was of courſe known to Baillie. Gov. Winſlow went on a miſſion to England in 1646, to defend the Maſſachuſetts government. In his *Briefe Narration* he claims that Preſbyterians as well as Anabaptiſts were allowed.—Young, *Chron. of Pilgrims,* 402. The ſtory of the treatment of Preſbyterians in Maſſachuſetts, is told in Palfrey, *Hiſt. of New England,* ii, 165–178.

the *paſſage* to *New England* ſhould change the *Judgment* or *Conſciences* of Men.

Truth. The Diſcuſſer profeſſeth (and I know in truth) to bewaile his *Ignorance* and *uncharitablenes*, yet upon a ſecond review of the words, it will be found there was not an *Imputation* of ſuch a *conceit*, to thoſe worthy *Authors*, or any man, but an *Item* unto all men, occaſioned by the *Confidence* expreſſed, that they doubted not, but thoſe godly brethren of *old England* ſhould agree with them here in *New*, if they were here in *New England* together. This *Item* or *Caveat* will appeare to be [276] given, not by way of poſitive *Charge*, nor in the leaſt derogating from the holy and bleſſed uſe of free and humble *Conference*, but to take off the *Edge* of ſuch *Conference* of agreeing in *New England*, when the *Differences* of *Gods* people have been and are yet ſo great in *Old* and *New*, and ſo many *Conferences* and *Diſputations* of *Truth* and *Peace* have not yet raiſed that bleſſed *Agreement* of which the *Anſwer* to the *Queſtions* would make no doubt.

Differences of Gods own children in *Old* and *New England.*

Peace. Me thinkes there ſhould be little hope of their coming to *New England* when the *New Engliſh Miniſters* had got the *Advantage* of the higher *ground*, and *Carnall Sword* for their *Religion* to Friend, and had expreſt their *Judgment* of their conceiving it not ſafe, that (if they ſhould not agree,) their ſeverall wayes of *Worſhipping God*, ſhould be permitted in one *Common-weale*.

Truth. Yea and I believe ſtill the *Conſequence* was truely gathered by the Diſcuſſer (how ever M[r] *Cotton* hath ſo charged his *Forehead* and *Heart* for it) to wit, that the *New Engliſh Miniſters* could not (as their *Conſcience* ſtood) adviſe the *Magiſtrates* of *New England* to permit that which their *Conſciences* and *Judgments* taught them was not ſafe, &c.

Peace. Theſe paſſages occaſion me to remember a ſerious *Queſtion* which many fearing *God* have made, to wit, Whether the promiſe of *Gods Spirit* bleſſing *Conferences*, be ſo comfortably to be Expected in *New England*, becauſe of thoſe many *publike ſinnes* which moſt of *Gods people* in *New England* lye under, and one eſpecially, to wit, the framing a *Goſpel* or *Chriſt* to themſelves without a *croſſe*, nor *profeſſing* nor *practicing* that in *Old* (except of late in times of *Libertie*) which they profeſſedly come over to enjoy with *Peace* and *Libertie* from any *croſſe* of *Chriſt* in *New*.

Profeſſion of Chriſt Jeſus in *New-England*, not ſo like to be true as that (which was perſecuted) in *Old*.

Truth. I know thoſe thoughts have deeply poſſeſſed, not a few, conſidering alſo the *ſinne* of the *Pattents*, wherein *Chriſtian Kings* (so calld) are inveſted with Right by virtue of their *Chriſtianitie*, to take and give away the *Lands* and *Countries* of other men; As alſo conſidering the *unchriſtian Oaths* ſwallowed downe, at their coming forth from *old Englana*, eſpecially in ſuperſtitious *Land* his time and domineering.

The great ſin of *New-Englands* former Pattents.

And I know theſe thoughts ſo deeply afflicted the Soule and [277] Conſcience of the Diſcuſſer in the time of his Walking in the Way of *New Englands Worſhip*, that at laſt he came to a perſwaſion, that ſuch ſinnes could not be *Expiated*, without returning againe into *England*: or a publike acknowledgement and Confeſſion of the Evill of

The Authors tryalls about the Pattents of *New-England*.

ſo and ſo departing: To this purpoſe before his *Troubles* and *Baniſhment*, he drew up a Letter (not without the *Approbation* of ſome of the *Chiefe* of *New-England*, then tender alſo upon this point beſore *God*) directed unto the *King* himſelfe, humbly acknowledging the *Evill* of that part of the *Pattent* which reſpects the *Donation* of *Land*, &c.

This *Letter* and other *Endeavours* (tending to waſh off *publike ſinnes*, to give warning to others, and above all, to *pacifie* and to give *Glory* unto *God*) it may be that *Councells* from *Fleſh* and *Bloud* ſuppreſt, and *Worldly policie* at laſt prevailed: for this very cauſe (amongſt others afterwards re-examined) to baniſh the Diſcuſſer from ſuch their *Coaſts* and *Territories*.[1]

[1] The letter on the Patents above referred to, was probably the treatiſe which he had drawn up while at Plymouth, as he ſtated, "for the private ſatisfaction of the Governour of Plimouth." It was probably never printed, although Coddington in 1677, charging him with being againſt the King's Patent and authority, said, he "writeth a large Booke in Quarto againſt it." Letter in *New-England-Fire-brand Quenched*, ſecond part: p. 246. This treatiſe was brought to the notice of the Governor and aſſiſtants of Maſſachuſets, Dec. 27, 1633, after Mr Williams had gone to Salem. "For this, taking advice with ſome of the moſt judicious miniſters, (who much condemned Mr Williams's error and preſumption) they gave order that he ſhould be convented at the next court, to be cenſured, etc." He wrote to the Governor and council "very ſubmiſſively," "withall offering his book, or any part of it to be burnt." Jan. 24, 1634 "the governour and council met, to conſider of Mr Williams's letter, etc., when with the advice of Mr Cotton and Mr Wilſon and weighing his letter, and further conſidering of the aforeſaid offenſive paſſages in his book, (which, being written in very obſcure and implicative phraſes, might well admit of doubtful interpretation,) they found the matters not to be ſo evill as at firſt they ſeemed. Thereupon they agreed, that upon his retractation, etc., or taking an oath of allegiance to the King, etc., it ſhould be paſſed over." *Winthrop*, i: 145, 147. Still Cotton declares that this was the firſt of two things "which (to my beſt obſervation and remembrance) cauſed the Sentence of his Baniſhment." *Anſwer* &c. 27. *Pub. Narr. Club*, ii, 44. It was not however contained among the final charges reported by Winthrop, as leading to his baniſhment, although Williams in the text admits that it was among the cauſes which led to it. *Winthrop*, I. 193.

Peace. But from *Violence* to the Diſcuſſer, or any other, Mr *Cotton* (in the next paſſage) proteſts his *Innocencie*, and inſinuates the Diſcuſſer to be no other then (a *Devill*) an *Accuſer* of the *Brethren*, for imputing to them any ſuch Evill, &c.

Truth. He that reads how hard the *Heart* of holy *David* grew, in the ſinne of *Whoredome* and *Murther*, untill the *Lord* awakened him, will leſſe wonder, that *Spirituall Whoredome* and *murtherous violence*, may poſſeſſe the *Hearts* of *Gods Davids* and holieſt Servants now, and that without bluſh, or ſhame, or leaſt appearance of *Relenting:* Doth not all this whole *Traverſe* of Mr *Cotton* maintaine a *perſecution* even unto Death, of ſuch whom the *Civill State* ſhall judge *Hereticks*, *Blaſphemers*, *Idolators*, *Seducers*, &c.

Gods children may be guilty of bloudy perſecution for the hiding of their ſpirituall uncleaneſſe.

Doth not this very Chapter expreſſely juſtifie *perſecution* upon the *Subverters* of the *Chriſtian Faith*, obſtinate after *Conviction?* upon *Blaſphemers*, *Idolators*, *Seducers?* And is Mr *Cotton* not informed, what ſucceſſe his *Doctrine* hath had, that (if a *mercifull God* had not prevented) nor *Courting*, nor *Fining*, nor *Impriſoning*, nor *Whipping*, nor *Baniſhing* had been *puniſhment* ſufficient, to men and women, for cauſe of *Conſcience* in *New-England*, but even Death it ſelfe, (according to the *principles* of *perſecution*) had been inflicted.

Gods mercy in ſtopping *New-Englands* perſecution, by the mercy of *old England*, the mother to diſſenting Conſciences.

Peace. Mr *Cotton* will urge that *Gods* people will not be ſuch *Hereticks*, &c.

278] *Truth.* I might urge Mr *Cottons* owne grant of ſuch ſinnes in *Gods* owne people, for which they may be juſtly *Excommunicated*; but I will rather

Holy *Cranmer* and *Cromwell* joyning with perſecutors of Chriſt Jeſus out of great weaknes in *H.* 8. his dayes.

produce an *Inſtance* in our Nation of *England.* None fearing *God* will eaſily deny the Eminent Godlines of *Cranmer* & *Cromwell* in King *Henry* the eight his dayes; At that very time when King *Henry* himſelfe diſputed in ſo famous an *Aſſembly* againſt the bleſſed *witneſſe* of *Chriſt Jeſus, John Lambert!* Finde we not alſo holy *Cranmer* diſputing before the *King* and that *Stately Aſſembly,* againſt this poore Servant of *God,* for that horrible and monſtrous *Idoll* of *Tranſubſtantiation?*

Peace. Finde we not then alſo holy and zealous *Cromwell* (at the *Kings command*) reading that bloudie *Sentence* of Death againſt that bleſſed Lambe of *Chriſt Jeſus,* who was thus worried to Death, not onely by the bloudie *Wolves* the *Biſhops,* but even by thoſe holy *Lambes* of *Chriſt, Cranmer* and *Cromwell* alſo!

The moſt famous paſſages of *Cromwell* & *Lambert* in *H.* the 8. his dayes.

Truth. This was that bleſſed *Lambert,* a true *Follower* of the *Lambe* of *God Chriſt Jeſus,* who cryed out in the midſt of the *Flames,* None but *Chriſt,* None but *Chriſt:* and well might he ſo cry: Not *Cranmer,* not *Cromwell,* who after ſo much *Light* in *Diſputations,* yet perſiſted in their *Hereſie* and *Idolatry,* and partaking with *violence* againſt this holy man, that he might well cry out, *None but Chriſt, None but Chriſt.*[1]

[1] This was the dying exclamation of John Lambert, who was burned at Smithfield, in 1538. His condemnation was read to him by Cromwell, by command of the King, as Fox ſuppoſes, at the crafty inſtigation of Gardiner, Biſhop of Wincheſter. The diſputations, &c., are given in Fox, *Acts and Monuments,* ii. 331–358.

Exam: of Chap. 77. *replying to* Chap. 80.

Peace. AS it is (Deare *Truth*) oftentimes in *Journies*, the *worst way* and *saddest weather* attends the *Journies End:* So here Mr *Cotton* (neere our close) chargeth upon the Discusser a threefold *wresting* of his words, and accordingly so much *false-dealing*.

Truth. It is sad on the Discussers part, if this be done by him, either by a *willfull* or a *negligent* hand.

Peace. Yea and it is sad on Mr *Cottons* part, if the *Charge* be not *reall* and *substantiall*.

Truth. Mr *Cotton* acknowledgeth his words to be these [The *Godly* will not persist in *Heresie* or turbulent *Schisme*, [279] when they are *convinced* in *Conscience* of the *sinfullnesse* of their way] The first charge therefore against the Discusser is that he confoundeth *Admonition* with *Conviction*, for (saith (Mr *Cotton*) *Admonition* ought not to be dispenced untill the *offendour* be *convinced* in his own *Conscience* of the *sinfullnesse* of his Way.

Truth. For answer hereunto the Discusser to my knowledge humbly appealeth to the *Searcher* of all *Hearts*, that he hath not *willingly* nor *wittingly* falsified Mr *Cottons* words in a *tearme* or *syllable*. And indeed whether he hath wronged him at all, or be not rather unjustly trampled under the feete of weake and *passionate charges*, the Discusser appealeth to Mr *Cottons* owne *Conscience*, awaked (if *God* so please) out of this *bloudie Dreame*.

Peace. Yea but (sayth Mr *Cotton*) *Admonition* is

Of Admonition and Conviction.

one thing, and *Conviction* in their owne *Conſcience* is another; for though ſayth he, *Admonition ought not to be diſpenced till after Conviction*, yet it may fall *out that the Church* (through miſtake) *proceedeth to Admonition* beſore the *offendour be convinced* in his own *Conſcience of the ſinfullneſſe* of his Way.

Truth. Paſſing gently by the want of *Equitie* in Mr *Cotton* to the Diſcuſſer, in condemning him of *falſhood*, for taking *Admonition* for *Conviction*, when he makes it but a *miſtake* in the *Church* to practice the one for, or beſore the other:

I anſwer, I know not that ſutable *Diſtinction* between *Admonition* and *Conviction*, as Mr *Cotton* carrieth it, ſaying, that how ever the *Church* may through miſtake practice *Admonition* before *Conviction*, yet *Admonition* ought not to proceede, untill after *Conviction* in a mans owne *Conſcience*, for finde we not the words *Reprooving*, *Rebuking*, *Admoniſhing*, *Exhorting* a brother, indifferently uſed both in the *Old* and *New Teſtament?* And doth not that very word ἔλεγξον (*Matth.* 18. Reprove him) imply *Conviction* as well as *Reproofe* or *Admonition*, for doth it not ſignifie *Convincingly* reprove him?

Conviction twofold.

Peace. I have heard indeed, that *Conviction* is two-fold:

Firſt, *Externall* and *legall* before men in *Civill* or *Spirituall judicature.*

Secondly, *Effectuall* and inward in the *Court* of a mans owne *Conſcience* before *God*, which internall, alwayes followes not the *Externall.*

280] *Truth.* No, ſuch *Externall Conviction* may be *legall* before men, but not in the ſight of *God*, and a mans owne *Conſcience*, as we ſee in the caſe of *Naboth*, who was legally convict of *Blaſphemy*, when acquitted by *God* and his owne *Conſcience:* As alſo in thoſe *Conſciences* (of which *Paul* ſpeakes) ſeared with hot irons, which *Conſciences* (notwithſtanding the abundance of *Light* from heaven *convincing*, yet) are not brought from believing *Lyes*.

Peace. Yea, but it ſeems by Mr *Cottons words*, that the *Church*, that is (according to his way) the *Major* part of the *Church* muſt judge that the *Heretick* is convinced in his own *Conſcience* of the *ſinfullneſſe* of his way before ſhe proceedeth to *Admonition*.

Of Conviction of Hereticks.

Truth. For my part I cannot *reconcile* theſe three *Propoſitions*, comprized by Mr *Cotton* in theſe few lines.

Firſt, the *Godly* will not perſiſt in *Hereſie* or turbulent *Schiſme*, when they are convinced in *Conſcience* of the ſinfullneſſe thereof.

Secondly, The *Church* is to judge of the *Conviction* of ſuch a *Godly* mans *Conſcience*.

Thirdly, Although ſuch a *Godly* man be convinced of the *ſinfulneſſe* of his way, yea although he will not perſiſt in *Hereſie* or turbulent *Schiſme*, when he is thus *convinced* in *Conſcience* of the ſinfulness thereof, yet then is the *Church* to proceede to *Admonition*. For thus he ſayth, *Admonition* ought not to be diſpenced till after *Conviction*.

Peace. If Mr *Cotton* ſpake of the firſt *Conviction*, to wit, the *Externall*, I could ſubſcribe, but now ſpeaking of that *internall* in a mans owne *Conſcience*, I ſee it pleaſeth *God*, moſt holy and onely

Conviction ſufficient, externall by the word, and efficient internall by Gods Spirit.

wiſe to permit the beſt and and wiſeſt of his Servants, to intrap, intangle, and bewilder themſelves, that they may learne to confeſſe him onely and infinitely wiſe, and be more humble in themſelves, as *fools* and *lyars*, and leſſe bitter in their Judgements and Cenſures on the poore *Underlings* and *Outcaſts*.

Chriſt Jeſus (accounted) the greateſt Heretick, Blaſphemer, Seducer, and Deceiver that ever was in this

Truth. O that Mr *Cotton* who grants the *Godly* may fall into ſuch fowle ſinnes of *Hereſie* and *Schiſme*, may also be godly jealous over himſelfe and others fearing *God* in *old* or *New England*, that, alſo poſſibly they may fall, into the very ſinne of *perſecuting* the Sonne of *God* himſelfe, eſpecially ſince it is the [281] *Lot* of *Chriſt Jeſus* (beyond all compare) both in *Himſelfe* and his *Followers*, to be accounted the greateſt *Heretick*, *Blaſphemer*, *Seducer* and *Deceiver*.

Peace. To the ſecond and third Charge Mr *Cotton* complains of falſe dealing, in that the Diſcuſſer ſhould render his *words*, as if he charged ſuch to be *obſtinate perſons*, that yeelded not to once or twice *Admonition*, and that for every *Errour*, when he ſpeakes onely of perſiſting in *Hereſie*, or turbulent *Schiſme*.

Truth. For anſwer, let Mr *Cottons Concluſions* in the beginning of this Booke be remembred. Wherein he maintaines that a *Man* of *Erroneous* and blinde *Conſcience* in *Fundamentall* and *weighty points*, and perſiſting in the *Errour* of his way, is not perſecuted for cauſe of *Conſcience*, but for ſinning againſt his *Conſcience*. Whence it followes that the *Civill Courts* of the *World* muſt judge: whether the *matter* be *fundamentall* and *waighty:*

whether the partie have been rightly once and twice *admoniſhed:* and whether he perſiſt in the *Errour* of his *Way:* that is, whether he be *obſtinate* after ſuch *Admonition*, and muſt then be *perſecuted*, though (as the *Concluſion* wofully concludeth) not for cauſe of *Conſcience*, but for ſinning againſt his *Conſcience*.

Peace. Yea but the Diſcuſſer (ſayth Mr *Cotton*) dealeth falſly, in carrying my words, as if I had ſaid, that *Godly perſons* in whatſoever *Errour* they hould, if they yeeld not to once or twice *Admonition*, they muſt needs be *obſtinate:* whereas (he ſaith) he ſpeakes not of every *Errour*, but of perſiſting in *Hereſie* and *turbulent Schiſme*.

Truth. The Diſcuſſer did not ſo ſay, or ſo carry it as Mr *Cotton* inſinuates, but this he ſaith, that even in the place of *Righteouſneſſe* and *Judgement* (as *Salomon* ſaith) *Iniquitie*, and ſuch *Iniquitie* (in all *civill Courts* of the *World*, and in all *Ages* of the *World*) uſually hath been found, that as in multiplying glaſſes a *Flea* is made an *Elephant*, &c. So the *poore witneſſes* of *Chriſt* have been *proclaimed* and *perſecuted* for *Hereticks*, *Blaſphemers*, *Seducers*, &c. not onely for houlding the *Popes Tranſubſtantiation*, *Auricular Confeſſion*, *Purgatorie*, and those waightier points of the *Beaſts worſhip:* but *reading* a piece of a Leafe of *Scripture* or any *good Booke* is *Hereſie:* Eating a piece of Fleſh in *Lent*, yea the ſlight breaches of the ſmalleſt *Traditions* of the [282] *Elders* and *State Worſhips*, accounted *Hereſie*, *Blaſphemie*, &c.

Small matters accounted Hereſies.

Peace. Hence it was I think, that the *Naturaliſt* could tell us in the *Fable* of the *Fox* and the *Lyon*, that the *Fox* ran not away in vaine upon the *Proclamation* of the departure of all *horned Beaſts*, as knowing that if the *bloudie perſecutors* of the *World* ſhall ſay, the *plaineſt Ears* are *hornes* (that is, the *ſmalleſt Errours*, yea the *plaineſt Truths* are *Hereſies*) it is in vaine for any *Innocent* to plead they are but *Eares*, &c.

The barbarous uſage of John Hus in the Councell at Conſtance.

Truth. Yea hence it was that in that famous, or rather moſt infamous *Councell* of *Conſtance*, the bleſſed *Servant* and *witnes* of *Chriſt Jeſus*, *John Hus*, was as it were ſtobd to Death (before his burning) with tearmes of *Hereſie*, *Heretick*, *Hereſiarck*, yea though he held as the *Pope* and the *Councell* held, even in thoſe points for which they condemned him, becauſe (beſide their hatred for his *Holines*, witneſſing againſt their *Filthines*) themſelues would ſay from his *writings*, that he did hould ſo and ſo againſt their *Popiſh Tenents*, which he he himſelfe profeſt he never did.[1]

Peace. In the next place (Deare *Truth*) are two Paſſages related by the Diſcuſſer from *New England*. to which Mr *Cotton* gives no credit.

2. He ſayth, If ſuch words were ſpoken, they might be ſpoken upon ſuch *waights* as might hould *waight*, &c.

[1] "He himſelf would never allow even to the laſt, that he had departed from the orthodox ſtandards of the Church,—the Scriptures, and the Fathers. In fact, with the exception of the views of Jacobel in regard to the communion of the cup, there was ſcarce a doctrine which he held, upon which he could not have found many members of the Council to agree with him. Many of the propoſitions attributed to him by the Council he publicly diſavowed, and others he explained in ſuch a manner that they could not properly be regarded heretical." Gillett, *Life and Times of John Huss*, ii: 74–75.

Truth. For the Stories and the Difcuffers mif-takes (willing *miftakes,* as M[r] *Cotton* feemes to in-finuate) I know the Difcuffer humbly defires like a true *Traveller* to his heavenly *Countrey,* to heare of, and fee and acknowledge, and forfake every *falfe path* and *ftep* (by the helpe of *Chrift*) that the poor-eft *childe* though but a *naked Pagan* fhall hint him of: But why fhould the *Stories* feeme incredible that fuite fo wofully fit with the *Common Tenents?*

Peace. It may be M[r] *Cotton* will not believe it, nor approve it: But there are not two, but ten wit-neffes, to teftifie fuch *Stories,* were it feafonable to relate and inlarge fuch *particulars.*

The bloudie Tenent deftroying civilitie and humane Societies out of the World.

Truth. Let M[r] *Cotton* then pleafe to underftand (to paffe by particular names of the former *Stories,* which are ready to be declared to any *charitable* and *loving Enquirie*) that his *bloudie Tenent* is a bitter *Roote* of many *bitter branches,* not onely bitter [283] to *fpirituall tafts,* but even to the taft of *Civilitie* and *Humanitie* itfelfe. But fince the names of per-fons are fo defired, I fhall relate (not out of any perfonall difrefpect to M[r] *Streete* and the *people* of *Cohannet, alias Taunton,* my loving friends) what many teftifie, that the faid (reputed) *Minifter* M[r] *Streete,* publikely and earneftly perfwaded his *Church-members* to give *Land* to none but fuch, as might be fit for *Church-members:* yea not to receive fuch *Englifh* into the *Towne,* or if in the *Towne,* yet not to Land, that if they lived in the *Towne* or place, yet they might be knowne to be but as *Gib-*

eonites, *hewers* of wood, and *drawers* of water for the ſervice of them that were of the *Church*.[1]

Peace. I know what *troubleſome Effects* followed in the ſame place, and what *Breaches* of *Civill* and *humane Societie?* What *Departures* of divers, and *Barres* to the *comming* oſ others, to the *ſpoile* and *hindrance* of a moſt likely and growing *Plantation.*

But to proceede (Deare *Truth*) you cannot more faithfully and carefully labour to diſcharge the Diſcuſſer of *falſhoods*, then Mr *Cotton* endeavours to lay them on: For to the former three, behould in the next paſſage foure more.

"For, firſt the Diſcuſſer is charged to report M^r^ "*Cotton* as expreſſing Confidence in this cauſe, "which Mr *Cotton* ſayth he expreſſed not.

"Secondly, He reports Mr *Cotton* to ſay, that he (to "wit, Mr *Cotton*) had removed the *grounds* of this "*Errour*, whereas Mr *Cotton* (ſaith he) ſaid not ſo, 's but that he had ſpoken ſo much for that *End.*

"Thirdly, He foiſteth in the name of *great Errour*, "which though it be ſo, yet Mr *Cotton* did not ſo "*ſtile* it.

"Fourthly, That Mr *Cotton* ſhould conclude, that

[1] Nicholas Street was inſtalled Teacher at Taunton, together with William Hooke as Paſtor. "What day that was, is aſked in vain" ſays Mr. Savage; *Gen. Hiſt. of N. E.* iv: 222. It was probably in 1637. Hooke went to New Haven ſeven years after, at which time Street ſucceeded him as Paſtor. In 1659 he alſo went to New Haven, as Mr Hookes ſucceſſor, and died there April 22, 1674. Emery, *Miniſtry of Taunton*, i: 156. *Baylies Memoirs of Plymouth Col.* i: 290–295. It is poſſible that the diviſion in the church which Leckford relates had ſome connection with the facts aſterted above. "Cohannet, alias Taunton, is in Plymouth Patent. There is a church gathered of late, and ſome ten or twenty of the church, the reſt excluded. Maſter Hooke Paſtor, Maſter Streate Teacher." *Plain Dealing*, 40. Baylies thinks it not improbable that Richard Williams, one of the firſt and leading ſettlers of Taunton was a relative, and perhaps brother of Roger. *New Plymouth*, i: 272, 284.

"to be a great *Errour*, that *perſons* are not to be "*perſecuted* for *cauſe* of *Conſcience*, when he ſtates "the *Queſtion* ſo, that none ought to be *perſecuted* at "all for *cauſe* of *Conſcience*, but for ſinning againſt "their *Conſcience*.

Truth. Sweet *Peace*, he that hath a minde to beate a *Dog*, will soone finde a cudgell, &c. If M[r] *Cotton* had not eſteemed the Diſcuſſer as a *Dog*, and had not had as great a minde as a *Dog* to uſe him, he would never have ſo catcht at every *line* and *word*, to finde out (ſuch) the Diſcuſſers *Lyes* and *Falſhoods*. [284] For, firſt, it is apparant that the Diſcuſſer here undertooke not to repeate M[r] *Cottons* words, but upon ſuch and ſuch words of M[r] *Cottons* (compared with all former *Agitations*) to collect according to his *underſtanding* ſuch a *Concluſion*.

Peace. But whether he hath rightly and without breach of *Truth* or *Love* ſo and ſo collected, let it be (briefly) in the feare of God *examined*.

All Men are confident in their owne opinions.

Truth. Firſt then, hath not M[r] *Cotton* through all this diſcourſe, expreſt a *Confidence* (ſome have called it *imperious* and *inſulting*) againſt the poore *Hereticks*, *Blaſphemers*, *Seducers*? And doe not theſe words [for avoyding the grounds of your *Errour*] import ſo much?

Secondly, Doth not M[r] *Cottons* words imply that in his *opinion* ſuch a *Tenent* is an *Errour*, and that by ſpeaking ſo much againſt it, he hath removed it, whatever his *opponent* thinkes to the contrary?

Thirdly, Why may not the Diſcuſſer or any man ſay, that M[r] *Cotton* counts that a great *Errour*, which M[r] *Cotton* endeavours ſo to repreſent to all men?

Peace. But the fourth (ſayth Mr *Cotton*) is an evident *falſhhood* in the Diſcuſſer to ſay, that Mr *Cotton* ſhould conclude this to be the great *Errour*, that *perſons* are not to be *perſecuted* for *cauſe* of *Conſcience*.

Truth. The Father of Lights hath of late been graciouſly pleaſed to open the *eyes* of not a few of his *ſervants* to ſee that Mr *Cottons Diſtinction* [of not *perſecuting* a man for his *Conſcience*, but for *ſinning againſt* his *Conſcience*] is but a *Figleafe* to hide the *nakednes* of that *bloudie Tenent*, for the *Civill Court* muſt then judge when a man ſinnes againſt his *Conſcience*, or els he muſt take it from the *Cleargie* upon truſt, that the poore reputed *Heretick* doth ſo ſinne.

Peace. Mr *Cotton* adds that it is *Aggravation* of ſinne to hould or practice *Evill* out of *Conſcience*.

The perſecutour of *Turks, Pagans, Jewes*, or *Antchriſtians*, is in a greater errour then any of them.

Truth. True, but I alſo aſke, Doth not that *perſecutour* that hunts or *perſecuteth* a *Turke*, a *Jew*, a *Pagan*, an *Antichrſtian* (under pretence that this *Pagan*, this *Turke*, this *Jew*, this *Antichriſtian* ſins againſt his owne *Conſcience*,) doth not this *perſecutour*, I ſay, hould a greater *Errour*, then any of the foure, becauſe he hardens ſuch *Conſciences* in their *Errours* by ſuch his [285] *perſecution*, and that alſo to the overthrowing of the *civill* and *humane Societie* of the *Nations* of the *World*, in point of *civill peace*?

Peace. Well you may (deare *Truth*) enjoy your owne holy and *peaceable Thoughts*, but Mr *Cotton* ends this Chapter with hope that the reputed *bloudie Tenent*, appeares not *whited* in the *bloud* of the

Lambe, and tends to ſave *Chriſts ſheepe* from *devouring*, to defend *Chriſts truth*, and to maintaine and preſerve *peace* in *Church* and *Common-weale*.

Truth. Sweet *Peace*, that which hath in all Ages powred out the *precious bloud* of the *Sonne* of *God*, in the *bloud* of his poore *ſheepe*, ſhall never be found *whited* (as Mr *Cotton* inſinuates) in the *bloud* of this moſt heavenly *Shepheard:* That which hath maintained the *workes* of *Darknes* 1600 *yeares* under the *bloudie Romane Emperours*, and more *bloudie Romane Popes*, hath never tended to deſtroy, but build and fortiſie ſuch *helliſh workes.* That which all Experience (ſince *Chriſts* time) hath shewen to be the great *Fire-brand* or *Incendiarie* oſ the *Nations*, hath powred out ſo many *Rivers* of *bloud* about *Religion*, and that amongſt the (ſo called) *Chriſtian Nations.* That *Tenent*, I ſay, will never be found a *preſerver*, but a *bloudie deſtroyer* both of *Spirituall* and *civill peace*.

The bloudie Fruits of the *bloudie Tenent.*

Exam: of Chap. 78. *replying to* Chap. 81.

Peace. WE are now (Deare *Truth*) through the *mercie* of the *Father* of *mercies*, arrived, at the laſt Chapter of this *Sorrowſull Agitation*: Mr *Cotton* finds nothing in this worth the while to ſpeake to ; yet thinkes he it good to finde time to blame the Diſcuſſer for ſelfe-*Applauſes*, vaine-glorious *Triumph*, and *confident perſwaſion*, which before he had noted Mr *Cotton* for.

Touching confidence in opinions.

Truth. That which was noted in Mr *Cotton* was not meerly a *perſwaſion* or *confidence*, but indeed an *imperious* and *inſulting confidence*, over the *poore* and *oppreſſed*, and an adding of *Vinegar* to the *Gall* of the *Sonne of God*, *perſecuted* in his poore *Saints* and *Members*.

286] *Peace.* But may there not ſeeme to be too in the Diſcuſſer, too great a *confidence* of the *converting* and turning of the *bloudie Storme* of *Warres* about *Conſcience*, into mercifull *calmes* of *peace*, and of the returne of *Chriſts dove*, with *Olive branches* of *civill peace?*

Freedome of Conſcience hath ever been a Pe ce-maker in all Natiōs where it hath appeared.

Truth. Then let thouſands and ten thouſands, *French*, *Polonians*, *Hungarians*, *Tranſylvanians*, *Bohemians*, *Netherlanders*, and others, and now at laſt (through Gods gracious ſmiling upon this holy *Truth* of his) I ſay, many thouſand *Engliſh* men ſet to their *ſeale* and *witnes*, to wit, that *Freedome* to the *Conſciences* of men, (from all other but *ſpirituall oppoſition*) hath ſtuck many *Millions* of *Browes* and *Houſes* with *Olive branches*, that were before beblubbered and overwhelmed with tears and bloud.

And eſpecially at this houre in *England*.

Peace. I cannot but confidently ſee and ſay, that doubtles, had not the *prudent* and *zealous care* of *Englands Parliament* and *Armie* ſubſcribed to this bleſſed means of *peace*, reſtored to *Lands* and *Counties embroyled* in *bloudie civill Warre*s about *Religion*, doubtles, the *streame* of *Warre* which hath run ſo long with *bloud* between the *Prelates* and the *Puritans* (ſo calld) had run as freſh and furious in all devouring *flames* between the *Preſbyterians* and the *Independents*.

Truth. Oh bleſſed be the *God* of *peace*, who hath more pitie upon the *unpeaceable Sonnes* of *Men*, then they have on Themſelves.

Peace. Mr *Cotton* in the next place addeth, that one paſſage he may not let paſſe, becauſe the name of *Chriſt* is intereſted in it, and diſhonoured by it. to wit, [*Chriſt* delighteth not in the *bloud* of men, but ſhed his own *bloud* for his *bloudieſt enemies:*] Mr *Cotton* anſwers; it is true that *Chriſt* delighteth not in the bloud of men, while they gainſay and *bloudily perſecute* him and his, out of *Ignorance:* but he delights in the *bloud* of ſuch, who after the *acknowledgement* of his *Truth,* doe tread the *bloud* of his *Covenant* under-foote, and *wittingly* and *willingly* reject him from raigning over them: The contrary whereof he ſayth Proclaimes the *Goſpel* to [be] the *ſeede* of the *Serpent: Sows pillowes* under all *ellbowes,* makes the *Heart* of the *Righteous ſad,* ſtrengthens the hand of the *wicked,* and proclaimes *peace* to *Jezabell,* and her *whoredomes* and *witchcrafts,* and concludes with *prayer* [287] againſt ſuch a bewitching of the *Whores Cup,* where, by open *profeſſion* ſhe is rejected, but let in by the *back-doore* of *Toleration.*

How Chriſt delights in bloud.

Truth. I perceive (Sweet *Peace*) that in the winding up of this *Diſcourſe* Mr *Cotton* winds up, reſolveth and reduceth his former pleaded for *perſecuting* of *Hereticks, Blaſphemers, Idolaters, Seducers,* into the perſecuting onely of *Apoſtates,* who after the acknowledging of the *Truth,* doe tread the *bloud* of *Chriſts Covenant* under foote, &c. To which I anſwer; If ſo then the diſcerning & judg-

Of perſecuting Apoſtates.

ing between ſuch as gainſay *Chriſt* and *blaſpheme* him out of *Ignorance*, (ſuch as Mr *Cotton* makes the *Jewes*, who put him to Death) and ſuch as *willingly* and *wittingly* reject him: I ſay the judging of this muſt then reſt at the *Barre* of the *Civill Courts* and *Judicatures* of the *World*, which neceſſarily implies a ſuppoſition of *power* of *Judging* in all the *Nations* of the *World*, and so conſequently in *Naturall* men contrary to the *Scriptures*, which conclude all *Mankinde* (while in their *naturall eſtate*,) uncapable of the things of Gods Spirit.

Peace. Yea and alſo (to my underſtanding) it implies, a *ſubmitting* and *ſubjecting* of the *Crowne* and *Sceptre* and *affaires* of *Chriſt Jeſus*, to the *Civill* and *humane Crownes* and *Scepters* and *Tribunalls* of the *Nations* of this *World*, and that in *ſpirituall* and *heavenly* things, the proper *affaires* of his owne *Spirituall Kingdome*, in which, the wiſeſt of this world are ignorant, and extreamly oppoſite.

A monſtrous ſuspenſion or hanging up of Magiſtrates.

Truth. For this, you know Mr *Cotton* hath a broken *Refuge*, to wit, [the *Nations* of the *World*, & *Naturall* men muſt not judge untill they be better informed] In which, what a wonderfull and *monſtrous ſuſpenſion* doth he put upon the *aſſaires* of *Chriſt Jeſus* all the world over, and leaves the *matters* of *Chriſt Jeſus* in worſe caſe, and more poorely provided for by *Chriſt Jeſus*, then the *matters* and *affaires* of any *King* or *Kingdome* in the *World*, beyond *compare* and *Imagination*.

Peace. Yet, me-thinks thoſe Scriptures quoted by Mr *Cotton Luc*. 17. [19: 27.] Thoſe mine *Enemies*, &c. and *Revel*. 16. [4-7.] *Bloudie vengeance* upon *Antichriſtian Emiſſaries*, are very conſiderable.

Truth. Doubtles all *Scripture* ſeriouſly alledged by the moſt *ignorant* and *unworthy* (how much more from ſo *learned* and *conſcientious*) ought ſeriouſly and awfully to be pondered in [288] the holy preſence of *God:* The *Warrants* and *Authorities* of *civill powers* (though but pretended) are not without due reſpect to be examined, although rejected (in the end) as inſufficient, &c. But conſider in the *Examination* of thoſe *Scriptures:* Is it credible that all that reſiſt *Chriſt Jesus*, his *Kingdome* and *Government*, are *Apoſtates* and *Antichriſtian Emiſſaries*, againſt whom he powres out that *Violl?* Have they firſt acknowledged the *Covenant* of *Jeſus*, and then trod the *precious bloud* of that *High Covenant* under feete?

Allegations of Scriptures ought ſeriouſly to be made and anſwered.

Millions of *Turks*, *Jewes* and *Antichiſtians* are far from the due charge of Apoſtacie.

Peace. The *Eaſt* is not ſo farre from the *Weſt*, as thoſe *Scriptures* from ſuch a *Concluſion*.

Truth. Yea how many hundreth thouſands of *Jewes* and *Turkes* and *Antichriſtians* periſh *temporally* and *eternally*, and that for refuſing *Chriſt Jeſus* to be *King*, and for ſhedding his *bloud* in his *ſervants*, who can never be brought under this guilt of *Apoſtacie*, after they have once acknowledged the truth of *Chriſts Government* and *Kingdome*.

Peace. Me-thinks to underſtand the *Scriptures* in Mr *Cottons ſence*, were a wonderfull *penning* up and *ſtraightning* the holy *Scripture*.

Truth. Sweet *Peace*, as ſoon may we *immure* the *glorious Sun* in a *darke dungeon*, as confine thoſe bright *Scriptures* in the dark *Cells* of *Apoſtacie:* but I further obſerve, that *Chriſt Jeſus* not only praid and dyed for his *Enemies*, who bloudily *per-*

ſecuted him and his out of *Ignorance*, but gave this reaſon againſt bodily Death to be inflicted on any for his cauſe and ſake, *Luc.* 9. [56.] The *Son* of *Man* is not come to *deſtroy Mens lives:* and I might returne the *Queſtion* to Mr *Cotton*, not unfitly, Are not theſe the words of *Him* that delighteth not in the *bloud* of his *bloudieſt enemies* and *Gainſayers?*

Peace. It will be said, What *ſlaughters*, what drinking of *Bloud* is that which *Chriſt Jeſus* in theſe *Scriptures* intendeth?

Truth. I anſwer, although the *Sword* of *Chriſts Kingdome*, that ſharpe *Sword* with two edges is a *Spirituall Sword*, and is carried in his *Mouth*, yet all power in *Heaven* and *Earth* being given into his hands by his *Father*, he *ruleth* and *over-ruleth* in a way of *power* and *providence*, all the *powers* of the *World*.

The myſterie of the red horſe of War.

There is therefore a great *Sword* given to him that rideth upon the *white Horſe*, (*Revel.* 6. [2.]) by which, for the reſiſting [289] of him that rideth upon the *white Horſe*, (in the *gainſaying* and *perſecuting* of *Chriſt* in his *Members*) *Chriſt Jeſus* takes *peace* from the *Earth*, and ſuffers the *Turkes* to plague the *Antichriſtian World*, (*Papiſts* and carnall *Proteſtants*) to plague each other, and to fill *Cups* of *Bloud* each to other, while they contend and fight, firſt againſt *God*, and then one againſt another, for their ſeverall falſe *Prophets* and *Religions*.

Peace. Me-thinkes then Mr *Cotton* might have ſpared to charge the Diſcuſſer with proclaiming of *peace* to *Jezabell*, &c.

Truth. There is a *Spirituall peace* in the *matters* of *Chrifts Kingdome* and *Worfhip*, and in the *particular Confciences* and *Soules* of his *Servants.* There is a *civill peace* in the quiet enjoyment of each mans *proprietie,* in the *Combination* of *Townes, Cities, Kingdomes,* &c. But neither of thefe three will Mr *Cotton* prove the Difcuffer proclaimeth to fuch *Antichriftians* or *enemies* of *Chrift Jefus,* who *perfecute* and *oppreffe Jew* or *Gentile* upon any *civill* or *spirituall pretence.*

A fpiritall and Civill peace.

'Tis true, the *Confciences* and *Worfhips* of all men *peaceable* in their way, he affirmes ought not to be molefted, and though not *approved* yet *permitted,* and (although no *fpirituall,* yet) a *civill peace* proclaimed to their *outward man* while *peaceable* in *civill commerce.*

To *perfecutours, he not onely proclaimes Gods Judgements fpirituall* and *eternall,* but *temporall* alfo, and affirmeth that all *perfecutours* of all *forts* (and efpecially the bloudie *Whore* of *Rome* (who hath so long been *drunk* with the *bloud* of the *Saints,*) ought by the *Civill Sword* to be *reftrained* and *punifhed* (as the *Deftroyers* of *Mankinde* and all *civill* and *peaceable* being in the *World,*) according to the hight of their *cruell* and *murtherous Oppreffions.*

Peace. But *Tolleration* of her (fayth Mr *Cotton* brings) her in at the back dore, and fo we may come to drink deeply of the *Cup* of the *Lords wrath,* and be filled with the *Cup* of her *plagues.*

Truth. There are two opinions which have bewitched the *Nations* profeffing the name of *Chrift.*

Two wofull opinions bewitching the Nations.

Firft, That a *Nationall Church* or *State,* is of *Chrifts appointing.*

290.] Secondly, That ſuch a *Nationall Church* or *State* muſt be maintained pure by the *power* of the *Sword.* While Mr *Cotton* prayes againſt the *bewitching* of the *Whores cup*, O that the *Father* of *Lights* might graciouſly please to ſhew him the depth of her *witchcrafts*, and his owne moſt *wofull Deluſions* in both theſe.

The 3 great Cauſes of the downfall of the Church of *Rome.*

In vaine doth Mr *Cotton* feare *partaking* of her *ſinnes* and *plagues* by a *tollerating* (meerly) of her *Worſhip* in a *civill State*, while he forgets the *three great cauſes* of her *downfall* and *deſolation*, and partakes of any of them (*Revel.* 18.) to wit, Her *worldly pompe* and *pleaſure:* Her *ſpirituall Whoredomes* and *invented Worſhips*, and her *crueltie* and *bloudſhed*, more eſpecially againſt the *Conſciences* of the *Saints* or *holy ones* of *Jeſus.*

Exam: of Chap. 79. *Touching the* Modell *of Church and Civill power, Examined in the firſt part of the* bloudie Tenent, *but not defended by* Mr *Cotton, or any, that the Diſcuſſer knowes of.*

Touching a *New Engliſh Modell* of Church and civill power.

Peace. I Had hoped (*Deare Truth*) that we had gained a *peaceable* and *quiet harbor*, after all our tempeſtuous *Toſſings* in the boyſterous Seas of this *bloudie Tenent*, yet now behold a *ſharpe* and *cutting winde* of Mr *Cottons* continuall *Cenſures*; For I was not (ſayth Mr *Cotton*) of thoſe that compoſed the *Modell:* and ſecondly, the *Miniſters* ſay it was not ſent by them to *Salem*, and therefore the *Diſcuſſer* is left of *God* to a double *falshood*,

Truth. *Sweete Peace*, till *ſweete Death*, in and (often) for *Chriſt*, cloſe up the Eyes of his *ſervants*, they muſt not expect to reſt fully from their *Labours*, and expect their *workes* to follow them.

Once againe therefore let us heare the Diſcuſſers *plea* for himſelfe againſt this bluſtering charge of double *falſhood*. Maſter *Cottons* owne words in the End of his *Anſwer* to the *Priſoners Letter*, are "theſe; I forbeare *adding Reaſons* to juſtifie the "*Truth*, becauſe you may finde that done to your "hand in a Treatiſe ſent to ſome of the Brethren, "late of *Salem*, who doubted as *you doe.[1]

291.] *Truth.* To my knowledge it was reported (according to this hint of Mr *Cottons*) that from the *Miniſters* of the *Churches* (pretended) ſuch a *Modell* compoſed by them was ſent to *Salem*: Hereupon it was that the *Diſcuſſer* wrote on purpoſe to his worthy friend Mr *Sharpe* (*Elder* of the *Church* of *Salem*, (ſo called) for the ſight of it, who accordingly ſent it to him.

*Writing to one Mr *Hall*.

Peace. If this *Modell*, of ſuch *conſequence*, were ſo *compoſed* and ſo ſent to *Salem*, if Mr *Cotton* directs others thither to *repaire* to make uſe of it, if he thus *approve* and *promote* it, I ſee not why it might not probably be *collected*, that Mr *Cotton* (not the laſt in ſuch *great* and *publike matters*) was amongſt, if not *chiefe* amongſt the *compoſers* of it, and that he and they were not ignorant of the *conveyance* of it to *Salem*.[2]

[1] *Pub. Narr. Club*, iii: 53.

[2] The *Model*, &c. ſeems to have originated in an Act of the General Court, paſſed March 4, 1634, in which they "entreate of the elders and brethren of every church within this juriſdiction that they will conſult and adviſe of one uniform order of diſſipline in the churches,

Deepe Cenſures for none or innocent miſtakes.

Truth. But grant M[r] *Cotton* ſhould have been imagined to have been left out in this ſo great and *publike* a *ſervice*, and that all the former *probabilities* faile: yet doubtles M[r] *Cotton* will be caſt at the barre of *Chriſtian Love* and *Moderation*, for ſo *bitter* a *charge* upon the poore *Diſcuſſer* for ſo eaſie and harmles *Miſtakes*.

Peace. Such fierce *flaſhes* might well iſſue from the bloudie *French Cardinall* againſt the poore *Hugenots*, from the *Engliſh bloudie Biſhops* againſt the poore *Lollards*, from the bloudie *Popes* againſt the *Hereticks* and *Lutherans*: but a gentler *Breath* and *ſtile* might well beſeeme a *Proteſtant* to a *Proteſtant*, engaged in *common principles* and *Teſtimonies* and *ſufferings* of *Jeſus* againſt thoſe *bloudie Tyrants*.

But to the *Modell*, M[r] *Cotton* ſeemes highly offended, that the *Diſcuſſer* ſhould ſay, that the *Modell* awaketh *Moſes* from his *unknowne Grave*, and denies *Jeſus* yet to have ſeene the *Earth*. For, *Moſes* his *Lawes* were of force (ſayth he) to the *Iſraelites* in the Land of *Canaan*, when *Moſes* was dead: and

agreeable to the Scriptures, and then to conſider howe farr the Magiſtrates are bound to interpoſe for the preſervation of that uniformity and peace of the churches." *Mass. Col. Rec.* I: 142. Cotton is very explicit in his denial of any part in its compoſition, "What other Miniſters of New England did in it, themſelves know: But for M[r] Cotton, I know, that he was none of them that compoſed it." *Bloudy Tenent Waſhed*, 192. That "M[r] Cotton ſhould have been imagined to have been left out in this ſo great and publike a ſervice" might well have ſeemed improbable.

He is equally explicit in his denial that it was ſent to Salem by its authors. "The Miniſters themſelves, that compoſed the Modell, doe deny it; Howſoever the Modell came to Salem, the Miniſters ſay it was not ſent by them." *B. T. Waſhed*, 192. Williams obtained a copy there from Samuel Sharpe, who came to Salem in 1629, and was a ruling elder in the Church. But Cotton does not actually ſay, as Williams implies, that he knew that it was ſent there. He only ſays that it was "ſent to ſome of the Brethren *late of Salem*."

In reference to Hall, Cotton's correſpondent, see p. 54 *supra*, and *Pub. Narr. Club*, iii: v.

againe, *Chriſt* came not to deſtroy the *Law* of *Moſes*, not the *Morall Law*, nor the *Judicialls*, ſuch as are of *common Equitie:* Or els (ſayth he) *the Conſcience of the Civill Magiſtrate could never doe any act of civill Juſtice out of Faith, becauſe he ſhould have no word of God to be the Ground of his Act, if the Lawes of Judgement were abrogated, and none extant in the New.*

Truth. I anſwer; that ſpeech of the *Diſcuſſer* was neither [292] *unreaſonable*, nor *untrue*, as M[r] *Cotton* alledgeth: for grant *Chriſt* came not to deſtroy the *Morall Law* of the ten *Commands* (for the *Subſtance* of it, for all *materiall circumſtances* therein M[r] *Cotton* will not urge nor practice). Nor ſecondly, the *Judicialls* of *Moral Equitie*, that is, ſuch as in deed concerne *Life* and *Manners*, according to the *Nature* and *Conſtitution* of the ſeverall *Nations* and *Peoples* of the *World.*

Touching *Moſes* his Judicialls.

Peace. Pardon me (*Deare Truth*) before you proceede, a word of *Explication:* your *Addition* [according to the *Nature* and *Conſtitution* of the *Peoples* and *Nations* of the *World*] will not be allowed of.

Truth. Without this I cannot allow of *Moſes* his *Judicialls* to binde all *Nations* of the *World*, then before, or ſince *Chriſt Jeſus:* my reaſon is: That people of *Iſrael* (to which thoſe *Judiciall Lawes* and *puniſhments* were preſcribed) was as I may ſay, a *miraculous people* or *Nation*, miraculouſly brought from one *Nation*, (the Land of *Ægypt*) into another the Land of *Canaan*) both types, a people furniſhed with *miraculous food* and *cloathing* during their ſortie yeares Travell through the *Wil-*

Iſrael in a kind a miraculou people.

dernes: The ſeaven *Nations* of *Canaan* wondrouſly and *miraculouſly* deſtroyed before them; Their *Lawes* and *Inſtitutions miraculouſly* delivered to them, &c.

Beſide (not to wade deeper into this *Controverſie*, as in the *Examination* of the *Modell* I have done) their Land was typically *holy*, and that people the *Church* of *God*, the onely *Church* of *God* in the *World*. And therefore being a people of ſuch *miraculous conſiderations*, *Meanes* and *Obligations*, the breach even of *Morall Lawes* concerning *Life* and *Manners* and *civill Eſtate*, might be more tranſcendently *heinous* and *odious* in them, then in the other ſeverall *Nations* and *peoples* of the *World*, many *thouſands* and *millions* whereof never ſo much as heard of the Name of the *God* of *Iſrael*.

Peace. If men ſee cauſe to ordaine a *Court* of *Chancery*, and erect a *Mercy-ſeate* to moderate the *rigour* of *Lawes*, which cannot be juſtly executed, without the moderate and equall conſideration of *perſons* and other *circumſtances!* Me-thinks, the *Father* of *Mercies* (though he be *Juſtice* it ſelfe, yet) cannot be juſtly imagined to carrie all *Judiciall* or *Civill Lawes* or *Sentences*, by one *univerſall ſtrictnes* through all the *Nations* of the *Earth*.

293] *Truth*. The *Lord Jeſus* tells us of a more tollerable *Sentence*, (even for the *Sodomites* in the day of *Judgment*, then for the *Jewes*, who were the *people* and *Church* of *God:* and *Paul* his ſervant layes heavier load (*Rom*. 2. [21, 22]) upon ſuch *Adulterers*, *Thieves*, as profeſſe to be *Teachers* unto others, &c. of the contrary *Graces* and *Vertues*.

Peace. Deare *Truth,* the *Scriptures* are full, and many Arguments might be drawne out this way, but pleafe you to pitch upon an *Inftance,* whereby we may the fooner finifh this *Digreffion.*

Truth, Take that great cafe of the *punifhment* of *Adulterie,* and I confidently affirme, that the *Confcience* of the *Magiftrate,* may out of *Faith,* execute other *punifhments* befide (ftoning to) Death, which was the *punifhment* of that *finne* in *Ifraell.* For although (as Mr *Cotton* fayth) That was the *Law* of *Judgement* in the *Old Teftament,* and there is no other *particularly* expreft in the *New,* yet the *Confcience* of the *Magiftrate* may know, Touching punifh-ment of Adulterie.

Firft, That the carriage of the *Lord Jefus* about this cafe, when the *Queftion* was precifely put to him, was *extraordinary* and *ftrange:* For (although unto other *Queftions,* even of the *Pharifees, Herodians, Sadduces,* the *High Prieft,* and *Pilate,* he gave more or leffe, firft or laft, punctuall *Refolutions,* yet) here, he *condemnes* the *finne,* yet he neither confirmes nor difanulls this *punifhment,* but leaves the *Queftion* (in all *probabilitie*) and leaves the *feverall Nations* of the *World,* to their owne *feverall Lawes* and *Agreements* (as is moft probable) according to their feverall *Natures, Difpofitions* and *Conftitutions,* and their *common peace* and *wellfare.*

Secondly, The *Lord Jefus* (1 *Pet.* 2. [13.]) approveth of the feverall humane *Ordinances* (or *Creations*) which the feverall *peoples* and *Nations* of the *World* fhall agree upon their *common peace* and *fubfiftence.* Hence are the feverall *forts* of *Governments* in the *Nations* of the *World,* which are not framed after All Civill Govern-ment Gods Or-dinance.

Iſraels Patterne. And hence conſequently, the *Lawes, Rewards* and *Puniſhments* of ſeverall *Nations* vaſtly differ from thoſe of *Iſraell,* which doubtles were unlawfull for *Gods* people to ſubmit unto, except *Chriſt Jeſus* had (at leaſt in generall) approved ſuch humane *Ordinances* and *Creations* of Men for their *common peace* and *wellſare.*

294] *Peace.* Me-thinks Mr *Cotton,* and ſuch as literally ſtick to the *puniſhment* of *Adultery, Witchcraſt,* &c. by *Death,* muſt either deny the ſeverall *Governments* of the *World* to be lawfull (according to that of *Peter*) and that the *Nature* and *Conſtitutions* of *peoples* and *Nations,* are not to be reſpected, but all promiſcuouſly forced to one *common Law,* or els they muſt ſee cauſe to moderate this their *Tenent,* which elſe proves as bloudie a *Tenent* in *civill affaires,* as *perſecution* in *affaires religious.*

True Republikes & Common weales without Kings.

Truth. Yea, of what *wofull conſequence* muſt this prove to the ſtate of *Holland* and *Low-Countries,* to the *State* of *Venice,* to the *Cantons* of *Switzerland,* to our owne deare *State* of *England,* and others who have no *King,* as *Iſraells* laſt eſtabliſhed *Government* had, eſpecially no *King* immediately deſigned, as *Iſraells* (in the *Roote*) was? Yea what becomes of all *Chriſtianitie,* and of *Chriſts Church* and *Kingdome* in the *World* for ever, if it want the *Government* of a *King:* for ſayth Biſhop *Hall* (in his *Contemplation* on *Michaes Idolatrie*) in plaine and expreſſe words: No *King,* therefore no *Church.*[1]

A wonderfull ſaying of Biſhop *Hall.*

[1] “It is no marvell if Levites wandred for maintenance, while there was no King in Iſrael. The tithes and offerings were their due: if theſe had been paid, none of the holy Tribe needed to ſhift his ſtation. Even when Royall power

Peace. To end this paſſage, upon the former grounds, me-thinkes the *Conſcience* of a *New Engliſh Magiſtrate* (being calld to be a *Magiſtrate* in *Old England*) may in *Faith* execute any other puniſhment (according to *Law* eſtabliſhed) beſide Death, upon *Adulterers.* And the *New Engliſh Colonies* may be exhorted to rectifie their wayes, and to moderate ſuch their *Lawes*, which cannot poſſibly put on the face of *morall Equitie* from *Moſes*, &c.

The State of *Iſrael.*

Truth. Your *Satisfaction* (Deare *Peace*) now præſuppoſed I proceed and grant (with that *Limitation* forementioned) that *Chriſt Jeſus* neither abrogated *Moſes Moralls* nor *Judicialls*, yet who will deny that *Moſes* eſtabliſhed, (beſide the two former) a third, to wit, *Lawes* meerly *figurative, typicall* and *ceremoniall*, proper and peculiar to that Land and people of *Iſrael?* Thoſe *Lawes* neceſſarily wrapt up that *Nation* and people in a *mixt conſtitution*, of *Spirituall* and *Temporall*, *Religious* and *Civill*, ſo that their *Governours* of *Civill State* were *Governours* of the *Church*, and the very *Land* and *People* were by ſuch *Governours* to be compelled to obſerve a *ceremoniall puritie* and *Holines:* But *Chriſt Jeſus* erected another *Common-weale*, the *Common-* [295] *weale* of *Iſrael, the Chriſtian Common-weale* or *Church*, to wit, not whole *Nations*, but in every *Nation* (where he pleaſeth) his *Chriſtian Congregation*, &c.

ſeconds the claime of the Levite, the injuſtice of men ſhortens his right. What ſhould become of the Levites, if there were no King? And what of the Church, if no Levites? No King, therefore no Church." *Contemplations.* Liber x. 940: ed. 1621.

Peace. Deare *Truth*, I cannot count him a *peaceable* childe of mine, that refts not herewith fatisfied: M[r] *Cottons* next *Exception* is againft your excepting againft a *Magiftrates* Memberfhip in a *Church-eftate*, joyned with a *Head-fhip* over it, to eftablifh reforme, &c. (as being impoffible that a *Magiftrate* fhould fit Head and Supreame on the *fpirituall Bench*, & yet ftand as a delinquent at the *fpirituall Barre* of *Chrift Jefus*) M[r] *Cotton* anfwers, that in feverall refpects, a *Magiftrate* may be a nurfing *Father* and *Judge* in caufes *Ecclefiaftiall*, and yet be fubject to *Chrifts* cenfure in the offenfive *Government* of *himfelfe* againft the *Rules* of the *Gofpel*. And where it might be faid, that the *Church* is fubject to the *Magiftrate* in *civill caufes*, and the *Magiftrate* is fubject to the *Church* in *fpirituall cafes*, M[r] *Cotton* anfwers, this eafeth not the *Difficultie*, for fuppofe, fayth he, the *Magiftrate* fall into *Murther*, *Adulterie*, &c. which are *civill Abufes*, fhall the *Church* tollerate him herein? And he concludes, Let the like *Power* be granted to the *civill Magiftrate* to deale faithfully with the *Church* in the notorious *Tranfgreffion* of the firft Table, as is granted to the *Church* to deale with the *Magiftrate* in the notorious *Tranfgreffion* of the *fecond Table*, and the *Controverfie* is ended.

Of *Magiftrates* being nurfing Fathers, &c.

Of *Magiftrates* Power in Spiritualls

Truth. This anfwer and inftance of M[r] *Cotton* carries a feeming *Beautie* with it, but bring it to the *Triall* of the *Teftament* of *Chrift Jefus*, and it will appeare to be, but a vanifhing *Colour*. For, there is a vaft *Difference:* The fins of each *Church-member*, whether againft the *firft* or *fecond Table*, are

Magistrates.

proper to the *Cognizance* and *Judgement* of the *Church*, as the *ſinne* of the *Inceſtuous* perſon was puniſhed by *Chriſts Ordinances* (in the *Church* at *Corinth*) as well as the Abuſe of the *Lords Supper*. But it is not ſo with the *civill Magiſtrate*, whoſe *Office* is *eſſentially civill*, one and the ſame, all the world over, among all *Nations* and *people:* For having no *ſpirituall power* (as the *Authours* of the *Modell* afterwards acknowledge) he cannot poſſibly act as a *Civill Magiſtrate* in *ſpirituall matters*, though as a *Church-member* he may in *Church-eſtate*, as alſo may the reſt of the Members of that ſpirituall Body.

A caſe touching the Magiſtrates puniſhing the Sin of Church members.

296] *Peace*. Me-thinks it is cleare as the Light, that if that inceſtuous perſon in the *Church* of *Corinth*, had beene a M*agiſtrate* in the *Citie* of *Corinth*, the *Church* might juſtly have proceeded againſt him, becauſe all ſinne is direcctly oppoſite to the holy *Kingdome* of *Chriſt*. But in that abuſe of the *Lords Supper* (which was meerly unchriſtian) neither that M*agiſtrate*, nor all the M*agiſtrates* of *Corinth*, or the *World* to helpe him, could juſtly puniſh the *Church*, becauſe that *Supper* (in the *Inſtitution* and *Spirituall* uſe of it) was not onely of the *Nature* of the *Suppers*, of the meates and drinks of the *Citie* of *Corinth*, but alſo of a *divine* and *ſpirituall Inſtitution*, of a heavenly and *myſticall Nature* and *Obſervation*. But to Conclude this piece and the whole, M[r] *Cotton* corrects himſelfe for putting in his *Sickle* into the *Harveſt* of his *Brethren*, unto whom he refers the defence of their M*odell*, and for himſelfe ends with deſires that *Chriſt Jeſus* would blaſt that peace which he ſayth the *Examiner* proclaimeth to all the wayes of falſe *Religion*, to *Hereſie* in *Doctrine*, &c.

Truth. If *Chriſt Jeſus* ſhall pleaſe (for the further *manifeſtation* of his holy *Truth* and *Glory*) to permit thoſe *able* and *worthy men*, to proceed to fortifie and defend their *Modell:* I hope he will alſo pleaſe to aſſiſt the *Diſcuſſer*, or ſome other of his poore ſervants, to batter downe (with the *Spirituall Artillerie* of his *Word* and *Teſtament*) ſuch weake and looſe and *unchriſtian Fortifications*.

Peace. But with what a *deepe* and *unrighteous charge* doth Mr *Cotton* end againſt the poore *Diſcuſſer*, as a *Proclaimer* of *peace* to all the *wayes* of falſe *Religion*, to *Hereſie* in *Doctrine*, &c.

Truth. Grant Mr *Cotton* (in many excellent *Truths* of *Jeſus*) a ſweet ſounding *Silver Trumpet:* Grant the *Diſcuſſer* as baſe a *Rams-horne* harsh and contemptible*:* Grant that (for the *peace* of the *Civill State*, the being of the *Nations*, and the *World*, the *ſafetie* of the good *Wheate* the *Righteous*, and the calling home of the Elect to *God*, *Jewes* and *Gentiles!*) the *Diſcuſſer* proclaimes a *civill being*, and *civill peace* to *Erroneous Conſciences*, not ſinning againſt humane and *civill Principles:* Yet what *Peace* hath this *Rams-horne* proclaimed (as Mr *Cotton* inſinuates) when throughout this whole Booke, from [297] firſt to laſt, the *Proclamation* ſoundeth out *open warre* againſt all falſe *Worſhippers*.

The direfull ſtate of falſe Worſhippers.

Peace. I am a joyfull *witnes* of *warre* proclaimed from the *God* of *Truth*, from the *Sun* of *Righteouſneſſe*, from the *Spirit* of *Holines*, from the ſlames of Fire, those mighty *Angels*, from all the *Saints* and

Witneſſes of *Jeſus*, from all his holy *Truths* and *Ordinances*. *Warre* to their *Conſciences*, *Preachings*, *Writings*, *Diſputations*, a *warre present*, a warre *perpetuall*, and (without *Repentance*) a warre *eternall* and *everlaſting*.

Truth. Deare *Peace*, our *goulden ſand* is out, we now muſt part with an holy *Kiſſe* of heavenly *Peace* and *Love*: Mr *Cotton* ſpeakes and writes his *Conſcience*: Yet the *Father* of *Lights* may pleaſe to ſhew him that what he highly eſteemes as a *Tenent* waſht white in the *Lambes bloud*, is yet more *black* and *abominable*, in the moſt *pure* and jealous *eye* of *God*.

Peace. The *Blackmores Darknes* differs not in the *darke* from the *fayreſt white*.

Truth. *Chriſt Jeſus* the *Sun* of *Righteouſneſſe* hath broke forth, and dayly, will, to a *brighter* and *brighter Diſcoverie* of this deformed *Ethiopian*: And for my ſelfe I muſt proclaime, before the moſt holy *God*, *Angells* and *Men*, that (what ever other *white* and heavenly *Tenents* Mr *Cotton* houlds) yet this is a *fowle*, a *black*, and a *bloudie Tenent*. The Portraiture of the *Bloudie Tenent*.

A *Tenent* of high *Blaſphemie* againſt the *God* of *Peace*, the *God* of *Order*, who hath of one *Bloud*, made all *Mankinde*, to dwell upon the face of the Earth, now, all *confounded* and *deſtroyed* in their *Civill Beings* and *Subſiſtences*, by mutuall flames of *warre* from their ſeverall reſpective *Religions* and *Conſciences*.

A *Tenent warring* againſt the *Prince* of *Peace*,

Chriſt Jeſus, denying his *Appearance* and *Comming* in the *Fleſh*, to put an end to, and *aboliſh* the *ſhadowes* of that *ceremoniall* and *typicall* Land of *Canaan*.

A *Tenent* fighting againſt the ſweete *end* of his
Luc. 9. *comming*, which was not to deſtroy mens *Lives*,
for their *Religions*, but to ſave them, by the meeke
Prov. 9. and peaceable *Invitations* and *perſwaſions* of his
peaceable *wiſdomes Maidens*.

The Portraiture of the *bloudie Tenent.* 298] A *Tenent* fowly charging his *Wiſedome*, *Faithfullnes* and *Love*, in ſo poorly providing ſuch *Magistrates* and *Civill Powers* all the *World* over, as might effect ſo great a *charge* pretended to be committed to them.

A *Tenent* lamentably guilty of his moſt precious *bloud*, ſhed in the *bloud* of ſo many hundreth thouſand of his poore *ſervants* by the *civill powers* of the *World*, pretending to ſuppreſſe *Blaſphemies*, *Hereſies*, *Idolatries*, *Superſtition*, &c.

A *Tenent* fighting with the *Spirit* of *Love*, *Holines*, and *Meeknes*, by kindling fiery *Spirits* of *falſe zeale* and *Furie*, when yet ſuch *Spirits* know not of what *Spirit* they are.

A *Tenent* fighting with those mighty *Angels* who ſtand up for the peace of the *Saints*, againſt *Perſia*, *Grecia*, &c. and ſo conſequently, all other *Nations*, who fighting for their ſeverall *Religions*, and againſt the *Truth*, leave no *Roome* for ſuch as feare and love the *Lord* on the Earth.

A *Tenent*, againſt which the bleſſed *Soules* under the *Altar* cry loud for *vengeance*, this *Tenent* having cut their *Throats*, torne out their *Hearts*, and powred forth their *Bloud* in all *Ages*, as the onely *Hereticks* and *Blaſphemers* in the World.

The Portraiture of the *bloudie Tenent.*

A *Tenent* which no *Uncleannes*, no *Adulterie*, *Inceſt*, *Sodomie*, or *Beaſtialitie* can equall, this *raviſhing* and forcing (*explicitly* or *implicitly*) the very *Soules* and *Conſciences* of all the *Nations* and *Inhabitants* of the *World*.

A *Tenent* that puts out the very *eye* of all true *Faith*, which cannot but be as free and voluntarie as any *Virgin* in the *World*, in *refuſing* or *embracing* any *ſpirituall offer* or *object*.

A *Tenent* loathſome and ugly (in the eyes of the *God* of *Heaven*, and ſerious ſonnes of men) I ſay, loathſome with the palpable *filths* of *groſſe diſſimulation* and *hypocriſie*: Thouſands of *Peoples* and whole *Nations*, compelld by this *Tenent* to put on the ſowle *vizard* of *Religious hypocriſie*, for feare of [299] *Lawes*, *loſſes* and *puniſhments*, and for the keeping and hoping for of *favour*, *libertie*, *wordly commoditie*, &c.

A *Tenent* wofully guiltie of hardning all falſe and *deluded Conſciences* (of whatſoever *Sect*, *Faction*,

The Portraiture of the *bloudy* *Tenent.*

Heresie, or *Idolatrie*, though never ſo *horrid* and *blaſphemous*) by *cruelties* and *violences* practiced againſt them: all falſe *Teachers* and their *Followers* (ordinarily) contracting a *Brawnie* and *ſteelie hardneſſe* from their *ſufferings* for their *Conſciences*.

A *Tenent* that ſhuts and bars out the gracious *prophecies* and *promiſes* and *diſcoveries* of the moſt glorious *Sun* of *Righteouſnes, Chriſt Jeſus*, that burnes up the holy *Scriptures*, and forbids them (upon the point) to be read in *Engliſh*, or that any *tryall* or *ſearch*, or (truly) free *diſquiſition* be made by them: when the moſt able, diligent and conſcionable *Readers* muſt pluck forth their own *eyes*, and be forced to reade by the (which ſoever *prædominant*) *Cleargies Spectacles*.

A *Tenent* that *ſeales up* the ſpirituall *graves* of all men, *Jewes* and *Gentiles*, (and conſequently ſtands guiltie of the *damnation* of all men) ſince no *Preachers*, nor *Trumpets* of *Chriſt* himſelfe may call them out, but ſuch as the ſeverall and reſpective *Nations* of the *World* themſelves allow of.

The Portraiture of the *bloudie* *Tenent.*

A *Tenent* that fights againſt the *common principles* of all *Civilitie*, and the very *civill being* and *combinations* of *men* in *Nations, Cities*, &c. by commixing (*explicitly* or *implicitly*) a *ſpirituall* and *civill State* together, and ſo confounding and overthrowing the *puritie* and *ſtrength* of both.

A *Tenent* that kindles the devouring *flames* of

combuſtions and *warres* in moſt *Nations* of the *World*, and (if *God* were not infinitely gracious) had almoſt ruind the *Engliſh*, *French*, the *Scotch* and *Iriſh*, and many other *Nations*, *Germane*, *Polonian*, *Hungarian*, *Bohemian*, &c.

A *Tenent* that bowes downe the *backs* and *necks* of all *civill States* and *Magiſtrates*, *Kings* and *Emperours*, under the proud feete of that *man* and *monſter* of *ſinne* and *pride* the *Pope*, and all [300] *Popiſh* and proud *Cleargie-men* rendring ſuch *Laicks* and *Seculars* (as they call them) but ſlaviſh *Executioners* (upon the point) of their moſt imperious *Synodicall Decrees* and *Sentences*.

A *Tenent* that renders the highest *civill Magiſtrates* and *Miniſters* of *Juſtice* (the *Fathers* and *Gods* of their *Countries*) either odious or lamentably grievous unto the very beſt *Subjects* by either clapping or keeping on, the *iron yoakes* of cruelleſt *oppreſſion*. No *yoake* or *bondage* comparably ſo grievous, as that upon the Soules necke of mens *Religion* and *Conſciences*.

The Portraiture of the *bloudie Tenent.*

A *Tenent*, all beſprinckled with the *bloudie murthers*, *ſtobs*, *poyſonings*, *piſtollings*, *powder-plots*, &c. againſt many famous *Kings*, *Princes*, and *States*, either actually performed or attempted, in *France*, *England*, *Scotland*, *Low-Countries*, and other *Nations*.

A *Tenent* all *red* and *bloudie* with thoſe moſt *barbarous* and *Tyger*-like *Maſſacres*, of ſo many thouſand and ten thouſands formerly in *France*, and other parts, and ſo lately and ſo horribly in *Ireland:* of which, what ever cauſes be aſſigned, this chiefly will be found the true, and while this continues (to wit, *violence* againſt *Conſcience*) this *bloudie Iſſue*, ſooner or later, muſt *breake forth* againe (except *God* wonderfully ſtop it) in *Ireland* and other places too.

The Portraiture of the *bloudie Tenent.*

A *Tenent* that *ſtunts* the *growth* and *flouriſhing* of the moſt likely and hopefulleſt *Common-weales* and *Countries*, while *Conſciences*, the *beſt*, and the *beſt* deſerving *Subjects* are forct to flie (by enforced or voluntary *Baniſhment*) from their native *Countries*; The lamentable proofe whereof *England* hath felt in the flight of ſo many worthy *Engliſh*, into the *Low Countries* and *New England*, and from *New England* into old againe and other forraigne parts.

A *Tenent* whoſe groſſe partialitie denies the *Principles* of *common Juſtice*, while *Men* waigh out to the *Conſciences* of all others, that which they judge not fit nor right to be waighed out to their owne: Since the *perſecu ours Rule* is, to take and perſecute all *Conſciences*, onely, *himſelfe* muſt not be touched.

301] A *Tenent* that is but *Macheviliſme*, and makes a *Religion*, but a *cloake* or *ſtalking horſe* to *policie* and *private Ends* of *Jeroboams Crowne*, and the *Prieſts Beneſice*, &c.

A *Tenent* that *corrupts* and *ſpoiles* the very *Civill Honeſtie* and *Naturall Conſcience* of a *Nation*. Since

Conſcience to *God* violated, proves (without *Repentance*) ever after, a very *Jade*, a *Drug*, looſe and *unconſcionable* in all converſe with men.

Laſtly, a *Tenent* in *England* moſt unſeaſonable, as powring *Oyle* upon thoſe *Flames* which the high *Wiſdome* of the *Parliament*, (by eaſing the yoakes on Mens *Conſciences*) had begun to quench.

In the ſad Conſideration of all which (Deare *Peace*) let *Heaven* and *Earth* judge of the *waſhing* and *colour* of this *Tenent*. For thee *ſweete heavenly Gueſt*) goe lodge thee in the *breaſts* of the *peaceable* and humble *Witneſſes* of *Jeſus*, that love the *Truth* in *peace!* Hide thee from the Worlds *Tumults* and *Combuſtions*, in the breaſts of thy truely *noble children*, who profeſſe and *endeavour* to breake the *irony* and inſupportable *yoakes* upon the *Soules* and *Conſciences* of any of the ſonnes of Men. Peace her Repoſe and Tabernacle.

Peace. Me-thinkes (Deare *Truth*) if any of the leaſt of theſe deepe charges be found againſt this *Tenent*, you doe not wrong it when you ſtile it *bloudie:* But ſince, in the wofull proofe of all *Ages* paſt, ſince *Nimrod* (the *Hunter* or *perſecutour* before the *Lord*) theſe and more are lamentably evident and undeniable: it gives me wonder that ſo many and ſo excellent *eyes* of *Gods* ſervants ſhould not eſpie ſo fowle a *monſter*, eſpecially conſidering the *univerſall oppoſition* this *Tenent* makes againſt *Gods Glory*, and the *Good* of all mankinde.

Truth. There hath been many fowle *opinions*, with which the *old Serpent* hath infected and be-

The *Bloudie Tenent* of perſecution compared.

witched the ſonnes of men (touching *God*, *Chriſt*, the *Spirit*, the *Church*, againſt *Holines*, againſt *Peace*, againſt *civill Obedience*, againſt *chaſtitie*) in ſo much, that even *Sodomie* it ſelfe hath been a *Tenent* maintained in print by ſome of the very *pillars* of the *Church* of *Rome:* But this *Tenent* is ſo univerſally oppoſite to *God* and *man*, ſo pernicious and deſtructive to both (as hath been declared) that [302] like the *Powder-plot*, it threatens to blow up all *Religion*, all *civilitie*, all *humanitie*, yea the very *Being* of the *World*, and the *Nations* thereof at once.

Peace. He that is the *Father* of *Lies*, and a *murtherer* from the beginning, he knowes this well, and this ugly *Blackmore* needs a *maſke* or *vizard.*

The maſkes and vizards of the *bloudie Tenent.*

Truth. Yea the *bloudines* and *inhumantie* of it is ſuch, that not onely Mr *Cottons* more tender and holy Breaſt, but even the moſt bloudie *Bonners* and *Gardiners* have been forced to arme themſelves with the faire *ſhewes* and glorious *pretences*, of the *Glory* of *God*, and *zeale* for that *Glory*, the *Love* of his *Truth*, the *Goſpel* of *Chriſt Jeſus*, *love* and *pitie* to mens ſoules, the *peace* of the *Church*, *uniformitie*, *Order*, the *peace* of the *Common-weale*, the *Wiſedome of the State*, the *Kings*, *Queenes* and *Parliaments* proceedings, the *odiouſneſſe* of *Sects*, *Hereſies*, *Blaſphemies*, *Novelties*, *Seducers*, and their *Infections:* the *obſtinacie* of *Hereticks*, after all *Meanes*, *Diſputations*, *Examinations*, *Synods*, yea and after *Conviction* in the poore *Hereticks* owne *Conſcience:* Add to theſe the flattring ſound of thoſe gloſing *Titles*, the *Godly Magiſtrate*, the *Chriſtian Magiſtrate*, the *Nurcing Fathers* and *Mothers* of the *Church*, *Chriſtian Kings* and

Queenes. But all other *Kings* and *Magiſtrates* (even all the *Nations* of the *World* over, as Mr *Cotton* pleads) muſt ſuſpend and hould their hands, and not meddle in *matters* of *Religion*, untill they be informed, &c.

Peace. The dreadfull righteous hand of *God*, the *Eternall* and avenging *God*, is pulling off theſe *maskes* and *vizards*, that *thouſands*, and the *World* may ſee this *bloudie Tenents Beautie.*

Truth & Peace, their meetings ſeldome and ſhort.

Truth. But ſee (my *heavenly Siſter* and true *ſtranger* in this Sea-like reſtles, raging World) ſee here what *Fires* and *Swords* are come to part us! Well; Our *meetings* in the Heavens ſhall not thus be interrupted, our *Kiſſes* thus *diſtracted*, and our *eyes* and *cheekes* thus *wet*, *unwiped:* For me, though *cenſured*, *threatned*, *perſecuted*, I muſt profeſſe, while *Heaven* and *Earth* laſts, that no one *Tenent* that either *London*, *England*, or the *World* doth harbour, is ſo *hereticall*, *blaſphemous*, *ſeditious*, and *dangerous* to the *corporall*, to the *ſpirituall*, to the *preſent*, to the *Eternall* Good of all Men, as the *bloudie Tenent* (how ever *waſh't* and *whited*) I say, as is the *bloudie Tenent* of *perſecution* for cauſe of *Conſcience.*

The Copie of a Letter of R. *Williams* of *Providence* in *New England*, to Major *Endicot*, Governour of the *Massachusets*,[1] upon *occasion of the late persecution against* Mr Clarke *and* Obadiah Holmes, *and others at* Boston *the chiefe Towne of the* Massachusets *in* New England.

SIR,

*Matters touching the peace of the *English* and *Indians*, about which the said Governour did write to *R. W.*[2]

HAving done with our transitorie Earthly *Affaires (as touching the *English* and the *Indians*) which in Comparison of heavenly and *Eternall* you will say are but as dung and drosse, &c. Let me now be humbly bold to remember that *Humanitie* and *pietie*, which I and others have formerly observed in you, and in that hopefull Remembrance to crave your gentle *audience* with *patience* and *mildnes*, with *ingenuitie*, *equanimitie*

[1] John Endicott was one of the six original patentees of Massachusetts. He arrived at Salem, Sept. 6, 1628. In the following year he was appointed Governor, and held the office until Winthrop's arrival in 1630. He was afterwards Deputy-Governor for four years, and was Governor for sixteen years. In 1645 he was put in command of the military force as "Sergeant-Major General," and hence prohably received the title with which Williams here addresses him. He had passed the sentence upon Clarke and Holmes, being Governor, at that time. *Ill Newes*, 4 *Mass. Hist. Coll.* ii. 31–39,

[2] Gov. Endicott writes to John Winthrop, jr., "Salem the 15, 6, 51," that is August 15, 1651: "I have written Mr. Williams an answer to his letter you were pleased to bring mee, and I hope to satisfaccon as much as lyes in mee. And I heartilie desire you that you will labour with the Sachems of the Narragansetts, Ninecroft and Mixam, till their complaints be heard and answered, &c." 4 *Mass. Hist. Coll.* vi: 153.

and *candour*, to him that ever truely and deeply loved you and yours, and as in the awfull preſence of his holy *Eye*, whoſe dreadfull *hand* hath formed us to the praiſe of his *mercy* or *Juſtice* to all *Eternitie*.

Sir, I have often feared and ſaid within my Soule, Have I ſo deeply *loved* and reſpected? Was I alſo ſo well *beloved?* Or was all *counterfeit*, and but guilded o'er with earthly Reſpects, Worldly ends, &c. Why am I ſilent? my Letters are not *Baniſhed!* may be wellcome, may be ſeene and heard, and if neither, yet will back againe (together with my *prayers* and cries) into my *Boſome*.

Great love formerly between the ſaid Governour *Endicot*, and *R. W.* before his Baniſhment.

Thus while I have ſometimes muſed and reſolved! *Objections*, *Obſtructions*, and a thouſand hindrances (I feare from *Sathan* as *Paul* ſaid) have preſt in, held my hand, &c.

Sir, it hath pleaſed the Father of *Spirits* at this preſent to ſmite my heart in the very breaking up of your Letter: This **Deaths Head* tells that loving *Hand* that ſeald it, and mine that opens your *Letter*, that our *Eyes*, our *Hands*, our *Tongues*, [304] our *Braines* are flying hence to the hole or pit of *Rottennes:* Why ſhould not therefore ſuch our *Letters*, ſuch our *Speeches*, ſuch our *Actings* be, as may become our laſt *minutes*, our *Death-beds*, &c.

*The Seale wherewith the Governours Leter to *R. W.* was ſealed.[1]

If ſo, how *meeke* and *humble*, how *plaine* and *ſerious*, how *faithfull* and *zealous*, and yet how tender and *loving* ſhould the *Spirits* and *Speeches* be of dying and departing Men?

Sir, While ſomething of this Nature I muſe over

[1] Endicott's ſeal was a death's head and croſs-bones, with the name of John Garrad in a circle round it. A facſimile of it is given in 4 *Maſs. Hiſt. Coll.* vi. Appendix ii.

your *Deaths head*, I meete (in the Entrance of your "Letter) with this paſſage [*Were I as free in my* "*ſpirit as formerly I have been to write unto you, you* "*ſhould have received another manner of Salutation* "*then now with a good Conſcience I can Expreſſe*; "*However God knoweth who are his, and what he is* "*pleaſed to hide from ſinfull man in this life, ſhall in* "*that great Day be maniſeſted to All.*]

Perſecutours conclude no *conſcience* in the whole world but their own.

Sir, at the reading of this Line, (I cannot but hope I have your leave to tell you) The ſpeech of that wiſe Woman of *Tekoah* unto *David* came freſh unto my Thoughts: Speakes not the *King* this Thing as one that is *Guiltie?* For will my honoured and beloved ſriend not know me for feare of being diſowned by his *Conſcience?* Shall the *Goodnes* and *Integritie* of his *Conſcience* to *God* cauſe him to forget me? Doth he quiet his minde with this; [*God* knoweth who are his? *God* hides from ſinfull man, *God* will reveale before All?] Oh how comes it then that I have heard ſo often, and heard ſo lately, and heard ſo much, that he that ſpeakes ſo tenderly for his owne, hath yet ſo little reſpect, mercie or pitie to the like *conſciencious* perſwaſions of othet Men? Are all the Thouſands of *millions* of *millions* of *Conſciences*, at home and abroad, fuell onely for a *priſon*, for a *whip*, for a *ſtake*, for a *Gallowes?* Are no *Conſciences* to breathe the *Aire*, but ſuch as ſuit and ſample his? May not the *moſt High* be pleaſed to hide from his as well as from the eyes of his fellow-*Servants*, fellow-*mankinde*, fellow-*Engliſh?* And if *God* hide from his, from any, who can diſcover? Who can ſhut when he will open?

and who can open when he that hath the key of *David* will ſhut? All this and more (honored Sir) your words will warrant me to ſay, without any juſt offence or ſtraining.

Object. But what makes this to *Heretickes, Blaſphemers, Seducers,* to them that ſin againſt their *Conſcience* (as Mr *Cotton* [305] ſayth) after *Conviction?* What makes this to ſtobbers of *Kings* and *Princes,* to blowers up of *Parliaments* out of *Conſcience?*

Firſt, I anſwer, He was a *Tyrant* that put an Innocent Man into a *Beares*-skin, and ſo cauſed him as a wild *Beaſt* to be baited to Death.

Secondly, I ſay this is the common cry of *Hunters* or *perſecutours* [*Hereticks, Hereticks, Blaſphemers,* &c.] and why, but for croſſing the perſecutours *Conſciences,* (it may be but their ſuperſtitions, &c.) whether *Turkiſh, Popiſh, Proteſtant,* &c.

All perſecutours render the moſt innocent moſt odious.

This is the Outcry of the *Pope* and *Prelates,* and of the *Scotch Preſbyterians,* who would fire all the world, to be avenged on the *Sectarian Heretickes,* the blaſphemous *Heretickes,* the ſeducing *Heretickes,* &c. had it not pleaſed the God of Heaven who bounds the inſolent Rage of the furious *Ocean,* to raiſe up a ſecond *Cromwell* (like a mighty and mercifull *Wall* or *Bullwark*) to ſtay the Furie of the *Oppreſſour,* whether *Engliſh, Scottiſh, Popiſh, Preſbyterian, Independent,* &c.

Cromwell the ſecond, a Refuge of the oppreſſed.

Laſtly, I have ſaid much and lately, and given particular Anſwers to all ſuch pleas, in my Second Reply or Anſwer to Mr *Cottons* waſhing of the *Bloudie Tenent* in the *Lambes* bloud, which it may be is not yet come to your ſight and Hand.

This Rejoynder was ſent to *England* long ſince, and hoped to have been publiſhed.

'Tis true, I have to ſay elſewhere about the *Cauſes* of my *Baniſhment*: as to the calling of *Naturall* Men to the exerciſe of thoſe holy *Ordinances* of *Prayers*, *Oathes*, &c. As to the frequenting of *Pariſh Churches*, under the pretence of hearing *ſome Miniſters*: As to the matter of the *Patent*, and King *James* his *Chriſtianitie* and *Title* to theſe parts, and beſtowing it on his Subjects by vertue of his being a *Chriſtian King*, &c.

At preſent, let it not be offenſive in your eyes, that I ſingle out another, a fourth point, a cauſe of my *Baniſhment* alſo, wherein I greatly feare one or two ſad evills, which hath befallen your *Soule* and *Conſcience*.[1]

The point is that of the *Civill Magiſtrates* dealing in matters of *Conſcience* and *Religion*, as alſo of perſecuting and hunting any for any matter meerly *Spirituall* and *Religious*.

The two Evills intimated are theſe; Firſt, I feare you cannot after ſo much *Light*, and ſo much profeſſion to the contrary (not onely to my ſelfe, and ſo often in private, but) before ſo many Witneſſes; I ſay, I feare you cannot ſay and [306] act ſo much, againſt ſo many ſeverall *Conſciences*, former and later, but with great *Checks*, great *Threatnings*, great *Blowes* and *Throwes* of inward *Conſcience*.

[1] *Mr Cottons Letter examined and anſwered*, pp. 4, 5. *Pub. Narr. Club*, i: 40, 41. Cotton gives his version of the cauſes of Williams' baniſhment in his *Anſwer* 27–31. *Pub. Narr. Club*, ii, 44-52. He ſays, "It is evident the two latter cauſes which he giveth of his Baniſhment," the ſecond and fourth named above, "were no cauſes at all, as he expreſſeth them. There are many knowne to hold both theſe opinions, and yet they are tolerated not only to live in the Commonwealth, but alſo in the fellowſhip of the Churches."

Secondly, If you ſhall thanke *God*, that it is not ſo with you, but that you doe what *Conſcience* bids you in *Gods* preſence, upon *Gods* warrant, I muſt then be humbly faithfull to tell you, that I feare your underprizing of holy *Light*, hath put out the *Candle*, and the *Eye* of *Conſcience* in theſe particulars, and that *Deluſions*, ſtrong *Deluſions*, and that from *God* (by *Sathan*s ſubtletie) hath ſeaſd upon your very *Soules* beliefe, becauſe you priz'd not lov'd not the indangered perſecuted Son of *God* in his deſpiſed *Truths* and *Servants*.

Abuse of light moſt dangerous.

Sir, With Man (as the *Lord Jeſus* ſaid of the *Rich man*) I know it is impoſſible for the (otherwiſe piercing) *eye* of your underſtanding to ſee into theſe things, for it is *diſcoloured*, as in ſome *Diseaſes* and *Glaſſes*; It is impoſſible for your *Will* to be willing to ſee, for that's in a thouſand chaines reſolved (as once you ſpake *heroically* and *heavenly* in a better way) to ſpend your deareſt *Heart bloud* in your way, &c. Yet with *God* all things are poſſible, and they that laughed the *Lord Jeſus* to ſcorne when he ſaid, the *Damſell* is not *dead* but *ſleepeth*, were afterwards confounded, when they ſaw her raiſed by his heavenly voice.

His holy pleaſure I know not, nor doe I know which way the *Glory* of his great Name will more appeare, either in finally ſuffering ſo great a *fall* and *ruine* of ſo ſtrong a *pillar*, that *Fleſh* may not *Glory*, but that his *ſtrength* and *Glory* onely may be ſeene in *Weakneſſe*. Or elſe in your holy *Riſing* and *Reviving* from the *Bed* of ſo much ſpirituall filthines, and from ſo *bloudie* a *minde*, and *lip*, and *hand*, againſt *all withſtanders* or *Diſturbers* in it. That ſo the ſhort *Remainder* of your *Candle* may hould out to the World, the *Riches* of his *Mercy*, at whoſe words the holyeſt of his Servants ought to tremble, and to work out their Salvation with feare and trembling: I ſay, I deſire to ſay it, tremblingly and mournfully) I know not which way he will pleaſe to raiſe his *Glory*) onely I know my *Dutie*, my *Conſcience*, my *Love*, all which enforce me to knock, to call to cry at the Gate of *Heaven*, and at *Yours*, and to preſent you with this loving, though lowd and faithfull noyſe and ſound of a [307] few Grounds of deeper Examination of both our *Soules* and *Conſciences* uprightly and impartially at the holy and dreadfull *Tribunall* of Him that is appointed the *Judge* of all the *Living* and the *Dead*.

Be pleaſed then (honored Sir) to remember that that thing which we call *Conſcience* is of ſuch a Nature (eſpecially in *Engliſh-men*) as once a *Pope* of *Rome* at the ſuffering of an *Engliſh-man* in *Rome*, himſelfe obſerved) that although it be groundles, falſe, and deluded, yet it is not by any *Arguments* or *Torments* eaſily removed.

The power of Conſcience though Erroneous

I ſpeake not of the ſtreame of the multitude of all *Nations*, which have their *ebbings* and *flowings* in *Religion*, (as the longeſt *Sword*, and ſtrongeſt *Arme* of *Fleſh* carries it) But I ſpeake of *Conſcience*, a *perſwaſion* fixed in the minde and heart of a man, which enforceth him to judge (as *Paul* ſaid of himſelfe a *perſecutour*) and to doe ſo and ſo, with reſpect to *God*, his worſhip, &c.

This *Conſcience* is found in all mankinde, more

or leſſe, in *Jewes*, *Turkes*, *Papiſts*, *Proteſtants*, *Pagans*, &c. And to this purpoſe let me freely without offence remember you (as I did Mr *Clarke* newly come up from his ſufferings amongſt you) I ſay, remember you of the ſame *Story* I did him, twas that of *William Hartly* in Queene *Elizabeth* her dayes, who receiving the Sentence of *hanging*, *drawing*, &c. ſpake confidently (as afterward he ſuffered) what tell you me of *hanging*, &c. If I had ten thouſand millions of *lives*, I would ſpend them all for the *Faith* of *Rome*, &c.[1]

True & falſe Witneſſes both Confident.

Sir, I am far from glancing the leaſt Countenance on the *Conſciences* of *Papiſts*, yea or on ſome *Scotch* and *Engliſh Proteſtants* too, who turne up all *Rootes*, and lay all *levell* and in bloud, for exaltation of their own *way* and *Conſcience*. All that I obſerve is, that *Boldnes* and *Confidence*, *Zeale* and *Reſolution*, as it is commendable in a kinde when it ſeriouſly reſpects a *Dietie*, ſo alſo, the greateſt *Confidence* hath ſometimes need of the greateſt *Search* and *Examination*.

I confeſſe, that for Confidence no *Romiſh Prieſt*, hath ever exceeded the holy *Martyrs* or *Witneſſes* of *Jeſus*: Witnes (amongſt ſo many) that holy *Engliſh Woman*, who cryed out, that if every *haire* of her head were a *life* or man, they ſhould burne

[1] William Hartley was of St. John's College, Oxford, and a Roman Catholic Prieſt. When Campian, the Jeſuit emiſſary, came to England in 1580, Hartley engaged in diſtributing one of his books. He was impriſoned, and being releaſed in 1584, left the kingdom. Wood, *Athenæ Oxon.* i: 474. I find mention of his impriſonment in Strype, *Whitgift*, i: 268. The accounts given of Campian and his trial and execution contain no reference to him, and I have found no alluſion to the fact named in the text.

[308] for the Name of the *Lord Jeſus:* But Sir, your *Principles* and *Conſcience* binde you, not to reſpect *Romiſh or Engliſh, Saints or Sinners: William Heartly*, and that *Woman*, with all their *lives*, you are bound by your *Conſcience* to puniſh (and it may be) to hang or burne, iſ they tranſgreſſe againſt your *Conſcience*, and that becauſe (according to Mr *Cottons* monſtrous *Diſtinction* (as ſome of his chieſe *Brethren* to my knowledge hath called it) not becauſe they ſinne in matters of *Conſcience*, (which he denies the *Magiſtrate* to deale in) but becauſe they ſinne againſt their *Conſcience*.

The Common Prayers & the Composers of it.

Secondly, It is ſo notoriouſly knowne, that the *Conſciences* of the moſt holy men, zealous for *God* & his *Chriſt* to *Death* and *Admiration*, yea even in our owne Countrey, and in Queen *Maries* dayes eſpecially, have been ſo groſsly miſlead by miſtaken *Conſciences* in matters concerning the *worſhip of God*, the comming out of the *Antichriſtian Babell*, and the *Rebuilding* of the ſpirituall *Jeruſalem*, that I need but hint who were they that pend the *Common prayer*[1] (in its Time, as glorious an Idoll, and as much adored by *Godly perſons*, as any *Invention* now extant) I ſay who they were that lived and dyed (five in the flames) zealous for their *Biſhopricks*, yea and ſome too too zealous for their Popiſh *Ceremo-*

[1] The Book of Common Prayer was firſt put forth in Engliſh, May 4, 1549. There were thirteen compilers, of whom Cranmer and Ridley are the moſt famous. Strype, *Ecc. Mem.* ii: 134. Short, *Hiſt. of Ch. of Eng.* p. 279. "Of the firſt compilers, Dr. Whitgift gave this character, that they were ſingular learned men, zealous in God's religion, blameleſs in life, and martyrs at their end. For either all, or the moſt part of them, had ſealed this book with their blood." Strype, *Life of Whitgiſt*, i: 175.

nies, againſt the doubting *Conſciences* of their Brethren: At which and more, we that now have riſen in our *Fathers* ſtead, wonder and admire how ſuch piercing *eyes* could be deceived, ſuch *Watchmen* blinded and deluded. But

Thirdly, We ſhall not ſo much wonder when we lift up our trembling *eyes* to *Heaven*, and remember our ſelves (poore duſt) that our *Thoughts* are not as the *Thoughts* of our *Maker*, that, that which in the eyes of man (as the *Lord Jeſus* tells us, *Luc.* 16. [15.]) is of high and ſweet eſteeme, it ſtincks and is abomination with *God:* Hence ſuch *Worſhips*, ſuch *Churches*, ſuch glorious *profeſſions* & *practices* may be, as may raviſh *themſelves* and the *behoulders*, when with the piercing *eyes* of the moſt *High*, they may look *counterſeit* and ugly, and be found but (ſpiritually) *Whores* and *Abominations*.

What's ſweet with man, ſtinks (often) in Gods noſ-trills.

Fourthly, Wiſe men uſe to inquire, what *Motives*, what *Occaſions*, what *Snares*, what *Temptations* were there, which mooved, which drew, which allured, &c. This is the *Apologie* [309] which the five *Apologiſts* (Mr *Goodwin*, Mr *Nye*, &c.) made to the *Parliament*, to wit, That they were not tempted with the moulding of New *Common-wealths*, after which they might be mooved to frame their *Religion*, &c.[1]

Surely Sir, the *Baits*, the *Temptations*, the *Snares*

[1] The five apologiſts, Thomas Goodwin, Philip Nye, Sidrach Simpſon, Jeremiah Burroughs and William Bridge preſented *An Apologetical Narration* to Parliament in 1643. In 1644 Williams publiſhed his *Queries of Higheſt Conſideration*, propoſed to theſe perſons and to the Scotch Commiſſioners in the Weſtminſter Aſſembly. *Pub. Narr. Club.* ii.

Sathans policie in propoſing Motives and Baits to wiſe and excellent Saints.

laid to catch you, were not few, nor *common*, nor laid to every foote. *Saul* pretended *zeale* to the Name of *God*, and love to *Iſrael* in perſecuting the poore *Gibeonites* to death, but Honour me before the people, was the maine *Engine* that turned the *Wheeles* of all his *Actions* and *Devotions*. What ſet *Jeroboams* braines to conſult and plot the *Invention* of a new *Religion*, *Worſhip*, *Prieſts*, &c. but *Honour*, & the feare of the loſſe of his gained *honour?* What moved *Jehu* to be falſe and halting with *God* after ſo much glorious *zeale* in the *Reformation?* Yea I had almoſt ſaid, what mooved *David* to ſtob *Uriah* (the fire of *God*) with his pen, but the feare of diſhonour in the Diſcovery of his ſin, though doubtles there was ſome mixtures of the feare of his *Gods* diſpleaſure and diſhonour, alſo?

Sir, it is no ſmall offer, the *choice* and *applauſe* and *Rule* over ſo many *Townes*, ſo many *holy*, of many *wiſe*, in ſuch a holy *way* as you believe you are in: To ſay nothing of *ſtrong drinkes* and *wines*, the *fat* and *ſweet* of *this* and other *Lands:* Theſe and others are ſnares which without abundant ſtrength from *God* will catch and hould the ſtrongeſt feete: Sir, I have knowne you ſtrong, in repelling ſtrong *Temptations*, but I cannot but feare and lament, that ſome of theſe and others have been too ſtrong and potent for you.

Spirituall Witchcraft.

Fifthly, We not onely uſe to ſay proverbially, but the Spirit of *God* expreſsly tells us, that there is a *minde-bewitching*, a *bewitching* of the very *Conſciences* and *ſpirits* of men. That as in *Witchcraft*, a *ſtronger* and ſupernaturall *power* layes hould upon the powers of *Nature*, with a ſuppreſſing or elevating of thoſe powers beneath or above themſelves: So is it with the very *Spirits* and *Conſciences* of the moſt *Intelligent* and *Conſcientious*, when the *Father* of *Spirits* is pleaſed in his righteous diſpleaſure and jealouſie, ſo to ſuffer it to be with ours.

Sir, I from my Soule *honour* and *love* the perſons of ſuch, whom I, you, and themſelves may ſee have been *Inſtrumentall* in your *bewitchin*. Why ſhould it be thought inconſiſtent with [310] the holy wiſdome of *God* to permit *wiſe* and *holy* and *learned* perſons to *wander* themſelves and *miſlead others*; when the holy *Scripture* and *Experience* tells us of the dangerous *Councells* and *wayes* of as *wiſe* and *learned* and *holy* as now breath in either *Old* or *New Engliſh* aire?

Sir, I had thought to have named one or two, who may juſtly be ſuſpected (though otherwiſe worthily beloved) but I have choſe rather to preſent an hint, for thats enough to ſo *intelligent* a Breaſt, if but willing to make an Impartiall *Review* and *Examination* of Paſſages between the moſt *High* and your inmoſt *Soule* in ſecret.

Therefore ſixthly, for a fixt ground of ſuſpecting your *Soule* and *Spirit* and *Conſcience* in this particular of *perſecution*, which I now inſtance in, may you pleaſe, Sir, without offence to remember, that as it is in ſuch as have exceeded in *Wine*, their *ſpeech* will bewray them: So is it in Spirituall *Cups* and *Intoxications*.

Myſticall Drunkenneſſe and drunken Language of it.

The *Maker* and *Searcher* of our hearts knowes with what *Bitternes* I write, as with *Bitternes* of

The Language of perſecutours.

Soule I have heard ſuch *Language* as this to proceed from your ſelfe and others, who formerly have fled from (with crying out againſt) perſecutours! [you will ſay, this is your *Conſcience:* You will ſay, you are *perſecuted*, and you are *perſecuted* for your *Conſcience:* No you are *Conventiclers, Hereticks, Blaſphemers, Seducers:* You deſerve to be *hanged*, rather then one ſhall be wanting to *hang* him I will hang him my ſelſe: I am reſolved not to leave an *Heretick* in the *Countrey*; I had rather ſo many *Whores* and *VVhoremongers* and *Thieves* came amongſt us:] Oh Sir, you cannot forget what *Language* and *Dialect* this is, whether not the ſame unſavourie, and ungodly, blaſphemous and *bloudie*, which the *Gardiners* and *Bonners* both former and later uſed to all that bowed not to the *State* goulden *Image* of what *Conſcience* ſoever they were. And indeed, Sir, if the moſt *High* be pleaſed to awaken you to render unto his holy *Majeſtie* his due praiſes, in your truly broken-hearted *Confeſſions* and *Supplications*, you will then proclaime to all the *VVorld*, that what profeſſion ſoever you made of the *Lambe*, yet theſe *Expreſſions* could not proceed from the *Dragons* mouth.

A price and a Heart bleſſed companions.

Oh remember, and the moſt holy *Lord*, bring it to your *Re-* [311] *membrance*, that you have now a great price in your hand, to bring great *Glory* to his holy Name, great *Rejoycing* to ſo gracious a *Redeemer* (in whom you profeſſe is all your *Healing* and *Salvation*) great *Rejoycing* to the holy *Spirit* of all true *Conſolation*, whom yet ſo long you who have grieved and ſadded, great *Rejoycing* to thoſe bleſſed

Spirits (attending upon the *Lambe*, and all his, and terrible to his *perſecutours*) great *Rejoycing* and *Inſtruction* to all that love, the true *Lord Jeſus* (notwithſtanding their wandrings among ſo many falſe *Chriſts*) mourning and lamenting after him in all parts of the World where his Name is ſounded: Your *Tallents* are great, your *Fall* hath been ſo: Your *Eminencie* is great, the *Glory* of the moſt *High* in *Mercy* or *Juſtice* toward you will be great alſo.

Oh remember it is a dangerous Combat for the *potſheards* of the Earth to fight with their dreadfull *Potter:* It is a diſmall *Battle* for poore naked *feete* to kick againſt the *Pricks*; It is a dreadfull *voyce* from the *King* of *Kings*, and *Lord* of *Lords*, *Endicot, Endicot*, why *hunteſt* thou *me?* why *impriſoneſt* thou *me?* why *fineſt*, why ſo bloudily *whippeſt*, why wouldeſt thou (did not I hould thy *bloudie* hands) *hang* and *burne me?* Yea Sir, I beſeech you remember that it is a dangerous thing to put this to the *may be*, to the *venture* or *hazzard*, to the *poſſibilitie:* Is it poſſible (may you well ſay) that ſince I *hunt*, I *hunt* not the *life* of my *Saviour*, and the bloud of the Lambe of *God:* I have fought againſt many ſeverall ſorts of *Conſciences*, is it beyond all *poſſibilitie* and *hazard*, that I have not fought againſt *God*, that I have not perſecuted *Jeſus* in ſome of them?

The horrible & dangerous path which all perſecutours and Hunters walk in.

Sir, I muſt be humbly bold to ſay, that 'tis impoſſible for any Man or Men to maintaine their *Chriſt* by their *Sword*, and to worſhip a true *Chriſt!* to fight againſt all *Conſciences* oppoſite to theirs, and not to fight againſt *God* in ſome of them, and to

The leaſt ſparke of perſecution tends to bloud, and will proceed, except God mightily ſtop it.

hunt after the precious life of the true *Lord Jeſus Chriſt*. Oh remember whether your *Principles* and *Conſciences* muſt in time and opportunitie force you. 'Tis but worldly *policie* and *compliance* with Men and Times (*Gods* mercy over-ruling) that houlds your hands from *murthering* of thouſands and ten thouſands were your *Power* and *Command* as great as once the bloudie *Roman Emperours* was.

The truth is (and your ſelfe and others have ſaid it) by your [312] *Principles* ſuch whom you count *Hereticks*, *Blaſphemers*, *Seducers*, to be put to *Death*; You cannot be faithfull to your *Principles* and *Conſciences*, if you ſatisfie them with but *impriſonment*, *fining*, *whipping* and *baniſhing* the *Hereticks*, and by ſaying that *baniſhing* is a kinde of *Death*, as ſome chiefe with you (in my caſe formerly) have ſaid it.

Sir, 'Tis like you knew or have heard of the man that ſaid he would never *Conforme* publikely, although he did *ſubſcribe* in private for his Libertie ſake of *Preaching*: That, although he did *conforme* in *ſome* things, yet in *all* he never would: That although he did *himſelfe* yeeld, yet he would not moleſt and *inforce* others: That although he yeelded, that *other*s did moleſt them, yet himſelfe would never *perſecute*, and yet did all.

But oh poore duſt and Aſhes, like *ſtones* once rolling downe the *Alpes*, like the *Indian Canoes* or *Engliſh Boats* looſe and adrift, where ſtop we untill infinite mercy ſtop us, eſpecially when a falſe fire of *zeale* and *Conſcience* drives us, (though againſt the moſt holy and eternall himſelfe?)

Oh remember the black *Catalogues* it hath pleaſed

the moſt jealous and righteous *God* to make of his ſierie *Judgements* and moſt dreadfull ſtoakes on Eminent and remarkeable *perſecutours* even in this life. It hath been his way and courſe in all Countries, in *Germanie, France* and *England,* (eſpecially) what ever their pretences have been againſt *Hereticks, Rebells, Schismaticks, Blasphemers, Seducers,* &c. How hath he left them to be their owne *Accuſers, Judges, Executioners,* ſome by *hanging,* ſome by *ſtobbing,* ſome by *drowning* and *poyſoning* themſelves, ſome by running *mad,* and ſome by *drinking* in the very ſame *Cup* which they had filld to others?

Gods moſt dreadful Judgements againſt perſecutours.

Some may ſay, ſuch *perſecutours* hunted *God* and *Chriſt,* but I, but we, &c. I anſwer, the *Lord Jeſus Chriſt* foretold how wonderfully the wiſeſt of the World, ſhould be miſtaken in the things of *Chriſt,* and a true viſible *Chriſt Jeſus!* When did we ſee thee *naked, hungry, thirſty, ſicke, inpriſon* &c. How eaſie, how common, how dreadfull theſe *miſtakes?*

Oh remember once againe (as I began) and I humbly deſire to remember with you, that every gray haire now on both our heads, is a *Boanerges,* a ſonne of *Thunder,* and a warning piece [313] to prepare us, for the waighing of our laſt *Anchors,* and to be gone from hence, as if we had never been.

Death is a *Boanerges.*

'Twas mercy infinite, that ſtopt provoked *Juſtice* from blowing out our *Candles* in our *youths,* but now the *feeding Subſtance* of the *Candles* gone, and 'tis impoſſible (without repentance,) to recall our *Actions!* nay with *repentance,* to recall our *minutes* paſt us.

Gray hayres are Gods Alarums.

Sir, I know I have much preſumed upon your many waighty *affaires* and *thoughts*, I end with an humble cry to the *Father* of *mercies*, that you may take *Davids Counſell*, and ſilently commune with your owne heart upon your *Bed*, reflect upon your owne *ſpirit*, and believe Him that ſaid it to his over-zealous *Diſciples*, You know not what *ſpirit* you are of: That, no ſleepe may ſeize upon your *eyes*, nor ſlumber upon your *eye-lids*, untill your ſerious thoughts have *ſeriouſly*, *calmely*, and *unchangeably* (through helpe from *Chriſt Jeſus*) fixed.

Firſt, On a *Moderation* towards the *Spirits and Conſciences* of all mankinde, meerly differing from or oppoſing yours with onely Religious and Spirituall *oppoſition*.

Secondly, A deepe and cordiall *Reſolution* (in theſe wonderfull ſearching, diſputing, and diſſenting times) to ſearch, to liſten, to pray, to faſt, and more fearefully, more tremblingly to enquire what the holy *pleaſure*, and the holy *myſteries* of the moſt *Holy* are; in whom I humbly deſire to be

Your poore fellow-Servant, unfainedly,

reſpective and faithfull,

R. VVilliams.

An *APPENDIX*.

To the *Cleargie* of the foure great *Parties* (profeſſing the Name of *Chriſt Jeſus*) in *England, Scotland,* and *Ireland,* viz. The *Popiſh, Prelaticall, Preſbyterian, and Independent.*

WORTHY SIRS;

I Have pleaded the Cauſe of your ſeverall and reſpective *Conſciences* (againſt the bloudie Doctrine of *Perſecution*) in my former Labours, and in this my preſent *Rejoynder* to Mr *Cotton* :

And yet I muſt pray leave without offence to ſay, I have impartially oppos'd and charg'd your *Conſciences* alſo, ſo farre as *Guiltie* of that *bloudie* Doctrine of perſecuting each other for your *Conſciences*.

You *foure* have torne the ſeamless Coate of the Son of *God* into *foure* pieces, and (to ſay nothing of former *Times* and *Tearings*) you *foure* have torne the three *Nations* into thouſands of *pieces* and *Diſtractions*.

The ſeameles Coat of Chriſt Jeſus torne into foure pieces, and the three Nations torne into thouſands.

The two former of you, the *Popiſh* and (*Proteſtant*) *Prelaticall*, are *Brethren* : So are the latter, the *Preſbyterian* and *Independent* : But, oh, how *Rara eſt*, &c? What *Concord*, what *Love*, what *pitie* hath ever yet appear'd amongſt you, when the *providence* of the moſt *High* and onely *wiſe* hath granted you your *Pattents* of mutuall and ſucceſſive *Dominion* and *precedencie?*

The Battles of the *Cleargie*.

Juſt like two men, whom I have knowne breake out to *Blowes* and *Wraſtling*, ſo have the *Proteſtant Biſhops* fought and wraſtled with the *Popiſh*, and the *Popiſh* with the *Proteſtant!* The *Preſbyterian* with the *Independent*, and the *Independent* with the [315] *Preſbyterian!* And our *Chronicles* and *Experiences* have told this *Nation*, and the *World*, how he whoſe *Turne* it is to be brought under, hath ever felt an heavie wrathfull hand of an *unbrotherly* and unchrſtian *perſecutour:*

All Court the Magiſtrate for his Sword,

Meane while, what *outcries* for a *Sword*, a *Sword* at any *price*, on any *Tearmes*, wherewith to take finall *Revenges*, on ſuch their *Blaſphemous* and *Hereticall* Adverſaries and Corrivalls?

&

Hence is it, that the *Magiſtrate* hath been ſo courted, his perſon *adored* and *Deified*, and *his Religion* magniſied and *Exalted*.

his Money

For which any perſon and Religion hath ſerv'd the Turne.

Amongſt the *People*, ſome have thought and ſaid, How hath the ſhining of the *Magiſtrates Money* and *Sword*, out ſhin'd the *Nobilitie* of his *perſon*, or the *Chriſtianitie* of his *Conſcience?* For when the *perſon* changes and *Religion* too, how groſſely notorious have been the *Cleargies* Changes alſo? For Inſtance, how have they *Pernified*,[1] tack't and turn'd about (as the wind hath blowne) from *Poperie* to *Proteſtaniſme*, from *Proteſtantiſme* to *Poperie*, and from *Poperie* to *Proteſtantiſme* againe, and this within

[1] For the meaning and derivation of this word, see p. 209 *supra*.

the Compaſſe of about a dozen yeares; as the *Purſe* and *Sword-Bearers* were changed, what ever the perſons of thoſe *Princes* (*male* or *female*, *Men* or *Children*, or their *Conſciences*, *Popiſh* or *Proteſtant*) were.

Yea, how juſtly in the late *Kings* book[1] (if his) are the *Cleargie* of *England* charged with horrible breach of *Vows* and *Oaths* of *canonicall* obedience to their *Fathers* the *Biſhops*, againſt whom (in the *Turne* of the *Times* and the *Sword-Bearers*) they turned to the *Scotch Preſbyters*, their fathers dreadfull Enemies and *perſecutours*?

The late K. charging his *Cleargie*, &c.

Now as to the *perſecuting* each of other, I confeſſe the *Wolfe* (the *perſecutour*,) devoures the *Goate*, the *Swine*, yea the very *Fox*, and other Creatures, as well as the inoffenſive *Sheepe* and *Lambe*? Yet (as the *Lord Jeſus* made uſe of that excellent *Fable* or Similitude of a *Wolfe* getting on a *Sheepes*-skin, ſo) may I not unſeaſonably make uſe of that of the *Wolfe* and the poore *Lambe* coming downe to drinke, upon the ſame Brooke and Streame together: The *Wolfe cruell* and *ſtrong* drinks *above* and aloft: The *Lambe innocent* and *weake*, drinks upon the Streame *below*: The *Wolfe* queſtions and quarrells the *Lambe* for corrupting and defiling

The *Wolfe* in plea with the *Lamb* will be alwaies Judge.

[1] *ΕΙΚΩΝ ΒΑΣΙΛΙΚΗ. The Portracture of his Sacred Majeſtie in his ſolitudes and ſufferings.* 1649. This work was attributed to Charles I., and the authorſhip has been the ſubject of much controverſy. Williams here intimates his doubt in regard to its being the King's. In 1650 he wrote to John Winthrop, jr., "The Portraicture, I gueſſe is Bp. Halls, the ſtile is pious and acute, very like his, and J. H. ſubſcribes the Epitaph:" 4 *Mass. Hiſt. Coll.* vi: 282. It was claimed by Biſhop Gauden. Mackintosh, Hallam and Macaulay are decided in aſcribing the book to Gauden alone. *Edin. Rev.* xliv: 1–47. *Introd. to Lit. of Europe*, iii: 661. *Hiſt. of Eng.* iv. 249.

the Waters: The *Lambe* [316] (not daring to plead how eaſily the *Wolfe* drinking higher might transfer *Defilement* downeward, but) pleads *Improbabilitie* and *Impoſſibilitie*, that the waters deſcending could convey defilement upwards: This is the *Controverſie*, This the *plea:* But who ſhall *judge?* Be the *Lambe* never ſo innocent, his plea never ſo juſt, his Adverſary the *Wolfe* will be his judge, and being ſo cruell and ſo ſtrong ſoon teares the *Lambe*, in pieces.

Thus the cruell *Beaſt* armed with the power of *Kings* (*Revel.* 17. [12]) ſits Judge in his owne Quarrels againſt the *Lambe*, about the drinking at the *Waters.* And thus (ſayth M[r] *Cotton*) the Judgement ought to paſſe upon the *Heretick*, not for matter of *Conſcience*, but for ſinning againſt his *Conſcience.*

Object. Me-thinks I heare, the great charge againſt the *Independent* partie to be the great pleaders for *Libertie* of *Conſcience*, &c.

Answ. Oh the horrible *Deceipt* of the hearts of the ſons of Men! And, what Excellent *Phyſick* can we preſcribe to others, till our Soule (as *Job* ſaid) come to be in their ſoules caſes? What need have we to be more vile (with *Job*) before God, to walke in holy ſence of ſelfe-Inſufficiencie, to cry for the bleſſed *Leadings* of the holy *Spirit* of *God*, to guide and leade our *Heads* and *Hearts* uprightly?

The wonderfull Myſterie of the Libertie of Conſcience.

For (to draw the *Curtaine*, and let in the *Light* alittle) doe not all *perſecutours* themſelves zealouſly plead for *Freedome*, for *Libertie*, for *Mercie* to Mens *Conſciences*, when them ſelves are in the *Grates*, and *Pits*, and under *Hatches*?

Doth not *Gesner*[1] tell us of a Gentleman in *Germanie*, who fitting his *Pitfall* for *Wilde Beasts*, found in the morning a *Woman*, a *Wolfe*, and a *Fox* in three severall Corners, as full of Feare, and as quiet, and as desirous of Libertie one as well as another?

Which all persecutours themselves (in their turnes) plead for.

Thus bloudie *Gardiner* and *Bonner* (prisoners, during King *Edwards* dayes) yea and that bloudie Queene *Mary* her selfe, all plead the freedom of their *Consciences*. What most humble Supplications, and indeed unanswerable Arguments for *Libertie* of *Conscience* have the *Papists* (when in Restaint) presented, (and especially) in King *James* his time? Yea what excellent *Subscriptions* to this Soule-Freedome, are interwoven in many passages of the late *Kings* Booke (if his)? Yea and one of his [317] *Chaplaines* (so cald') Doctor *Jer. Taylour*, what an Everlasting Monumentall *Testmonie* did he publish to this *Truth*, in that his excellent Discourse, of *the Libertie of Prophesying*?[2] Yea the (formerly) Non-conforming *Presbyterian* and *Inde-*

K. *Charles* and his Chaplains forced to subscribe to Libertie of Conscience.

[1]Conrad Gesner, was born at Zurich, March 26, 1516, and died Dec. 15, 1565. His History of Animals, from which Williams probably quotes, Cuvier says "may be considered the basis of all modern zoology." *Biog. Univ.* 17 : 247. Hallam speaks of him as "that prodigy of general erudition." *Int. to Lit. of Europe*, ii: 465–469. Sir W. Jardine gives an account of this work in a memoir in *Naturalist's Library*, xx: 29–39.

[2]This work was published in 1647. Williams sent a copy of the present work to Mrs Sadleir, which she returned, declining to read it. He replied "since you please not to read mine, let me pray leave to request your reading of one book of your own authours. I meane The Liberty of Prophesying, penned by (so called) Dr Jer. Taylor, in which is excellently asserted the toleration of differing religions, yea, in a respect, that of papists themselves, which is a new way of soule-freedom, and yet the old way of Christ Jesus, as all his holy Testament declares. I also humbly wish that you may please to read over impartially Mr Milton's answer to the King's book." *Elton's Life*, p. 97.

pendent, *Scotch* and *English*, *Old* and *New*, what moſt humble and pious Addreſſes have they made before the whole World, to *Princes* and *Parliaments*, for juſt mercy (in true Petitions of Right) to their *Conſciences?* But, let this preſent Diſcourſe, and Mr *Cottons* Fig-leave *Evaſions* and *Diſtinctions:* Let the *practices* (of the *Maſſachuſets*) in *New England*, in twenty yeares *perſecution:* and this laſt of Mr *Clarke*, *Obadiah Holmes*, and others be Examined: Yea let the *Independent Miniſters* late Propoſalls be waighed, with the double waight of *Gods* Sanctuary, and it will appear what *Mercy* the poore Soules of *all* Men, and *Jeſus Chriſt* in any of them, may expect from the very *Independents Cleargie* themſelves.

About Twenty years perſecution in *New England.*

Object. But doth not their *Propoſalls* provide a *Libertie* to ſuch as feare *God*, viz. that they may freely preach without an *Ordination!* and that ſuch as are not free to the publike *Aſſemblies* may have Libertie to meete in private.

Anſw. It may ſo pleaſe the *Father* of *Lights* to ſhew them that their *Lines* and *Modells*, and *New Englands* Copie alſo (after which they write and penſill,) are but more and more refined *Images*, whereby to worſhip the *Inviſible God:* and that ſtill (as before) the *Wolſe* (the *perſecutour*) muſt judge of the *Lambes* drinking!

The perſecution of the *New* and *Old Engliſh Independent Cleargie.*

For inſtance; *New Englands* Lawes lately publiſhed in Mr *Clarks Narrative*,[1]) tell us *how free* it ſhall be for people to gather themſelves into *Church-*

[1] Extracts from the laws of Maſſachuſetts on theſe ſubjects were printed in *Ill Newes*. 4 *Mass. Hiſt. Coll.* ii. 65–70.

eſtate? *how free* to chooſe their owne *Miniſters?* *how free* to enjoy all the *Ordinances* of *Chriſt Jeſus*, &c? But yet, provided, ſo- and ſo (upon the point) that the *Civill State* muſt judge of the *Spirituall*, to wit, *Whether* perſons be fit for *Church*-eſtate, *Whether* the *Gathering* be *right*, *Whether* the peoples *choice* be *right*, *Doctrines right*, and what is this in truth, but to ſwear that blaſphemous *Oath* of *Supremacie* againe, to the *Kings* and *Queenes* and *Magiſtrates* of this and other Nations in ſtead of the *Pope*, &c?

Into theſe *Priſons*, and *Cages*, doe thoſe (otherwiſe worthy and excellent Men, the) *Independents*, put all the Children of [318] *God*, and all the Children of *Men* in the whole World, and then bid them *flie* and *walke* at *Libertie* (to wit, within the Conjured *Circle*) ſo far as they pleaſe.

To particularize briefely: When they have in their ſix ſeverall *Circuits* ejected (according to their Propoſalls) it may be hundreths, it may be thouſands (if impartiall) of *Epiſcopall* and *Presbyterian Miniſters*, and that without & againſt their *Peoples conſent*, to the preſent Diſtreſſing of thouſands, and inraging (through ſuch *Soul-oppreſſions*) the whole *Nation!* Then, ſay they, it ſhal be free for all that be able, &c. to be *Preachers*, though not ordained, &c. But, provided, that two *Miniſters* hands (at leaſt, which upon the point, is inſtead of an *Ordination*) be to their *Approbation*, &c. Upon this *lock* any ſhall be free to preach *Chriſt Jeſus*, upon this *point* of the *Compaſſe* (as I may in humble reverence, and with ſorrow ſpeake it) the *Spirit* of *God*

A briefe touch of upon the 15 Propoſalls of the (ſo calld) *Independent Miniſters.*

The *Independents* implicitly and ſilently challenge the power of Ordination.

ſhall be free to *breathe* and *operate* in the Soules of Men! By this *Plummet* and *Line*, *Rule* and *Square*, and (ſeeming) *Goulden Reede* and *Meetewand*, the *Sanctuary* muſt be built and measured, &c.

But further, if any ſhall be of tender *Conſciences*, and that the common ſize will ſerve their *foote*, if they ſhall thinke the *Independents Foundations* too *weak*, or it may be too *ſtrong* for their weake *Beliefe*, if they cannot bow downe to their Goulden *Image*, though of the fineſt and lateſt *Edition* and *Faſhion*: Why *God* forbid they ſhould be forc'd to *Church* as others, they ſhall enjoy their *Libertie*, and meeteapart in private: But, provided, they acquaint the Civill *Magiſtrate*, that is, as it may fall out, (who knowes how ſoon?) and too too often hath faln out, the poore *Sheepe* and *Deere* of *Chriſt* muſt take *Licence* of and *betray* themſelves unto the *pawes* and *jawes* of their Lyon-like *perſecutours*.

The Danger of pawning ſpirituall Liberties to Civill powers.

Heare Oh *Heavens*, give Eare O *Earth!* What is this but like the Treacherous *Dutchmen*, who Capitulate of *Leagues* of *Peace* and *Amitie*, with their *Neighbour Engliſh*, and in the midſt of *State Complements* (ſome ſay, out of malicious *wrath*, others ſay twas out of drunken *Intoxications* at the beſt) thunder out *Broad-ſides* of Fire and Smoake of *perſecution?*

The *Dutch* Attempts, and the *Independents*, on their Friends, compared.

Object. Some poſſibly may ſay, Your juſt ſuffring from the *Independents* in *New England* makes you ſpeake *Revenges* againſt them in *Old*.

[319] *Anſw.* What I have ſuffred in my *Eſtate*, *Body*, *Name*, *Spirit*, I hope through helpe from *Chriſt*, and for his ſake I have deſired to beare with

a *Spirit* of *patience* and of *reſpect* and *love*, even to my *perſecutours*. As to particulars, I have, and muſt (if God ſo will) further debate them with my truely honoured and beloved *Adverſarie* M[r] *Cotton*.

But as to you, worthy Sirs, (men of *Learning*, and men of perſonall *Holines* many of you) I truely deſire to be far from envying your *Honours*, *pleaſures*, and *Revenues*, from whence the two former *Popiſh* & *Prelaticall* are ejected, unto which the two later *Preſbyterian* and *Independent* are advanced: Nor would I move a *Tongue* or *pen* that any of you now poſſeſſed, ſhould be removed or diſturbed, untill your *Conſciences* by the holy Spirit of *God*, or the *Conſciences* of the *people*, to whom you ſerve, or miniſter, ſhall be otherwayes (then as you are yet) perſwaded.

The Authours deſire as to the Miniſtrie of the Land now poſſeſſed.

Much rather would I make another humble *plea* (and that I believe with all the *Reaſon* and *Juſtice* in the World) that ſuch who are ejected, undone, impoveriſhed, might ſome way from the *State* or *you* receive *reliefe* and *ſuccour*: Conſidering, that the very *Nations* Conſtitution hath occaſioned *parents* to traine up, & *perſons* to give themſelves to *ſtudies* (though in truth, but in a way of *Trade* & *Bargaining*, before *God*) yet, 'tis according to the *Cuſtome* of the *Nation*, who ought therefore to ſhare alſo, in the fault of ſuch *Prieſts* and *Miniſters* who in all changes are *ejected*.

And as to that Ejected.

I end with humble begging to the *Father* of *Spirits*, to perſwade and poſſeſſe yours with a true ſence of three *particulars*.

The Authour begs three things of *God* for the *Cleargie* of *England*.

Firſt, of the *yoakes* of *Soule-oppreſſion*, which lye

upon the necks of moſt of the *Inhabitants* of the 3 *Nations*, & of the whole world: as if *Chams* Curſe from *Noah* were upon them, *Servants* of *Servants* are they, and that in the matters of the *Soules* Affection unto *God*, which call for the pureſt *Libertie*: I confeſſe the *World* lyes in *wickedneſſe*, and loveth darkneſſe more than *light*: but why ſhould you helpe on thoſe *yoaks*, and force them to receive a *Doctrine*, to pray, to give thanks, &c. without an *Heart?* yea and (in the many changes and caſes incident) againſt their *Heart* and Soules Conſent?

Soule-Bondage the greateſt.

Secondly, of the *bloudines* of that moſt bloudie *Doctrine* of *perſecution* for cauſe of *Conſcience*, with all the *Winding Staires* and *back dores* of it, &c. Some *profeſſors* true and falſe, *Sheepe* [320] and *Goats*, are daily found to differ in their *Apprehenſions*, *perſwaſions*, *profeſſions*, and that to Bonds and Death.

What now, ſhall theſe be wrackt, their *Soules*, their *Bodies*, their *purſes*, &c? Yea if they refuſe, deny, oppoſe the *Doctrine* of *Chriſt Jeſus*, whether *Jewes* or *Gentiles*, why ſhould you call for *Fire* from *Heaven*, which ſuits not with *Chriſt Jeſus* his *Spirit* or *Ends?* Why ſhould you compell them to come in, with any other *Sword*, but that of the *Spirit* of *God*, who alone perſwaded *Japhet* to come into the Tents of *Shem*, and can in his holy ſeaſon prevaile with *Shem* to come into the Tents of *Japhet*?

The Bloudineſſe of the *Bloudie Tenent.*

Thirdly, Of that *Biaſs* of ſelfe-love which hales and ſwayes our minds to hould ſo faſt this bloudie *Tenent*: You know it is the *Spirit* of *Love* from

Christ Jesus, that turns our feete from the *Tradition* of *Fathers*, &c. That sets the *Heart* and *Tongue* and *Pen* and *Hands* too (as *Pauls*) day and night to work, rather then the *progresse* and *puritie* and *simplicitie* of the *Crowne* of *Christ Jesus* should be debased or hindred.

Little of the Spirit of Love from Christ Jesus yet extant, and our selfelove biasseth us to conventions, traditions, and Doctrines of persecutions.

This *Spirit* will cause you leave (with joy) *Benefices*, and *Bishopricks*, *Worlds* and *Lives* for his sake: the *Heights* and *Depths*, *Lengths* and *Breadths*, of whose Love you know doth infinitely passe your most knowing *Comprehensions* and *Imaginations*. There is but little of this *Spirit* extant, I feare will not be, untill we see *Christ Jesus* slaine in the slaughter of the *Witnesses*: Then *Joseph* will goe boldly unto *Pilate* for the slaughtered *bodie* of most precious *Savior*: and *Nicodemus*, will goe by day, to buy and bestow his sweetest *spices* on his infinitly *sweeter* Soules *beloved*. The full breathings of that heavenly *Spirit*, unfeinedly and heartily wisheth you,

Your most unworthy countriman,

R. Williams.

FINIS.

The Principal

CONTENTS.

FINIS.

ERRATUM.

In note, p. 423, read *The Ploughman's Tale* for *Piers Ploughman's Tale.*